THE CZECH RENASCENCE OF THE NINETEENTH CENTURY

ESSAYS PRESENTED TO OTAKAR ODLOŽILÍK
IN HONOUR OF HIS SEVENTIETH BIRTHDAY
EDITED BY PETER BROCK & H. GORDON SKILLING

THE CZECH

RENASCENCE

OF THE NINETEENTH CENTURY

UNIVERSITY OF TORONTO PRESS

Copyright Canada 1970 by
University of Toronto Press

Printed in Canada by
University of Toronto Press
Toronto and Buffalo

ISBN 0-8020-5233-9

PREFACE

IN COMPILING THIS VOLUME of essays on the Czech national renascence of the nineteenth century we have had two objects in mind. In the first place we desire to honour, on the occasion of his seventieth birthday, an outstanding Czech scholar. Secondly, we hope that through its pages English-speaking readers, scholars and laymen alike, may become better acquainted with selected topics in the history of the Czech awakening and of the Czech national movement, which finally led, with the collaboration of the closely related Slovak people, to the establishment of the independent republic of Czechoslovakia in 1918.

We have not attempted to put together a comprehensive history of the Czech revival. However, some – though, of course, by no means all – of its most important aspects are dealt with in the pages that follow. Many of the essays centre on the second quarter of the nineteenth century, for the events of 1848 and the preceding two decades were indeed of vital importance to the development of the Czech renascence. The work of its first outstanding figure, Josef Dobrovský, in the earlier period and the emergence in Bohemia of modern Czech political parties in the last two decades of the nineteenth century are among the other themes treated.

Otakar Odložilík, to whom our volume is dedicated, was born at Kostelec, near Holešov in Moravia, on 12 January 1899. For many years, however, he has made his home on the North American continent, from which most of our contributors are drawn (though scholars from Europe, including his native country, have also joined us in our tribute). Until 1948, apart from the period of the Second World War which he spent in America, he taught history at Charles University in Prague where he had carried out his undergraduate and doctoral studies and eventually held a chair. Then, in 1948, he left Prague to take up permanent residence in the United States, where he was appointed to a professorship of Central European history first at Columbia University and then at the University of Pennsylvania.

A glance at the extensive, yet selective bibliography of his writings, which is to be found at the end of this volume, will show that Otakar Odložilík has concentrated his professional interests on two major periods of his people's history. In the years before 1939 his publications were centred mainly in the late fourteenth, fifteenth, sixteenth, and early seventeenth centuries, that is, in the epoch stretching from the first beginnings of the great reform movement, which ultimately crystallized around the figure of Jan Hus, up to the disaster of the Battle of the White Mountain in 1620 and the dark decades that followed for the Czech people.

In his New World environment Odložilík did not abandon his deep interest in the Hussite and Reformation eras in Czech history. His full-length biography of the Hussite king, George of Poděbrady, which he published in English in 1965, indicates his continued concern for what many Czechs consider a golden age in their history. But a new dimension emerged in his research – one that had existed earlier, but had remained subordinate to his interest in the late mediaeval and early modern centuries. In the United States he started to work on the history of that rebirth of the Czech nation which had begun towards the end of the eighteenth century, and the completion of which he himself had witnessed as a young man. A series of thoughtful and penetrating studies bear witness to their author's intimate knowledge and understanding of the subject. It was indeed no mere chance that the historian of Hussite Bohemia should turn his attention, in the trying days of the Second World War and during the tribulations of the post-1948 era, to the emergence of his people as a modern nation. The Hussites' passionate quest for religious truth and the democratic humanism of Tomáš G. Masaryk, the greatest protagonist of modern Czech nationalism, are both reflected in Odložilík's writings.

One of the editors (Skilling), who first met Odložilík in Prague in 1937 and saw him often during the subsequent years of crisis, remembers him as a thoughtful adviser on his country's history and a friendly guide to the Prague and Bohemia he loved so much. Odložilík seemed to belong to Prague and to epitomize the intellectual side of Czech life. The tenor of his ways was rudely upset first by Munich and the German occupation, and then by the 1948 overthrow. Out of his natural element, and far from his beloved homeland, Odložilík continued to manifest his intellectual integrity, his stubborn realism, his devotion to his nation, and his personal modesty and wit. He is not the first, nor the last, Czech exile who, by his work abroad, has contributed greatly not only to his new country but also to the land of his birth.

We wish to express our gratitude to the following persons and institutions: the Canada Council for a special grant for preparation of the manuscript; the Centre for Russian and East European Studies of the University of Toronto for administrative assistance; Miss Francess Halpenny, Dr R. M. Schoeffel, and Miss L. Ourom, all of the University of Toronto Press, for help at various stages in production; Professor Josef Anderle for his extensive and valuable comments on the manuscript; Dr Ann Keep for compiling the index; Professor Gleb Žekulin for advice in regard to Czech style; Mr Dalibor Chrástek for aid in drawing up the select bibliography of Otakar Odložilík's writings. This work has been published with the help of a grant from the Humanities Research Council of Canada using funds provided by the Canada Council, and with the aid of the Publications Fund of the University of Toronto Press.

The contributions were all assembled by mid-1968. However, unforeseen circumstances have considerably delayed the appearance of the volume, which we had originally hoped might coincide with the celebration of Odložilík's seventieth birthday.

PETER BROCK

H. GORDON SKILLING

October 1969

CONTENTS

Preface / v

Contributors / x

1

The Periodization of Czech Literary History, 1774–1879
WILLIAM E. HARKINS / 3

2

Changing Views on the Role of Dobrovský in the Czech National Revival
ROBERT AUTY / 14

3

Locus Amoenus: An Aspect of National Tradition
MILADA SOUČKOVÁ / 26

4

The Social Composition of the Czech Patriots in Bohemia, 1827–1848
MIROSLAV HROCH / 33

5

The Matice Česká, 1831–1861: The First Thirty Years of a Literary Foundation
STANLEY B. KIMBALL / 53

6

Jan Ernst Smoler and the Czech and Slovak Awakeners:
A Study in Slav Reciprocity
PETER BROCK / 74

7

Metternich's Censors: The Case of Palacký
JOSEPH F. ZACEK / 95

8

Karel Havlíček and the Czech Press before 1848
BARBARA KOHÁK KIMMEL / 113

9

The "Czechoslovak" Question on the Eve of the 1848 Revolution
THOMAS G. PEŠEK / 131

10

German Liberalism and the Czech Renascence:
Ignaz Kuranda, *Die Grenzboten*, and Developments in Bohemia, 1845–1849
FRANCIS L. LOEWENHEIM / 146

11

The Preparatory Committee of the Slav Congress, April–May 1848
JOHN ERICKSON / 176

12

The Czechs and the Imperial Parliament in 1848–1849
STANLEY Z. PECH / 202

13

America and the Beginnings of Modern Czech Political Thought
JOSEF V. POLIŠENSKÝ / 215

14

The Hussite Movement in the Historiography of the Czech Awakening
FREDERICK G. HEYMANN / 224

15
Masaryk's National Background
THOMAS D. MARZIK / 239

16
The Politics of the Czech Eighties
H. GORDON SKILLING / 254

17
Kramář, Kaizl, and the Hegemony of the Young Czech Party, 1891–1901
STANLEY B. WINTERS / 282

Selected Bibliography of the Publications of Otakar Odložilík / 315

Index / 327

CONTRIBUTORS

ROBERT AUTY
Professor of Comparative Slavonic Philology, University of Oxford

PETER BROCK
Professor of History, University of Toronto

JOHN ERICKSON
Professor of Politics, University of Edinburgh

WILLIAM E. HARKINS
Professor of Slavic Languages, Columbia University

FREDERICK G. HEYMANN
Professor of History, University of Calgary

MIROSLAV HROCH
Docent in History, Charles University of Prague

STANLEY B. KIMBALL
Associate Professor of History, Southern Illinois University, Edwardsville

BARBARA KOHÁK KIMMEL
Columbia University

FRANCIS L. LOEWENHEIM
Associate Professor of History, Rice University

THOMAS D. MARZIK
Columbia University

STANLEY Z. PECH
Associate Professor of East European History, University of British Columbia

THOMAS G. PEŠEK
Assistant Professor of History, Washington State University

JOSEF V. POLIŠENSKÝ
Professor of History, Charles University of Prague

H. GORDON SKILLING
Professor of Political Science and Director of the Centre for
Russian and East European Studies, University of Toronto

MILADA SOUČKOVÁ
Visiting Professor, University of Chicago

STANLEY B. WINTERS
Professor of History, Newark College of Engineering

JOSEPH F. ZACEK
Associate Professor of History, State University of New York at Albany

THE CZECH RENASCENCE OF THE NINETEENTH CENTURY

The Periodization of
Czech Literary History, 1774–1879

WILLIAM E. HARKINS

THE DIVISION of Czech literary history into periods has, as is generally the case with such classifications, given rise to difficulties in the form of arbitrary terms or inconsistencies, or produced evasive reactions on the part of literary historians aware of the difficulties but unable to solve them. The present paper is devoted to the periodization of Czech literary history during the national renascence and the subsequent decades down to 1879. Before focusing more closely on the problems involved, however, let us see what methods of dividing Czech literary history into periods have been used in the more important literary histories.

The history of Czech literature by Václav Flajšhans[1] offers us three periods within the time span indicated: 1774–1815 ("Vzkříšení jazyka i písemnictví/Resurrection of the Language and Literature), 1815–48 ("Období předbřeznové"/The Pre-March Period, i.e. the period before the uprising of March 1848), and 1848–79 ("Od počátku ústavního života moderního až po naše dni; první květ"/From the Beginning of Modern Constitutional Life to Our Days; the First Flowering). The last caption seems inadequate, but its motivation becomes clearer when we note that Flajšhans's history was published in 1901. The choice of initial and terminal dates for the periods is explained by the author at the opening of the relevant chapters (though

1 Václav Flajšhans, *Písemnictví české slovem i obrazem od nejdávnějších dob až po naše časy* (Prague, 1901).

several of them are obvious to anyone with a slight knowledge of Czech history):
1774 is the year of the foundation of public schools, in which German was the language of instruction; 1816 is the year of certain concessions to the use of Czech in
public schools and government offices (Flajšhans's explanation of the dividing date
hinges on this fact, though the year actually chosen for division is 1815); 1848 is,
of course, the Year of Revolution and of the Prague uprising; finally, 1879 (a date
the significance of which Flajšhans does not bother to explain) is when a Czech
delegation re-entered the Austrian Parliament after a twelve-year boycott, following on the coming to power of the new government of Count Eduard Taaffe, who
was more favourably disposed toward the Slavic peoples of the empire.

It can be seen that Flajšhans's dates are dates of either political history (1848,
1879) or cultural history (1774). It is true, of course, that all these dates had certain implications for intellectual history and even for literature in the narrower
sense, though these may not always be so obvious: the exclusion of Czech from the
new public schools probably (if paradoxically) caused a reaction in favour of the
use of Czech in speech and writing among the growing circles of Czech patriots,
and 1848 brought the eventual shut-down of the Czech newspapers and the virtual
suppression of Czech national thought in literature (though it is true that complete
censorship was instituted only at the very end of 1851). The only date whose
choice remains questionable is 1815, and Flajšhans gives a motivation for this
choice, rather curiously, by pointing out that 1816 (sic) is the date of official concessions to the use of Czech in the schools and public offices of Bohemia. 1815 itself
may actually be a date chosen from literary and cultural history, rather than political
history, for it marks the beginning of Josef Jungmann's stay in Prague and of his
intensive activities on behalf of the use of spoken and written Czech. But it may
also be a date from political history: 1815 is the year of the foundation of the
German Confederation, into which the Austrian provinces, including Bohemia,
were incorporated in spite of their traditional and constitutional autonomy; the year
marks the end of even the pretext that Bohemia was a separate and independent
state. This tendency to prefer dates from history, at times cultural history but most
often political history, has been very strong in Czech literary historiography.

Both Jaroslav Vlček[2] and Jan Jakubec[3] avoid the problem of division into periods
in their histories, preferring an approach based on subjects which divide literary
periods topically rather than strictly chronologically. Vlček's history features such
chapter headings for the period in question as "Od osvícenství k nacionalismu"
(From the Enlightenment to Nationalism), "Poetický návrat k přírodě" (The Poetic
Return to Nature – Jungmann, Matěj Polák, etc.), and "Idea slovanská v poesii"
(The Slavic Idea in Poetry), and Jakubec's history gives us (as parts of longer and

2 Jaroslav Vlček, Dějiny české literatury, II, pt. 2 (Prague, 1914).
3 Jan Jakubec, Dějiny literatury české (Prague, 1911); enlarged edition, 2 vols. (Prague, 1929–34).

more involved chapter titles) such headings as "Jungmann a jeho škola" (Jungmann and His School), "Vrchol slovanské idey v české literatuře" (The Culmination of the Slavic Idea in Czech Literature), and "České básnictví pod vlivem poesie lidové" (Czech Poetry under the Influence of Folk Poetry).

The history in German by Jakubec and Arne Novák[4] avoids the use of period headings, like Jakubec's history, and rather employs subject categories without precise dividing dates. On the other hand, the German language history written by Arne Novák on his own for Oscar Walzel's *Handbuch der Literaturwissenschaft* and subsequently translated into Czech,[5] has period chapter headings, such as "Reformace, renasance a baroko" (Reformation, Renaissance, and Baroque), "Literatura národního obrození" (Literature of the National Renascence), and "Realisté a novoromantikové" (Realists and Neo-romantics), but also lacks precise dividing dates. Jan V. and Arne Novák's history in Czech, which has appeared in a number of editions and reached its culminating version in the edition of almost 1800 pages published in 1936–9,[6] presents us with the best-defined scheme of any history of Czech literature. The Nováks devote more than two pages to the periodization of literary history from 1774 to 1859,[7] and distinguish the following periods:

(a) Osvícenství (1774–1815)/Enlightenment,
(b) Klasicismus (1815–1830/Classicism,
(c) Starší romantika (1830–1848)/Early Romanticism,
(d) Pozdní romantika (1847–1859)/Late Romanticism.

The period 1860–79, defined by the phrase "Tendenční realismus v duchu světoobčanském" (Tendentious Realism in a Cosmopolitan Spirit), is characterized separately.[8]

The dividing dates are explicitly described by the authors (see footnotes 7 and 8). 1774 is again the year of the opening of German public schools, with the consequent exclusion of Czech from public life. 1815 is specifically identified with the coming of Jungmann to Prague. 1830 is defined rather apologetically: "Around 1830, when new currents and models penetrated to Bohemia, the ideological, literary and stylistic force of the classicist generation achieves its culmination in principle, even though the leaders of the [classicist] school only later publish their especially significant works." But, in spite of this statement, one wonders whether it is not really the Polish revolt of 1830, dividing certain members of the younger generation of

4 Jan Jakubec and Arne Novák, *Geschichte der čechischen Literatur* (Leipzig, 1907).
5 Arne Novák, "Die tschechische Literatur," pp. 1–114 in vol. XVIII, *Handbuch der Literaturwissenschaft*, ed. O. Walzel (Potsdam, 1931); Czech version as *Dějiny českého písemnictví* (Prague, 1946).
6 Jan V. and Arne Novák, *Přehledné dějiny literatury české* (Olomouc, 1936–9).
7 *Ibid.*, 216–18.
8 *Ibid.*, 474–5.

patriots, especially Karel Hynek Mácha, from their elders, which motivates the choice of the year. A suitable date for a purely literary division could hardly be found much earlier than 1836, the year of the publication of Mácha's *Máj*, if it is a question of dividing generations. 1848 is again the Year of Revolution, 1859 is the year of the fall of the reactionary Bach government with its notorious censorship, and 1860 is the year of constitutional reform granting new liberties of expression, and of the foundation of Czech nationalist newspapers. Finally, 1879 is, as has been noted above, the year of a decisive political change in the Czech nationalist movement, which then began a new relation of cooperation with the Austrian government.

We shall return later to a discussion of the Nováks' terms and periods, to which the bulk of the present study is devoted. But there remains one more literary history to be mentioned, the recently published three-volume history of the Czechoslovak Academy of Sciences.[9] The second volume (covering the era between the 1770s and the end of the 1850s), in contrast to the two other volumes of the work, is carefully divided into periods carrying precise names. The period from the 1770s to 1805 is called "Základy obrozenské literatury" (Foundations of Renascence Literature); that from 1806 to 1830, "Zrod obrozenské ideologie v literatuře" (The Birth of Renascence Ideology in Literature); from 1830 to 1848, "Sblížení obrozenské literatury se životem" (The Coming Together of Renascence Literature and Life); and 1848 to the end of the 1850s, "Obrozenská literatura v době revoluce 1848 a v boji proti reakci let padesátých" (Renascence Literature at the Time of the Revolution of 1848 and during the Struggle against the Reaction of the 1850s). The subsequent period, treated in the third volume, witnessed the rise of socialist and, eventually, Marxist thought, and the maintenance of period categories therefore becomes more difficult, since it is important to keep the rising radical movement separate from the predominant current of "bourgeois" literature. The editors refer to the period of the 1860s and 1870s as that of "Rozvoj demokratické literatury" (The Development of a Democratic Literature), presumably because the main figures in Czech literature of this period, such as Jan Neruda, were liberal but not yet socialist.

The introduction to the second volume tells us quite candidly that the editors really have non-literary criteria in mind in their period divisions and titles, and we are treated to a separate list of terms, taken from Czech Marxist historiography, which actually explain the choice of dividing dates. This makes us wonder how serious the editors really are, for though the "literary" period names are different from the "historical" ones, by some incredible coincidence the dates for the two series coincide exactly! But at least they are franker than the "bourgeois" literary historians in admitting their preference for historical rather than literary dividing lines. The historical periods which determine, for the Marxists, the parallel division into "literary" periods are:

9 *Dějiny české literatury*, 3 vols. (Práce Československé akademie věd, Prague, 1959–61).

1   The period of absolutist reforms and the inception of the national movement (from the 1770s to 1805),
2   The time of the Napoleonic Wars and of reactionary absolutism following the Congress of Vienna (from 1806 to 1830),
3   The time of the inception and development of revolutionary forces in the period 1830–48,
4   The time of the revolution of 1848 and the period of its premature suppression in the 1850s.[10]

The third volume of the Academy's History, though it introduces all sorts of material from political, social, and economic life, avoids any commitment to specific dates.

It is the classification of Jan V. and Arne Nováks' 1936–9 history to which I wish now to return, for this is obviously the most serious and thoughtful effort to establish a chronology of named periods for modern Czech literature; its only possible competitor in this respect, the Academy's History, which attempts to apply Marxist historiographical labels to literary history, comes close to being a parody of the method (or, rather, several types of parody, since the treatments in the separate volumes of the work are distinct in approach).

The proper subject of literary history is vague and flexible. To what extent, for example, is the literary historian to treat materials which have importance for cultural history as documents, but have no marked or obvious literary quality, such as fictive character, stylistic adornment, or formal organization? The usual solution is to err on the side of inclusiveness for older stages of a literature (particularly the Middle Ages, the Renaissance, and Humanism), but to become more strictly aesthetic in point of view as one approaches the modern era. Czech literary history is, however, saddled with an additional burden, that of the national idea, its pathos and ultimate triumph, and so even the treatment of literature during the nineteenth and twentieth centuries can hardly be purely aesthetic. It is not only that certain writers, such as Jan Kollár, František Ladislav Čelakovský, and Svatopluk Čech, are so heavily imbued with a nationalist or pan-Slavic content. Certain chapters and figures from national history have become firmly imbedded in literary history, so that they cannot be dislodged from it, even if anyone wished to do this: Karel Havlíček as a political journalist and Josef Václav Frič in 1848; later Tomáš G. Masaryk and Realism as a political and social movement; and so on. Indeed, the Nováks' *Přehledné dějiny literatury české* is in actuality a great intellectual history, which treats even certain scholars, journalists, statesmen, legal theorists, or natural scientists. It is true that most of these figures occupy less than proportionate space compared with the authors of *belles lettres*, but still they are there, and in several cases at least (František Palacký, Pavel Josef Šafařík, and Masaryk) the treatment is full and abundant.

10 *Ibid.*, ii, 9.

It is obvious that such a history as the Nováks' can hardly give an answer to the theoretical question: "What is Czech literature?" The answer cannot be all writing in Czech which is somehow worthy of honour, for the authors also include some writing in Latin and, in spite of their announced title, following a long tradition, they treat Slovak writers using the Slovak language (though the tradition which is followed here is doubtless paternalistic and even imperialistic). If the Nováks had intended their book to be a reference book (which is probably the best kind of use to which their volume can be put), we could hardly quarrel with its conception: the more useful information there, the better. But intermingled with the author entries we find paragraphs and even whole subchapters characterizing literary periods and discussing general trends, not only for literature itself but for intellectual history as a whole. The Nováks have thus attempted to give us a synthetic work as well as a reference book, though it is hard to imagine a reader (unless he were a student cramming for an exam) who would read continuously beyond the frequently able period characterizations and through very many of the individual author entries, with their endless catalogues of dates and titles. In spite of its pretensions to being the history of a literature, the Nováks' huge volume is in fact an encyclopaedia of that literature.

Still, the Nováks' history has influenced a whole generation, and their terms are so frequently employed that one can hardly help but reflect on them and take exception to them. First, however, we must make a terminological digression: what are we to denote by such terms as "classicism," "romanticism," "realism"? It would be easy to refer the reader to some of the very copious literature on the subject, and to the mass of definitions by various authorities, which are often contradictory. Another and even easier escape would be to seize, arbitrarily, on some working definition advanced by a single distinguished authority, e.g., René Wellek in his *Concepts of Criticism* (New Haven and London, 1963), or make a rhetorical appeal to some sense (no doubt illusory) of a "common denominator" of understanding by either the literary historians or the educated reading public. I have preferred to take another tack (one which is perhaps as rhetorical and as arbitrary): to try to formulate working definitions which correspond to notable tendencies of the periods in question, and which are dialectically as simple and as comprehensive as possible. "Classicism" (or better, "neo-classicism") I call that literary tendency which accepts (or supposes that it accepts) the authority of classical antiquity in matters of genre (especially hierarchy of genres), style, metrics, etc. "Romanticism" is that movement which breaks away from the authority of classicism, replacing the models of classical antiquity with those derived elsewhere, whether (seemingly) from an inner subjectivity, from the inspiration of nature, folklore, or mediaeval art, or from contemporary music and painting. The common denominator of all this is perhaps to be found in a tendency to blur hierarchies and limits, whether imposed by authority or by "reason" (i.e., common sense). "Realism" is likewise dialectically opposed to "romanticism," and seeks its grounding in an illusion of reality, maintained above all in narrative tone (the writer does not betray his presence in the work), as well as in the use of specific detail. The close relation of literary "realism" to the new positivist sciences, particularly sociology and psychology, and to journalism, is also important.

These terms have a certain universal application, no doubt, but I mean them first and foremost to apply to the trends predominant in specific periods: "neo-classicism" to the late seventeenth and eighteenth century; "romanticism" to the end of the eighteenth and early nineteenth centuries; "realism" to the second half of the nineteenth century. The dates are of course very approximate, and somewhat later for Bohemia than for western Europe. To make these concepts too abstract would be to rob them of much of their meaning in the time stream of literary history.

Although the development from one movement to another occurs for the most part dialectically, i.e., by "leaps" and oppositions, and not by smooth transition from generation to generation, still, intermediate stages, the results of incomplete opposition, are found: these we shall call "pre-romanticism" and "pre-realism"; their precise nature will be indicated later.

In turning now to analyse the Nováks' period terms, we are first struck by the fact that their categories are inconsistent. To repeat their classifications: (a) Enlightenment (1774–1815), (b) Classicism (1815–30), (c) Early Romanticism (1830–48), (d) Late Romanticism (1848–59). "Enlightenment" is a term taken from philosophical and intellectual history, while "classicism" and "romanticism" are terms of literary history proper. Is this not actually a confession that in the so-called period of the Enlightenment (1774–1815) there was very little artistic literature as such? But was there in fact so little? Václav Thám's early verse collection, *Básně v řeči vázané* (Poems in Rhythmic Speech), often considered to mark the beginnings of modern Czech literature, appeared in 1785, and the period up to 1815 is crowned by the odes of Antonín Puchmajer and the first version of Polák's magnificent nature poem *Vznešenost přírody* (The Sublimity of Nature), which appeared in 1813. What is particularly disturbing, too, is the fact that these works are largely "classicist," more so, indeed (at least in so far as their form is concerned), than those of the period 1815–30 which the authors label as "classicism." Puchmajer's odes, recalling those of Klopstock, Lomonosov, or Derzhavin, perpetuate the classic genre of the ode (and, like their predecessors, are baroque in their emphasis on the contrast of man's world and God's); Polák's concern for "sublimity" as well as his special blend of poetry and science both go back to classic antiquity.

On the other hand, how "classicist" is the period 1815–30, which the Nováks actually label "classicism"? By the term the authors mean "an intellectual and literary trend ... which sought to revive and elevate national literatures and legislate for them in the spirit of the ideological and artistic heritage of classic antiquity; it lasts from the seventeenth century up to the threshold of the nineteenth."[11] Their definition, it can be seen, is not very far from our own. Further on they present the

11 *Přehledné dějiny*, 264.

reader with an impressive list of the achievements of Czech and Slovak classicism, including the discovery of the forged *Královédvorský rukopis* (The Manuscript of Dvůr Králové; 1817), the theoretical writings of Palacký and Šafařík on Czech verse (1818), the work of Josef Jungmann, and especially the publication of his *Slovesnost* (Literature; 1820), a theoretical treatise on poetics and rhetoric with examples, as well as his article "O klasičnosti v literatuře" (On Classicism in Literature; 1827), and the poetry of Kollár and Čelakovský.

It is quite true that in Slovakia (as in Hungary) the use of Latin and the influence of classical literary models persisted very late, and the epic poetry of Jan Hollý is one of the Nováks' best examples. Otherwise their most convincing examples are drawn from the realm of literary theory (Palacký and Šafařík, Jungmann's *Slovesnost*, etc.), though Jungmann's article on classicism in literature actually defines classicism as the balance of form and content, and not merely the influence of classic models. But Jungmann was a complex figure of many aspects: as early as 1805 he published his Czech translation of Chateaubriand's *Atala,* a novel usually considered as pre-romantic, and even markedly so. In fact, most of the poets cited by the authors in this list could more logically be classified as pre-romantic (a concept which the authors do not use) than as classicist. If by pre-romanticism we mean the appearance of certain marked traits of romanticism (e.g., meditative poetry in which subjectivity is emphasized, an interest in nature landscape and in painting the "moods" of nature, the influence of folk poetry), then most of their poetic examples (as opposed to their theoretical ones) turn out to be pre-romantic rather than purely classicist.

What were the most important literary works of the period 1815–30? No doubt the forged manuscripts ("discovered" by Václav Hanka in 1817 and 1819), and the early poetry of Kollár and Čelakovský; in prose there is little enough, to be sure, but we might conceivably mention Josef Linda's novel *Záře nad pohanstvem* (Dawn over Paganism; 1818). Kollár has often been characterized as a typical devotee of classicism, and in fact his elaborate attempt to create a Slavic patriotic "mythology" might seem classicist in spirit. But his use of sonnet form, his intense patriotism and nationalism, the cast of his pan-Slavic ideas – all these strike us as more typical of romanticism than of classicism. This could be debated, it is true, but one underlying image definitely seems to make Kollár a romantic: his identification of sexual love (Minna) with the love of nation and the Slavic world. This motif, which was continued in a later period by Čelakovský in his *Růže stolistá* (The Hundred-Petalled Rose; 1840), is doubtless romantic and not classicist, for it is an illogical but metaphorically effective blending of logically distinguishable emotions; it seeks to enlist for the national cause the strongest private and subjective emotion of which a human being is capable. Its roots are in the baroque (the love of God, sometimes contrasted with, sometimes likened to sensual love), and not in the Renaissance or the world of classic antiquity.

But what of the other works mentioned above? The forged manuscripts may represent an attempt to give the Czechs their own mythology and antiquity, but this effort is romantic in character, and not classic as the authors suggest: the antiquity which it seeks to create is that of the mediaeval world and not the classic world as such. Its model is to be found in the work of James Macpherson, whose forgeries of the poetry of Ossian (*Fingal*, 1761) open the pre-romantic era in England and constitute, along with the poetry of James Young and Thomas Gray, one of its most typical examples. Related to this Ossianic wave is Linda's novel *Záře nad pohanstvem*, which also seeks to create a romanticized past for the Czech nation. The folk influence is strong in the forged manuscripts, and the discovery and celebration of national folklore is another pre-romantic trait; certainly it is not typical of classicism, with its intellectualism and its hierarchic view of literary values.

Besides *Růže stolistá*, Čelakovský's most important poetic works are his two collections of *ohlasy*, poems in the spirit of Russian and Czech folk songs, the *Ohlas písní ruských* (Echo of Russian Songs; 1829) and the *Ohlas písní českých* (Echo of Czech Songs; 1839). These poems are not classicist in any sense: they have no genre models either in classic antiquity or in the neo-classical period in western European literature; their form and lexicon are free, spontaneous, improvised, tending occasionally even towards a rhapsodic quality; their content, with its idealization of a heroic Russian tradition or a colourful Czech present, is not a whit classicist.

To the period 1815–30 I would rather give the name "pre-romanticism," reserving "classicism" for the preceding era (1774–1815).[12]

The Nováks' division into "Early Romanticism" (1830–48) and "Late Romanticism" (1848–59) also raises certain questions, for the second period is that of most of the novels and tales of Božena Němcová (1820–62) and of Karel Jaromír Erben's *Kytice* (The Bouquet; 1853). Are these really works of a "late romanticism"? Erben's models and parallels are found in such figures as the Brothers Grimm or Bürger. (Of course, many of the individual ballads of *Kytice* were published before 1848.) Němcová might well be called the Czech George Sand, without intending thus to belittle her own significance. Only in her strong ethnographic interest, stronger than its parallel in the work of Sand, does she seem to be moving away from romanticism to a kind of realism, but her love plots are hardly "late" romantic. And, if the period 1848–59 is to be regarded as "Late Romanticism," what are we to say in regard to the period after 1860? Are Vítězslav Hálek and Karolina Světlá not also romanticists? True, the Nováks begin realism with 1860, and give the rather heavy name of "Tendentious Realism in a Cosmopolitan Spirit" to the era of the 1860s and 1870s. One may be disturbed to learn that the significant models for this "tendentious realism" include Béranger and Heine, along with the movement of Young Germany. We may even ask if "tendentious realism" is realism at all, assum-

12 Felix Vodička also prefers the term "pre-romantic" rather than "classicist" for early Czech prose. See his study, *Počátky krásné prózy novočeské* (Prague, 1948), 315ff.

ing that the typical "realist" quality of assumed objectivity eliminates the possibility of tendentiousness, at least in manner. There is no doubt, of course, that the writing of the 1860s and 1870s had certain realist features: it depicted contemporary society, it emphasized typical details of colloquial speech and manners, and it took for its subject matter social and even economic problems of the here and now: the rights of women, the emerging proletariat, the democratization of society, etc. Its principal writers, Neruda, Světlá, Gustav Pfleger-Moravský, even Hálek in his ballads and prose works (though his lyrics and those of Adolf Heyduk are still closely tied to romantic sources and themes), all show this interest in problems of contemporary Czech society. Elsewhere I have proposed the term "pre-realism" for the era of the 1860s and 1870s,[13] preferring to retain "realism" for the more self-conscious movement which began later under the influence of the western realist and naturalist movement, under the aegis of Masaryk and the journal *Čas* (Time), founded by Jan Herben in 1886. "Pre-realism" is by analogy with "pre-romanticism," and implies a mixture of romantic and realistic traits; rather than a sharp and conscious break, it denotes a more gradual transition, a partial shifting of literary interests, but without a complete discarding of the forms or even the language and imagery of romanticism.

There is of course no great virtue in labels, and a literary history which deals only or chiefly in them will be devoid of content. Between those critics and literary historians who seek to generalize and to classify, and those who seek to find distinction, originality, and uniqueness, there will always be a conflict. Yet in the end the activity of literary history would seem to draw us more in the direction of intellectual generalization, while that of criticism would lead us rather toward discovering what is unique in a particular writer and work. If literary history is to be possible, then, we must make some effort to find a scheme or pattern.

In summary I would suggest, I hope modestly and tentatively, my own scheme for the periods in question:

1 Neo-Classicism (1785–1816),
2 Pre-Romanticism (1817–35),
3 Romanticism (1836–57),
4 Pre-Realism (1858–79).

In all cases except the final date of 1879, I have chosen literary events for the dating, rather than political ones. 1785 is the year of the publication of Thám's anthology, *Básně v řeči vázané*. 1817 is the year of the discovery of the forged *Královédvorský rukopis* (one might conceivably date the beginnings of Czech pre-romanticism as early as 1805, with the publication of Jungmann's translation of Chateaubriand's *Atala*, but this clearly was an isolated event). 1836 is the year of the publication of Mácha's poem *Máj*, a dynamic work which shocked the older, pre-romantic generation by its exaggerated individualism and subjectivism, its pessimistic fatalism, and its radically new use of iambic metre in Czech verse. (Though Mácha was writing

13 William E. Harkins, ed., *Anthology of Czech Literature* (New York, 1953), 100–3.

early in the 1830s, comparatively little of this work was published before 1836, and that which was did not inspire the same violent reaction.) Finally, 1858 is the year of the appearance of the first of the five successive *Máj* almanacs which brought Hálek and Neruda to the fore.

The year 1879 is simply the terminal date for the entire epoch I have been considering, and I do not propose it seriously as a boundary between literary periods. The following epoch, known typically, in the Nováks' as in other histories, as the period of the "Struggle between Nationalism and Cosmopolitanism," is a complex era which requires further and much closer examination than is possible here. For this yet another study would be required.

Changing Views on the Role of Dobrovský
in the Czech National Revival

ROBERT AUTY

Tam se w Bruně we hrob uložilo
Tělo otce Slawů učených,
Moře zásluh jeho wznešených
Na Europu celau působilo;
Zwláště český jazyk zpowinnilo
K činění mu díků skraušených,
An se tři sta roků ztracených
Tímto mužem jemu nawrátilo:
Zrozen w Uhřích; bydlel w Čechách; spatřil
Rusko, Polsko; zemřel w Morawě,
Aby tak náš celý národ sbratřil;
Proto zde si potomkowé jeho
Přisahejte lásku ke Sláwě,
Nebo toť jest oltář Dobrowského.

Jan Kollár, *Slávy dcera*[1]

This study was written in the spring of 1968 while the author held a visiting professorship at the University of California, Los Angeles.
1 1852 edition, sonnet 252: "There in Brno the father of learned Slavs has been laid to rest;

THE FIRST PERIOD of the Czech national revival is dominated by the figure of Josef Dobrovský (1753–1829); and for many who have studied him and his work with attention it is hard to dissociate him from the portrait by František Tkadlík, painted in Vienna in 1821 and now preserved in the museum (Památník národního písemnictví) at Strahov. In it the great scholar is brilliantly depicted gazing with a glance at once questing and sceptical at whatever of the real world reveals itself to him. We are reminded of the bust of Newton in Trinity College, Cambridge. Dobrovský too voyaged "through strange seas of thought, alone," even though his work was of less general import than that of the English astronomer. Understandably, this withdrawn and magisterial figure has attracted the close attention of scholars in every generation of his fellow-countrymen in the period since his death in 1829. Their assessments of the nature of his thought and achievement, and their analyses of his exact significance in the life of the nation, have varied very considerably. No attempt will be made here to enumerate all these different judgments; but a few representative assessments will be examined, ranging from 1833 to 1964, in the hope that some elements of the permanent value of Dobrovský's work in the cultural history of the Czechs may be singled out from those elements which, in different periods, were viewed subjectively through the eye of the beholder and not in an objective manner.

Immediately after Dobrovský's death the Royal Bohemian Scientific Society (Královská česká společnost nauk), of which he had been one of the earliest members, entrusted the historian František Palacký with the task of writing a biographical appreciation. The result was a 64-page essay that appeared in 1833, based on careful research among Dobrovský's own papers and on the reminiscences of his friends.[2] This elegant work, in which the dispassionate approach of the historian is supplemented by the warm affection of the friend and pupil, has scarcely been bettered by later writers, even though the details of Dobrovský's biography have been considerably supplemented by subsequent research. Palacký prefixed to his account the brief but penetrating sentences in which Goethe, who had himself died a few months earlier, summed up the achievement of the Czech scholar:

Abbé Joseph Dobrowsky, der Altmeister kritischer Geschichtforschung in Böhmen, dieser seltene Mann, welcher frühe schon dem allgemeinen Studium slawischer Sprachen und Geschichten mit genialem Bücherfleiss und herodotischen Reisen nachgegangen war, führte jeden Ertrag immer wieder mit Vorliebe auf die Volks- und Landeskunde von

the ocean of his noble merits has influenced the whole of Europe. The Czech language is under an especial obligation to offer him humble thanks, for through this man three hundred lost years were returned to it. Born in Hungary, he lived in Bohemia, visited Russia, Poland, died in Moravia, in order thus to bring together our whole nation in brotherhood. Therefore you, his descendants, should pledge love to Slavdom, for this is the altar of Dobrovský."

2 *Joseph Dobrowsky's Leben und gelehrtes Wirken, geschildert von Franz Palacky, ordentlichem Mitglied der königl. böhmischen Gesellschaft der Wissenschaften* (Prague, 1833).

Böhmen zurück, und vereinigte so mit dem grössten Ruhm in der Wissenschaft den selt-
neren eines popularen Namens. Wo er eingreift, da ist gleich der Meister sichtbar, der
seinen Gegenstand überall erfasst hat, und dem sich die Bruchstücke schnell zum Ganzen
reihen.[3]

We do not know how familiar Goethe was with Dobrovský's writings, but his
appreciation combines an understanding of the Czech scholar's work with a
characteristic Goethean approval of the "morphological" approach which had enabled Dobrovský, like Goethe, not merely to identify the partial elements with
which his investigations were concerned, but to envisage the whole which they constituted. It was entirely appropriate that Palacký should, at the opening of his study,
associate Dobrovský with Goethe. Their life-spans coincided almost exactly
(Goethe lived from 1749 to 1832) and, although Dobrovský totally lacked the imaginative gift which made Goethe into a great poet and novelist, his interests in
scholarship were of a similar breadth to those of the German writer. Both were
among the last representatives of the universal, polymathic approach to scholarship
and literature which did not survive the early nineteenth century. It may be supposed, also, that the two men shared certain attitudes as a result of the fact that
they were coevals in the civilization of central Europe. "Das Klassische nenne ich
das Gesunde," Goethe once said, "und das Romantische das Kranke."[4] What we
know of Dobrovský's attitude to the romantic generation of Václav Hanka and Josef
Jungmann would lead us to believe that he would have strongly approved this
judgment.

Palacký's account is very factual, but he permits himself a number of significant
statements which enable us to see what precisely he considered to be of value in the
life and work of Dobrovský. Fundamental is his statement that Dobrovský, though
sometimes describing himself, according to his place of birth, as *Ungarus Jerme-
tensis*,[5] and sometimes ascribed to the German nation by virtue of his education and
the language which he used most frequently in his vernacular writings, always considered himself a Czech: "Er selbst bekannte sich jedoch stets zu den Böhmen, und

3 "Abbé Joseph Dobrovský, the supreme master of critical historical research in Bohemia,
  this remarkable man, who had from an early age pursued the broad study of Slavonic
  languages and history through brilliant study and Herodotean travels, loved always to direct
  all the fruits of his learning towards the people and province of Bohemia; in this way he
  united with the greatest fame in scholarship the rarer fame of a popular reputation. His
  touch is everywhere that of the master who has embraced every aspect of his subject and
  for whom the disparate parts are quickly ordered into a whole." F. Palacký, *Joseph Dobrowsky's Leben*, 5, quoted from *Berliner Jahrbücher für wissenschaftliche Kritik* (March
  1830).
4 "I call classical what is healthy, romantic what is sick." (*Gespräche mit Eckermann*, under
  2 April 1829.)
5 Dobrovský was born at Gyarmat near Ráb in Hungary, where his father was then serving
  as a non-commissioned officer in the Dragonerregiment Erzherzog Joseph.

nannte das Böhmische ausdrücklich seine Muttersprache."[6] This statement is an indirect criticism of Jungmann who, in a bitter moment, had referred to Dobrovský as "ein slavisierender Deutsche."[7] It was not nationality but generation that caused Dobrovský to use the German language for his scholarly writings.

Palacký notes, without special emphasis, Dobrovský's intention, expressed in his review of Czech literature for the year 1779: "bloss referiren [sic], nicht raisonnieren."[8] This approach to his material remained characteristic of Dobrovský throughout his life. He was concerned with facts, not theories. His friend and disciple, Jernej Kopitar, echoed his master's words when he said: "Fakta entscheiden hier [scil. in the study of language], nicht Räsonnements."[9]

In one crucial question the witness of Palacký, the contemporary and admirer of Dobrovský, is of the first importance. He discusses, as was unavoidable, the question of Dobrovský's views on the future of the Czech language. "Dass er bei all seiner Liebe zu dieser Sprache," Palacký wrote, "dennoch so wenig böhmisch schrieb, kam daher, weil er die Hoffnung eines Wiederauflebens der böhmischen Nationalliteratur längst aufgegeben hatte, und auch später immer der Ansicht war, dass dieselbe sich höchstens nur als genuine Volksliteratur ausbilden könne."[10] Dobrovský's doubts about the future of the Czech language were clearly expressed in the first edition of his *Geschichte der böhmischen Sprache und Literatur* (History of the Czech Language and Literature; Prague, 1792). It has sometimes been asserted that his omission of these sentiments from the later edition (*Geschichte der böhmischen Sprache und ältern Literatur*, Prague, 1818) is a proof that he had changed his mind as to the future prospects of his native language. The testimony of the sober and sympathetic Palacký speaks against such an interpretation.

Palacký, though no philologist, recognized accurately the specific merit of Dobrovský's work on the Czech and, in general, the Slavonic languages. "Dobrovský war der erste Forscher," he wrote, "dessen Blick ins Innere des wundersamen Organismus der slawischen Sprachen eindrang und ihn aufdeckte."[11] Although Palacký does not support this judgment in detail, it would be possible to do so. Dobrovský was not concerned with isolated details of vocabulary, such as had been the pre-

6 *Joseph Dobrowsky's Leben*, 7: "He himself always declared his allegiance to the Czechs and expressly stated that Czech was his native language."

7 "A Slavicizing German." See J. Hanuš *et al.*, *Literatura česká devatenáctého století*, 1 (2nd ed., Prague, 1911), 286.

8 *Joseph Dobrowsky's Leben*, 15: "Simply to report, not to argue."

9 "Facts decide here, not arguments." Bartholomäus [Jernej] Kopitar, *Grammatik der slavischen Sprache in Krain, Kärnten und Steyermark [sic]* (Ljubljana, 1808), XLVI.

10 *Joseph Dobrowsky's Leben*, 37: "The fact that for all his love for this language he wrote so little in Czech was because he had long since abandoned the hope of a revival of the Czech national literature, and even later on was always of the opinion that it could at best be cultivated as a simple literature of the common people."

11 *Ibid.*, 47: "Dobrovský was the first scholar who penetrated the innermost being of the marvellous organism of the Slavonic languages and revealed it to view."

occupation of the fantastically puristic Pohl.[12] To Dobrovský the Czech language was indeed an organism, not an assemblage of individual items; and in his grammar[13] he characterized this organism – the classical Czech language of the sixteenth century. Furthermore, in his Old Church Slavonic grammar[14] he showed his awareness of the existence of laws which governed and regularized the relationship of the Slavonic languages ("dialects") to one another.

"Ihm galt überall die Wahrheit," Palacký wrote, "andere Absichten kannte er nicht."[15] Dobrovský could not have wished for a better epitaph.

Three years after Dobrovský's death Jan Kollár published, in the second edition of his *Slávy dcera* (Daughter of Sláva), the sonnet which has been quoted as an epigraph to this article. The first three lines of the sestet seem to be an expansion of the elegant Latin epitaph which was inscribed on the tombstone erected in Brno by the munificence of Count Hugo von Salm-Reiferscheid:

HUNGARIA. ME. GENUIT.

BOHEMIA. SIBI. LITERISQUE. VINDICAVIT.

MORAVIA. REGENDIS. SACRORUM. ALUMNIS. QUONDAM. ADHIBUIT.

NUNC. PIA. COMPOSUIT.

SLAVICA. QUA. PATET. TERRA. NON. IGNORAT.

AMICI. LUGENT.

E. QUEIS. HUGO. COMES. DE. SALM. HOC. MONUM. P.[16]

In his tribute to Dobrovský's role in the revival of the Czech language Kollár spoke, with an acceptable poetic hyperbole, of the "three hundred lost years" that, through Dobrovský's work, had been returned to the Czech language. The appreciation is entirely just. But for Dobrovský the "lost years" would hardly have been recovered; the Czech language might well have been revived, but not in the classical form which he restored to it. Reading Kollár's sonnet in the light of our knowledge of Dobrovský's own views and practice we can appreciate the historical irony of the fact that the man who was concerned only with "referiren [sic], nicht raisonnieren," and who had no confidence in the restoration of the Czech literary language to its ancient status among the tongues of Europe, was in fact one of the chief agents in the process which led to just that restoration.

12 Jan Václav Pohl, the author of a grammar whose third edition, *Neuverbesserte böhmische Grammatik*, published in 1783, was sharply criticized by Dobrovský in his *Literarisches Magazin von Böhmen und Mähren* (Prague, 1786–7) pt. 3, 136–40.

13 First edition: *Ausführliches Lehrgebäude der böhmischen Sprache* (Prague, 1809); second edition: *Lehrgebäude der böhmischen Sprache* (Prague, 1819).

14 *Institutiones linguae slavicae dialecti veteris* (Vienna, 1822).

15 Palacký, *Joseph Dobrowsky's Leben*, 53: "For him the truth was always paramount; other aims were unknown to him."

16 "Hungary bore me; Bohemia claimed me for herself and for letters; Moravia at one time gave me the duty of teaching students of religion and now in pious duty has received my remains; my name is known to the wide lands of the Slavs; my friends mourn; and one of them, Hugo Count of Salm, has erected this monument."

In his poetical reconstruction of Dobrovský's epitaph Kollár interprets Dobrovský's journeys through the Slavonic lands as a contribution towards the unification, or at least reconciliation, of the Slavs. The clause introduced by *aby* is ambiguous: it may be final or consecutive, so that we are not sure whether Kollár was ascribing to Dobrovský the intention of increasing brotherly feelings among the Slavs or whether he was simply stating that such feelings had been in fact intensified as a result of his life and work. Here again it would seem that Dobrovský achieved results which were no part of his intentions. His "herodotische Reisen" had severely practical aims: they were made for purposes of scholarship and not in the pursuit of Slavonic brotherhood. Kollár's phrase seems to claim Dobrovský's travels as in some way foreshadowing the poetical pilgrimage that forms the subject of *Slávy dcera*. As a poetical conceit the idea is attractive and justifiable, but if it was ascribing an intention to Dobrovský it was not a faithful reflection of the historical reality.

In 1883 V. Brandl published the first full-length biography of Dobrovský.[17] As a purely factual account it has still not been superseded. It is a typical product of the positivist school of literary or cultural history, and none the worse for that. All later writers on Dobrovský are in Brandl's debt. At the end of his study the author adds to the purely factual account of Dobrovský's life and writings a chapter in which he attempts to characterize the great scholar. The sobriety and rational objectivity of his thought and writing, sometimes developing into coldness, are justly stressed. We gain the impression, however, that Brandl felt it necessary to defend his subject against possible attacks. He almost overemphasizes the fact that Dobrovský, despite his critical and often negative spirit, loved his nation; and he seems to be trying to persuade a sceptical public that Dobrovský, though no romantic enthusiast, nevertheless deserved the admiration and affection of his fellow-countrymen. "Rozumová, nepoetická povaha jeho jest na příčině, že *cit* potomkův raději se ohlíží po Kolarovi [*sic*], Jungmannovi atd.; ale když *věda* česká a slavistika vůbec za našich dnů zpátečnou cestu koná k původu a počátku svému, všudy po té pouti září jí vstříc slavné jméno *Josefa Dobrovského* a povždy zářiti bude.[18]

In 1895 T. G. Masaryk published his work on the "Czech question" (*Česká otázka*, Prague, 1895),[19] the most important of the series of studies in which the great Czech thinker and statesman sought to re-evaluate his nation's history and draw lessons from it for future action. The first chapter of this work deals with the first period of the Czech national revival, extending in Masaryk's conception to 1811, and is entitled "The Age of Dobrovský." The Czech revival is here viewed as a process leading to the development of a specifically Czech ideology of Slavonic humanism

17 V. Brandl, *Život Josefa Dobrovského* ("Sborník Matice moravské," ɪ; Brno, 1883).
18 *Ibid.*, 277: "His rationalistic and unpoetical nature is the reason why the *feelings* of his successors are rather drawn to Kollár, Jungmann, etc.; but now that Czech *scholarship* and Slavonic studies in general are in our time finding the way back to their original source they see shining towards them on that path the glorious name of *Joseph Dobrovský* whose lustre will never be dimmed."
19 References to this work are made from the reprint that appeared in Prague in 1948.

ultimately deriving from the ethical concepts of the Hussites and the Unitas Fratrum (Bohemian Brethren). The importance of Dobrovský's historicism is correctly, if briefly, noted when the author characterizes one of the aims of the Czech movement of the revival period as the endeavour to forge links with the past;[20] and the fact that the great scholar was firmly rooted in the beliefs and practice of the Enlightenment is clearly brought out, with specific mention of the importance of Josephinism and the free thought of the eighteenth century for the formation of his attitudes and methods of work.[21] A new concept, fundamental to Masaryk's theory of the Czech revival, is expressed rather more schematically: the belief that the rational free thought of the Enlightenment in Bohemia was in some way descended from the ideas of the Czech reformation.[22] To this, Masaryk added the further assertion that Dobrovský carried on the idea of *Humanität* which was evolved by Herder. This assertion is not precisely documented or substantiated; and it would seem that Masaryk was here projecting back to Dobrovský ideas which were in fact formulated by the following generation, by Kollár and his contemporaries. It is certainly correct, as Masaryk wrote, that Dobrovský felt and thought as a Slav and that in certain of his writings he spoke warmly of the "Slavonic mind" (*um*), but it is anachronistic to ascribe to Dobrovský the kind of Slavonic humanism that was formulated in the writings of Kollár.

Masaryk felt it necessary to defend Dobrovský against the charge of lacking faith in his nation. Here he thought that Brandl had not gone far enough. Dobrovský was not isolated in his pessimism as to the future of the Czech language: it was shared, at various times, even by Jungmann, Pavel Josef Šafařík, and Kollár.[23] Very important is Masaryk's recognition that at the time of Dobrovský nationality was not yet – at any rate in Bohemia – conceived solely in terms of language and that the fact that he wrote for the most part in German was no sign of any lack of patriotism.[24]

Much of the picture of Dobrovský drawn by Masaryk can be accepted by the impartial historian; nevertheless, the picture remains slightly distorted by the desire to assimilate the liberal Catholic of the Enlightenment to a supposed continuous stream of ethical humanism deriving from the Czech reformation and handed on by the German thinkers of the eighteenth century.

Despite the attempts of Brandl and Masaryk to modify the "coldly respectful"[25]

20 *Česká otázka*, 8.
21 *Ibid.*, 12ff.
22 *Ibid.*, 14.
23 *Ibid.*, 37f.
24 *Ibid.*, 40ff.
25 "Protože ve vědě vláda romantiky trvá u nás o dvě pokolení déle než v poesii, zůstával poměr k Dobrovskému málem šedesát let uctivě chladný, a lesk jeho jména byl zastiňován trojhvězdím Jungmann, Šafařík, Palacký, bylo třeba naukového převratu, aby se Josefu Dobrovskému dostalo nového triumfu" (Arne Novák, *Josef Dobrovský* [Prague, 1928], 5)/"Owing to the fact that in scholarship the reign of romanticism lasted two generations longer in our country than it did in poetry, the attitude to Dobrovský remained one of cold respect for almost sixty

attitude to Dobrovský, this attitude continued to be held by many Czechs well into the present century. Even some of the publications which were inspired by the centenary of his death in 1929 still reflect a certain unease and lack of warmth. One such is the study of Arne Novák of 1928.[26] He pointed out that Dobrovský's reputation had risen again after the victory of reason over romanticism in the "Manuscripts" controversy, but that it was nevertheless still necessary to present a clear image of the great scholar to the Czech public, to transform him from a legend into a reality: "Bylo by nejčestnějším výtěžkem stého výročí smrti Josefa Dobrovského, kdyby úcta chovaná k jeho jménu byla naplněna konkrétním obsahem, a kdyby jeho mohutná osobnost vystoupila před nás do plného jasu z teplé a nazlátlé mlhy domněnek legendárních, kterou ji obklopila nejprve obraznost básnická a později konstruktivní horlivost myslitelská."[27] Despite his good intentions it cannot be said that Arne Novák did justice to the historical Dobrovský. The reason seems to lie in Novák's own distaste for the ideals and atmosphere of the Enlightenment, which in any case he misinterpreted in some respects.

Most surprisingly, Dobrovský is criticized for being "unhistorical": "A přece i jako jazykovědec byl Dobrovský věrným synem osmnáctého století, vyznavačem osvícenských zásad, stoupencem nehistorické metody: nevystoupil ze své doby, ač vytušil mnohé, k čemu mohly soustavně přikročiti teprve generace pozdější."[28] This remark must be taken in conjunction with another passage in which Novák describes the age of Maria Theresa and Joseph II as "unhistorical, indeed antihistorical."[29] It is to be feared that he is here falling into the same error of which he accuses Dobrovský: it is the twentieth-century literary historian who has failed to rise above his own age and to understand the past in its true essence. One of the principal characteristics of the eighteenth-century intellectual movement in central Europe was its historicism. Preoccupation with the past, and in particular with the documents of the past, was a dominant feature among the intellectuals of Bohemia in the second half of that century. Gelasius Dobner, Fortunát Durych, Adaukt Voigt, Karel Ungar, František Martin Pelcl, Dobrovský, all bear witness to this

years and the brilliance of his name was overshadowed by the constellation of Jungmann, Šafařík, and Palacký: a revolution in scholarship was needed for Josef Dobrovský to achieve a new triumph."

26 *Josef Dobrovský*.

27 *Ibid.*, 6: "The most honourable possible result of the centenary of Josef Dobrovský's death would be for the respect men feel towards his name to be given a concrete content, and for his tremendous personality to emerge before our eyes into full brightness out of the warm, gold-tinged haze of legendary imaginings with which it has been enveloped first by poetical fantasy and then by the constructive fervour of thinkers."

28 *Ibid.*, 38: "And yet, even as a philologist, Dobrovský was a faithful son of the eighteenth century, professing the principles of the Enlightenment and practising an unhistorical method: he never emerged from his own age, although he sensed much which could be systematically achieved only by later generations."

29 *Ibid.*, 46.

trend. The fact that these scholars exercised their historical techniques on specific texts rather than on vague traditions and a priori conceptions speaks for, not against, their "historical method." It is possible to criticize Dobrovský for excessive caution in his approach to historical material, but to accuse him of an "unhistorical" approach is unjustifiable. Arne Novák no doubt felt that Dobrovský was lacking in that imaginative gift which can reconstruct past periods of history; but such a gift is of no avail if the primary sources have not first been studied and evaluated. This was the task that Dobrovský and the other Enlightenment scholars in Bohemia and elsewhere in central Europe set themselves.

In Novák's study Dobrovský is further criticized for having failed to produce a universal system of Slavonic orthography, to engage in a more profound study of Slavonic mythology, and to write the history of Slavonic Bible translations. The first of these three tasks would have been otiose. Despite the insistence of Kopitar there is not the least hope that the awakening Slavonic nations would have agreed to any such arbitrary unitary system. In view of the encyclopaedic breadth of Dobrovský's preserved writings, we can only deplore the censorious tone of a critic who blames him for not having produced even more.

The bicentenary of Dobrovský's birth in 1953 brought forth a further series of tributes. The collective volume *Josef Dobrovský 1753–1953*, edited by Bohuslav Havránek and Julius Dolanský,[30] contains a number of valuable factual studies which are of permanent importance to any student of Dobrovský. In addition to these, there are two essays, by Dolanský and Milan Machovec, which attempt a general characterization of Dobrovský and his work from a Marxist standpoint. Dolanský's essay[31] very rightly points out the basic trends of Dobrovský's work: the desire to attain truth[32] and the historical principle.[33] It is, however, mainly concerned to interpret his work in accordance with Marxist theory as practised in the late Stalinist period, and in consequence reaches a number of erroneous conclusions. Dobrovský, we are told, was aware of the principles governing the formation of nations which had more recently been authoritatively formulated by J. V. Stalin, even though he had not been able to formulate them in the correct Marxist terms.[34] On several occasions the author claims that Dobrovský's views tended towards philosophical materialism.[35] This view seems wholly to misinterpret the eighteenth-century deism which is displayed in many of Dobrovský's writings. The denial of divine intervention in human affairs was by no means unusual among the progressive Christians of the eighteenth century and is, indeed, already implicit in the systems of Leibniz and Wolff. There is no reason whatever to describe Dobrovský as a materialist or a potential materialist.

30 Published by the Czechoslovak Academy of Sciences in 1953.
31 Julius Dolanský, "Zrození buditele," in *Josef Dobrovský 1753–1953*, 11–45.
32 *Ibid.*, 13.   33 *Ibid.*, 27ff.
34 *Ibid.*, 26.   35 *Ibid.*, e.g., 28, 35, 45.

Milan Machovec, in his article in the same volume,[36] is concerned to represent Dobrovský, if not as a materialist, then as one who approached close to this desirable state: "Dobrovského odklon od katolictví – protože byl odklonem ne theologa, ale vědce – není odklonem k protestantismu, ale k materialismu." "Když Dobrovský pracuje – tíhne k materialismu." Nevertheless, Machovec admits that Dobrovský remained a deist.[37] The victory of Marxism in the Slavonic countries is seen as a realization of Dobrovský's visions.[38] It is sad to observe these attempts to interpret a historical figure in such an unhistorical way. It is the right of a Marxist to interpret historical events and personages in accordance with the categories on which he bases his approach; but it is unjustifiable to interpret the thoughts and words of a past age in accordance with the ideological systems of today. The historian should attempt, to the limit of his capacity, to understand past ages in their own terms before subjecting them to his categories. The application of a priori concepts easily leads to the involuntary distortion of facts. Thus Machovec states: "... od smrti Josefa II. cítil k reakční rakouské vládě jen odpor a pohrdání."[39] Such an assertion is bewildering when we consider that on 25 September 1791, fifteen months after the death of Joseph II, Dobrovský delivered, in the presence of the new emperor Leopold II, his famous oration "Über die Ergebenheit und Anhänglichkeit der slawischen Völker an das Erzhaus Österreich" (On the Devotion and Attachment of the Slavonic Peoples to the Ruling House of Austria). That Dobrovský's attitude, like that of many others, changed after the untimely death of Leopold in 1792 is likely enough, but the statement by Machovec cannot be substantiated.

"Nikoli upadající kosmopolitní buržoasie, překrucující jeho dílo, ale jedině my máme právo se k němu hlásit," Machovec states towards the conclusion of his article.[40] This is a considerable claim. The right to declare allegiance to Dobrovský cannot so easily be withdrawn from past generations, from Palacký and Kollár, from T. G. Masaryk, Jan Jakubec, and Arne Novák. It may even be suggested that some Slavonic philologists who are neither Czechs nor Marxists have the right to declare their allegiance to the founder of their discipline.

Eleven years later Milan Machovec published a fuller study of Dobrovský[41] in which some, though not all, of his earlier essay was incorporated. Many of the ex-

36 Milan Machovec, "Filosofický význam díla Josefa Dobrovského," in *Josef Dobrovský 1753–1953*, 46–86.
37 *Ibid.*, 65, 67, 68. The Czech passages run as follows: "Dobrovský's move away from Catholicism – because it was that of a scholar, not of a theologian – is not a move towards Protestantism but towards materialism." "When Dobrovský is at work he tends towards materialism."
38 *Ibid.*, 78, footnote 174.
39 *Ibid.*, 79: "... after the death of Joseph II he felt only disgust and scorn for the reactionary Austrian government."
40 *Ibid.*, 86. "It is not the decadent cosmopolitan bourgeoisie, who distort his work, but we alone who have the right to declare allegiance to him."
41 Milan Machovec, *Josef Dobrovský* (Prague, 1964).

treme formulations to which exception has been taken above were removed, and the work shows evidence of a more tolerant and more genuinely historical approach. The roots of Dobrovský's thought in the historicism of the Central European Enlightenment and in the liberal Christian ideology of Josephinism, interpreting that term in its widest sense (*katolické osvícenství*), are accurately and skilfully characterized. Although the author still speaks of "materialist elements" in Dobrovský's thought, he freely admits that he never became a materialist and indeed specifically states that religion always remained a necessity for him and that he never ceased to be a Christian.

It is refreshing to read the statement that it is nonsensical to interpret Dobrovský's work on narrow class lines.[42] On occasion, however, even in this new work, Machovec seems to allow a priori assumptions to distort his picture of the great scholar. While admitting that Dobrovský was a Josephinist in the wider sense, he is at pains to claim that he did not identify himself with the concept of the state as applied by Joseph II and his advisers (*étatistické pojetí osvícení*). It would be wrong, he argues, to describe Dobrovský as "simply a Josephinist." This leads to a very complicated justification of Dobrovský's acceptance of a state function as director of the *Generalseminar* of Olomouc.[43] At this point in his career, we are told, he gave preference to the atmosphere of Josephinism rather than to that of the patriotic nobility. It is surely only as a result of subsequent historical analysis that such clear alternatives can be posited. There is no need to suppose that Dobrovský had to make a choice between the *Landespatriotismus*, which was no doubt expressed in the salons of the Nostic and Kinský families who gave him such generous patronage, and support of the imperial reorganization of the church in the Habsburg realms. Dobrovský was not without ambition for advancement in the church; and the opportunity afforded him in Olomouc to influence the younger generation in no way precluded a *landespatriotisch* rather than a centralistic approach to the cultural problems of Bohemia and Moravia. Such a combination of local nationalism and loyalty to the dynasty is moreover apparent in Dobrovský's loyal speech to Leopold II, though Machovec is fully justified in noting here a shift to the idea of the Slavonic nation, as against the Bohemian province, as the basis of Dobrovský's loyalties.[44] The fact that these loyalties are subordinated in explicit terms to the House of Habsburg needs no excuses or explanations. In the context of the age such an attitude was a normal one for any Czech intellectual, and Machovec does not do justice to it by speaking of it as being "veiled in the form of 'Austro-Slavism'" or by the deprecatory phrase "'pečet' austroslavismu a tím určité 'loyálnosti.'"[45] Such expressions are anachronistic when applied to the atmosphere of 1792.

Despite these survivals of dogmatic views from an earlier and unhappier period of Marxist thought, Machovec's study must be welcomed as a thoughtful and posi-

42 *Ibid.*, 85.   43 *Ibid.*, 82, 84ff.
44 *Ibid.*, 113ff.
45 *Ibid.*, 115: "the seal of Austro-Slavism and thus of a sort of 'loyalism.'"

tive contribution to our knowledge and understanding of Josef Dobrovský. The field remains open for a full critical biography of the unwitting founder of the Czech national revival, based on the extensive documentation now available. Such a work would have to be based on a deep and sympathetic understanding of the intellectual and social conditions of eighteenth-century Bohemia against the wider background of central European and especially German scholarship and literature at this time. To "see Dobrovský plain" and not in the light of our own problems and prejudices remains an important task for Slavists and historians.

Locus Amoenus:
An Aspect of National Tradition

MILADA SOUČKOVÁ

THE CZECH NATIONAL ANTHEM is not tuned to the thunder of marching steps, nor is its melody built upon majestic harmonies characteristic of some others of its kind. Words like *tsar*, expressions like *enfants de la patrie* or *Gott erhalte*, are not to be found in its text. It lives by a lyrical mood.

> Kde domov můj?
> Hučí voda po lučinách,
> bory šumí po skalinách,
> v sadě skví se jara květ,
> zemský ráj to na pohled!
> A to je ta krásná země –
> země česká – domov můj![1]

The poem was written by Josef Kajetan Tyl (1808–56), for the musical *Fidlovačka aneb žádný hněv a žádná rvačka*, which had its première in December 1834. As its title suggests, it had as model *Leopold's Tag oder weder Menschenhass noch Reue* (1820) by Adolf Bäuerle, the popular playwright of post-Napoleonic Vienna.

---

1 This is the original text, which differs from the present text as it is sung. "Kde domov můj?" (Where Is My Home?) became the official national anthem of the Czechoslovak Republic in 1918.

The composer of the music for Tyl's play was František Škroup (1801–62), and one may say that it was the music, and especially the song "Kde domov můj?," which won the acclaim of the public. The song penetrated into the fashionable music circles of the period: the Czech singers Jan Kř. Písek (1814–75) and Karel Strakatý (1809–68) introduced it to the guests of the Rothschild salons, to the English court, and to the international society in Marienbad; the violinists Ondříček and Kubelík played the catchy melody in their concerts, and Dvořák used the motif for the incidental music of a play about the composer Škroup.[2] The song, the *quodlibet* as it was called then, was performed on the stage by the blind violinist Mareš accompanied by his daughter Bětuška, who played the horn; they joined in the *dohrávka*, the coda played by instruments particularly capable of sustaining a lyrical mood. The critic of *Bohemia*, the official Prague German newspaper, also praised the music but attacked the tendency of the play.[3] The audience of the first night of *Fidlovačka* must have been unaware that the pleasant melody of "Kde domov můj?" might contain emotions transcending the moment. Their patriotic reaction – if they had any – was connected with those parts of the play which were not to the taste of the reviewer in *Bohemia*. Tyl himself, of course, had no intention of writing anything like a national hymn. If he had, he probably would have brought forth some pompous verses of the same character as the incidental poems by his better-known contemporaries Karel Hynek Mácha and Karel Jaromír Erben.[4]

If one leaves aside the respect and awe due to a national hymn and reads "Kde domov můj?" as a poem, its lines 2–5 offer the reader the image of a landscape fashioned after the current pattern of the romantic song. Still, whence come the meadows, the pines on the rocks, and the murmur of the stream, which all had the power to coalesce into the image of *patria*?

The Czech literary historians tried to find an answer. Professor F. Strejček interpreted lines 2–5 as a poetic sublimation of the Prague pastoral of that time. He thought that "voda hučí po lučinách" was in reality the brook Botič in the valley of Nusle, where the yearly fiesta *Fidlovačka* took place. He also related the line "v sadě skví se jara květ" to Wimmerovy sady, a renowned park of Romantic Prague.[5] Guided by these interpretations, the author of a book about the Czech national anthem, J. V. Šmejkal, read "po lučinách" as the meadows of the Vltava island Císařská louka and "bory" as the pines of the valley Šárka.[6] But the anthem's image of fatherland was not born from the idealized and poeticized description of Šárka, Císařská louka, Nuselské údolí, or any other similarly popular site of Prague. The

2 J. V. Šmejkal, *Píseň písní národa českého* (Prague, 1935), 58–62; cf. Miloslav Hýsek, *J. K. Tyl* (Prague, 1926), 40–5.

3 Hýsek, *J. K. Tyl*, 110; *Bohemia*, 1834, no. 153: "... das ganze dreht sich um einem Gendanken, welcher bei den jungen böhmischen Schriftstellern zur fixen Idee zu werden droht nämlich dass es eine Schande sei, in Böhmen nicht böhmisch zu sprechen ..."

4 K. H. Mácha, *Na příchod krále* (1835); K. J. Erben, *Věštba* (1854).

5 F. Strejček, *Naše řeč*, 18/8 (Prague, 1934), 225–9; cf. Hýsek, *J. K. Tyl*, 56–67.

6 *Píseň písní národa českého*, 56–7.

antecedents of "Kde domov můj?" should be sought in another and less positivist direction.

At the end of the eighteenth and during the first decades of the nineteenth century, the Czech national idea was alive and spoke with eloquence in scholarly and literary works. The cultural situation of those days was limited, and yet the scholars succeeded in their determination to revive the literary monuments of the Czech mediaeval past and to find an interested public for them. Among those works published *ad maiorem patriae gloriam* was also the Latin chronicle by Cosmas Pragensis, in the first volume of *Scriptores rerum bohemicarum*, edited by Josef Dobrovský and Martin Pelcl in 1783. The Cosmasian epic about the foundation of Bohemia, about Krok and his three daughters, soon became national property and in a simplified form entered the imagination of Czech people. Tyl was not an exception and he knew of course more than the average *vlastenec* (patriot). Although he was not a scholar like Václav Hanka, who had mediaeval texts at his fingertips, he was familiar enough with Cosmas' epic to write the short story "Čech a Lech" (Čech and Lech), published in the magazine *Květy* in 1835; its subject is the arrival of the two brothers, Čech and Lech, in the territory which was and is known as Bohemia.

Tyl's narrative reminds one of Josef Linda's *Záře nad pohanstvem* (Dawn over Paganism; 1818) and its stylistic mannerisms as they were worked out by the early Czech romantics, with Josef Jungmann and his translation of Chateaubriand's *Atala* at their head. Tyl conceived the story of the forefather Čech as a part of the sixth-century European migration – "v tom věku se hýbal ... rozlehlý a slavný národ Slovanů"[7] – one cannot miss the touch of modern history and of Panslavic ideology. These Slavic people were coming from their old far-away homesteads – "národ na tomto tahu z domů dávnověkých"[8] – until the leader stopped, arrested by the view of pleasant meadows, woods, rivers, and brooks. In this passage it is not difficult to relate "Čech a Lech" with Cosmas' *Chronicon*. The mediaeval historiographer was geographically more precise and made the Slavic *dux* stop "circa montem Rzip, inter duos fluvios, scilicet Ogram et Wltavam,"[9] whereas Tyl used the fairy-tale style: "... přecházeli vrchy, lesy a řeky a pouště, až se přibrali k vysoké hoře" (they crossed mountains, woods, rivers and deserts, until they arrived at a high mountain).[10] Cosmas' and Tyl's descriptions of the territory have parallel elements: "... serae sylvarum innumerae ... et bestiarum gregibus vix sufficiebat tellus ... Aquae illic perspicuae ... Similiter et pisces suaves ..."[11] – "Vidí stinné háje ... procházela se po ní [úrodné půdě] tučná stáda ... hojnost potoků rybních ..."[12] Tyl also took

7 *Sebrané spisy J. K. Tyla*, pt. II (Prague, 1908), 83.
8 *Ibid.*, 80.
9 *Cosmae Ecclesiae Pragensis Decani Chronicon Bohemorum, Scriptores rerum bohemicarum*, I (Prague, 1783), 7.
10 *Sebrané spisy J. K. Tyla*, 81.
11 *Chronicon*, 6.
12 *Sebrané spisy J. K. Tyla*, 81, 83.

over the eponym – "quia tu(o) Pater diceris Bohemus, dicatur et terra Bohemia?":[13] "zemí Čechovou čili českou, a sebe Čechy"[14] – and added Herderian overtones: Czechs were peace-loving people (*lid mírumilovný*).

Cosmas, the original poet of the Czech fatherland, was not entirely self-sufficient either, at least as far as rhetoric is concerned. His image of the settlement of the Czech nation depended largely on the teaching of the mediaeval *ars grammatica*. As little as we know about him, we do know – for he tells us so in the concluding parts of his chronicle – that he studied in Liège; but even without this biographical information we must recognize in him a man steeped in mediaeval learning, whether taught from *Donati de partibus orationis ars minor* or the work of some other standard Latin grammarian in current use in mediaeval schools. Cosmas' style was formed on examples from Cicero, Suetonius, Livy, Horace, Terence, and of course Virgil. The *Prisciani Partitione duodecim versum Aeneidos* was a text-book teaching Latin with the help of the twelve cantos of the *Aeneid*; the *Eclogues* and *Georgics* served to train the student in the description of the pastoral.

The Czech scholars give as the model for Cosmas' chronicle the Bavarian Regino (d. 915) and his *Abbatis Prumiensis Chronicon*, well known during the early Middle Ages. However, the similarities between Regino's and Cosmas' work in many cases might be reduced to the cultural compactness of their centuries, Regino's tenth and Cosmas' twelfth. Cosmas' invocation of the Muse – to give an example – depends much more on the mediaeval tenets of style than on Regino. On the other hand, the oral tradition (hearsay) – Regino's *narratione seniorum* and Cosmas' *senum fabulosa narratio* – must indeed be considered an influence; yet, at the same time and under closer investigation, it is precisely the comparison of the two expressions which tells the difference between them. Regino speaks simply about persons older than he and therefore able to know or remember events more distant in time than he can. Cosmas, though his expressions preserve Regino's meaning, goes beyond it in the direction of poetry; the word *senum* in the vicinity of *fabulosa* (*narratio*) suggests more than one person or persons old enough to remember the remote past or familiar with its traditions. Cosmas' *senes* are prophets of biblical age and memory and sybiline power, and not merely old people. Cosmas' poetic intent is present in the Virgilian hexameters – over two hundred of them – which are interspersed in the prose of his *Chronicon*.

There is nothing comparable in Regino, whose prose operates with a constant calendar formula *Anno domini incarnationis*, which is much less conspicuous in Cosmas' text. Regino attempted to write the "world's history," whereas Cosmas restricted it to the minimum, to a few sentences – *Post deluvium effusione* ... The epic art of *Chronicon Bohemorum* is striking in its beginning; only later does it acquire those characteristics for which it was rightly or wrongly compared with Regino, and where it is essentially a record and comment on events, whether a

13 *Chronicon*, 7.
14 *Sebrané spisy J. K. Tyla*, 83.

hard winter or a political situation. The *senum fabulosa narratio*, on the contrary, signals an original epic, and this even if one allows a margin for its existing oral tradition – Virgil's story of Aeneas too drew on folk tradition. Cosmas' Libussia, Lubussa – the modern Libuše – exists primarily as a Virgilian Sibyl, the Sibyl of Aeneid and in a way that of the Fourth Eclogue: *Libussia fuit Pythonissa ut Cumae Sibylla.*[15] For Cosmas it must have mattered that Sibylla was connected with the settlement of Aeneas in Italy, with the prediction of the Roman empire and perhaps also of the coming of Christ. Cosmas' choice of Sibylla-Libuše as the dominating figure of his myth-history was poetically proper and the propriety was tested by modern Czech intellectual history. The Czechs never lost Cosmas' myth from their mind's horizon. Cosmas witnessed an overwhelming historical process: the gradual change from paganism to Christian society, from decentralized local political power to organized feudal society. His book was composed in the spirit of this great vision. And it was this spirit and its temper which the Czech literary renascence adopted.

Cosmas conceived the arrival of Čech in the territory of Bohemia along the lines of the Virgilian epos. The Roman nation descended from a fugitive exile from Troy; the Czech nation and its abodes were founded by a fugitive who sought a better future for himself and for his progeny. Like Aeneas, Čech was seen by Cosmas in the perspective of the political and cultural expansion of his times. The Czech patriots of the nineteenth century could embrace Cosmas' epic because it suited their ambitions; all the glory was in the past, yet it might be recaptured again. The Cosmasian epic came from that climate where nations are established and states created, where men are called from the plough to reign. *Dux vester duobus variis bubus arat.*[16] The mythical founder (Prziemysl, Primizl) of the historical dynasty of the Přemyslids was an *arator*; so he was portrayed by Cosmas and so he appears –clad in *veste principali* – on the twelfth-century fresco in the Romanesque chapel of St. Catherine in Znojmo.[17] "Interea Aeneas urbem designat arato ..."[18]

The modern Czech poets and their public assimilated Cosmas' myth-epic, and Tyl's "Čech a Lech" is merely a minor instance of its many transpositions into Czech literature and art. And the *patria*, its *locus amoenus* to which the forefather Čech has led his people, was also the traditional force behind the song "Kde domov můj?"

From the time of the Greek and Latin classics until the late Renaissance, *locus amoenus* meant the ideal and beautiful countryside. In the tenth chapter of his *Europäische Literatur und lateinisches Mittelalter*, Ernst Robert Curtius defined it as the "Ideallandschaft ... Seine minimum Ausstattung besteht aus einem Baum (oder mehreren Bäumen), einer Wiese und einer Quelle oder einem Bach." Curtius also cited classical references: *Dignus amore locus, molle gramen inter herbas*;

15 *Chronicon*, 11.
16 *Ibid.*, 15.
17 Jiří Mašín, *Románská nástěnná malba v Čechách a na Moravě* (Prague, 1954), 21.
18 *Aeneid*, v, 775.

amoena loca dicta; quod amorem praestant, iocunda, viridia; deliciis plenus locus.
He referred to Theocritus' concept of *locus amoenus* as a pleasant place surrounded
by a wooded wilderness.[19] This image may have determined Cosmas' choice of
locus amoenus as the back-drop for the epic of the foundation of Bohemia. The
forefather Čech was seeking a new *patria* and he had to look for it in no man's land,
which at that time was mostly woodland in those parts of Europe. For the mediaeval
man woods were ominous even if useful places, but unsuitable to inspire the confidence necessary for the choice of a settlement. The tenets of mediaeval rhetoric,
however, offered a solution for the adoption of a land "nectare mellis et lacte
humida ... ad habitandum aere locunda"[20] – the Virgilian pastoral looms distinctly
behind Cosmas' landscape of the primaeval Bohemia. And similarly, as under an
old fresco X-rays discover layers of previous paintings, so under the romantic song
"Kde domov můj?" traces of the twelfth-century epic are still discernible.

In his story about the forefather Čech, Cosmas used the figure called *prosopopeia*
or *suasoriae*,[21] the stylistic device which gives the word to a person who is fictitious
or absent. The forefather Čech addressed his people: "Haec est illa, haec est illa
terra (quam saepe me vobis promisse memini)."[22] In listening carefully one hears
the echo of these words in "a to jest ta [krásná] země." *Krásná země* preserves also
one of the classical meanings associated with *locus amoenus*: Elysium.

> Devenere locos laetos et amoena virecta ...[23]
> Zemský *ráj* to na pohled ...

In the story "Čech a Lech," the forefather Čech dreams about orchards in bloom:
"[ouval požehnaný] květy ... po travnatých sadech."[24] "... v sadě skví se ... květ."
Čech's invocation before the view of the promised land – "Tu, nám dejte, dobří
bozi býti domovem" – reappears in "Země česká *domov* můj!"

The last Czech translation of Cosmas' *Chronicon* (1929, 1950) supplied for the
Latin *Oreades, Dryades, Hamadryades* the collective *víly*; Cosmos called the three
daughters of Krok (Croccos, Crecko, Croh) *tres Eumenides*, and the translation
gives *tři hadačky*. Both expressions, *víly* and *hadačky*, have the flavour of a folk
tale and much less of Greek and Latin deities, which were a part of the mediaeval
poetic imagination. Such discrepancies may occur in translations, even if there is no
gap of centuries to bridge as there has been in our case. Thus, it also happened
that the translation-transposition of Cosmas' epic into the modern Czech linguistic

19 Ernst Robert Curtius, *Europäische Literatur und lateinisches Mittelalter* (Bern, 1948), 200–5:
   "The ideal landscape ... Its minimum ingredients comprise a tree (or several trees), a meadow
   and a spring" (transl. by W. R. Trask, *European Literature and the Latin Middle Ages* [New
   York, 1953], 195).
20 *Chronicon*, 7.
21 Quintilian, in Edmond Faral, *Les arts poétiques du XIIe et du XIIIe siècles* (Paris, 1924), 72.
22 *Chronicon*, 7.
23 *Aeneid*, VI, 638.
24 *Sebrané spisy J. K. Tyla*, 81.

medium changed the classical *locus amoenus* into a romantic idyll. The mediaeval *locus amoenus*, the *digne amore locus*, possessed the lasting beauty of classic poetry, its poise and clear contours; the romantic transposition stressed the lyrical singing sentiment. In the experience of the poets of the Czech literary renascence, sentiment and fatherland were inseparable.

This essay tends not so much to give an account of the Czech national anthem as dependent on Cosmas' epic and through it on mediaeval classics. Rather, the investigation is directed towards another literary phenomenon: the memory of literary tradition and its ability to carry certain words, groups of words, their imagery and their concepts, far beyond their original milieu even if the line may be occasionally broken, hidden, or disappear entirely. That such literary evolution has a super-individual character need hardly be mentioned. Achilles' shield survives in the poem by W. H. Auden, Cosmas' epic is alive whenever Smetana's *Libuše* is performed on the stage of the Národní divadlo. Writing the *quodlibet* "Kde domov můj?," Tyl was probably unaware of the evolutionary phenomenon in his work. Yet it touched and reproduced with a rare clarity the *locus amoenus* as it lived in the poetry of the Middle Ages and as it was handed down to him through the centuries by Cosmas' epic.

The Social Composition of
the Czech Patriots in Bohemia, 1827–1848

MIROSLAV HROCH

MUCH RESEARCH has been done on the Czech national renascence which tells us in great detail about the development of the national programme, about how Czech patriots (*vlastenci*) thought, what books they printed, and how they organized their activity. However, we know less about the structural changes undergone by Czech society during the first half of the nineteenth century. So far, the question of who these patriots were, what social groups they came from, and in what social environment they moved, has been almost entirely neglected. Yet, it is necessary to obtain the most concrete knowledge possible regarding the social composition of the widest circle of activist patriots in order to gather more reliable data on the causes and social presuppositions of the birth of the modern national movement – not only in Bohemia but in all small European nations.

This essay is an attempt to characterize the community of Czech patriots from several points of view: (a) social composition, (b) territorial distribution, (c) occupation of parents (i.e. social origin), and (d) environment in which they spent their youth. For the execution of such a task, it is first necessary to obtain the largest possible number of individuals with national consciousness and then to gather biographical data for them. The criterion used here for inclusion of an individual in the group is whether he engaged in public patriotic activity or gave active and

Translated from the Czech.

conscious support to such activity – be it in the form of financial subventions for patriotic purposes, collaboration with patriotic journals, or membership in patriotic organizations. The period chosen for concentrated study is a key one in the Czech national movement. It is a period of successful national agitation displaying great tenacity of purpose. It followed a time of predominantly scholarly interest and preceded the beginning of the mass national movement, which first manifested itself in the revolutionary year of 1848. It is in our limited period that the activity of the small patriotic group was of special significance.

A number of sources can be used to determine the social composition of patriots between the 1820s and 1840s. During this period some periodicals were already being published in the Czech language and a relatively large number of publications were put out at irregular intervals. Needless to say, not every periodical in the Czech language can be regarded as a patriotic one, and not every reader as a patriot. Only some of the Czech periodicals had a wider impact on the Czech renascence. One of these was the *Časopis Českého musea* (Journal of the Czech Museum; 1827 ff.), which had as its aim to gather around itself the Czech patriotic public and thus distinguished itself from the very beginning from contemporary periodicals of other nations. Even the act of subscribing to this periodical was of significance. For other periodicals, however, only the contributors should be considered significant.

For our purposes, the most valuable sources of identification of Czech patriots are, however, the lists of members and collaborators of the Czech Literary Foundation, the Matice česká. This institution, from the beginning of the 1830s, served as a centre for those who favoured and supported Czech patriotic literature and, before 1848, it became the central organ of Czech patriotic activity (especially for southern Bohemia, although the Matice was weak there).[1] Because of its solely patriotic preoccupation, the Matice differed from an analogous organization publishing religious literature in the Czech language, the Dědictví svatojanské (The Heritage of St. Jan Nepomuk), in which the Catholic aspect took precedence over the patriotic. The Matice was generally recognized as the main institution for the publication of Czech books, as can be verified from its lists as well as from private correspondence of Czech patriots, and the funds required to finance their publication came solely from the voluntary contributions of those who shared the Matice's aims. Fortunately for our present study, the names of the contributors to the Matice were regularly published as an appendix to the "Journal of the Czech Museum," along with the occupation and domicile of the donor. This appendix, which at the time of its origin aimed especially at propaganda goals, has preserved source

1 On the activity of the Matice cf. K. Tieftrunk, *Dějiny Matice české* (Prague, 1881); *Stolet Matice české, 1831–1931* (Prague, 1931); W. Nebeský, *Geschichte des Museums des Konigreichs Böhmen* (Prague, 1868), esp. chap. III. Stanley B. Kimball presents more detailed data on the publishing and organizational activity of the Matice in the following study in the present volume.

material of singular value, since the contributors were necessarily backers of the Matice's stand. Of course, the publication of the names also served a practical purpose: it was a check on book-keeping (and on the basis of random checks we can say that the lists are reliable). The fact that the contributions were perhaps partly motivated by personal vanity, by the attempt to keep up with the neighbours, and so on, is not of too great consequence to our study, since we start with the assumption that national consciousness is not in itself a proof of the personal noble-mindedness and unblemished character of the individual. Vanity, too, must undoubtedly be considered as an expression of national consciousness – rejoicing in the publication of one's own name in the pages of a patriotic journal, side by side with well-known patriots – especially if popularization in such manner carried with it some risk of social or even political discrimination.

The publication of lists of contributors to the Matice in the "Journal of the Czech Museum" was not entirely accidental, for the Matice was closely linked to the Museum from its beginning. The lists of contributors followed directly the lists of subscribers to the Journal. During the twenty years from 1827 (the year in which publication of the Journal was started) to 1847, both institutions underwent a number of changes. The programme of their activities turned increasingly from scholarly patriotic efforts to patriotic work for the benefit of the popular reader, as expressed by a new conception of the Matice's editorial policy from the beginning of the 1840s. We can assume, therefore, that the representation of the educated public during the earlier period is exaggerated and that only in the 1840s does the composition of contributors begin to encompass the whole patriotic community. The composition of patriots obtained from these lists is distorted, however, because the contributions to the Matice were relatively high (the smallest recorded contribution of an individual was five florins) and poorer patriots would not have appeared often since they would have had to save for a long time to be able to send this amount to the Matice. The results of this analysis have therefore to be verified by comparison with another patriotic enterprise, where property was not an obstacle to such an extent. We refer to collections on behalf of the Czech industrial high-school, taken on the eve of 1848 and later up into the early 1850s. Again, in individual cases, there could be distortion because of personal reasons or reasons of principle. For scholarly and artistic circles, this difficulty can be overcome by supplementing the lists with data in the *Riegrův naučný slovník* (Rieger Dictionary).

During the pre-March period, renascence passed through Moravia considerably later than, and on the whole independently of, the development in Bohemia. Therefore, the lists of the Matice cannot be considered as reliable in identifying Moravian patriots as in identifying Czechs of Bohemia. Since, in addition, we do not have other sources of similar character for this period, we have disregarded the Czech renascence in Moravia before 1848 and have concentrated on the renascence in Bohemia.

Having made the above remarks by way of introduction, we may now turn to consider the results of our analysis of the social composition of patriots in Bohemia. A picture of the variable part played by individual social groups, which is the easiest problem to survey, emerges from a review of the social composition of contributors to the Matice (and until 1833 also of subscribers to the Journal) on the basis of individual years in which they sent in their contributions (cf. Table 1). In analysing the figures of Table 1 it should, of course, be remembered that individual contributors could appear on the lists several times, either in one year or over several years, although they could appear at most five times if they wished to become founding members.[2] It is difficult to say whether such distortion has a greater effect on the figures for the more propertied or for the poorer strata of the patriots. Some of the more propertied ones contributed a lump sum of fifty florins and as a result appeared only once on the lists, but others paid ten florins on five occasions and appeared five times. In spite of numerous considerations of this sort, Table 1 does demonstrate a number of explicit changes in the representation of individual groups. In the period in which the main body of patriots consisted of the subscribers to the "Journal of the Czech Museum" (i.e. to 1833) men of education of the old type predominate among the subscribers; the proof is to be found in the relatively high proportion of the gentry and the relatively low proportion of students in comparison with the later period. However, the interest expressed by bourgeois circles is surprising. The beginnings of the Matice (i.e., the 1830s) are characterized by an increase in the proportion of students and a sharp decrease in that of the gentry and also – a fact which is as yet difficult to explain – of the burghers. The change in the orientation of the Matice in the early 1840s manifested itself above all in a growth of interest among the ranks of officials and professional people, and a temporary drop in that of students and a permanent one in that of the clergy.

A more thorough analysis on a more reliable basis can, of course, only be made through the compilation of a broader list of patriots. This we drew up after adjusting the lists of contributors to the Matice on the basis of the criteria mentioned above. An analysis of the social composition of almost 2800 patriots, as indicated in Table 2, confirms the basic trends of development apparent in Table 1, i.e. a strong participation of students, clergy, and officials (especially seigniorial officials).[3] Not all groups shared equally in the sharp numerical increase of contributors.

As shown in Table 3, typical features are the relatively insignificant increase in the number of gentry, clergy, and to some extent also those in professional occupations, and the considerable dynamism of the students, officials, and the popular strata (whose numbers were, of course, insignificant in the earlier stages). The

---

2 M. Hroch and A. Veverka, "K otázce sociální skladby české obrozenecké společnosti," *Dějepis ve škole* (Prague, 1957), 155ff.

3 The classification of social groups is arranged on the twofold basis of division into basic social classes and division according to professional groups and is done in more detail for the members of the intelligentsia.

TABLE 1

Social composition of contributors to the Matice česká, 1827–48 (per cent)

YEAR	Gentry	Professional occupations	Officials	Teachers	Students	Merchants, burghers, artisans	Peasants	Workers	Clergy	TOTAL NUMBER OF CONTRIBUTORS
1827	8.5	7.5	11.5	5.5	10.0	6.0			45.0	375
1828	9.0	8.0	13.0	8.5	6.0	11.0			45.0	173
1829	10.0	7.0	14.0	8.0	7.5	8.5			45.5	140
1830	8.5	8.5	14.0	8.5	5.0	9.5			44.5	157
1831	13.5	12.0	9.0	9.0	5.5	5.5			44.5	134
1832	9.5	7.0	17.0	8.0	9.5	8.5			40.0	279
1833	2.0	6.5	12.0	7.0	23.0	5.5			44.0	223
1834	1.0	6.0	11.5	9.5	25.5	5.5			41.5	222
1835	1.0	8.0	12.0	6.0	23.0	6.0			44.0	227
1836	4.0	5.0	14.5	7.0	23.5	4.0			42.0	183
1837	7.5	8.5	13.0	5.0	10.5	6.5	1.5		41.0	219
1838	3.0	11.0	12.5	3.0	18.5	5.0		0.5	47.0	125
1839	2.5	8.5	13.0	7.0	22.0	6.5	1		39.0	74
1840	4.0	10.0	8.0	4.0	20.0	6.0			48.0	49
1841	2.5	12.0	22.0	4.0	14.0	4.0	1.5		40.0	76
1842	4.0	16.5	20.0	8.5	13.0	10.0			28.0	231
1843	2.5	15.5	16.5	7.0	17.0	12.5	0.6	0.5	28.0	381
1844	1.5	15.0	18.0	4.0	22.0	11.0		0.5	28.0	517
1845	0.5	11.0	18.0	6.0	22.0	8.5		0.5	33.5	917
1846	1.5	6.0	20.0	6.0	24.0	12.5	1.5	2.0	30.5	1157
1847	1.5	3.5	20.0	7.0	23.5	11.5	1.0	2.0	29.0	1443
1848	0.1	1.0	16.5	7.5	30.0	11.0	1.5	2.5	29.0	1135

TABLE 2

Social composition of Czech patriots, 1827–48

	Prague		Towns, pop. over 5000		Towns, pop. 2000–5000		Towns, pop. 1000–2000		Villages and small towns		TOTAL	
	1827–41	1842–48	1827–41	1842–48	1827–41	1842–48	1827–41	1842–48	1827–41	1842–48	1827–41	1842–48
Gentry, land-owners, high officials	54	28	6	4	3				6	12	69	44
Merchants	5	19	3	17	10	12		7		4	18	59
Entrepreneurs	1	8	1	3	4	3		2			6	16
Artisans	14	34	9	13	15	42	2	16	7	31	47	136
BURGHERS, TOTAL	20	61	13	33	29	57	2	25	7	35	71	211
Doctors	19	26	1	7	7	17		3		3	27	56
Lawyers	17	8	1	1							18	9
Artists, etc.	33	21	5	2		1					38	24
PROFESSIONALS, TOTAL	69	55	7	10	7	18		3		3	83	89
Seigniorial officials	4	4	2	4	15	38	14	20	40	79	75	145
Other officials	21	59	5	23	19	26	1	19	3	24	49	151
OFFICIALS, TOTAL	25	63	7	27	34	64	15	39	43	103	124	296
Clergy	20	21	13	29	72	85	44	70	164	248	313	453
High-school teachers	6	16	6	9	8	12	1				21	37
Other teachers	13	25	3	11	9	11	1	8	8	25	34	80
TEACHERS, TOTAL	19	41	9	20	17	23	2	8	8	25	55	117
Officers, soldiers	4	8		4	1	5		1			5	18
Students	113	257	14	77	28	107	1	9	4	40	160	490
Millers	1	7		2		2		2	2	15	3	28
Peasants								1	2	28	2	29
Wage labourers	1	5		2	2	2		4	2	10	5	23
Women, etc.	3	10	3	6	2	14		1	2	15	10	46
TOTAL	329	556	72	214	195	376	64	163	240	534	900	1843

TABLE 3

Social composition of Czech patriots according to period when contributions were begun
(percentage of total in category in parentheses)

	1827–34	1835–41	1842–48	TOTAL
Landowners and gentry	27 (41)	9 (13)	30 (46)	66 (100)
Merchants and artisans	63 (23)	8 (3)	213 (74)	283 (100)
Professional occupations	54 (30)	31 (17)	91 (53)	176 (100)
Officials	112 (25)	35 (8)	307 (67)	456 (100)
Clergy	268 (34)	64 (8)	461 (58)	793 (100)
Teachers and high-school teachers	46 (27)	10 (6)	120 (67)	176 (100)
Officers and non-com. officers	5 (21)		18 (79)	23 (100)
Students	122 (17)	41 (7)	483 (76)	646 (100)
Peasants and millers	5 (9)		57 (91)	62 (100)
Servants and workers	4 (14)	2 (3)	23 (83)	28 (100)
Other and undetermined	8 (13)	2 (4)	48 (83)	58 (100)
TOTAL	714 (26)	202 (7)	1851 (67)	2767 (100)

speed of growth in the participation of the burghers was somewhat above average. An over-all survey can be obtained by gathering all social groups into larger entities according to the degree to which a particular group was linked to the old society and partly also according to its living standard.[4] The average ratio of the number of patriots up to 1841 to those after is 33:67. Considering the groups linked with the old society, the ratio of "notables" (291 patriots) was 53:47, and that of the other groups, especially the clergy (i.e., altogether 1081 patriots), was 39:61. For groups linked with production (artisans, burghers) the ratio was 24:76, and for petty intelligentsia and students (1000 patriots) it was 23:77. The national movement was, then, clearly losing ground among the "notables," whose position was, as can be seen elsewhere, close to the provincial patriotism (*Landespatriotismus*) of the eighteenth century, and, by contrast, it was gaining ground among the young intelligentsia and among the burghers.[5] If medical doctors are not counted among the "notables," the increase in their number would be even less, the ratio becoming 63:37.

As can be seen from Table 2, the great majority of the patriots lived in the towns, and in Prague and medium-sized towns they were especially strong. That merely one-quarter of the patriots were active in the villages is certainly surprising in

4 Among the patriots whom we equate with the "old pre-industrial society" we include as "notables" the gentry, high officials, and the elite of the educated of the old type; clergy, seignorial and other officials, and officers belong to the other group. By "phase B" we understand the period of conscious national agitation directed towards the broad masses in an attempt to win them for the programme of national, cultural (and eventually even political) emancipation, i.e. the period which superseded that of scholarly concern for the nation ("phase A"). The period of mass nationalist activity is designated as "phase C." In Bohemia "phase B" may be dated from the 1820s to 1840s, and 1848 marks the beginning of "phase C."
5 This fact reflects the change in attitude of the broader patriotic strata towards the Matice during the 1830s.

view of the agrarian character of Czech society. We would at least expect this proportion to grow during phase B, but this was not the case. Although the ratio of growth for Prague was indeed actually below average (it was 38:62, clearly because of the decrease in the representation of the "notables"), in other cities it was slightly above average (ratio 30:70), and in the villages it remained average (31:69).

Now we can finally consider the distribution of the relevant social groups among the various types of settlement (cf. Table 4). The majority of those belonging to the professional occupations and the majority of students lived in Prague. By contrast, more than half of the patriotic clergy were active in the countryside; they formed the majority of village patriots. Seigniorial officials formed the second largest group of village patriots. The rest of the officials, as well as artisans and burghers, were distributed on the whole among the various types of settlements in roughly the same proportion as the over-all distribution of patriots, which was: Prague, 31:5 per cent; larger towns, 10.5 per cent; medium-sized towns, 21 per cent; small towns, 8 per cent; and villages, 28 per cent.

The data obtained regarding the social composition of our community of patriots will now be compared with the corresponding figures for the social composition of the reading public of two popular reading enterprises of the pre-March period, and with the composition of contributors to the Czech industrial school before 1848. The lists of the supporters of the Dědictví svatojanské could be analysed as has been done for the Matice lists, but we shall be satisfied with a basic classification according to social groups, and with the trends of development.[6] The percentages for the various groups (considerably rounded off) are given in Table 5. The proportion of artisans and burghers was roughly the same as in our previous analysis, but the proportion of secular intelligentsia decreased sharply and was on the whole insignificant. The predominance of clergy is not surprising; however, the sharp decrease, caused by the mass influx of the peasantry into the Dědictví, is surprising. It is an incontestable expression of the penetration, if not of the national awakening, then of education to the peasant masses. This development is the basis for our periodization of the beginning of phase c in Bohemia (cf. footnote 4).

The social composition of subscribers to the popular journal Večerní vyražení for the year 1831 gives us the picture shown in Table 6. It is surprising how close the social composition of the readers of Večerní vyražení is to that of our community of patriots at the time of the founding of the Matice; we find here a similarly low proportion of students and peasants and a roughly similar distribution for the various types of settlements. Only the proportion of artisans and burghers is considerably higher, and the proportion of the clergy is considerably lower.

From the end of phase B lists of contributors to the Czech industrial school have been preserved. The complicated problem of analysing these lists would require

6 Cf. lists in K. Borový, Dějiny Dědictví svatojanského (Prague, 1885).

TABLE 4

Social composition of patriots according to the size of their place of activity

	Prague	Towns, pop. over 5000	Towns, pop. over 2000	Small towns, pop. over 1000	Villages and small towns, pop. up to 1000	TOTAL	Per cent
Landowners and gentry	46	46	1		18	66	2.3
Merchants and artisans	81	17	86	27	42	283	10.2
Professional occupations	124	44	25	3	3	176	6.3
Officials	110	42	99	54	146	456	16.8
Clergy	55	29	158	124	412	793	28.7
Teachers and high-school teachers	60		40	10	33	176	6.3
Students	360	91	135	10	44	646	23.3
Officers	12	4	6	1		23	0.8
Peasants and millers	8	2	2	3	47	62	2.2
Servants and workers	6	2	4	4	12	28	1.0
Other and undetermined	13	9	16	1	17	58	2.1
TOTAL	875	286	572	237	774	2767	100.0

TABLE 5

	1834–40	1841–45	1847–48
Artisans and burghers	9	15	12
Officials, professionals, teachers	16	8	6
Clergy	65	60	21
Peasantry	3	11	54
Other	7	6	7
TOTAL	100	100	100

an independent study.[7] For our purposes, a rough break-down of the social composition of the first contributors in 1847 will suffice.[8] The burgher and artisan subscriptions make up 32 per cent, the secular intelligentsia, 24 per cent; students, only 3.5 per cent; clergy, 8 per cent; and peasants, 14 per cent. In the course of the following years workers especially were added to the subscription lists; otherwise the relative proportions were substantially maintained. Here we encounter, then, a social structure which is characteristic of phase c of the national movement in Bohemia. It should be noted, however, that this structure differs from the composition of readership of the *Večerní vyražení* only by having a lower proportion of the clergy and a higher proportion of peasants.

On the basis of the above data we consider the decisive proportion of urban patriots in the Czech national renascence to be incontestable. This determines the basic ratio in the analysis of "patriotic topography," the geographic distribution of patriots on the territory of Bohemia. Did all towns participate more or less equally in national activity? In which regions do we find the largest number of patriots? To find the answers to these questions we have gathered the data on contributors to the Matice and projected them on the "map" of Bohemia. At the same time we have taken into consideration patriotic groups – even those found in the countryside. A

TABLE 6

Social composition of subscribers to the journal *Večerní vyražení* in 1831 by place of activity (per cent)

	Prague	Towns	Countryside	Undetermined	TOTAL
Artisans and burghers	13.0	10.0	0.5	6.0	29.5
Officials, professional occupations, teachers	9.0	9.0	8.0	6.0	32.0
Clergy	2.0	6.0	10.0	0.5	18.5
Students	3.0	0.5		4.0	7.5
Peasants and millers	0.5		2.0		2.5
Undetermined	1.5	0.5	6.0		8.0
TOTAL	29.0	26.0	26.5	16.5	98.0

7 See E. Mandler, "Počátky Jednoty pro povzbuzení průmyslu v Čechách," unpublished dissertation, University of Prague, 1956.

8 Cf. also lists published regularly in the issues of *Časopis Českého musea* for the year 1847.

town or a community is considered to be a seat of a patriotic group when we have proof that it has had at least three contributors to the Matice in the same period, or two contributors of different occupations in the same period and another in the period immediately preceding or following. We wish to ascertain which environment was more favourable for national awakening, if we can ascertain any regularities at all in this direction. The designation "patriotic community" for a three-member group of contributors is in no way exaggerated. We assume logically, and we know from some partial regional studies, that patriots gathered around themselves others who were interested, and that journals and books were lent and borrowed, or collectively read.[9] However, we must not overestimate the significance of the geographic distribution of those patriotic groups which were composed predominantly of persons unable to decide for themselves where they would be active and about whom we have no proof that they grew up in the place of their activity. The clergy, in particular, and partly also high-school teachers and to a lesser degree officials, belong to this category. Accordingly, we need only to summarize some basic facts.

The size of the patriotic groups was not directly proportionate to the population in the localities where the patriots were active. The patriotic communities were not distributed evenly over the territory of Bohemia. On the basis of the density of distribution of patriots in towns (and in larger village patriotic groups), we can distinguish three regions in Bohemia: (a) areas where patriotic groups were active in all towns and small towns with population over 1000 (central Polabí, Pojizeří, eastern Bohemia), (b) areas where we find patriotic groups only in larger towns and in some administrative or governmental centres (above all in southwest and west Bohemia), (c) areas with single patriotic groups fairly remote from one another (southeast Bohemia, south Bohemia). Interpretation of these facts will be possible only on the basis of a comparative study. In the meantime we can only express some negative judgments. The density of the patriotic communities did not depend on their location relative to language frontiers; sometimes at such a frontier we find a dense network of communities, while at other times we find only single contributors. The density did not even depend on the location in Bohemia; e.g., the southern part of central Bohemia was almost inactive. Finally, it did not even depend on the degree of language purity; sometimes we find patriotic communities in linguistically mixed areas, and in contrast a number of solidly Czech regions remained aloof.

Patriotic groups differed from one another not only in size but also in social composition. We shall attempt, therefore, to characterize briefly the types of patriotic communities with regard to both social composition and location. Without

9 Patriotic activity of local groups is described with reference to Nové Město nad Metují in Z. Nejedlý, *Bedřich Smetana*, III (Prague, 1929), 447ff. Activity in Polička is described in J. Růžička, *O Drašarovi a poličských buditelích. Román a skutečnost* (Polička, 1966), esp. chap. I.

a detailed enumeration of the names of localities, we can draw the following conclusions on the basis of detailed research:

1 Groups in the nationally more active regions of Bohemia were composed, more often than elsewhere, of members of all basic social elements (i.e., officials, burghers, and clergy).

2 Burghers were represented most strongly in patriotic groups in east Bohemia and in the eastern parts of central Bohemia (Polabí), but are scarcely represented at all in patriotic groups in the nationally less active territories of Bohemia.

3 Officials were strongest in patriotic groups in nationally active territories, which stretched from west Bohemia to the basin of the river Jizera in northern Bohemia.

4 Small patriotic groups in nationally passive regions were most often composed mainly of clergy, with sometimes some officials.

The question of the social origin of the patriots, or to put it more accurately the patriotic intelligentsia, is not one which has gone unnoticed in Czech literature. Most authors see in Czech patriots the sons of peasants who went to Germanizing or Germanized towns for education and there began their national awakening,[10] but E. Chalupný has pointed out that a number of patriots came from the towns.[11] Although such statements have been made, no reasonably accurate or concrete analysis has yet been carried out. However, from the catalogues of students at the University of Prague and at theological seminaries outside Prague very valuable material on the social origin of the patriotic intelligentsia can be obtained.[12] These catalogues make it possible to ascertain the occupation of parents and the birthplace of almost all students after 1815. With the exception of some catalogues in which the birth-place is indicated only by the name of region, we have at our disposal reliable and carefully kept source materials.[13]

A somewhat more serious distortion may arise as a result of our inability to identify all members of the intelligentsia. Out of a total number of 1800 members of the intelligentsia and students we succeeded in ascertaining complete data for 800

10 E. Denis, Čechy po Bílé Hoře, II/1 (Prague, 1931), 14: K. Krofta, Dějiny selského stavu (Prague, 1949), 349; A. Klíma, Rok 1848 v Čechách (Prague, 1949), 16.

11 E. Chalupný, Havlíček (Prague, 1929), 133.

12 The sources for the identification of the origin of the patriotic intelligentsia are the lists of students of individual university faculties and of diocesan theological seminaries, which, from the second decade of the nineteenth century, carefully noted such data as father's employment (and changes of employment where these occurred), the place and date of birth, and high-school education. The lists are in the Archives of Charles University in Prague.

13 Since the majority of entries were made on the basis of data given by the students, the possibility that there is some distortion "upwards" of the social composition cannot be excluded. A random check of the data on the social origin of a student given in different catalogues of the same faculty or in catalogues of different faculties (e.g. philosophy and law), however, showed that the data are very reliable. Substantial fluctuations are evident only in two areas: between the general designation "burgher" and the concrete designation of craft, or father's trade, and between the term Bauer and Landmann and occasionally also Gutsbesitzer.

patriots, while for 140 patriots the data are incomplete. The success, however, varied considerably from one individual group of the intelligentsia to another. The social origin of almost all university students was ascertained, as well as of a majority of doctors and lawyers and a large part of the clergy. In contrast to this, we did not succeed in identifying the majority of officials, probably because by no means all of them had a university education or were educated at the University of Prague. The older generation of patriots, born roughly before 1795, though small, is also poorly represented in our sample, since complete catalogue lists had not been established at the time they pursued their studies. With these exceptions, however, we can consider the sample of identified patriotic intelligentsia as sufficiently representative.

Again, as in the case of the social composition of the patriots, we shall be interested first in social origin (i.e., occupation of parents) and in place of birth. Table 7 is constructed on the basis of these indicators.[14] The largest part of the patriotic intelligentsia came from artisan or burgher families, while not quite one-fifth came from peasant families. Similarly, a majority of the patriots were born in towns and only one-quarter in villages. The relatively low percentage of sons from doctors' and lawyers' families is not surprising, and the very low percentage of patriots from teachers' families only confirms the insignificant representation of this stratum in the national renascence. The figure for sons of seigniorial officials in the countryside is also surprisingly low, but this may not reflect the true state of affairs since we succeeded in identifying the social origin of only a small part of patriotic officials. Only an insignificant proportion of Czech patriots came from families which we could classify as among the "notables," while the highest proportion came from urban and rural families of small manufacturers. The insignificant proportion from the ranks of the poor in the towns and in the countryside can be explained by the relatively low influx from these strata into institutions of higher learning. The nature of the data obtained above forces us to re-examine critically the traditional view, which is still held, that thatched-roofed cottages were the cradle of Czech patriots. They also lead us to adopt a position of scepticism in regard to traditional conceptions about the social origins of patriots in other nations as well.

We can establish, to some extent, the degree of validity of our findings so fas as the social origin of single generations of the patriotic intelligentsia is concerned. To do this, we must take into consideration the distortion in the figures due to gaps in the data given in the catalogues, and eliminate as much as possible the oldest patriotic generation. For this reason we take as our first dividing line the year 1810, and as our second the year 1820; the older generation will then be composed of patriots who studied during the beginning period of phase B; the middle

14 Social groups are determined on the basis of the same criterion as social origin. Sons of non-gentry landowners and sons of officers are listed under "other." The size of places is determined on the basis of the year 1844; according to F. Palacký, *Popis království Českého* (Prague, 1848).

TABLE 7

Social origin of patriotic intelligentsia according to size of birth-place
(figures in parentheses are the percentage share, of the total, of each occupation in each category)

OCCUPATION OF PARENTS	Prague	Towns, pop. above 4000	Towns, pop. 1500–4000	Small towns, pop. under 1500	Villages	Undetermined birth-place	TOTAL
Merchants	17 (1.8)	8 (0.8)	16 (1.7)	6 (0.6)	9 (1.0)	7 (0.7)	63 (6.7)
Artisans and burghers	37 (3.9)	76 (8.1)	118 (12.5)	57 (6.1)	36 (3.8)	26 (2.8)	350 (37.1)
Professional occupations	12 (1.2)	4 (0.4)	10 (1.1)		1 (0.1)		27 (2.8)
Officials	32 (3.4)	17 (1.8)	25 (2.7)	9 (1.0)	17 (1.8)	3 (0.3)	103 (10.9)
Teachers	5 (0.5)	1 (0.1)	5 (0.5)	8 (0.9)	13 (1.3)	9 (1.0)	41 (4.3)
Millers	3 (0.3)	8 (0.9)	6 (0.6)	5 (0.5)	18 (1.9)	13 (1.3)	53 (5.6)
Peasants		1 (0.1)	2 (0.2)	9 (1.0)	119 (12.6)	30 (3.3)	161 (17.1)
Employees and workers	9 (1.0)	4 (0.4)	2 (0.2)	7 (0.8)	7 (0.8)	6 (0.6)	35 (3.7)
Other and undetermined	19 (2.0)	19 (2.0)	30 (3.2)	15 (1.5)	24 (2.1)		107 (10.2)
TOTAL	134 (14.2)	138 (14.6)	214 (22.7)	116 (12.3)	244 (25.8)	94 (10.4)	940 (100)

TABLE 8

Social origin of patriotic intelligentsia according to date of birth

OCCUPATION OF PARENTS	Born up to 1810			Born 1811–20			Born 1821–30			TOTAL (per cent)
	number	A*	B†	number	A	B	number	A	B	
Merchants	20	6.2	2.5	21	7.9	2.6	14	6.3	1.7	6.8
Artisans	141	44.3	17.6	92	35.5	11.5	75	33.3	9.4	38.5
Professional occupations	4	1.2	0.5	14	5.5	0.7	8	3.6	1.0	3.2
Officials	22	6.4	2.6	38	14.6	4.7	34	15.1	4.2	11.5
Teachers	12	3.8	1.5	12	4.6	1.5	6	2.2	0.7	3.7
Millers	13	4.0	1.6	15	5.8	1.9	12	5.1	1.5	5.0
Peasants	36	11.4	4.5	34	13.1	4.2	49	21.8	6.1	14.8
Employees and workers	6	1.8	0.7	12	4.8	1.5	11	4.6	1.4	3.6
Other and undetermined	66	20.1	8.3	21	8.2	2.6	16	7.3	2.0	12.9
TOTAL	320	100	39.8	259	100	32.2	225	100	28.0	100

*A = percentage share of the patriots of the age group.
†B = percentage share, in the total group, of each occupation in each age group.

OCCUPATION OF PARENTS	Per cent born up to 1810	Per cent born 1811–20	Per cent born 1821–30
Merchants, artisans, millers	21.7	16.0	12.7
Peasants	4.5	4.2	6.1
Officials, professional occupations	3.1	6.4	5.2
TOTAL	39.8	32.2	28.0

generation, of those who reached maturity after the revolutionary years 1830–1, and the youngest generation, of those who had already begun their studies during the decline of phase B.[15] The social composition of the members of these three, numerically roughly equal generation groups, set out in Table 8, shows an interesting and rather pronounced trend of development.

Although from the end of the eighteenth century artisan production developed significantly and the towns grew along with the growth in the non-agricultural population, the number of patriots increased through an influx of those who came from peasant families. From the older generation, in which only a little over one-tenth of the patriots came from peasant families,[16] to the youngest generation, their proportion almost doubled. The increase in the proportion from the ranks of the officials and from the ranks of the professional occupations, especially in the older and middle generations, is even greater. An over-all trend emerges more clearly when we combine the data in larger social groups, as shown in the tabulation above.

It is of interest to see how the proportions of those joining the patriotic ranks from towns and countryside correspond to this picture. Table 9 confirms a growing influx of patriots from the countryside and a decrease in the proportion of patriots from towns – with the exception of Prague, whose proportion, on the contrary, grew. This trend is exactly the opposite of that revealed by the analysis of the social composition of the patriotic community. As a result, although the number of patriots domiciled in Prague increased considerably more slowly than the number domiciled in other towns, the number of patriots born in Prague increased, whereas the number born in other towns decreased relatively. The number of patriots who came from small towns with over 1000 population fell especially sharply.

The picture of the social origin of those participating in the Czech national renascence corresponds, then, less and less to traditional conceptions. On the basis

15 When dividing into generation groups we have also tried to arrange that the individual age groups are roughly equal numerically; this demand is met by taking as dividing line the years 1810 and 1820.

16 The relatively high percentage of persons whose type of employment in this age group is unknown is to a large extent made up of those born in towns who studied before 1815, i.e. before the column on parents' employment was in general use in university catalogues, and whose birth-place was determined from other encyclopaedic and biographic manuals. The real proportion of patriots from peasant families in this age group should, therefore, be under 10 per cent.

TABLE

Place of origin of patriotic intelligentsia according to date of birth
(column percentage in parentheses)

	Born before 1811	Born 1811–20	Born 1821–30	TOTAL
Prague	44 (13.8)	47 (18.1)	41 (18.2)	132 (16.4)
Towns with pop. over 4000	57 (18.2)	46 (17.8)	31 (14.0)	134 (16.6)
Towns with pop. 1500–4000	93 (29.2)	59 (22.7)	51 (22.6)	203 (25.4)
SUBTOTAL	194 (61.2)	152 (58.6)	123 (54.8)	469 (58.4)
Small towns	51 (16.0)	35 (13.6)	24 (10.8)	110 (13.6)
Villages	75 (22.8)	72 (27.8)	78 (34.4)	225 (28.0)
SUBTOTAL	126 (38.8)	107 (41.4)	102 (45.2)	335 (41.6)
TOTAL	320 (100)	259 (100)	225 (100)	804 (100)

of these conceptions we would assume that the patriotic spirit expanded from the countryside to the towns; in reality, however, our figures show a decline of the originally very high proportion of patriots from the urban environment and a growth of the originally small proportion from the villages. Similarly, until now, we have assumed a large proportion of patriotic men of education coming from families of the intelligentsia in the older patriotic generation and a decline of this proportion in later generations in favour of patriots of popular origin (artisans and burghers). However, we now find the exact opposite: the proportion of patriotic intelligentsia coming from small urban artisan families declined, while the proportion of patriots coming from families of men of education (doctors and officials) increased considerably. It would seem that here, in the middle and in the youngest groups, the effect of the ascendence of the third generation, for whom there was a growth in the proportion of officials during phase B, has been felt.

Of course, the results of the study of the social origin of the patriots need verification and refining. To do this, the extent to which the social origin of the patriots and the changes in it over the course of time reflected only the social origin of Prague students in general would have to be considered. But this would require a systematic elaboration of the social origin of all students – a sufficient topic for an extensive and independent study. Let us be satisfied, therefore, with a random comparison of some years in various faculties.[17]

These comparisons showed that the proportion of students of peasant origin was generally higher, especially in theological seminaries, than that of the intelligentsia of peasant origin among the patriots: the proportion fluctuated between 15 and 20

17 A comparative analysis was done with students of philosophy and theology in 1819 and 1823, with theologians in Prague in the year 1831, in Hradec Králové in 1834–5, and in the law faculty in Prague in 1827.

per cent in philosophical faculties and between 20 and 30 per cent in theological faculties. The proportion of students from artisan and merchant families fluctuated considerably between 40 and 60 per cent, but there is nothing to support the view that it fell so distinctly that we could deduce any over-all trend of development from the declining influx of patriotic intelligentsia from these strata. Students from the ranks of the intelligentsia were found in theological seminaries only in very small numbers (about 10 per cent), but in the medical and law faculties their number was, understandably, considerably higher (about 40 per cent) and higher proportionally than the number of patriotic doctors and lawyers coming from the ranks of the intelligentsia. Roughly then, the social origin of patriots corresponded to the over-all picture of social origin of the university-educated intelligentsia in Bohemia during the pre-March period. Any deviations from the basic ratios are generally in just the opposite direction from the one we would expect on the basis of the summary estimates: the percentage of intelligentsia from peasant strata who joined the patriots was smaller than that of students of peasant origin in the whole student body; the percentage of patriots from the ranks of the intelligentsia (with the exception of doctors and lawyers), on the contrary, was above the over-all average. Our data, then, underline the significant role played by the artisan and urban environment in the birth of the Czech patriotic intelligentsia.

Another useful check will be a comparison of the social origin of the patriots with the social origin of a group of students – on the basis of a criterion close to, but not identical with, the criterion of patriotism. Such a group were the students of the Czech language in the philosophical faculty of the University of Prague. We certainly cannot consider as patriots even those among them who successfully passed the examinations, although we can, of course, consider the passing of these examinations as a criterion of Czech nationality in most cases. However, the environment in which these students moved was saturated with patriotic impulses and was the optimal environment for national awakening.[18] Hence we are interested not only in the over-all percentages on the basis of social origin but also in their evolution during the 1820s to 1840s (cf. Table 10). This table confirms the results of the analysis of the patriotic intelligentsia only in that it also registers the decrease in the proportion of students from artisan families. By contrast, the proportion of students from families of the intelligentsia increased, but that of students of peasant origin did not. This finding is also confirmed by the basic percentages of students of the Czech language according to their birthplace:[19]

18 The lists of students of the Czech language are in the catalogues of the so-called liberal philosophical studies. From 1826 all those who sat for examinations were listed in these catalogues, and before this date all those who registered for lectures. The numerical difference is considerable.

19 Here we omit the detailed tables for each year, but choose the totals for six-year periods roughly corresponding to the above-differentiated age groups.

PLACE OF BIRTH	1826–31	1832–37	1842–47
Prague	19.5	18	22.5
Towns and small towns	41	43	40
Villages	39.5	39	37.5

The proportion of village students did not therefore increase, but was from the beginning considerably higher than that of the educated of village origin among the members of the national renascence. As with the patriotic intelligentsia, here too the (somewhat smaller) growth in the 1840s of the proportion born in Prague is partly a reflection of the increase in the proportion of students from the families of officials.

On the basis of both sets of data, we can now state that the intelligentsia coming from villages and from peasant families were, in the older generation (i.e. those born before 1820), relatively more immune to patriotic agitation and, in general, to a patriotic environment. Only after the national awakening spread and the social prestige of the patriot increased did the nationalistic activity of the intelligentsia of peasant origin increase to the point where they were reasonably represented among the educated. No less explicit resistance to the patriotic environment was shown – but only in the older generation – by the educated from the families of officials and from the families of doctors and lawyers, but for them the situation was already changing during the 1830s. Therefore, it is still valid to say that the educated from the ranks of small artisan manufacturers and tradesmen were relatively more sensitive to patriotic impulses and participated in the national movement considerably more vigorously than one would have expected, judging by the over-all picture of the social origin of students.

Of course, we do not intend to exaggerate the significance of social origin, but it is of interest to know the environment that produced those of the educated with the highest qualifications who participated in the national movement and who were relatively most receptive to national interests. Because of the incompleteness of material we unfortunately cannot construct a table showing the relation between the social origin of the intelligentsia and the place where they received their high-school education, but we can make some use of the location of the birth-places on the "map" to obtain further information. First of all, we can already state that a considerable part of the patriots (also of those who came from places other than Prague) graduated from Prague high-schools. Furthermore, many were graduates from high-schools in Slaný, Rychnov, and understandably in Hradec Králové, where there was also a lively activity in the theological seminary, but in the seminary in Litoměřice we find only a few patriots, and the seminary in České Budějovice became activist only in the 1840s. Indeed, only in the case of České Budějovice is the traditional notion which we have subjected to criticism valid: namely, that those students who came from the villages to the German urban environment became

TABLE 10

Social origin of students of the Czech language at the University of Prague
(column percentage in parentheses)

OCCUPATION OF PARENTS	1826–31	1832–37	1842–47
Landowners	4 (0.8)	8 (1.6)	2 (0.2)
Merchants	27 (5.3)	25 (4.9)	40 (4.3)
Artisans	202 (38.3)	191 (36.8)	249 (28.8)
Professional occupations	13 (2.6)	10 (1.9)	52 (5.6)
Officials	58 (11.2)	71 (13.6)	129 (13.2)
Teachers	11 (2.1)	30 (5.8)	26 (2.8)
Millers	20 (3.8)	22 (4.2)	22 (2.4)
Peasants	69 (13.3)	67 (12.8)	144 (15.4)
Servants and workers	14 (2.8)	23 (4.3)	32 (3.4)
Other and undetermined	103 (19.8)	72 (14.1)	212 (22.9)
TOTAL	521 (100)	519 (100)	908 (100)

nationally awakened. The majority of patriotic theologians in České Budějovice
came from peasant families.

In regard to the school and living environment in which the patriots moved
during their youth, we can also make a contribution by projecting their birth-place
on the "map." These places were not distributed at all equally over the territory of
Bohemia. The places from which most patriots came are to a large extent identical
with the places where we found the largest patriotic groups and their thickest network. This is especially true of Polabí and northern Bohemia, while in western
Bohemia the birth-places of a larger number of patriots reached farther south and
southeast. The distribution of birth-places follows the network of high-schools
only to the extent that all places with high-schools were also at the same time birth-
places of the larger groups of patriots. National activation of those born in towns,
near a place with a high-school, clearly depended on other factors as well, however.
The area with the largest density of village birth-places roughly corresponds to the
area of largest density of urban birth-places.

Let us finally ask at what average age the patriots began to support the Matice.
We have ascertained that the average age of the groups of patriots clearly differed
according to the social environment from which they came. Even if we could
theoretically assume that the wealth of parents played a decisive role here, we still
could not but be satisfied with the finding that the patriots who came to study from
families without higher education merged into the national activity faster and at
an earlier age than the patriots who came from educated families. An explanation
on the basis of parents' wealth would give exactly the opposite result.

In conclusion, let us summarize the results of our analysis of the social composition
of Czech patriots in Bohemia as follows:

1 The largest patriotic group at the beginning of phase B was composed of the

clergy; towards the end of phase B, however, their proportion decreased and became nearly equal to that of the students and officials (of the latter, one-half were seigniorial officials).

2   The proportion of small merchants and small artisan manufacturers among the contributors to the Matice followed only behind that of the intelligentsia. Control analyses of the social composition of participants in other patriotic activities or in activities close to the national movement have drawn attention to the fact that the participation of artisans among the patriots equalled that of the secular intelligentsia, and that the decrease in the participation of the clergy towards the end of phase B should have been more pronounced than numbers in the basic table indicate.

3   The largest proportion of patriots was active in the towns; the proportion in Prague was higher at the beginning of phase B, but decreased towards its end.

4   The distribution of patriotic activity over the territory of Bohemia was very uneven. It was strongest in central Polabí and adjacent regions of eastern and northern Bohemia. In contrast, we find a very weak participation (on the basis of contributions to the Matice) in the southern parts of Bohemia, roughly behind the line of the river Sázava to the Brdy mountains.

5   Patriotic groups with a high proportion of artisans and merchants were concentrated especially in the nationally active region of Polabí and they combined with the influential secular intelligentsia among the patriots of western and northern Bohemia. Clergy predominated in most groups in southern Bohemia and in the southeast (with the exception of towns with high-schools).

6   Most patriots came from an urban environment, and from the point of view of social origin sons of artisans and merchants formed the largest group. The proportion of patriots from peasant families and from families of the intelligentsia, however, grew significantly in the youngest generation.

7   Birth-places of the patriotic intelligentsia were concentrated roughly in the regions where the network of patriotic communities was thickest and also in the towns with high-schools.

A more thorough explanation and interpretation of the results of our analysis can, of course, only be given by a comparative analysis, by a consideration of these results in the light of what we know about the social composition of analogous patriotic communities in other small nations of Europe. In this sense, the present article is only a preparatory and partial study.[20]

20 Cf. M. Hroch, "Die Vorkämpfer der nationalen Bewegung bei den kleinen Völkern Europas. Eine vergleichende Analyse zur gesellschaftlichen Schichtung der patriotischen Gruppen," *Acta Universitatis Carolinae, Philosophica et Historica, Monographia* XXIV (Prague, 1968).

The Matice Česká, 1831–1861:
The First Thirty Years of a Literary Foundation

STANLEY B. KIMBALL

FORMATION

THE VITAL ROLE played by language and literature in the various Austro-Slav revivals of the nineteenth century has been studied exhaustively and is well known and appreciated. Little, however, has been written about the many institutions which promoted and supported the literary renascences. Probably the most famous of such institutions was the Matice česká, or the Czech Literary Foundation, which the great historian František Palacký organized in 1831 as a special committee of the Bohemian Museum for the purpose of the scholarly fostering and revival of the Czech language.[1]

1 The term *matice* or *matica* is difficult to translate. It is a generic term meaning many things such as "queen-bee," "mother," "river-bed," or "screw" and implies protection or embracing care. It can also signify a society, association, or more precisely a foundation – an institution for applying private wealth to public purposes. Its probable origin is from the Old Slavonic *mat'* ("mother"), with the added suffix *ica*.

The basic bibliography of the Czech Matice includes the following works: *Slovník naučny*, v (Prague, 1866), 167–76; *Jména p.p. zakladatelův Matice české na konci r. 1868* (Prague, 1869), which is a pamphlet presenting a complete listing of 2765 individual and 132 institutional founding members, plus the names of 591 deceased founding members; Karel Tieftrunk, "O vynikajících momentech dějin Matice české," *Časopis Českého musea*, LV (1881), 353–66; Karel Tieftrunk, *Dějiny Matice české* (Prague, 1881); *Ottův slovník naučny*, XVI

Even though learned societies had existed in the lands of St. Václav for nearly a century, and in spite of the fact that Czech savants for more than thirty years had been trying to organize formally a "Czech [language] Society" (*Společnost česká*), the Matice was the first institution to promote successfully the revival of Czech. It was also the first independent Czech cultural institution to advance nationalism, the first modern institution of a purely Czech character, one of the first and strongest supports of the modern Czech nation, and the most important legal centre of the Czech national movement to 1848.

By 1829 a group of Czech savants and writers led by Palacký, the physiologist Jan Svatopluk Presl, and the philologist Josef Jungmann organized informally to consider ways and means of promoting the revival and survival of the Czech language, which at that time was in great need of modernization, standardization, and fashioning into a fit instrument for the rebirth. They also decided to try to publish a Czech encyclopaedia to bring the reviving Czech culture and intellectual life more into line with western European developments. Subsequently, on 6 January 1830, Palacký went before the Museum Board with a proposal to organize formally as a committee of the museum. He pointed out that such a committee could and should be created in accordance with the museum's by-laws of 1818, especially section 12 which stated that the museum would advance knowledge of all kinds, and 13 which insisted that "All members of the museum must [at least] understand Czech and the secretary must [also] be able to read and write it."[2]

His proposal was quickly adopted and on 11 January a Committee for the

(Prague, 1900), 981–7; Josef Hanuš, *Národní museum a naše obrození*, II (Prague, 1923), 412–42; Antonín Grund, *Sto let Matice české 1831–1931* (Prague, 1931); Jaroslav Prokeš, "Z těžké doby 'Matice české', 1850–60," *Časopis Národního musea*, cv (parts 1 and 2, 1931), 1–40; "Storočina Matice českej," *Slovenské pohľady*, XLVII (1931, no. 5), 335–6; Jaroslav Prokeš, "The Centenary of the Matice česká," *Slavonic and East European Review*, x (Dec. 1931), 420–7; František Kop, *Národní museum* (Prague, 1941), chap. 2; M. Hroch and A. Veverka, "K otázce sociální skladby české obrozenské společnosti: Rozbor společenského složení vlastenců kolem Českého musea a Matice české v letech 1827–48," *Dějepis ve škole*, 4 April 1957, 153–9; S. E. Mann, "'The Journal of the Czech Museum' and František Palacký," *Slavonic and East European Review*, XXXVI (Dec. 1957), 81–93; Pravoslav Kneidl, *Časopis Národního musea 1827–1956: rejstřík 125 ročníků Muzejního časopisu*, 2 vols. (Prague, 1961–3); Jaroslav Vrchotka, "Matice česká a Národní muzeum," *150 let Národního muzea v Praze*, ed. Miroslav Burian and Jiří Spět (Prague, 1968), 83–90.

For nearly 25 years, between 1925 and 1948, Professor Odložilík was connected with both the Matice česká and its sister organization, the Matice moravská. He first published in the *Časopis Matice moravské* in 1925, and from 1931 to 1938 and 1946 to 1947 he was on its editorial board. He also contributed to the *Časopis Českého musea* (which was published by the Czech Matice) and was on the governing board of the Czech Matice from 1945 to 1948 and senior editor of a series of monographs called *Naše minulost* (Our Past) published by the Czech Matice for a while after 1945.

2 These by-laws are reprinted in Hanuš, *Narodní museum*, II, 102–4, and in Kop, *Národní museum*, 177–9. The stipulation in section 13 seems absurd today, but it is very revealing of the neglected condition of Czech at the beginning of the national revival.

Scholarly Fostering of Czech Language and Literature (Sbor k vědeckému vzdě-lávání řeči a literatury české) was made an agency of the Museum Board. To fur-ther their goals more effectively the new committee set up a foundation called the Matice česká which commenced activity on 1 January 1831.

Palacký's sources and inspiration for the Matice came from domestic and foreign institutions going back nearly one hundred years. Among the domestic sources the earliest was the Societas incognitorum (Gesellschaft der Unbekannten/Society of Unknowns), the first learned society in the Czech lands. It was founded in Olo-mouc (Olmütz) in 1746 chiefly through the efforts of Josef Freiherr von Petrasch, who was well educated, had traveled widely in western Europe, and was acquainted with the activities of learned societies there. He wanted to do something similar for his own country and people. Petrasch, therefore, gathered around him some like-minded individuals, and they founded the society, which was housed in his home in Olomouc where it met quarterly.

Its most significant activity was the publishing of a monthly journal, the *Monat-liche Auszüge, Alt- und neuer-belehrten Sachen*. This journal was a frank imitation of similar western journals, such as the *Journal des sçavans* and the *Philosophical Transactions of the Royal Society*, both of which were published as early as 1665 and are probably the earliest examples of learned journalism in Europe, and the German *Acta Eruditorum* published from 1682 in Leipzig.

The *Auszüge* published the papers of the society's members, necrologies, "news," and such information as is found in most scholarly journals of earlier and later date. The society and the journal lasted only until 1751, when Petrasch left Olomouc. It was not a national society at all, or even necessarily patriotic, and it was strictly German in spirit. In reality it was the extension of one man's desire to see a learned journal published in his homeland.

Not for close on twenty years was another learned society organized in the Czech lands – the Gelehrte Privatgesellschaft (Soukromná společnost učená/The Private Learned Society), which was organized in 1770 in Prague by Ignaz, Knight of Born and a few like-minded friends.[3] Their most important activity was the publication of the first scholarly journal in Bohemia – the *Prager gelehrte Nachrichten*, a book-review periodical which reviewed publications throughout the empire. The journal, however, lasted only two years, 1771–2. This society also published an important journal of research, *Abhandlungen*, from 1775.

Until 1784 the society was simply a private organization embracing a small group of men influenced by the spirit of the English and French Enlightenment (rather than the romantic nationalism of Herder), who were interested in intellectual pur-

3 See Arnošt Kraus, "Kdy byla založena 'Soukromná společnost v Čechách,'" *Český časopis historický*, XLII (April 1936), 56–76. There is some question about the date of the founding of this society. Other writers suggest it may have been founded in 1769, 1771, 1772, or even in 1774. See Joseph F. Zacek, "The *Virtuosi* of Bohemia: The Royal Bohemian Society of Sciences," *East European Quarterly*, II (June 1968), 147–59.

suits. Even so it contributed considerably to the cultural reawakening of Bohemia. In 1784 it received permission from Joseph II to organize as a public institution with the name Böhmische Gesellschaft der Wissenschaften (Česká společnost nauk/ Societas Scientiarum Bohemica/The Bohemian Society of Sciences), and Prince Karl Egon of Furstenberg became its first president. Finally in 1790 it took the name by which it is generally known, the Königlich-böhmische Gesellschaft der Wissenschaften (Kralovská česká společnost nauk/The Royal Bohemian Society of Sciences), and became one of the earliest academies in central Europe.

From the beginning this society was strictly aristocratic, intellectual, and patriotic rather than national in spirit. It was patriotic to the extent that it was interested in producing a critical history of the Czechs, but not national enough to foster Czech language and literature. Despite its non-national character, it became and remained the centre of Czech intellectual life until the museum was founded, and even thereafter it continued to grow and flourish. In 1840 it was divided into four sections: mathematics, natural history, history, and Czech philology.[4]

Towards the end of the eighteenth century, other similar societies for special interests were organized – K.K. Patriotischökonomische Gesellschaft (C. k. vlastenecká hospodářská společnost/The Royal-Imperial Patriotic Economic Society) in 1769 for example, and somewhat later the Privatgesellschaft patriotischer Kunstfreunde (Společnost vlasteneckých přátel umění/The Society of the Patriotic Friends of Art) in 1796. Since these societies were largely aristocratic and provincial, rather than national, in spirit, and since their language was German, at the end of the eighteenth century a group of Czech savants including the philologist Josef Dobrovský, the historian František Martin Pelcl, and the publicist Václav Matěj Kramerius began vain attempts to found a "Czech Society" (mentioned above) in order to promote the sadly neglected and deteriorated Czech language and literature in the same way as the other societies were promoting science, economics, and art. They also hoped to publish a Czech dictionary and to improve the unsatisfactory conditions of book publishing in the Czech lands.

At that time most publishing was in the hands of booksellers who were interested mainly in profit and not in advancing any cause. Not many Czech books were printed because of the small market for them, and those few which were printed were mainly of the type which could sell fast – almanacs, religious works, and popular songs and stories. Often even these books were published only if there was a prepaid subscription list.[5] Nor was there much financial inducement for authors to produce manuscripts. They were seldom paid for their work, and usually only received a few free copies.

---

4 Even after the Czech Academy of Emperor Francis Joseph I for Science, Literature, and Art was organized in 1890 (called simply the Czech Academy of Arts and Sciences after 1918) the Learned Society held its own. Finally, in 1952, both the Learned Society and the Czech Academy were merged into the newly organized Czechoslovak Academy of Sciences.

5 Such lists are helpful today in reconstructing the history of the early Czech national revival.

Another domestic activity which may also have influenced Palacký was the reading societies (sing. *čtenářský spolek/Leseverein*). Such societies had been known in western Europe since the beginning of the eighteenth century. Among the earliest were the French *cabinets de lecture* (one is known to have existed in 1701). The first English Reading Room or Circulating Library was founded in Edinburgh in 1726, and the Germans organized *Lesegesellschaften* as early as 1771 in Vienna and 1779 in Stralsund, Prussia. The basic idea of these societies was to arrange with one or more publishers to buy copies of books at a reduced price. These books would then circulate among members and later be placed in a library, along with journals and newspapers to which the society subscribed, for the future use of the members.

An early attempt among the Czechs to emulate this western European idea, but for the fostering of nationalism, was made by Antonín Puchmajer, a priest and poet, in 1818 in the town of Radnice near Plzeň in western Bohemia.[6] A professor in Plzeň, Josef Vojtěch, became very enthusiastic over the work of Puchmajer and through the pages of Kramerius's *C. k. vlastenecké noviny* (Royal-Imperial Patriotic Journal) he appealed to his countrymen to follow this example and set up other reading societies. Not much came of this suggestion, however. Only about ten or so were founded in small cities and towns throughout the Bohemian countryside. Their activities were very tame and consisted mainly of subscribing to Czech books and journals and making them available to all members in a central reading room. They also provided a few modest and innocuous social and cultural activities with only slightly nationalistic tendencies. Their main significance was to unite the countryside more closely with the great cultural and national centre in Prague.[7]

Palacký also may have been influenced by the Dědictví svatojanské (The Heritage of St. Jan Nepomuk), a Catholic publishing society organized in 1829 to distribute good, cheap books in Czech, such as bibles, catechisms, legends, and other entertaining and useful literature. This venture was very popular. It sold membership cards at prices ranging from ten to forty florins and soon had over 20,000 members of all classes throughout the Czech lands.[8]

6 For the earlier history of related activities see Josef Volf's *Dějiny veřejných půjčoven knih v Čechách do r. 1848* (Prague, 1931). From the Czechs the idea spread to the South Slavs – to the Croats in 1837, to the Serbs in 1841, and to the Slovenes in 1860. Having no great centre like Prague or other important learned societies, they founded dozens of the simple and easily organized *čitalnice* and *čitaonica* throughout their territories. Cf. also the Bulgarian *čitališta* beginning in 1856.

7 Prague played a much greater role in the Czech national movement than Zagreb in the Croatian, Ljubljana in the Slovenian, Lwów (Lviv) in the Polish and Ruthenian, Bratislava in the Slovak, or Belgrade in the Serbian. None of the other Austro-Slav groups was so centralized or compact a national, ethnic, political, and geographic group as the Czech. The others were divided geographically and politically, sometimes into as many as six divisions.

8 See K. Borový, *Dějiny Svatojanského dědictví* (Prague, 1885). This society was a successor to the Dědictví svatováclavské (Heritage of St. Václav), which had been founded by the Jesuits in Bohemia in 1669 and which had been active in the same field up to 1773. During the nineteenth century similar societies were organized by the other Austro-Slavs: the Slovene

Among the foreign influences on Palacký were the eight or ten literary and learned societies organized by the Slovaks since 1785 – especially the Catholic Anton Bernolák's Literata slavica societas (Slovak Literary Society) organized in 1793 in Trnava, the first real national-cultural organization among the Slovaks.[9] Bernolák used it to foster a Western Slovak dialect as the literary language for the Slovaks separate from literary Czech. The Protestant Spolek literatury slovenské (Slovak Literary Society; the name was later latinized into Institutum linguae et literaturae slavicae), founded in Bratislava in 1801 in connection with the Lutheran Lyceum (an autonomous secondary school) there, was also influential. In 1803 this society founded a chair for the study of Slovak language and literature. Under the direction of Juraj Palkovič this society (which lasted into the 1840s) became a great force in making the Lyceum a centre of the Slovak national revival, which influenced not only a whole generation of Slovak patriots, but also Palacký, who had studied there prior to going to Prague in 1823.

Palacký may have also been influenced by the linguistic reforms of the Serb Vuk Karadžić and the Croat Ljudevit Gaj. By far the most important foreign influence on Palacký, however, was the older Matica srbska, founded in Pest in 1826 by the Serbs in the Austrian empire (it later moved to Novi Sad in 1864). This matice, which became the prototype of all the various matices subsequently founded by the Austro-Slavs,[10] was organized by a nationally minded lawyer in Pest, Jovan Hadžić-Svetić, and six young, wealthy Serb businessmen, also of Pest, in order to foster and promote Serbian culture and literature in all ways, especially by publishing.

Palacký was acquainted with this foundation both through correspondence with his friend Pavel Josef Šafařík, who was at that time director of the Serbian Gymnasium in Novi Sad and who also had been loosely connected with the organization of the Serbian Matice, and through the gift copies of its publication *Ljetopis* (Yearbook) which were sent to the Bohemian museum.

Society of St. Hermagoras, 1852; the Ruthenian Society of St. Basil, 1865; the Croatian Society of St. Jerome, 1868; and the Slovak Society of St. Adalbert, 1870.

9 This society, also known as the Bernolák Society, the Slowenské učené Towarišstwo, and the Towarišstwo literného uměna, lasted over fifty years and was successful in setting up branches and bookstores in five towns – Nitra, Rovne, Banská Bystrica, Rožňava, and Košice.

10 Subsequently the following maticas were founded: the Matice česká in 1831, the Matice moravská in 1836 (known as the Jednota moravská during 1848–9, as the Národní jednota moravská Sv. Cyrilla a Methoda for the period 1849–53, and thereafter again as the Matice moravská), the Matica ilirska in 1842 (which changed its name to Matica hrvatska in 1874), the Matice slovenska in 1863, the Matica dalmatinska in 1863 (which became a branch of the Croatian matica in 1912), the Slovenska matica in Ljubljana in 1864, and the Macierz polska in 1882 in Lwów. (Actually the Polish Ossolineum of 1829 in Lwów was in some ways comparable to the other matices.) Cf. also the Lusatian Maćica Serbska of 1847 and the Bulgarian Knizvno druzestvo of 1869. There is a large bibliography on the Serbian Matica. The latest Serbian work is Živan Milisavac, *Matica Srpska* (Novi Sad, 1965). See also my study "The Serbian *Matica* – Prototype of Austro-Slav Literary Foundations: The First Fifty Years 1826–76," *East European Quarterly*, III (September 1969), 348–70.

However much all these domestic and foreign societies and activities may have influenced Palacký, it was the founding of the Bohemian Museum which gave him the first real opportunity to act and to institutionalize his ideas. The hopes of those working for the "Czech Society" had indeed almost gone, when their cause was resuscitated by the founding of the museum in 1818.

The museum was organized by certain members of the Czech nobility who, though largely Germanized, had been working carefully for some time to secure more autonomy from Vienna and had developed a kind of *Landespatriotismus* – a territorial or Bohemian patriotism which was neither German nor Czech in orientation. (In 1783, to give one example of this attitude, Count Franz Anton Nostitz-Rieneck, the Highest Burgrave [*Nejvyšší purkrabí český*] of Bohemia, built the Gräflich Nostitzsches Nationaltheater – in 1797 renamed the Estates Theatre [Standestheater/Stavovské divadlo] – as an act of moderate resistance to Joseph II's centralization.) These nobles slowly and cautiously began to cooperate with the growing number of middle-class intellectuals, who were becoming increasingly nationalistic and who were beginning to challenge the centralist, absolutist, and Germanized Austrian state as epitomized by Emperor Francis I, his chief minister Prince Clemens Metternich, and Count Josef Sedlnitsky, head of the powerful Polizei- und Censor-Hofstelle, through the only means possible – cultural activity.

In 1814 another Highest Burgrave of Bohemia, Count Franz Anton Kolovrat, inspired by the founding of the Magyar National Museum in 1802 and the Johanneum (a museum founded in Graz in 1811 by Archduke Johann) as symbols of provincial autonomy, requested Count Kašpar Sternberg to investigate the Johanneum and report whether such an institution could be organized successfully in Prague. Count Sternberg's report was in the affirmative and in 1808 Kolovrat (spurred to action by the organization of the Franciscium, a museum named in honour of Francis I in Brno earlier that same year) petitioned Vienna for permission to organize a museum in Prague.

Because of the cumbersome and suspicious Austrian bureaucracy, it took two years for the petition to be processed, but finally in June 1820 permission was granted to organize the Gesellschaft des vaterländischen Museums in Böhmen (Společnost vlastenského musea v Čechách/Society of the Patriotic Museum in Bohemia), which, although it was as conservative, aristocratic, and patriotic as the earlier learned societies, did differ significantly from them in that its leaders insisted that all members at least understand Czech.

Count Kašpar Sternberg was elected the first president and provided space for the society in his palace. In 1847 it moved to the Nostić palace, and finally in the 1890s to the present monumental structure at the top of Václav Square in the heart of Prague.

For the first few years the museum society accomplished little. Its first significant activity was the publication of two journals, beginning in 1827 – a monthly in German, the *Monatschrift der Gessellschaft der vaterländischen Museums in Böhmen* and a quarterly in Czech, the *Časopis Společnosti vlastenského museum v Čechách* (Journal of the Society of the Patriotic Museum in Bohemia).[11]

To be editor of both publications the leaders of the museum chose the Moravian Palacký – evidence of the growing rapprochement between some of the patriotic nobles and the nationally minded intellectuals. Palacký had come to Prague in 1823 at the age of twenty-four with the desire of writing Hussite history. There he made friends with Dobrovský, who helped him secure employment as keeper of the family archives of Count František Sternberg, older brother of Kašpar. Through Sternberg's influence Palacký was later (in 1829) appointed by the Diet to the honorary position of "Historiographer of the Bohemian Estates," although this was not confirmed until 1838.

Through Palacký's efforts as editor, the *Časopis* fostered Czech and became the first real "beach-head" of the Czech campaign for national rights, the first organ for the fostering of the Czech language, the official representative of Czech culture and scholarship, and one of the chief means of spreading knowledge of past and present Czech culture and history among the people.

It was not edited for a small group of scholars, as were other journals such as the *Abhandlungen* of the Royal Bohemian Society of Sciences, but for the widest possible audience of intelligent readers in Bohemia, Moravia, and Slovakia. It carried all kinds of articles, not just scientific ones, and especially contributions on literature – samples of old Czech literature, new poetry and prose, translations from German and other Slavic tongues – and such features as "news" and book reviews. No other Czech journal has ever had such a deep and lasting influence.[12]

Following the organization of the Czech Matice as a committee in 1831 the Museum Board appointed the Prince-patriot Rudolf Kinský as its agent or curator of this new committee and called Palacký, Jungmann, and Presl to work with him as an "agency" (*jednatelství*) or sort of executive committee. Thus the Museum Board had turned the direction of the Matice over to such leaders of the new national Czech spirit who, though genuinely interested in promoting Czech language and literature, were also politically minded and who realized the necessity in the police state in which they lived of disguising their national and political efforts as literary activities. This fact proved as fortunate for the institutionalizing of Palacký's ideas as it was further evidence of the cautious but real support given to the Czech revival by some of the Czech nobility at that time.

11 The German journal changed its name to *Jahrbücher des böhmischen Museums für Natur und Länderkunde, Geschichte, Kunst und Literatur* in 1830, but it was short-lived and soon ceased publication for lack of subscribers (it expired in 1832). Few Czechs, of course, subscribed to it and Germans were apparently satisfied with the *Abhandlungen* of the Royal Bohemian Society of Sciences. In 1831 the Czech journal became the *Časopis Českého musea*, in 1855 the *Časopis Musea království českého*, and finally in 1923 the *Časopis Národního musea*, the name it still bears.

12 For the complete bibliography of this journal see Kneidl, *Časopis Národního musea 1827–1956*.

The Matice officially began its activities immediately by issuing on 1 January a public announcement[13] to "the Patriots of National Literature" calling for a general collection of funds to establish a treasury called the Matice česká (a name which was soon applied to the whole committee). This fund was to be used for the publishing of "good Czech books of a useful, scholarly, and belletristic kind." Those who contributed at least fifty florins[14] were considered as supporting members entitled to one free copy of each publication. The first announcement also stressed that the initial major goals of the Matice would be to publish a large Czech-German dictionary and an encyclopaedia.

The most important and active period during the more than 100-year life of the Matice was from 1831 to about 1861. After that, the relative freedom of constitutionalism enabled the formation of so many new societies that it slowly shrank in importance and activity to a publishing house. For this reason this study will concern itself with the pre-1861 period, which may be broken into three roughly equal ten-year periods: 1831–40, which was a period of organization and development; 1841–51, which represented the time of its greatest flourishing and significance; and 1852–60, which was a period when its activities were severely curtailed by absolutism.

During these thirty years the Matice engaged in many different kinds of activity to foster the Czech language and literature, to increase national consciousness, and to raise cultural standards among the masses. Such activities included publishing books and journals, raising standards of literary criticism, promoting spelling reforms, awarding prizes for outstanding Czech manuscripts, making book grants, and promoting the use of Czech in schools and public life. It also engaged in such related activities as establishing book and journal exchanges with similar societies, and actively promoting Slavic reciprocity.

DEVELOPMENT

During its first decade the Matice's activities and successes were rather limited and unspectacular and membership and funds grew slowly. Membership records reveal that during its first year there were only 35 individual founding members and 134 donors (those who gave less than fifty florins). By 1834 these figures had increased to a total of 359 founding members and 858 donors. By 1840 there were a total of 522 founding members and 1735 small contributors. The Matice's funds correspondingly increased from 2363 to 11,795 florins and then to 18,794 florins – a modest amount, far short of the 50,000 florins considered necessary to publish an encyclopaedia.

This slow beginning can be explained by the fact that national life was just beginning to stir, that the Matice limited its appeal to the public almost exclusively

13 Reprinted in Tieftrunk, *Dějiny Matice české*, 264–6.
14 One florin was worth approximately 0.48 (1850) dollars, and 50 fl. represented the average workingman's pay for nine days.

to announcements in the *Časopis*, that its programme and publications did not appeal to the masses, that the fifty-florin membership fee was beyond the budget of most Czechs, that some overzealous members of the museum worked against the Matice for fear it would compete with the museum, and finally that Vienna did not favour the rise of Czech nationalism and harassed the Matice in the beginning. The committee, for example, was not even allowed to use the term Matice česká during the years 1835–41.

A detailed analysis of membership figures reveals that throughout this decade about 40 per cent of all support came from the clergy (especially the lower clergy – the priests, chaplains, and theological students); about 20 per cent from students, mainly at the university level; and the remainder from businessmen, officials, professional men, the literati, and the nobility. Peasants, workers, and tradesmen were hardly represented at all.[15]

Among the noble founding members were Thuns, Kolovrats, Kinskýs, Sternbergs, Krakovskýs, Černíns, Lobkovics, Clam-Martinics, Schwarzenbergs, and Furstenbergs. But since none of these were able to commit themselves wholly to the national cause, they made no large gifts to the Matice in any way comparable to the 118,000 florins contributed in 1825 to found the Magyar Academy by Counts Széchenyi, Károlyi, Vay, and Andrássy, or even to the 10,000 florins donated by Bishop Strossmayer to found the South Slav Academy in 1867. Even Prince Kinský gave only 1000 florins and Counts Kašpar Sternberg and Alois Kolovrat-Krakovský, Archbishop of Prague, gave only token gifts of 100 florins each.[16] Most donations were between five and fifty florins. Other important early founding members, besides Palacký, Jungmann, and Presl, included the poet and philologist Václav Hanka, the physiologist Jan Evangelista Purkyně, the strong nationalist Josef Václav Frič, the future political leader František Ladislav Rieger, and the Slovak poet Jan Kollár.

The publishing activity of the Matice began in 1832 when it assumed publication of the *Časopis*, which at that time became the mouthpiece of the Matice as well as

15 See Hroch and Veverka, article in *Dějepis ve škole*, cited above in note 1.
16 Further evidence of the well-known difference between the highly nationalistic Polish and Magyar nobility and the conservative, provincially patriotic at best, Bohemian nobility is provided by the following figures concerning the contributions to the Czech Museum during its first four years. At the end of the first year (1818), all contributions totalled only 98,079 florins. Four years later, at the end of 1822, the figure was 168,113 florins – or only about 40 per cent of the amount to be contributed to the Magyar Academy in the one year 1825 by just four noblemen. The largest single contribution to the Czech Museum in the beginning was 10,000 florins from Prince Ferdinand Kinský. Other large gifts during the first four years came from Prince Václav Leopold Chlumčanský (8000 fl.), Count Josef Vratislav (7500 fl.), the Duchess Katherin of Sagan or Zaháň (7500 fl.), Prince Ferdinand Trautmannsdorf (5000 fl.), Count Michal Kaunic (5000 fl.), Count Jan Filip Stadion (5000 fl.), Prince Josef Schwarzenberg (4000 fl.), and Archduke Karl (4000 fl.). All the Černíns, Furstenbergs, Harrachs, Sternbergs, Thuns, Kolovrats, Lobkovics, Nostics, and Kolovrat-Krakovskýs together contributed only 18,350 florins by the end of 1822. These figures are based on membership lists given in Hanuš, *Národní museum a naše obrození*, II, 52–6.

the organ of the museum. (Further evidence of the neglected state of Czech book production is the fact that this journal was printed by Jan Pospíšil in Hradec Králové, who published as many Czech books as all the Prague printers together.) Its first two editors were Palacký (who had edited the journal since its founding in 1827 and continued to do so under the new auspices until 1838) and Šafařík (1838–42). Under their editorship its circulation increased from 500 to 1000. They worked hard to purify and standardize the language and to initiate some modest spelling reforms – against the wishes of antiquarians who wanted to preserve some old-fashioned elements from the sixteenth century. (In all, only four orthographic changes were made in the early 1840s: *j* for *g*, *i* for *j*, *ou* for *au*, and *v* for *w*.)

During its first decade the Czech Matice published very little. Owing to lack of sufficient funds, the condition of the language, and the need for a great deal of preparatory work, little further was said about the publishing of the encyclopaedia. In addition to nine volumes of the *Časopis*, the Matice published only six other works during this decade, of which four were not of much importance.[17] In 1832 and 1835 pamphlets were printed in honour of Francis I and Ferdinand I. In 1833 a useful and popular book *Domácí lékař* (Home Physician) by Jindřich Felix Paulický was published, and in 1832 a seven-page survey by Palacký about court and provincial officials of the Czech kingdom from earliest times (*Přehled saučasný neywyššjch důstognjků a auřednjků zemských i dworských we králowstwj Českém* ...). Had it not been for two other books the publishing activities of the first decade of the Matice could be ignored. But these two publications established its scholarly reputation. They were Jungmann's five-volume *Slownjk česko-německý* (Czech-German Dictionary), 1835–9, and Šafařík's *Slowanské starožnitnosti* (Slavic Antiquities), 1837.

Jungmann's work, which fulfilled one of the original major goals of the "Czech Society" and the Matice, was the result of over thirty years' labour. It became one of the foundation-stones of the language rebirth and considerably enriched the native vocabulary and demonstrated its latent potential as a living literary language. Šafařík's work, the first publication in the Czech language to have important European influence, became a source of argument and ammunition for the Czechs in their struggle against the Germans. Its main thesis was that before the Christian era the Slavs had settled all lands between the Baltic, Black, and Adriatic seas and between the Vistula and Danube rivers, thus giving the Slavs an old and respectable pedigree. The work was soon translated into Russian, Polish, and German. The publication of the "Dictionary" and "Antiquities" had some negative side-effects, however. Their cost was so great that the Matice actually acquired a debt of 750 florins in order to complete their publication, and furthermore their very scholarliness became a factor hindering mass participation in the Matice.

17 All bibliographical citations are from Grund, *Sto let Matice české*, and those published before the spelling reforms of the 1840s are given in their original spellings. Personal names, however, have been modernized.

The merits of the Matice at this time, however, do not lie entirely in its publishing activities. One of its greatest achievements was the bringing of Šafařík from Novi Sad to Prague. In 1830 Šafařík had been dismissed as director of the Gymnasium because he was a Protestant, and in correspondence with Palacký he indicated his interest in coming to Prague if he could make a living and support his family there. Palacký, realizing what an important contribution Šafařík was capable of making to the Czech rebirth and national movement, secretly arranged with nine wealthy patriots to guarantee that the Matice could make him an offer of 480 florins a year for five years to assist with the publishing of the *Časopis*. The offer was made, and accepted, and Šafařík moved his family to Prague in May 1833, where he remained until his death twenty-eight years later in 1861. Because of his influence and his many Russian, Polish, and South Slav connections he helped make Prague the main centre of Slavic studies and Slavic "reciprocity."

EFFLORESCENCE

The 1840s proved a new and much more vigorous decade for the Matice. It was in fact the most important decade in its history of over one hundred years. In December 1841 the Matice published a new announcement or appeal written by Šafařík for more support, contributions, and members.[18] Jan Norbert, Knight of Neuberg, a nationally minded and sympathetic member of the Czech nobility, became the new curator. (Prince Kinský had died in 1836 and Count Hanuš Kolovrat-Krakovský, who succeeded the prince as curator, had resigned in 1841 because of "frequent travelling.") The Executive Committee was also enlarged by adding leading patriots, scholars, and writers such as Šafařík and Hanka in 1841, and later Count Lev Thun, Josef Frič, Václav Vladivoj Tomek, František Ladislav Čelakovský, Karel Jaromír Erben, Purkyně, Josef Čejka, Václav Staněk, and Jan Erazim Vocel (who also edited the *Časopis* from 1843 to 1849).

In an effort to improve its publishing programme and to attract a wider audience and membership than such scholarly works as the "Dictionary" and "Antiquities" had done, five new publishing series were inaugurated in 1841. They were intended not only to aid Czech literature and science, but also to meet the more popular and general needs of the people. The five series consisted of the Staročeská bibliothéka (Old Czech Library) of standard classics up to the eighteenth century, the Novočeská bibliothéka (New Czech Library) of new works in the fields of science and belles-lettres, the Bibliothéka klassiků (Classical Library) of translations of important past and present world literature, and finally the Domácí Bibliothéka (Domestic Library) for popular and useful works. In the following year another series, the Malá encyklopaedie nauk (Small Encyclopaedia of Science), which was to function as a sort of a substitute until the Matice could produce a real encyclopaedia, was commenced.

18 Reprinted in Tieftrunk, *Dějiny Matice české*, 266–7.

A good gauge of the success of the Matice's activities at this time, and evidence that this was a fruitful period, can be found in the detailed membership and financial records, which show that the number of new members (who after 1840 paid as little as five florins) rose during the year from an all-time-low of 10 in 1840 to 48, and increased steadily thereafter to 490 in 1851, when there was a grand total of 3773 individual and 95 institutional memberships. A few important non-Czech founding members such as Prince Miloš Obrenović of Serbia and the Russian Minister of Culture, Sergei Semionovich Uvarov, joined during this decade.

Finances showed a commensurate growth from 19,309 florins in 1841 to 62,912 florins by the end of 1851. Furthermore, the Matice's publications were now being printed in increasingly large numbers – from 1000 copies in the beginning to 3000 copies. Slowly the Matice earned for itself the position of the chief representative of Czech scholarship and culture in general, not only at home but also abroad, especially among the other Austro-Slavs. It also began to approximate an academy of science in spite of the existence of the Royal Bohemian Society of Sciences.

The response of official Vienna is of some interest. Even though during the 1830s the Matice published two honorific volumes – one in honor of Francis I in 1832 and one in honour of Ferdinand and Marie Anna in 1835 – not a kreutzer was donated to the Matice from Vienna. It was not until 1840 that Archduke Franz Karl gave a niggardly 100 florins. The only other gift from the "Haus, Hof, und Staat" was a trifling fifty florins from Archduke Stephan in 1845. Nevertheless, in 1851 the Matice was required, as were all other publishing concerns throughout the empire, to send one copy of all its publications to the Imperial Court Library and the Imperial Academy of Science in Vienna and to the libraries of the University of Prague. Of much more significance, however, than the trifling note which Vienna did take of the Matice is the fact that Vienna did not seriously hound and persecute it.[19]

In 1844, at the suggestion of Palacký, the Matice initiated a programme of offering prizes for worthwhile books written in good Czech. The books could be written anywhere or published anywhere. There were two classes of prizes: for books about Czech language and literature, fifty florins, and for books on other subjects, twenty-five florins. During the initial year no first prize was awarded, but the dramatist Josef Kajetán Tyl received a second prize for his novel *Poslední Čech* (The Last Czech), written in the historical spirit of Sir Walter Scott.

During this period the Matice also began a programme of book grants. The first grant was made to a Czech regiment in Mainz in 1844. Others followed to the Imperial Hospital in Vienna and to the Soldiers Hospital in Prague. During the revolutionary era of 1848–9 books were distributed to poor students, and a copy of each

19 A search in the Haus-, Hof-, und Staatsarchiv and the Verwaltungsarchiv in Vienna failed to turn up any significant documents on the Matice. Much, of course, was destroyed by the fire of 1927, but even the various indexes hardly mention it. The archive of the Matice itself is in the Central State Archives in Prague as a part of the Archiv Národního musea, Registratura NM.

publication was donated to a group of revolutionary students called Slávia (the Slavic Brotherhood). During the period 1850–1 several book grants were made to the Protestant Theological Seminary in Vienna and to a local library in Celje, Styria.

At this same time the Matice began exchanging books and journals with institutions such as the Ossolineum in Lwów (Lviv, Lemberg), the Library of the University of Cracow, the Kievan Society of Antiquities, the Copenhagen Society of Antiquities, and with such Polish publications as the Lwów *Rozmaitości* (Miscellanies), the Przemyśl *Tygodnik* (Weekly), and the *Biblioteka Warszawska* (The Warsaw Library). Similar book exchanges were arranged with the Royal Academy of Munich, the Imperial Society of History and Antiquities of the University of Moscow, and the St. Petersburg Archaeological Society. The Matice was also careful to set up exchanges with sister organizations in Moravia, Croatia, and among the Ruthenians. Through such exchanges the Matice furthered and strengthened Slavic reciprocity and solidarity.[20]

In 1849 an exchange programme was arranged with the recently established (1846) Smithsonian Institution in Washington, D.C. By 1852 the Matice had received from the Institution among other things volumes I and II of the *Smithsonian Contributions to Knowledge*, the *History, Conditions and Prospects of the Indian Tribes in the United States*, a *Report on the Discovery of Neptune*, and the *Ephemeris of Neptune for 1852* and had in turn sent to Washington some of its publications by Palacký, Jungmann, Čelakovský, Tomek, Vocel, and a nearly complete run of its journals published to that date.[21]

In 1845–6 the Matice began specific activities to help Czech students in the Germanized middle schools become better acquainted with their mother tongue, chiefly by publishing special cheap editions of appropriate books. They made available, for example, Jungmann's *Slowesnost* (Literature, i.e. a textbook with literary excerpts; first edition 1820) for one florin in 1845, volume I of Josef František Smetana's *Wšeobecný dějepis občanský* (Universal History) for 36 kreutzers in 1846, and a special German-Czech dictionary of scholarly terminology in 1851. In addition, a few years later, in 1856 the Matice entered the lists as a champion for the preservation of a common Czech and Slovak literary language by publishing a work entitled *Hlasowé o potřebě jednoty spisowného jazyka pro Čechy, Morawany, a Slowáky* (Voices Concerning the Need for a Unity of the Written Language for Czechs, Moravians, and Slovaks). This remarkable little book cited a formidable list of thirty-one Czech, Moravian, and Slovak authorities and their arguments against a separate Slovak language. Its publication was occasioned by various individuals

20 The documents pertaining to these exchanges are in the Archiv Národního musea, Registratura NM, S-3-7.
21 Archiv Narodního musea, Registratura NM, S-7, 20–49, 51, 64. My correspondence with the Smithsonian Institution has failed to turn up any further documents on this interesting Czech-American exchange of publications. Most likely these documents were lost in the fire of January 1865, which destroyed all the official records of the Smithsonian Institution.

and groups among the Slovaks, especially Anton Bernolák and Ľudovít Štúr, who were advocating either a Western Slovak dialect (*bernoláčina*) or a Central dialect (*štúrovčina*) in place of Czech.

In 1844 the Matice had also begun to collect manuscripts and rare books for the museum. Among their acquisitions was a fourteenth-century manuscript of Tomáš Štítný and a copy of the rare fifteenth-century Krumlov Bible. They also provided funds to help support the research and work of Šafařík in preparing a fount of Glagolitic type, which at that time did not exist in Europe.

Towards the end of this decade the Matice once again seriously began to work on the encyclopaedia. They commenced by preparing an index of all the articles to be included, and by the end of 1851 they had about 700 covering "A" through "Al." (The following year, however, when Bach's absolutism began in earnest, the government refused to let them proceed further.) Aside from political considerations, the Matice was constantly frustrated in its attempt to produce an encyclopaedia by the lack of funds and of co-workers and editors for such an enormous undertaking. Furthermore, the great proponent of the encyclopaedia, Palacký, turned more and more from the frustrating work of editing an encyclopaedia to the successful publishing of his "History." (The Matice never did fulfil its goal. The first Czech encyclopaedia was the *Slovník naučný*, published between 1860 and 1874 without Matice support and under the editorship of Rieger.)

The most important activity of the Matice during this decade was, of course, its publishing. For the first time original and scholarly works in various fields in Czech began to appear regularly. Between 1841 and 1851, in addition to the *Časopis*, it printed thirty-seven books. The subjects of history, natural history, and belles-lettres dominated, but some works were published in the fields of law, geography, travel, and pedagogy. Some important maps and atlases were also published.

Of these thirty-seven publications, eighteen should be noted. In 1841 a fifteenth-century Czech legal classic was reprinted. This was the work of the great Czech humanist Viktorín Kornel of Všehrd, *Knihy dewatery o práwiech a súdiech i o dskách země české* (Nine Books on Laws, Verdicts, and Records of Bohemia; 1st ed., 1499; enlarged, 1502–8). Also in 1841 the first of three works to be published by Jungmann during this decade was published – his *Sebrané spisy weršem i prosau* (Collected Writings: Poetry and Prose). In 1845 and 1846 the Matice brought out a revised and corrected second and third edition of his important *Slowesnost*. Finally, in 1849, a second, enlarged and revised edition of his famous *Historie literatury české* (History of Czech Literature), which was first published in 1825, appeared. This was the first modern history of Czech literature written in Czech.

In 1842 the first of four works by the historian and disciple of Palacký, V. V. Tomek, was published. This was his *Krátký wšeobecný dějepis* (Short Universal History), which was followed in 1843 by his *Děje země České* (History of the Czech Lands), in 1845 by his *Děje mocnářství Rakauského* (History of the Austrian Empire), and finally in 1849 by the first volume of his important *Děje uniwersity Pražské*

(History of the University of Prague) in honour of its 500th anniversary.

The most important publication of 1845 was volume I *of Výbor z literatury české* (An Anthology of Czech Literature), which was intended to range from oldest times to the present. It was collected and edited by Palacký, Šafařík, Hanka, and Jungmann, who served as the chief editor. This first volume, covering the period up to the beginning of the fifteenth century, is still considered one of the best anthologies of early Czech literature.

One year later, in 1846, the first of two important works in the field of natural history was published – Presl's greatest work *Wšeobecný rostlinopis* (General Botany). In 1848 the Matice also published his *Počátkové rostlinosloví* (Introduction to Botanical Terminology) as a companion to the first work.

In 1847 the most important of the several books of belles-lettres published during this decade appeared. It was *Spisů básnických knihy šestery* (Six Books of Poetic Writings) by the famous Czech poet Čelakovský.

Three important translations were published during this period: Milton's *Paradise Lost* by Jungmann in 1843, Shakespeare's *Romeo and Juliet* by František Doucha in 1847, and Virgil's poems by Karel Vinařický in 1851. Jungmann's translation of *Paradise Lost* (Ztracený ráj) was extremely important in that it proved conclusively that the Czech language was capable of grace and power and could express lofty thoughts.

However, the most important publications of the Matice since Jungmann's "Dictionary" and Šafařík's "Antiquities" were two volumes in Palacký's by then famous *Dějiny národu českého* (History of the Czech Nation): volume I, part 1, appeared in Czech in 1848 and volume III, part 2, in 1851. This history, Palacký's real life work, which made him the "father of his people," restored to the Czechs their forgotten history, and gave them pride in the past and hope and courage for the future. Each volume of this monumental work, of course, had to be approved by the office of the censor, but even so it became one of the great foundation-stones of the whole Czech rebirth.[22]

During the revolutionary period of 1848–9 the Matice as an institution accom-

22 Palacký began publishing his history in German as *Geschichte von Böhmen*, the first volume of which appeared in 1836. The first part of volume I of the Czech edition in 1848 was a rewriting of the German. Thereafter, Palacký wrote in Czech, and the parallel publication of the German version was translated from the Czech. By 1864 four volumes of the work had been published. These were volumes I, III, IV, and V, which brought the story to 1526, the beginning of the Habsburg rule in Bohemia. Between 1874 and 1876 Palacký finished the Czech edition by bringing out the missing volume II covering the period 1253–1403, from the beginning of the reign of Přemysl Otakar II to the early career of Jan Hus. For various reasons Palacký never went beyond 1526. He had not intended in the first place to go beyond the Czech loss of independence in 1620. Furthermore, he assumed that the authorities would make access to the requisite documents for the critical century between 1526 and 1620 difficult. And, finally, by the time censorship was relaxed in the 1860s he was too involved in public affairs to continue his historical researches.

plished little. Many of its leaders, who were as interested in politics as in culture, eagerly seized this opportunity to pour their energies into genuine political activity. At least five members of the Executive Committee, Palacký, Šafařík, Vocel, Čejka, and Staněk, were members of the Kroměříž Diet. As a result they temporarily neglected the cultural activities of the Matice.

REPRESSION

After the failure of the revolutionary phase of the "Spring of the Peoples" the political-cultural leaders of the Matice returned to the offices of the Matice in the Nostic palace to preserve and advance the national movement as best they could through purely cultural activities. The new absolutism which was instituted by the end of 1851 by Alexander Bach, the minister of the interior since 1849 who functioned as the real head of the Austrian government after the death of Prince Schwarzenberg in April 1852, proved to be more rigid than that of Metternich. Prague lay under a state of siege until 1853, Czech "home rule" was negligible, Bach's Press Law (Pressordnung) and Law of Associations (Vereingesetz) firmly curtailed most national activities, and all forms of particularism were suppressed.

The most feared problem of the monarch at this time was nationalism, and one of the most alarming varieties was the Czech. The leaders of the Matice, especially Palacký and those who had been to Kroměříž, were closely watched. Leopold von Sacher-Masoch, director of the Prague police, was particularly interested in forcing Palacký out of the museum and the Matice.[23] And not only was Sacher-Masoch successful in this, but in 1852 he also arranged for the conservative Count Kristián of Valdštejn, who had previously not even been a member of the museum, to replace Jan of Neuberg as the museum's president. Even after Sacher-Masoch was transferred to Graz in 1854 things did not improve, for Vienna saw to it that his place was taken by Anton Paumann who was just as thoroughly anti-Czech as Sacher-Masoch and who saw to it that the museum and Matice were directed by conservatives and that their more liberal members were muzzled.

Although the Matice never regained the unique position it had held during the 1830s and 1840s, the relative lack of other political and cultural activity during the bleak 1850s caused it, because of its publishing activities, to become the foremost

23 Because of the political activities of some of its leaders and because of articles about the Slav Congress of 1848 and letters of Hus which had appeared in the *Časopis Českého musea*, the Matice was compromised in the eyes of Vienna. Palacký, as editor of the *Časopis*, and as an active participant in the Slav Congress, was particularly watched by Vienna. Furthermore, the publication by the Matice in 1851 of volume III, part 2, of his "History," which treated the Hussite Wars (from the death of Žižka in 1424 to the beginning of the reign of Ladislav Posthumous in 1439) and thus did much to revive national feelings, angered Vienna. So complete was Sacher-Masoch's victory over Palacký that Palacký, who had been a member of the museum board for thirty-four years, was not even thanked formally or recognized for his service by the museum.

champion of the Czech national movement during that decade[24] (if we disregard the committee to build the National Theatre).

One of the first acts aimed at curtailing its importance and influence occurred in April 1852 when it was told that henceforth it would be required to notify the Municipal Captaincy (*Hejtmanství/Hauptmannschaft*) of its meetings, so that a representative of the *Hejtmanství* could be present. This form of police supervision lasted until as late as 1866. Subsequent laws and requirements were initiated both to neutralize increasingly the museum and to turn the Matice simply into a section of the museum, that is, the Matice was no longer to remain an independent society.

In July 1852, Jan, Knight of Neuberg, resigned as curator and was replaced by Professor Purkyně, who was assisted by Šafařík, Erben, Frič, Hanka, Tomek, Vocel, and Nebeský who then served as secretary and editor of the *Časopis*. (Jungmann, Presl, and Čelakovský had by then died and Palacký had been forced out.)

The new by-laws of this period necessarily stressed that the main goal of the Matice was the scholarly fostering of the Czech language and literature. The government required that it become completely subservient to the museum and that it request permission from the latter for each publication. Thus by strictly controlling the conservative museum, the government also controlled the Matice.

The Law of Associations in 1852 required that the name of the museum be changed from National Museum to the Museum of the Bohemian Kingdom and that the Matice be reduced from an independent committee to a subordinate section.

The negative features of absolutism are clearly revealed in the membership and financial records of the Matice. Membership fell from a total of new members for the year 1852 of 327 to 31 in 1860, and contributions correspondingly fell from 14,635 florins in 1852 to 3542 florins in 1860. The modest support of the patriotic nobility all but ceased after 1849. Still, in spite of the decrease of the annual number of new members and contributions, the total membership grew from 4105 members in 1852 to 4655 plus 142 corporations in 1860, and the funds from 57,791 florins in 1852 to 79,120 florins in 1860. The annual decrease reflects the ravages of absolutism, the discontent of many Czechs with the greatly curtailed activities of the Matice, and the general discontent with all national life at this time, while the over-all increase suggests the importance of the Matice as one of the few outlets for Czech national aspirations.

Apart from the publication of books and journals the activities of the Matice were extremely limited in this period. It made a few book grants and arranged for some book and journal exchanges. For example, books were given to several Czech gym-

24 In 1850, to help compensate for the failure of 1848–9, a committee was founded to build a Czech national theatre, of which Palacký was also president. By the time of the first opening of the National Theatre in 1881 (it burned and had to be reopened in 1883) the committee had raised nearly two million florins. See my study *Czech Nationalism: A Study of the National Theatre Movement, 1845–83* (Urbana, Ill., 1964).

nasia and to some Slovak libraries. Books were also sent to the Bavarian Academy, the Lusatian *Maćica*, and the Royal Bohemian Society of Sciences. Exchanges were arranged with the St. Petersburg Academy, the Danish Archaeological Society, the Ossolineum in Lwów and the Society of Learning in Cracow.

As a result of Bach's absolutism it is not surprising that most of the publications in this period were scholarly, practical, and neutral. The Matice had to be very careful to stay away from political and religious subjects. For example, in 1856, when it wanted to publish Jan Krejčí's *Geologie* (Geology), it had to take care that there was nothing in the manuscript against religion, and even then it was not finally published until 1860–3. Works about and by Hus were, of course, not permitted.

Under the dead hand of absolutism it is not surprising that the Matice shifted thus towards more neutral ground and restricted its publishing primarily to harmless works on botany, health, travel, and translations of Shakespeare's plays, of which eight (*Richard III, Hamlet, King Lear, Cymbeline, The Merry Wives of Windsor, Coriolanus, Henry IV Part 1*, and *Henry V*) were published by 1859. Although such works, especially the Shakespeare translations, caused no problems with the censor's office, and extended the Czech's acquaintance with a great poet of the non-German world, they did not do much to increase interest and participation in the Matice, which became more and more a simple printing society.

Nevertheless, even under these dreary circumstances the Matice managed to publish some important works. In addition to the eight plays of Shakespeare its most important publications were Čelakovský's *Mudrosloví národu slovanského ve příslovích* (The Wisdom of the Slavic Nation in Their Proverbs) in 1852, the Slovak Ľudovít Štúr's *O národních písních a pověstech plemen slovanských* (National Songs and Stories of the Slavs) in 1853, volume i of the twelve-volume *Dějepis města Prahy* (History of Prague) by Tomek in 1855, and in 1857 and 1860 volume iv, parts 1 and 2, of Palacký's "History," which brought the narrative through the reign of Jiří of Poděbrady, the last native Czech king, and to his death in 1471.

The Matice also initiated the publication of two new journals in addition to the *Časopis*: *Živa* and *Památky*. In 1852 the great scientist Purkyně had suggested that something practical be published, primarily on science for the use of teachers in the Czech secondary schools. This led to the founding of a periodical for this purpose, a natural history journal for which permission was received in December 1852. It was called *Živa* (Czech name for Ceres, the goddess of agriculture; from *život*, meaning life) and was edited by Purkyně and Krejčí. Although called a "Natural History Magazine," it was actually a yearbook averaging about 300 pages an issue. It was an immediate success and soon had 1500 subscribers; indeed it was largely self-supporting, and lasted for twenty-five years (1853–78).

The success of *Živa* caused the archaeological section of the museum to want to set up its own journal. This section complained that the *Časopis* did not devote enough of its space to archaeology and claimed that its members had all kinds of articles to publish. Therefore, two years late, in 1855, the museum authorized, and the Matice published, another learned journal devoted to archaeology and geography. It was called *Památky archaeologické a místopisné* (Archaeological and Topographic Monuments) and, like *Živa*, it appeared annually and was sold at half price to Matice members. *Památky*, edited by Karel V. Zap, was also successful, but not nearly so successful as *Živa*, because of the nature of its materials. By the end of 1854 it had 569 prepaid subscribers. (It continued to be published by the Matice until 1892, when the Czech Academy took it over.) In 1855 the Matice tried to stabilize the number of copies of each of these two journals – publishing 1000 of *Živa* and 800 of *Památky*. The *Časopis* was still appearing also, but in 1857 the number of copies had to be cut from 4000 to 3500 as a consequence of the competition provided by the two other journals.

Slowly the three journals began to specialize: the *Časopis* concentrated on literature, philology, and philosophy; *Památky* published primarily archaeological and historical articles; and *Živa* took the field of natural history. Such were the activities of the 1850s.

Because of its important pioneering activities up to 1848 and the suppression of the bleak 1850s, which limited its contribution to the cause of Czech nationalism, it is surprising that the Matice did not experience a period of great growth and activity after the fall of Bach in 1860 and with the subsequent freedom of the age of constitutionalism initiated by the October Diploma of 1860 and the February Patent of 1861. Though surprising, this development is, however, rather easily explained. After 1860 there were simply too many political opportunities and too much freedom for Czech patriots to continue to rely so much on cultural substitutes for political activity. (This is a characteristic feature not only of the Czech national movement but of the whole Austro-Slav national revival – while cultural advancement remained as important a desideratum as ever, as soon as political tools became available, cultural tools were no longer considered so politically and nationally important.) Furthermore, by 1862 other societies and institutions, such as the Umělecká beseda (Artists' Union), the choral society Hlahol, the gymnastic society Sokol, and the literary society Svatobor were founded, each of which either took over a part of the activities of, or drew away members from, the Matice. New popular publishing concerns were also founded. One of the most important of these was the Matice lidu (People's Foundation), organized by several patriots in 1867 for the purpose of publishing good, popular books as cheaply as possible – for one florin members received six publications annually. Soon the activity of the Czech Matice was reduced almost exclusively to the publishing of scholarly books.

Thereafter, under the aegis of men of the calibre of Erben, Rieger, Tomek, Alois Jirásek, Jan Jakubec, and Lubor Niederle, the Matice continued to contribute to the mainstream of Czech cultural development by publishing books and journals; it advanced education by making generous book grants to schools in Bohemia, Moravia, and among the Slovaks, and it strengthened Slavic reciprocity by developing publication exchange programmes with other matices, libraries, and institutions throughout the Slavic world. After the restructuring of Czech intellectual and cultural life following the Second World War the Matice ceased to exist, though its name is still preserved by a lecture society.

The Matice česká was an important pioneering society, which fostered the Czech revival at an early and difficult time. It prepared the way for other national societies, and helped to lay the foundation for the later and fuller development of Czech national and cultural life.

6

Jan Ernst Smoler and
the Czech and Slovak Awakeners:
A Study in Slav Reciprocity

PETER BROCK

THE CZECH AWAKENING, as it gained strength and direction during the first half of the nineteenth century, exercised a powerful influence over the emergent national consciousness of other, less nationally developed Slav peoples. In turn, the national renascences of these peoples helped to strengthen the Czechs' confidence in their own ability to attain a level of civilization equal to that of the most advanced European nations. The call went out from the Czech-speaking intelligentsia for "Slav reciprocity," for the free circulation of cultural values and the sharing of cultural achievements among the various Slav groups. Nowhere did the Czechs find a more enthusiastic response than among members of the struggling intelligentsia of the Lusatian Serbs, a small Slav-speaking people set down amidst a sea of "Germandom."

The Lusatian Serbs were partitioned politically between the kingdoms of Prussia and Saxony and divided in literary language between speakers of the Upper and more vigorous, and of the Lower and increasingly moribund, variants of their tongue; they were also separated along confessional lines. Owing to divergent systems of writing their language (which is closely related to both Czech and Polish) the somewhat meagre literature published by Protestants or Roman Catholics was unintelligible to the other party. If we add to numerical weakness[1] and cul-

1 The earliest official estimates of the number of Lusatian Serbs were – in round figures –

tural fissiparousness the fact that the Lusatian Serbs were overwhelmingly a peasant people only just beginning at that time to emerge from centuries-long serfdom, there is little wonder that their intelligentsia, made up of a few hundred pastors and priests and a handful of nationally conscious school-teachers, should grasp eagerly at the outstretched hand of their Czech brothers. True, the Lusatian Serb renascence of the nineteenth century had its roots in the western Enlightenment, which had reached Lusatia in the previous century through its German protagonists.[2] German liberalism and romanticism of the pre-1848 era had likewise been a factor in stimulating interest in the Lusatian Serb *Volk*. And, even though they were as yet scarcely aware of their nationality, the Serb-speaking countryfolk themselves, of course, provided the essential base on which all the efforts of future awakeners must build. But, largely owing to the close linguistic kinship as well as to the missionary zeal of the Czech cultural nationalists, it was in the Czech (and Slovak) lands that the Lusatian Serb awakeners found the most effective inspiration for their own activities.

This influence can be seen nowhere more clearly than in the life of Jan Ernst[3] Smoler (1816–84), the "Father" of his people – as his grateful admirers came to call him – and the man who, for nearly fifty years, carried, with only a few co-workers, the burden of keeping alive the still tender culture of the nation. In his home Smoler learned respect for his native tongue, and in the Upper Lusatian village of Łaz (Lohsa) where his father was a humble school-teacher he grew to know and to love the ways of the Serb countryfolk. Although throughout his life he remained a loyal citizen of his German state – at first of Prussia, under whose rule he was born, and from 1850 onwards of Saxony – he was, seemingly from his earliest years, conscious of the difference between himself and his German-speaking fellow citizens and, as he grew up, increasingly – almost defiantly – proud

---

127,000 in 1832, 140,000 in 1849, 160,000 in 1858. Smoler in his own calculations around the beginning of the 1840s arrived at a figure of 164,000. See Ernst Tschernik [Černik], *Die Entwicklung der sorbischen Bevölkerung von 1832 bis 1945: Eine demographische Untersuchung* (Berlin, 1954), 20, 35, 43. In Tschernik's view "die Schätzungen bei Schmaler [Smoler] etwas zu hoch erscheinen lässt" (35). The difficulty of setting up completely reliable criteria for determining whom one should consider a Lusatian Serb has caused wide variation in the assessment of numbers at any given time. The most recent demographical study is by Frido Mětšk, "Serbow rěčna přestrěn a jich ličba w 19. lětstotku," *Rozhlad: Časopis za serbsku kulturu* (Budyšin/Bautzen), XVIII/4 (1968), 140–4.

2 Josef Páta, "Lužickosrbské národní obrození a československá účast v něm," *Slavia* (Prague), II/2–3 (1923), 355.

3 Today Lusatian Serb writers always use the indigenous form "Arnošt." In fact Smoler, when writing in Lusatian Serb, signed himself "Jan Ernst." See Lucija Hajnec, "Jan Arnošt Smoler," unpublished PH.D. dissertation (written in Upper Lusatian), University of Prague, 1952. His visiting card is preserved in the Literární archiv památníku národního písemnictví, Strahov, Prague (formerly the Literary Archive of the National Museum). Evidently intended by Smoler for foreign acquaintances, the card is inscribed on one side in Russian; on the other there is written in the Lusation Serb language: "Jan E. Smoleŕ, Serb-Łužičan."

of his membership of the tiny ethnic group that was only gropingly and with great difficulty reaching towards a national identity. While he was a boy still in the high school (*gymnasium*) at Bautzen, the chief town of Saxon Upper Lusatia, we find him – with the director's permission, for Smoler always cleaved to legality – organizing classes for his fellow Serb students in their own tongue where they could exercise in reading, writing, and speaking a language which then found no place in the official curriculum. Frustrated by a ruling of the Prussian government in his efforts to gain admittance to the Saxon University of Leipzig where a Lusatian Serb student society had existed since 1716, Smoler chose Breslau as his university after hearing that there the Polish students had organized a patriotic society.

Polish was the first Slav language that Smoler learned (apart of course from his native Lusatian Serb), for after entering Breslau University in 1836 he had begun to take Polish lessons from one of his student acquaintances. But it was not so much Smoler's Polish contacts that were to mark an epoch in his life and to convert him into an ardent exponent of Slav reciprocity as the only policy open to a small and culturally backward people like his own Lusatian Serbs. It was his meeting in 1838 with the famous Czech physiologist Jan Evangelista Purkyně (1787–1869), which first truly opened out before his eager young mind the potentialities inherent in membership of the world of Slav culture. Smoler himself fully recognized his debt: as he wrote a decade later, in addition to many other kindnesses he had to thank Purkyně especially for his "first general introduction to Slavdom."[4] For Purkyně, who since 1823 had occupied a chair at Breslau University, was not only eminent in his professional field, he was an ardent Slavophil with a genuine interest in, and a wide knowledge of Slav literatures, folklore, and history, and himself something of a poet. His contacts embraced the whole Slav learned and literary world.

Smoler had chosen to study Protestant theology, since the ministry seemed the most obvious calling for one who wished to devote his life to the welfare of the devout Lusatian countryfolk. It was a public lecture Smoler gave in Breslau in August 1838 to mark the official inauguration of the "Society for Lusatian Language and History," which he had been instrumental in setting up among students from his native province, that brought the obscure young theology student to the notice of the professor of physiology. Purkyně then took Smoler under his wing. He placed him in charge of his very extensive Slavic library and entrusted him with the

---

4 *Tydźeńske Nowiny* (Budyšin, 15 Dec. 1849), quoted in J. Páta, *Z čěskeho listowanja Jana Arnošta Smolerja: Přinošk k stawiznam čěsko – serbskich počahow* (Budyšin, 1919), 12. This volume of Smoler's correspondence is the main source for his relations with the Czech (and Slovak) awakeners. I cite it below in abbreviation as Smoler-Páta. The older literature on Smoler is discussed by Páta on pp. 7–9. A three-volume popular biography of Smoler is at present in preparation by Jan Cyž: *Jan Arnošt Smoler: Wobrys jeho žiwjenja a skutkowanja*. The first volume (covering the period before 1848) appeared in Budyšin in 1966. See also L. Heine [Hajnec], "Jan Arnošt Smoler – Verfechter der Idee von der slavischen Wechselseitigkeit in der Lausitz," *Zeitschrift für Slawistik* (Berlin), III/2–4 (1958), 534–42.

education of his two young sons. In addition, Smoler was invited to join the Sunday morning class in Czech that Purkyně had been holding in his home. And finally the young ordinand was received into Purkyně's household to live as a member of the family.

"Purkyně's library," wrote Smoler in his autobiography,[5] "opens the door [for me] to the literature of all the Slavs."[6] Visiting Slav scholars and literati were frequent guests at the Purkyně's hospitable house: here Smoler became personally acquainted with Poles and Czechs, Russians and South Slavs. A more vivid realization of the size of the Slav world, a growing confidence in its intellectual vitality and its spiritual depth, and an ardent belief in the Slav future, and in the future of his own small Lusatian Serb nation as a part of the Slavic whole, resulted from Smoler's membership of the Purkyně household. In particular he came to learn in detail the story of the Czech awakeners' efforts, dating back to the latter years of the previous century, first to revive a seemingly expiring language and then to go on to build, on the basis of painstaking philological research, a new literature and a modern learning. Czech culture was being adapted to the needs of a nation which aimed to secure a place for itself in contemporary European civilization. Smoler rejoiced at the successes already won by the Czechs and dreamed of similar victories for his own people, while scheming at the same time how to set in motion a movement among them that might eventually achieve a national renascence of their own.

Smoler, for all his idealism as to ultimate ends, remained throughout his life a realist in regard to means.[7] This moderation showed itself in two of his earliest projects: the publication of a scholarly edition of Lusatian Serb folk-songs and the devising for Upper Lusatian of an orthography that would bridge the gap

5 The complete version of Smoler's autobiography, written towards the end of his life, is seemingly no longer extant. Two shorter versions have been published. One is in German (possibly a translation from Smoler's Lusatian original) as Appendix II of a volume by Smoler's colleague, pastor H. Immisch [Imiš], *Deutsche Antwort eines sächsischen Wenden: Der Panslavismus, unter den sächsischen Wenden mit russischem Gelde betrieben und zu den Wenden in Preussen hinübergetragen* (Leipzig, 1884). The other is in Upper Lusatian: "Autobiografija J. E. Smolerja," ed. Adolf Černý, *Časopis Maćicy Serbskeje* (Budyšin, 1917). The editor also published this in Czech translation as "Vlastní životopis Jana Arnošta Smolefa," *Slovanský přehled* (Prague), XII (1910), 6–11, 62–9, 204–12.

6 "Autobiografija," 8.

7 The contrast has often been pointed out between Smoler's moderation and the ebullience of his contemporary Jan Pětr Jordan (1818–91), the other great figure in the Lusatian Serb awakening and a Roman Catholic (unlike Smoler who came from the Protestant majority of the Lusatian Serbs). Smoler moved slowly but surely towards some modest goal: Jordan, more ambitious in his schemes than Smoler, at the same time lacked the temperament to carry them to success in the face of the obstacles with which he inevitably met on the way. During the 1840s the two men collaborated from time to time in various literary efforts but their relationship, while always correct, lacked warmth of feeling. For Jordan, see my article "J. P. Jordan's Role in the National Awakening of the Lusatian Serbs," *Canadian Slavonic Papers* (Toronto), X, 3 (Autumn 1968), 312–40.

between Protestant and Catholic and thus make possible the creation of a common literary heritage. Smoler was engaged in working out these schemes during the years he spent as a guest of Purkyně and, if they did not actually originate from the Czech's inspiration, his projects received momentum from the latter's support and encouragement.

Collection and publication of national folk-songs, along with the oral tales, riddles, and proverbs of the people, was a task undertaken by the early ideologists of all the emergent national movements in central and eastern Europe. For in folk literature cultural nationalists saw a priceless treasure, the hidden wisdom of the nation, which the simple people had preserved uncontaminated by corrupt civilization and by debasement through foreign influences. While still a boy in school Smoler had begun to explore the countryside around his native village in search of folk creativity; he jotted down words and melodies in notebooks he kept for this purpose, until his collection reached substantial proportions and came to include samples not only from Upper, but from Lower Lusatia as well. It was now that his contact with Purkyně proved providential for, as we have seen, it was Purkyně who introduced him to the rich folk literature which Czech and other Slav scholars had been publishing over the previous decades. Thus Smoler's horizon as a folklorist was widened from a narrow, local antiquarianism to embrace a general view of Slav ethnography, and the scholarly value of the work which he eventually produced[8] was greatly enhanced. As editor he was now able to take into consideration the findings of other scholars and to compare the texts of the folk literature of his Lusatian Serbs with the songs and tales of the other Slav peoples. It was in Purkyně's private library that Smoler found the volumes of song collections that were essential for his studies; it was to Purkyně's aid that Smoler had recourse when, back in his home village, Łaz, and therefore far from the resources of any library, he needed the loan of books to carry on his folklore studies.[9]

Again, owing largely to Purkyně's urgings, to his reminders that the Lusatian Serbs formed part of a wider all-Slav cultural community and that, not far to the south across the mountains, their writings might find eager readers, too, among the Czechs of Bohemia, Smoler, in his efforts to reform Lusatian Serb orthography,

8 *Volkslieder der Wenden in der Ober- und Nieder-Lausitz*, i: *Pjesnički* (Grimma, 1841); ii: *Próznicki* (Grimma, 1843). The volumes also bear the name of pastor Leopold Haupt as co-editor, but in fact Haupt's contribution was minimal.

9 For example, in a letter from Łaz, dated 11 December 1839, Smoler, back at home for several months to prepare for his final examinations in theology, asks Purkyně *inter alia* for the loan of both a Czech and a Polish dictionary to help him continue his folklore researches. His knowledge of Czech and Polish, only recently acquired, was evidently insufficient at that date to cope with the unusual words that cropped up in the folk literature he was studying. See J. Páta, "Jan Ev. Purkyně a lužičtí Srbové," in *Jan Ev. Purkyně 1787–1937: Sborník statí*, ed. Fr. Páta *et al.* (Prague, 1937), 270. An appendix to this essay prints the correspondence between Smoler and Purkyně in a more accurate transcription than in the earlier Smoler-Páta edition.

modelled himself on the example of the Czechs (and to a lesser degree the Poles). The written language, disguised – as it then was – in the cramping Gothic black-letter type and using an orthography that was adopted from German and was indeed ill adapted to a Slavonic tongue, appeared to Smoler a poor instrument with which to forge a new literature. It could never help to create an audience embracing the many Slav peoples. His new, "analogical" orthography was, there-fore, designed to serve the policy of Slav literary reciprocity, to set before the educated Slav world the products of their neglected Lusatian brothers. Among a people like the Lusatian Serbs, whose books could necessarily enjoy only a very small circulation if confined within their own nation, a people moreover who did not yet possess its own journal of opinion, it was of vital importance, wrote Smoler to Purkyně on 16 June 1841,[10] to get other Slavs to read and to buy their works. Thus Smoler was proving an apt pupil of his Czech master.

Some Slav scholars were indeed already familiar with the language and litera-ture of the Lusatian Serbs.[11] Back in the late eighteenth century the great Dobrov-ský, forerunner of the Czech awakening, had shown interest in their fate. Pavel Josef Šafařík (1795–1861), in his influential *Geschichte der slavischen Sprache und Literatur nach allen Mundarten* (A History of the Slav Language and Litera-ture in All Dialects), also included a section, not without some serious errors of fact, on the Lusatians. Probably Smoler knew this work of Šafařík before he made Purkyně's acquaintance, but other writings by Šafařík, which Smoler now found in Purkyně's library – for instance, the "Slav Antiquities" (*Slovanské starožitnosti*), published in 1836–7 – must have been among the most telling influences on the Lusatian student's intellectual development.

In March 1840 Smoler received a letter from Šafařík's fellow Slovak, Ľudovít Štúr (1815–56), who was studying at that time at the University of Halle.[12] On behalf of "our great Šafařík" Štúr asked Smoler to send him as detailed information as possible concerning Lusatian Serb place-names, which the older scholar needed for an ethnographical map of the Slavs then in the last stages before publication. As a result of this introduction Smoler now entered into direct correspondence with one of the leading figures in the Slav scholarly world. The following year Smoler was able to be of further assistance to Šafařík, who was then bringing out his famous textbook of Slav ethnography (*Slovanský národopis*, 1842), by loaning him the demographic maps of Upper and of Lower Lusatia, which Smoler had compiled, and by passing on to Šafařík statistical information relating to the

10 Páta, "J. E. Purkyně a lužičtí Srbové," 273. It should be noted that, quite independently, Jordan was also working at this time on a very similar "analogical" system of orthography. The orthography of modern Upper Lusatian is based on a fusion and extension of the principles devised by Smoler and Jordan.

11 See J. Páta, *Zawod do studija serbskeho pismowstwa* (Budyšin, 1929), *passim*.

12 Letter dated 17 March 1840, Smoler-Páta, 26. See also Karel Paul, "P. J. Šafařík a lužičtí Srbové," pt. i, *Časopis pro moderní filologii* (Prague), xvii/3 (March 1931), 180–2.

demographic position of the Lusatian Serbs.[13] From all this Šafařík gained a very positive opinion of the young Lusatian's scholarly ability, which was confirmed after the publication of Smoler's two volumes of Lusatian Serb folk-songs. An "important work" was how Šafařík described it in a letter to the Russian scholar O. M. Bodianskii. "It ... is," he went on, "indispensable for every Slav scholar, who wishes to study the Lusatian language and folk poetry."[14]

From Šafařík, on the other hand, Smoler was able to obtain valuable assistance in his own researches. In 1840 Smoler had gained an influential benefactor in the person of the *Viceoberceremonienmeister* of the royal Prussian court, Baron von Stillfried, the descendent of an ancient Czech noble family and a patron of Lusatian local history. It was the baron who got a grant for Smoler from the king's private purse that enabled the young man to continue at Breslau University after the completion of his theological studies in 1840 and to devote himself for the next four years exclusively to slavistics. In his private archives the baron possessed a copy of his family chronicle and other old Czech documents, which he asked Smoler to translate and edit. To Šafařík Smoler now turned with a series of questions connected with the historical background to the Stillfried chronicle and various linguistic problems connected with its text.[15] The works of the great Slovak ethnographer and cultural historian remained thereafter one of the chief sources for Smoler's more modest and localized studies in these fields.

Smoler, however, was by no means a dry-as-dust antiquarian; despite his temperate political views, he was a true son of the romantic era. In his youth he had enthused over the sentimental poetry of another and equally famous Slovak, Jan Kollár (1793–1852), whose *Slávy dcera* (Daughter of Sláva; 1824–32) lamented the tragic fate of the Polabian Slavs. The programme elaborated in a later prose work by Kollár, which he published in German in 1837 (*Über die literarische Wechselseitigkeit zwischen den verschiedenen Stämmen und Mundarten der slavischen Nation*/Concerning Literary Reciprocity between the Various Races and Dialects of the Slav Nation), became for Smoler a model for his own political and cultural activities during the rest of his life. In Purkyně's library Smoler found Kollár's edition of Slovak folk-songs published in 1834–5. These songs proved

13 Smoler-Páta, 33. Jan Petr in his article "Šafaříkův přínos k rozvoji sorabistiky," *Acta universitatis Carolinae – Philologica 3 – Slavia Pragensia* III (Prague, 1961), 36, 37, points out that the figures then given to Šafařík by Smoler differed from those which the latter published in his collection of Serb *Volkslieder* – and appear in fact to have been more accurate. To Šafařík, for instance, Smoler gave a total round figure of 142,000 Lusatian Serbs, while in his published work he reached a somewhat inflated figure of 164,000. It should be noted that it it was through Smoler's instrumentality that Šafařík was now able to present more accurate population statistics concerning the Lusatian Serbs than he had been able to give in his *Geschichte der slavischen Sprache und Literatur* of 1826.

14 Letter dated 18 September 1844, *Korespondence Pavla Josefa Šafaříka*, ed. V. A. Francev [Frantsev], I (Prague, 1927), 83.

15 Smoler-Páta, 46, 47, 76.

extremely valuable to him as material for comparison with the songs of the Lusation Serbs.[16]

Direct contact between the two men came only in 1840 and it resulted from a
previous correspondence, which Kollár had struck up with the Lusatian-speaking
high-school students of the Bautzen *gymnasium*. In 1838, largely under Smoler's
influence, the boys revived his earlier society for practising the Lusatian language
(Societas slavica Budissinensis they now rather grandiloquently named it). In
their letters to Kollár they told him of their older contemporary's investigations
into Lusatian Serb folklore and Smoler, too, wrote to Kollár of his present project
and future plans.

Kollár, in his reply, dated from Pest 12 February 1840, expressed his joy in learning of Smoler's efforts to forward such an important aspect of national culture as
the preservation of the oral literature of the folk. He went on:

I would be happy to receive a short and concise account of the present state of the Lusatian Serbs. Namely, how many of them roughly are there still in both Lusatias? Which
towns and villages are still purely Lusatian and which are now mixed or Germanized?
How does the present administration deal with the Serb language? Who among the
schoolmasters and preachers are fairly ardent patriots and nationalists? Which denomina-
tion, Catholic or Evangelical, loves its nation and language more, and how many adherents are there of each?

He encouraged Smoler to continue with his folklore researches and to proceed,
once he had brought out his song collection, to the publication of a companion
volume of proverbs and popular sayings together with fairy stories and folk tales.

Only through the sun [wrote Kollár] do we see sunlight: in the same way, too, through
the people and the things treasured by the people do we exert influence on the nations.
Since your landowning class and nobility, as with us [Slovaks], take no heed of the
nation or despise it and merge themselves with aliens, so it is your task, you school-
teachers and religious preachers, jointly to become cultivators of nationality and protectors of the language against all enemies.

Kollár urged Smoler and his colleagues to maintain close contact with Prague
and the Czechs, both by correspondence and by sending every year several of
their young men to Bohemia – and even to Pest (where presumably Kollár and
the Slovaks resident in this Hungarian town would watch over their Slav education). Finally, Kollár begged Smoler, if he should get the opportunity, to visit "our
Slovaks" then studying at the University of Halle and to exchange frequent letters
with them. "Such reciprocity," he added, "while it may be tiresome, is absolutely
essential above all for our flowering."[17]

Of the three Slovak students whom Kollár named in his letter, the one with

16 *Ibid.*, 14, 16, 17, 21.
17 *Ibid.*, 20–2.

whom Smoler became most closely acquainted was L'udovít Štúr, who was at Halle from 1838 to 1840.[18] While Šafařík and Kollár, though of Slovak background, used Czech – along with German – in their literary work, Štúr was soon to come forward as the creator of modern written Slovak. At this date, however, he still used Czech, and it was in this language that he carried on his correspondence with Smoler and other nationally minded young Lusatian Serbs.

Like Kollár, Štúr first heard mention of Smoler's name from the Lusatian Serb high-school boys when he visited Bautzen in the spring of 1839. During his stay in Lusatia he was entertained in Łaz by Smoler's parents, who welcomed their Slovak visitor with truly "Slavonic friendliness."[19] Smoler was away from home at this time; the two men, however, may have met personally before Štúr finished his studies at Halle. Štúr had been overjoyed, as he told Smoler,[20] to discover such enthusiasm for Slavdom "in your forsaken Lusatias," and he congratulated the latter for his part in stimulating this spirit. He adjured Smoler and his associates to watch over their nationality so that, far from being extinguished, it would gain new strength at a time when a fresh spirit – "a spirit full of goodwill, full of hope and noble deeds" – was reinvigorating all Slavdom. "Have you to lag behind your brothers who are waking to a new life? No! Your enterprise is an assurance to us that this will not be so."

From the same letter it is clear that Smoler was already contemplating the publication of a regular periodical in Lusatian Serb. A project of this kind, although not easy to realize, Štúr welcomed as an important aid in awakening Lusatian nationality.[21] Through a journal of opinion in your own language, he went on, "you would join in a literary covenant with other Slavs: which reciprocity would be very beneficial for us – but especially for you." "You and your young friends represent our finest hopes," Štúr concluded.

A dedicated Slav – he stated in a later letter to Smoler,[22] who had become worried at his Slovak friend's long silence – could never cease to think of his brothers "now just awakening from a long sleep." Forgetful of his own shortcomings as a correspondent, Štúr lectured Smoler on the essential role which frequent exchange of letters among Slavs should play as the most easily applied form of reciprocity.

18 The other two Slovaks were Benjamín Pravoslav Červenák (1816–41), before his premature death the author of a work on Slovak antiquities, and the poet and Czechophil, Jonáš Záborský (1812–76), who later wrote in literary Slovak.

19 L. Štúr, "Cesta do Lužic (Wykonaná z gara 1839)," Časopis Českého musea, xiii/4 (1839), 474, 488.

20 Letter dated Halle, 5 January 1840. Printed in Páta, "Dodawk k čěskemu listowanju J. A. Smolerja," Časopis Maćicy Serbskeje, lxxv (1922), 72–4, and again in Listy L'udovíta Štúra, ed. Josef Ambruš, i (Bratislava, 1954), 171–3.

21 Cf. Smoler-Páta, 29. The year 1842 marks the beginning of the modern Lusatian Serb press: Smoler played an important role in these ventures. See Walter J. Rauch, Presse und Volkstum der lausitzer Sorben (Würzburg, 1959), 35ff.

22 Letter dated 17 March 1840. Printed in Smoler-Páta, 25–7, and again in Listy L'udovíta Štúra, i, 173–6.

"Activity must be their chief password," he told the Lusatians, congratulating them at the same time on their willingness to read books and journals put out by Czechs and Poles, Russians and "Illyrians," and to widen their contacts with their Slav brethren.

It was indeed as an aid to intercommunication between Slavs of various tongues that Štúr viewed Smoler's proposed reform in Lusatian Serb orthography. The changes were soon accepted by the youth groups at the universities of Breslau and Leipzig as well as by the Lusatian society at the Bautzen high school.[23]

All Slavs here [wrote Štúr from Halle] have rejoiced with all their heart seeing that you have decided to adopt Latin letters, as well as Czech orthography in place of the hitherto Germanized one. Your proposal for this orthography I thoroughly approve; I only add some observations designed to keep you from straying greatly from the Czech ... if you are successful in introducing this reformed orthography, you will have made an important contribution both to Lusatia and to Slavdom as a whole.

Another Slavophil scholar who warmly welcomed these attempts at purging Lusatian Serb orthography of its Germanisms and at bringing it closely in line with the Czech was František Ladislav Čelakovský (1799–1852), poet, folk-song collector, philologist, and literary historian. Čelakovský had become interested in the dialects and folk culture of the Lusatian Serbs in the late 1820s and soon began to express in print the need for a spelling reform of the kind Smoler now recommended. In 1841 Čelakovský, who had previously sought vainly an academic position in the Habsburg realm or in Russia, was appointed by the Prussian government to the newly founded chair of slavistics at the University of Breslau, and he arrived in that city to take up his post in May of the following year.

Now, in addition to Purkyně, a second major influence appears to shape Smoler's intellectual growth. Smoler immediately became Čelakovský's closest and most devoted student. "I continually offer thanks to God," Smoler was to write to Purkyně, with a slight note perhaps of self-satisfaction,[24] "that he permitted me to come to know you and Mr. Čelakovský. Indeed, if this had not happened, then our Serbdom would never have progressed as today we can congratulate [ourselves] that it has done. Therefore, I must avow: We owe our wisdom to Bohemia [Čechy] and the most valuable assistance comes to us from the Czechs." Smoler continued to work on his orthographic reform under Čelakovský's guidance. "When I introduced our new orthography," the former wrote,[25] "I stood alone and no one knew how to advise me." Now Smoler could turn to Professor Čelakovský with his long experience and knowledge of all the Slav languages, and Čelakovský would assist him in his task of making Upper Lusatian a serviceable instrument for a literature

23 See Pawoł Nowotny, "L'udovít Štúr pola Łužiskich Serbow," *Lětopis Instituta za serbski ludospyt* (Budyšin), ser. A, no. 4 (1956–7), 92. Cf. *Listy L'udovíta Štúra*, III (1960), 18.
24 Letter dated 22 March 1846, in Páta, "J. E. Purkyně a lužičtí Srbové," 278.
25 Letter to František Doucha, dated 4 July 1844, Smoler-Páta, 70–2.

that would find a worthy, if modest, place in nineteenth-century European culture.

Writing to Čelakovský from his home at Łaz in the spring of 1845, after the formal completion of his studies in the faculty of philosophy at Breslau in the previous year, Smoler expressed his debt to his teacher in these words:

What I particularly regret [at having to remain at home] is that in this way I cannot be for some time an auditor at your lectures, since I am unwilling to let slip even one word of your teachings ... I hope that in due course you will allow me to read everything that I have missed. As a Serb I have indeed still much to learn, and there is nowhere in the world that I can better obtain this knowledge than from you. Therefore, I have many questions for you when I return; for here what I cannot resolve by myself, no one else knows how to solve for me.[26]

Two years earlier, in the late summer of 1843, master and pupil had made a pilgrimage to Prague together during the long vacation. For Čelakovský, of course, the visit was to familiar places, to the city where he had spent the most productive years of his life. On the other hand, to Smoler, who saw Prague and the Czech lands for the first time, everything was new – and immensely stimulating. The novelty and excitement of all he saw and heard is mirrored in his correspondence. "When ... I reflect on Prague," he wrote nearly two years later,[27] "I recall days that I number among the finest and dearest of my life." In Prague Čelakovský had found him lodging in the house of the professor's future son-in-law, Dr. Václav Staněk (1804–71). By profession a physician and by avocation a practitioner of Slav reciprocity, Staněk entertained as guests in his home a whole series of visitors from other Slav lands. He showed them round the city, introduced them to the leading Czech awakeners, with most of whom he was on friendly terms, and, after the visitors' return to their own country, continued to maintain contact with them by correspondence, each side writing in his native Slav language. Through Staněk and Čelakovský Smoler during his visit gained not only first-hand knowledge of the cultural monuments of the Bohemian past, but also a more intimate acquaintance with the contemporary leaders of Czech national life, whether in Prague or in the provinces, than he could possibly have acquired in his native Lusatia or even from Slavophil circles at the University of Breslau.

Like Purkyně, Čelakovský held a high opinion of the scholarly abilities of his Lusatian pupil, whose edition of the folk-songs of his people he described as "a work which, in regard to its poetic contents and range, ... is outstanding and which,

26 *Ibid.*, 93, 94 (Letter dated 27 May 1845).
27 *Ibid.*, 91 (Letter to Václav Staněk, dated 14 February 1845). Not long before his departure for Bohemia Smoler wrote: "I rejoice exceedingly [at the prospect], particularly because I shall get to know in person all those with whom I have for so long been in friendly correspondence and will be able to converse with them face to face" (Letter to Doucha, dated 13 August 1843, in Smoler-Páta, 61). Cf. *Korrespondence a zápisky Frant. Ladislava Čelakovského*, ed. František Bílý, III (Prague, 1915), 124, 127. Čelakovský describes his young companion as "a worthy Serb and agitator or awakener in the Lusatias" (124).

from the ethnographical standpoint, constitutes a rich mine [of information]. From every angle it deserves to be placed alongside the finest monuments of their inner life, which other nations possess." He praised the knowledge of Slav languages and philology which Smoler had acquired through hard work and attendance at his professor's lectures.[28] And Čelakovský gladly granted Smoler permission to carry out, with the assistance of another of his Lusatian Serb pupils, Jan Awgust Wárko (1821–62), an Upper Lusatian translation of his own poetic variations on Russian folk poems.[29]

Čelakovský also gave assistance and encouragement around this time to another of Smoler's translating ventures: the rendering into Upper Lusatian of the allegedly ancient Czech epic poem, which in 1817 the eminent slavist Václav Hanka (1791–1861) had presented to an astonished public as the literal transcript of a manuscript found in a church at Dvůr Králové (Königinhof).[30] Hanka's fame was then at its height: as director of the Bohemian Museum, he occupied a key position in the Czech national movement, in which historical and philological studies still played a vital role. Suspicion as to the authenticity of Hanka's manuscript discoveries existed even during his lifetime, but it was not until after his death that the certainty of their forgery eventually gained almost universal acceptance. Smoler seems to the end of his life to have remained a believer in Hanka's integrity. Naturally the young scholar from provincial Lusatia had grasped eagerly at the opportunity of contact with the man who stood at the very centre of the West Slavic intellectual world. Their correspondence begins around the year 1840 and continues into the next decade.

Dobrovský, Hanka's original mentor, had first interested him in the fate of the Lusatian Serbs by putting him in touch with the students at the Lusatian Roman

28 *Korrespondence Čelakovského*, IV (1933), ed. F. Bílý and Václav Černý, 190–2. Cf. Karel Alois Vinařický, *Korrespondence a spisy pamětní*, ed. Václav Otakar Slavík, II (Prague, 1909), 532, for a very positive evaluation of Smoler's Serb *Volkslieder* from another eminent Czech awakener.
29 The translation was published in Prague in 1846 in 300 copies under the title: *Fr. Lad. Čelakowskjeho Wothłós pěsni ruskich*. See *Korrespondence Čelakovského*, III, 419.
30 Smoler-Páta, 60, 61 (Smoler's letter to Doucha, dated Breslau, 13 August 1843). Smoler's translation, published – likewise in Prague – under the title *Kralo-dwórski rukopis: Zebrane lyricko-epicke pěsnje a spěwy* and with a preface by Hanka himself, did not appear until 1852. Numerous translations of this and the Zelená Hora (Grünberg) manuscript, equally famous in its day, appeared in Slav and other languages. Smoler in his letter to Doucha records his surprise at the similarity between modern Upper Lusatian and the old Czech language of the Dvůr Králové manuscript: a similarity that was in fact not so surprising since this supposed Old Czech, as it later transpired, was in fact the product of a contemporary pen. In her unpublished dissertation on Smoler (p. 115), L. Hajnec notes that Smoler's translations from the Czech (and later from the Russian) served, as Jungmann's earlier translations from west European languages into Czech had done, to create a literary terminology for a language spoiled hitherto by "Germanisms" and scarcely rising above the level of a peasant dialect. In addition, Smoler was enriching Lusatian Serb culture by introducing to his readers important works in contemporary Slav literature.

Catholic seminary in Prague's Malá strana. Hanka liked to visit them often; he tutored them in Czech and Old Slavonic and, especially after Dobrovský's death, took a fatherly interest in the students' welfare. Among the latter it was Smoler's contemporary, Jan Pětr Jordan, who remained closest to Hanka even after the termination of formal studies at the seminary. The somewhat cool relationship existing between the two young Lusatian awakeners, Smoler and Jordan, seems to have been reflected in the relations of Smoler with Hanka.[31] They lacked entirely the intimacy and warmth of Smoler's friendship with such older scholars as Purkyně or Čelakovský. Nevertheless, Smoler on occasion sought to enlist Hanka's support for the cultural development of the Lusatian Serbs and to interest him in his own publications and in his reformed Lusatian orthography. Smoler sometimes asked Hanka's assistance in getting materials printed in Prague if lack of suitable type prevented this from being done properly at home, and he consulted him from time to time in connection with various points of historical and literary research.[32] In 1852 we find Smoler seeking Hanka's advice in regard to possible Czech and Russian contributors to the new series of the Slavonic *Jahrbücher* (Yearbooks) that he was about to commence with the hoped-for collaboration of writers from all the Slav lands.[33]

When Hanka died, Smoler wrote to the poet and antiquarian Karel Jaromír Erben (1811–70) that the Lusatian seminary in Prague had thereby lost its foremost protector. "All [Lusatian] Serbs, Catholic *as well as Evangelicals* [my italics], mourn his loss with all their heart and pray God to again raise up for the Prague Serbs a man who would care for the development of their nationality [*kiž by so narodnje wo nich starał*]." He asked Erben himself to take a friendly interest in "the Slav studies" of the seminarists after the example left by Dobrovský and Hanka, whose Slavophil sympathies had led them to support the students' "national aspirations."[34]

Among the Czechs of Bohemia and Moravia, however, it was not so much Hanka but a rather lesser figure, František Doucha (1810–84), who was chiefly instrumental in placing the emergent Lusatian Serb culture before the Czech literary public. Doucha, a Roman Catholic clergyman, was not only a minor poet but also a prolific translator and an accomplished bibliographer. His interest in the Lusatian Serbs was first aroused by conversations with J. P. Jordan, whom he met in 1839 while taking a cure at Liebwerda, and from that time on Doucha con-

---

31 See Miloslava Lorencová, "Václav Hanka a lužičtí Srbové," *Lětopis Instituta za serbski ludospyt*, ser. A, no. 3 (1955), 186–90.

32 See, for example, Smoler's letter to Hanka, dated 6 October 1841, in Smoler-Páta, 45–9.

33 *Ibid.*, 138 (Letter to Hanka, dated 8 August 1852).

34 Letter to K. J. Erben, dated 21 March 1861, ms. in Literární archiv památníku národního písemnictví, formerly the Literary Archive of the National Museum. Erben in fact did step into Hanka's position as unofficial mentor of the seminarists' Slav studies and interests (see Smoler-Páta, 155). In a letter to Adolf Patera, dated 15 January 1861 (ms. in Literární archiv), Smoler wrote: "Hanka's death, the news of which I received an hour ago, has overwhelmed me."

tinued to keep a watch on cultural developments in Lusatia, inserting articles from time to time in the Czech press on the latest publications in Lusatian Serb. He had welcomed the heralded publication of Smoler's *Volkslieder*, and this prompted their author to express his appreciation of Doucha's support for his nation's cultural strivings. He was happy, Smoler wrote to Doucha, that in him "Serbdom ... had gained a very valuable friend." "Only if the other Slavs support [Lusatian] Serb literature," Smoler went on, "can it in its regeneration grow and blossom and our Serb people be preserved in their nationality."[35]

For Smoler Doucha soon became the main channel through which he sought to mobilize support in the Czech community behind his own cultural programme for the Lusatian Serbs. He assisted Doucha, who was at first far from a master of the Lusatian tongue and who always preferred Smoler to append a German translation of the Upper Lusatian text of his letters, in numerous translations into Czech, translations that now made accessible to the Czechs the first fruits of the Lusatian literary revival. He supplied Doucha with factual information, which the latter could use in his contributions to the periodical press. For instance, the greater part of Doucha's article "On the Development of Nationality among the Lusatian Serbs" ("O postupu národnosti Srbů Lužických"), which he published in 1845 in the influential journal of the Bohemian Museum (*Časopis Českého musea*), was taken – with the writer's permission – almost word for word from Smoler's letter of the previous October. In this letter Smoler had sketched in outline the endeavours of the young, nationally conscious Lusatian Serb intellectuals over the previous decade or so to stem Germanization and to prevent total submergence in the dominant German cultural milieu. "True, we cannot report any earth-shaking events," Smoler wrote. "The [Lusatian] Serbs, however, are only a tiny folk among the peoples [*nur ein Völkchen unter den Völkern*]." "Apart from 72 clergymen and 122 teachers almost the whole Serb population belongs to the peasantry."[36]

For the Lusatian Serb intelligentsia at this time the publicity thus given to their movement in the Bohemian Museum's journal, which was widely read not only by Czech but by other Slav intellectuals, could prove immensely serviceable in the future development of Lusatian cultural nationalism.

On 17 October 1845 Smoler and his friends, among whom the most active in this venture was the composer Karl August Kocor (1822–1904),[37] succeeded in holding in Bautzen the first of a long series of national song festivals (*serbische Ge-*

35 Letter to Doucha, dated 6 January 1841, Smoler-Páta, 38, 39.
36 *Ibid.*, 81–9 (Letter to Doucha, dated 20 October 1844). Another figure whom in the early 1840s Smoler supplied with information concerning Lusatian Serb history and literature was the historian and philologist Alois Vojtěch Šembera (1807–82). Šembera used this information in his lectures and writings. See *ibid.*, 54.
37 In his old age Smoler was to be instrumental in introducing the second leading personality in Lusatian music, Bjernat Krawc (1861–1948), to the music of the great Czech composer Smetana. See B. Krawc, "Bjedrich Smetana a jeho poćahi k serbskej Łužicy a k łužiskim Serbam," pt. I, *Łužica* (Budyšin), 1923, no. 4, 98.

sangfesten), which acted both as a demonstration to friends and opponents alike of the flexibility and poetic qualities of the Lusatian language and as an opportunity for social intercourse between members of the nationally conscious intelligentsia (especially the school-teachers). Doucha was asked by Smoler to write a full report of this first festival in a leading Czech literary journal, *Květy*, and also, where possible, to insert accounts in other Prague papers.[38] The following year Smoler asked a similar favour of Doucha in connection with the second annual song festival held on 7 August 1846.[39]

Although Doucha was not to report on subsequent festivals, perhaps because the song festival soon became an established institution among the Lusatian Serbs, and although after 1852 direct contact between him and Smoler appears to have ceased, the Czech continued his interest in Serb Lusatia, publishing translations from its growing literature and writing appreciatively of its cultural achievements. Doucha may indeed be considered the first of a distinguished line of Czech interpreters of Lusatian cultural aims that includes the names of Adolf Černý, Josef Páta, and Antonín Frinta.

Among Smoler's major successes was the establishment in 1847 of a central institution to unite the cultural efforts of his people: the Maćica Serbska. Doucha had been extremely helpful in arousing support for Smoler's efforts in the Czech lands, and he was the first person outside Lusatia to donate books to the Maćica's library.[40] But Smoler's chief inspiration in this work came from the example of František Palacký (1798–1876),[41] who on several occasions during the mid-1840s visited Bautzen in connection with the research for his great history of the Czech nation (for the Lusatias had for several centuries formed part of the Bohemian crown-lands). Whether at this time he actually met Smoler, whose activities as a journalist and cultural organizer were centred in Bautzen only from 1848, is unknown. Palacký was certainly in touch with members of Smoler's circle.

38 Letter to Doucha, dated 26 October 1845, Smoler-Páta, 98–103. Among the works sung at the festival was Smoler's own adaptation of the Czech national hymn: "Kde domov můj?" In Smoler's version ("Hdźe statok mój?"), the query – "Where is my country?" – is answered by the assertion: "The Serbian land is my country." Smoler also translated or adapted other songs and poems from the Czech.

39 Letter to Doucha, 15 August 1846, *ibid.*, 116–19.

40 *Ibid.*, 134.

41 Adolf Černý, "Palacký a łužiscy Serbja," pt. I, *Łužica*, XVII/7 (July 1898), 75, quotes Smoler's own words spoken at the celebrations in Prague on 23 April 1876 to honour the completion of Palacký's history of the Czech nation to 1526: "It was particularly Palacký after whose example the [Lusatian] Serbs founded the Serb Maćica." (This article has recently been reprinted in an Upper Lusatian translation in a volume entitled *Adolf Černý: Antologija jeho dźěłow* [Budyšin, 1958], 173–7.) Smoler, in his obituary of Palacký, who died on 26 May 1876, called him "one of the finest and most active awakeners of Czech nationality and thus also one of the most meritorious architects of Slavdom" (*Łužičan* (Budyšin), no. 6 [June 1876], 95). See also J. Petr, "Serbja a Palackeho swjatočnosće lěta 1876 w Praze," *Rozhlad*, XVIII/4 (1968), 144–9.

Smoler's whole thinking, moreover, was impregnated with the concepts which were being elaborated in the successive volumes of Palacký's history. In particular, Palacký's idea of the peaceful role of the Slav peoples throughout history over against the more warlike Germanic folk (an idea that he derived from the German romantic Herder) proved immensely attractive to Smoler. Thus, with Smoler, admiration for Palacký the historian was naturally accompanied by a desire to emulate the achievements of Palacký the patriot and of his colleagues in the Czech cultural awakening. True, the examples of the southern Serb Matica, which was founded in Pest in 1826, and of an Illyrian Matica, which the Croats set up in Zagreb in 1842, were also influential on Smoler and his friends when in April 1845 they took the first steps towards the establishment of their own Lusatian Serb Maćica.[42] But it was Palacký and the Czechs with their Matice česká of 1831 who provided the Lusatian Serbs both with the immediate incentive and the best model for future activity. Smoler, for long well instructed by friends like Purkyně, Čelakovský, and Kollár as to the central role played by the Matice česká in the burgeoning Czech national movement, firmly believed that the cultural awakening of his own people would make no progress "until," as he told Čelakovský,[43] "we have our Maćica according to the example of the Czechs." Smoler was responsible for the wording of the Maćica's statutes (*Wustawki*), which had then to be presented to the Saxon and Prussian governments for approval before the Maćica could function in their respective territories.

Smoler enlisted Čelakovský's aid in framing these statutes,[44] which were drawn up in 1845. "God grant that Slavdom assist us to push the work to completion," Smoler had confided a little earlier to his mentor.[45] At first Smoler could feel fairly optimistic concerning the response his efforts evoked in Prague, where he was likely to draw most Slav support. Šafařík wrote to assure him of his moral backing: "When your *Maćica Serbska* starts to function, send us word and a summons to join; I do not doubt that here, too, members will be found." Yet, after the Maćica came formally into existence, Šafařík's name is not to be found in the list of its foreign members. Apart from Palacký, Hanka, and Doucha and a few other enthusiasts, Prague in fact remained indifferent, and Smoler's appeals for help passed for the most part unanswered.[46]

Smoler expressed the need for outside support, if his Maćica was to fulfil its purpose properly, in the following words:

42 See A. Černý, "Matice srbská v Budyšíně," pt. I, *Slovanský sborník* (Prague), IV (1885), no. 4, 199.
43 Letter dated 27 May 1845, Smoler-Páta, 94.
44 *Ibid.*, 106 (Letter dated 8 November 1845).
45 *Ibid.*, 94.
46 *Ibid.*, 107 (Šafařík's letter to Smoler, dated 22 February 1846); K. Paul, "P. J. Šafařík a lužičtí Srbové," pt. I, 181. On 29 April 1847 Smoler told Čelakovský (Smoler-Páta, 123): "From the Czech lands we can expect some [financial] support" for the Maćica. See also Smoler-Páta, 123–7.

Although we believe that our [Lusatian Serb] fellow-countrymen will give to the Maćica, each according to his possibilities, and will thus assist Serb literature and, thereby, Serb nationality according to the need, at the same time we also know that all our effort will have only poor and inconspicuous results, if other Slavs do not come to our aid. Therefore, as in other matters, now in this affair, too, we turn to our Czech brothers to support us willingly and in a friendly spirit in this venture, which will prove so important for the future of our nation ... and we hope that you will want to comply in brotherly fashion with our most loving and heartfelt request.[47]

The task of Smoler and his associates was considerably more arduous than had been the work of Palacký and the other Czech awakeners in setting up their Matice.[48] The nationally conscious Czech community at that date was numerically very much larger than the Lusatian Serb. It possessed at least some wealthy and influential patrons as well as a tradition of uninterrupted cultural endeavour going back several generations, which was far stronger than the tradition inherited by the puny Serb national movement. This movement was totally without support among the Lusatian nobility, and it had failed so far to expand much outside a narrow circle of clergymen, school-teachers, and students. It is not surprising, therefore, that in the creation of the Lusatian Maćica Smoler turned repeatedly to the Czechs and the other Slavs for moral – and sometimes material – assistance.

The year 1848, which saw in February the appearance under Smoler's editorship of the first number of the Maćica's journal, brought revolution in March to Saxony and Prussia as to other areas of central and eastern Europe. The Lusatian Serbs, a peasant people remote from the major urban centres which formed the arena of revolutionary struggle, did not participate actively in the overthrow of the *ancien régime*. In fact, during the revolt in Dresden in May 1849 Serb soldiers in the royal Saxon army formed the mainstay of the king's body-guard and protected him and his family against the assaults of the republicans. Nevertheless, the "Springtime of the Peoples" witnessed for the first time a blossoming of political life among the Lusatian Serbs. For the first time in their history they were now free to discuss political events in Lusatian-language papers and to organize for political purposes. One group among the intelligentsia supported a republican constitution and the German left. However, the majority of Lusatian Serb intellectuals, and Smoler among them, came out in favour of constitutional monarchy and sought allies in the German liberal movement (in so far, that is, as anti-Slav feeling on the German side allowed). It was Smoler's group that controlled most of the farmers' associations, which sprang up in the villages of Serb Lusatia. Leading members of the group gave final form to a petition (sometimes known as the "Maćica petition," since it was this institution that sponsored it) which was presented by the Serbs in July 1848 to the Saxon administration in an attempt to use the revolutionary up-

47 Letter to Doucha, 1 May 1847, Smoler-Páta, 125.
48 A. J. Parczewski, *Jan Ernest Smoler: Ustęp z historyi narodowego odrodzenia Górnych Łużyc* [Warsaw, 1883], 39.

heaval to obtain language equality in Lusatia in respect to church, school, legal system, and public office. Smoler and his associates constantly stressed their loyalty to the Saxon (and Prussian) states, rejecting the call from Prague to participate officially in the Slav Congress of June 1848, despite the fact that among the organizers of the Congress was Smoler's old colleague, the Lusatian Serb J. P. Jordan.

This refusal did not signify any wish to cut ties with the Czech nationalists; it meant only a desire to avoid action which could be construed as subversive, as hostile to existing state structures, or as an alliance with "Panslavism." In fact Smoler felt very close in his political views to the Czech liberal party led at this juncture by such men as Palacký and Karel Havlíček (1821–56).[49] Smoler became a devoted reader of Havlíček's *Pražské noviny* (Prague News) soon after Havlíček had taken over the post of editor at the beginning of 1846 and proceeded to transform it into an organ of democratic opposition to Habsburg absolutism and of a liberal Czech nationalism. "The spirit of his *News* I like very much," Smoler told Doucha, "the only trouble is that I so rarely get hold of it."[50] Though Smoler and Havlíček had met at least once earlier, by 1848 the two men do not appear to have been any longer in contact with each other.[51]

Smoler, however, was in touch with Palacký during the revolutionary year, and he sought the Czech leader's advice at one crucial moment during that exciting spring. Uncertain how to proceed with the drawing up and presentation of the "Maćica petition," Smoler wrote (in German) to Palacký. The Serb spoke warmly of "the sympathies which we cherish in regard to our Slav brothers and which we wish to learn are reciprocated by them." "We Lusatian Serbs," he stated further, "seek to act according to the new principles followed by Slavdom as a whole." He asserted the Serbs' desire to frame their demands, which represented the collective will of their community (*sie sich einmal als Ganzes fühlen und als Ganzes zeigen*

49 Smoler was also acquainted with one of the future leaders of the Czech left of 1848, Josef V. Frič (1829–91). In his memoirs (*Paměti*, new Prague ed., ed. Karel Cvejn, I [1957], 173) Frič writes of his visit to Lusatia as a schoolboy in the summer of 1845. "In Boleslav, indeed, I did not by chance find Mr. Smoler at home. At my uncle Čelakovský's I had become friendly with him as the most enthusiastic of my uncle's four students, whom he preferred to teach at his house rather than at the university in an otherwise empty lecture hall." The youthful Frič's radical democratic creed, as it had evolved by 1848, cannot have been very palatable to a conservatively minded liberal like Smoler, and the two men do not appear to have been in contact with each other at this date.

50 Letter dated 11 July 1846, Smoler-Páta, 115. In a letter to Purkyně dated 22 March 1846 (in Páta, "J. E. Purkyně a lužičtí Srbové," 278), Smoler expressed his appreciation of the value of the press in other Slav lands, and of Czech newspapers in particular, in informally educating young Lusation Serb nationalists, who seized avidly every opportunity to obtain copies of such journals. Several decades later, when the period of Bach absolutism had ended, we find Smoler writing to Adolf Patera as follows: "The *Národní listy* [of which the first number appeared on 1 January 1861] is at this moment my chief daily recreation and I wish it all future success" (Letter dated 4 February 1861, ms. in Literární archiv, Prague).

51 Páta, "K. Havlíček a lužičtí Srbové," pt. I, *Národní listy: Večerní vydání* (Prague), 15 November 1921.

können), in consonance with the political programme of the Slav world. Palacký, therefore, was requested to send as soon as possible his suggestions for incorporation into the final draft of the petition.[52]

Between mid-1848 and 1852 correspondence between Smoler and his Czech friends almost ceased: at least few letters have been preserved from this period. Perhaps, as Páta suggests,[53] this silence was a result of pressure of his journalistic and organizational work on Smoler at this time or of his fear, during a period of deepening reaction, of associating too closely with the Czechs, whom the powers that be suspected of revolutionary and Panslav sympathies. More probably the silence stemmed from Smoler's increasing independence of judgment. He was no longer the immature young scholar constantly in need of the advice, support, and encouragement of his older, more influential, and more experienced Czech friends. True, the Czech national movement remained for him a model worthy of imitation by the struggling Serb nationalists of Lusatia, and he did not cease to seek Czech help in the national awakening of his own people.[54] But Smoler, it is evident, now felt more autonomous, better able to stand on his own – despite the continued weakness of the cultural nationalism of the Lusatian Serbs.

In the 1850s and 1860s he even attempted to make Bautzen a centre of intercommunication between the cultures of the various Slav peoples. To this end he first revived the *Jahrbücher für slawische Literatur, Kunst und Wissenschaft* (Yearbooks for Slav Literature, Art, and Learning) (1852–6), which he had taken over from Jordan in 1848 and edited until the journal had to cease publication in the following year; then in the 1860s he started up an entirely new publication,[55] which likewise, through the common medium (somewhat ironically) of the German language and through the publication of current listings of all serious publications in Slav languages, attempted to make known Slavic literary and artistic achievements to Slav and non-Slav alike. The venture was ultimately a failure, for a small German country town like Bautzen was scarcely suited for the role of a cultural capital of the Slav world. Yet, if Bautzen was unlikely to replace Prague as hub of at least West Slav literary and scholarly endeavours, Smoler's activities

52 Letter dated 4 May 1848, ms. in Literární archiv (Prague). It has been transcribed by Hajnec in an appendix to her unpublished doctoral dissertation on Smoler. See also Smoler-Páta, 132.
53 *Ibid.*, 133.
54 Smoler, for example, was a great admirer of the movement for a Czech national theatre, and in May 1868 he was present in Prague at the ceremonies connected with the laying of the theatre's foundation-stone. (See Stanley B. Kimball, *Czech Nationalism: A Study of the National Theatre Movement, 1845–83* [Urbana, Ill., 1964], 108, 109.) For Smoler's interest in developing a theatrical tradition among his own people patterned on that of the Czechs, see A. Černý, "Narodne dźiwadło w Praze a Serbja," reprinted in *Adolf Černý: Antologija jeho dźělow*, 187–90; J. Petr, "Serbja na swjatočnosćach Narodneho dźiwadła lěta 1868 w Praze," *Lětopis Instituta za serbski ludospyt*, ser. A, no. 10 (1963), 177, 181. See also Smoler-Páta, 66, 67.
55 At first called *Zeitschrift für slawische Literatur, Kunst und Wissenschaft* (1862–4), it was later transformed into the *Centralblätter für slawische Literatur und Bibliographie* (1865–8).

witness to the independent position he now felt able to occupy in regard to Slav cultural interchanges.

In the years following mid-century, death removed from the scene several of Smoler's Czech and Slovak friends of the 1840s. Čelakovský and Kollár died in 1852, Štúr in 1856, and Hanka and Šafařík in 1861. After 1850 we find only two new names in the roster of Smoler's Czech correspondents: Adolf Patera (1836–1912) and František Jezbera (1829–1901).[56]

Smoler's first extant letter to Patera dates from August 1860, soon after Patera, still a student, had visited Lusatia during his summer vacation. With Hanka's death in the following year Patera, who was then working in the Bohemian Museum's library (of which he was eventually appointed director), then became Smoler's main channel of contact with Prague.[57] Patera helped him to raise money and to enlist subscribers for his Lusatian-language periodical *Łužičan* (The Lusatian), which Smoler had founded in 1860. "I hope," wrote Smoler on 15 January 1861,[58] "that you will want to continue to be active on behalf of *Łužičan* and to gather money for it." Patera also kept Smoler in touch with prominent Czech writers and scholars and with eminent literati from the rest of the Slav world. Smoler from time to time requested his assistance in carrying out small commissions in Prague, questioned him in regard to recent Czech cultural developments and the latest books published in the Bohemian capital, and asked him to find Czech contributors for Smoler's German-language periodicals.

Czech awakeners of the middle decades of the nineteenth century, from Purkyně to Patera, found in Smoler the exponent of a cultural nationalism that they discovered had much in common with their own, especially in the earlier stages of its development.[59] Their interest in the national awakening of the smallest Slav

56 Smoler's advocacy from the late 1850s of the Russian language as a Slav *interlingua* and of the use of the Cyrillic alphabet for all Slav vernaculars was in part the result of Jezbera's influence. For Smoler's views on nationality, see my article "Smoler's Idea of Nationality," *Slavic Review* (Seattle, Washington), xxviii/1 (March 1969), 25–47.

57 The Literární archiv in Prague possesses 37 items (letters, postcards, etc.) written by Smoler to Patera – either in Upper Lusatian, Russian, or German – between the years 1860 and 1879. The correspondence is of considerable interest and publication in the immediate future was promised by L. Heine [Hajnec] in her article "J. A. Smoler," *Zeitschrift für Slawistik* (1958), 537; however, to my knowledge, nothing has yet appeared in print.

58 Letter to Patera, ms. in Literární archiv (Prague). In a further letter of 12 February 1862 we find Smoler thanking Patera for his efforts to help not only *Łužičan* but also Smoler's latest venture in Slav cultural reciprocity, his Slavonic *Zeitschrift*. See also Smoler to Patera, letter dated 19 April 1862. On 6 August 1865 Smoler writes to Patera to tell him that in place of the now defunct *Zeitscrift* he will be publishing from the beginning of October its continuation under the title *Centralblätter*. He hopes thereby "to be able to effect something worthwhile for Slav reciprocity."

59 Smoler from his side was also keenly aware of this similarity in development (*mutatis mutandis*) between the Czech and Lusatian Serb national awakenings. This awareness comes out, for instance, in an article he wrote for *Łužičan* (no. 7, July 1873, p. 111) in celebration of the hundredth anniversary of Josef Jungmann's birth. Praising the Czech's efforts to revive

ethnic group derived from a desire to strengthen Slav culture even at, indeed especially at, its weakest and most threatened point. By supporting the aspirations of the Lusatian Serbs Czech and Slovak awakeners believed that they would ultimately be strengthening both the Czech position vis-à-vis the Germans and that of the Slovaks in relation to the Magyars. In acting as interpreters of the Lusatian Serb awakening to the rest of the Slav world they would, if indirectly, be contributing to the establishment on a firmer foundation of the *raison d'être* of their own cultures.[60] From Smoler, in particular, they were able to obtain accurate knowledge of, and informed opinion on, developments taking place among the Serbs of Lusatia.

Smoler, on the other hand, hoped to reap more direct and more concrete advantages for his people from his cultural intercourse with the Czech and Slovak awakeners of his time. He cultivated relations with the intellectual leaders of the Slav peoples more systematically and in greater depth than any of his predecessors in the Lusatian Serb awakening had done.[61] He viewed Slav reciprocity, and its most effective manifestation in his case in a close relationship with the leaders of Czech cultural life, as a means whereby the Lusatian Serbs in their struggle to keep their young culture alive in face of the crushing weight of the German environment could draw upon resources, both moral and material, that were much greater than anything they could muster on their own.[62] As Smoler grew older, he was able to emancipate himself to some extent from the perhaps excessive influence exercised on him at first by the Czech cultural model. But, for Smoler, the assistance and support of the Czechs remained an essential element in his programme for the national renewal of the Lusatian Serbs.

---

the expiring language and national consciousness of his people, Smoler pointed out that Jungmann had met with derision not merely from the outside world but within the Czech-speaking community, just as he himself and his associates were now meeting with scorn and opposition from some Serb speakers within Lusatia. "Therefore," he concluded his evaluation of Jungmann's achievements, "it is right and proper that Jungmann's memory should be revered worthily not only among the Czechs but also among other Slavs" like the Lusatian Serbs. Strangely enough, although Jungmann did not die until 1847, there are no recorded contacts between him and Smoler.

60 See in this connection the conclusion to Páta's article on "Lužickosrbské národní obrození a československá účast v něm," *Slavia* (1923), 369, 370.

61 However, the poets Handrij Lubjenski (1790–1840) and Handrij Zejler (1804–72) were in contact with the Czechs and, of course, Smoler's contemporary, J. P. Jordan, cultivated Slav reciprocity as assiduously as Smoler himself.

62 An eloquent acknowledgment from Smoler's pen of the Lusatian awakening's, and his own, debt to such men as Purkyně, Čelakovský, and Štúr is to be found in the first paragraph of his letter, dated 5 July 1844, to the poet, antiquarian, and Slavophil Father Karel Alois Vinařický (1803–69), in Smoler-Páta, 73. His people, Smoler writes, had now begun to feel themselves "an inseparable part of the whole of Slavdom." "We are not only Serbs, but Slavs as well": this knowledge, which contact with the Czechs and other Slavs had brought them, was – he goes on – a tremendous encouragement in face of almost overwhelming German cultural predominance.

Metternich's Censors:
The Case of Palacký

JOSEPH F. ZACEK

THE PROSPECT which faced the tiny band of Czech "national awakeners" at the beginning of the nineteenth century was a dismaying one. For almost two centuries, since the disaster of the Thirty Years' War, Czech culture in Bohemia had been moribund. Written Czech, the *Rebellen-Sprache* arrested in its development since the sixteenth century, was too antiquated to cope with modern concepts; spoken Czech was largely the mutilated tongue of servants and peasants. The number of Czech inhabitants of the kingdom who possessed a strong national consciousness was pathetically few – so few that, as the contemporary wits put it, they could all congregate in a single room and be buried, together with all hopes of a Czech revival, by a falling ceiling. The Bohemian nobility, to a large extent of foreign origin, had developed a certain territorial patriotism by the late eighteenth century but little sympathy for Czech culture. And what remained to the Czechs of their past literature and history, especially of the proud Hussite period, had been thoroughly denationalized by the Jesuit counter-reformers and the Enlightened Despots who followed them. How a few dedicated men met this dishearten-

This is a revised and expanded version of a paper presented at the 1966 meeting of the Pacific Coast Branch of the American Historical Association. It is the partial result of research done under a grant-in-aid from the Joint Committee on Slavic Studies of the American Council of Learned Societies and the Social Science Research Council in 1965.

ing challenge and revived the Czech nation *en masse* in a half-century is so impressive an achievement that it may almost be ranked in Czech history with the Hussite Revolution itself. The achievement is all the more impressive because it took place during the repressive times of Francis I and Metternich, with their paranoid fear of all innovations, of Slavdom and Panslavism, of the possible political consequences of historical writing – in short, of the very tactics and goals of the Czech "national awakeners." Against them, the absolute state mobilized its many resources – its bureaucracy and police, its spies and *provocateurs*, and especially its comprehensive system of censorship.

The *Zensur*, one of the most notorious aspects of the *Vormärz* period in the Habsburg Empire, has not lacked for researchers, particularly scholars who have based their studies chiefly on the fragmented testimony of its victims and have been been disposed to condemn it outright. Far fewer authors have comprehensively surveyed the entire complicated system and have presented it from the point of view of the regime.[1] The case study offered here, based on the experiences of the famous historian and statesman František Palacký, would seem at first glance to fall neatly into the first category. That is not entirely so, however. Though Palacký was clearly one of the more abused victims of the censors, a detailed examination of his relations with them shows that, at least in practice, they were formidable but not indomitable opponents. And for both critics and defenders of the system, the material connected with Palacký's case provides additional primary evidence of particular value. Palacký was one of the most prolific writers of the empire, and one-half of his activity fell within the difficult "Age of Metternich." His troubles with the imperial censors in Prague and Vienna, and his attempts – successful and unsuccessful – to avoid deletions, interpolations, and outright prohibitions of his writings are well recorded in his correspondence and in his published works.[2] Moreover, his works themselves, the classic "History of Bohemia" as well as the host of studies preceding and accompanying it, were both scholarly and nationalistic in nature, and thus came up squarely against the political and religious taboos of the empire. Palacký's case thus provides an unusually comprehensive illustration of the Austrian censorship in action in the half-century before 1848 and of the obstacle it posed to the Czech national revival.

1 The most significant work of this type is Julius Marx, *Die österreichische Zensur im Vormärz* (Vienna, 1959). The long study by Miloslav Novák, "Rakouská policie a politický vývoj v Čechách před r. 1848," *Sborník archivních prací*, III (1953), 43–167, presents a Czech Marxist, not a pro-Habsburg point of view. It gives a detailed description of the police and censorship mechanism and activity specifically in Bohemia in the Metternich period.

2 Palacký's observations are quite scattered, however. The only previous attempt at a synthesis is Karel Köpl, "Palacký und die Censur," *Památník na oslavu stých narozenin Františka Palackého* (Prague, 1898), 646–88. This old study is still valuable, for Köpl has combined part of Palacký's own account with data gleaned from the official correspondence between the Bohemian Landespraesidium, censorship headquarters in Vienna (the Polizei- und Zensurhofstelle), and the provincial branch of the censorship organization in Prague (the k. k. Bücherrevisionsamt). It thus gives an especially detailed account of the tortuous passage of manuscript material through the censorship labyrinth.

Writing in retrospect, Palacký minced no words in characterizing the first half of the nineteenth century in the Habsburg monarchy. In the reign of Francis I the empire was "a focus of old absolutism, a nest of reaction, and the Eldorado of the bureaucracy," "a realm of darkness and slavery of every kind." Metternich himself was not only "the greatest enemy of freedom, but also the most ferocious, dedicated enemy of all Slavic nationalities in Austria."[3] Scholarship under such conditions was burdensome, even dangerous, for history, philosophy, and theology were considered "contraband." As for history in particular, only dynastic, not national histories were acceptable to the Habsburg regime. "Without doubt," wrote Palacký, "that government was well aware that its past conduct in Bohemia would not meet with the approval it desired before the judgment seat of history ... No wonder, then, that it was devoted not to furthering but rather to hindering historical studies."[4]

Palacký's first recorded comment upon the Habsburg censorship dates from 1825, two years after he arrived in Prague to seek a career. Professor Johann Gottfried Eichhorn of Göttingen had requested the young scholar to contribute a survey of Czech literature to his literary history. Palacký wrote to Eichhorn from Dresden, explaining why he had not yet finished the assignment and why only his great respect for Eichhorn could induce him to attempt it at all: "It is not at all pleasant to write about our literature, long connected so closely with the political history of the land, at a time when the domestic censorship persecutes all old national memories, even the most innocent ones, not only with anxiety but with unheard-of high-handedness, when everything that the Czechs from Hus to Comenius thought, suffered, and did is condemned *a priori*."[5]

Palacký's serious contacts with the imperial censors began in 1826, when he accepted the position of editor of two new journals established by the Royal Bohemian Museum.[6] Published respectively in German and Czech, the journals had the twin functions of popular enlightenment and the fostering of a Bohemian territorial patriotism (and in the case of the Czech journal, a Czech cultural self-consciousness, as well). Both journals began publication in 1827 but soon suffered different fates. The German *Monatschrift der Gesellschaft des vaterländischen Museums in Böhmen* (Journal of the Society of the National Museum in Bohemia) was first reduced from a monthly to a quarterly in 1830, and then abandoned entirely in 1831. On the other hand, its Czech counterpart, the quarterly *Časopis Společnosti vlastenského museum v Čechách* (Journal of the Society of the Patriotic Museum in Bohemia), thrived and, indeed, has continued in existence

3 Palacký, *Gedenkblätter* (Prague, 1874), 183 and 153.
4 Palacký, *Zur böhmischen Geschichtschreibung* (Prague, 1871), 2. (This work is cited below as *Zur böhm. Gesch.*)
5 Palacký to Eichhorn, 13 August 1825, in Vojtěch J. Nováček, *Františka Palackého korrespondence a zápisky*, III (Prague, 1911), 103.
6 See V. E. Mourek, "Palacký jako vydavatel německého časopisu vlasteneckého musea v letech 1827–1831," *Památník Palackého*, 268–89; and Josef Hanuš, *Národní museum a naše obrození*, II (Prague, 1923), 329–35, 392–4.

under slightly variant titles to the present day. Why did the German periodical, deliberately favoured over the Czech one by the more serious nature and quality of its content and the frequency of its publication, fail? Both Count Kašpar Stern-berg, the president of the museum, and Palacký attributed this primarily to the effects of the severe imperial censorship.

To be sure, Count Josef Sedlnitzky, the head of the Polizei- und Zensurhofstelle in Vienna, had agreed to permit the publication of the periodicals only on the condition that "articles destined for the periodicals be subjected to careful and rigorous censorship, and that articles which touch upon political conditions, in a historical connection or any other, not be allowed into print without higher permission."[7] But the project had powerful protectors. The political loyalty of the museum and its president, Sternberg, was above reproach.[8] Count Franz Anton (František) Kolovrat, the Highest Burgrave of Prague (i.e. governor of Bohemia) and one of the founders of the museum, gave the venture his hearty support and ordered the Prague Bücherrevisionsamt to speed submitted articles through the censorship process.[9] And when Kolovrat moved in 1826 to Vienna as Staats- und Konferenz-minister, his successor as governor of Bohemia, Count Karel Chotek, continued to try to aid and shield the periodicals. In 1829, for example, he attempted to assume the censorship of articles for both periodicals personally, insisting that the order that all historical articles be censored only in Vienna endangered the regular publication of the German periodical.[10]

Despite such impressive support, and despite his own extreme editorial caution which went so far that it began to alienate his friends, Palacký was not spared by the censors. The German periodical, in particular, had difficulty in attracting contributors and subscribers, for the censors would only allow the publication of such materials as held no interest for the cultivated readership for whom this journal

7 Sedlnitzky's memorandum of 11 February 1826, quoted in Hanuš, ii, 313.
8 The museum wished to establish a special committee to watch over the periodicals and screen contributions to them. Palacký welcomed the idea: "Since the committee would thus form a first and ... most conscientious office of censorship, perhaps the local governing authorities could be requested to arrange matters so that the editor would be protected to some degree against possible erroneous interpretations and misunderstanding by the censors." Quoted in Hanuš, ii, 326. The committee was named but never met.
9 Kolovrat to Sternberg, 23 February 1826, copy by Palacký in Nováček, ii (Prague, 1902), 252–3. Articles touching upon political matters were to be sent on to him together with a preliminary judgment by the Prague censorship office. The intervention of Kolovrat, Metternich's ambitious competitor, in the censorship process was not always a benefit to Palacký. In November 1826, he complained to a friend in Vienna that, in the previous month, Kolovrat had insisted on taking three articles destined for the first issues of the journals with him to Vienna, promising to bring them back in censored form when he returned. He had not done so, and Palacký had to wait in "painful uncertainty" as to whether the first issues would actually go to press as scheduled. Palacký to Carl Georg Hoppe, 19 November 1826, in Nováček, iii, 119–20.
10 Hanuš, ii, 333–4; Mourek, *Památník Palackého*, 288.

had been intended. Palacký wrote to Count Evžen Černín in 1830: "Indeed, I do not know how it will end when we cannot write about anything except cook-books and prayer-books, fairy-tales and charades."[11] More crucial, the success of the German periodical was predicated upon its securing a sizable number of foreign subscribers in the Germanies, as well, and this – despite the personal efforts of Goethe himself to publicize it there – never materialized, chiefly because of the distrust and distaste of the German reading public for the heavily censored Austrian publications and the ill will of the German booksellers, who resented the difficulties the Austrian censorship caused them. Palacký complained to Jernej Kopitar:

Many German booksellers believe they are making reprisals against the censorship prohibitions of our government by interfering with the sale of Austrian publications ...; some told us this explicitly, most proved it by returning our packages unopened and unexamined. Goethe wrote that the prejudice of the north Germans against us and against all literary products of our empire is greater and more derogatory than he dares to say, and Böttiger [Böttinger?] confessed to me sincerely that the ill will of our German comrades toward Austrian literature is unmatched.[12]

Forced to depend exclusively upon a small domestic readership, the German periodical was reduced in size and price, changed from a monthly to a quarterly, and finally – after an unsuccessful attempt to turn it over to a commercial publisher – entirely abandoned. In late 1831, Palacký informed Sternberg that he had lost all desire to try to continue with it under such unpromising circumstances:

During the past three years, the severity of our censorship authorities has increased in striking measure; and although I often cherished the hope that it had reached its peak, I have seen myself disappointed anew in this respect with every new half-year. The most unpleasant consequence of this is the alienation of my best German collaborators, who no longer care to present their writings to the censor under such conditions. Even I must confess that it is often difficult for me to find new topics for the German journal ... which could be worked up freely without giving offense to the present censorship and still be of some interest to a public pampered by foreign, uncensored periodicals.[13]

That foreign suspicions were not unjustified is illustrated by the treatment

11 Quoted in Hanuš, II, 334.
12 Palacký to Kopitar, 5 November 1829, quoted in Mourek, *Památník Palackého*, 285; similarly in his autobiography (1864–5) in Jaroslav Charvát, ed., *Dílo Františka Palackého* (Prague, 1941), I, 44. Sternberg complained in the same vein to Goethe that the Germans could not be convinced that a sensible, free word could be published in the Austrian states and that the German booksellers had sworn to handle all publications sent to them from Austria as if they were crabs (Sternberg to Goethe, 22 January 1829 and 4 February 1830, quoted in Mourek, *Památník Palackého*, 285, 286).
13 Palacký to Sternberg, 16 October 1831, in *Gedenkblätter*, 65–6; similarly, Palacký to C. J. Czoernig, 3 September 1832, quoted in Mourek, *Památník Palackého*, 288–9.

accorded by the censors to two articles destined for the German periodical. In July 1829, Palacký was informed by the Viennese authorities that, in order to be allowed publication, an article by C. J. Czoernig entitled "Albrecht von Waldsteins Versuch eine ständische Verfassung in seinem Herzogthume Friedland einzuführen" (Albrecht of Wallenstein's attempt to Introduce a Constitution and Diet in His Duchy of Friedland) would have to be retitled "Albrecht von Wallenstein's Documentarily Proven Attempt to Convert the Duchy of Friedland into an Independent Territory and to Separate It from the Bohemian Crown." Also, the document in question was to be notarized and printed in full along with the article. Palacký complied.[14] The next year, Palacký presented his own "Zur Geschichte der Unterthänigkeit und Leibeigenschaft in Böhmen" (On the History of Vassalage and Serfdom in Bohemia), which fared much worse. Like many of his romantic contemporaries, Palacký was prone to strain the slender evidence and to idealize the ancient politico-economic institutions of the Slavs, insisting that they had originally enjoyed freedom and democracy, and that slavery and serfdom had been fastened upon the Bohemian peasants only after the Hussite Wars by an ascendant nobility under the weak king Vladislav (Jagiełło) (1471–1516). The work was rejected for publication by the Viennese censors, "so that such welcome materials could not be misused by the secret scribblers about the countryside to inspire complaints (already numerous enough) by the Bohemian serfs against their masters."[15] It was not printed until 1874, when Palacký included it in his collection of minor works entitled *Gedenkblätter*.[16]

Palacký's *bête noire* in the matter of the periodicals, and in general until the mid-1830s, was a local official, the chief of the imperial censorship in Prague, a priest and Knight of the Cross, Father Jan Václav Zimmermann. "I do not know," he wrote to Czoernig, "what reason Zimmermann had to be especially severe with the museum periodicals which I edited, but he himself admitted that, in fact, he had been. If he had at least been sensible and impartial about it, his severity would not have embarrassed me so often with my collaborators."[17] A stream of bitterness against Zimmermann's behaviour runs through Palacký's correspondence. As early as 1824 he complained to Jan Kollár, the Slovak poet who was then living in Pest, of

14 See Mourek, *Památník Palackého*, 288. The article appeared in the *Monatschrift*, III (Dec. 1829), 447–61.
15 *Gedenkblätter*, 94.
16 *Ibid.*, 93–103.
17 Palacký to Czoernig, 3 September 1832, quoted in Mourek, *Památník Palackého*, 288–9. There may have been personal malice behind Zimmermann's behaviour. In 1826, Palacký had completed and presented for approval a critical synthesis of the seventeen anonymous chronicles known as the *Staří letopisové čeští od r. 1378 do 1527*. Zimmermann himself had published an edition of one of the chronicles in 1819 which Palacký criticized as faulty. As censor, Zimmermann held up the publication of the work until 1829 and subsequently, in Palacký's opinion, revenged himself "with a carpenter's severity" by hewing away at the periodicals. See Václav Chaloupecký, *Fr. Palacký* (Prague, 1912), 55. There is a sharply etched portrait of Zimmermann, as an accused forger of historical manuscripts, in I. J. Hanuš, *Die gefälschten böhmischen Gedichte aus den Jahren 1816–1849* (Prague, 1868), *passim*.

"the daily tragicomedy [with the censorship], performed not on orders from above ... but because of the haughtiness and extreme foolishness of our chief censor, Zimmermann, who behaves like an autocrat, knowing as a state official that the police will take his part against all complaints."[18] In 1830 he reported to Kollár that the sale of the latter's Panslav poem *Slávy dcera* (Daughter of Sláva) was handicapped in Bohemia by the fact that it had not been advertised or displayed openly at the booksellers, for fear that Zimmermann would give orders to his underlings to move against it.[19] In 1831, Palacký wrote to the German poet Karl Egon Ebert: "The tyranny of Pope Zimmermann's censorship has finally become unbearable to me,"[20] and in 1835 satirically to the Moravian historian Antonín Boček, that Zimmermann had agreed to permit the printing of Ludwig Spohr's oratorio, *Des Heilandes letzte Stunde* (The Saviour's Last Hour), only if the name "Jesus" were everywhere removed.[21]

Yet, by his own admission, the censorship authorities were not always so officially troublesome and unapproachable.[22] Looking back upon his career in 1874, Palacký granted that they had often shown goodwill toward his complaints and had even sent him their preliminary opinions and requests for further clarifications before they arrived at a final decision. Palacký's replies in two such cases illustrate, among other things, the types of arguments deemed to be efficacious against the censor's criticisms and against total prohibition of the printing of a submitted manuscript.[23]

In February 1834, in connection with a manuscript-source which had recently

18 Palacký to Kollár, 22 January 1824, in Nováček, II, 164.
19 Palacký to Kollár, 8 July 1830, in A. J. Vrťátko (ed.), "Dopisy Františka Palackého k Janu Kollárovi," *Časopis Českého musea* (ČČM), LIII (1879), 467.
20 Quoted in Jaroslav Goll, "František Palacký," *Český časopis historický*, IV (1898), 228.
21 Palacký to Boček, 25 November 1835, in Boh. Navrátil, ed., "Listy Palackého Bočkovi," *Časopis Matice moravské*, XXV (1901), 123.
22 Nor apparently on a personal level, either: Palacky's diary for several years after he arrived in Prague in 1823 (Nováček, I) records that he and Zimmermann often met in polite Prague circles and even went out socially together. Some of Palacký's closest friends became Slavonic censors themselves: Jernej Kopitar, the Slovene philologist, worked in Vienna, and Pavel Josef Šafařík, the Slovak authority on Slavonic antiquities, became the censor of Czech periodicals at the Bohemian *gubernium* in 1837. Palacký also tried to ingratiate himself with no less a figure than Sedlnitzky himself, sending him luxuriously bound copies of the journals. In 1841 he visited Sedlnitzky in Vienna and apparently tried to convince him that Austro-Slavism would provide a shield for the government against the Magyars and foreign enemies. Sedlnitzky presented Palacký with his portrait in a gilded frame and pretended to be convinced. Palacký's future son-in-law, František Rieger, received a letter from a friend in Vienna which stated: "Palacký has been to see Sedlnitzky, who told him that the government is glad to see that the Czechs wish to remain Czechs ... He [Sedlnitzky] conversed with him for more than a half-hour, telling him at the conclusion that whenever he [Palacký] was subjected to any pressure or injury he was to turn directly to him." Josef Podlipský (?) to Rieger, 6 March 1841, in Jan Heidler, ed., *Příspěvky k listáři Dra Frant. Lad. Riegra*, I (Prague, 1924), 7. See also Novák, *Sborník archivních prací*, III, 109.
23 They are reprinted in *Gedenkblätter*, 103–9, and should be supplemented with additional pertinent primary materials in Köpl, *Památník Palackého*, 647–56.

been discovered in Russia and which had already been published in the Czech periodical of the museum in 1830, Palacký offered to that journal a critical evaluation of the old Slavonic legend about the martyrdom of St. Václav (Wenceslaus). The censor returned the manuscript with the tentative verdict of *Damnatur*, charging that Palacký had not represented Drahomíra, the mother of St. Václav, as a heathen and co-author of the murder of the holy martyr. This was in conflict with two old, established chroniclers, with Roman and Czech breviaries, and with centuries-old popular religious belief. In his polite, almost unctuous reply, Palacký carefully answered these charges. Against the chronicles he skilfully marshalled the judgments of two more recent and highly respected authorities, both churchmen-historians – Gelasius Dobner and Josef Dobrovský. He had no quarrel with popular belief, he wrote, adding however, "I only fear that if the verdicts of later legends and general popular faith are set up as rules for history, all historical research will come to an end. That surely cannot be either among the principles of our enlightened government or the intentions of the highly cultivated censor." He argued that the article was a purely learned discourse of the type clearly permitted by the censorship laws and that it would appear in a periodical read by a limited number of the educated, not the general public. Drahomíra obviously was not a woman of good character, but would it not deeply offend the religious feelings of "our people" to have her unjustly accused of the most fundamental, most monstrous crime, the murder of her son? Finally, he warned, the complete prohibition of the article would do serious harm to the national reputation abroad. It would stimulate the unjust opinion there that the Czechs were people without knowledge and sense enough to appreciate so precious a discovery, so ancient a fragment of old Slavonic and Bohemian literature. Although declaring himself ready to make any changes deemed absolutely necessary (as he always did in such cases), Palacký apparently did not get satisfactory results with his plea and withdrew his manuscript before a final decision was made. Not till the fall of 1836 did his patron, Kašpar Sternberg, reactivate the matter on his behalf with Sedlnitzky. Finally, in 1837, after Palacký had satisfied his religious critics, including the Consistory of Prague, the study was at last permitted to appear in the Czech journal of the Bohemian Museum – but with the unfortunate Drahomíra still depicted as a heathen and murderess. The full, uncensored version was printed only in 1872, in the collection of Palacký's smaller works entitled *Radhost*.[24]

In the second case, Palacký came to the assistance of his friend Václav Hanka, who in 1839 wished to publish an edition of Viktorín Kornel of Všehrd's famous early sixteenth-century treatise on the laws and judicial procedures of the Kingdom of Bohemia (*O práwiech, o súdiech i deskách zemie české knihy dewatery*). Although the Bücherrevisionsamt in Prague (under Šafařík's influence) recommended its approval, the Polizei- und Zensurhofstelle in Vienna dissented and returned a verdict of *Non admittitur*. Sedlnitzky pointed out to Count Chotek that,

24 "O umučení sv. Václava, podlé legendy slovanské, úvaha kritická," ČČM, XI (1837), 406–17; *Radhost*, II, 131–45.

originating in a period when Bohemia was not yet under the Austrian sceptre, the document was written in a spirit of intolerance and hatred for the Germans and was therefore ill-suited to contemporary conditions in the empire. He added, however, that as an important historical source it could certainly be used without restriction in historical research. Chotek asked Palacký to reply,[25] and the latter again tendered the familiar arguments against total prohibition of publication. He pointed out that Všehrd had originally dedicated his work to King Vladislav II himself, and he assured the censor that the few and insignificant passages revealing Czech-Utraquist bias could be efficiently deleted, altered, or "neutralized with contrary annotations" (a surprising concession from such a usually conscientious and "scientific" historian). Both the archaeological-legal character of the topic and the antiquated language would make the study of interest only "to an already cultured audience, hence certainly to a limited one among the Czechs." Changes in the judiciary since its day made the treatise largely useless for Bohemian lawyers. Furthermore, in view of the current interest in the study of Slavic laws in Poland and Russia, the work would surely be quickly published there if prohibited in the empire. And such a prohibition would only lend support to the opinion, already stimulated by several similar recent incidents, that the government wished to diminish the national monuments and memories of the Czechs: "The spreading of this belief would be more harmful to the interests of this state than the printing of this work ..." Palacký's plea was successful, in that an altered text was granted publication in 1840, although with the warning that the "old national character" of the work was to be preserved and no modernization of the orthography or content allowed. This version appeared in 1841, but an uncensored edition appeared only in 1864.[26]

Two further altercations with the imperial censorship apparatus in which Palacký became involved as secretary of the Royal Bohemian Society of Sciences (Královská česká společnost nauk) display an increasing audacity on his part.[27] In 1842, Palacký again had to intercede on behalf of Hanka, who had published in the society's Transactions some sample passages from a Church Slavonic evangelium sent to him from Paris. This codex, believed to have been written by St. Prokop himself, had been a gift from Charles IV to the Slavonic monastery in Prague and had made its way to France, where it had been much prized before being lost during the Revolution. Hanka expressed his joy at the rediscovery of this monument to the Slavonic rite in the Czech lands, which had been preserved in spite of unending Catholic hostility to it. In a footnote, he also printed an excerpt, in Cyril-

25 The work was to be published by the Matice česká, the institution devoted to publishing scholarly works in the Czech language, of which Palacký was a founding member. Palacký himself had already published part of the Všehrd work in the Czech journal of the Bohemian Museum: "Viktorina Kornelia ze Všehrd o právích země České kniha čtvrtá (ze starého rukopisu)," ČČM, x (1836), 13–39.

26 The 1841 version included an introduction on the work and its author by Palacký. Despite the censor's warning, the old orthography was not maintained.

27 See Josef Kalousek, Děje Královské české společnosti nauk (Prague, 1884), 167–9.

lic, from a Russian legend about Cyril and Methodius, which castigated "the Latin Vojtěch," "who abolished the orthodox faith, rejected the Russian script, elevated the Latin script and faith, burned the pictures of the true faith, and cut down and dispersed the bishops." On 21 August 1842, the Prague Bücherrevisionsamt informed the society that Vienna had been alerted to an offprint of Hanka's work as well as its "audacious Slavonic character." Hanka's comment was viewed as offensive, "and especially the appended Russian legend ..., in a theological sense (considered from the Roman Catholic standpoint) and even somewhat in a political sense (considering the known endeavours of the Russian church)." Because the topic involved "higher political interests," the society was required to inform the censors promptly whether the contents of the offprint corresponded to the oral presentation before the society and to the account printed in its Transactions.

As secretary of the society, Palacký replied three days later, describing the procedure followed in all matters of publication and defending Hanka against any evil intent. As to the fragment of the Russian legend, he insisted that it required a deep knowledge of Slavonic philology to read the Cyrillic script and to understand the various abbreviations in the passage, a knowledge rare in Bohemia and even in Vienna – "in all Vienna, there is scarcely anyone, with the exception of Mr. Kopitar, who could correctly translate and explain it." In this way, Palacký attacked the informer who had alerted Vienna and whom he suspected of being Kopitar, acting out of personal spite. In late November, Palacký was further required to explain who had been responsible for permitting the publication of the separate offprint (since the *imprimatur* had been granted only for the Transactions of the Society) and to state the number of offprints which had been published. Palacký replied that since 1800 the Transactions of the Society consisted only of separate offprints in the number of 500 copies, 150 of which were bound in the volumes of the Transactions and 350 of which were given to the author in lieu of an honorarium. The matter seems to have stopped there.

One final incident concerns Palacký's own writings and the sensitive subject of Hussitism, the topic which, when presented at length in the *Geschichte von Böhmen* (History of Bohemia), was to provoke his most memorable combat with the Austrian censors.[28] In October 1842, Palacký addressed the historical section of the society on the precursors of Hussitism in Bohemia, and a year later presented the work to it for publication. The *Předchůdcové husitství v Čechách* introduced and presented excerpts from the writings of such fourteenth-century reformers as Konrad Waldhauser, Jan Milíč of Kroměříž, Matěj of Janov, and Jan of Štěkna. Despite Šafařík's own ardent approval of the study, the censor, acting on the advice of

28 See Kalousek, 169, and Jiří Beran, "František Palacký jako sekretář Královské české společnosti nauk," in Jiří Beran, ed., *Akademiku Václavu Vojtíškovi k 75. narozeninám* (Prague, 1958), 119–20, in which Beran cites documents in the Archive of the Czechoslovak Academy of Sciences and the Literary Archive of the National Museum (Literární archiv Národního musea, cited below as LANM.)

religious officials, refused permission to publish it without major revisions. Palacký defended himself boldly: "The judgment of the Most Reverend Consistory on my "Precursors of Hussitism" not only destroys all critical historiography but makes all historical writing in general impossible ... If everything that properly characterizes these men is struck out of my essay, it not only loses all value but its publication would comprise a falsification, a sin against history."[29] When the censors would not budge, Palacký withdrew his manuscript and gave it to a Lusatian Serb friend, Jan Pĕtr Jordan, who published it under his own name in German (*Die Vorläufer des Hussitenthums in Böhmen*), in Leipzig in 1846. A new German edition appeared in Prague under Palacký's name only in 1869; the original Czech edition finally appeared in *Radhost* in 1872.[30]

All of the foregoing must be considered only a preliminary to the major bout between Palacký and the imperial censors over his major work, the famous *Geschichte von Böhmen*.[31] Dealing with the period to 1526, when the Czechs were still their own masters, and centred on the "heretical" Hussite Revolution, it automatically awakened their keen attention and close criticism. Indeed, long before he actually began writing the first volume in the fall of 1832, the project seemed ill-omened. Originally, the Bohemian Estates had simply sought someone to continue the *Chronologische Geschichte Böhmens* (Chronological History of Bohemia) (10 vols., 1770–1801) which František Pubitschka had advanced to 1618 before his death. But candidate after candidate refused, some of the chief reasons being the fear of government censorship and of ill will toward those researching the sensitive period following the battle of White Mountain.[32] In 1829, when Palacký agreed to

29 Quoted in Kalousek, 169.
30 *Radhost*, ii, 297–356. The ruse apparently was successful: Köpl (*Památník Palackého*, 661) was unable to find any documentary evidence that the censors had noticed "Jordan's publication."
31 The best primary account of this struggle is in Palacký's *Zur böhm. Gesch.*, 94–107. Selections from this work have been published in English translation by Count Francis Lützow, *Lectures on the Historians of Bohemia* (London and New York, 1905), 95–7, and in his *History of Bohemian Literature* (London, 1907), 396–8. The best secondary account is Köpl, *Památník Palackého*, 661–88. The latter draws heavily upon Palacký's manuscripts, citing censored passages copiously and even reprinting some of those which were altered or expunged as they originally appeared (see especially 684–7, note 63). Since the censored instalments of the *Geschichte von Böhmen* were never reprinted as Palacký had originally written them (Palacký simply lost interest in the German edition of his history after 1848), Köpl's article is an indispensable supplement for those using this version instead of the Czech one, the *Dějiny národu českého*.
32 Palacký gave a more specific reason. The unpublished part of Pubitschka's manuscript ended with the dismissal of Wallenstein from his generalship in 1630. "In the public opinion of Bohemia in the years 1820–1830, the controversy over the guilt or innocence of the Duke of Friedland formed the most delicate and sorest point of all Bohemian history. Everyone feared to compromise himself, either with the public or the government, through a critical investigation of the subject. That was the peculiar reason why everyone chose to refuse the ticklish offer." *Zur böhm. Gesch.*, 12.

take the job (promptly electing to compose an entirely new history), these fears seemed substantiated. The promised appointment of Palacký as official Historiographer of the Bohemian Estates was refused by Francis I in 1830, ostensibly because the domestic treasury of the Bohemian Estates already showed a considerable deficit for 1831. Popular opinion, and Palacký himself, attributed the decision rather to the aversion of the emperor and Metternich for innovations, especially one instituted for a Bohemian Protestant. The angry Estates had to content themselves with simply commissioning Palacký to write his history for an annual retainer. The title of historiographer was granted him officially only in 1838 by the new emperor, Ferdinand, after seven years of industrious, highly praised, and demonstrably *loyal* research and writing on his part.

Nevertheless, with the enthusiastic support and influence of the Estates, especially of Count Chotek, the first two volumes of the work and the first instalment of the third were handled speedily and quite leniently by Vienna (1836–43). Instalments generally made the circuit from Prague to Vienna and back in a month or less, and only a few minor changes were required.[33] Even the covert condemnations of the work by a busy informer, Josef Leonhard Knoll, apparently could not seriously impede the project. Knoll, a professor of history at Prague and Vienna and ostensibly Palacký's friend, was a self-motivated and passionate defender of a centralized and Germanized Austrian empire, and ever vigilant for any sign of a cultural or political revival on the part of the Czechs, whom he considered potential traitors to the House of Habsburg. As part of a long series of secret communications to the Highest Chancellor, Count Anton Friedrich Mitrowsky, he urged, when the first volume of the *Geschichte* appeared, that it be suppressed before it created "thirteen million Slavs burning with national fanaticism and hatred against the Germans."[34] From the start, Chotek continually beseeched Sedlnitzky for speed, in the hope that the

33 Köpl (*Památník Palackého*, 661, n. 28) has prepared a table showing when sections of the work were submitted by the Landespraesidium to Vienna and returned to it by the Zensurhofstelle. Sample changes required: "das ihm *vom Volke* anvertraute Land" was replaced with "von den Böhmen," to avoid any reference to *Volks-Souveränität*; and "Missbräuche *in der Kirche*" was changed to "in den böhmischen Kirchen."

34 See the study of Knoll's activities, based on his previously secret correspondence, by František Dvorský, "František Palacký a náš nepřítel," *Památník Palackého*, 443–72; and Palacký's own *Gedenkblätter*, 129–31. In 1844, after Mitrowsky's death, the custodian of his papers showed Palacký Knoll's secret denunciations. Palacký found them very amusing, with only one serious consideration involved: "Were such Knolliads really the secret levers that set our governmental apparatus in motion? Then woe not only to the nation but above all to the government itself that uses them!" (*Gedenkblätter*, 131). The network of informers, so closely tied to the censorship authorities, enraged Palacký as early as 1826, when he complained to Kollár of being surrounded by ignoble people who, eager to earn more than thirty pieces of silver, betrayed their fatherland by turning the government's mistrust toward the most innocent of acts (Palacký to Kollár, 28 September 1826, in Nováček, II, 282). There is strong evidence that Knoll himself was a paid agent of Sedlnitzky and that Captain Josef Hoch, the director of the Prague police, even tried once to persuade Palacký to inform on a fellow author. See Novák, *Sborník archivních prací*, III, 113, 118.

entire first volume might be published in time for the impending coronation of Ferdinand (scheduled for 7 September 1836), and this tactic, possibly a stratagem, may have encouraged the rapid progress of the censoring process. However, Chotek's offer to save time by doing the censoring personally in Prague was not accepted because, in Sedlnitzky's words, the work in question dealt with important issues of constitutional law and imperial and domestic interests and therefore had to pass the scrutiny of the *geheime Haus-, Hof- und Staatskanzlei*.[35]

Not even Chotek's successor, Archduke Stephan, could shield Palacký when in November 1843 he submitted the second section of volume III, dealing with the beginnings of Hussitism (1403–14). The manuscript was returned to Archduke Stephan the following March with a great number of alterations and excisions required, chiefly on theological grounds.[36] While admitting that it was difficult for a Protestant to depict the period in a manner completely palatable to Catholic readers, and that the author's facts and language were generally fair, Sedlnitsky nevertheless charged that Palacký's over-all treatment was highly subjective as well as unfriendly and injurious to Catholicism.[37] Archduke Stephan was informed: "The Austrian government, as the chief protector of the Catholic church, cannot allow that in a work appearing under its censorship periods of domestic history be treated in a spirit hostile to the ruling religion." Referring to "the previously noticeable inclination of the author to Czechism at the expense of the German element," Sedlnitzky also warned: "In a state where many nations are united under one sceptre and give their allegiance to a ruler of German blood, it cannot be allowed that one nationality attack, disparage, or undermine the others, especially not the ruling one."[38] Archduke Stephan was instructed to inform Palacký of this "general line," so that further actions and reminders on the part of the censors would be unnecessary.

35 Or, in Palacký's words, "Provincial insight in such things was deemed insufficient and inadmissible" (*Zur böhm. Gesch.*, 94).
36 "As long as I had to contend only with political censorship, things went well; but now that theologians have been called in to decide on my description of Hussitism, many errors and shortcomings are being discovered," Palacký wrote to an unknown correspondent (quoted in Chaloupecký, *Palacký*, 152).
37 More specifically, he charged, for example, that the church hierarchy was depicted as of no value to religious faith; that Palacký sought to "excuse" the Hussite movement by referring to its many predecessors; and that Palacký claimed that the Protestant reformation was an act of Providence to halt the stagnation of the church.
38 Quotes from Köpl, *Památník Palackého*, 669–71. Though Sedlnitzky agreed in general with the theologian-censor's evaluations, he was, nevertheless, conscious of the problems Palacký faced. In a letter of 25 February 1844 to the k. k. geheime Haus-, Hof- und Staatskanzlei about this manuscript, he pointed out how difficult Palacký's task was to describe the confused Bohemian religious conditions in this period accurately, and asserted that a certain forbearance was necessary on the part of the censors if such historical writing were not to be made completely impossible. The letter is reprinted in Jos. Volf, "Palackého dějiny a censura," ČČM, LXXXVII (1913), 157–8.

The next instalment (1414–19), including the description of Hus before the Council of Constance, fared even worse. Palacký submitted it at the end of June 1844, with the plea that the censoring be expedited so that he could oversee the printing of the manuscript before he left Prague with his ailing wife for Nice at the beginning of October.[39] It was not returned until the very end of September.[40] The censor, a professor of political economy Gustav Franz von Scheiner, had reportedly urged that the entire manuscript be suppressed, charging that it was "sometimes an open, sometimes a concealed apology for Hus and his cause" and that the author was acting as "Hus's attorney," swaying the reader in his favour, discrediting his Catholic accusers and judges, and seeking to paint him as without faults and as a martyr. The case was ultimately referred to Metternich himself, who decided that the author was to be allowed to state facts but was to avoid all *missliebige Raisonnements*. Scheiner thereupon demanded a long series of changes to ensure that the work would be acceptable and not misleading to Catholic readers or damaging to the Catholic cause. For example, in reply to Palacký's statement that even Hus's enemies had admired his courage before the Council, he wrote: "The Catholic church does not discern in [Hus's attitude] unshakeable courage but insolence and obstinacy founded on deep delusion." As for the famous letter from the papal secretary, Poggio Bracciolini, to Leonardo Aretino, praising the life and death of Hus's colleague, Jeroným (Jerome) of Prague (d. 1416), which Palacký had cited, Scheiner doubted both its authenticity and the credibility of its author. At any rate, in his view the letter was a one-sided judgment and thus misleading.[41]

When the mutilated manuscript reached Palacký on 30 September 1844, he was in the midst of last-minute preparations for the trip to Nice. Before he left, however, he penned a long, detailed, and unusually emotional and sharply worded reply. He insisted that the censor kept seeing meanings he had not intended. He disclaimed any intention of misleading Catholic readers: "My wife and children and many of my closest friends are ardent Catholics, and it has never occurred to me to wish to offend them or divert them from their faith." He had even solicited opinions about the manuscript from his Catholic friends before submitting it for censorship. If, despite his wish to give both sides their due, he had given Hus more virtues than

---

39 See the draft of Palacký's letter (no addressee), 30 June 1844, in the collection of his manuscript materials entitled "Historiographica," in LANM, Palacký Collection, sign. 11 D 17.

40 Palacký to Jan Evangelista Purkyně, 24 September 1844, in "Několik listů Fr. Palackého k prof. J. Purkyňovi," ČČM, LIV (1880), 422: "The printing of the new volume of my history, extending from 1378 to 1419, is not complete because the section of the manuscript including the years 1414–19 has been stuck in the censorship in Vienna for a quarter-year."

41 Among numerous additional criticisms, Scheiner cited various "hateful expressions," criticized Palacký's overreliance on Protestant sources and those favourable to Hus, objected to Palacký's point that contemporary Catholic opinion had varied as to Hus's orthodoxy, and warned that Palacký's statement that the Council had lost authority with the people because of its treatment of Hus implied a dangerous right of the people to judge the actions of Councils.

faults, it was partly because the most detailed sources had been provided by Hus's adherents, partly because of "the undeniable importance and worth of the man."

According to my innermost convictions and, I think I may add, according to the verdict of every *impartial* judge, Hus intended only good, even though the means which he chose were not all free of sin and therefore not completely blameless. In this sense, I have tried to write about him with the greatest possible impartiality and I believe that my account is quite compatible with a genuinely devout Catholic interpretation. If I have been mistaken in certain details, I will gladly yield to correction. I cannot, however, believe that it is indispensable to Catholicism that every deed and thought of Hus be condemned *a priori*, that he be painted entirely in black, and that all circumstances which appear to favour him, even if they are completely corroborated historically, should be suppressed. Such a one-sided and unjust presentation would no longer be history but a party-pamphlet. Unfortunately, the censor seems to expect something of that nature from me. Should this apprehension be justified, I regret to have to declare that I cannot and will not ever accede to such a demand. I would rather give up all my work and withdraw my hand from the writing of history. For a historian also has his high and extensive obligations, which must be sacred to him as are, for instance, those of a professor of dogmatics or an inquisitor.[42]

Passage by passage, Palacký replied to Scheiner's charges and, like a retreating general, yielded up less essential positions while doggedly insisting that he be referred to superior source materials when crucial changes were demanded. The professional historian found himself forced to plead repeatedly that objectionable passages were "generally known fact." He was amazed, for example, that Scheiner was not acquainted with the Bracciolini letter, since it had been cited by Aeneas Sylvius (later Pope Pius II) himself in his well-known *Historia Bohemica* and had since been passed by the censors and reprinted many times. "If contemporary Catholic theologians appear so much more anxious about judging their adversaries than popes and papal secretaries of the fifteenth century, should I not conclude that their anxiety goes much too far?"[43] Having made his defence, he bowed to the inevitable and declared himself ready to make all changes deemed absolutely imperative. He asked only that the final decision not be left to Scheiner but "to another, reasonable man, who knows how to combine the necessary Catholic zeal with a little Christian love."[44] In his absence, the changes were made by his authorized assistants, Václav V. Tomek and Karel J. Erben, with the guidance of Pavel Josef Šafařík. According to Tomek,[45] the most extensive change required by the

42 *Zur böhm. Gesch.*, 101–2.
43 *Ibid.*, 105.
44 *Ibid.*, 106.
45 See especially the three letters on the subject from Tomek to Palacký, 26 November 1844, 14 January 1845, and 7 March 1845, LANM, Palacký Collection, sign. 11 B 9; also Tomek *Paměti z mého života*, I (Prague, 1904), 198–9, and his "Styky mé s Palackým do roku 1862," *Památník Palackého*, 69.

new censor concerned the Bracciolini letter, which could not be printed in its entirety but only in excerpts which mentioned those merits of Jerome (e.g., as a dialectician and ortator) which had no bearing on his relations with the church.[46] As for the other disputed passages in the manuscript, almost all of them were left entirely as Palacký had suggested in his reply, except that in every case a word had been altered somewhere "so that the author would not have it completely as he wished."

Widespread public knowledge of Palacký's spirited wrangling with the censors made him a celebrity for a time, and the new volume of the "History" was awaited with even greater eagerness because of the difficulties it had encountered. Diverse rumours circulated in Prague about the matter, wrote the amused Tomek to Palacký: "Some think that the publication of the *History of Bohemia* has been completely forbidden and stopped forever, and they are glad to have something to talk and argue about; others say that because of this you have emigrated from Bohemia and that you will do your writing abroad, and they are all the happier for this ..."[47] But Sedlnitzky was not amused. In November 1844, he wrote to Archduke Stephan, stiffly protesting the unsuitable tone of Palacký's reply and his vehement remarks against a censor who was simply performing his duties conscientiously. Archduke Stephan was instructed to inform Palacký of the official displeasure at his mode of writing. The archduke passed the instructions on to the executive committee of the Bohemian Estates, which refused to administer the rebuke on the grounds that Palacký was not one of its officials. Archduke Stephan then left the matter to the Prague police, who duly reprimanded Palacký when he returned home in May 1845.

This seems to have been the last of Palacký's major troubles, at least as a scholar, with the imperial censors. The next section of the *Geschichte* did not appear until 1851, and neither it nor its Czech counterpart, the *Dějiny národu českého* (which only began publication in 1848, after the first suspension of censorship), apparently suffered much from the renewed censorship after the Revolution.[48] The next time Palacký's writings were censored and prohibited, it was at the hands of the Nazis in the Protectorate of Bohemia-Moravia.

46 Tomek believed that even this required change was the result of a misunderstanding on the part of the new censor in Vienna, who apparently had not read the entire text but only the disputed passages, and who considered the Bracciolini letter simply as a supplement which could be eliminated without detriment to the text and not as an integral part of the text itself. The efforts of the Prague Bücherrevisionsamt to explain this to Vienna were, however, unsuccessful. Tomek to Palacký, 14 January 1845, LANM, Palacký Collection, sign. 11 B 9.

47 *Ibid.*

48 Church and state had to find other, indirect means to protect themselves against the work. Palacký's correspondence after 1848 indicates that the executive committee of the Bohemian Estates sometimes balked and held up the publication of instalments of the *Geschichte*, probably in fear of Vienna's displeasure, and the Prague Consistory allegedly considered forbidding faithful Catholics to read the work. See, for example, Palacký to his son Jan, 16 February 1860, in Čeněk Zíbrt, ed., "Z dopisů Františka Palackého synu Janovi, 1848–1874," *Osvěta*, XXXIX (1909), 156.

Though Palacký the historian breathed easily after 1848, Palacký the politician – the additional role he had assumed in that year – was not yet finished with the other aspects of the Habsburg censorship, such as the censoring of newspapers and personal correspondence. To be sure, he had been well aware even earlier of how thoroughly censored the Bohemian newspapers were,[49] but after 1848, as leader of the Old Czechs and political spokesman for the Czech nation, he had to cope with this form of censorship personally and frequently. One of the tactics he used successfully to circumvent it was to append his views on contemporary political affairs to collections of scholarly writings. Thus his two famous "political testaments" of the 1870s appeared as epilogues to the collections *Radhost* and *Gedenkblätter*.[50] The censorship of his personal correspondence, despite his use of such well-known tactics as sending letters with travelling friends or to innocuous addressees by whom they were sent on, could not be avoided easily[51] and provoked the elegantly mannered Palacký to anger and coarse invective. Thus, he apologized to Karel Havlíček in 1855 for writing so seldom, attributing it to his disgust: "What I send you from a fervent heart should be sniffed by the dogs-_____, to see if it smells according to their regulations ... Whenever I feel like writing, I am seized by rage that [my letter] should be read not only by you but also by _____ in human likeness, and then I hear the biblical 'Do not cast pearls before _____.' "[52]

In the light of Palacký's experiences with the imperial Habsburg censorship, an evaluation of that institution in practice must be carefully qualified. Palacký's case amply illustrates that the *Zensur*, although extremely comprehensive, was not the

49 In 1832, for example, he wrote to Kollár that no mature man wanted to lower himself to write for the newspapers any longer; in 1833 he wrote in a similar vein to Šafařík, who wanted to return to Bohemia from Novi Sad and was seeking employment, discouraging him from wasting his time and frustrating his soul by accepting the proffered editorship of the heavily censored *Pražské noviny*. Palacký to Kollár, 19 July 1832, in Vrťátko, ČČM, 411, 474; Palacký to Šafařík, 19 March 1833, in V. Bechyňová and Z. Hauptová, eds., *Korespondence Pavla Josefa Šafaříka s Františkem Palackým* (Prague, 1961), 156.
50 Palacký admits to this tactic in a letter to his daughter Marie, 9 May 1874, in Karel Stloukal, ed., *Rodinné listy Františka Palackého dceři Marii a zeti F. L. Riegrovi* (Prague, 1930), 280.
51 In the late 1820s, Palacký had corresponded covertly with the "political apostate," Josef Freiherr von Hormayr, himself an Austrian censor and official historiographer of the empire before he fell out with Metternich and moved to Bavaria. The letters were sent by each party via the wife of the Royal Bavarian Legationsrat in Vienna. Nevertheless, even such "diplomatic" correspondence apparently was systematically detained and opened at the Postlogen, and Palacký was warned by Sedlnitzky, through the chief of the Prague police, of the danger of his connections with Hormayr. See Jos. Volf, "Sedlnitzky zapovídá Palackému styk s Hormayrem 1829," in ČČM, LXXXVII (1913), 463–5.
52 Palacký to Havlíček, 3 September 1855, in Bohumil Novák, ed., *Karel Havlíček Borovský, 1856–1956* (Prague, 1956), 56. At the very end of his life he wrote similarly to Louis Léger: "From 1831, when I first learned and proved that the Austrian police were opening all of my letters at the post office, even those I sent to my own wife, I took a dislike to all correspondence by post..." Palacký to Léger, 17 March 1876, LANM, Léger Collection, sign. 20 P 71 (original); Palacký Collection, sign. 11 C 11 (copy).

brutally uncompromising, flawlessly efficient, totalitarian machine its enemies have depicted. Yet the dogmatism, narrowness, and incompetence which usually have been charged against it are also much in evidence. In one respect, however, this case study is unequivocal. It demonstrates incontestably how very difficult it was for a historian to follow the principles of modern historical research in Metternich's Austria. For a historian like Palacký, who attempted to combine scientific historiography with nationalist exhortation, the obstacles were even greater – but even they were not insurmountable. The success of the Czech national revival, in which Palacký and his "History" played so conspicuous a role, is proof of that.

Karel Havlíček and the Czech Press before 1848

BARBARA KOHÁK KIMMEL

IN THE YEARS PRECEDING 1848 newspapers and magazines, just as plays and novels, presented a means of reviving the Czech language as well as of educating the people.[1] In the 1820s and the 1830s a number of both scholarly journals and papers of a more popular nature came into existence in Czech.[2] Of the latter, *Pražské noviny* (Prague News) and its literary supplement *Rozličnosti* (Miscellanea) enjoyed the greatest longevity.

Most of the popular papers were printed at irregular intervals and in limited editions, and tended to be mere compilations of news and anecdotes with little or no comment. The *Časopis pro katolické duchovenstvo* (Journal for the Catholic Priesthood), a Czech magazine published by the consistory of the archbishopric of Prague, was, however, of a different character. It dealt with the problems of the priesthood, and also represented the clergy's position toward the Czech renascence, which was often a very sympathetic one. This magazine had a wide circulation

1 For a general history of Czech journalism during the periods before and after 1848, see Josef Volf, *Dějiny novin do r. 1848* (Prague, 1930); František Roubík, *Časopisectvo v Čechách v letech 1848–1862* (Prague, 1930); Milena Beránkova, *České novinářství národního obrození* (Prague, 1965).
2 Two of the former were of lasting significance: *Časopis Českého musea* and *Technologie*. The best known of the latter were: *Hyllos, Dobroslav, Jindy a nyní, Večerní vyražení, Poutník*, and *Paleček*.

among both priests and laymen. Another timely publication, which appeared in 1820–5, was the periodical *Čechoslav* (Czechoslav), which contained essays on contemporary Czech problems. This was continued in the next few years first as *Čech*, then *Sám*, and finally *Krok*.

Soon after the appearance of *Čechoslav*, still greater vitality was brought to Czech journalism by Josef Kajetán Tyl,[3] who became the editor of *Jindy a nyní* (Then and Now) in 1834. Tyl purposely tried to stay away from translations of German literary pieces and hoped to raise the standard of Czech literature by publishing original contributions. He therefore encouraged young writers to submit their work, and served as an example by his own prolific production.

Tyl changed the journal's name to *Květy* (Flowers), and it soon became the place for young, new writers to get a start.[4] It also became the organ of national life: it reported on national progress, such as the building of theatres, libraries, and schools, and it carried on propaganda for the national cause. This journal was not without competition, however. Its strongest competitor, for a time, was *Rozličnosti*, which came under the editorship of the poet František Ladislav Čelakovský in 1834. Under the new name *Česká včela* (The Czech Bee) this soon became the model of proper Czech usage, for, unlike Tyl, Čelakovský stressed style and substance rather than originality for its own sake. The contest did not last long, however. In 1836 Čelakovský was dismissed as editor for printing a harsh critique of a speech of the tsar, and without his leadership, *Česká včela* fell into mediocrity. *Květy*, although it was written in the popular idiom, maintained its position as the leading literary magazine until 1848.

The original writing that Tyl sponsored had its faults. It often lacked the quality needed to raise the literary standards of Czech literature at that time. Also it often contained much sentimental patriotism. Many Czechs felt that they had to prove their national zeal by writing, whether or not they possessed any talent. Indeed, the bulk of Czech writing at this time tended to be marked by the fanciful and vague phraseology common in the romantic era. The appearance of Karel Havlíček (1821–56)[5] on the scene provided just the boost that was needed. When he delved into this genre, he became convinced that much of it was not good literature and that it was not, as many supposed, an efficacious means of arousing patriotic feeling. He felt that the romantic style which had been borrowed from the Germans was too far removed from Czech idiom. Desiring to introduce into Czech writing a simpler, clearer style which would be closer to the speech of the people, he came to Prague in the spring of 1845, hoping to find a position on the staff of some Czech journal.

3 For a standard biography of Tyl, see J. L. Turnovský, *Zivot a dílo Josefa Kajetána Tyla* (Prague, 1892).

4 Karel Havlíček's first work, a description of an examination in the Czech language which he had witnessed in Moscow, appeared in *Květy*, 22 July 1843.

5 Three major studies on Havlíček are Karel Tůma, *Karel Havlíček Borovský* (Kutná Hora, 1883); Emanuel Chalupný, *Karel Havlíček* (Prague, 1911); Tomáš G. Masaryk, *Karel Havlíček* (Prague, 1920 ed.).

This was not his first visit to the capital. After completing his studies at the Piarist gymnasium of Německý Brod in southeastern Bohemia, as a young man of seventeen, he had come to the city in 1838 to continue his education, and had found the atmosphere of the city and his encounter with the national awakening a very stimulating experience. Following a two-year philosophy course,[6] he had decided to serve his country as a priest, and in October 1840 he had entered the Archbishop's Seminary in Prague, a devout Catholic. From early childhood he had held the priesthood in high esteem and he began his studies with the belief that the priesthood would offer him the best opportunity for self-expression. Within a year, however, he became disenchanted; the regimentation of life in the seminary along with the emergence of religious doubt on his own part led him to return to a secular life.

Havlíček had then turned to a firm rationalism which contained strong anticlerical overtones. He hoped to become a writer and a teacher, and when his efforts to secure a teaching position failed, he remained in Prague for further study on his own. He read European literature and learned Slav languages, especially Russian and Polish, which he had begun studying in the seminary. At this time he was most influenced by Voltaire, whose stories he liked to translate into Czech, and by Lamennais' *Paroles d'un croyant*. The works of Slav authors, too, were not neglected. Adam Mickiewicz's *Księgi narodu polskiego i pielgrzymstwa polskiego* (Books of the Polish Pilgrimage; Paris, 1832), which he read in Polish, was a source of inspiration, and he was much impressed by the work of Jan Kollár and his ideas of Slav reciprocity. Havlíček read every Czech book and journal available to him; and he became deeply interested not only in the national renascence itself but in the awakening of the Slav world as a whole. In the library of Charles University, where he spent most of his time, he became acquainted with the leading men of the Czech movement. Josef Jungmann and Pavel Josef Šafařík, two of the foremost among these, saw great promise in the young man.

In the fall of 1842 Šafařík, knowing of Havlíček's growing interest in Slavdom, offered him the post of a tutor in Moscow. Havlíček accepted and journeyed to Russia. In his capacity of tutor in the home of Stepan Shevyrev of Moscow University, he had access to the libraries of many prominent families, which enabled him to become well versed not only in Russian literature but also in that of the French Enlightenment. While in Russia Havlíček began to do some writing of his own and worked on the translations of the Russian author whom he admired the most, and who was to leave his stamp on Havlíček's own style, Gogol. He valued Gogol's realism, an element which Havlíček found sadly lacking in contemporary Czech literature.

6 A two-year philosophy course was an intermediary stage between the six-year gymnasium course and the university. This period of study often meant the first assertion of independence for Czech students; they usually left home and lived on their own. These two years also served as a preparation for adulthood during which the young men chose their future professions.

In the summer of 1844, upon his return from Russia, Havlíček spent a year in Německý Brod with his family before making the decision to engage himself fully in the Czech renascence. The following spring, as mentioned above, he came to Prague. Although his hopes of obtaining a position on a Czech newspaper went unrealized, he did, almost immediately, make himself known in literary circles by his critique of the latest romance of Tyl, *Poslední Čech* (The Last Czech), which appeared in *Česká včela* on 5 July 1845. This review also brought the newcomer into public notice.

Tyl was the most popular Czech author of his day, and *Poslední Čech* had been well received by the public and had been awarded a prize for excellence by the Matice česká (Czech Foundation). Havlíček was, however, repelled by the superficial nationalism represented by the novel, and therefore he chose to strike at the heart of this movement by criticizing it. His very frank discussion of the style and content of the book was interpreted by many as an affront to a patriot of high standing in Czech society.

Ostensibly, the book aimed to enlist the interest of the Bohemian nobility in the Czech national movement. To be successful in this, Havlíček claimed, the author would have had to become thoroughly familiar with the life of the nobility, and this Tyl had neglected to do. As an obvious illustration of this failure Havlíček cited an instance in which a minstrel appears and addresses his noble host in the familiar form. The style of the book Havlíček found equally unsatisfactory: it was too theatrical, too unreal. It was his conviction that the first sign of mastery in an author was simplicity, the ability to write clearly in everyday language.

Within the framework of his review of Tyl's book, Havlíček took the opportunity to analyse the entire literary awakening of the Czechs. He remarked caustically that it was easier to die for one's country than to torture oneself by reading some of the patriotic literature being produced.[7] It seemed to Havlíček that anyone who professed his love for his country by the use of his pen was automatically acclaimed a great writer no matter how impoverished his style. As he stated:

Everyone is becoming weary of perpetual speeches about patriotism and of patriotic romances with which our authors pursue us incessantly, in prose and poetry. It is high time that our patriotism pass from our lips to our hands, so that we might do something to show our love for the country instead of only talking about our love and devotion to it. We spend so much time exuding patriotic sentiment, we hardly have time left for educating ourselves. If the time and effort we spend on persuading people to read Czech patriotic works were expended on translating good foreign literature or genuinely improving our own, we would be acting far more wisely.[8]

7 "Kritika Tylova *Posledního Čecha*," in Havlíček, *Korespondence Karla Havlíčka Borovského*, ed. Ladislav Quis (Prague, 1903), 379. Quis includes in this volume the full exchange of words: Havlíček's review as it appeared in *Česká včela*, nos. 52, 53, 1 and 4 July 1845; Tyl's answer from *Česká včela*, nos. 56, 57, 15 and 18 July 1845.
8 Havlíček, *Korespondence*, 380.

The best-remembered phrases of the whole review, sentiments which Havlíček himself was to repeat many times, were the appeals to the nation to stop talking and writing about love of country and to start translating this feeling into hard work. Although the young man's critique did acquire these wider implications, Tyl interpreted Havlíček's indictment of mediocre, sentimental literature as represented by his novel in strictly personal terms and submitted a bitter reply to *Česká včela*. Tyl was offended by the daring of a man, as yet almost completely unknown, who criticized a writer of his own stature in such a manner. The controversy that followed divided the patriotic camp into two factions for some time to come. Havlíček stood his ground and, in the long run, not only won the argument but also much respect among the Czechs.

The conflict made Havlíček's name just as much a household word as Tyl's had been earlier. National societies such as the Matice česká took notice of the newcomer. His immediate gain was a most cordial invitation by *Česká včela* for contributions. Only a month earlier, in June 1845, it had published one of his articles about Russia and it was now eager to publish more of his work and to pay him well for his contributions.[9]

Havlíček had just begun his freelance work when he was approached by the publishing house of Haase brothers about the possibility of editing a new Czech literary, apolitical magazine.[10] At the same time, it happened that another publisher, Medau, was looking for someone to fill the job of editor for the bi-weekly *Pražské noviny* and its supplement *Česká včela*. The former, though the only political newspaper in the Czech language, was looked upon as an uninteresting paper because it often carried news long after the event with no editorial comment; it also carried little weight with Czech nationalists in comparison with its supplement.

It was for the position of editor of both the paper and the supplement that František Palacký, who had been impressed by Havlíček's writing up to that time, recommended him to Medau. Havlíček, however, hesitated to accept because of his inexperience. He was willing to undertake the direction of the literary supplement, since he had become acquainted with its management as one of its contributors,

9 In 1843–6 Havlíček wrote a number of articles which he called "Obrazy z Rus" (Pictures from Russia). They were published in a number of Czech magazines, and are collected in Havlíček, *Obrazy z Rus*, ed. Miloslav Novotný (Prague, 1948).
10 There were at this time four firms in Prague which published Czech books. The oldest was that of Bohumil and Ondřej Haase, which had been in the family from 1798 and remained in existence until 1871. In 1833–45 it published *Pražské noviny* and a humorous magazine *Poutník* besides its German publications, *Prager Zeitung* and *Bohemia*. Karel Medau, a firm publishing Czech books of general interest, took over the publication of *Pražské noviny* in 1846. Martin Neuretter published prayer-books and literature for youth; and Václav Spinka, employed by a wealthy widow, Josefina Vetterlová, published patriotic literature. Outside of Prague an influential publication centre developed in Hradec Králové where Jaroslav Pospíšil had a publishing house. In the 1820s this became a literary centre for the Czechs, but the quality of the writing was frequently low because Pospíšil was willing to publish any patriotic effort.

but he was cautious about undertaking the editorship of a political newspaper. Palacký finally succeeded in persuading him to accept full responsibility for the editing of both, and loaned him, perhaps as a model to copy or just for general assistance, several yearly volumes of the political journal that was then read most widely by the Czech middle class, the *Augsburger Allgemeine Zeitung* (Augsburg Universal Newspaper). Havlíček assumed editorial work on 1 January 1846, at the age of twenty-four.

Fluent in German as the Czechs were, they read the *Augsburger Allgemeine Zeitung* and the *Grenzboten* (The Border Messengers) of Leipzig. Both came to Prague several days after issue but were eagerly awaited in the coffee houses. Unlike *Pražské noviny*, they were newspapers of substance with not only wider coverage of news events but also much comment on European developments. They carried articles about Czech literature and the whole cultural revival, too. The hold which these two German papers had on the Czech bourgeoisie was broken after Havlíček assumed the editorship of *Pražské noviny*. The Czech middle class found in it a quality newspaper of their own, a newspaper with good coverage and plenty of interesting editorial comment as well. Up to that time Czech journals had done much in reviving the Czech language and literature, but politically they had been silent. Havlíček wanted to make *Pražské noviny* the instrument through which the Czechs could not only follow political developments in other countries, but also prepare themselves for the day when the exercise of political power would be theirs. He thought that the political education of the people was indispensable since the Czechs had had no experience of self-rule since 1620. To this purpose he committed himself irrevocably.

Havlíček wished for his *Pražské noviny* to serve as a "diary of the times," a faithful echo of everything which was taking place at the time.[11] Besides giving a thorough coverage of all domestic and foreign news events, Havlíček made other innovations in both papers. To *Česká včela* he added a satirical column appropriately titled "Žihadlo" (Stinger); in *Pražské noviny* he introduced a humorous column and in every issue he included an article of an educational nature, usually a lengthy discussion and comment on a social or political problem of the day. Havlíček's style was a lively one, but seldom was it sensational. In all his writings he employed Czech exclusively. By casting German aside completely, he hoped to encourage the Czech bourgeoisie, who still customarily used German in their discussions of politics, to widen their own usage of the Czech language and to reach a larger public. In this he succeeded; by December 1847, the number of subscribers

11 Havlíček, *Politické spisy*, ed. Zdeněk V. Tolbolka (Prague, 1903), I, p. iv. *Politické spisy* is a three-volume collection of Havlíček's articles and editorials from the three journals that he edited: *Pražské noviny*, *Národní noviny*, and *Slovan*. Volume I covers the period of *Pražské noviny* (1846–8), volume II *Národní noviny* (1848–50), volume III *Slovan* (1850–1), and in addition his *Epištoly Kutnohorské* and two articles from *Česká včela* (1848). Each volume is enriched by an introductory chapter and explanatory notes by Tobolka.

to *Pražské noviny* rose from the 200 it had when he took over the editorship, to 1500,[12] and he was able to enlarge its format.

The task of educating the nation in matters of politics which he had thus begun, Havlíček believed to be an intrinsic part of the general education of a citizen. "No power," Havlíček was to write, "can hold an enlightened, educated citizenry in bonds."[13] He hoped that such an education would come through rational explanation of issues and opinions given, and not in the form of agitation. With this in mind he wrote simply and succinctly, trying to appeal to reason and common sense, not to emotions. In every column, though not all were written by him, his spirit came through. He was always ready with a suggestion, an analysis, a comment on a situation.

On the general question of education Havlíček himself wrote a number of contributions. In the first issue of *Pražské noviny* under his editorship he published an article concerning vocational education, entitled "Potřebnost průmyslové školy české" (The Need for a Czech Industrial School),[14] which he had written in support of a proposal for a Czech industrial school made by the Průmyslová jednota (Industrial Union).[15] At this time there were seven industrial schools in Bohemia, but in all of these, as indeed in all secondary education, German was the language of instruction. A Czech could get instruction in his own language only on Sundays in Prague, where the Industrial Union sponsored afternoon courses in various trades in both languages, German and Czech. The Industrial Union felt this was inadequate preparation for young Czechs, and wanted to raise a new working class that would not be ashamed of its national identity or of its language. The type of school it envisioned was a full-time school where a craft could be learned and a general education obtained as well, but the foremost consideration was that the language of instruction should be Czech.

Havlíček himself supported these ideas, and in *Pražské noviny* he gave full coverage to a fund-raising campaign initiated by the union. In his article, he insisted that the training received in the existing schools was ineffective, primarily because of the fact that the Czechs were handicapped by having to master a foreign language and to learn their trade in that language instead of their own. He believed that a

---

12 Havlíček, *Politické spisy*, ɪɪ, 875.

13 *Ibid.*, ɪ, 15.

14 *Ibid.*, ɪ, 1. For a survey of education in Bohemia at this time, see J. Šafránek, *Vývoj soustavy obecného školství v král. českém od r. 1769–1895* (Prague, 1897).

15 The Industrial Union can best be described as a society for the promotion of both industry and industrial education. It was founded in 1829 and its membership consisted of industrialists and interested parties of both nationalities. At first the German element was the dominant one, but in 1833 the union began the publication of a Czech scientific journal *Technologie*. The magazine covered both the physical and natural sciences and played a significant part in developing Czech technological terminology. By the 1840s the Czechs in the union had fully asserted themselves and taken over its leadership. Havlíček himself joined the union in 1845.

Czech school would make better craftsmen out of its students since the time spent learning German could be devoted to better mastery of their trade. These opinions were in harmony with Havlíček's firm hope that the Czech language would not remain either the jargon of servants or the ornament of an educated few, interested in reviving Czech literature. In the establishment of an industrial school Havlíček perceived an opportunity to educate a Czech labour force and thereby to take a big step toward regaining national self-respect.

Havlíček dealt with the subject of education again in a series of articles which began in *Pražské noviny* on 29 January 1846, under the title "Něco pro učitele a o učitelích" (Something for and about Teachers).[16] In these articles he took a sharp look at the teaching profession and its status. He argued that teachers tended to be inferior because they were inadequately trained and poorly paid. He boldly attacked the complacent attitude which prevailed throughout the country in this matter and which also obtained on the question of raising educational standards. Havlíček felt that there was enough money to build better community schools: what was lacking was a communal spirit on the part of the citizenry of most towns.

Until we can think beyond our own doorstep, there can be no progress made; we have not learned, as yet, what a common goal and purpose can mean to the citizenry. There has not yet appeared among us that spirit which drives an individual to work as hard as he can for the good of all as he would for himself. If a town were to levy a specific school tax there would be no end of grumbling, but no one ever thinks of the great good that would come of such a tax to his own children.[17]

Of the leading personalities of the Czech revival, Havlíček stood alone in applying self-criticism to the Czechs. He realized that much could be done on the local level to improve the state of the nation. Unlike many Czechs, he did not blame either foreign control, the church, or the nobility for the nation's cultural and political weakness. Though he knew well the obstacles that all of these represented to the Czech renascence, he wanted to examine his own fellow-countrymen first.

"Who is the greatest enemy of our nationality?" Havlíček asked. "We are ourselves! The government cannot wipe us out, it cannot stamp out our language if we use it. In time, it will even have to protect it. Who can keep us from learning Czech? And yet only a few hundred know it well enough so that they can use it in discussion and professional writing!"[18] This was the strongest criticism that Havlíček could have levelled at his own nation.

Only a year after his polemic with Tyl about the shoddy romanticism prevailing in Czech literature, he attacked a political variation of romanticism among the Czechs, Panslavism.[19] Many Czechs, seeing themselves helpless in the face of a

16 Havlíček, *Politické spisy*, I, 13.
17 *Ibid.*, 25.   18 *Ibid.*, 127.
19 The standard work in English on Panslavism is Hans Kohn, *Pan-Slavism: Its History and Ideology* (New York, 1960 ed.). For its influence on the Czechs and Slovaks see part I, 3–30.

strong, even if politically disunited Germany, sought refuge in a vague concept of Slavdom, a spiritual union of Slavs from which moral and material strength could be drawn. Among the first exponents of these ideas in the Czech language was Jan Kollár, who spoke and wrote in terms of a cultural reciprocity that would eventually create a feeling of spiritual unity and kinship among the Slavs. Though they would still be separated from each other by the boundaries of the different political systems under which they lived, they would gain an inner strength from this spiritual union. A period of cultural reciprocity among the Slavs would usher in a great new era of Slav greatness which Kollár foresaw in the future. The poet envisioned a day when the Slavs would experience their kinship most keenly through the use of one literary language.

Havlíček, as we have seen, had also been influenced, at first, by Kollár's ideas. Like many Czechs of his generation he was a Polonophil and felt that the attainment of Czech autonomy and Polish independence were closely related.[20] While still in the gymnasium he had been inspired by the Polish revolution of 1830 and had held a favourable view of the entire Polish movement.[21] This attitude was intensified by his friendship with Polish students in Prague and a trip to Poland during the summer vacation of 1842. At Cracow Havlíček wept at the tomb of Kościuszko.

But this warm sympathy for the Poles and their cause cooled after Havlíček became acquainted with some of the Polish nobility during a month-long stay in Lwów on his way to Russia late in 1842. He found the Polish nobility to be an arrogant, self-centred class of people who thought of themselves exclusively as representing the Polish nation. In Russia Havlíček became similarly disillusioned with the Russian aristocracy. Although the very word "Slav" had a magic charm in it for many Czechs who associated it with ideas of love and brotherhood, to Havlíček, after his experiences in Poland and Russia, the word had a false ring. Instead of finding a spirit of cooperation and brotherhood among Slavs there, he found a feeling of mutual distrust and hate. In "Slovan a Čech" (The Slav and the Czech)[22] he wrote:

So intense is the hatred between these two peoples that they exclude each other from a Slav brotherhood! The Poles claim the Russians are Mongolians while the Russians call the Poles Sarmatians. The main bone of contention which has divided every generation of

20 A generation earlier, after the Napoleonic wars, the Czechs tended to espouse an uncritical Russophilism, but this was altered by the events of 1830 when Russian troops suppressed Polish insurgents.
21 In 1838, Havlíček had translated a *Polenlied* by Julius Mosen, "Die letzten Zehn vom vierten Regiment," into Czech. Though the translation was a rough one, his text became popular with his classmates. See Tůma, *Karel Havlíček*, 16–17.
22 "Slovan a Čech" formed a series of eight articles Havlíček published in the February and March 1846 issues of *Pražské noviny*. The articles are reprinted in Havlíček, *Politické spisy*, ɪ, 28–70. Extracts have been printed in translation in H. Kohn (ed.), *The Mind of Modern Russia* (New York, 1962 ed.), 83–90.

Poles and Russians is the possession of the Ukraine. Both the Poles and the Russians claim this land on the basis of related nationality. The Russians point to the fact that they share the same religion with the Ruthenes; the Poles retort with the formation of the Uniate church. At present the Russians hope to acquire the Ukraine by Russifying the people as the Poles have been able to Polonize the Lithuanians, by alienating the upper classes from the rest of their own people.

Havlíček dubbed this discourse between the Russians and the Poles "a fable of two wolves." "If there is a lamb in the picture," he went on, "it is the Ukrainian."[23]

Havlíček, having shown the conflict that existed between two of the Slav nations, stressed that Slavs in fact form distinct, very different nations, among whom the centrifugal forces are far stronger than the centripetal. He repudiated the idea that the Slavs ever could become one nation; he was well aware that, although related, they varied greatly among themselves in culture, government, history, and were, as he had shown, often each others' enemies. He felt that any Slav nation must first educate itself and broaden its own horizons before embarking on any kind of cultural or political venture with other Slavs. Havlíček was asking the Czechs to take a more realistic view of their relationship to the rest of Slavdom. Unlike many patriots who placed their faith in Russia as the protector and redeemer of other Slavs, he interpreted Russian Panslavism as an opportunist expansionism and called it "Panrussism." He wrote:

The Russians delight in the idea of being our brothers; they have become particularly friendly with the Illyrians and with us because they assume that we want to live under their rule. In a song that is called "The Freeing of the Slavs" we are all liberated by the Russians. The "Slav" countries included are Hungary and Prussia! The Russian design is not an honest one of mutual cooperation and partnership with other Slavs; it is imperial in nature. For myself I prefer the Magyars, who persecute us openly, to the Russians who come to us with a Judas' embrace – only to swallow us up. We Czechs are of Czech nationality and want to remain so; we do not want to become Germanized or Magyarized, but neither do we want to become Russians; therefore, let us remain cool to the Russians and their overtures to us.[24]

The only group of Slavs with whom Havlíček believed the Czechs could have a cordial relationship were the South Slavs (or "Illyrians," as they were then called). He thought that the two sides could have a prosperous cultural exchange and could help toward each others' goals because neither presented a threat to the other. They both faced similar problems: uniting very closely related peoples and gaining autonomy within the structure of the empire. For it was within a strong Austria that Havlíček thought both the Czechs and the South Slavs would find the best guarantee of their nationality and traditions. In closing "Slovan a

23 Havlíček, *Politické spisy*, I, 63.
24 *Ibid.*, 67.

Čech" he boasted: "With great national pride I say, 'I am a Czech,' but never, 'I am a Slav!' "[25]

This explosive conclusion brought rebuke from many a patriot who thought that the idea of Slavdom had been degraded and cheapened. At this time it was not unusual among the more ardent nationalists to address each other as "Slavs" and "Czechs" interchangeably. Jakub Malý[26] and other Slavophils felt that the whole national movement had been badly damaged by Havlíček. A bitter polemic was waged between Havlíček and Malý.[27] Once again, as in the earlier confrontation with the established nationalists who defended romantic patriotism, Havlíček emerged better known and more respected, particularly by those who had themselves become suspicious of the nebulous idea of Slavdom as a panacea for Czech problems. In "Slovan a Čech" Havlíček recognized the difficulties of survival that a small nation such as the Czechs faced and he offered the concept of a new, federalist Austria as a solution to the problem. After Jungmann's work on the Czech language,[28] "Slovan a Čech" became the second cornerstone of Czech national and political policy.

It is probable that Havlíček's anti-Slav attitude gave him a freer rein as editor of *Pražské noviny* than he had previously enjoyed. Whereas his earlier Panslavist sympathies made him somewhat suspect to the authorities, the publication of "Slovan a Čech" dispelled this impression.[29] These articles he followed up with a number of suggestions about strengthening the empire from within by transforming it gradually into a democratic society. He was convinced that the beginnings of self-government must come about inconspicuously, that the process must start in the little-known villages up and down the country.

Accordingly, in articles called "Co je Obec?" (What Is a Community?)[30] he sought to show that even under the yoke of absolutism much self-improvement

25 *Ibid.*, 70.
26 Jakub Malý (1811–85), Czech journalist and writer. He had issued one of the first Czech grammar books and was editor of *Květy* in 1846. He is best known for his accounts of this period, *Vzpomínky a úvahy starého vlastence* (Prague, 1872) and *Naše znovuzrození*, in 6 parts (Prague, 1880–4).
27 Malý published his criticism in *Květy*, 7, 9, 11, 16, 23, and 28 April 1846. Havlíček answered in *Pražské noviny*, 3 May 1846 and again in the 17 and 21 May 1846 issues. The polemic ended by Malý's declaration in *Květy* on 26 May 1846, in which he stated that he would not waste any more time and effort dealing with a senseless agitator. This whole exchange is reprinted in Havlíček, *Politické spisy*, I, 70–103.
28 Josef Jungmann, *Dvojí rozmlouvání o jazyku českém* (Prague, 1806).
29 The conception of Havlíček as a Panslavist came from three letters he had written from Russia which had been confiscated by the Austrian police. All three were written in a Slavophil spirit. The letters are reprinted in Karel Kazbunda, "Karel Havlíček a c. k. úřady v době předbřeznové," *Český časopis historický*, XXXII (Prague, 1926), 52–61.
30 'Co je Obec?" appeared in the following issues of *Pražské noviny*: 8, 12, 19, and 22 November 1846, and 13, 17, 20, 24, 27, and 31 December 1846. They are reprinted in Havlíček, *Politické spisy*, I, 126–52.

could be achieved. Havlíček suggested that his readers ask themselves the question he was now posing: Why do you live together in a town, a village? In exploring this question they would see that living next door to one another without any feeling of mutual concern is not what is meant by community. The very reason for the appearance of communities in history was to serve the individuals inhabiting them, particularly in such matters where they were helpless by themselves. Of greatest significance to Havlíček was the fact that men joined voluntarily to form a community, and therefore all members were willing to sacrifice something of themselves for the common good. "In such a situation each man knew the laws, his own duties and his rights."[31] He went on rather despairingly:

On the other hand, when people live in a community without participating in its affairs, they do not usually know its government and they are not citizens in the true sense. The end result we know full well. People become interested exclusively in their own property; they live for themselves alone, and they cheat the state at every opportunity because they consider it their enemy. Such people have no notion of a civic spirit. When this is lacking no one will undertake anything for the common good, the good of anyone other than himself, and when employed as a public servant a man will do the minimum that he thinks the state requires of him. This attitude does most damage among civil servants. But in a community where citizens rule themselves, the people know the laws and customs of the town, they know their duty, and there a civic spirit reigns. Here people are willing to sacrifice of their time and talent for the community at large, because they know that the benefits of any enterprise will be shared by all. In such a state of affairs progress is made at every level; there are better schools, better libraries, better recreational areas.[32]

Havlíček believed that there was much that people could do on the local level even though the country's government was not one of self-rule. He was critical of the opinion held by many people that the activities of municipal governments throughout the country must be totally dependent on orders from the central government. Havlíček hoped to change this feeling by imbuing the people with the spirit of self-help. He recommended a number of projects to which patriots could direct their efforts: raising money for the founding of libraries, for increasing teachers' salaries, for buying freedom from patrimonial lords. "What have been the obstacles to the realization of such ideas?" asked Havlíček. "There is just one, but it is an enormous one, the utter lack of a communal spirit, a spirit of self-help."[33] Havlíček returned to this idea of cooperation and united effort when he focused on the question of serfdom itself early in 1847.[34] In the form of a review of

31 Havlíček, Politické spisy, I, 137.
32 Ibid., 142.   33 Ibid., 152.
34 In Bohemia, as in the rest of the Austrian Empire, the manorial system of the Middle Ages survived until 1848. The legal position of the peasant had been improved at the end of the eighteenth century by the Josephinian reforms which granted him a certain amount of mobility, choice of occupation for the children, marriage without the lord's authorization, and

a recent study of peasant conditions in Bohemia,[35] he discussed the peasant question in a number of articles in *Pražské noviny*.[36] As a man devoted to the idea of equality, he considered the abolition of serfdom a necessary condition for the establishment of autonomy in Bohemia. Typically, he urged the Czech farmers to take the initiative and begin the process of buying out their *robota* (corvée),[37] though he was aware of the difficulty involved when he wrote: "The root of our problem is that only an educated people knows how best to take advantage of union and how to work effectively together."[38]

Although the Czechs had begun to fight for an industrial school, nothing had been done for the farmers. Not only was the peasant neglected in education, but greater damage had been done by the spiritual down-grading of the simple peasantry that had gone on for many years. Havlíček felt this reflected on the entire nation. He stated: "As long as the peasant is ashamed of his own name, the nation cannot raise itself!"[39] He reminded his readers that is was precisely this labouring class that had done most to preserve the nationality because it had never discarded Czech in favour of German.[40] He looked upon the Czech farmer as the embodiment of national virtues and strength.[41] Therefore he scorned the condescending

---

some protection against an abusive landlord. But, owing to strong opposition from the landlords and ignorance on the part of the peasants, the reforms were never fully realized. For the most part the peasantry remained overworked and overtaxed. By the 1840s, however, a complex hierarchy existed within the peasant estate ranging from the simple field hand to the steward. Though it was possible to improve one's position, to enter into a contract with the lord to pay off the *robota*, the very existence of the manorial system as such, irrespective of the character of the lord, was strongly resented throughout the countryside.

35 František A. Brauner, *Böhmische Bauernzustände* (Vienna, 1847). Brauner was one of the leaders of Czech national society. He had the book published in Vienna after the Prague censor refused to release it. Brauner exposed the conditions of the peasantry and recommended ways of reducing the peasants' burden without actually asking for emancipation. Havlíček had much praise for the book and its thorough coverage of the Czechs' most pressing problem.

36 "O našich selských záležitostech," which came out in the January and February issues of *Pražské noviny* and are reprinted in *Politické spisy*, i, 158–75.

37 In Bohemia, ever since 1798 contracts could be made between peasants and landlords for this purpose.

38 Havlíček, *Politické spisy*, i, 165.

39 *Ibid.*, 163.

40 After the Battle of White Mountain in 1620, the Czech nobility was drastically reduced and a foreign upper class, mostly German, was settled in the place of the Protestant Czech nobility. For the next two centuries the German language of this new class permeated all upper and middle class society. Nearly all of the cities were also Germanized, but this was not true of the countryside. There the one-time greatness of the nation lived on in folk-songs and legends which were retold by the peasantry.

41 This point of view is representative of the Czech "awakeners," who tended to idealize the peasant. They had not only been influenced by the ideas of the Enlightenment and its concepts of the noble savage, but many of them were themselves sons of simple people. Jungmann, son of a shoemaker, for example, called the farmer the most important citizen.

attitude that many city people and nobility assumed in their dealings with the peasantry. He pointed sharply to the irony of the situation: "What is the difference between so-called 'free' city people and country folk? The latter is subjugated to the landlords, the former to the magistrates!"[42]

In looking beyond emancipation, Havlíček hoped that, given an education, the common man could take full part in a new democratic system. He especially looked forward to the development of a self-sufficient farming class, which he considered the happiest and the most important component of a free society; for while they were not very wealthy they were well off to a degree that enabled them to devote much time to community affairs. To ensure the growth of such a class Havlíček warned against fragmentation of land and urged that family lots be passed on to the eldest son intact. As free men he anticipated that the farmers would not only take care of their own land, but also any communal properties such as pasture and roads.[43] Through the management of common land they would strengthen the spirit of cooperation that Havlíček felt was so sorely needed. It was within such free farming communities that he thought the roots of self-government should be planted.

From these beginnings of autonomy on local levels, self-rule might be achieved throughout the Austrian Empire. As a liberal interested in such a development, Havlíček followed progressive movements outside of Bohemia as closely as possible. He was most attracted by the Irish movement for home rule, "Repeal," because the Irish situation provided a good analogy to the Czech one. In June 1847, Havlíček published five articles dealing with Ireland.[44] They have often been referred to as forming a kind of first political textbook for the Czechs; Havlíček used the story of Ireland and its dilemma as an object lesson to the Czechs themselves.

The articles cover the period of Irish greatness in the Middle Ages, then the decay which set in after that, accompanied by a gradual loss of nationality, and finally the struggle of the Irish to regain their national identity which was being led by Daniel O'Connell. The entire Irish problem gave Havlíček an opportunity to examine a process similar to the Czech experience: the loss of nationality. Using

42 Havlíček, *Politické spisy*, I, 162.
43 *Ibid.*, 166–8.
44 The articles were entitled "Daniel O'Connell" and they appeared in *Pražské noviny*, 13, 17, 20, 24, and 27 June 1847. They are reprinted in Havlíček, *Politické spisy*, I, 194–215. Havlíček had already printed shorter reports concerning events in Ireland which won him much popularity. These were datelined Cork or Tipperary and attacked English policy in Ireland. The reports were so skilfully written that the reader knew the criticism was really directed at Vienna, not England. The public had little difficulty translating "Ireland" and "Repeal" into Bohemia and its struggle for a national rebirth. Even the story of O'Connell itself was not entirely unknown among Czech nationalists, because it had been dealt with by a German radical, Uffo Horn, in some lectures presented to the Industrial Union in 1845. The slogan "Repeal" became so popular with Czech youth that it was adopted as the name of a loosely organized political club in Prague. For a history of the Czech Repeal, see Karel Slavíček, *Tajná politická společnost: Český Repeal v roce 1848* (Prague, 1947).

Ireland as an example, Havlíček showed how a nation begins its journey into oblivion. Whatever may have been the original cause of this decline, history shows, according to Havlíček, that the consequences tend to be the same. First the dominant or ruling nationality incorporates all the resources of the country as its own, leaving to the native, now subordinate group only those positions which wield no power and have little or no status attached to them. At this point many people abandon their own identity and join the ruling nation; they adopt the language of the masters and rise in society. Their alienation from their former nationality is complete, and they are often ashamed of their origin. Henceforward the awakening of the people's dormant nationalism becomes an immense undertaking and such a nationality is in danger of extinction.

From this general theoretical statement, Havlíček turned to a discussion of Ireland's plight: its loss of political and economic independence. And, finally, he gave a painstaking description of the fight O'Connell was then leading among the Irish to revive their identity and, hopefully, their one-time greatness. What impressed Havlíček most about O'Connell was his method, the constant reliance on legal means of opposition. O'Connell resorted to the use of petitions, newspapers, pamphlets, public meetings, and organizations, all ways of exposing his people's plight. Whether through the Catholic Union[45] or Repeal,[46] O'Connell marshalled public opinion for the objectives of Irish nationalism, always working within the boundaries of the law.

It was this legal opposition and the constitutional framework within which O'Connell worked that Havlíček admired. Under a similar system Havlíček hoped that his own press could become the avenue through which Czech demands would be made known. Until such a time he continued his self-imposed task of providing some political education for the Czechs. Havlíček knew full well that prudent parliamentary action would demand political awareness on the part of the masses.

With this in mind, in the beginning of the new year, 1848, he concentrated on defining the vocabulary and concepts of political democracy as he understood them. In the manner of eighteenth-century encyclopaedists Havlíček gave full definitions of words such as "constitution," alerting people to all the connotations such a term might carry. The two most significant editorials that he wrote at this time were devoted to a discussion of political parties and the best forms of government.[47] Havlíček pointed out the difference between a monarchy, an aristocracy, and a republican form of government, but stressed what to him was decisive in judging the worth of a government: the spirit that was found behind the form. He

45 The Catholic Union was an organization which had worked for the emancipation of Catholics in Ireland. Emancipation was achieved in 1829.
46 The name Repeal referred to the hoped-for dissolution of the union between Ireland and England concluded in 1801.
47 These editorials appeared in the 2 and 6 January 1848 issues of *Pražské noviny*. They are reprinted in Havlíček, *Politické spisy*, I, 222–8.

reminded his readers that words were sometimes used as labels and could be very deceptive:

Every government, every party can be good or bad, depending much on the particular circumstances that a country happens to be in, but most of all ... its quality hangs on one characteristic, the honesty that a government or party displays in its dealings with the people. It is possible to prosper under all governments, whether they be monarchies or republics, if they observe the basic principles that governments are instituted for the people, not the people for governments, and if they abide by the moral principles imposed by God through eternal laws on both individuals and society.[48]

These statements constitute the first expression of democratic thought in a Czech newspaper. They show Havlíček's debt to the Enlightenment, and they reflect in some measure the momentum which the Czech revival was gaining. The Czech national awakening was now changing its character from a primarily cultural phenomenon to a political movement as well.

Havlíček's advocacy of constitutionalism and the strong backing that *Pražské noviny* gave to national activities made a clash with the authorities inevitable.[49] His frank manner of reporting brought him to the attention of Josef Heyde, the chief of police in Prague. In May 1847, Havlíček received a warning from Heyde which referred to the tenor of his writing and the general tone of the paper as too bold. In July of the same year, this was repeated.[50] Heyde was especially suspicious of Havlíček's sustained effort on behalf of the Průmyslová jednota's campaign for a Czech industrial school. He saw it as a part of a greater plan for the weakening of the central government by the establishment of strongly separatist institutions.[51] After the second warning, *Pražské noviny* was placed on probation; any extravagance of political expression would jeopardize Havlíček's position. In spite of this threat, Heyde, well aware of Havlíček's growing popularity, feared that his dismissal might turn the editor into a martyr for the Czech cause, which would create a more explosive situation than his propaganda in *Pražské noviny*.[52] Nevertheless, Havlíček tells us that by the spring of 1848 his fate had been sealed and he was to have been removed for a sympathetic portrayal of the new liberal

48 Havlíček, *Politické spisy*, i, 227.
49 In Austria the fear on the part of the government of any repercussions of the French Revolution had demanded a strict censorship of the press. But since proficiency in a given language was necessary for the censor, it was not inconceivable for the censor to be sympathetic to a cultural and national awakening. This was certainly true of Pavel Josef Šafařík, who held the post of censor of newspapers when Havlíček became editor of *Pražské noviny*.
50 Karel Kazbunda, "Karel Havlíček," 37–40.
51 *Ibid.*, 55–61. Havlíček's propaganda on behalf of a Czech industrial school contributed to the dismissal of Šafařík from the post of censor on a charge of leniency. Kazbunda traces Šafařík's exchange with the police, his attempt to defend himself and Havlíček, his plea for a review of the case, and the rejection of the appeal. Šafařík was replaced by P. J. Koubek (1805–54), a minor poet and professor of Czech and Russian literature at Charles University.
52 *Ibid.*, 61.

Pope Pius IX and of the Italian national movement.[53] This time Havlíček was saved by the fall of Metternich and the declaration of the freedom of the press which came on 15 March 1848.

Havlíček availed himself of the new freedom immediately. With great enthusiasm and a sense of readiness to tackle the problems that faced the Czechs, he wrote: "Yesterday we were children, today we are grown and free men ... let us forget any thought of revenge; the past is gone, on with the future!"[54] Only four days after the promulgation of freedom of the press and the promise of a constitution for Austria, Havlíček published an exposition of the main objectives of Czech nationalism:[55] dissolution of the bond that existed between Bohemia and the German Bund; a constitution together with administrative autonomy for the Bohemian crown-lands (Bohemia, Moravia, and Silesia); complete equality of the Czech and German languages, not in name only; and a new provincial Diet based on a broadened suffrage. He called upon the nobility to take the lead by pressing for equal treatment of the two languages wherever they could. In addressing them, he wrote: "this is your last chance to show the nation whether you are friends or enemies of the country."[56] Building on the foundations he had already laid down in "Slovan a Čech," Havlíček wrote: "Austria is our only association, there is no place for us in any German union. In Austria we are together with other Slavs, we [Slavs] can develop our nationalities and yet benefit from the protection that our empire can provide. We want to work for a greater Austria!"[57] For the fulfilment of these ideas Havlíček worked relentlessly; this was, in essence, the programme that he was to defend in his own daily, *Národní noviny* (National News), from 1848 to 1850.[58]

Havlíček's significance before 1848 lies in the success he had in arousing political awareness among the Czechs. He was able to break the political silence of Czech journalism and give the nation a new paper of its own that could compete effectively with German newspapers. The courage he displayed as editor of *Pražské*

53 Havlíček, *Politické spisy*, II, 876.
54 Havlíček, "Bratří," in *Česká včela*, 17 March 1848. This article is reprinted in *Politické spisy*, III, 1545.
55 Havlíček, "Korouhev naše," in *Pražské noviny*, 19 March 1848. Reprinted in *Politické spisy*, I, 239–45.
56 Havlíček, *Politické spisy*, I, 241. In Bohemia, in contrast to Poland where the nobility were national leaders, most of the nobility were tied by blood and tradition to the German Habsburgs. Though some did support the national awakening, for the most part they remained aloof or professed a provincial patriotism, a loyalty to the land, not the nation.
57 *Ibid.*, 243.
58 Havlíček had felt that, since up to 1848 *Pražské noviny* had been the only political newspaper approved by the authorities, it would now become the government's organ. He was afraid that if this happened the editor would have to defend government policies at all times. Since he did not wish to be hemmed in by any restrictions, he decided to launch a newspaper of his own, through which he could support the Czech liberal programme. The newspaper first appeared on the newstands on 5 April 1848.

noviny endeared him to the people. By expressing faith in the people themselves, Havlíček did much to restore self-respect and dignity among the Czechs. His concept of self-help and self-reliance bolstered the confidence of the nation in the Czech revival.

Havlíček revolutionized the Czechs' outlook by being critical and by going beyond the abstract patriotism of many of them. In his journalism he shunned romanticism of any kind and aimed at presenting a realistic picture of the Czechs' situation. His common sense approach, his wit, and the easy command of the Czech language which he possessed soon made him the people's favourite. Through his sober writing came a sincere concern for the nation and its everyday problems. It was his firm belief that the nation should draw strength from a good grasp of the present, of the realities of the day, rather than from the glories of the past or dreams of the future. In his insistence on the study of the present and the need to prepare for the future, Havlíček championed constitutional opposition such as exists in a political democracy. He was neither a romantic nor a revolutionary, but a dedicated reformer. Therefore he placed such strong emphasis on education for all, which he considered the prerequisite for any radical changes in Czech society and its government.

In Havlíček's egalitarianism the people recognized something deeply Czech, something rooted in the Czech national tradition as exemplified by Hus and Komenský.[59] Though political journalism might be silenced time and time again, the impact of Havlíček's work on the Czechs remained. Several decades after his death, it was the idea of self-help and hard work for the nation that was to attract his greatest disciple, Tomáš G. Masaryk.

59 Throughout his life Havlíček pressed for the elimination of class barriers and for equality of nationalities. He went beyond most liberals when he endorsed the idea of universal suffrage. See Havlíček, *Politické spisy*, III, 346.

The "Czechoslovak" Question on the Eve of the 1848 Revolution

THOMAS G. PEŠEK

ONE OF THE MOST STRIKING FEATURES of the history of east-central Europe has been the fact that diverse peoples which today inhabit the same countries and share common political destinies frequently placed greater value on associating with one another prior to their unification than in the period following the achievement of national statehood. In the first decades of the nineteenth century, political realities in the Austrian Empire created among the Slavic peoples living there a strong attraction to the notion of "cultural reciprocity" and the advantages it might bring. The Congress of Vienna of 1815 had led to Great Power reaffirmation of the principles of dynastic legitimacy and prerogative, which in turn denied subject nationalities any meaningful voice in affairs of state or deviation from narrowly prescribed social and political norms; for in the post-Napoleonic era, deviation meant internal instability and internal instability in turn endangered the status quo and the peace of the entire continent. Yet, at the same time, Slavic intellectuals had retained an admiration for the ideals of the French Revolution and, more important, were now coming under the influence of German romantics who, in idolizing rural *Volk*, had envisioned a

This article is based in part on the author's unpublished doctoral dissertation, "Karel Havlíček and the Origins of Czech Political Life" (Indiana University, 1969), and on research carried out in Czechoslovakia in 1964–5 under the auspices of the Inter-University Committee on Travel Grants.

glorious destiny for the Slavic peoples. The result was a growing estrangement on the part of Slav intellectuals from the system of absolutism which controlled the fortunes of their peoples. Deprived of legal and direct outlets for promoting national advancement, they came to feel that the Slavs of the Habsburg Monarchy had to fall back on themselves and place their hopes for the future in the collective strength of the Slavic world.

Prior to 1848, disciples of "Slavism" were relatively few in number, at least compared to their counterparts in the latter half of the century. Yet their pioneering contributions to the Slavic cause proved invaluable.[1] In the Balkans, the Croat Ljudevit Gaj fostered and led the Illyrian movement for South Slav unity, while the Slovene poet Stanko Vraz extolled Slavic culture in his lyrics. Among the Czechs to the north, the philologist Josef Jungmann, publishing in 1825 a monumental history of Czech literature, began to urge the adoption of a common Slavic literary language.[2] His work complemented the efforts of such individuals as Josef Dobrovský and František L. Čelakovský in the fields of linguistics and poetry. The Slovak Lutherans Jan Kollár and Pavel Josef Šafařík also achieved renown, the former with his *Slávy dcera* (Daughter of Slava) by prophesying a union of all Slavs who in time would replace the Germans as the dominant force in central and eastern Europe,[3] the latter through his *Slovanské starožitnosti* (Slavic Antiquities) in which he stimulated interest in the origins, early history, and culture of the Slavic peoples.[4] Only the fact that their Slavism contained little that was of a political nature obscured and lessened their impact. Being products of a politically stagnant society, they had little comprehension of, or desire to become involved in, political issues as they existed at that time in the Austrian Empire and the rest of Europe. In fact, had they openly issued a call for political unity, especially to kinsmen outside the empire, they would most certainly have evoked an immediate reaction from conservative authorities and

1 The complexities of Slavic thought, which culminated in the second half of the nineteenth century in a full-fledged ideology of political Panslavism, are treated extensively in two excellent monographs: Michael B. Petrovich, *The Emergence of Russian Panslavism, 1856–1870* (New York, 1956) and Hans Kohn, *Pan-Slavism: Its History and Ideology* (New York, 1960). A useful discussion of a somewhat more general nature is in Miloš Weingart, *Slovanská vzájemnost* (Bratislava, 1926).

2 Ernest Denis and Jindřich Vančura, *Čechy po Bílé hoře* (Prague, 1911), II, pt. 1, 75–6, 101–2.

3 Jan Novotný, "K některým problémům slovanské myšlenky v českém národním hnutí v době předbřeznové," *Historický časopis*, VIII (1960), 267–8. As early as 1821, Kollár had formulated the idea of one Slavic nation with four branches: Russian, Czechoslav (including the Slovaks), Polish, and Illyrian (South Slavs). His *Slávy dcera*, which represented a poetic elaboration on these concepts, had an immediate and rather considerable impact on members of the Czech national intelligentsia, as is borne out by Palacký's remark to Kollár in a letter dated 28 September 1826: "... it [*Slávy dcera*] resounds everywhere throughout Bohemia, even if only in the hearts of patriots who have not forsaken their country." Cited in Novotný, "K některým problémům slovanské myšlenky," 269.

4 Denis and Vančura, *Čechy po Bílé hoře*, II, part 1, 179ff. The activities of Kollár and Šafařík are also covered in Thomas Čapek, *The Slovaks of Hungary: Slavs and Panslavism* (New York, 1906), 18–30, and in Milan Prelog, *Slavenska renesansa* (Zagreb, 1924), 55ff.

jeopardized all they had painstakingly worked to construct. As a result, they limited the substance of their appeal to a general revival of Slavic literary creativity which, they hoped, could be achieved through a single written language, an aroused national and Slavic consciousness, and closer cultural contacts among all the Slavs.[5]

Ultimately, the most useful function performed by the concept of Slavic solidarity among Austrian Slavs in the first half of the nineteenth century was the psychological uplift it gave its propagators. As an ideological form, it justified the feeble struggles of national "awakeners" and helped them overcome feelings of despair brought on by their awareness of monumental, and seemingly insurmountable, problems they had yet to face. It was a convenient crutch which sufficed to sustain national spirit when other more practical programmes and activities appeared futile. The efforts of Slavic intellectuals – individuals who had found themselves more and more drawn into the vortex of nationalism, but increasingly frustrated in their attempts to respond to it – could now be augmented by a new feeling of reliance on the greatness and strength of the Slavic world, particularly tsarist Russia.[6] Yet their cause remained a tenuous one. To protect their lofty mission, supporters of "Slavdom" were necessarily forced to guard against all internal separatist tendencies, against any inclination to question basic premises and assumptions which would make it impossible for the Slavic ideal to progress beyond its initial stage. Challenges from without could scarcely be avoided; those from within would destroy the movement and had to be summarily stopped.

The main subject of this discussion, the so-called "second Czech-Slovak linguistic split," constitutes one of those internal challenges to Slavic unity.[7] When, in the mid-1840s, a small group of Slovak Protestant intellectuals decided to abandon Czech as their literary language and adopt instead a new Slovak tongue based on spoken

5 Kohn, *Pan-Slavism*, 11–12.
6 See Václav L. Beneš, "Bakunin and Palacký's Concept of Austroslavism," *Indiana Slavic Studies*, II (1958), 80, for a similar approach, applied to the Czechs in particular.
7 The first break was instigated by the Slovak Catholic priest Anton Bernolák who, in the last decade of the eighteenth century, codified the spoken Slovak language by devising letters for specifically Slovak sounds and by discarding letters of the Czech orthography (ř, ě, ů) not sounded in Slovakia. On the basis of these changes, the Western Slovak dialect of the Trnava region was then made to serve as a separate Slovak literary medium, ending centuries of Slovak use of Czech.
   The principal reasons for the split appear to have been the ever increasing antagonism between Slovak Catholics and Protestants and Bernolák's desire to provide Catholics with a means of exercising a greater influence in Slovak cultural affairs, heavily dominated to that time by Protestants. In a sense, however, the second split came to be considered even more important than the first because Bernolák's innovations had failed to gain broad popular acceptance (the Protestants remained faithful to Czech) and many peoples of both nationalities continued to hope for a complete reconciliation. See Čapek, *The Slovaks of Hungary*, 116–20.
   Precise percentages on the relative strength of Catholics and Lutherans in Slovakia in the 1840s do not exist; Hungarian census figures of the time provide a breakdown of religious

dialects of central Slovakia, they precipitated an action which could not help but have consequences for the emergence of Czech and Slovak political life in the nineteenth century. It brought on an immediate and embittered response from prominent older Slovaks and leading Czechs, who saw in the rejection a division of common forces and a weakening of traditional ties of nationality on which both peoples had depended for support in their respective national struggles. But the new language was not the only issue at stake. What in reality divided the two camps and made the episode an event of historic importance was a series of deeper questions involving differences of attitude toward two elemental issues: the over-all purpose of inter-Slavic relations and the nature of the tactics to be utilized by the two groups in attempting to resolve their problems as national minorities within the framework of the Habsburg Monarchy. The bitter polemics caused by the "secession" split the intellectual leadership of both nations when neither could afford it and caused a rift which would endure up to the convening of the Prague Slav Congress in 1848.

The background to the second Czech-Slovak linguistic split lies in the wave of Magyarization which swept the Hungarian lands of the Austrian Empire during the 1830s and 1840s. As early as 1830 the Hungarian Parliament had extended the jurisdiction of the Magyar language by making knowledge of it compulsory for all holders of public office in the lands of St. Stephen. Six years later it became, together with Latin, the language of laws and, beginning in 1840, the official language of government.[8] Knowledge of Magyar was further made binding on clergy of all denominations. Finally, in 1843, it was proclaimed the sole language of legislation and official business and, in principle, of public instruction as well.[9] So controversial were these innovations that they ignited a series of bitter exchanges between prominent individuals on both sides of the issue, the most noteworthy being the correspondence between Count Leo Thun, governor of Bohemia, and the Magyar publicist Francis Pulszky.[10]

The attempts at Magyarization fell hard on the Slovaks. They were assailed in the early 1840s at a General Assembly of the Lutheran church at which Hungarian leaders proclaimed Magyar to be "the truest guardian and protector of the liberty of our country, of Europe, and of the Protestant cause."[11] There followed an attempt to exclude the Czech language from Lutheran synods, with Louis (Lajos) Kossuth

---

affiliation only for Hungary as a whole. It is generally conceded, however, that the Catholics constituted a large majority – at least 75 per cent.

Unlike the Czech national awakening, on which there exists a copious literature, the Slovak national awakening has yet to be treated exhaustively. For the latter, the best monographic studies are those of the eminent Slovak historian Daniel Rapant. For a more recent work, see J. Butvin, *Slovesnské národnozjednovacie hnutie* (Bratislava, 1965).

8 Robert W. Seton-Watson, *A History of the Czechs and Slovaks* (London, 1943), 259–62.

9 *Ibid.*, 260.

10 See Oscar Jászi, *The Dissolution of the Habsburg Monarchy* (Chicago, 1961), 309.

11 Seton-Watson, *Czechs and Slovaks*, 260.

himself demanding the banning in Lutheran schools of all Slav societies, which were considered to be "breeding grounds of Panslavism."[12] Other Hungarian leaders, notably Count Karol Zay, general inspector of the Lutheran church in Upper Hungary, and Francis Kazinczy, supported Kossuth's stand by holding Magyarization of the Slovaks necessary in the interests of a unified land, religion, and culture.[13] On the other side of the issue certain Magyars, including Stephen (István) Széchenyi, denounced the action being directed against non-Magyars as chauvinistic and detrimental to Hungarian interests. But Kossuth and his followers prevailed, so much to the detriment of the Slovaks that their national cause declined rapidly throughout the decade.

In this precarious situation, the Slovaks found three able leaders to champion their interests: Ľudovít Štúr, Jozef Miloslav Hurban, and Michal Miloslav Hodža. Štúr, however, was by far the most dynamic and articulate and, as events turned out, he was to become the pre-eminent figure of the separatist movement. Like Kollár, he had been an ardent supporter of Slavic unity in his youth and in 1836, at the age of twenty-one, was appointed assistant to the aged Slavicist, Jur Palkovič, at the evangelical *lyceum* in Bratislava.[14] It was here that he distinguished himself as a young intellectual of some promise and most likely made the acquaintance of his two close friends Hurban and Hodža, both Lutheran pastors. In 1844 he was dismissed from his post because of alleged anti-Magyar agitation among students and subsequently became editor of the Slovak newspaper *Slovenskje národňje novini* (Slovak National News). Hurban, who was to collaborate closely with Štúr in resisting Magyar policies among the Slovaks, became editor of the literary supplement to Štúr's paper, *Orol Tatránski* (Eagle of the Tatras).

That Štúr was acting from the highest motives when he now began to foster yet another literary tongue has been well established. He was deeply concerned about the plight of his people, about their uncertain status as a small national minority in the Magyar-dominated lands of the empire; and his desire to devise a bulwark against the thrust of Magyarization, more than anything else, led him to take action. But the problem involved more than just the attempted denationalization of one ethnic group by another. If the Slovaks were to solve permanently the question of their position in a multinational Hungary, they would first have to achieve a semblance of internal unity, which in the past had been sorely lacking. Long-standing divisions along confessional and social lines, especially in terms of Protestant-Catholic friction and the dissociation of the upper native nobility from Slovak nationality, had

12 *Ibid.*
13 Albert Pražák, *Národ se bránil: Obrany národa a jazyka českého od nejstarších dob po přítomnost* (Prague, 1945), 245–6.
14 For a concise discussion of Štúr's early career see Ľudovít Holotík, "Ľudovít Štúr – bojovník proti národnému a sociálnemu útlaku," in the collective work *Ľudovít Štúr: Život a dielo, 1815–1856* (Bratislava, 1956), 504–6.

made progressive national development difficult. At the same time, there was an obvious need to retain the allegiance of lower social groups and sections of the country where Slovak was still spoken and respected, lest they too become disaffected. In Štúr's mind, the solution to all these problems lay in the creation of a new literary language.

References to these problems abound in Štúr's correspondence. Writing, for example, to the distinguished pioneer of Russian Slavic studies I. I. Sreznevskii, he lamented the adverse effect Catholic-Lutheran antagonism was having on Slovak unity. Such discord was to be deplored at any time, but it was especially harmful in its current phase, he intimated, because it coincided with a new and crucial need of the people to marshal all forces and resources in order to preserve their identity as a nation.[15] Having a common literary medium, the two hostile factions might well bring themselves to tone down their differences; yet he doubted – and here history supported him – that the Catholic bernolákčina could effectively serve as a means. At the same time, he took cognizance of traditional Slovak Catholic aversion to Czech, identified as it was with the Hussite Reformation, and rejected it also as a possible solution.[16] The answer had to lie in something new.

On the other side of the ledger, Štúr was forced to weigh a number of attendant social problems. During the course of their early awakening to national consciousness, many peoples in the eastern and southeastern parts of Europe had at one time been shaken from their political lethargy through the instrumentality of their native aristocracy. Among the Poles, for instance, the szlachta had come to dominate the national movement under the rule of the partitioning powers. In Slovakia, however, the situation was different. The upper nobility had been largely Magyarized and most of Štúr's followers, including Štúr himself, had abandoned hope of reclaiming them. "Those [nobles] who are inclined toward us are all older; all the younger ones are against us," he complained.[17] The new language, however, could still hopefully be used with effect among the lower nobility, the more national-conscious bourgeoisie, and perhaps some elements of the peasantry. Here even its partial success would make the venture worth while. In the meantime, with the aristocracy reproaching Slovak intellectuals for not adhering more to Hungary and for seeking instead, through language and literature, to join themselves to the Czechs, with

15 Štúr to Sreznevskii, 18 April 1844; cited from V. A. Frantsev, Cheshsko-slovenskii raskol i ego otgoloski v literature sorokovych godov (Warsaw, 1915), 5.
16 Ibid. Štúr's doubts as to the efficacy of the bernoláčtina stemmed from a realization that, if the Slovaks had to abandon Czech, Bernolák's Western dialect would not be much help because it was closest to Czech and only slightly better understood than Czech by simple people in central and eastern Slovakia. For this reason, he selected a Middle Slovak dialect (Zvolen district) for his new literary language, hoping it would be comprehensible to Slovaks everywhere.
17 Štúr to Staněk, September 1841; F. Kleinschnitzová, Z listov štúrovcov, Sborník Matice slovenskej (Turčiansky Svätý Martin, 1929), 157.

whom indeed there was little hope of political unification, the separatists could logically proclaim that Slovak nationality would once again become "domesticated" and no Slovak need look any longer to Bohemia-Moravia in order to find a homeland.[18]

Štúr's only comprehensive attempt to justify the new language on somewhat more philosophical grounds appeared in 1845 in an article carried by *Orol Tatránski*. The Slovaks, no less than the Poles, Russians, Czechs, and South Slavs, he insisted, were a distinct branch of the Slavic race with their own distinct dialect (*nárečie*) and had every right to exploit it in order to ensure their national identity, cultural development, and, by implication, their political well-being as well.[19] But what was more important in his mind was the fact that peculiarity and uniqueness of language denoted a broader and yet more significant quality without which no human aggregate could call itself a nation. This he termed *kmenovitosť*, or the collective personality of a people which results from participation, through language, in common endeavours on all planes of human life. Politics, social norms, moral outlook, biases, and temperament – all formed part of it and served to make those who shared in it a separate "tribe" (*kmen*) rather than just an adjunct or extension of another. The greatest responsibility of a nation, he concluded, lay in recognizing and developing this personality, just as an individual would be obliged to recognize and develop his own; otherwise it would surely atrophy and die.[20] Here was a clear-cut challenge not only to Kollár's concept of one Slavic nation with but four branches, but to the feeling, still widespread at the time, that the spiritual, cultural, and political interests of the Slavic peoples could be best served by the adoption of a single literary language.

Yet in spite of the repercussions which would certainly result from his actions, including strong opposition among Czechs and Slovaks alike, Štúr continued to hope that his critics would see the wisdom of his policy. He repeatedly denied throughout the course of the ensuing controversy that he was apathetic toward Slav aspirations in the monarchy or that he had any desire to minimize traditional Czech-Slovak contacts, as was charged by some Czechs. Such contacts had proliferated greatly in the preceding decades through the exchange of periodical and other literature, journeys of Czech students to Slovakia and Slovak students to Prague, and the cooperative efforts of the two nationalities in a wide variety of scholarly endeavours. And this intercourse, Štúr realized, was invaluable to the Slovaks in their attempts to raise the cultural and intellectual level of their nation. "Whoever seeks to break from his [Czech] brother at this time will incur the most serious rebuke of our people," he wrote in 1846, adding that he hoped the Czechs too would profit from any good he might accomplish and that the unity of the two peoples, at

18 See Albert Pražák, "Československá otázka u Havlíčka," *Památce Havlíčkově* (Německý Brod, 1924), 26–7.
19 "Hlas k rodákom," *Orol Tatránski,* 12 Sept. 1845, no. 6, p. 42.   20 *Ibid.*

least in spirit, would continue as before.[21] For the moment, then, all he could do was continue to assert his open-mindedness and benevolence toward his detractors. When at a later time Czechs themselves were confronted by the demands of certain Moravian spokesmen for greater provincial autonomy for the Moravian Estates and *de facto* recognition of the administrative divisibility of Bohemia-Moravia, Štúr spoke out strongly against the movement. Such was his way of reaffirming his desire to retain the goodwill of the Czechs and his refusal to support any kind of centrifugal tendencies among individual Slavic nations.

In examining Czech opposition to Štúr, together with the factors that lay behind it, one finds a series of arguments and rationalizations only slightly less varied and involved than those which led the "separatists" along their path of action. Social, political, and cultural considerations, all cited by Štúr to justify his actions, were in turn used by the Czechs in an attempt to dissuade him from them. Yet, as events materialized and the controversy wore on, little understanding was ever reached and, rather than diminishing, intransigence continued to mount on both sides. What few people at the time realized was that the failure of Czechs and Slovaks to resolve their differences in an amicable way was a result of the fact that both based their tactics and programmes on conditions peculiar to their own parts of the monarchy and failed to comprehend attitudes reflecting problems that were current elsewhere.

To the majority of Czechs conversant with the issue, as well as to Slovaks of Kollár's generation, Štúr's new course was an ill-conceived one for the simple reason that it violated the historical development of the two peoples. From earliest times, they held, there had always lived in Bohemia, Moravia, Silesia, and Slovakia one people, possessing but one language, one cultural tradition, and a strong sense of belonging together. "It has been and is my firm conviction," stated Šafařík characteristically, "that from the Ore Mountains ... to Humenné above the Laborec in Hungary and transversely from the Krkonoše to the Danube at Komárno ... there reigns one and the same Slavic tongue, ... the surest proof [of which] is the reciprocal intelligibility of common speech among people inhabiting those ... districts."[22] Such uniformity was deemed a source of strength and cited as the factor which had enabled the people to survive great crises and achieve rapid cultural advancement. To destroy it was to take a step backward, to retreat as it were "from the white to the black, from the Iliad to the alphabet."[23]

21 L. Štúr, *Nárečia slovenskuo a potreba písaňja v tomto nárečí* (Prešpork, 1846), as cited in Josef Kočí and Jan Novotný, "L'udovít Štúr a česko-slovenské vztahy," *Štúr: Život a dielo*, 348. Similar denials were also voiced already two years earlier in letters to Hodža and a Czech friend Josef Staněk; see *Listy L'udovíta Štúra*, ed. Jozef Ambruš (Bratislava, 1956), II, 38 and 42.

22 *Hlasové o potřebě jednoty spisovného jazyka pro Čechy, Moravany a Slováky* (Prague, 1846), para. 68; cited in Pražák, *Národ se bránil*, 245. Also Pavel Josef Šafařík, *Slovanský národopis* (Prague, 1842), II, para. 21.

23 Pražák, *Národ se bránil*, 245. The words are Šafařík's.

Similar thoughts were also expressed by František Palacký, historian of the Czech people and leading Czech spokesman of his time. He too viewed the past as an argument for Czech-Slovak unity, finding its clearest manifestation in the Great Moravian Empire of the ninth century. Here singleness of culture and liturgy, the tradition of Cyril and Methodius, had welded the people into one and made them great. Only because of the coming of the Magyars to central Europe and the accompanying destruction of Great Moravia was this development aborted and the nation split into its two branches. The Hussite Revolution eventually renewed a consciousness of unity among the people, which then survived until the Counter-Reformation when efforts by the Jesuits to supplant the Protestant Slavic heritage of Bohemia and Moravia led to the rapid Germanization of indigenous culture.[24] But even at that time, unity was not disrupted altogether; for the "Czechoslav" tradition lived on in Slovakia and there managed to survive even the Theresian and Josephine reforms of the eighteenth century. As for Bernolák's new orthography, its disruptive influence was, in Palacký's estimation, minimal. It produced disaffection only among Catholics who were not, generally speaking, among the nation's most advanced social elements. The majority of educated Slovaks continued to write in Czech, and it was through them that the centuries-old tradition of linguistic and cultural unity was preserved.

Whatever may be their historical validity, these sentiments reflected a fundamental fear which possessed all politically conscious Czechs in the 1840s: that Slovak linguistic separatism would not remain confined to matters of language – ultimately a secondary issue – but would invariably disrupt relations between the two peoples on other and more important planes as well. As a rule, Czechs were reluctant to recognize differences between their own national predicament in Austria and that of the Slovaks in Hungary. Both peoples, they felt, faced threats to their national identity from politically stronger forces, notwithstanding the fact that the Slovaks, because of Magyar reforms, might be temporarily in a weaker position.[25] One had only to consider that in the Czech lands German predominated as the language of administration and that only the lower classes felt socially safe to identify with Czech nationality and culture to see a similarity of problems. In this situation, what was needed, in the Czech view, was unity and a common front of opposition, not particularism and independent solutions.

As for Štúr himself, few of his critics doubted his good intentions. Most, in fact,

24 See in particular Palacký's two articles "O Českém jazyku spisovném" and "O národech Uherských, zvláště Slovanech," which appeared in the *Časopis Českého musea* in 1832 and 1829 respectively. Important excerpts are contained in Josef Fischer, ed., *Z politického odkazu Františka Palackého: Výbor statí* (Prague, 1926); see especially pages 145–51.
25 Jan Novotný, *O bratrské družbě Čechů a Slováků za národního obrození* (Prague, 1959), contains much valuable information on every important facet of this problem. A work of considerable depth, it is the best treatment of Czech-Slovak relations to come out of Czechoslovakia since 1945. The mild Marxist bias of the author detracts little from its reliability.

considered him at worst a misguided and inexperienced individual and felt that his policies might even temporarily slow down Magyarization pressures against the Slovaks. But success on a permanent basis they doubted he could achieve. Palacký, for one, maintained that, in order for it to achieve lasting results, the *štúrovčina* would have to secure some standing as a language of education, administration, and legislation; and this, quite obviously, the Magyars would never permit.[26] Excluded from a role in public life and lacking a strong historical tradition, it could then only with great difficulty serve as a medium for the creation of the native Slovak literature Štúr so desperately wanted. A major portion of the educated classes which would be called on to use it, the aristocracy, had already adopted Magyar, while others would scarcely understand it.[27] Granted the persistence of internal divisions and the improbability that Štúr's language could succeed in overcoming them, the Slovaks were advised to retain those symbols of unity they possessed in the past and which had proved their resilience in maintaining the vitality of the nation.

A closer look at the works of Czech liberal writers reveals that some Czech leaders were also attempting to justify their stand on Slovak separatism on what might be termed a broader philosophy of national development. Once again it was Palacký who took the lead, stating a principle which was to become a corner-stone of his later thought; namely, that a nation is fully a nation only when it has achieved political life. Deprived of its right to engage in political activity, a people could never hope to function as an organic whole, let alone maintain indefinitely its national existence, even if it were to achieve great things on other levels of human activity.[28] The implications of the argument were clear: not just the Slovaks, but all Slavs of Austria, faced deprivation of political power, the total loss of which "no known cure on earth" could remedy.[29] To gain political rights, Austria's Slavs would have to begin acting in concert, for none were sufficiently strong to force concessions independently.

This finally pointed to what was in fact the major issue of the entire controversy: Štúr's implication that, from a political point of view, the Slovak question was insoluble outside Hungary. As far back as the 1820s, and even earlier if one considers the psychological propaganda which preceded their actions, the Magyars had begun to lay the plans for administrative reform designed to make them masters in their own half of the monarchy. The abolition of Latin as the official language of Hungary was only a prelude to the complete denationalization of non-Magyar peoples, a process which in itself would entail even more comprehensive changes.

26 Josef Fischer, *Myšlenka a dílo Františka Palackého* (Prague, 1926), ɪ, 241.
27 *Ibid.*
28 *Františka Palackého spisy drobné*, ed. Bohuš Rieger (Prague, 1898), ɪ, 115–16.
29 *Ibid.*, 116.

As long as the Vienna Court retained effective control over affairs of state in Hungary, Croats, Serbs, Slovaks, and Rumanians could reasonably hope that the dynasty would protect their national individuality. Certainly in the past the Habsburgs had found it in their interest to favour temporarily the interests of weaker subject groups against those of stronger nationalities so as to prevent open challenges to dynastic authority. But as time elapsed and the efforts of Magyar reformers produced their first notable successes, it became increasingly evident that Vienna either would not, or momentarily could not, halt the rise of a Magyar national state. It is at this point that Štúr most likely decided to act.[30] If some form of Austro-Hungarian dualism in the Habsburg Monarchy was imminent and inevitable, as indeed it must have seemed likely to Štúr by 1844, the Slovaks would no longer be able to call on the Czechs for support. Instead they would have to place proportionately greater, if not all, reliance directly on themselves and other nationalities faced with the same prospect of a Magyar-dominated Hungary.[31]

To the Czech liberals, these thoughts were inadmissible. Far from ridiculing Štúr's apprehensions, they too felt that a *détente* between the Magyars and Vienna was more than a remote possibility. But those who stood to lose by it were not just Slovaks. A break-up of the monarchy into coequal Austrian and Hungarian parts would isolate the Czechs in the west and there force them to bear the brunt of a movement equal to that of the Magyars in the vehemence of its opposition toward Slavic aspirations. This force, the *Grossdeutsch* nationalism of German liberals, was of relatively recent origin; but it had already begun to make incisions into the political fabric of Austria.[32] With this danger in mind, Czech spokesmen again reproached Štúr for suggesting that national oppression was peculiar only to certain Slavs and that it could be solved through independent action. The problem was universal in Austria; and if it were ever to be resolved successfully, it would have to be met with a common programme coordinated among all Austro-Slavic peoples.

Such a programme Czech liberals had already begun to devise in the mid-

30 This theory has been proposed in slightly different forms by many Czech historians, including Albert Pražák, perhaps the most prolific of all who have written on Czech-Slovak relations. See his *Národ se bránil*, 262. The idea is an interesting one and attractive, especially since it goes far toward explaining Štúr's timing of the break. Its only short-coming is a lack of evidence sufficient to support it fully.

31 In September 1846, Štúr in effect admitted this to be the case when he wrote in his newspaper: "In a political sense we are truly nothing [when] separated from the other inhabitants of our homeland ... In this sense *we are Hungarian citizens; we are Hungary.*" "Naše položeňja vo vlasťi," *Slovenskje národňje novini*, no. 119, p. 475. The italics are mine.

32 See Novotný, "K některým problémům slovanské myšlenky," 275ff., as well as his "Příspěvek k vzájemným vztahům Čechů a Slováků v první etapě revoluce roku 1848," *Historický časopis*, XI (1963), 366–7.

1840s in the form of the complex, but relatively sophisticated, ideology of "Austro-Slavism."[33] The integrity of Austria had to be preserved at all cost and the empire democratized through a federation of equal subject nations, insisted Palacký and the young journalist Karel Havlíček, the chief propagators of the plan. In a truncated, divided monarchy, the Slavs would remain weak forever, dominated by Germans or Magyars, or even by Russians who would not hesitate to betray their brothers, given the chance to incorporate them into a universal Slavic empire under tsarist control.[34] In a united Austria, however, the Slavs were a majority, and through federation they could achieve liberty and the relative dominance rightfully theirs by reason of their superior numbers. All that was needed was for the dynasty to recognize its true calling in central Europe as a bulwark against Russian expansionism, Prussian hegemony, and the divisive forces of Magyar and Great German nationalism. This done, it would see the Slavs as its only true supporters, grant their demands, and the ideal would become reality. Štúr's great sin was his failure to appreciate the dream. He had, in effect, denied that its realization was possible.

By the end of 1845, Štúr had gained a large following in many Slovak districts, especially among students and scholars. Fearing his success would produce a change of attitude among the Czechs, the anti-secessionists, both Czech and Slovak, increased the intensity of their attacks. Early in 1846 they published a lengthy tract entitled *Hlasové o potřebě jednoty spisovného jazyka pro Čechy, Moravany a Slováky* (Voices on the Need for Unity of a Written Language for Czechs, Moravians, and Slovaks), again calling on Štúr to desist from his actions. The fact that the document appeared under the sponsorship of the prestigious "Matice česká" in Prague gave it additional force.[35] At the same time, Štúr's most outspoken opponent, Havlíček, joined the controversy in an independent journalistic capacity, proclaiming Slovak linguistic separatism to be no longer a verbal game, but a serious cultural and political problem.[36] Dire results would come about from a permanent separation of Czechs from Slovaks, he maintained, feeling again perhaps that Czechs in particular would become conscious of the significance of the split only when it was too late to heal. He added: "Then we will look around ourselves in pain; our numbers will seem to us scanty before our powerful and inimical neighbours, and we will yearningly stretch out our

33 This programme is discussed here only in so far as it relates to the main topic of this paper. The author recognizes, however, that Austro-Slavism is not, strictly speaking, a uniform body of thought and that variations of it can be found among writers belonging to classes other than the bourgeoisie.

34 Beneš, "Bakunin and Palacký," 83–6.

35 Palacký, Kollár, and Šafařík all contributed to the tract. Havlíček did not, but associated himself with it shortly afterwards by reprinting excerpts from it in the official *Pražské noviny* (Prague News), of which he was chief editor. See Zdeněk V. Tobolka, ed., *Karla Havlíčka Borovského politické spisy* (Prague, 1900), I, 103–18.

36 Jan Jakubec, *Dějiny literatury české* (Prague, 1934), II, 948.

arms to Slovakia; but perhaps it will already be too late if we neglect [to take action at] this decisive time."[37] Neither Havlíček's protestations nor the injunctions of the *Hlasové*, however, produced any change in the situation.

Journalistic charges and countercharges continued for the remainder of 1846, with each side soliciting additional support from various writers and public figures. In 1847, the controversy subsided somewhat. Then, in the spring of 1848, Štúr made a final effort to clarify the motives behind the new language; but by that time the *štúrovčina* had already taken root in Slovakia and rancour was too strong to allow for compromise.

Writing in Havlíček's own *Národní noviny* (National News), Štúr admitted that he had acted largely for political reasons.[38] He first reiterated his often-stated desire to devise a compromise literary language which Slovaks of all religious faiths could accept, thus symbolizing the linguistic and confessional unity of the nation. Using the language as a political tool was logically the next step. If indeed the Slovak nobility had become Magyarized to a point where their redemption was no longer posible, the *štúrovčina* would serve to weaken their vast influence in the country by providing a new standard around which to awaken the politically insensitive middle and lower classes. In this manner the "secessionists" would have secured dominant control in Slovakia through the active backing of majority social elements and could then demand that Magyarization be stopped. The final result would hopefully be the eventual granting of full nationality rights to the Slovaks, commensurate with their numerical strength.

A fair assessment of this controversy from the standpoint of those most involved in it is difficult to reach because the contentions of leading spokesmen on both sides were frequently marred by *ad hominem* attacks and unfounded statements which tended to obscure the real issues. Harrassed by opposition from many quarters and often unsure of himself as the dispute wore on, Štúr had accused the Czechs, before Slovak Catholics, of being Hussites, while in other parts of Slovakia he ranted against them as "Germanized ghosts."[39] Havlíček, on his part, went so far as to label the new Slovak literature "Tartar" and characterized both Štúr and Hurban as individuals who were seeking self-aggrandizement and who, to this end, would openly join the Magyars against the Czechs.[40]

It is indeed ironical that, in the wake of these charges which caused so much bitterness, neither side ever really accomplished what it considered to be its

---

37 *Ibid.* The source is Havlíček's *Česká včela*, literary supplement to the *Pražské noviny*, 1846, 236.

38 L. Štúr, "Pohled na hýbání západních a jížních Slovanů," *Národní noviny*, 2 May 1848. Especially enlightening is the commentary on this article in Pražák, "Československá otázka," 26–7.

39 Pražák, "Československá otázka," 25.

40 *Česká včela*, 20 Jan. and 27 Feb. 1846, as cited in Emanuel Chalupný, *Havlíček: Prostředí, osobnost a dílo* (Prague, 1929), 92.

major goals. Though at times there were indications that Štúr might reconsider his position, the Czechs ultimately failed to convince him and his followers that they should return to the use of Czech as their sole literary language. Furthermore, events in the ensuing years, at least until 1867, generally proved that Czech concern over Slovak separatism was groundless. The attempt of the "secessionists" to strike a more independent course in linguistic and literary matters remained at best a "Hungarian" phenomenon and had little appreciable impact on the movement of Czechs in Bohemia and Moravia for more substantial national and political rights.

Even more paradoxical was the end result of the movement initiated by Štúr. Having broken with the Czechs, he never succeeded in uniting the Slovaks behind his new literary medium. Partly because the new language was based on a dialect of the central lower Tatras which was relatively unaffected by outside influences, it was often unintelligible to Slovaks in districts to the east and west and hence became unacceptable to them. More important, however, proved to be the reluctance of some religious groups and members of the intelligentsia to abandon their traditional way of writing. As a result, instead of one common literary language, the Slovaks now possessed three: young Protestants generally adopted the new *štúrovčina*, but Catholics continued to use the *bernoláčtina* and older writers like Kollár and Šafařík remained faithful to Czech.

A final word remains to be said about the enigmatic role of certain leading members of the Czech bourgeoisie, particularly Palacký and Havlíček. Although conspicuous for their liberal stand on most other political issues of the time, they displayed what might in retrospect be considered a certain narrow-mindedness and lack of perspective in their unwillingness to concede the Slovaks the right to their own literary language.[41] Yet, considering the peculiar state of Czech political affairs in the mid-1840s, the circumstances of the dispute, and, above all, their own obviously sincere belief in the ethnic oneness of Czechs and Slovaks, their approach is entirely understandable, even if somewhat ill-advised.

Slovak linguistic separatism, although on the whole not adversely affecting the national movement in Bohemia and Moravia, had a cataclysmic effect on the evolution of political ideas among Czech liberals. As a development which substantially altered Czech views on relations with another Slavic people, its impact can be compared to that of the Russian suppression of the Polish uprising of 1830–1. The latter bluntly exposed to Czech intellectuals the shortcomings of uncritical Russophilism, which had taken root in Bohemia following the Napoleonic wars, and demanded of them a radical reassessment of their concept of the

41 See V. A. Francev [Frantsev], "Štúrovo 'schisma' a jeho ohlasy," *Časopis pro moderní filologii a literaturu*, IV (1914), 16; also *Cheshsko-slovenskii raskol*, 24, by the same author. For a Marxist interpretation, critical of Havlíček's actions as a "manifestation of the nationalism of Czech liberals," see Jarmila Tkadlečková, "Názory a činnosť Karla Havlíčka Borovského z hľadiska vývoja česko-slovenských vzťahov," *Historicky časopis*, VI (1958), 38.

tsar as a potential liberator of Austrian and Hungarian Slavs. Slovak separatism, if it had no other greater effect, brought to Czech leaders the realization that reciprocal Slavic relations, when and where they existed, derived not from some philosophical conviction of ethnic oneness, but from the conveniences of practical politics and the chance identity of national self-interests.

Confronted now with the determination of the Slovaks to act more independently of Bohemia and Moravia in seeking national and political rights in Hungary, Czech leaders reluctantly recognized the probability that direct Czech influence in Slovakia would to some extent decrease. At the same time, they never abandoned hope that the two peoples would act in unison, should the opportunity for joint political action present itself in the future. As for the main protagonists, Štúr and Havlíček, considerable bitterness remained between them. Only in June 1848, with the calling of the Slav Congress in Prague, did there occur a partial reconciliation,[42] and then only when it became evident to both that greater issues were at stake.

42 It should be pointed out that the question of Czech-Slovak linguistic and ethnic unity remained open long after the revolutionary years of 1848–9. In the decade following the revolution, Kollár used his influence to reintroduce Czech into certain Slovak areas where younger writers had earlier abandoned its use. In the 1890s, Hurban attempted to introduce a new Slovak journal, *Slovenské pohledy*, in Czech and even Štúr on occasion published in the old language. What occurred in 1848 was but a gentlemanly moratorium, brought on by the need for spokesmen on both sides to consider more pressing problems.

German Liberalism and the Czech Renascence: Ignaz Kuranda, *Die Grenzboten*, and Developments in Bohemia, 1845–1849

FRANCIS L. LOEWENHEIM

THE HISTORY of modern Europe knows few greater tragedies than the seemingly endless hostility of German and Slav, and the history of the nineteenth century, in particular, knows few more unfortunate developments than the almost simultaneous rise and bitter frustration of German liberalism and the Czech renascence.

It is one of the strange gaps of central European historiography that the relationship between these two epochal developments has yet to be fully explored, but it is one of the notable achievements of the distinguished scholar and teacher to whom this volume is inscribed that he has, in both capacities, contributed significantly to our knowledge and understanding of the liberal and national forces in those hopeful days[1] before "iron and blood" became, in large parts of central Europe, the intellectually respectable method for bringing about its long needed and widely desired national reconstruction.

No one who has read or thought much about the history of Czech-German relations in the middle of the nineteenth century, and who approaches that vital subject in the spirit of liberal nationalism, can fail to be dismayed by the inability of men of goodwill, in Bohemia, in Austria, and in Germany proper, to resolve

1 Otakar Odložilík, "A Czech Plan for a Danubian Federation – 1848," *Journal of Central European Affairs*, I (1941); "Storm over the Danube," *ibid.*, VIII (1948); and "The Czechs on the Eve of the 1848 Revolution," *Harvard Slavic Studies*, I (1953).

the national problem in those areas in a peaceful and generally accepted manner. To be sure, some German historians, for instance Hans Rothfels, would have us believe that such a settlement was never a serious prospect, and that the only real hope for lasting peace in central Europe lay in some sort of loose, German-dominated confederation.[2]

In one sense, of course, Rothfels and others agreeing with him seem to have been proved right by events. For there never was, either in 1848 or 1918 (or for that matter in 1938 and 1945), a peaceful or freely accepted settlement between Germans and Czechs. But why was this? Why indeed were the Czech and German (as well as Austrian) liberals unable to reach a lasting accommodation in the middle of the nineteenth century, and what light does that calamitous failure throw on the history of the Czech renascence and on that of German liberalism?

Although much has been written, especially since the First World War, on the inner development of Bohemia – on the economic, social, intellectual, and political aspects of the Czech renascence – the linguistic limitations of many Western historians have, in effect, made much of this scholarship inaccessible to them. As a result, many widely read Western accounts of the Czech renascence hardly go beyond the conventional treatments of a generation or more ago. These Western accounts usually recall, for instance, František Palacký's famous letter to the Frankfurt *Vorparlament* (Pre-Parliament), dated April 1848, declining Czech membership in any predominantly German assembly; the short-lived Slav Congress that convened in Prague early in June 1848; and Windischgrätz's brutal bombardment and occupation of that city thereafter. But almost everything that preceded and followed these admittedly historic events remains largely obscure. This not only need not be. It must not be. For to fail to understand the course of Czech-German relations before the rise of the Czech independence movement at the close of the nineteenth century is to overlook one of the most significant and prophetically tragic aspects of modern history – and perhaps not only modern European history.

Ranke, in an often-quoted phrase, once remarked that, after all the conflicting opinions on a particular subject had been heard, it was all the more necessary to go back to the original sources, to see what actually happened.[3] It should be

2 Hans Rothfels, "1848 – One Hundred Years After," *Journal of Modern History*, xx (1948); *Ostraum, Preussentum, und Reichsgedanke* (Leipzig, 1935), and the second edition thereof *Bismarck, der Osten, und das Reich* (Stuttgart, 1960), which omits some of the more flagrantly nationalistic formulations of the first – but see esp. pp. 4ff., 14ff. (with the ironic dismissal of the great French slavicist Louis Eisenmann), and 270ff. See also his essay "Das erste Scheitern des Nationalstaats in Ost-Mittel-Europa 1848/49," in Rothfels and Werner Markert, eds., *Deutscher Osten und slawischer Westen* (Tübingen, 1955), which concludes blandly that Schwarzenberg's New Absolutism "pushed aside" the hopeful beginning made at Kremsier – conveniently overlooking the fact that Schwarzenberg's repressive nationality policies were an integral part of the post-1849 reaction in Austria.

3 Leopold von Ranke, in *Zur eigenen Lebensgeschichte*, ed. Alfred Dove (Leipzig, 1890), 569.

added that this is especially appropriate in this case, since the passage of time has clearly not brought about a cooling of nationalist passions, but, on the contrary, has led to the further distortion and obscuring of many important aspects of the Czech-German relationship.[4]

Fortunately, in the case of the Czech renascence and its relationship with German liberalism, we are by no means lacking in significant contemporary evidence. One of the most valuable sources on the subject, as has long been recognized, is the political and literary weekly *Die Grenzboten* (The Border Messengers) founded in Brussels in October 1841 by Ignaz Kuranda. Probably the most widely read German journal of its time, it was from the beginning designed to serve as an intellectual bridge between the Habsburg Empire and Germany proper. To be sure, that was anything but an easy or enviable task, either in the last dreary years of Metternichian Europe, or even in the stormy period that followed the Austrian chancellor's overthrow in March 1848. It is, indeed, something of a reflection of the lagging state of central European scholarship in the United States that, as late as 1969, no pre-1845 copies of *Die Grenzboten* existed in any American library. Yet the years between 1845 and 1849, for which it is available in its entirety, have a unity and importance all their own; and a closer look at *Die Grenzboten* for those years goes a long way toward illuminating the history of the Czech renascence and its fateful connection with the rise and defeat of German liberalism.[5]

KURANDA AND PREREVOLUTIONARY BOHEMIA

In an important essay written shortly after the centennial of the revolutions of 1848, Professor Odložilík has noted that "in March 1848 the Czech people returned on stage as a political unit,"[6] and he went on from there to discuss, in interesting and significant detail, the social and intellectual development of the Czech people in the crucial decades before the outbreak of the mid-century revolutions. To be sure, both the Viennese government and the other great powers of Europe – that is, Britain, France, Russia, and Prussia – might have refused, in those days, to acknowledge the awkward fact that there was once more a "Czech problem." But both in a constitutional and intellectual sense that problem had clearly begun to emerge some time before March 1848, and the pages of *Die Grenzboten* contain considerable evidence on the mounting crisis in Bohemia, and why the Czech-German relationship tended to follow the tragic course that it did after March 1848.

4 See Bibliographical Postscript at the end of this essay.
5 No detailed studies of *Die Grenzboten* exist. Josef Matl, "Die 'Grenzboten' und die Slawen-frage – Ein Beitrag zur Geschichte der öffentlichen Meinung Mitteleuropas," *Sisičev Zbornik* (Zagreb, 1929) (reprinted, in extended form, in his collected essays *Südslawische Studien* [Munich, 1965]) concerns mostly *Die Grenzboten*'s comments and reporting on South Slav affairs betwen 1844 and 1849.
6 Odložilík, "The Czechs on the Eve of the 1848 Revolution," 178.

No one, of course, can approach the liberal discussion of pre-March Bohemian conditions, or the general state of Czech-German relations during those years, without understanding something of the circumstances under which that discussion necessarily proceeded. Those conditions, it cannot be sufficiently emphasized, were highly unfavourable; indeed, they contributed materially to the subsequent course of revolutionary politics and national understanding. The fact of the matter is that, despite everything that has been written by Srbik and other Metternich apologists since the 1920s,[7] the Austrian and (Metternich-inspired) German censorship and other forms of literary control prevailing in the *Vormärz* period were such as to render all frank and serious discussion of national and political issues extremely hazardous.[8] In other words, not only did the rulers of central Europe in those years seek to preserve the status quo at almost any

7 Heinrich Ritter von Srbik, *Metternich – Der Staatsmann und der Mensch* (vols. I and II: Munich, 1925; vol. III: Munich, 1954). In some ways the last volume is an even more remarkable work than the first two. In it Srbik proved to his own satisfaction that almost everything written about Metternich since 1925 either confirmed what he had written in his own biography or what he had believed all along. It is interesting to note that Srbik refers to what he calls "the honorable will to improvement [on the part] of the moderate-constitutional Kuranda and his 'Grenzboten'" (II, 218), but then, in characteristic Srbik fashion, says nothing whatever about the things that Kuranda and *Die Grenzboten* had been publishing about Metternichian Austria for some years, much less about the Austrian government's strenuous efforts to keep this admittedly well-intentioned journal from circulating within its borders. What Metternich thought about the Czechs (and not even Srbik, II, 188, or III, 174, makes him out to be a friend of the Czech renascence) is revealed by a remark of his quoted by his biographer, Guillame de Bertier de Sauvigné. "Czech patriotism," Metternich is supposed to have said, "is an urge which gives rise to unimportant aberrations when things are moving along in their usual rut, but at times of great excitement it has as much influence on men as a salad of beans in an outbreak of cholera" (*Metternich and His Times* [London, 1962], 166). All this should be kept in mind since it is perfectly clear that, just as Bismarck stands at the centre of German and European history during the second half of the nineteenth century, so Metternich does during the first. Until his work and significance have been properly reassessed, no tenable history of the nationality problem in central Europe – including the Czech renascence – can be written. Perhaps the first, and a long overdue, step in this direction would be the publication of a comprehensive documentary history on Metternich and Bohemia to parallel Friedrich Walter's important two-volume administrative history of the Austrian central government from 1792 to 1848 (*Veröffentlichungen der Kommission für neuere Geschichte Österreichs*, XLII, XLIII [Vienna, 1956]), which unfortunately, however, deals only briefly with the 1840s.
8 Cf. *Die Grenzboten* (hereafter abbreviated D.G.), 1847/I, 167, 557ff.; 1847/II, 417ff.; 1847/III, 480ff.; and 1848/I, 376ff. See also Julius Marx, *Die österreichische Zensur im Vormärz* (Vienna, 1939); "Die amtlichen Verbotslisten – Neue Beiträge zur Geschichte der österreichischen Zensur im Vormärz," *Mitteilungen des österreichischen Staatsarchivs*, XI (1958), 444; and "Johann Gabriel Seibt als Zensor," *Jahrbuch des Vereins für Geschichte der Stadt Wien*, XV–XVI (1959–60), esp. 255, 260ff. See further Viktor Bibl, *Die niederösterreichischen Stände im Vormärz – Ein Beitrag zur Vorgeschichte der Revolution des Jahres 1848* (Vienna, 1911), 320ff.; *Der Zerfall Österreichs* (Vienna, 1924), II, 67, 81ff.; and *Metternich – Der Dämon Österreichs* (Leipzig and Vienna, 1936), esp. 320ff.

price; they were equally determined to prevent even the discussion of existing conditions, lest such discussion serve to undermine them. Little wonder then that the revolutionaries of 1848, whether in the Habsburg Monarchy or in the German states, were, first of all, concerned with matters of political reform, especially with the establishment of effective guarantees of political freedom on the British and, more especially, the American model.[9]

Die Grenzboten was a product of those stifling *Vormärz* days. It commenced publication, as already noted, in Brussels in October 1841. Its founder and first editor was Ignaz Kuranda, a young Jewish liberal, himself born in Prague, whose steadfast courage and devotion to the cause of free discussion kept the magazine alive in the face of repeated Austrian, Prussian, and other conservative efforts to destroy it. It is perfectly clear how these governments felt about *Die Grenzboten*, or, for that matter, why they felt as they did. In Austria, where the government exercised the harshest and crudest form of censorship, it was long and repeatedly banned, and available only, with the greatest difficulty, in the restricted quarters of a few highly selected reading societies.[10] The Prussian government, for its part, even after the accession of the supposedly more enlightened Frederick William IV in 1840, first managed to force Kuranda's move from Brussels to Leipzig in 1842,[11] and then, when Kuranda came to Berlin for

9 The outstanding account of the mid-century revolutions in central Europe, their origins, course, and consequences, is now William L. Langer, *Political and Social Upheaval 1832–1852* (New York, 1969). On American politics as a constitutional model in 1848, cf. Eckhardt G. Franz, *Das Amerikabild der deutschen Revolution von 1848/49* (Heidelberg, 1958); Rudolf Ullner, *Die Idee des Föderalismus im Jahrzehnt der deutschen Einigungskriege, dargestellt unter besonderer Berücksichtigung des Modells der amerikanischen Verfassung für das deutsche politische Denken* (Lübeck and Hamburg, 1965); and Günter Moltmann, "Amerikanische Beiträge zur deutschen Verfassungsdiskussion 1848" and "Zwei amerikanische Beiträge zur deutschen Verfassungsdiskussion," *Jahrbuch für Amerikastudien*, XII (1967). A detailed study of the American impact on the central European revolutions has not yet been made, but see also Anton Ernstberger, "Charles Mackay und die Idee der Vereinigten Staaten von Europa im Jahre 1848," *Historische Zeitschrift*, CXLVI (1932), and Robert C. Binkley, "The Holy Roman Empire versus the United States – Patterns for Constitution Making in Central Europe," in Conyers Read, ed., *The Constitution Reconsidered* (New York, 1938).

10 D.G., 1847/II, 117. As R. John Rath has pointed out, *Die Grenzboten* "soon ... became the rallying point for the various opposition groups in the Habsburg monarchy, and its influence was tremendous" (*The Viennese Revolution of 1848* [Austin, 1957], 20). On the importance of the Viennese reading societies at this time, see Friedrich Engel-Janosi, "Der wiener juridisch-politische Leseverein – Seine Geschichte bis zur Märzrevolution," *Mitteilungen des Vereins für Geschichte der Stadt Wien*, IV (1923), and Minna R. Falk, "Alexander Bach and the *Leseverein* in the Viennese Revolution of 1848," *Journal of Central European Affairs*, VIII (1948). Even in southeastern Europe *Die Grenzboten* was then avidly read; cf. Josef Matl, "Weg und Wirkung der deutschen Sprache und Literatur in Südost- und Osteuropa," *Südostforschungen*, XXIII (1964), 312.

11 That Kuranda chose to settle in Leipzig where he remained for half a dozen years (he also took time out to get a doctorate in philosophy at the university there) was hardly

a brief visit in 1846, treated him with (even for Prussia) rare bureaucratic arbitrariness and forced him to leave the Prussian capital in short order.[12] Whatever the growing strength of liberal opinion in Germany's largest state, it was unmistakably clear then that its government was no more prepared than its Viennese counterpart to facilitate the work of liberal journalists within its borders.

Such obstacles, however, never seemed to discourage Kuranda. He exercised complete and effective control over his journal until the beginning of 1848, when the outbreak of revolution led him to devote most of his time and energy, first, to the organization and deliberations of the Frankfurt Assembly (to which he was elected from a Bohemian constituency), and later to developments in Vienna, which he rightly regarded as of crucial importance to the success of the whole central European revolution. During the first months of 1848, therefore, Kuranda began to share editorial direction of Die Grenzboten with two other rising liberal writers and critics, Gustav Freytag and Julian Schmidt, and in July 1848 the latter pair assumed full editorial control of the journal, with Kuranda remaining as occasional contributor.[13]

Although, like other formerly liberal German papers, Die Grenzboten became increasingly conservative and nationalist in its views after the 1870s,[14] it would be inaccurate to say that there was a noticeable change once the editorship had passed from Kuranda's hands. The dominant note of Die Grenzboten had always been liberal-constitutional rather than social-radical. Its primary concern had always been with practical political and cultural problems as against more purely theoretical or speculative questions. Nor did Kuranda's resignation of the

---

surprising, for that Saxon city, close to the Bohemian border, was well known for its rather liberal censorship regulations, and was also rapidly becoming an important centre of Slavic scholarship and publication. Thus the Lusatian Serb Jan Pětr Jordan, a slavicist at the University of Leipzig, published his *Jahrbücher für slavische Literatur, Kunst und Wissenschaft* there from 1843 to 1848, and the leading Slav publishing house of Ernst Keil & Company was also located in the city. Cf. Josef Pfitzner, "Die grenz- und auslandsdeutsche Bewegung des Jahres 1848," *Historische Zeitschrift*, CLX (1939), 318ff., and Eberhard Wolfgramm, "Die Rolle der Universität Leipzig bei der nationalen Wiedergeburt der slawischen Völker besonders in der Periode des Vormärz," *Karl Marx Universität Leipzig 1409–1959 – Beiträge zur Universitätsgeschichte*, I (Leipzig, 1959).

12 D.G., 1846/III, 501ff., 543ff.

13 *Ibid.*, 1848/III, 1ff.

14 For Freytag's interesting account of his editorship of Die Grenzboten, which he held (alone or with others) until 1870, see his *Erinnerungen aus meinem Leben* (Leipzig, 1887), chap. ix, and Hans Lindau, *Gustav Freytag* (Leipzig, 1907), chaps. vi–xii, neither of which, unfortunately, devotes much attention to his attitude toward the Habsburg Monarchy and its nationality problems. Although in later years Freytag was inclined to disparage the political wisdom and insight of his *Grenzboten* years (cf. for instance [Hermance Strakosch-Freytag, ed.] *Gustav Freytag Briefe an seine Gattin* [Berlin, 1912], 39, 40, 43), in his memoirs he rightly put great emphasis on Die Grenzboten's increasingly outspoken *kleindeutsch* position after mid-1848, for which he was largely responsible, including the advice to the Habsburg government to reach a just and lasting settlement with its constituent nationalities.

editorship lead to a declining interest in Austrian – and especially Bohemian – affairs.

It was hardly surprising that *Die Grenzboten* should have devoted considerable attention to such matters in the first place. Ignaz Kuranda was a quite remarkable young man.[15] He was born in Prague on 8 May 1811. About his family background not much is known. His father owned a modest second-hand bookshop. Ignaz first attended school in Prague, and in 1834 went to Vienna, where he studied philosophy at the university, and began his literary career as drama critic for the *Telegraph*, and also wrote a play of his own, *Die letzte weisse Rose* (The Last White Rose), based on an unfinished Schiller text. The Viennese Court Theatre, however, refused to produce the play for fear of possible conflict with the censor, but it was soon produced in Stuttgart, Karlsruhe, and Frankfurt. In 1838 Kuranda himself moved for a time to Stuttgart and then to Tübingen, where he studied history and literature and also met some of Germany's leading young liberal and radical writers and philosophers, including Robert Mohl and David Friedrich Strauss. In 1839 he journeyed briefly to Paris, and the following year he moved to Brussels, where the comparative freedom of the Belgian *charte* seemed to offer the best possible opportunity for the liberal political journal he was planning to publish.[16]

Although Kuranda – who lived a long and fruitful life, and died a much honoured man, in Vienna, on 3 April 1884[17] – spent few of his later years in his native Bohemia, his Prague background stamped his new journal from the beginning. It reported as did no other publication of the day the course of politics and society in his native land. Hardly a month passed without one or more lengthy reports from his several correspondents there; and the Viennese authorities were doubtless all the more concerned since Kuranda's correspondents

15 No detailed study of Kuranda, his life and work, exists. For brief biographical sketches, see Constantin von Wurzbach, *Biographisches Lexicon des Kaiserthums Oesterreich*, XII (Vienna, 1865), and *Allgemeine deutsche Biographie*, LI (Leipzig, 1906). The important new work of Stanley Z. Pech, *The Czech Revolution of 1848* (Chapel Hill, 1969) makes only passing reference to Kuranda. Hugo Hantsch, *Die Nationalitätenfrage im alten Österreich – Das Problem der konstructiven Reichsgestaltung* (Vienna, 1953), and Karl Eder, *Der Liberalismus in Altösterreich – Geisteshaltung, Politik und Kultur* (Vienna and Munich, 1955), say nothing about Kuranda or *Die Grenzboten* and relegate the mid-century nationality problem to a few routine paragraphs. Georg Franz, *Liberalismus – Die deutschliberale Bewegung in der habsburgischen Monarchie* (Munich, 1955), adds a few interesting details on what he calls "Young Austria," together with a plethora of anti-Czech remarks and a few anti-Semitic overtones that betray the 1942–3 origins of the work. Most suggestive for the intellectual background of Kuranda is Adam Wandruska, "Die Männer von 1848 – Die Zwiespalt im österreichischen Liberalismus," *Wort und Wahrheit*, II (1947).

16 For Kuranda's autobiographical account of his earlier career, see D.G., 1845/I, 345ff.

17 Kuranda's later career included extended membership in the Landtag of Lower Austria and the Austrian House of Representatives, in whose deliberations he participated with great vigour and distinction until a few weeks before his death.

included such leading liberal aristocrats as Count Friedrich Deym, Baron Dobblhoff, and Freiherr von Stift, not to mention that *Die Grenzboten* also soon began to publish the prose and poetry of such rising Bohemian writers as Moritz Hartmann, Uffo Horn, Alfred Meissner, and Josef Rank who in 1845, for instance, contributed a shattering account of his imprisonment in Prague.[18]

In his important work *The Age of the Democratic Revolution*, R. R. Palmer has pointed out that one of the great weaknesses of the *ancien régime* was its great (and frequently unnecessary) penchant for secrecy concerning public and governmental affairs.[19] In the case of the Habsburg Monarchy in the 1840s, however, there was doubtless good reason for such secrecy, and though for much of the time *Die Grenzboten's* reports from Prague and other parts of Bohemia consisted mostly of straightforward accounts of conditions obviously known to local residents, it is not difficult to understand why even such prosaic and circumspect reports chagrined and embarrassed the Viennese authorities, and led them to do almost everything possible to discourage and obstruct circulation of the journal.[20]

The fact of the matter is that in the 1840s Bohemia was, for a number of reasons, in a distinctly pre-revolutionary situation. To begin with, there were growing (mainly German) aristocratic demands for political liberalization, aiming in the first place at a meaningful restoration of the moribund provincial estates (concerning these demands, which it reported at length, *Die Grenzboten*, with its strong Josephinist overtones, had distinct reservations).[21] Secondly, there was increasingly widespread disaffection with the government's evident inability to provide effective leadership in the realm of economic and social policy and

18 On Hartmann, for instance, see also D.G., 1845/I, 128ff.; 1846/I, 80ff.; and 1847/III, 36–7.
19 R. R. Palmer, *The Age of the Democratic Revolution – A Political History of Europe and America, 1760–1800* (Princeton, 1959), I, 86–7. Cf. also D.G., 1847/III, 230. As late as February 1847 the *Kölnische Zeitung*, the leading voice of Rhenish Prussian liberalism, was still banned in Austria, although it should be added that, on the whole, censorship in Prague was probably milder than in Vienna. See D.G., 1845/III, 275ff., and 1846/I, 118.
20 "Secrecy is Austria's hereditary disease," *Die Grenzboten* observed in 1846 (II, 444), "and every concession which it makes in that respect is a significant step forward, since what is most lacking is the knowledge of things required to discuss affairs with success and precision."
21 It should be noted that, *pro forma* at least, the Bohemian estates had never completely lost their powers even in the dark days following 1620. But their remaining prerogatives, formally reaffirmed by royal edict in 1627, lay largely dormant until 1845 when the estates began to demand such things as additional representation for the towns, closer control over budgetary matters, and introduction of Czech into the higher schools. Since even in the 1840s, however, the Bohemian aristocracy was still largely German, it would be difficult to discern a distinctly Czech nationalist motive behind such demands. On the other hand, the estates were doubtless well aware of the increasing national consciousness and restlessness among the Czech population, and were increasingly prepared to exploit such feeling for their own purposes. Cf. D.G., 1846/I, 131ff.; 1846/II, 8ff.; 1846/III, 67; 1847/II, 223; 1847/IV, 347ff.; as well as Anton Springer, *Geschichte Oesterreichs seit dem wiener Frieden 1809* (Leipzig, 1863), I, 509ff., and Ernest Denis, *La Bohême depuis la Montagne-*

development (disaffection which, it appears, also came largely from German-speaking circles).[22] And, finally, there was also a significant rise in Czech national consciousness, reflected for instance in the growing activity of such native institutions as the National Museum, the Royal Bohemian Society of Sciences, the appearance of Palacký's pathbreaking "History of Bohemia,"[23] and the publication of important literary works by some of the outstanding Czech scholars and writers of the day, including Josef Jungmann (d. 1847), František Ladislav Čelakovský (d. 1852), Jan Kollár (d. 1852), Josef Kajetán Tyl (d. 1856), and Pavel Josef Šafařík (d. 1861).

Blanche (Paris, 1903), II, chaps. i, iii. Perhaps it would be most accurate to say that in the pre-revolutionary atmosphere of the 1840s the (largely German) nobility in Bohemia and the (slowly but increasingly Czech) middle and upper-middle classes reached something of an informal political and intellectual understanding – a relationship which, however, came quickly apart in the revolution of 1848, contributing significantly to the failure of the revolution. Cf. Friedrich Prinz, "František Palacký als Historiograph der böhmischen Stände," *Probleme der böhmischen Geschichte* (Munich, 1964), 89ff., esp. 92. It seems worth noting that *Die Grenzboten* observed reformist tendencies in Prussia, though largely muted since the great days of Stein and Hardenberg, with rapt attention and no little envy. On the other hand, it viewed the revival of the Bohemian estates – weak, divided, ineffectual, and apparently largely the spokesman of special class privilege – with considerable scepticism. Cf. D.G., 1845/II, 578; 1846/IV, 191; 1857/I, 300, 349ff. On the revival of the *Vormärz* estates, their membership, and debates see also Bibl, *Die niederösterreichischen Stände im Vormärz*, 308ff.

22 If, statistically speaking, it would seem that the Austrian economy had been performing fairly well, this is not how many contemporaries viewed the situation. Cf. D.G., 1845/I, 470ff.; 1845/II, 188ff., 578ff. "Anyone travelling through Bohemia now," reported a *Grenzboten* correspondent, "might think he was back in the aftermath of the Thirty Years' War" (*ibid.*, 1847/I, 188). On the government's wavering course concerning abolition of the hated labour services (the *robota*), cf. *ibid.*, 1847/I, 44, and 1847/II, 202–3, all of which should be compared with the valuable studies of Jerome Blum, "Transportation and Industry in Austria 1815–1848," *Journal of Modern History*, xv (1943), and *Noble Landowners and Agriculture in Austria, 1815–1848* (Baltimore, 1948), esp. 87–90, 199–200, 215ff., 224, 230ff., 243–6. How little even a dedicated Habsburg civil servant could accomplish in the way of economic and social improvement is made clear, *inter alia*, by the sympathetic study of Christoph Thienen-Adlerflycht, *Graf Leo Thun im Vormärz – Grundlagen des böhmischen Konservatismus im Kaisertum Österreichs* (Graz and Vienna, 1967), esp. 153ff.; but just how much work needed badly to be done is shown by the important study of Julius Marx, *Die wirtschaftlichen Ursachen der Revolution von 1848 in Österreich* (Vienna, 1965).

23 Palacký's "History of Bohemia" had first appeared in a German, censorship-abridged, edition between 1836 and 1867. An edition in Czech appeared between 1848 and 1867. When the fifth and last volume (apart from two supplementary sections published in 1870 and 1876) of Palacký's appeared in 1867, G. H. Pertz, the famous German mediaevalist, wrote to him: "Accept my heartiest congratulations on the completion of your great patriotic work. *Exegi monumentum sere perennius* is your immortal slogan." (Quoted in Hans Raupach, *Der tschechische Frühnationalismus* [Essen, 1939], 149). More recent German scholarship has adopted a less generous atttitude toward Palacký's work; cf. Kurt Oberdorffer, "Der Verein für Geschichte der Deutschen in Böhmen 1862–1938," *Bohemia*, III (1962), 9ff. For Palacký the historian and the Czech renascence, see the essay by F. G. Heymann below.

It is important to note that, of all these developments, *Die Grenzboten* significantly – and, as events were seen to show, rather fatefully – took the least notice of those within the Czech community. The most important of such developments was the growing separation of the Czech and German cultural consciousness and community that had been an increasingly important aspect of the Bohemian scene since Joseph II, and which continued apace at the very time when it was most desirable to move toward a much closer understanding and relationship between German and Czech cultural, social, and political interests. What produced such comparative disinterest on the part of *Die Grenzboten?* Was it rising German national consciousness on the part of Kuranda himself? In the light of subsequent events, that seems rather difficult to believe.[24] Was it due to the fact that most, perhaps all, of his Bohemian correspondents were Germans? Perhaps that had more to do with it. In any case, *Die Grenzboten's* probably unconscious selectivity in reporting Bohemian developments augured ill for the future. For, not the least reason for the fateful Czech-German crisis of 1848 was that the Germans, in particular, had not been prepared, and had not prepared themselves, for what lay ahead in Bohemia.[25]

On the other hand, it seems fair to say that *Die Grenzboten* was unsparing in

24 It seems clear that most German liberals and intellectuals had little interest in Bohemian history and politics before 1848 (a notable exception is the article on Bohemia in the Rotteck-Welcker *Staats-Lexicon* [Altona, 1848]), x, 389ff., and few German historians ever showed much interest in Czech history before the First World War (cf. the bibliography of Harald Bachmann, *Adolf Bachmann – Ein österreichischer Historiker und Politiker* [Munich, 1962]). "The Austrian share in writing the history of other nationalities was comparatively small," Alfons Lhotsky has written. The Slavs, among others, "have taken care of themselves, even in German." (*Österreichische Historiographie* [Vienna, 1962], 217.) What Lhotsky wrote about the Austrians applies, by and large, also to the Germans. It seems not to have occurred to him however, much less yet does he ask, what such indifference – or hostility and condescension in works that were published – meant to the Slavic intellectual elite, who were surely aware of such sentiments and their symbolic significance.

25 One exception, evidently, was Kuranda, who continued to travel and to correspond widely throughout the 1840s. His correspondence remains uncollected, but the following letter, sent to an unidentified friend from Dresden in March 1847, is further evidence of his continuing search for a lasting Czech-German accommodation. He was, he wrote, looking forward to his next trip to southern France, two months hence, and especially to his journey to Provence. Kuranda continued: "I am much less drawn to Provence – please do not look down at me – because of its burning sky and the poetic survivals of the old troubadors, than for reasons of political study, pertaining to my old fatherland; I want personally to learn the means by which France has overcome the linguistic differences of its provinces ... Provence is richer in literary and national monuments than Bohemia and other Slavic-German provinces. Why has the linguistic debate become extinguished there, and why has it flared up here? Or has it not turned to ashes there either? Or has France got magic means? And how might these be used by us?" Othmar Feyl, "Unveröffentlichte Bohemica der Vormärzzeit und verwandte Briefe aus der Universitätsbibliothek Jena," *Jahrbuch für Geschichte der deutsch-slawischen Beziehungen und Geschichte Ost- und Mitteleuropas,* II (1958), 388–9.

its comments on non-Czech problems and developments, and anyone reading its weekly reports must have wondered just how much longer the current state of affairs could go on unchallenged. Moreover, *Die Grenzboten* did not, as might have been expected from its predominantly middle-class orientation, limit itself largely to political or constitutional issues. Thus from early 1845 on, for instance, it published regular reports from Prague (as well as Vienna) on such subjects as growing industrial unrest in Bohemia (the aftermath of the 1844 disorders[26]), Austrian technological backwardness and economic isolation from Germany proper[27] (*Die Grenzboten* watched the *Zollverein*'s development with due appreciation of its economic and political possibilities[28]), and the government's evident inability to handle urgent problems of flood control and railroad construction.[29] Repeatedly, *Die Grenzboten* drew attention to continuing unemployment in Bohemia, to the lagging cause of land and social reform there since Joseph II (*Die Grenzboten* being strongly Josephinist throughout this period), to the government's failure to provide adequate credit for economic development, or its inability to cope with the almost continual rise in food prices that was one of the main causes of popular unrest in Bohemia as it was elsewhere in Austria and Germany.[30]

This is not to say, however, that *Die Grenzboten* was wholly oblivious to the growing national problem in Bohemia. To be sure, in some ways Bohemia seemed somewhat better off than Vienna or Lower Austria generally. For instance, despite Josef Rank's flagrant imprisonment in 1844[31] – an action that caused a national scandal and was widely publicized by *Die Grenzboten*[32] – censorship in Prague, on the whole, was probably more lenient than it was in Vienna. It was easier even to obtain a copy of *Die Grenzboten* in Prague, and since the Austrian authorities did not yet sense the dangerous implications of the Czech renascence, no overt action was taken against the leading Czech writers

26 On the industrial disorders and their aftermath, see D.G., 1845/I, 470ff.; Friedrich Walter, "Die böhmischer Arbeiterunruhen des Jahres 1844," *Mitteilungen des Instituts für österreichische Geschichtsforschung*, Supplement XI (1929); Eberhard Wolfgramm, "Der böhmische Vormärz, im besonderen die böhmischen Arbeiterunruhen des Jahres 1844 in ihren sozialen und politischen Zusammenhängen," in Karl Obermann and Josef Polišenský, eds., *Aus 500 Jahren deutschtschechoslowakischer Geschichte* (Berlin, 1958), 199ff.; Ernest Paul, "Industrialisierung und soziale Frage in den böhmischen Ländern," *Bohemia*, II (1961); Rudolf Wierer, "Das nationale Problem in den Anfängen der tschechischen Arbeiterbewegung," *ibid.*, III (1962); and Julius Marx, *Die wirtschaftlichen Ursachen* ... , 57ff.
27 D.G., 1845/III, 548ff.
28 *Ibid.*, 1845/I, 21, 600ff.; 1845/III, 533ff.; 1846/I, 3ff.; 1846/II, 264ff.
29 *Ibid.*, 1845/I, 600ff.; 1845/II, 188ff.; 1847/IV, 546ff.
30 *Ibid.*, 1847/III, 124ff., 160ff.
31 Anton Ernstberger, "Josef Rank in Zensurhaft Prag 1844," *Festschrift für Erich Gierach* (Prague, 1942); reprinted in Ernstberger, *Franken-Böhmen-Europa* (Erlangen, 1959).
32 Rank published a deeply moving account of his imprisonment in *Die Grenzboten*, 1845/IV, 158ff.

and intellectuals on account of their nationalist leanings.[33] Still, the sources of Czech disaffection were numerous enough, including rampant clericalism, bureaucratic stagnation, and a hopelessly stymied land reform.[34] For decades, the imperial motto had appeared to be "Ich brauch keine Gelehrten, ich brauch nur gute Unterthanen" (I don't need scholars, I only need loyal subjects).[35] Now Czechs as well as Germans found that patronizing attitude increasingly intolerable.

Die Grenzboten reported such conditions and sentiments, for the most part, in a straightforward and unxenophobic manner. But here and there the first signs of growing Czech-German hostility and conflict were beginning to appear. There was resentment, for instance, at the government's more liberal treatment of the Czech as against the German press. There were some indications of developing linguistic conflicts between the two peoples, and there was increasing criticism of Czech linguistic nationalism, and of what *Die Grenzboten's* correspondents regarded as unwise government concessions to such nationalism.[36] On several occasions, *Die Grenzboten* published reports on growing anti-Semitism among the Czech population, about the distribution of anti-Jewish pamphlets, and on government efforts to improve conditions in the Jewish ghetto in Prague (efforts, which, so *Die Grenzboten's* reports suggested, met with little favour on the part of many Czech nationalists).[37]

Did the Czechs, in those increasingly agitated times, already hope for restoration of their old political independence? *Die Grenzboten's* reports include no evidence to that effect. On the contrary, as early as the fall of 1847, *Die Grenzboten* noted that, given their numerical strength in the Habsburg Monarchy, the interests of the Slav and Magyar peoples would best be served by a policy of Austro-Slavism. *Die Grenzboten* left little doubt that *that* was not its own preferred vision of the Habsburg future.[38]

THE CRUCIAL MONTHS

Had Kuranda and his journal foreseen the revolutionary shape of things to come? For all the critical reports on the Habsburg state that had appeared in *Die Grenzboten* before February 1848, it seems highly unlikely; and when the sudden overthrow of the Orleanist regime in France led to the rapid appearance of revolutionary outbreaks throughout Germany and Austria,[39] Kuranda and his

33 *Ibid.*, 1846/I, 356.

34 *Ibid.*, 1845/II, 76ff.; 1845/III, 132; 1847/IV, 258ff.

35 *Ibid.*, 1846/III, 304.

36 *Ibid.*, 1846/I, 114ff., 323ff., 379ff., 431ff., 499ff.; 1845/II, 579. See also Pech, *Czech Revolution of 1848*, 90ff.

37 *Ibid.*, 1846/IV, 262ff., 300ff., 375ff.; 1847/I, 297, 535ff.; 1847/II, 494ff.

38 *Ibid.*, 1847/IV, 75ff.

39 On the inner history of the Bohemian revolution, see – in addition to the older standard works of Anton Springer and Ernest Denis, cited above, and of Josef Redlich, *Das österreichische Staats- und Reichsproblem – Geschichtliche Darstellung der inneren Politik*

correspondents seemed as uncertain as everyone else as to what to propose next.[40]

Hardly had Metternich resigned and fled, in disguise, to England, than Kuranda himself returned to Vienna. But his stay there was not to be protracted. A few weeks later he was one of seven Austrian liberals selected as members of the Austrian delegation to the Frankfurt Vorparlament, and for the next six months or so, Kuranda was to devote himself mostly to German or Central European rather than purely Austrian or Bohemian affairs.[41]

Nevertheless his considerable activities in that regard deserve more than passing notice, for – despite the growing Czech-German antagonism that was soon to break out into the open in Bohemia – Kuranda sought, during the next few months, to bring about a generous reconciliation between the nations and peoples of central Europe, a lasting settlement which would allow them all a truly free and suitably autonomous development. Since the late Sir Lewis Namier, in his distinctly one-sided, yet widely accepted account of German-Slavic relations in 1848,[42] did so much to launch a new legend of German liberal and revolutionary

der Habsburgischen Monarchie von 1848 bis zum Untergang des Reiches, I: Der dynastische Reichsgedanke und die Entfaltung des Problems bis zur Verkündigung der Reichsverfassung von 1861 (Leipzig, 1920), esp. 135–88 – also the following more recent studies: Karl Hugelmann, "Die österreichischen Landtage im Jahre 1848" (part III), Archiv für österreichische Geschichte, cxv (1940); J. J. Udalzov [Udaltsev], Aufzeichnungen über die Geschichte des nationalen und politischen Kampfes in Böhmen im Jahre 1848 (Berlin, 1953); Karl Kreibich, Die Deutschen und die böhmische Revolution 1848 (Berlin, 1958); Friedrich Prinz, Hans Kudlich (1823–1917) – Versuch einer historisch-politischen Biographie (Munich, 1962); Peter Burian, Die Nationalitäten in "Cisleithänien" und das Wahlrecht der Märzrevolution 1848/49 – Zur Problematik des Parlamentarismus im alten Österreich (Graz and Cologne, 1962); Friedrich Walter, Die österreichische Zentralverwaltung, part III: Von der Märzrevolution 1848 bis zur Dezemberverfassung 1867, I, II (Vienna, 1964), and his essay "Die 'Böhmische Charte' vom April 8, 1848," in Beiträge zum deutsch-tschechischen Verhältnis im 19. und 20. Jahrhundert (Munich, 1967); and Ernst Karl Sieber, Ludwig von Löhner – Ein Vorkämpfer des Deutschtums in Böhmen, Mähren und Schlesien 1848/49 (Munich, 1965); Friedrich Prinz, "Die böhmischen Länder von 1848 bis 1914," in Karl Bosl, ed., Handbuch der Geschichte der böhmischen Länder, III (Stuttgart, 1968); the superb analysis of Langer, Political and Social Upheaval, and the important work of Pech, Czech Revolution of 1848, both cited above.

40 Cf. the interesting essay "Die neuen Anforderungen des deutschen Liberalismus," D.G., 1848/I, 455–6, 466–7. For a more detailed constitutional programme for Austria – whose avowed purpose was to conciliate and compromise the desires of "diverse and hostile nationalities," and which included such features as a single-house legislature, fully responsible government, revitalized estates with added middle-class representation, and freedom of religion and the press – see ibid., 499ff.

41 Allgemeine deutsche Biographie, LI, 447.

42 Sir Lewis Namier, 1848 – The Revolution of the Intellectuals ("Transactions of the Royal Academy," xxx [London, 1944]), esp. 258ff. Namier, it should be noted, was also quite critical of the Czech leadership. "Palacký and Šafařík," he wrote, "were great savants, of outstanding merit in their services to the Czech revival, but timid politicians" (p. 263). Not surprisingly, Namier's views have been generally approved by such anti-liberal German historians as Hans Rothfels (cf. his comments in Journal of Modern History, xix [1947], 167–9).

xenophobia, it seems especially desirable to draw attention to Kuranda's persistent efforts to prevent a fatal split between the German and Slavic peoples.[43]

Thus as early as mid-April 1848, Kuranda pleaded with the members of the Frankfurt Vorparlament, saying: "we wish, in the German constitution, to declare the maintenance and respect of foreign nationalities and hereby set an example to the world of humanity and higher constitutional law,"[44] and he vigorously supported a motion made by Victor von Andrian-Werburg, the famous aristocratic critic of the Metternich regime,[45] that it "be one of the first tasks of the National Assembly legally to recognize the inviolability of all nationalities on German soil." Indeed, it was Kuranda who first suggested to the Vorparlament that it invite Palacký to come to Frankfurt to take part in its deliberations – the invitation which Palacký subsequently declined in his famous letter of 11 April.[46]

Palacký's letter did not, however, end the matter. Soon after, the Vorparlament delegated Kuranda and two other members to travel to Prague, to persuade Palacký to change his mind. By the time Kuranda reached the Bohemian capital the situation there was, however, beyond negotiation. Czech-German street clashes were becoming a regular occurrence, and the Czechs – who had already twice asked Vienna for authority to elect their own assembly[47] – seemed deter-

43 Cf. D.G., 1848/I, 528–9, and Friedrich Prinz, "Die Sudetendeutschen im frankfurter Parlament," *Zwischen Frankfurt und Prag* (Munich, 1963), 103ff. Since recent Marxist scholarship has made much of the alleged social and philosophical differences and dissensions in the Czech ranks – the rally at the St. Wenceslas (St Václav) Baths being a good example – it should be said that *Die Grenzboten* contains almost nothing on this point. Its correspondents and editors either saw no such divisions, or thought them unimportant in the over-all scheme of things, or in any case of no particular interest to their readers.

44 Quoted in *Allgemeine deutsche Biographie*, LI, 447.

45 D.G., 1847/I, 517. In 1845–7 *Die Grenzboten* had devoted considerable space to Victor von Andrian Werburg's (anonymously published) two-volume work *Österreich und dessen Zukunft* (Austria and Its Future), which the Austrian government was making strenuous efforts to suppress, but about which – because of the work's strong aristocratic overtones – *Die Grenzboten* had considerable reservations of its own. Cf. D.G., 1845/II, 579; 1846/II, 235ff.; 1846/III, 349; 1847/I, 297, 399ff., 516ff., 558. See also Bibl, *Die niederösterreichischen Stände im Vormärz*, 279ff.

46 "The rulers of our people," Palacký wrote in his letter, "have for centuries participated in the Federation of the German Princes, but the people never looked upon itself as part of the German nation ... When I direct my view beyond the frontiers of Bohemia ... I turn it not towards Frankfurt but towards Vienna ... Indeed, if the Austrian Empire did not exist, it would, in the interest of Europe, no, of humanity, be necessary to make haste and create it." A complete translation (by William Beardmore) of Palacký's letter appears in *The Slavonic and East European Review*, XXVI (1948).

47 R. W. Seton-Watson, *A History of the Czechs and Slovaks* (New York, 1943), 185ff.; and D.G., 1848/I, 604ff. "Today," *Die Grenzboten* reported prophetically from Prague on 28 March, when the first deputation returned from Vienna with some of its principal demands unmet, "is an important turning point in Bohemian history." Especially enraged were the Prague University students, who had sent a delegation of their own, along with that of the citizenry, asking that the university's course of study be completely modernized and that universities on the latest German model be introduced in Bohemia. This student deputation

mined not to permit elections for the Frankfurt assembly to be held in Bohemia.[48] A mass meeting that Kuranda was to address on the subject of Slav relations with the Frankfurt assembly was broken up by the Czech National Guard. Kuranda and Palacký did meet to discuss the situation several times, but nothing came of their talks, and in mid-July Kuranda had to report back to the Frankfurt assembly that his mission to Prague had failed.[49]

In May 1848 Kuranda was elected a member of the Frankfurt Parliament from a German-speaking district in Bohemia, and he spent part of the summer in Frankfurt, seeking vainly to interject a note of conciliation into its increasingly acerbic and fruitless discussions of nationality problems. But Kuranda's efforts proved largely unsuccessful, and perhaps his heart was never in those parliamentary struggles and manoeuvres in any case. Be that as it may, in September he returned to Vienna, and having meanwhile, as already noted, given up editorial direction of *Die Grenzboten*, in October he launched a new journalistic venture, a daily newspaper named *Ostdeutsche Post* (East German Mail), which soon became a leading voice of liberal political and social reform, and – save for interruptions by counter-revolutionary suspensions – soon achieved an honourable record of trying to advance the cause of constitutional and national equality within the Habsburg Monarchy.[50]

In short, the tragic events of the summer had not at all diminished Kuranda's abiding faith and confidence in the universal applicability of human freedom and national autonomy. Accordingly, this is how he summed up his political creed in the first issue of the *Ostdeutsche Post*. He was, he wrote there, a strong supporter of constitutional monarchy on the broadest possible democratic base. The concept of freedom and nationality must, in Austria, be synonymous. He now

---

returned completely empty-handed. Thus began the dangerous polarization of Czech-German opinion in Prague. The Czechs began to accuse the Viennese government of "selling them out to the Germans," while the Germans in Prague (as one report to *Die Grenzboten* put it) believed that "the government in Vienna is in Slavic hands; the Habsburgs, who don't care that they are German princes (?) as long as they are princes at all – whether on a Czech or West Slavic throne – have a special tenderness for the Czechs" (*ibid.*, 1848/II, 199).

48 For the Czechs' refusal to permit elections to the Frankfurt Parliament to be held on Bohemian soil, cf. *ibid.*, 1848/II, 146ff., 179ff., 199. See also Ottokar Weber, "Die prager Revolution 1848 und das frankfurter Parlament," *Festschrift des Vereins für Geschichte der Deutschen in Böhmen* (1902), and Josef Pfitzner, "Die Wahlen in die frankfurter Nationalversammlung und der Sudetenraum," *Mitteilungen des Vereins für Geschichte der Deutschen in Böhmen*, LXXIX (1942).

49 Prinz, *Hans Kudlich*, 110ff. See also D.G., 1848/II, 199; and Pech, *Czech Revolution of 1848*, 92ff.

50 It is interesting to note that the biographical sketch of Kuranda that appeared in the Austrian biographical dictionary, published in Vienna in 1865, makes no mention of these suspensions, but that they are frankly discussed in the account of his career in the *Allgemeine deutsche Biographie*, published in Leipzig in 1906 (pp. 448–9).

opposed – as Palacký had always opposed – the merger of Austria into a new German state. To be sure, he stated, "Austria – the real Austria – has always been German and must remain German for all time," but, he added, "there was very serious question whether we are not of more use to the great German fatherland by bringing to it the combined military and economic power of 30 million allied Slavs, Magyars, Poles, Italians, Wallachians, and Germans."[51]

By October 1848 such hopes of Slavic-German cooperation, on a free and liberal basis, must have seemed very unpromising even to Ignaz Kuranda, and some of the principal reasons for the failure of his hopes and expectations may be gleaned from a closer look at the journal that he left behind, and at how *Die Grenzboten* viewed developments in Bohemia – and Bohemian affairs in the larger perspective of Austrian and central European affairs – during 1848 and 1849.

THE DEFEAT OF LIBERAL NATIONALISM

Perhaps the first point to be made concerning *Die Grenzboten*'s correspondence and commentary on Bohemian developments during these revolutionary years is that *Die Grenzboten* had already, some years before, noted the increased tempo of Czech national activity. "The Czechs," it had reported as early as April 1845, "labour incessantly for the development of all causes that may advance their nationality."[52] And in an important article, entitled "Austria and Its Unity," published in November 1847, it had once more drawn the attention of its readers to Bohemia's strategic place in Austria's past and present:

Bohemia had either to conquer Austria, at which task [Přemysl] Otakar [II] had failed, or it had, sooner or later, to become Austrian; since, for Bohemia, Austria was, of all its neighbours, the most dangerous, no less than the richest and the most attractive – for Austria, however, Bohemia and Moravia were a prerequisite for its consolidation and its rounding-off, especially when Hungary was also taken into account.[53]

To be sure, *Die Grenzboten*'s correspondents probably underestimated the growing significance of Czech cultural nationalism – just as the Viennese authorities seemed largely oblivious to its various manifestations during the 1840s – and so, when revolutionary disorders first broke out in Prague in early March

---

51 *Ibid.*, 448. Kuranda's liberal national ambivalence suffused the whole editorial. "The German nationality is the pillar of freedom in Austria," Kuranda wrote, "not only for us Germans, but also for our non-German political comrades [*Staatsgenossen*], the surest guarantee against the resurgence of absolutism." But if there was the slightest danger to the German nationality, or of the monarchy's falling into Slavic hands, "then the monarchy might as well go to pieces, and it would be our most sacred duty to do as the Italians and Croats have done against their oppressors ... Austria, the real Austria, has always been German, and must remain so for all time."
52 D.G., 1845/II, 78.
53 *Ibid.*, 1847/IV, 495.

1848, *Die Grenzboten* appeared rather hopeful that German-Czech amity could be maintained.[54] These hopes, however, proved rather short-lived, and by the end of March, *Die Grenzboten* published the first of a long and increasingly intemperate series of dispatches strongly suggesting that Czech and German national interests were indeed far from synonymous.[55]

If the editors of *Die Grenzboten*, like most of their countrymen, seemed at this stage of the revolution rather uncertain as to what kind of new Germany they wished to see come into being, they had little doubt as to what sort of Austria or Bohemia they did *not* wish to see.[56] The Czechs, for their part, were making no secret of the fact that they had no desire to see Bohemia included in any Greater German state. On the contrary, they now began vigorously to press their policy of Austro-Slavism, a course of action which the Bohemian Germans (including *Die Grenzboten's* correspondents in Bohemia) considered to be little more than a thinly veiled cover for a "Slavic Austria," which was entirely unacceptable to them.[57] Thus *Die Grenzboten* began to describe in increasingly lurid

54 *Ibid.*, 1848/ɪ, 513ff., 559ff., 602ff. "Austria has risen!," Franz Schuselka wrote from Hamburg under the headline "New Austria," on 16 March 1848. "Yes, Unity in Freedom. Universal Forgetting and Forgiveness, a brotherly League of Nations! [The inhuman policy] has collapsed, and joyfully the Germans, Hungarians, Slavs, and Italians join hands for the great work of political and human deliverance. No other conflict shall henceforth exist among us than noble competition for the good, the beautiful, the great. We shall have the same goal, freedom; we all have the same enemy, tyranny ..." *Ibid.*, 548–9.

55 *Ibid.*, 1848/ɪ, 557ff.; 1848/ɪɪ, 75ff. See also, however, *Die Grenzboten's* increasingly anti-Slavic tone already some weeks earlier (esp. 1848/ɪ, 378); indeed, as early as the spring of 1846 it had passed on to its readers indication of growing tensions between Czechs and Germans in Bohemia, as for instance in an article on "The Czech National Ball," which, interestingly, the *Prager Zeitung* had refused to publish. "A large part of those whose mother tongue is Czech," this article declared, "or who for other reasons devote themselves to the advancement of this language, look with pride and hostility beyond their German-speaking and German-educated fellow-citizen, who shares with them joy and sorrow, law and government, toward those millions who, although geographically and politically separate, speak a language akin to their own. This part, this party wishes to appear as a nation, to act like a nation within a nation ... [but] overlooks the practical requirements of nationality, which unite them with the German-Bohemians living in the same country, and it seeks to make the German Bohemians into strangers in their own country, where, like their Czech brethren, they have lived for centuries and [which they have] likewise defended with their blood and decorated and elevated with their diligence and intelligence. But we shall not give way without a struggle. We close, however, with confidence in a peaceful understanding, whose assurance is the sound noble sense of our Czech fellow-citizens, whom we well know how to differentiate from ... certain activists and misguided men." D.G., 1846/ɪ, 433ff. See also *ibid.*, 1846/ɪᴠ, 560; 1847/ɪ, 130; 1847/ɪᴠ, 405; and 1848/ɪ, 165ff.

56 *Ibid.*, 1848/ɪ, 566ff.; 1848/ɪɪ, 83ff.

57 *Ibid.*, 1848/ɪɪ, 135ff. "It is possible to criticize the concept of Austro-Slavism from the vantage point of the present, but it is not easy to question it as a policy for 1848 ... On the evidence then available, Austro-Slavism was the [Czech's] only realistic policy" (Pech, *Czech Revolution of 1848*, 339).

and hostile tones such manifestations of Czech nationalism as the famous gathering at St. Wenceslas baths in mid-March.[58] By early April *Die Grenzboten* was contending that the Slavs were openly getting the better of the government in Vienna, and declared that the reported plan to appoint Palacký a minister of the crown was a national affront, and announced that the appalling weakness of the authorities in Bohemia – for instance, in allowing the Czechs to interfere with the election of representatives to the Frankfurt Parliament (only three people reportedly showed up to vote for such delegates in Prague!) – only sowed the seeds of future civil war.[59]

In the light of such stiffening national attitudes, it was hardly surprising that *Die Grenzboten* reported all manifestations of Czech national sentiment and activities in increasingly critical terms – it published, for instance, detailed reports of Czech revolutionary anti-Semitism (most Prague Jews being distinctly pro-German)[60] – and that it viewed the forthcoming Slav Congress with an ominous mixture of disdain, fear, and contempt.[61] To be sure, as one of its new editors, Julian Schmidt, pointed out on one occasion, it was necessary to make some concessions to the Czechs,[62] but most of the time *Die Grenzboten* took the position that the grasping ambitions of demagogic Czech politicians went far beyond anything remotely justified by history or more recent experience.[63] And once the Slav Congress actually began to gather in the Bohemian capital, *Die Grenzboten's* derision and abuse knew no bounds. It repeatedly ridiculed the dress, the speech, the manner and appearance of the assembled delegates. Why, the only language many of the delegates could communicate in was German! Was there better evidence possible of the Slav Congress's arrogant purpose and presumption?[64] "Die Nemesis kann und wird daher nicht ausbleiben" (Nemesis cannot and will not, therefore, be long delayed), *Die Grenzboten* concluded.[65]

58 *Ibid.*, 1848/II, 179ff.
59 *Ibid.*, 1848/II, 199ff., 227ff., 267ff., 277, 308ff., 317, 360. On the Sudeten German choices for the Frankfurt Parliament, see above, note 48 and Josef Pfitzner, "Zur nationalen Politik der Sudetendeutschen in den Jahren 1848–1849," *Jahrbuch des Vereins für Geschichte der Deutschen in Böhmen,* III (1934).
60 D.G., 1848/II, 200.
61 *Ibid.*, 1848/II, 383ff.
62 *Ibid.*, 1848/II, 413ff.
63 *Ibid.*, 1848/II, 436ff. Nor did *Die Grenzboten* show much interest in, or solicitude for, the anguished dilemma of such leading Czech scholars as the philosopher Augustín Smetana, who in April 1848 was elected rector of Prague University, and who was both a devout cultural Germanophil and true Czech patriot, passionately devoted to the political resurgence of his own people. Cf. Eberhard Wolfgramm, "Augustin Smetana, der Philosoph der tschechischen revolutionären Demokratie," *Jahrbuch für Geschichte der deutsch-slawischen Beziehungen und Geschichte Ost- und Mitteleuropas,* II (1958).
64 D.G., 1848/II, 442.
65 *Ibid.*, 1848/II, 445ff. It should be noted that, even at this time, there was by no means general agreement among liberal Germans in Frankfurt and Prague as to what ought to be done about Bohemia. Thus *Die Grenzboten* carried a report from one of its correspondents

This was indeed a prophetic analysis, and the Nemesis of the Slav Congress was, of course, General Alfred Windischgrätz. It is interesting to note that, if there were any contemporary rumours about a possible military action by the Austrian government – then in exile in Innsbruck – against the Slav Congress, there was no indication of it in *Die Grenzboten*. But once Windischgrätz appeared on the scene, *Die Grenzboten* welcomed him and his bloody triumph with great enthusiasm.[66] In a long series of reports from Prague, it described the alleged brutalities of the Czech revolutionaries, which in effect left Windischgrätz no choice but to proceed with decisive and overwhelming force.[67] Indeed, *Die Grenzboten* believed that if Windischgrätz had not arrived to save Prague from the Slav Congress, the job would surely have been done by Bavarian, Saxon, and Prussian troops stationed just across the Bohemian frontier.[68]

Although *Die Grenzboten* generally supported Windischgrätz's harsh policy of retribution, this is not to say that, over the summer months, it also uncritically endorsed the Austrian government's increasingly open counter-revolutionary course. It recognized, for instance, that the Czech people had suffered considerably during the Metternichian era[69] – more ancient wrongs, especially their brutal repression in the period after 1620, *Die Grenzboten* seemed much less concerned about – and that the time had clearly come for a new spirit of reconciliation, a new beginning between the peoples of Bohemia.[70]

---

in Prague, dated 15 March, saying: "One thing is certain: things have gone so far that they cannot be resolved without a bloody struggle. The longer the decision is delayed, the more dreadful, violent, and brutal the battle will be" (1848/II, 310). But two weeks later Julian Schmidt, writing from Frankfurt, confessed that if all Germans were to be united in one new political unit, "the same right must be accorded the Poles, Czechs, Slovaks, and others." And, in any case, Germany could not permit herself "to become involved in a war of conquest against Bohemia, or any other province determined not to join Germany" (1848/II, 417).

66 In that respect *Die Grenzboten* probably echoed Vienna opinion more closely than sentiment in any other German city, and it was one of the great ironies of that revolutionary year that the city Palacký said in his famous letter he was most looking toward took so disdainful a view of the Czechs' and the other nationalities' struggle for freedom. Cf. R. John Rath, "The Viennese Liberals of 1848 and the Nationality Problem," *Journal of Central European Affairs*, xv (1955), 237, 238. As Stanley Pech has pointed out: "By every criterion, the German radical press in Vienna was the most brutally and offensively anti-Czech and anti-Slavic in the monarchy" (*Czech Revolution of 1848*, 90).

67 D.G., 1848/II, 488ff., 524ff.; see also Schmidt's more critical view of official government policy toward the Czechs, *ibid.*, 1848/IV, 49ff.

68 *Ibid.*, 1848/II, 524ff.

69 For Kuranda's moving autobiographical recollections of pre-revolutionary Bohemia, and how he gradually became aware of the Habsburgs' degradation of the Czech people and their culture, see *ibid.*, 1848/III, 44ff.

70 *Ibid.*, 1848/III, 80, 93ff., 405, 429ff. That the events of the previous few weeks, including Windischgrätz's brutal occupation of Prague, had by no means diminished the urgent need for a better understanding between Czechs and Germans was also the view of Bernard Bolzano. See Eduard Winter and W. Zeil, eds., *Wissenschaft und Religion im Vormärz – Der Briefwechsel Bernard Bolzano mit Michael Josef Fesl 1822–1848* (Berlin, 1965), 420.

Indeed, as the Frankfurt Parliament's fumbling, dissension, and general ineffectiveness became ever more evident, *Die Grenzboten*'s point of view, once distinctly *grossdeutsch*, became increasingly similar to the position Palacký and other leading Czech Austro-Slavs had held since the outbreak of the revolution – namely, that a reformed and moderately centralized Austria was very much in the best interest of its various constituent nationalities.[71] As Julian Schmidt put it in an open letter to Palacký in December 1848:

If Austria wishes to fulfil its great mission, the development of a democratic league of nations, it must have free hands ... Unfettered by dead parchments! There is no need for a paper agreement between Germany and Austria ... the Slavic nightingale (and this is addressed to you, distinguished Sir!) will not always twitter war songs against the German brethren. Enough of this false game! I do not for a moment ascribe all outrages to the [Czech] party; I know that every political aspiration seeks a meaningful outlet, a popular response, ... But it would be dangerous to permit this blind game to go on unchecked indefinitely, for it transfers political development into the wilderness of dreams and myths. Only as Austrian can the Czech realize his political goals; only in close association with German culture can he achieve his honoured place among the nations ... Monarchy is quite compatible with a free constitution; but a republic of monarchies, extended over more than sixty million people of the most diverse tongues, would stifle all living aspirations [*Lebenskeime*], until, in a wild explosion, these artificially united forces would once again separate from each other. Austria can only remain truly great and free if it remains independent and does not interfere with Germany's independence; it can only remain in a lasting relationship with Germany if it is not formally chained to the latter.[72]

By this time, of course, *Die Grenzboten* was confronted with a very different political situation from that which had prevailed nine or even six months earlier. For, in mid-October, Windischgrätz had surrounded, shelled, and conquered Vienna, as he had previously conquered Prague (it had apparently not occurred to *Die Grenzboten* that what Windischgrätz could do to the Bohemian capital, he might then proceed to do to the Austrian).[73] The Austrian National Assembly

71 D.G., 1848/III, 169, 300, 401ff., 425ff.; 1848/IV, 276ff., 308ff. For Freytag's judgment that Austria had nothing to fear from such an arrangement, see *ibid.*, 1848/IV, 217.

72 *Ibid.*, 1848/IV, 490ff. See also, however, Schmidt's open letter to Kuranda, *ibid.*, 1848/IV, 47ff., and 1848/IV, 308ff.

73 Not all liberal or radical newspapers were similarly myopic. "The Bohemians are being shot down like dogs," the Vienna correspondent of the *Berliner Zeitungshalle* reported on 20 June, "and when the opportune time has come there will be a move against *Vienna*" (italics in the original), and the *Neue rheinische Zeitung* reported from Prague on 25 June that Windischgrätz's troops regarded the attack on Prague "only as a prelude to the firing and storming of Vienna." Quoted in Roman Rosdolsky, "Friedrich Engels und das Problem der 'geschichtlichen' Völker (Die Nationalitätenfrage in der Revolution 1848–1849 im Lichte der 'Neuen rheinischen Zeitung')," *Archiv für Sozialgeschichte*, IV (1964), 95. (A few months later, however, the attitude of Marx's famous paper toward the Czech revolution underwent a profound change: it became extremely hostile.)

was forcibly prorogued to the small Moravian town of Kremsier (Kroměříž), and in December the emperor Ferdinand abdicated in favour of his eighteen-year-old nephew Francis Joseph.[74]

It would be pleasant to be able to say that Die Grenzboten's comments and reports on this dramatically changed situation – especially in so far as the new situation affected the future position of Bohemia – were more perspicacious than they had been in previous months. But this was hardly the case. To be sure, Die Grenzboten urged the newly restored German elements in Bohemia not to make a vainglorious show of their regained power.[75] On the other hand, it proceeded to treat the Kremsier Parliament, which operated under great difficulties and which was indeed one of the Habsburg Monarchy's last best hopes, with airy indifference, and it dismissed the viewpoints and role of such leading Czech members of that assembly as Palacký and Rieger with little more than polite bemusement.[76] (When Palacký, in February 1849, introduced his famous motion asking for clarification of the government's position on the nationalities issue, Die Grenzboten roundly denounced him.[77]) Not until the Habsburg government, in March 1849, suddenly – though hardly surprisingly – dissolved the Kremsier Parliament,[78] and decreed still another constitution of its own (the third such in

74 D.G., 1848/IV, 119ff., 169ff., 246ff., 273ff., 324ff., 448ff. For a good account of developments in the Austrian capital, see Rath, The Viennese Revolution of 1848, and "The Viennese Liberals of 1848 and the Nationality Problem," cited above, and his other articles, "Public Opinion during the Viennese Revolution of 1848," Journal of Central European Affairs, VIII (1948), and "The Failure of an Ideal – The Viennese Revolution of 1848," Southwestern Social Science Quarterly, XXXIV (1953), all generally critical of the more radical elements. See further Joseph Redlich, Emperor Francis Joseph of Austria (New York, 1929), chaps. I and II, and Paul Müller, Feldmarschall Fürst Windischgrätz – Revolution und Gegenrevolution in Österreich (Vienna, 1934), 139ff.

75 D.G., 1848/III, 492. "We do not wish to expect too much," Die Grenzboten declared late in the summer of 1848, "we also do not wish any discriminatory legislation against the Czechs, and would not wish to take from them the smallest of those rights that Germany has accorded to all nationalities and languages within the Reich." See also ibid., 1848/IV, 169ff., 247ff. Events in Vienna in October 1848 had a very sobering effect also on the Germans in Bohemia, and, as the fortunes of the Viennese revolution waned, Die Grenzboten's attitude toward the aims and experiences of the Czechs earlier in the year appeared to become, for a time at least, somewhat more sympathetic again (cf. ibid., 1848/IV, 340ff).

76 Ibid., 1849/I, 39ff., 98ff., 121ff., 196ff. This attitude was shared by not a few German liberals in Bohemia. Cf. J. Loužil, "Franz Thomas Bratranek – Ein Vermittler der deutschen Philosophie im böhmischen Vormärz," in W. Steinitz, P. N. Berkov, B. Suchodolski, and J. Dolanský, eds., Ost und West in der Geschichte des Denkens und der kulturellen Beziehungen [Festschrift für Eduard Winter zum 70. Geburtstag] (Berlin, 1966), 610. See also Heinrich Friedjung, Österreich von 1848 bis 1860 (Stuttgart and Berlin, 1908), I, 155ff.

77 D.G., 1849/I, 394ff.

78 That the Kremsier Parliament was never a serious threat to the political structure and territorial integrity of the Habsburg Monarchy, and that Schwarzenberg and the young Francis Joseph were only looking for a convenient pretext to prorogue the assembly is strongly indicated by Friedrich Walter, "Fürst Felix Schwarzenberg im Lichte seiner Innenpolitik,"

less than a year), did *Die Grenzboten* finally begin to understand the full dimensions of the political and national disaster that had befallen the Habsburg Monarchy.[79]

Thus from the spring of 1849 on, *Die Grenzboten*'s attitude toward the Austrian government and the whole nationality problem began, once more, to undergo a marked and significant change. The new spirit of reaction, which soon approached flood tide, was bound to produce a new wave of Slavic solidarity, with all the perils that implied.[80] Thus *Die Grenzboten* reported with respectful sympathy, for instance, the passing of Jan S. Presl, a leading Czech scholar and distinguished professor of natural history at Prague University.[81] It denounced the government for calling in Russian troops to quell the Hungarian revolution[82] (the Austrian government had also obtained a large loan in St. Petersburg, for the purpose of meeting some of its extraordinary expenses in putting down domestic disorders – a transaction *Die Grenzboten* likewise viewed most critically[83]).

Needless to say, the Austrian government was not in the least concerned over this kind of criticism in *Die Grenzboten* and, not surprisingly, the summer and autumn of 1849 were anything but pleasant in Bohemia. In May, for example, the Habsburg authorities reimposed martial law in Prague, and strong pressures were brought to bear upon the Roman Catholic hierarchy to use all its moral and psychological influence and powers of persuasion to get the Czech people to

---

Bericht über den siebenten österreichischen Historikertag ... August 1962 ("Veröffentlichungen des Verbandes österreichischer Geschichtsvereine," xv, 1963), 151–2, and by Friedrich Prinz, "Die deutsche Nationalversammlung in Frankfurt und der Reichstag in Kremsier," *Beiträge zum deutsch-tschechischen Verhältnis im 19. und 20. Jahrhundert* (Munich, 1967), 23ff., 30. The ostensible reason for dissolving the Kremsier Parliament was that it had "failed to complete" its work: an accusation, Friedrich Walter has written, "whose untruth ... was perfectly clear" ("Österreichische Verfassungsentwicklung 1848–1859," in *Die Entwicklung der Verfassung Österreichs vom Mittelalter bis zur Gegenwart* [Graz and Vienna, 1963], 78). On the contrary, on 1 March 1849 the Parliament had unanimously approved the "Kremsier Constitution," envisaging, as Langer has pointed out, "a liberal representative system and at the same time a federal organization based on the historic lands with a large measure of local self-government and full scope for national self-expression. This was probably as close to a satisfactory solution of the nationalities problem as one could hope to come" (*Political and Social Upheaval*, 487).

79 D.G., 1849/ɪ, 406, 447, 454ff., 502ff.; 1849/ɪɪ, 21ff., 25ff., 308. "Austria," noted *Die Grenzboten* about this time, "has relapsed into the terror of a mediaeval state" (*ibid.*, 325). Lest this seem somewhat of an extreme statement, one may refer to the private sentiments of a leading Austrian government official, Freiherr von Kübeck, before March 1848 president of the court chamber (*Hofkammer*) and after December 1850 again a top member of Francis Joseph's government, as quoted from his private diary in April 1849 by F. Walter, "Karl Kübeck Freiherr von Kübeck und die Aufrichtigung des franzisko-josephischen Neuabsolutismus," *Südostforschungen*, xɪx (1960), 195.

80 D.G., 1849/ɪɪ, 30ff., 341ff., 377ff.

81 *Ibid.*, 1849/ɪɪ, 170ff.

82 *Ibid.*, 1849/ɪɪ, 213ff., 337ff., 377ff.

83 *Ibid.*, 1849/ɪɪɪ, 315ff.

accept the new counter-revolutionary state of affairs. (The hierarchy, it should be added, did not resist, and perhaps could not resist, such pressures.[84]) And while *Die Grenzboten* doubtless disliked some of the more flagrant manifestations of Habsburg restoration, before long it also seemed to be slipping back into something like its *Vormärz*, anti-Slav posture. Thus in July 1849, for instance, it published the first of a series of articles on leading Czech scholars – including Palacký, Šafařík, and Hanka, the last of whom it singled out for his "non-political" attitude[85] – but these pieces contained none of the illuminating detail and critical acumen which it had recently lavished on Lamartine's *Histoire des Girondins* or Macaulay's history of England, the first two volumes of which had just appeared in German translation.[86] It was fairly clear, then, that *Die Grenzboten* and its correspondents continued to take Czech intellectual life and achievement far less seriously than they did comparable developments in Britain and France, and in this posture of thinly disguised condescension lay the seed of much future recrimination and cultural conflict between the Czech and German peoples.[87]

In October 1849 *Die Grenzboten* published a long article analysing what it regarded as the principal reasons for the failure of the Czech revolution the year before, but once more its general tone was clearly unsympathetic.[88] It was one of the saddening aspects of *Die Grenzboten* that, even as its own disenchantment with, and bitter opposition to, the ministry of Prince Felix zu Schwarzenberg continued to mount, its attitude toward the Czech people and their problems became no more probing or sympathetic than it had been before March 1848. To the very end of 1849, then, *Die Grenzboten* seemed generally unaware, or at least unwilling to consider for more than a brief moment, that the Czech people and enlightened Germans in the Habsburg Monarchy had much in the way of common interests, and that the two peoples would either cooperate effectively, or would be separately and savagely repressed by the unchecked tide of counter-revolution.[89]

To be sure, concerning that unchecked course of counter-revolution, *Die Grenzboten*'s anger and outrage knew no bounds. In a series of detailed reports, courageously sent through the unashamedly opened mails, *Die Grenzboten* described, month after month, the incredible police and military brutality that

---

84 *Ibid.*, 1849/III, 34ff.
85 *Ibid.*, 1849/III, 70ff., 358ff. On Václav Hanka, see Seton-Watson, *A History of the Czechs and Slovaks*, 178–9.
86 Cf. D.G., 1847/II, 566ff., and 1849/II, 332ff., for *Die Grenzboten*'s extended comments on German editions of Alphonse de Lamartine's *Histoire des Girondins* (3 vols.; Leipzig, 1847), and Thomas Babington Macaulay's *Die Geschichte Englands seit dem Regierungsantritt Jakob's* II, translated by Friedrich Bülau (2 vols.; Leipzig, 1849).
87 Cf. D.G., 1848/III, 176, and 1849/IV, 95ff. The passage of time has done little to reduce such condescension.
88 D.G., 1849/III, 375ff.
89 See, for instance, *ibid.*, 1849/II, 377ff.

reigned unchecked in Vienna following on Windischgrätz's occupation of the city. "The ministry, and especially Schwarzenberg," it reported as late as September 1849, "have got the young Emperor convinced that he should not interfere with the executioner, and the Emperor, having been brought up in the military tradition, accepts this counsel."[90] How much better things were in the Prussian capital, even in the face of the martial law existing there![91]

But however brutal and bloody the Austrian government's repression of the slightest political opposition, the existing political and economic situation of the country seemed beyond its power – or readiness – to correct. The new constitution of March 1849 was an unworkable sham,[92] and, even more serious perhaps, the financial condition of the government bordered on complete disaster. Forced loans and repeated depreciation of the currency afforded the government only a short period of grace. The fact of the matter was that Austria was basically a rich country, whose wealth had yet to be fully developed, and it was most unfortunate, declared *Die Grenzboten*, that – as in Bohemia in the dark years after 1620 – the Austrian government was now resorting in Hungary to the confiscation of landed estates in order to meet its immediate financial needs.[93] Indeed, in an ominous forecast of impending Austrian economic-political (and military) decline, *Die Grenzboten* reported, in late 1849, that Schwarzenberg, Alexander Bach, the minister of the interior, and Philipp von Krauss, the minister of finance, had formally warned the emperor Francis Joseph that unless the army was rapidly demobilized, the Austrian government would be completely bankrupt within two years.[94]

One might have thought that such gloomy but rather accurate forecasts, to say nothing of the actual course of revolution and counter-revolution over the preceding eighteen months, would have sufficed to persuade the Austrian government that the time had come to adopt a more moderate attitude toward the political, economic, and nationality problems confronting it; and that, along with the editors and correspondents of *Die Grenzboten*, the German-speaking inhabitants of Bohemia had learned something from their recent experiences. But this was far from being the case. Thus *Die Grenzboten*'s reports from Prague in the

90 *Ibid.*, 1849/ɪɪ, 373ff.; 1849/ɪᴠ, 278ff. See also Walter, "Österreichische Verfassungsgeschichte 1848–1859," 79ff.

91 ᴅ.ɢ., 1849/ɪɪ, 111.

92 *Ibid.*, 1849/ɪɪɪ, 232ff., 496ff.

93 *Ibid.*, 1849/ɪɪɪ, 304ff.; 1849/ɪᴠ, 345ff.

94 *Ibid.*, 1849/ɪᴠ, 519. *Die Grenzboten*'s revealing account was later confirmed by the highly informed work of Adolf Beer, *Die Finanzen Österreichs im XIX. Jahrhundert* (Prague, 1877), but seems to have escaped the simplistic, but highly acclaimed, work of Helmut Böhme, *Deutschlands Weg zur Grossmacht – Studien zum Verhältnis von Wirtschaft und Staat während der Reichsgründungszeit, 1848–1884* (Cologne, 1966). On the problems faced by the Austrian minister of finance, see further the valuable account of Maria Woinovich, "Philipp Freiherr von Krauss, Finanzminister im Jahr 1848," *Mitteilungen des österreichischen Staatsarchivs* (Gebhard Rath Festschrift), xɪᴠ (1961).

summer of 1849 make melancholy reading indeed. Not surprisingly, Czech anger and despair ran very deep.[95] Worse yet, the philistinism of the self-satisfied Germans seemed unbounded. As one report noted:

The [German] aristocrat's olympian repose has returned in full measure ... He was earlier torn from his traditional (*standesgemässen*) contempt for the world in such disagreeable fashion; he could no longer remain indifferent to the agitated masses, for he was forced to confront them. Now however he can, for a while, smile benevolently once more on the seriousness agitating the masses, without the anxiety of former days, which showed itself in pale countenances, contrasting with such irony. He can once more devote himself to the arcadian pleasures of his *ipso facto* valuable existence, and quietly, as in former days, take care of his zoos, his stables, and picture galleries. For he alone has not yet lost that paradise in which man lives alone, in holy community, with God and the animals.[96]

It seems only fair to note that such smug self-satisfaction among the German middle (or upper) class was too much even for some *Grenzboten* reporters. "I know one businessman in Prague, who is also an amateur musician," one correspondent reported drily at the end of 1849, "whom, after every important event, I always ask about his feelings. So I asked him after March 4 [i.e. the dissolution of the Kremsier Parliament]: 'Now, how do you feel, Herr G.?' 'Since yesterday,' he replied, 'I feel well; now the stocks will go up again.' I asked him the same question after the state of siege was reimposed. 'I am quite satisfied,' came the reply this time, 'now I can quietly practice a Chopin sonata, without having to worry about noise from the street.' "[97]

Sanguine, too, seemed to be the mood of Prague's restored Habsburg masters. While reflective Czechs doubtless wondered how they could have escaped such a malign fate, the former emperor Ferdinand took up residence in the Hradčany, the castle overlooking the city, from where Windischgrätz had shelled Prague into submission. In late 1849 the emperor, Francis Joseph, announced that he would make a state visit to the Bohemian capital.[98] Not surprisingly, the Austrian authorities were concerned to make the visit a grand and auspicious occasion. The whole city was festively lit up, but the oppressive state of siege was not lifted, and the city's harsh military commandant, General Franz von Khevenmüller, made no other gestures of goodwill to the local population – sensing, correctly no doubt, that while he might have conquered them physically, the independent spirit of the city still remained.

All the same, the mayor, members of the city government, and other selected notables were to greet Francis Joseph upon his arrival at the Prague railroad station, and some of the city's most beautiful young women were to pay homage

95 D.G., 1849/III, 375ff. 96 *Ibid.*, 1849/II, 461.
97 *Ibid.*, 1849/II, 462–3.
98 *Ibid.* The whole episode is described in 1849/IV, 395ff.

to him. It was all so fastidiously planned, but it ended almost in disaster. The mayor, for instance, had prepared a few innocuous words of greeting. But these had to be approved in advance by the local government authorities – and they disapproved. Thus he was forced to greet His Imperial Majesty with no more than a silent smile. Even the young maidens could not carry out their tribute as planned. Their spokesman had planned humbly to address Francis Joseph: "Your grace, so young in years, yet so aged in experience." That also seemed too suggestive to the authorities.

Thus at the end of 1849 Czechs and Germans in Bohemia faced the future with much bitterness, with little awareness as to why they had failed to reach their goals during the preceding two years, and with really not much better understanding of each other's hopes and desires for the future.[99] This was especially true regarding German awareness and understanding of the Czech people. The essential facts of Czech political life, of course, were quite simple and they remained at the end of 1849 much as they had been throughout the 1840s. Bohemia was and continued to be, as it had been since 1620, an occupied province. Because of the devotion and perseverance of its sturdiest elements, stimulated by the romantic revival, and by the cultural reawakening brought about, in part, by men like Herder,[100] the Czech people had, in the 1830s and 1840s, acquired a renewed national consciousness. It was one of the specially unfortunate consequences of the Metternichian era that their German neighbours remained largely indifferent to that important development, and that the German people's own unsuccesful quest for freedom and national unity, in 1848–9, made them even more indifferent to the similar fate of smaller, still less fortunate, nationalities around them.[101]

99 *Ibid.*, 1849/III, 503; 1849/IV, 99ff.
100 Cf. Matthias Murko, *Deutsche Einflüsse auf die Anfänge der böhmischen Romantik* (Graz, 1897); Konrad Bittner, *Herders Geschichtsphilosophie und die Slawen* (Reichenberg, 1929); Josef Pfitzner, "Heinrich Luden und František Palacký – Ein Kapitel deutsch-slawischer Kulturbeziehungen," *Historische Zeitschrift*, CXLI (1929); Ernst Birke, "Herder und die Slawen," in Walther Hubatsch, ed., *Schicksalswege deutscher Vergangenheit – Festschrift für Siegfried A. Kaehler* (Düsseldorf, 1950); and S. E. Mann, " 'The Journal of the Czech Museum' and František Palacký," *Slavonic and East European Review*, XXXVI (1957). See also Hans Kohn, *The Idea of Nationalism* (New York, 1944), 437. Herder, moreover, left no doubt what he thought of a multinational state: "The most natural state [he wrote] is *one* people with *one* national character ... Nothing therefore appears so directly opposed to the end of government as the unnatural enlargement of states, the wild mixture of various breeds and nations under one sceptre ... Such monstrosities are pieced together like the Trojan horse ... being destitute of national character, there is no life in them ... But history sufficiently shows that such instruments of human pride are formed of clay, and, like all clay, will dissolve or crumble into bits." *Sämmtliche Werke*, XIII, 384–5, quoted in Carlton J. H. Hayes, "Herder and the Doctrine of Nationalism," *American Historical Review*, XXXII (1927), 735.
101 Cf. Josef Hemmerle, "Die tschechische Wiedergeburt und die Fälschungen nationaler Sprachdenkmäler," *Stifter Jahrbuch*, VII (1962), 77. This continued lack of interest is further

It is perilous, perhaps, to try to sum up the state and direction of the Czech political mind at the close of the revolutionary years. Yet for all the turmoil and debate beneath the surface,[102] and despite all the bitterness and repression of the past year, it should be remembered that leading intellectuals and public men like Palacký and Rieger were still pleading for Czech-German cooperation, and were continuing to advocate a policy of Austro-Slavism that would safeguard Czech freedom and national development within a reformed and properly federalized Habsburg Empire.[103] But the Habsburg Monarchy, freshly if bloodily restored to something like its old authority, saw no need for such cooperation. It missed the last best hope for a great and generous national reconciliation, and within two years of Francis Joseph's death in November 1916, the empire over which he had presided from December 1848 was in its grave.

Once more, in the autumn of 1918 hope of new freedom and national independence seemed to sweep over Bohemia. Once more tragedy was to ensue. But the struggle and disaster of the Czechoslovak Republic[104] might have surprised few men who remembered Ignaz Kuranda, *Die Grenzboten*, and developments in Bohemia in 1845–9.

BIBLIOGRAPHICAL POSTCRIPT

"Interpretation of the national past," as Hans Kohn once pointed out in an important essay on "The Historical Roots of Czech Democracy," "serves to answer the question of the meaning and the destiny of the national existence of a people, as a symbol around which the national cultural life is integrated and by which the vision of the

confirmed by Freytag's brief mention of the subject in his memoirs, published in 1887. After their own shattering experiences in the 1860s and 1870s the German liberals (and, possibly, radicals and socialists, too) were perhaps either too defeated by Bismarck, or caught up in their own unsolved domestic problems, or culturally and intellectually too desensitized by the rise of integral nationalism after the 1860s, to devote much time and energy to the struggle of smaller, still more unfortunate peoples such as the Czechs. This, too, is a legacy of the Bismarckian era about which his historian-admirers have been notably silent.

102 D.G., 1849/IV, 397ff., 523.

103 The history of "Austro-Slavism" from Palacký to Masaryk remains to be written, but see Emil Schieche, "Edvard Beneš und die slawischen Ideen," *Zeitschrift für Ostforschung*, IV (1955), 196; Eberhard Wolfgramm, "Deutsche und tschechische Demokraten im Jahre 1850 – Die Korrespondentenberichte aus Prag in der 'Deutschen Monatsschrift,'" in H. H. Bielfeldt, ed., *Deutsch-slawische Wechselheitigkeit in sieben Jahrhunderten* [Festschrift für Eduard Winter] (Berlin, 1956), 456ff.; and Rudolf Wierer, "Das Böhmische Staatsrecht und der Ausgleichsversuch des Ministerium Hohenwart-Schäffle," *Bohemia*, IV (1963). For a German nationalist view of this important subject before the Second World War, set forth with the thoroughness and intellectual arrogance characteristic of his school of thought, see Eugen Lemberg, "Der Staat im Denken des tschechischen Volkes," *Jahrbücher für Geschichte Osteuropas*, III (1938).

104 Cf. Francis L. Loewenheim, ed., *Peace or Appeasement? Hitler, Chamberlain, and the Munich Crisis* (Boston, 1965).

future is determined" (in Robert J. Kerner, ed., *Czechoslovakia*, 3rd ed. [Berkeley and Los Angeles, 1949], 93). Given the fact of what Hans Kohn has rightly termed as German "ancestor-centered nationalism" (*Living in a World Revolution – My Encounter with History* [New York, 1964], 183), it is not surprising, but nevertheless of great importance, that the historical study of Czech-German relations has long been caught up in a kind of "intellectual cold war," and that these relations, including relations in the crucial mid-nineteenth century discussed above, cannot be fully understood without awareness of that long-standing – and still continuing – acrimonious debate.

The purpose of this essay, then, has been twofold: first, to give an account and explanation of *Die Grenzboten's* views and reporting on Bohemian affairs before and during the mid-century revolutions, with special reference to the background, intellectual outlook, and political views of its founder and first editor, Ignaz Kuranda; secondly – since the nature and details of the important historiographical struggle about mid-nineteenth century Czech-German relations are so little known and appreciated in the West – to give some account also of that distinctly unhappy story. Unfortunately for over half a century (that is, ever since the end of the First World War), many German scholars – and especially historians – both in Czechoslovakia and in Germany have engaged in a systematic campaign of intellectual warfare against the Czechoslovak state and people, a campaign that reached its logical conclusion in 1938–9.

As examples of this literature betwen the two world wars, see for instance the voluminous publications of Konrad Bittner, Alfred Fischel, R. F. Kaindl, Eugen Lemberg, Paul Molisch, and Josef Pfitzner, and especially Wilhelm Wostry, "Das Nationalitätenstaatsproblem in der böhmischen Revolution des Jahres 1848," *Auslandsdeutsche Volksforschung*, II (1938); Hans Lades, *Die Tschechen und die deutsche Frage* (Erlangen, 1938); Hermann Aubin, "Deutsche und Tschechen," *Historische Zeitschrift*, CLX (1939); and Hans Raupach, *Der tschechische Frühnationalismus* (Essen, 1939). "Nowhere is a viable people's [*lebensfähiges Volkes*] right to live more respected than in National Socialist Germany," Raupach wrote in 1936, "and in German scholarship, which, with striking selflessness, made intellectually possible and nurtured this [Czech] national awakening a hundred and fifty years ago" (*Jahrbücher für Geschichte Osteuropas*, I [1936], 470). What German control of Czechoslovakia actually did to that country's historical scholarship already during the first years of Nazi occupation was reported by Professor Odložilík in 1941. "On vital problems," he wrote, "such as the relation of medieval Bohemia to the Empire, the Czech struggle for independence, the domestic and foreign policy of the Republic, only German-speaking historians are allowed to express opinions which, needless to say, agree to the minutest point with the ideology fabricated for the conquered nations in Berlin. There is no discussion concerning the views of the self-appointed interpreters of the political and spiritual tradition of the Czech people, because any discussion would constitute a political crime. Enchained Clio looks silently upon her German sister, dancing obsequiously to the tune from the Berlin Ministry of Propaganda." ("Clio in Chains – Czech Historiography in 1939–1940," *Slavonic and East European Review*, XX [1941], 336.)

Needless to say, this German intellectual warfare – or worse – has been toned down somewhat since the Second World War, but it has by no means abated altogether. See, for instance, Hermann Münch, *Böhmische Tragödie – Das Schicksal Mitteleuropas im Lichte der tschechischen Frage* (Braunschweig, Berlin, and Hamburg, 1949), probably the best German treatment of modern Bohemian history, and interestingly enough the work of a private scholar; Eugen Lemberg, *Geschichte des Nationalismus in Europa* (Stuttgart, 1950), "Das Geschichtsbewusstsein der Sudetendeutschen," *Stifter Jahrbuch*, ɪᴠ (1955), and "Das Bild des Deutschen im tschechischen Geschichtsbewusstsein", *Ostdeutsche Wissenschaft* [Festgabe für Max Hildebert Boehm], ᴠɪɪɪ (1960); Helmut Preidel, ed., *Die Deutschen in Böhmen und Mähren*, 2nd ed. (Gräfelfing bei München, 1952); H. Aubin, "Die Deutschen in der Geschichte des Ostens," *Geschichte in Wissenschaft und Unterricht*, ᴠɪɪ (1956); Hellmut Diwald, "Deutschböhme, die Deutschen Prags, und das tschechische Wiedererwachen," *Zeitschrift für Religions- und Geistesgeschichte*, x (1958); Friedrich Prinz, "Studien zur Gestalt Hans Kudlichs," *Zeitschrift für Ostforschung*, ᴠɪɪɪ (1959); Franz Seibt, "Der Nationalitätenkampf im Spiegel der sudetendeutschen Geschichtsschreibung 1848–1938," *Stifter Jahrbuch*, ᴠɪ (1959); Ernst Birke und Kurt Oberdorffer, eds., *Das böhmische Staatsrecht in den deutsch-tschechischen Auseinandersetzungen des 19. und 20. Jahrhunderts* (Marburg, 1960); Wenzel Jaksch, *Europe's Road to Potsdam* (New York, 1963); and the numerous publications of the Sudeten German Collegium Carolinum in Munich, of which F. Prinz, "Probleme der böhmischen Geschichte zwischen 1848 und 1914," *Bohemia* [Jahrbuch des Collegium Carolinum], ᴠɪ (1965), is a representative example. But see also Ludwig Gogolák, "Deutschland und die Deutschen im Geschichtsbild der Slowaken," *Südostdeutsches Archiv*, ɪɪɪ/1 (1960); the moderate essays of Friedrich Walter, Friedrich Prinz, and Karel Lisický, in *Beiträge zum deutsch-tschechischen Verhältnis im 19. und 20. Jahrhundert* (Munich, 1967); the important (if thus far rather isolated) revisionist study of Karl Bosl, "Deutsche romantische-liberale Geschichtsauffassung und 'Slawische Legende,'" *Bohemia*, v (1964); and Hans Lemberg, in *Archiv für Sozialgeschichte*, v (1965), p. 543. For the continuity of Eugen Lemberg's views, for instance, see his articles "Der Staat im Denken des tschechoslowakischen Volkes," *Jahrbücher für Geschichte Osteuropas*, ɪɪɪ (1939), and "Volksbegriff und Staatsideologie der Tschechen," *Zeitschrift für Ostforschung*, ᴠɪɪɪ (1950), and see further the discussion of his paper "Vorraussetzungen und Probleme des tschechischen Geschichtsbewusstseins," in Ernst Birke and Eugen Lemberg, eds. *Geschichtsbewusstsein in Ostmitteleuropa* (Marburg, 1961), 106f., not the least remarkable comment being Birke's: "I believe that we Germans do not have a very good idea how the Czechs developed themselves as a nation and as a social organism over the past hundred to a hundred and thirty years ... [of course] the Czechs as a people are very young, and this has probably produced a whole series of excesses and contradictions." See also Birke's essay "Das neue Europa in den Kriegsdenkschriften T. G. Masaryks," in Wilhelm Berges and Carl Hinrichs, eds., *Zur Geschichte und Problematik der Demokratie – Festgabe für Hans Herzfeld* (Berlin, 1958), wherein Birke quotes Masaryk's famous lecture at the opening of the School of

Slavonic Studies at the University of London in October 1915: "How then can Germany or any other nation claim for herself this right [of national unity], and at the same time refuse it to others?" It is a question that few German scholars have asked themselves over the past half century, much less answered.

It seems only fair to add that East German, Soviet Russian, and Czech (Communist) scholars have sought to place rightful emphasis on the positive side of Czech-German relations over the centuries, although their work has, perhaps inevitably, suffered from a heavy dose of Marxist jargon and interpretation. Thus František Kavka (*An Outline of Czechoslovak History* [Prague, 1960]) has written of the post-1848 period that "the Czech bourgeoisie now stood for 'Austro-Slavism,' i.e., it was convinced that the Austrian Empire was the best guarantee for the preservation of the Czech nation against the pressure of the German bourgeoisie" (p. 81). See also J. J. Udalzov [Udaltsev], *Aufzeichnung über die Geschichte des nationalen und politischen Kampfes in Böhmen im Jahre 1848* (Berlin, 1953); K. Ksyrslová, "Friedrich Schiller und die tschechische nationale Wiedergeburt," *Zeitschrift für Slawistik*, I (1956); Alois Hofmann, *Die prager Zeitschrift 'Ost und West' – Ein Beitrag zur Geschichte der deutschslawischen Verständigung im Vormärz* (Berlin, 1957); Herbert Paukert, *Die Slawen der Donaumonarchie und die Universität Jena 1700–1848 – Ein Beitrag zur Literatur und Bildungsgeschichte* (Berlin, 1957); Hubert Rösel, *Dokumente zur Geschichte der Slawistik in Deutschland*, pt. I: *Die Universitäten Berlin und Breslau im 19. Jahrhundert* (Berlin, 1957); Karl Kreibich, *Die Deutschen und die böhmische Revolution 1848* (Berlin, 1958); Karl Obermann and Josef Polišenský, eds., *Aus 500 Jahren deutschtschechoslowakischer Geschichte* (Berlin, 1958); Eduard Winter, "Die tschechischen radicalen Demokraten," *Zeitschrift für Geschichtswissenschaft*, VII (1959); Eberhard Wolfgramm, "Zur Parteienbildung im Vormärz, besonders im Hinblick auf die nationale Entwicklung in Ost- und Südeuropa," *Jahrbuch für Geschichte der UdSSR und der volksdemokratischen Länder Europas*, V (1961); Hans Holm Bielfeldt and Karel Horálek, eds., *Beiträge zur Geschichte der Slawistik* (Berlin, 1964); and Manfred Jänichen, *Zwischen Diffamierung und Widerhall – Tschechische Poesie im deutschen Sprachgebiet 1815–1867* (Berlin, 1967), esp. 20–83. In 1955 a joint East German–Czechoslovak Historical Commission was created, whose studies proved of considerable, if also widely varying, quality. Its work seemed to fade out in the early 1960s, however, to be replaced by a new series of meetings of Czech and East German "Bohemianists." For a report on their first meeting at the Karl Marx University of Leipzig, see *Zeitschrift für Geschichtswissenschaft*, XIV (1966).

The Preparatory Committee of the Slav
Congress, April–May 1848

JOHN ERICKSON

LATE IN APRIL 1848, when the idea of a "Slav assembly" or a "Slav congress" was first suggested from at least three different quarters – Poznań, Prague, and Zagreb – the Slavs both within and without the Austrian empire found themselves faced with an increasingly dangerous situation, menaced by Germans and Magyars alike. For one intoxicating month they had stood "on the threshold of Paradise," as the poet Ferdinand Freiligrath subsequently described the sweep of the revolution, but too soon "the gates had slammed shut." The euphoria of March 1848, the excitement generated by the dismissal of Metternich, the invigoration of pressing demands upon "the kind Emperor," and the prospects for the Polish cause, apparently miraculously improved by insurgency in Berlin and its seeping into Prussian Poland, had all begun to fade; the artificial friendships which momentarily smothered nationalist competition were already splintered or falling apart.[1]

The Magyars, granted an independent Hungarian ministry on 17 March, set about enacting through their Diet at Bratislava (Poszony, Pressburg) the thirty-one bills which represented "the wishes of the nation," a striking liberal reform of "the Constitution," though it was Magyar liberalism thoroughly impregnated with feverish nationalist chauvinism which blocked any concessions to the non-Magyars of Hun-

1 See R. John Rath, *The Viennese Revolution of 1848* (Austin, Texas, 1957), chap. 4. Also L. B. Namier, *1848: The Revolution of the Intellectuals* (London, 1944; 3rd impression, 1950), 17–53.

gary: what Lajos Kossuth arrogated to the Magyars he refused to countenance in any form for the non-Magyars: Croats, Slovaks, Serbs, Germans, and Rumanians. Late in March the Croats assembled a great delegation and set it marching on Vienna, there to demand another independent ministry, one of the thirty points of their petition.[2] The Hungarian Serbs, also petitioning Vienna, sent yet another delegation from Novi Sad to the Hungarian Diet at the beginning of April, seeking autonomy for the province in which they formed the majority, only to be met with a fiery refusal. The Hungarian Slovaks also demonstrated for "the rights" of Slovak nationals, while the Rumanian majority of Transylvania took little comfort in the "invitation" issued by the Hungarian Diet and accepted by the Transylvanian Diet (representing only Magyar-speaking elements) for union. The iron ring of Magyarism was closing round all the lands of the Hungarian crown.

The ragged line of Slav political activity and interests, running from Poznań, Cracow (Kraków), and Lwów (Lviv), to Prague, Brno, and Bratislava, on to Ljubljana, Zagreb, and even Belgrade, was also entangled with the German search for unity, the wind of change blowing through "the dark night of Germany": on 5 March, a meeting of "German notables" at Heidelberg determined to convene a "Pre-Parliament" (*Vorparlament*), to prepare the way for an elected German National Assembly (*Nationalversammlung*) using the German Confederation as its territorial basis, which not only raised the question of the positions of Austria and Prussia but also the whole range of the mutual relationships of the Germans with other nationalities, principally the Slavs. Amidst an atmosphere of enthusiasm and excitement, five hundred delegates to the *Vorparlament* assembled at Frankfurt, the prelude to "the parliament of professors"; although invitations to participate in the elected German assembly had already been dispatched, just where the writ of this would-be Germany ran proved to be an awkward and vexatious question. Only one segment of the Austrian empire, the western provinces (which also included the Czechs and Slovenes), belonged to the German Confederation; augmented by these Slav constituents, Austria would have enjoyed a representation in the German assembly superior to that of Prussia, but on 11 April František Palacký for the Czechs refused the "invitation" to participate in these deliberations, arguing in his famous letter[3] that the proposal for so unifying the Czech nation with the German was one which had "no legal basis." To undermine Austria as "an independent empire" endangered the security not only of the Czechs but of all Europe, indeed of "mankind and civilization itself": to check Magyar predominance, to bar aggressive Germanism, to thwart Russian Panslavism, Palacký aimed to reinforce Austria through reorganization on the lines of a federation of equal nationalities.

In Bohemia itself the Czech-German "united front," fragile as it was, had already

---

2 Cf. *Correspondence Relative to the Affairs of Hungary, 1847–49.* Laid by the Crown, 15 August 1850 (Blue Books, vol. 58, 1851), 37–50. Also "Illyrische Nation," Haus-Hof-Staatsarchiv, Vienna. Nachlass Schlitter; Konferenz 1848/1241/432.

3 F. Palacký, *Spisy drobné:* pt. 1: *Spisy a řeči z oboru politiky,* ed. B. Rieger (Prague, 1898), 16–22.

178 / JOHN ERICKSON

begun to fracture and the Czech claims for the rights of their "Bohemian nationality," as well as the refusal to participate in a German assembly, speeded the break.[4] The imperial rescript of 8 April 1848 promised, in response to the petition of 29 March, a common administration for the three lands of the Bohemian crown, equality between German and "Bohemian nationality," and further liberal reform. The German protest was immediate and violent: on 9 April, a counterpetition insisted on the adherence of Bohemia to the German Confederation and denounced the status given to "Bohemian nationality" as inimical to German interests.[5] Ten days later the Prague Germans set up their own "representative body," the Konstitutioneller Verein (Constitutional Union), though on 10 April elections to the Národní výbor, the National Committee, had produced a mixed Czech-German representation of 126 delegates. The life of Prague became organized increasingly on divergent Czech and German lines and towards the end of the month there descended on Prague the emissaries of the Vorparlament, the three-man "Schilling committee," determined to browbeat the Czechs into joining the deliberations at Frankfurt. As Czech-German relations degenerated, Poles and Prussians had already come to blows, all the hopes raised by the Berlin revolution of 18 March being completely dashed.[6] In Galicia the Polish movement, which came to centre in the Polish National Committee (Rada Narodowa) in Lwów, sagged almost from the start; in Poznań it was shot to pieces.

Poznań Poles and Czechs alike were facing an adamantine German nationalism: Croats, Slovaks, and Serbs had to reckon with an unrelenting Magyar chauvinism. Neither the Germans nor the Hungarians could enlist the sympathy of the Slavs, to whom they denied what they asked for themselves. Now as never before was the time to prove that the Slavs were united, capable of combined action more effective than any German-Magyar alliance. A Slav assembly, albeit impromptu and not a little festive, there had already been, when the various delegations crowded into Vienna at the end of March; the Slav delegates first met as a body on 2 April when Ljudevit Gaj, Vuk Karadžić, Ľudovít Štúr, Josef Václav Frič, and "others too numerous to mention" crammed the hall in the Sperlgasse for an evening's conviviality, enlivened by speeches, patriotic declamations, and songs. Štúr's speech received a rapturous reception: the "Illyrian address" ended with shouts of "Sláva! Živio!"; the young Frič sang and the whole company joined in singing Hej Slávové![7] After the week-end, on Monday 4 April, another meeting convened, described by Frič as "an all-Slav assembly at the Sperl," a more restrained occasion with Štúr and Fran Kurelac as the main speakers, urging "Slav cooperation" and discussing the variety

4 See O. Odložilík, "The Czechs on the Eve of the Revolution of 1848," Harvard Slavic Studies, I (1953), 179–219.

5 Boj za právo: Sborník aktů politických v věcech státu a národa českého od roku 1848, ed. J. Černý (Prague, 1893), 110–11.

6 C. E. Black, "Poznań and Europe in 1848," Journal of Central European Affairs, 8/2 (1948), 191–206. Also Namier, 1848: The Revolution of the Intellectuals, 57–65.

7 See D. Rapant, Slovenské povstanie roku 1848–49: Dejiny a dokumenty, (Turčiansky Svätý Martin, 1937), I/II, Doc. no. 13, p. 64.

of problems facing the Slavs within the Austrian empire.[8] Throughout the month of April reports of the Sperlgasse meetings continued to drift back from Vienna to the provinces.

The first formal suggestion of a Slav "congress" or "parliament" came on 20 April with the publication of the Croat Ivan Kukuljević-Sakcinski's article "Kakva treba da bude u obće naša politika" (What Our General Policy Should Be) in the Zagreb newspaper *Novine Dalmatinske-Horvatske-Slavonske* (Dalmatian-Croatian-Slavo-nian News), recommending an assembly – *sabor* – made up of Slavs drawn from Russia, Poland, Serbia, Montenegro, Bosnia, and Bulgaria, with representatives of the Slavs of Saxony, Prussia, and the Austrian empire in attendance: let all attend, wrote Kukuljević, "whether of the great branch [of Slavs], whether living under this or that sovereignty, whether speaking with northern or southern accent." Where the Slavs would gather, be it "golden Prague" or some other city, was for the majority to decide.[9] Three days later, this time from Poznań, came another initiative: writing from Berlin Street on 23 April, Jerzy Moraczewski in Poznań suggested in a letter to Dr. František Brauner in Prague that "some kind of assembly" of Slavs, Czechs, Poles, Moravians, "Illyrians," and Serbs – possibly the Slovaks of Hungary and the Ruthenes – might be convened. In his subsequent account of the Slav Congress, Moraczewski indicated that his initiative was no mere personal whim but was known to the Komitet Narodowy, the Polish National Committee in Poznań;[10] a "common front" of Poles and Czechs menaced by Germans was not inconceivable and Moraczewski's first letter emphasized the common threat. Meanwhile in Prague the talk began to turn on more or less the same lines, a Slav "assembly," a proposal assiduously canvassed by Štúr, who returned to Prague on 20 April; before Easter (that is, before 23 April 1848) a "confidential meeting" was held to discuss Slav cooperation.[11] Štúr declared himself in favour of Czech-Slovak *rapprochement*. Vilém Gauč – staunch supporter of the radical organization Český Repeal – offered his assistance; Czech "specialists" in Slav affairs, Jan Erazim Vocel, Karel Jaromír Erben, Karel V. Zap, and Jan Pětr Jordan (an expatriate Lusatian Serb, then resident in Prague), also contributed their advice and views. While Czech societies in the city split off in deliberate separation from German bodies, plans went ahead to set up a new Slav society, the Slovanská orlice (The Slav Eagle), whose inspiration was Slav solidarity.

What precipitated a decision, however, was the arrival in Prague of the "Schilling committee," the emissaries from Frankfurt, who on 29 April tried both to cajole and to bully the Czechs into sending delegates to the German parliament. Introduced

8 See *Slovanský sjezd v Praze 1848: Sbírka dokumentů*, ed. Z. Tobolka and V. Žáček (Prague, 1952), I, 11. Rapant, *Slovenské povstanie roku 1848–49*, 65, prints the same letter, ascribing it to J. L. Stájský. *Slovanský sjezd* (as this volume will be cited henceforward) does, however, use the original spelling and identifies "fr." as J. V. Frič.

9 *Slovanský sjezd*, 18–21.

10 J. Moraczewski, *Opis pierwszego zjazdu słowiańskiego* (Poznań, 1848), 8.

11 J. V. Frič, *Paměti* (Prague, 1886), III, 21.

to the "Foreign Affairs" section of the Národní výbor, the three men from Frankfurt provoked a verbal brawl: introduced by Dr. Karl Georg von Wächter, Dr. Ernst Schilling – "the brazen Viennese" (*der schamlose Wiener*) – launched into a furious attack on the Slavs, taunting them with wanting to found a "Slav empire" only to destroy Hungary, all this by a people which had no capacity for freedom. If the Czechs were at all realistic, they must see that their best hope lay in sending deputies to Frankfurt: Bohemia and Prague were German. Schilling was roundly answered, not least by František Ladislav Rieger who insisted on absolute equality between nationalities in the Austrian empire, for this alone would compel the Germans and Hungarians to abandon the notion of hegemony over the Czechs and Slovaks.[12]

The confrontation with the Schilling committee was decisive in crystallizing Czech interest in a Slav "united front." The next day (30 April) Karel Havlíček-Borovský's *Národní noviny* (National News) carried a translation of Kukuljević's article calling for a "Slav congress": at ten o'clock in the morning, at Vocel's house in Cracow Street, a score of men assembled to discuss such a congress.[13] Karel Zap read out Kukuljević's article and its suggestion that Prague might be the *venue*; Jordan mentioned that the Poznań Poles were interested; Štúr, who had been a prime mover in the earlier initiative, spoke passionately of the need for a general Slav conference. More than that, he produced a "manifesto," its text already drafted, summoning the Slavs to an assembly, opening on 21 May and to be convened in "time-honoured Slavonic Prague."[14] Zap and Vocel warmly supported Štúr's proposal; after a short debate, the draft "manifesto" was agreed upon, with the suggestion that Pavel Josef Šafařík, Palacký, and members of the Bohemian nobility should sign it. (Since Šafařík was in Vienna, Jan Norbert, Knight of Neuberg intended to post it to him for signing.) At this the meeting adjourned.

At three o'clock in the afternoon a second meeting convened, this time in the Měšťanská beseda, a more formal affair devoted to electing a committee to handle the business of the "Slav assembly." Four lists of names were proposed for membership of the committee: members of the standing committee, substitute or co-opted members (*náhradníci*), representatives of the city, and "parties to the undertaking." In the voting for the first group Zap obtained 20 votes, Karel Ignác Villani, Václav Svatopluk Štulc, Rieger, Neuberg, and W. Grzybowski (a Pole resident in Prague) 16 votes, Vojtěch Deym, Palacký, and Vocel 15 votes, and Erben and Jordan 15. Brauner, Karel Boleslav Štorch, Havlíček, and Jan Slavík were elected to the second list with 13 votes. Martin Karel Brabec (10 votes), Karel Hugo Kašpar and Fran-

12 See *Constitutionelles Prager Zeitung*, 10 May (*Mittwoch*), no. 73: *Extrablatt*. The German delegation met with Sections 9–10 of the Národní výbor. See *Extrablatt*, paras. 1–5.

13 See H. Traub, "O přípravách k Slovanskému sjezdu v Praze 1848 … ," *Časopis Českého musea*, 1918, 246ff. Entry by date of meeting, minutes of the Prague Preparatory Committee. Here p. 249.

14 This is the very first text of the "manifesto" summoning a Slav congress. Reprinted in *L'udovít Štúr. K přátelům, k bratrům* (Prague, 1955), 269.

tišek S. Kř. Jaroš (6 votes), Pavel Mnouček and Jan Rypota (2 votes) were elected as "city representatives." Baron Robert Hildprandt and the counts Rummerskirch, Hanuš Kolovrat-Krakovský, and Vincenc and Kristián Valdštein were included under "parties to the undertaking,"[15] the seal of respectability supplied by the Slavophil Bohemian aristocracy.

The one name not included under any category was that of L'udovít Štúr, who, two hours before this meeting began, had gone to the St. Wenceslas Baths, there to take part in the inauguration of the new Slav society, Slovanská lípa.[16] Here his speech very closely resembled the draft "manifesto" he had produced earlier that same morning at Vocel's house. His plea, as ever passionately declaimed, was for the Slavs to mobilize their strength – "our dispersal was our weakness, our weakness was the strength of our enemies." It was a fiery address and one which threw the charges of "dangerous Panslavism" back in the teeth of its propagators.[17] Neuberg meanwhile sent Štúr's original "manifesto" by post to Šafařík in Vienna, together with an account of the day's proceedings: "a nucleus of spirited patriots," Neuberg wrote, have on this day taken a positive stride towards "saving Austria, greater Austria" and attached to the letter Šafařík would find the "manifesto" summoning "a congress of all Slavs in Austria" to Prague for 21 May, all other Slavs being invited as guests. Neuberg seemed hugely optimistic; this congress would supply the counterweight to Germany, it would guarantee the integrity of Austria and the national rights of the Slavs, it would "solve the important and difficult Polish problem on terms favourable to Austria and to the Slavs." It was "the sacred mission" (*die heilige Aufgabe*) of "patriots" to mobilize such strength for the Austrian empire.[18]

The last day of April, bearing its many portents for the Slavs within and beyond the Austrian empire, had become a watershed. In Vienna itself, the pro-German Austrians grew angry with the Czechs for their unwillingness to join with Germany, and the announcement of the Slav Congress could only raise monstrous pictures in their minds of Czech perfidy, as well as bringing back the hoots and jeers about the *Slawenreich*. This juncture of rival passions and supposed loyalties had to take only a very short step to outright hatred. The "counter-revolution" was creating itself in these purely national terms at a very early stage, though the critical point had not yet come. Into this menacing situation the Prague meeting had struck its plan for a

15 Traub, "O přípravách," 249.
16 For the Slovanská lípa, see *Slovanská lípa*, Protocols (Microfilm), Národní Museum (Prague): Literární Archiv (now known as Literární archív památníku národního písemnictví). The society became formally organized, and held its second meeting on 21 May, when its committee was announced. The constitutional principles were written, and dated 24 May, signed by J. P. Šafařík and W. Gauč, see Protocols (Microfilm). See *Slawische Jahrbücher* ... , ed. J. P. Jordan (Leipzig, 1848), 130, under Slovanská lípa.
17 See *L'udovít Štúr. K přátelům, k bratrům*, 267; cf. Frič, *Paměti*, III, p. 44, on Štúr and Slovanská lípa. For details of the Slovanská orlice, see Protocols, *Slov. lípa*. (Microfilm), Nár. Mus.: Lit. Archiv.
18 Neuberg-Šafařík correspondence, Neuberg to Šafařík, 30 April 1848, Nár. Mus.: Lit. Archiv.

Slav congress limited to Austrian Slavs, designed to save the empire from its Germanist malefactors. On and after 1 May, the Prague committee had to face two opponents, one pro-German, pro-Magyar, and anti-Slav, the other pro-Slav and anti-German, both seeking to determine the fate of the Slav Congress. The struggle was inevitably concentrated in the "Preparatory" or "Organizing" Committee and opened – symbolically – with a Polish voice raised at the session of 1 May. The beginning of dissension had taken merely twenty-four hours.

The monolithic unity which was implied in Neuberg's description of "the nucleus of ardent patriots" present on 30 April was somewhat misleading. The Preparatory Committee which had been brought into being by the voting that day was the very centre of Congress activity, yet the presence of town representatives and nobility indicated wider ramifications. Slávia, Měšťanská beseda, and the newly formed Slovanská lípa, all had their men near the seat of this new "Austro-Slav" power. Slávia sent J. V. Frič, J. Vodek, K. J. Lambl, M. Panić (a Serb), and V. Kleinert. The Měšťanská beseda dispatched D. Loos, P. Richter, and K. Kinzelberg, and Slovanská lípa was represented by F. Fingerhut, V. J. Rott, J. A. Gabriel, and K. Svoboda. These names are significant, for it is very probable that the proposed "congress" had been talked over among many of them before the meeting of 30 April. Among them, especially in the persons of the men from Slávia, a strong democratic interest was represented, as well as a faith in the Slav cause which was more expansive than the strict political necessities of Austro-Slavism.

The "nucleus of patriots" (and we must bear in mind Neuberg's special definition of the duty of a patriot) had decided upon the limitations that they wished to set upon the congress. Their chief preoccupation was with the publication of the manifesto to draw the Slav nations to Prague. On 1 May, at the afternoon meeting in the Měšťanská beseda, Karol Malisz presented himself with the request that the Poles might be allowed to join in the deliberations. He was met with the reply that these deliberations were designed solely to secure the salvation of Austria.[19] Since no reply had yet been received from Šafařík in Vienna, nothing further was decided at this meeting. The net result was a rebuff to the Poles, not only to Malisz, but to the plans of the Poles for participation in the Congress.

Štúr meanwhile had not been silent. In an article on the South Slav movement ("Pohled na hybání západních a jižních Slovanů"), dated 1 May and published on the 2nd in Národní noviny, he discussed the theme of inter-Slav cooperation. In five concluding points, Štúr suggested periodic Austro-Slav meetings, a general Slav cohesion based on close contact and fraternity, Slav "societies" on the lines of Slávia and Slovanská lípa, mutuality, and an interchange of newspapers and journals,[20] stressing the leading role which the Czechs had to play. The Czech Committee had every intention of claiming the primacy which Štúr had accorded them. Šafařík's letter of 2 May from Vienna left no doubt that the issue of "loyalty to Austria"

19 Traub, "O přípravách," minutes for 1 April, p. 250.
20 See L'udovít Štúr. K přátelům, k bratrům, 254–65; here 264–5.

had to come first. He had already spoken to the minister of internal affairs, Franz Pillersdorf, who was concerned with the effect that the Slav Congress would have on the Germans. In regard to the first draft of the "manifesto" Šafařík insisted that it was too "Panslav," and as such it would only be used as a weapon. Non-Austrian Slavs could only be invited privately (*privatim*), and it must be shown that they were present at the Congress only as guests and observers (*Zuhörer*).[21]

On 2 May, the Prague Committee debated the objections which Šafařík had raised, adding the invitation to the non-Austrian Slavs at the end of the manifesto. The manifesto was to be published in Czech, German, Polish, "Illyrian," and Lusatian Serb, Štúr being responsible for the Czech and "Illyrian" texts, Jordan for the German and Lusatian Serb, Grzybowski for the Polish.[22] On 3 May, Šafařík wrote a letter from Vienna which was to compensate for the haste of his letter of the 2nd, rushed as it was into the post. Dr. A. J. Beck had taken his first letter somewhat late to the post, hence Šafařík's anxiety. Šafařík repeated the details of his conversation with Pillersdorf; in spite of his fears, the minister told Šafařík to proceed with the Congress, adding: "we [the Slavs] should do what we think proper and purposeful ..." Those with whom Šafařík had talked in Vienna were enthusiastic about the Congress – a good idea come well-nigh too late, for the situation would have been better if Slav representatives were now sitting in Prague. However, all the more reason for speed. Neuberg should have men like Palacký, Antonín Strobach, Wocel (*sic*), and others read the manifesto through once again, word for word, before it was committed to print, but the actual invitation to the non-Austrian Slavs must be revised: Pillersdorf was visibly shocked that Russians might attend – "Also auch Russen!"[23]

Šafařík's emphasis on the public declaration of the aims of the Slav Congress was certainly a very relevant point, for there is some reason for believing that certain ideas about the form of the Congress had already taken some shape. The plans were not centred on a specific programme, but on the choice of particular persons to bring the whole purpose of the Congress to life. Prelog has referred to papers of the Preparatory Committee which contain the lists of names of possible guests to the Congress.[24] These lists were compiled in the very first days of May, and though they were never officially used by the Preparatory Committee, they were the basis on which enquiries to individuals were made. This fact must account for the mention of isolated names in later proceedings of the Preparatory Committee, as if parts of a list were recalled or thought suitable.

Two lists were circulated. One was the directory compiled by Václav Hanka, who drew it up in the first few days of May. It is most comprehensive and included

21 Šafařík to Neuberg, letter of 2 May, Nár. Mus.: Lit. Archiv.
22 Traub, "O přípravách," 251.
23 Šafařík to Neuberg, letter of 3 May, Nár. Mus.: Lit. Archiv.
24 See M. Prelog, *Slavenska renesansa, 1780–1848* (Zagreb, 1924), 286. He uses the phrase "na jednom sačuvanom papiru" – a point elucidated in *Slovanský sjezd*, 225–7.

Russians: "M. Rajevsky, Count Uvarov, Professor Sreznevsky, Professor Kassovsky, Malevsky [these last four names represented St. Petersburg], Professor Pogodin, Katkov, Professor Bodiansky [representing Moscow], Professor Grigorović, Count Działynski, Wolański, Muczkowski, Helcel, Wiszniewski, Cybulski, Demidov, Mickiewicz, Lipiński, Sawiczewski, Zubricky, Caf, Kojsević."[25] These names represented Russian, Polish, Ruthene, and Slovene interests. Among the Poles there were non-Austrian Poles. The poet Adam Mickiewicz was then in Florence, as was Demidov, a Russian diplomat and a patron of the arts. This "Hanka committee" has its own history, for the Polish and Ruthene names were used once again in drawing up a provisional Polish-Ruthene delegate list. This list, which never became effective, also included other Polish names, and this would coincide with the existence of yet another guest-list, which was prepared at the beginning of May. This directory is of greater interest, for in it were entered all those names used by K. V. Zap to circulate the manifesto dated 5 May.

All the Russian names have now disappeared. There is a striking preponderance of newspaper editors, and though this list does not appear to have been formally discussed in the Preparatory Committee (it does not appear in the minutes), it makes its appearance in the to-and-fro correspondence between Zap and the Slav newspapers, as well as in occasional letters. The list reads as follows: P. J. Ohéral (editor), J. Bleiweis (editor), A. Kuzmanić (editor), T. Pavlović (editor), L. Gaj (editor), S. Vraz (editor), M. Popović (editor), J. Dobrzański (editor), the editorial board of the *Gazeta Krakowska* (Cracow Gazette), A. Klodziński, J. Muršec, M. Majer, P. Jawornik, M. Malinowski, the Serbian Metropolitan in Dolni Karlovci (*sic*), W. I. Menzel, L. Klucký, F. Čelakovský, J. Purkyně, J. Kollár, and J. Lubomirski.[26]

There is a great deal of deliberate rearrangement in this second directory. The principle of Austrian Slavdom is quite rigidly adhered to, and not only the Russians but the representatives of the Poznań Poles have been eliminated. Zubritskii has been replaced by Malinowski, a priest of the Uniate church and secretary of the Holovna Rada Rus'ka (Chief Ruthenian Council), which was set up by the Ruthenes.

The Committee meeting of 3 May did not depart from principles already laid down. The enactments of the Committee were to be registered through the chancellory of the Prague Měšťanská beseda.[27] A second version of the minutes indicates that there was some discussion about the details of the Congress. Palacký thought that it might be considered as a closed meeting to devise means to defend Slav nationality. Vocel suggested organization on the lines of the German *Germanistenverein*, while Štúr stressed the time factor. The manifesto was prepared for

25 *Slovanský sjezd*, 225–6. [Names in Czech transliteration.]
26 *Ibid.*, 226–7; also Prelog, *Slavenska renesansa*, 286.
27 Traub, "O přípravách," 251. This was the first meeting where Count J. M. Thun was mentioned in connection with the presidency.

printing on thin paper.[28] Šafařík wrote to Neuberg on 4 May from Vienna, reporting on the Viennese aspects of the Congress situation. This is a very interesting letter, for he suggested a method of organizing the Congress, as well as including a survey of the opposition to the Congress. On its organization, Šafařík sought for order in the Congress proceedings; there could be two types of session, "Round table Sessions" (Circularsitzungen) for each national group, organized in three sections – the first being Bohemians, Moravians, Silesians, the second composed of Poles, the third South Slavs, namely Slovenes, Croats, and Serbs. There could be more if the occasion demanded – should the Ruthenes attend, there could be some arrangement to fit in their dialect. These "Round table sessions" must be closed sessions. "General assemblies" (Generalsitzungen) would be open to all; hence non-Slav languages might be used, German or Latin perhaps, so that general discussions would be possible.[29]

Now the great anti-Slav press war had begun; Šafařík admits that it was only to be expected. Yet another point of resistance could be found in the preparations for the coming elections to the Reichstag. Šafařík quoted the fact that one of the ministers said to him that in this assembly (namely, the Reichstag) the Slavs would be in the majority, so that they could well defend their national interests; but Šafařík could not share this sentiment.[30]

On 5 May, the Preparatory Committee held three meetings to settle the business of the manifesto.[31] At the morning meeting, new signatures were added, those of J. Lubomirski, J. Dobrzański, Stefan Aranitskii, Maxim Papić, Hanuš Kolovrat-Krakovský, Robert Hildprandt, J. Dvoráček in Vienna, Count Vincenc Valdštein, and Count Rummerskirch. The other question of publishing an announcement in the German newspapers in Prague was raised, and Palacký read his text, designed to "reassure the non-Slav citizens of the Empire about the intentions of the Slav Congress." The three points emphasized that the Congress was committed to full and unchanging support of the House of Habsburg, that charges of separatism, Panslavism, and "Russianism" were lies and slander, and that the Slavs would not oppress their non-Slav fellows, being concerned only with the equality of national rights.[32]

28 Ibid.
29 Šafařík to Neuberg, letter of 4 May, Nár. Mus.: Lit. Archiv.
30 Ibid.
31 The dates of these three meetings are in doubt. Slovanský sjezd prints three records for 5 May, one of which was a Protokol, presented for the 5th; this proclamation to the other nationalities was prepared on the advice of Šafařík, transmitted by letter. Šafařík's letter of 3 May to a member of the Committee contained a suggestion of the text, including the words "proti veřejnému obviňování nás německého tisku z panslavismu, separatismu a russismu." These very words appear in the German-language Erklärung. The letter must have arrived on the 5th and been immediately acted upon.
32 See Časopis Českého musea (1848), Appendix 2, p. 18: "Provolání k neslovanským národům v Rakousku." Published in Národní noviny for 7 May, also as a broadsheet in German by Bohumil Haase in Prague.

The influence of Šafařík's letters was marked. The Prague meeting of 5 May had debated the wording of this text to the non-Slavs very extensively, so that several versions had been offered. Erben, Václav Vladivoj Tomek, Vocel, Deym, Rieger, Jordan, and Palacký himself had gone over the terms which they intended to use to describe themselves and their intentions. Grzybowski expressed some concern at the fulsome pro-Austrian sentiments, but the issue was finally settled.[33]

On 5 May, the manifesto of the Committee to the Slavs announcing the Congress was published in *Národní noviny*. Announcing that the Congress would be convened on 31 May, and now incorporating Šafařík's amendments, the published text carried Štúr's first draft only so far as his first two paragraphs. The published text merits close examination. Of even greater interest are the signatures appended to it. The original handwritten draft of the text contained the signatures of Deym, J. M. Thun, Malisz, Neuberg, Hanka, Grzybowski, Štúr, Jordan, Zap, Rieger, Štulc, Palacký, Wocel (*sic*), and Panić.[34] The additional signatures of the 7th were those of S. Aranitskii, Dr. J. Dvoráček, J. Lubomirski, Jan Dobrzański (*"jako pełnomocnik rady narodowej lwowskiej"*), Count V. Valdštein, and Maxim Papić. On the 12th the names of Kolovrat-Krakovský, Robert Hildprandt, and Rummerskirch, all of whom belonged to the nobility, were added.[35] The manifesto was translated into Polish, Croat, Lusatian Serb, and German. In Štúr's handwritten translation of the text into Croat there are no signatures to it. Slovene and Serb translations and an unofficial French version were also produced,[36] though these were not mentioned in the translating arrangements made by the Preparatory Committee.

Although the immediate problem was to circulate the manifesto to the Slavs and take those final steps which would result in a Slav Congress, yet another Congress had assembled on 5 May. The assembly in question was the Wrocław (Breslau) Congress, gathered in Wrocław because this city occupied a central position among the Poles of Galicia, Poznań, Cracow, and the Congress Kingdom.[37] By the end of the meetings, on 9 May, there were almost sixty Poles assembled, but the Congress failed in its purpose of implementing general Polish unity; it was, in effect, ruined by dissension and mistrust.[38]

33 The minutes are given by Traub, "O přípravách," 252, and in *Slovanský sjezd*, 69–70. Cf. Namier, *1848: The Revolution of the Intellectuals*, 106, where he states that Palacký proposed the *Erklärung* on the 5th.

34 Original draft, Nár. Mus.: Lit. Archiv. See also *Časopis Českého musea* (1848), Appendix 1, p. 17.

35 See *Slovanský sjezd*, 82, for note on dates of signatures. What is confusing is the appearance of Dvoráček's name later, though duly sent by Šafařík. It is possible to assume that much confusion attended the publication, for only a few days had elapsed since it had first appeared in any form. Dobrzański was in Vienna with the Lwów delegation.

36 *Slovanský sjezd*, 83–7.

37 H. Meciszewski, *Zjazd polski we Wrocławiu na dniu 5 – go Maja 1848 r* ... (Lwów, 1849), 10. See also M. Tyrowicz, *Polski kongres polityczny we Wrocławiu 1848* (Cracow, 1946), *passim*. See also M. Kukiel, *Czartoryski and European Unity 1770–1861* (Princeton, 1955), 251–76, on Prince Adam Czartoryski's position.

38 See General Dembiński's papers in the Archiwum domowe Czartoryskiego (Cracow), 43ᵉ

On the Slav Congress, the Wrocław Congress prepared a manifesto which was drawn up in Polish and Czech (dated 9 May) and signed by K. Libelt, R. Raczyński, W. Lipski, A. Cieszkowski, R. Berwiński, J. Lubomirski, and M. Darowski. The significant absence here was of any support for the (Prague) Congress by the Cracow Poles. While approving of the idea of a general assembly of delegates to talk over matters relevant to Slavdom, the Wrocław text took issue with the original Czech limitations; Poles could not be divided up geographically or linguistically.[39] The Wrocław text, carrying the names of the Poznań Poles, who were manifestly not Austrian Slavs, was a direct challenge to Czech leadership. Florian Ziemiałkowski, the future Galician conservative, had heard explanations of the Czech intentions at the meetings in the Sperlgasse. He had not been impressed by either the motives or the explanations, and in his *Memoirs* he accused the Czechs of having set out to save the Metternich system, in order that they might rule. Malisz had signed the text of 5 May in the name of the Polish deputation but Ziemiałkowski was curious to know what the Poles could do in a Congress where Czechs, Moravians, and "Illyrians" were playing the main role and where all wanted to struggle for the salvation of Austria.[40]

While the Poles were beginning their meeting in Wrocław, and the call to the Austrian Slavs made its appearance, Zap was sending letters to the Slav newspapers with copies of the manifesto. He wrote to Ante Kuzmanić of *Zora Dalmatinska* (The Dalmatian Dawn), to L. Gaj in Zagreb, to T. Pavlović and the Hungarian Serbs in Pest, to Jan Ohéral in Brno.[41] On 6 May, K. J. Erben wrote to Stanko Vraz, enclosing the text and urging him to press the matter of the Slav Congress upon the South Slavs.[42] Neuberg's letter to Šafařík of 6 May reported that the manifesto was now printed; this letter made an interesting reference to matters not directly connected with the Congress but bearing closely upon its fate, the rise of unrest and disorder in Vienna. The "Serenades" in Vienna had taken on a grimmer cast,[43] and dissatisfaction on the part of the Vienna radicals had increased since the beginning of May. Neuberg observed that any outbreak of "terrorism" in Vienna would make a "directory" in Bohemia inevitable.[44] This supposed Czech separationist tendency,

partie – "Mémoires du général sur ... les conférences de Breslau." Also 44ᵉ partie – "Divers écrits polonais et français ... relatifs aux évènements de 1848 et aux conférences de Breslau," pp. 355–7 on the aims of the Congress, p. 369; R41 and R42, Dembiński's letter drafts on the proposed Congress; R43, Dembiński's letter to the Congress. Also H. Meciszewski, *Zjazd polski*, 30.

39 W. T. Wisłocki, "Kongres słowiański roku 1848 i sprawa polska," in *Rocznik zakładu narodowego im. Ossolińskich*, I/II (Lwów, 1928), 157–8.

40 *Pamiętniki Floryana Ziemiałkowskiego: Rok 1848* (Cracow, 1904), 30ff.

41 *Slovanský sjezd*, 229–31.

42 *Ibid.*, 232.

43 Literally serenades, rowdy musical political concerts, held in the evenings, outside the houses of unpopular government officials and ministers, and later outside taverns and shops. The origin of this kind of demonstration can be traced to a play in Vienna, where a mock serenade took the students' fancy. It was good pantomime, where the audience joined in.

44 Neuberg to Šafařík, letter of 6 May, Nár. Mus.: Lit. Archiv.

which so alienated the Vienna liberals from the Czechs and rendered the Poles so deeply suspicious of the Czech motives, had evidently already made its appearance. Leo (Lev) Thun had to invoke measures to put down persecution of the Jews (*Judenverfolgung*) and attacks on bakeries. Peace, however, returned to Prague.[45]

In addition to the letter, Neuberg included the definitive list of the membership of the Preparatory Committee and the Slav Congress Committee. The president of the Preparatory Committee was Count J. M. Thun, the vice-president was Neuberg, with Villani, Rieger, Štulc, Hanka, Palacký, Deym, Vocel, Jordan, Erben, and Zap as members, plus Brauner and Štorch. Five members of the nobility were acting as guarantors. The second inclusion was a text which was later published as a pamphlet under the title *Ein Wort zur Verständniss über Slavenversammlung in Prag* (A Word in Explanation Concerning the Slav Congress in Prague). This declared the Austrian Slav strength – 18 million Slavs in Austria, whose "kind Emperor" had broken their chains and where the Constitution made them free men.[46] The appeal for a German-Slav unity fell on deaf ears, as the fear of some great Slav "conspiracy" grew in Vienna, as well as in Pest and in Frankfurt. In his letter of 6 May, Šafařík had told Palacký of the growing anti-Slav feelings, of "agitations and disturbances," and reported that he had heard that Count Lajos Batthyány, three days previous, had come to ask for troops against the Serbs and Croats.

Šafařík's letter of 8 May to Neuberg developed this theme of the growing opposition to the Slavs, especially in the pro-German press. *Die Constitution* led the attack, as indeed it excelled in vicious polemics and journalistic abuse. Šafařík suggested that the Preparatory Committee might find itself permanent premises, as well as setting up a small exchequer (*Cassa*), where voluntary contributions could be taken. The main thing was to get the appeal to the Slavs out and circulated as quickly as possible. The press persisted with its attacks, Šafařík went on: it had been suggested that 200 ducats should be put on Štúr's head. The change of residence of the Court was not much discussed, yet this was an event which could bring calamity down on all heads. Šafařík asked Neuberg what he thought of the chances of the implementation of the new constitution in Bohemia, a question prompted perhaps by the realization that revolutionary times were changing and paper promises were but weak instruments.[47]

While Šafařík was writing his letters from Vienna, progress was being made with the circulation of the appeal to the Slavs. On 8 May, Jan Ohéral replied to Zap's invitation of 5 May with a letter which indicated that the Moravians had already picked their delegation to the Congress.[48] On 9 May, the Vienna Czechs and Moravians sent a letter of congratulation to the Preparatory Committee in Prague. The translation of the appeal to the Slavs from *Národní noviny* had appeared in the

45 *Ibid.*
46 Printed in *Slovanský sjezd*, 44–6.
47 Šafařík to Neuberg, letter of 8 May, Nár. Mus.: Lit. Archiv.
48 *Slovanský sjezd*, 232–3.

Wiener Zeitung on 9 May. The congratulation was mixed with ominous complaint against the Poles, especially the Polish students in Vienna. The motive for the Polish dissent lay with Galicia, while the vexed question of the Czech officials in Galicia was being used by the Poles to abuse the Czechs. Already, misgivings were being voiced at the fateful combination of the Czechs, loyal to Austria, and the Poles. The letter asked that some announcement – designed to allay both suspicions and fears – be made.[49]

By the first ten days of May the reaction of both the Slavs and the non-Slavs to the idea of the proposed Congress was becoming clearer. The appeal to the Slav nations had appeared in the Vienna press. There had been the first replies to Zap's circular of 5 May. The Poles, both Austrian and non-Austrian, had made it plain that they would not be denied a place in the Congress and certainly desired an active role in its preparation. Šafařík himself had urged the greatest speed in bringing the business of the Congress to a successful conclusion, yet the actual arrangements for a Congress proceeded relatively slowly. The Congress had become a very significant item of discussion beyond the doors of the Preparatory Committee in Prague and by bodies less concerned with its welfare.

Before the fateful meeting of 13 May, when the Preparatory Committee debated the Polish question, the anti-Slav press in Vienna had continued its assault on the Slavs, while the Vienna Ministerialrath had also brought the matter up for serious discussion. Šafařík had already been visibly alarmed at the tone of the press. *Die österreichischdeutsche Zeitung*, on 8, 10, and 12 May, ran a series of articles under the evocative title of *Das lustige alte Wien* (Gay Old Vienna).[50] The Viennese were warned explicitly to guard their capital against a very dreadful fate; readers were advised to consider the present events in Prague and there they would find a picture of the fate in store for them. Prague had become the focal point of this huge new Slav empire, and it would be suicide for Vienna to give that helping hand to the foundation of the Slav empire, an assistance which Palacký had been seeking. On 10 May, *Der Freimuthige* (in an article called "Slavischer Volkstag in Prag") lashed out viciously at the Slav Congress. The article began by saying that the counterblow to Frankfurt had long been awaited – now it had come, and with it the long-feared clash between the Western Slavs and the Germans. These Slav leaders were banking on the outbreak of revolutionary movements in Russia, on blending the speakers of many Slav dialects into one combination, into a Slav republic which would stretch from the coast of the White Sea to the Bosphorus. Their talk of "loyalty to the monarchy" could not be taken seriously, for the monarchy had never had deep roots in the Slav peoples. The Congress should be banned.[51]

While sections of the Vienna press were shouting for government action against

49 The letter from Vienna is printed in *Slovanský sjezd*, 155–7.
50 Numbers 18, 20, and 22 of the newspaper. Before 14 April, the newspaper had been called *Die österreichische konstitutionelle deutsche Zeitung*.
51 *Der Freimüthige*, 10 May, no. 34, p. 137.

the Slavs, and as the Prague Preparatory Committee was itself preoccupied with the question of the governmental attitude, the meeting of the Council of Ministers of 10 May, attended by Pillersdorf, F. Freiherr von Sommaruga, P. Freiherr von Krauss, Count Theodor Latour, Anton Freiherr von Dobblhoff, and officials from other ministerial councils, raised the matter of the Slav Congress. The minister of internal affairs, Pillersdorf, was to contact Count Leo Thun and pursue the question of the legality of the Congress, as well as any other relevant matters.[52] On 11 May, Pillersdorf wrote to Count Leo Thun, pointing out that the political freedom of the Slavs – and the Germans – was secured by the Constitution. The exact significance of the forthcoming Slav Congress was somewhat hard to divine, giving rise to the fear that it might not be merely an attempt to draw level with the Germans, but a combination designed to bring the Germans into subservience. The tension between the Czechs and Germans of Bohemia had been very severe, and now this new step could bring the danger of "serious clashes" (*ernster Collisionen*) nearer. Pillersdorf requested that further information might be supplied to him by Leo Thun, for here was a Slav assembly in Prague drawing to itself not only Austrian but non-Austrian citizens. Though the right of assembly had been guaranteed, it was the duty of the government to see that this was not abused.[53]

On 12 May, the session of the council of ministers heard Pillersdorf advise that the Congress must not become a danger to the German population. The gubernial-president of Bohemia, Leo Thun, must be informed that this projected Congress could not be permitted to develop into a kind of Slav parliament with delegates from every Slav nation. In other words, the Austrian authorities would not hamper a Czech national demonstration, provided that it did not provoke German counter-action, but a general Slav assembly could not be tolerated. As German counter-action was likely, the Congress could not be regarded very favourably by the Vienna authorities. The legal pretext for objecting to the proposed Congress was that the vagueness of its intentions might lead it into paths which could abuse the freedom of assembly (*Assotiationsrecht*) granted by the Constitution.

On 13 May, Pillersdorf wrote once more to Leo Thun about the legal position of the Congress. The minister suggested to Leo Thun that he might find it more effective to set up a joint German-Slav Committee, under his presidency, which could arbitrate between the nationalities in this matter.[54] The next discussion of the Congress by the Council of Ministers was to be held on the 19th, when they were obliged to discuss the Magyar protest against the events in Prague.

The early efforts of the Prague Preparatory Committee now assumed a momentum which caused reactions far from the centre. One of the problems which faced

52 Minutes printed in *Slovanský sjezd*, 213.
53 *Ibid.*, 214–15, from Ministry of the Interior (Prague) archives, original ref. PG 1846–1849 fs. 15c/28, no. 6196.
54 *Ibid.*

the Committee was to contact the Croats and the Serbs, who were faced with a rapidly developing and dangerous situation. The Slovak situation was increasingly tense. On 2 May in Bratislava, and 10 May at Liptovský Svätý Mikuláš, the Slovaks had once again reasserted the demands which had been suppressed during the last days of March.[55] True to their established principles, the Slovaks were intent on gaining the constitutional guarantee of their nationality, which alone could provide the safeguards against Hungarian encroachment. On 9 May the Polish delegation in Vienna had sent the Rada Narodowa in Lwów news of the Slav Congress; the message, signed by L. D. Borkowski and W. Zbyszewski, assumed that the Rada would probably wait to choose its delegation to the Congress. On the 10th, Šafařík wrote to Gaj in Zagreb about the forthcoming Congress. His letter pointed out that the Congress would probably coincide with the Croat parliament's sessions, but "the eyes of Europe" were on Prague and the Croats could find men to attend.[56] The letter to Gaj reported that Palacký had come to Vienna to see the minister (Pillersdorf). The same day Šafařík had written to Neuberg, announcing Palacký's arrival in Vienna on the 9th, and commenting that the government in Vienna was loosing its grip on affairs.[57] Šafařík was clearly disturbed over the course which events were taking.

The Preparatory Committee had much to discuss on the morning of 11 May when they assembled at Neuberg's house. Palacký had left for Vienna; F. Zach reported in writing from Zagreb on conversations with the Croats. The meeting opened with the reading of Šafařík's letters of 4, 7, 8, and 9 May. Zach had written from Zagreb that the Serbs and Croats were effecting some *rapprochement*, though Gaj himself had lost much of his popularity. The main question at the meeting was whether or not the Germans should be invited to the Congress, whether by formal invitation or by having them discuss relevant matters with the Slavs. Jordan and Kašpar raised the question, Rieger suggested the compromise of joint discussion, Deym pointed out that this would change the Slav Congress; the majority opposed a formal invitation to the Germans to attend the Slav Congress.[58]

The idea of a proclamation to the citizens of Prague (the actual text of which was prepared later and dated 21 May) was raised as an item for discussion, as was that of finance; Erben and Kašpar were appointed to the exchequer. The meeting had reported no contact yet with La Société slave de Paris, although a copy of the manifesto to the Slavs about the Congress had been sent to them. In short, the

55 See Rapant, *Slovenské povstanie roku 1848–49*, i/ii, no. 48, 167–70, and no. 66, 202–6, under "Žiadosti slovenského národa."

56 "Pisma pisana Dr. Ljudevitu Gaju i neki njegovi sastavci (1826–1850)," in *Grada za povijest književnosti* ..., vi, ed. V. Deželić (Zagreb, 1909), 200.

57 Šafařík to Neuberg, letter of 10 May, Nár. Mus.: Lit. Archiv.

58 See Traub, "O přípravách," 254 for the minutes of the meeting. The question of an invitation to the Germans was an important element in the viewpoint of those who wished to see the Congress less aggressively Slav.

session of 11 May was a business meeting with little or no hint of the storm which was to burst upon the Committee on the 13th, when the Polish question was discussed.

On 4 May, Havlíček-Borovský had arrived in Cracow. His account of his visit to Galicia appeared in *Národní noviny* on 12 May, under the title "Rakouská vláda a Poláci" (The Austrian Government and the Poles). Characteristically, it was a brilliant and penetrating analysis of the Polish situation showing the many complexities of Polish thought and the possibilities of Polish policy, yet it was a bitter attack on the Poles, on Polish arrogance and impatience.[59] There was much justice in Havlíček-Borovský's favourable remarks about the Ruthenes, the same Ruthenes whom he had so admired in 1844. The old Polish dream of an empire running from the Baltic to the Black Sea was still dominant – "a distant path, a vain wish," was Havlíček-Borovský's comment on this. This article, in many ways, summed up the Czech view of the Poles and the consequences of their participation in the Slav Congress. Conversely, opinion among the Poles was not inclined to be gentle to the "Czech Ulysses," seeming to seek nothing less than hegemony of the Slav race. The Poles sneered at the Czech programme which clung so obstinately to the salvation of Austria; the Czechs feared and almost despised the Polish arrogance and their automatic claim to supremacy among the non-Russian Slavs.

The Czech-Polish question was debated by the Preparatory Committee on 13 May.[60] This was the critical meeting, and marked the end of the untrammelled Czech control of the Congress movement. The Czechs had known that they would have to face the animosity of the Frankfurt Germans, proof of which they had had with the Schilling committee. The pro-Frankfurt Vienna liberals had not taken kindly to the idea of the Slav Congress, and Šafařík had indicated in his letters that the Hungarians would take the same view. All this the Committee could deduce from the situation itself. The Polish participation now threatened to be Polish intervention. The president of the Committee, J. M. Thun, could only reaffirm the main objective of the Congress – the salvation of Austria. Palacký, who had returned from Vienna, had met Havlíček-Borovský who was on his way to Zagreb after visiting Galicia. Palacký's advice to the Committee was that they should not reject the "respectable" Polish faction.[61] The question of the participation of the Galician Poles was one which included a variety of factors: the aristocrats, the democrats, and the role of the *émigrés*. There could be considerable differences of interpretation about this situation. Jordan spoke – at some length – about the Poznán Poles and the virtues which could be ascribed to them. Zap pointed out that

---

59 Printed in *Politické spisy K. Havlíčka-Borovského*, ed. Z. Tobolka (Prague, 1901), II, no. 5. See shortened edition of his writings in *Duch Národních novin*, ed. M. Novotný (Prague, 1948).

60 Traub, "O přípravách," 319.

61 *Ibid.* The phrase used was "Dobré frakci polské musime ruku podati."

some agreement between the Poles and the Ruthenes must be arranged. The "Polish debate" developed into an interchange of views about the Poles, in which Rieger put his finger on the crux of the matter by pointing out that the Czechs were torn between the Poles and the empire. Brauner told his story of travelling in San-decki (i.e. the Nowy Sącz area) in 1846, and the question he put to the peasants: "Were they Poles? No, they were peaceful people. Were they Germans? No, they were honest men."[62] The discussion closed without any definite result, except per-haps a general realization that the Poles themselves were the major difficulty facing Czech control of the Congress. Rieger recalled the Sperlgasse conversations of 7 April, when the second Czech delegation talked with the Poles – Dobrzański, W. Biesiadecki, and T. Wolański – about their views of the situation in general.

Meanwhile in Galicia the Lwów Rada Narodowa noted in its minutes of the evening meeting of 12 May that the summons to the Slav Congress had been read. The meeting of the 15th decided that no further action would be taken to select a delegation to the Congress until they had heard more from the Vienna deputation. This had been the advice in the message sent to the Rada Narodowa from Vienna on 9 May by the delegation.[63]

There were difficulties not only in Galicia. Šafařík's letter of 14 May to Neuberg indicated that after the announcement of the 5th, and the rumours of the Court's move to Prague, the opposition to the Slavs had taken on a very bitter tone; he was not impressed with the list of new ministers which was being currently circulated (and his comments on the candidates betrayed a strong touch of anti-Semitism). Šafařík advised Neuberg that he hoped soon to be returning to Prague; Havlíček had left for Zagreb, but Šarařík thought that it would be useful to send a represen-tative from Bohemia to Karlovci to the National Assembly there on 27 May, and to Zagreb to the Diet on 1 June.[64] The Serbs were holding their assembly (*skupština*) in Novi Sad from 13 to 15 May, but this was a preliminary gathering for the Na-tional Assembly. Šafařík urged upon Neuberg that the Czechs should send represen-tatives to these meetings, so that they might inform Prague of the turn of events among the South Slavs. This, in fact, was partly accomplished, when Erben and Lambl were chosen to attend the Croat *sabor* as Czech observers.[65]

The Preparatory Committee in Prague did not meet again until 19 May. The last session of the 13th had left the Congress question very much in the air, since the participation of the Croats and Serbs had yet to be arranged, and the intervention of the Poles was still only a threat. Only the Moravians had whole-heartedly ac-cepted and chosen their delegation at the same time. There existed a shadow Polish

62 *Ibid.*, 320.
63 *Slovanský sjezd*, 237.
64 This letter is printed in *Slovanský sjezd*, 58–9.
65 See Deželić, *Grada za provijest književnosti*, VI, 200–1, Šafařík to Gaj, on Erben and Lambl being chosen to attend the *sabor* as Czech representatives. Dated 25 May.

"committee," and the Wrocław Congress had meanwhile committed the Poles to attendance at Prague, but the issue still had to be thrashed out by the separate National Committees in Galicia and Poznań. The Lwów Rada Narodowa did not tackle the business of sending representatives to the Congress until 17 May.

But beyond the channels of councils and committees, the Slav and non-Slav press was taking the Congress very seriously. The Congress had already had its journalistic baptism of fire by 10–11 May. While the advisory or executive agencies set up by the various Slav nationalities were slower in reacting, Slav patriotic societies were quicker to respond to the Prague Committee. The "Czech-Slovak-Illyrian" society in Graz sent a congratulatory message to the Czech Committee on 13 May. Signed by J. Dragoni-Křenovský, a Moravian, the address waxed most enthusiastic about the possibilities of the gathering of the Slavs of the Austrian empire, yet it expressed this enthusiasm in terms of an all-Slav politics which manifestly contradicted the original terms of the appeal of 5 May from Prague.[66] This reaction was typical, for the Congress had not become ordered and arranged as the expression of a particular policy. It was all things to all Slavs, if they chose to make it so. The vagueness had encouraged the Vienna authorities to question the whole undertaking on the grounds of a technical legality. The anti-Slav Vienna press did not choose to discriminate on the fine points of Austrian and non-Austrian Slav. The *Wiener Schnellpost* (writing on 13–14 May about "Das slavische Parlament") attacked the Congress bitterly, and with it the Bohemians, who did not indeed seem to realize that the "Slavicizing" of the Austrian Germans would be resisted. The anti-Slav press played a major role in exciting hostile passions which alienated sympathy and clouded understanding of the issues of the revolution still at stake.

The Lwów newspaper *Postęp* (Progress) (organ of the left-wing magnate Count Leon Rzewuski, who was sympathetic to the Ruthene cause) printed the Prague manifesto on the 5th, adding its own comment on the Congress. It was published in Lwów on the same day that the Polish participation was being debated in Prague. *Postęp* insisted that the Rada Narodowa must send representatives of both Polish and Ruthene nationality to Prague.[67] The Rada Narodowa proceeded to make up their minds about this double representation, but they no longer retained all the initiative, since Zap had already written to Iakiv Holovatskii about the Congress and the possibility of the Ruthenes attending.[68]

The situation of the Congress by mid-May was still confused. The attitude of the pro-German Vienna "liberals" was clear from the outset, though they had advanced from scornful comment to thinly veiled threats, with reference to armed force which

---

66 Printed in *Slovanský sjezd*, 157–60.

67 Quoted in I. Bryk, "Slavyanskiy z'izd u Prazii 1848 r ... ," in *Zapiski naukovoho tovarystva im. Shevchenka*, 129 (Lwów, 1920 [in Ukrainian]), 158. Bryk is still the best compilation of Polish newspaper material on the Ruthene question, though he chose his quotations with a ready eye to demonstrate the worst aspects of the Polish case.

68 See *Slovanský sjezd*, 228.

alarmed Šafařík. There is no doubt that there was genuine fear of Russian intervention;[69] further, the well-nigh traditional fear of a "Panslavistic combination," discussed long before 1848, could be emphasized to a public well-conditioned to the danger.

It is clear from the Slav reaction to the early announcements about the Congress that two views predominated, one prepared to support the Bohemian lead and to follow this approach, the other which saw in the manifesto a chance to organize a general Slav assembly. The whole awkward paradox was how the Slav Congress might be a "Slav Congress" without the active participation of a significant number of the Slavs. The Preparatory Committee did not delude itself that it had solved this dilemma. While it was prepared to invite individuals from the non-Austrian Slavs, this concession would not hold back the insistence of the Poles that they should be permitted to assist in the preparation of the Congress. Up to the middle of May, the Preparatory Committee had a very tight control upon the destiny of the Congress. This was virtually a negative benefit, for the matter had not gone beyond announcement and discussion. The Preparatory Committee was most anxious to ensure the attendance of the Croats and the Serbs, yet there was the difficulty of the clash of date with the South Slav National Assemblies.

Up to this point, by mid-May at the latest, the Preparatory Committee in Prague could persuade itself that it still possessed the initiative in Congress matters, and could count upon sufficient support to justify its steps. But the creation of a Slav front could not always suit the particularities of the Bohemian situation. The attempt to create a Slav front involved the Committee, Slavs both Austrian and non-Austrian, as well as parties antagonistic to the whole dangerous scheme. To the ranks of German antagonists were to be added the Magyars.

The question remained now how much control Prague could retain.

Time, it seemed, was no friend to the organizers of the Slav Congress. Although Šafařík had written early in May that the situation might well be more favourable if the delegates to the Congress were actually in session, the whole scope of the Congress had become much more complex and more dangerous. The paradox was that the Slav Congress could not be what it proclaimed to the world without large-scale Slav participation, yet this deliberate extension presented a range of new problems. The question of the participation of the non-Austrian Slavs had been left hanging in the air, but this was the crux of the whole Congress matter, especially in non-Slav eyes. All that the Wrocław Congress had established was that no single body of Poles would attend in Prague to speak for Poland and the Polish cause, though the same body, admittedly only in the name of certain participants, had endorsed the necessity of Polish attendance in Prague. And while the Preparatory Committee was attempting to break down "the Chinese walls" which slowed inter-Slav contacts, the government of Hungary was making a determined effort to rebuild these barriers.

69 Cf. Rath, *The Viennese Revolution,* 182.

It was quite consistent that the Magyars should try to prevent the organization of the Slav Congress, committed as it was to the salvation of the empire, embodying as it did all the numerical preponderance of the Slavs. On 16 May Batthyány sent to Prince Pál Eszterházy, Hungary's representative for "Foreign Affairs" at the Vienna Court, Hungary's protest over the Congress; this was to be transmitted to the authorities in Vienna.[70] The Magyar argument was very specific, and aimed at cutting the ground completely from under the feet of the Congress planners in Prague. The Congress, the Magyars argued, was merely a provincial assembly in Bohemia, so that the Galicians should be forbidden to attend.[71] Any encouragement to the Congress could only help "Panslavism." The protest was duly considered by the Ministerialrath on 19 May, when Pillersdorf answered the Magyars with yet another reference to the rights guaranteed to the nationalities by the Constitution.[72] Although Hungary's protest was serious, it amounted in this formal state to mere obstructionism, an extension of Hungary's intervention of 15 April, demanding for Galicia the rights given to Bohemia. But the Magyars had struck at the weak spot in the Congress armour, the participation of the Poles and the status of the Congress without them.

The Preparatory Committee met again on 19 May at Neuberg's house. There seems to be some confusion about the date of this meeting. In their documentary collection, Tobolka and Žáček print this as 9 May, yet the agenda of the meeting indicates that events which happened after the 9th were discussed. Traub prints the same meeting as one held on the 19th. In addition to the standing members of Committee, Kolovrat-Krakovský, Baron Aehrenthal, Vincenc Valdštein, Prince Leon Sapieha, and Antoni Walewski were present, the last two men intimates and representatives of Prince Adam Czartoryski.[73] Count J. M. Thun was in the chair.

The minutes record that Zap read a letter from Šafařík to Neuberg. (Tobolka and Žáček suggest that this might be the letter of the 14th, as the date is illegible in the written minutes.) Zap then read another letter from Šafařík, where the date is also illegible. This letter suggested that the Preparatory Committee might send two delegates to the Serb assembly at Sremski Karlovci. Šafařík made this suggestion in his letter of 14 May, when he said that the same delegates could then travel on to Zagreb for the Croat assembly on 1 June; the delegation must include, Šafařík

70 Rapant, *Slovenské povstanie roku 1848–49*, I/II, no. 79, 225–6. Also in L. Steier, *A tót nemzetiségi kérdés 1848–49-ben* (Budapest, 1937), no. 36, 66–7. A Czech translation is given in Černý, *Boj za právo*, no. 98, 262–3 (without a date).
71 Rapant, *Slovenské povstanie roku 1848–49*, 225–6.
72 *Slovanský sjezd*, 218.
73 Traub, "O přípravách," 321, dates it the 19th; *Slovanský sjezd*, 70–2, dates it the 9th. The texts are exactly the same. Walewski did not arrive in Prague in the first ten days of May. The conclusive point that *Slovanský sjezd* has made a considerable error is to be found in Prelog, *Slavenska renesansa*, 307 – the same additional members are mentioned as having been present. The exact similarity of the texts in Traub and *Slovanský sjezd* does not make it conceivable that there was a meeting on the 9th.

added, someone who can speak "Illyrian." When Zap read this letter out to the Committee, Neuberg added that there was no one who could speak "Illyrian," consequently they would be obliged to send instructions to Stanko Vraz.[74] The letters which Zap read were from Šafařík, and these were therefore written on 10 and 14 May respectively. (The meeting of 11 May had already heard the Šafařík letters of 4, 7, 8, and 9 May.) As Zap is recorded as having read two letters, they were presumably those written after the 9th; none of Šafařík's letters are recorded as having been read at the "Polish meeting" of 13 May.

Yet another topic at the meeting of the 19th suggests that this was indeed the date upon which it was held. Count J. M. Thun reported upon the recent events in Vienna, referring to the flight of the emperor from Vienna, which took place after 15 May.[75] The flight brought fear to conservative and radical alike in Vienna. On the afternoon of 17 May the emperor and empress drove to Schönbrunn, and drove on in the same light carriage to Sieghartskirchen. Then the emperor was informed by the empress that their destination was Innsbruck. On 19 May the royal family arrived in Innsbruck. News of the flight, which was carefully planned, leaked out on the night of the 17th in Vienna. The emperor entrusted affairs of state to the Ministerialrath, the actual decree for which was published on 20 May. The meeting of the Preparatory Committee in Prague was told by J. M. Thun that Leo Thun would not accept decrees from Vienna which contradicted the desires of the emperor; he would wait for instructions from Linz. This could only have been discussed on the 19th, and not at any time before the 15th. Apart from this momentous news, the meeting was devoted to details of the current Congress business. Jordan wondered about the delegates to the Serbs, who were possibly not acquainted with all the undertakings in Prague.[76] Palacký suggested that a letter from Šafařík would amend this. The agenda must also wait upon Šafařík.

Against a background of rising tension, the Croats and the Serbs were being pressed to attend the Slav Congress. On 10 May, Šafařík had written to Gaj asking him to be sympathetic to the question of sending representatives to the Congress, even though the dates of the Croat and Prague assemblies might clash. Erben had written to Vraz about the Congress.

The Slovenes showed the most unconditional enthusiasm for the Congress. The congratulatory letter of 13 May from Graz had shown that the idea had been well received, and the day previously Oroslav Caf had written to J. Muršec about the names of Slovenes concerned with the Congress.[77] The Slovenes in Vienna were also inclined to participate, but the efforts of the Slovene society Slovenija had

74 Traub, "O přípravách," 321–2.
75 Ibid.
76 Cf. "Kabinetts-Akten (Geheim)," Schwarzenberg Nachlass: Haus-, Hof-, Staatsarchiv, Vienna, p. 15, which is a copy of Der Serbe reporting extensively on Die National-Versammlung der Serben in Karlowitz.
77 Printed in Slovanský sjezd, 240.

been delayed by the illness of Franz Miklosich (Miklošić). Peter Kozler, writing to Muršec on 25 May, intimated that three or four Slovenes would still travel to Prague, notwithstanding this unfortunate occurrence, and "other patriots" might be found in Steyermark and Krain.[78]

Oroslav Caf wrote to the "Slav Committee" in Prague, wishing the Congress well, but saying that he himself would be unable to attend as he had no money.[79] He took this opportunity for giving his views about the Congress and the attitude of the Slovenes in a sensible and constructive letter. The first point touched on the German question, expressing the unwillingness to be a part of the new German unity which was in the making: the third point expressed a desire for closer unity with the Croats, the "Illyrians." Caf also stressed the Slovene demands for national rights in education, and in the use of the national language. To further the cooperation of the Austrian Slavs a Slav journal should be founded. Point 10 stressed that a general unity (*vzajemnost obca*) should be effected between the Czechs, the Poles, and the "Illyrians."[80]

The Dalmations had decided on 21 May, in an announcement (headed "Dalmatinci plemeni tomu odboru za skupštinu slavjanksu u Zlatnom Pragu"), that they would be unable to attend the Congress, since they had had so little time in which to prepare.[81] The announcement, signed by a most impressive list of names headed by Professor Ante Kuzmanić, was printed in *Zora Dalmatinska* on 29 May. Spiro Popović sent the Preparatory Committee a letter of friendship and support on 26 May.[82]

Meanwhile the Preparatory Committee in Prague had been thinking about the organization of the Congress. The delegates who had already been chosen had been nominated to attend what appeared to be a general Slav assembly. No word of the agenda had yet appeared. The Preparatory Committee meeting of 24 May heard Zap read the plan of the organization of the Congress, a draft which had been prepared by Jordan.[83] This set up an organization based on three national committees or sections, for (1) Czechs, Moravians, Silesians, and Slovaks, (2) Poles and Ruthenes, (3) Slovenes, Croats, Serbs, and Dalmatians.[84] The list of members of the sections was to be handed in to the assembly of the 31 May. As for the work of the sections, each section was to nominate two officers who could speak in their name to the other sections; the whole was an elaborate arrangement of interrelated committees, so that no chance could be lost for providing for common discussions. The work of the sections was an adjunct to the work of the main assembly of the Congress. Rieger pointed out that this depended on each nationality settling itself in

78 *Ibid.*, 249. 79 *Ibid.*, 207–9.
80 *Ibid.* 81 *Ibid.*, 205–6.
82 *Ibid.*, 203–4.
83 Traub, "O přípravách," 323.
84 This referred to Jordan's "Porządek Zjazdu Słowianskiego w Pradze," which consisted of twenty-two paragraphs. Printed in *Slovanský sjezd*, 382–5. The organization was taken from Šafařík's idea of *Cirularsitzungen* and *Generalsitzungen*.

properly. Zach added that each section, however, would have nominated a provisional committee. The question of the election of three trusted officers from the separate national committees was left to the sections themselves, after some discussion of the matter. Paragraph 2 of the original draft by Jordan was accordingly amended.[85] The sections were therefore not predetermined, but it was left to them to arrange their own affairs.

This was the decision which virtually rendered all efforts to control and direct the Congress quite ineffective. The composition of the Congress was crucial where it touched the Polish section, and especially in the organization of the Polish-Ruthene membership. The decision to leave the choice of membership of the section to the nationality concerned permitted the Poles to draw non-Austrian Poles (and others) into the real work of the Congress.

The formality of the proceedings to organize the Congress is, in fact, somewhat deceptive. There is much to be admired in the drafts of organization and programmes which were flaunted in the meetings of the Preparatory Committee, but the "Congress" – as literally an assembly of Slavs – was taking shape out of the prejudices and ambitions of parties not intimately concerned with the doings in Neuberg's house. It is hard to resist the impression that the rather conservative Czech committee members were behind the times, times which were dominated by rapid changes of mood and alignment in both the Slav and non-Slav world. The original invitation to the Slavs had been much disputed and had not made the best of even one world. The decision of 24 May can only be explained by the same indecision which marked yet another question, the invitation to the Germans, which had been debated on the 11th. The same rumour about an invitation to the Magyars was circulated; this would certainly have been to the taste of the Lwów Poles.

The days before the meeting of the 24th had been taken up with certain local arrangements for the assembly of the delegates to the Congress on 31 May. On 19 May, the hall of Žofinský ostrov (Sophia Island) had been provisionally booked, so that there should be no clash with a public concert;[86] two days later the Preparatory Committee in collaboration with the representatives of the city drew up a proclamation to the people of Prague about the reception of the Slav delegates, even as the vilification of the Congress continued in Vienna. The attempt to appoint Palacký to the cabinet as minister of education had inflamed anti-Czech passions, already aroused by the Czech refusal to serve on the Frankfurt Committee of Fifty. The Czech invitations to the emperor to move his residence to Prague, where he would have complete freedom of action, had not improved the opinions of the Czechs held in some sections of Vienna. On 20 May Count Leo Thun publicly announced that he would not obey orders from Vienna which were in opposition to the wishes of the emperor. This confirmation of Czech separatism was held as further proof of the diabolical intentions of the Czechs. The added effect of the

85 Traub, "O přípravách," 323.
86 *Slovanský sjezd*, 291.

preparations of the Congress was to widen this fear of the conspiracy against the empire; the Czechs were suspected of intriguing with the Court to destroy the Germans, using the *Camarilla* and allying with the aristocracy to blind the German provinces and thus capture the empire. The only alternative was to seek that close union with Germany which would avert this catastrophe. The last two weeks of May were the period of the beginning of that temper which led to military action in Prague and the first, fatal, and massive blow at revolution in central and eastern Europe.

The proposed Congress had its legion of enemies. The fortunes of the Slav front had not fared very well in the days after the middle of May. The Czechs had almost carelessly surrendered their prerogative over the form – and hence the fate – of the Congress by turning over the composition of the sections to the individual nationals involved, thus decentralizing the Congress into a number of committees and solving the problem by intricate arrangements for inter-section and inter-committee liaisons. The restriction of active membership to Austrian Slavs had been simply and directly overridden by the Poles, who were as suspicious of the Czech motives as many of the declared enemies of the Congress.

On 26 May J. M. Thun wrote to Palacký that he would be obliged to withdraw himself from the presidency of the Committee and the Congress.[87] Šafařík, Neuberg, and Rieger had requested Thun to speak to Vojtěch Deym about the possibility of his taking the presidential position, but Deym had declined because of his lack of languages, and also because "all the Poles knew him as policeman" (Deym had been state commissioner in Cracow in 1846). Deym's presidency of the Congress could perhaps supply a pretext for the opponents of the assembly to link the loyalty to Austria with a reactionary interpretation of this position. Thun told Palacký that he had had his eye on Šafařík and then on Palacký. As for himself, he had willingly given his name for the support of the declaration of 5 May, but he could go no further. While Thun would willingly continue as a member of the Czech section, he could not undertake further duties. A further reason for this lay in his infirmity, since the previous day an attack of gout had incapacitated him.

There remained but a few days to the assembly of the Congress which was due to open on 1 June. Already several forceful opinions on the role of the proposed Congress had been advanced, but the one thing conspicuously lacking was any certainty over its real aims. Enthusiasm there was, but also confusion and contradiction. The Czechs were clearly disturbed at the prospect of direct Polish intervention in the affairs of the Congress, yet it was the Preparatory Committee itself which had done much to clear the way for this eventuality. Czech representatives were due to attend the Croat *sabor*, an encouraging sign and a significant step, but there was much to be done to realize any effective collaboration between Czechs and Croats. And now at the end of the month not a few individuals,

87 *Ibid.*, 60.

as well as members of various delegations, had actually begun their journey to Prague in order to attend the first functions of the Slav Congress – yet at this acutely late hour, in spite of all the persistent Czech statements that the forth-coming Congress was to be essentially a demonstration of "Austro-Slavism," the all-important agenda, the pivot upon which the entire Congress turned, still waited to be fixed.

These were dangerous days indeed. In one revolutionary centre, Vienna, the populace were fearful of the aftermath of the emperor's flight, at which the grim word "republic" had been uttered. In Prague, which had severed itself from the movement in Vienna, the atmosphere was becoming increasingly tense. The mili-tary commander of Bohemia, Prince Alfred Windischgrätz, kept close contact with other imperial commanders who were smashing the Italian rising. And behind the scenes, the councils of the Polish *Emigracja* weaved their schemes which might or might not draw the Congress into a wider European revolution-ary context. The balance was finely drawn.

The Czechs and the Imperial Parliament
in 1848–1849

STANLEY Z. PECH

FROM THE DOWNFALL of Metternich in March 1848, the Czechs looked with anticipation to the Bohemian Diet, which was supposed to meet as soon as the necessary
preparations were made and an election was held. The Diet was to be the embodiment of the idea of Czech self-rule and a consummation of the political hopes of
an entire generation of national awakeners. It was expected that it would become
the principal instrument through which Czech leaders would press for ever increasing concessions for their nation.

These fond hopes were not to be realized. The shock of the "March Days"
began to wear off and the central government in Vienna developed second
thoughts about the many promises that had been made to the various protest
groups in the first weeks of the constitutional era. As early as 8 June it concluded that it was "most desirable" to postpone the meeting of the Bohemian
Diet until after the meeting of the Imperial Parliament.[1] The Prague Uprising
which broke out four days later (12 June) furnished the government with an
excuse to postpone the meeting indefinitely, although the election for it had
already been held in most parts of Bohemia.

1 Karel Kazbunda, *České hnutí roku 1848* (Prague, 1929), 283. For a detailed study of events
in Bohemia and Moravia in 1848–9, see my *Czech Revolution of 1848* (Chapel Hill, 1969).

Having thus lost an opportunity to express their political will through this channel, the Czechs transferred their expectations to the Imperial Parliament which opened in Vienna on 22 July (after several days of preliminary meetings). From this time until its dissolution, the Imperial Parliament was the most important forum through which the Czechs could make their opinions felt and through which they could help shape the uncertain course of Austrian politics.[2] The Imperial Parliament was a one-chamber body representing "Cisleithania" only. The electoral law provided for a very wide suffrage, though it was ambiguous enough to exclude from the right to vote a considerable segment of the working class.[3] The total number of deputies as laid down by the electoral law was 383, of which Bohemia had 90, Moravia 38, and Silesia 10.[4]

What was the nationality of the deputies? To enquire into the ethnic background of deputies presents a special difficulty, since some deputies did not identify themselves with a nationality but with the province which they represented. Of the ninety Bohemian deputies, a majority – about fifty or more – identified themselves with the Czech national cause. In Moravia, the Czechs were favoured far less; nominally twenty-two Moravian deputies – out of the total of thirty-eight – belonged to the Czech nationality, but only perhaps one-third of these identified themselves actively with the Czech national cause. Of the ten Silesian deputies, only one is believed to have been of Czech sentiment, the remainder being German.[5] In Parliament as a whole, the Germans constituted the largest single group, the Czechs the second largest. If we count all Slavic groups together (this is the way the Slavs preferred their statistics), the Slavs outnumbered the Germans. Although it is impossible to offer exact figures, both Slavic and German deputies agreed that the Slavs had a little over 190 deputies; this gave them a slight edge, since the chamber never had the total of 383 deputies provided for by law. As soon as the Slavs' numerical preponderance became known, the issues of some Viennese radical newspapers

2 For the record, it should be mentioned that, unlike the Bohemian Diet, the Moravian Diet was permitted to meet and was in session throughout most of the 1848–9 revolutionary era; its last meeting was held on 24 January 1849.

3 After several revisions, the electoral law allowed "independent workers" to vote. This presumably excluded workers receiving a daily or weekly wage, but there was much confusion on this point. See *Constitutionelles Blatt aus Böhmen*, 23 June 1848, Supplement.

4 For a complete list of Moravian and Silesian deputies, see *Národní noviny* (hereafter NN), 27 July 1848. A partial list of Bohemian deputies is given in NN, 14 July 1848. For a later date, see the complete list of deputies from all provinces of "Cisleithania" in NN, 26 Jan. 1849. The election took place in most regions in June; in Bohemia the June Uprising forced a postponement and the balloting took place on 8 and 9 July.

5 *Přehled československých dějin*, II/1 (Prague, 1960), 64, states that the number of Czech deputies from Bohemia was fifty-six and this is probably a fair estimate. As for Moravia, the number of Czech deputies from this province was twenty-two (out of a total of thirty-eight); see NN, 27 July 1848. For the Silesian situation, see J. Vochala, *Rok 1848 ve Slezsku* ... (Opava, 1948), 38.

appeared with black borders to indicate mourning; other radical Viennese newspapers contented themselves with diatribes against the Slavic "barbarians."[6]

From the point of view of occupation or social structure, the parliamentary delegation from Bohemia-Moravia was clearly middle class. From Bohemia (taking the Czechs and Germans together), there were lawyers, officials, physicians, writers, high-school teachers, and professors. The Czech journalist Karel Havlíček had advised his readers to elect to Parliament educated men who would have the resource to defend the Czech nationality in a hostile environment, and the readers had clearly heeded his advice. At the same time, there were almost no aristocrats. Moravia sent not a single aristocrat or clergyman to Vienna. Peasants were few. From Bohemia and Moravia (with Silesia) combined, the number of peasant deputies was seventeen.[7] Naturally, no woman or worker deputy had been elected from any province of the Habsburg Monarchy.

In time, the deputies formed political groupings known as "right," "left," and "centre," terms derived from the position each group occupied in the chamber.[8] These terms, however, do not entirely correspond to present-day usage. The most conservative was the Centre, consisting of die-hard champions of the status quo, bureaucrats and members of the Roman Catholic hierarchy. The Centre was the "right-wing" of modern political parlance. Ethnically, it was largely German, but its spirit was decidedly pro-Austrian rather than in favour of a Greater Germany. It was the most reliable supporter of the government. The Right consisted of groups that would in present-day terminology be described as moderate or middle-of-the-road. A majority of the Right were Slavs, the dominant and numerically strongest groups being the Czechs, but there were also a few Germans. The Right was politically liberal in the nineteenth-century sense of the word: it was committed to the principle of constitutional government and to other basic gains of the revolutionary era. On the national question, it was in militant opposition to the Frankfurt Parliament, which sought to incorporate Bohemia and Moravia in a new Germany. The Left in Vienna was the left of modern parlance; it was predominantly German, but included also several Polish democrats and radicals from Galicia. It was dominated by a spirit of German nationalism and was strongly anti-Slavic. The support of a few Poles did not dull its anti-Slavic edge any more than the support of a few Germans modified the anti-German sentiment of the Right.

Finally, no discussion of the Imperial Parliament would be complete without mentioning the German Viennese radicals. The German Left had a radical wing which, though it had few deputies in Parliament, nevertheless had a decisive impact on Austrian politics. The radicals' domain was Vienna and, though only five of the fifteen Viennese deputies were radical, the radicals controlled almost entirely the

6 A. Springer, *Geschichte Österreichs seit dem Wiener Frieden 1809*, II (Leipzig, 1865), 404.
7 V. Klimeš, *Česká vesnice v roce 1848* (Most, 1949), 344. Estimates for the proportion of various occupational groups vary, since the available data are not always clear.
8 See Havlíček's description in NN, 1 Aug. 1848.

Viennese press and also maintained a strong hold over the workers and students in the imperial capital. They were the most democratic of all political groups in the Habsburg Monarchy. They were also the most strongly nationalist and most vituperative in the treatment of their opponents. They were violently anti-Slavic and the most uncompromisingly centralist in their views. Their centralism clashed with the federalist views as espoused by the Slavs.

What was the relationship of the central government to the three political groups? It could hardly hope to rely on the support of the Left. Domestically the government pursued a moderate-to-conservative course, and such a course was obviously not acceptable to this party. More importantly, the government was dedicated to a preservation of the integrity of the monarchy, and its policies in this respect conflicted with those of the Left, which flirted with Magyar separatism and Frankfurt nationalism. By contrast, the Centre was a dependable force: it was German, but not too offensive in its Germanism. It advocated a strong monarchy, but did not regard moderate federalism (desired by the Right) as a bar to the monarchy's strength. Unfortunately, though a sound and logical ally, the Centre was too weak in numbers to furnish a parliamentary majority. This precarious position compelled the government to look for another ally and this it found in the Right, with the Czechs as its backbone.

The Czech parliamentarians were progressive, but moderate, and their views were unequivocally anti-"Frankfurt." Their staunch Austro-Slavism was a useful antidote to the menace of "Frankfurtism" and Magyar separatism. Their moderation, and their high intellectual calibre, would, it was hoped, prove equal to the pressure of the Left, especially to the fury of its radical wing. As the parliamentary session progressed, the government and the Czechs "discovered" each other, recognized each other's usefulness, and gradually concluded a marriage of convenience in which the missing element of romance was filled by the persuasive link of self-interest.[9] This placed the Czechs in the position of key actors in the bitter drama that unfolded in the parliamentary chamber in the ensuing weeks and months. In fact, it might be said without undue exaggeration that from the opening date until the outbreak of the October Revolution in Vienna, parliamentary deliberations reduced themselves to a contest between Czech and German nationalism. The Czechs were confident that their support of the government would bring them important political concessions. The quality of their confidence was rooted in the quantity of their votes: Havlíček wrote quite openly that the Slavs with their majority "have a hope of controlling the direction of the whole Parliament."[10] They felt that their votes, combined with those of their allies, were bound to defeat the German Left and, equally, to supply the lever with which to exert pressure on the government. However, in the existing circumstances, with the forces of reaction still entrenched just beneath the surface, such calculations were fraught with perils. It might easily

9 See, for instance, Havlíček's reflections from Vienna, in NN, 30 July 1848.
10 NN, 30 July 1848.

happen that by supporting the government the Czech leaders would, unless they exercised utmost vigilance, strengthen the forces of reaction.

The Czechs sent to Vienna a high-powered delegation. Its leading intellect was the famous historian František Palacký, and its voice the orator František Ladislav Rieger (Palacký's future son-in-law). The political hue of the Czech delegation was liberal; it included only a few radical democrats whose calibre could not match that of the liberals. The best-known radical deputy was František Havlíček (no kin of Karel Havlíček), but his contribution to parliamentary debates was modest.

The great issue of the revolutionary era in the Habsburg Monarchy was the abolition of the last remaining vestiges of serfdom, and the subject was placed on the agenda of the Imperial Parliament a few days after it opened. No deputy questioned the necessity of doing away with serfdom once and for all. It was the manner in which this should be carried out that became the subject of passionate controversy. Some deputies held that the peasants' *robota* duties and other obligations should be abolished without any compensation to the landlords. Others insisted that for some duties compensation should be paid. In the next weeks the term "compensation" became something of a shibboleth used by the partisans in the controversy, one side calling for "abolition without compensation," another for "abolition with compensation." Those opposing the compensation were the radicals of whatever nationality, those favouring compensation (a moderate one) were conservatives and liberals.

Most Czech deputies, including Palacký, Rieger, Karel Havlíček, and František Brauner favoured compensation. The leading spokesman for the Czech parliamentary group was Brauner, who was one of the monarchy's outstanding experts on peasant conditions. He delivered the main speech from the Czech side (23 August 1848) and supported the principle of compensation[11] as did the Czech liberal deputy Alois P. Trojan.[12] Neither Brauner, nor Trojan, nor the majority of Czech deputies, were willing to accept a compromise solution under which compensation would be instituted but would be paid by the state rather than directly by the peasant.[13] The gist of the arguments in favour of compensation was that to deny it would constitute a violation of accepted rules of law and justice. It is to be noted that the Imperial Government and the Court supported the idea of compensation (not by the state) as had been made clear by a government spokesman in Parliament on 26 August.[14] In the final vote on this question which took place on 31 August, "moderate compensation" received the endorsement of the majority, with 174 deputies for, 144 against, and 36 abstaining. Of the total of seventy-eight deputies who could be identified as Czech-speaking, fifty-three voted for compensation,

11 *Verhandlungen des österreichischen Reichstages nach der stenographischen Aufnahme* (5 vols., Vienna, 1848-9), II, 4-8.
12 *Ibid.*, I, 533-7.
13 Such a compromise was favoured by the young and personable Bohemian deputy Klaudy, a German by origin, a Czech by choice. See Klimeš, *Česká vesnice*, 371.
14 The spokesman was Minister Alexander Bach; *Verhandlungen*, II, 84.

fourteen against, and eleven abstained.[15] Palacký, Rieger, and many Czech leaders voted with the majority though Brauner, curiously, abstained. An interesting aspect of the voting is that the majority of those abstaining were deputies from Bohemia and Moravia, both Czech and German. Of the thirty-six abstentions, fully two-thirds (24) were Czech and German deputies from these two provinces (of the twenty-four, eleven, as noted above, were Czech). Whatever their reasons, Bohemian and Moravian deputies made themselves conspicuous as the largest parliamentary group that declined to take a stand – a performance that occasioned caustic comment at the time.[16] It would go beyond the scope of this paper to decide the question as to whether or not compensation was justified. However, it is legitimate to pose another question: in voting for compensation did the Czech deputies in fact represent the wishes of their constituents, most of whom were peasants? The roll-call in the crucial vote indicates that those deputies who were themselves peasants voted decisively against compensation. This suggests that in this particular instance the Czech deputies did not express the wishes of their constituents.[17]

Another conflict that dominated parliamentary debates involved the Magyars. The relationship between the central government and the Magyars had been deteriorating rapidly. During the early days of the constitutional era, Hungary had succeeded in exacting from the government spectacular concessions which had given it a large measure of autonomy. Yet, the Magyar leaders displayed an alarming tendency to demand more concessions, and, in late summer, the government finally resolved to deal firmly with the Magyar question and reforge the links between Pest and Vienna which the Magyar separatists had all but destroyed. With the emperor's acquiescence, the Croatian Ban Josef Jelačić crossed the river Drava (11 September), invading Hungary and signalling the beginning of an open war between Hungary and its nationalities, the latter supported by the central government. As disaster loomed, the Magyars decided to take an unusual step. They dispatched a delegation to Vienna which, instead of knocking humbly at the gate of the Imperial Palace, was supposed to bring its cause directly to the Imperial Parliament. Within this august body, the Magyars could count on the aid of their allies, the German Left (and also the Poles). The Magyars and the German Left had been drawn together by their common aversion to the smaller Slav peoples.

Arriving in the Imperial capital on 18 September, the Magyar delegation requested leave to enter the parliamentary chamber and address the deputies. For Parliament to permit this would have required setting aside, for this instance, the

15 Klimeš, *Česká vesnice*, 384. For a complete list of names of deputies, grouped according to their vote, see *Verhandlungen*, II, 163–4.

16 Springer, *Geschichte Österreichs*, II, 426.

17 As nearly as I could determine, the Galician peasants, the largest peasant block in Parliament, voted as a group against compensation; there was apparently not even an abstention. See *Verhandlungen*, II, 163–4, to be read in conjunction with the list in NN, 26 Jan. 1849, which gives the occupation of deputies. These sources indicate that most of the Czech peasant deputies also voted against compensation; see also Klimeš, *Česká vesnice*, 384–5.

rules of procedure, and the resulting debate turned upon this question of procedure – whether the rules should be set aside or not. The debate proved to be one of the most bitter and impassioned in the life of the Imperial Parliament during the 1848–9 era.

By their stand on this issue, the Czechs cut perhaps more deeply into the mainstream of Austrian politics in 1848–9 than on any other occasion. Though the debate lasted only one day (19 September), it developed into a breath-taking spectacle and trial of strength between the Right and the Left, the former opposing and the latter favouring the Magyars. The Czechs as members of the Right opposed the Magyars almost without exception. The Magyar separatist policy inevitably possessed revolutionary overtones and this only strengthened the fascination their cause held for the Left. But this same separatism endangered the whole policy of Austro-Slavism pursued by the Czechs and other Slavs (the Poles again excepted), and this threat to Austro-Slavism only reinforced the resolve of the Czechs to prevent the Magyars from achieving their objectives.

Within that one day all the prominent Czech deputies took the floor, with Rieger as one of their star spokesmen. They taxed the Magyars with national egotism. They drove home relentlessly the point that the Magyar delegation contained not a single representative of non-Magyar groups, groups that constituted half of Hungary's population. "Did [the Magyars] come to give us an assurance that they will render justice to all the peoples of Hungary?" cried Rieger. "Did they come in order to declare before this House that these peoples will from now on enjoy a complete equality? No, they did not."[18] The arguments of the Right were answered in a moving address delivered by the Bohemian German Ludwig von Löhner, the most eloquent orator of the Left.[19] Löhner was one of the most belligerently anti-Slavic deputies, but for this occasion he shed his anti-Slavic mantle and presented the case for the Magyars in terms of a threat which was hanging not only over the Magyars but over all other peoples of the monarchy. He voiced his anxiety at the growing intervention of the military in the affairs of the monarchy and at the menacing shadow the generals were casting over the lives and freedoms of its peoples. But Löhner's moving plea could not move the Czechs, who had little reason to hope that the Magyars would ever treat their nationalities as their equals. After what was probably the most exhausting day the deputies had undergone till then, a vote was taken at eight o'clock that evening, the vote being important enough to warrant a roll-call. The Magyar request was rejected by a safe majority of 186 to 108.[20] The

18 *Verhandlungen*, II, 472.
19 *Ibid.*, II, 480ff.
20 *Ibid.*, II, 523–4. It may be pointed out that a Croatian parliamentary deputation arrived in Vienna in July 1848, hoping to receive a hearing in Parliament. It was not admitted. The case was not entirely identical with that of the Magyars, but it lent cogency to the arguments of those who opposed the Magyar request. See J. Šidak, "Poslanstvo hrvatskog sabora austrijskom parlamentu g. 1848," *Radova filozofskog fakulteta u Zagrebu, Odsjek za povijest*, III (1960), 9ff.

majority was much larger than on the question of "compensation." Significantly, only one deputy abstained this time. The Czechs, with only one or two exceptions, voted against the Magyars.

The vote was the greatest triumph the Czechs ever scored in the Imperial Parliament. This fact was not lost on the Viennese radicals; it was on this occasion, more than before or since, that the anti-Czech voices of the radicals rose to a shrill crescendo of abuse. To them the Czech parliamentarians became the lackeys of absolutism and the very incarnation of reaction.[21] The Czech radicals at home (in Prague) endorsed the anti-Magyar vote, but did so with less enthusiasm than the liberals. These radicals saw the clouds of reaction gathering in the distance and were becoming uneasy at the support the Czech liberal deputies were giving the government.

Even before the vote on the Magyar request, tempers in Vienna were running high. Chronic unrest spread especially among students and workers, the latter being affected by unemployment. The Viennese radicals fed the flames of discontent with demagogic speeches and after their allies, the Magyars, were rebuffed by Parliament, their fury knew no bounds, and events hurtled toward the final catastrophe. On 24 September, Count Franz Lamberg, the imperial commissioner in Hungary, was murdered by a mob in Pest. On 4 October the government answered with a declaration of martial law over "entire Hungary." Two days later a group of workers in Vienna, their emotions whipped up by the radicals, lynched and murdered the minister of war Count Theodor Latour, hung his already lifeless body on a lamppost, and mutilated it.[22] On the following day the emperor fled the city. This was the beginning of the October revolution.

The October revolution called forth another military intervention, led by the same man who had bombarded Prague into submission in June, General Alfred Windischgrätz. After the outbreak of the revolution, a large number of deputies left, among them almost all Czechs, but a rump Parliament continued to sit in Vienna throughout the period of the revolution. Czech liberal deputies condemned the revolution outright as a German-Magyar onslaught on Slavdom and as a conflict between nationalities. Again, Czech deputies found themselves supporting squarely the government and the court circles, but this time they provoked dissent within the Czech ranks. Czech radicals in Prague, though they opposed German-Magyar nationalist policies, nevertheless hesitated to accept as simple an explanation of the conflict as the liberal deputies offered. The radicals realized that if the revolution won, the Magyars and the Germans would reign supreme and the Czechs and other Slavs would be the losers. But they also feared that if the revolution were defeated, the forces of reaction might be dangerously strengthened.

By contrast, the Czech liberal deputies permitted themselves few such doubts and reservations, at least for the record. As they saw it, the struggle was one between

21 See Havlíček's complaint after the vote in NN, 29 Sept. 1848.
22 R. J. Rath, *The Viennese Revolution of 1848* (Austin, 1957), 323, 329.

nationalities, pure and simple. The revolution had to be quelled whatever the means and consequences, and Windischgrätz was quite suitable for the job. So it was with considerable satisfaction that they received the news of Vienna's defeat at the hands of Windischgrätz at the end of October. Whatever their private thoughts, in public the liberal deputies, with hardly an exception, claimed to see no danger to freedom in the reliance upon Windischgrätz. Havlíček boldly editorialized: "Don't fear for your freedom: neither the court nor the army will or will want to disturb our constitution."[23] This was tantamount to giving Windischgrätz a clean bill of health as a protector of constitutional freedom – a charitable view of the general which was belied by his record in Prague after the June Uprising. At that time, the Czech deputies had criticized him frequently for his disregard of constitutional principles. Now they seemed to be accepting him as a defender of such principles.

Yet, the private beliefs of the deputies did not always match their public pronouncements. They could hardly be unaware of persistent rumours that the court would exploit the situation in order to do away with the Imperial Parliament altogether.[24] Palacký himself conceded publicly (15 October) that he did "not conceal it from himself that the imperial family will be susceptible to military influence"; this is apparently the only example of such a fear being openly expressed by any of the Czech leaders during that period.[25] Nevertheless, it must have been privately shared by other leaders, for in the end they decided to dispatch a two-man delegation to the emperor (now residing in Olomouc) which was supposed to dissuade the court circles and the government from any possible plans to dissolve the Imperial Parliament.[26] It is probable that although at least some deputies were aware of the threat of reaction, they believed that the reaction would not be strong enough to assert itself and that the threat could be held in check by the vigilance of the constitutionally minded deputies.

The Imperial Parliament reconvened on 22 November in the Moravian city of Kroměříž (Kremsier). The political groups were roughly the same, but there was a difference: the Left was held responsible for the murder of Latour and its temper was subdued. The Czechs felt correspondingly more vigorous and self-confident. In Kroměříž as in Vienna, the Czech deputies continued basically to support the government, but this support was less unqualified and on occasion the Czechs went into opposition.

Almost from the outset, the session in Kroměříž was a series of shocks and surprises for the Czechs and for all constitutionally minded deputies. Even before Kroměříž there had come the first warning: a new government had been formed at

23 NN, 11 Oct. 1848.
24 Rumours in J. A. Helfert, "Erlebnisse und Erinnerungen," *Die Kultur*, II (1900), 272.
25 *Noviny Lípy slovanské*, 19 Oct. 1848.
26 On 17 October 1848, Brauner, who was one of the two delegates, wrote to Rieger from Olomouc: "... the military and the nobility wanted to dissolve Parliament, by this I swear – we have enough evidence to prove it"; J. Heidler, ed., *Příspěvky k listáři Dra. Frant. Lad. Riegra*, I (Prague, 1924), 46.

the end of October, headed by the conservative Prince Felix Schwarzenberg. It bore a stamp of "dynasticism" and its generally conservative character augured ill for the future of parliamentary government. It soon began to take important measures without consulting the Imperial Parliament and in general showed itself contemptuous of the principle of constitutional government. At the beginning of December, the Schwarzenberg government announced the abdication of Emperor Ferdinand and the succession to the throne of Francis Joseph. The Imperial Parliament was presented with a *fait accompli*; on a matter of supreme importance for the future of the monarchy, it had not even been forewarned, let alone consulted. With the new emperor at the helm, laws and measures designed to curb the opposition and infringe on personal rights and freedoms followed one another in quickening pace. There could be no mistaking the direction in which the new emperor and the new government intended to lead their people. At the beginning of January 1849, a decree was issued which obliged the editors of "political" newspapers to submit a copy of each issue to an appropriate government office in advance of publication so as to make it possible for this office to confiscate an "offensive" issue.[27] In February began a major recruitment drive; the recruitment became an instrument for removing radical students from civilian status. It is to be noted that the recruitment drive was authorized by a law of 5 December 1848, which had been issued without any reference to the Imperial Parliament.

How little respect the government had for democracy was shown during the debate in the Imperial Parliament on Article One of the proposed constitution (the article proclaimed the principle of popular sovereignty). Commenting on Article One, Minister Franz Stadion questioned this principle (4 January 1849), the tenor of his remarks being that popular participation in government was not the right of the people but a favour bestowed on the people by a gracious ruler.[28]

Stadion's overbearing speech had a stunning effect on the deputies, most of whom were sincere believers in the principle of popular sovereignty. Stadion's words were a challenge which could only be met by an even greater challenge, and for a time it seemed that the Imperial Parliament would rise to the occasion. Aroused and angered by the minister, 178 deputies affixed their signatures to a protest drafted by the Czech deputy Adolf Pinkas; this represented a majority of the 332 deputies present at the meeting at which the protest was submitted (8 January).[29] Later at this same meeting the protest was approved by 196 votes against 99 (with some abstentions), a seemingly crushing defeat for the government. The defeat seemed confirmed by a full-fledged debate on Article One that followed. The most prominent speaker in defence of Article One was the Czech Rieger, and his speech on that occasion became the most famous one of his life. Stadion's speech had been an attack on the sovereignty of the people. Rieger replied by what amounted to an

27 NN, 2 Jan. 1849.
28 *Verhandlungen*, IV, 267.
29 *Ibid.*, IV, 277. Text in NN, 9 Jan. 1848.

attack on the sovereignty of the monarch. He was impassioned and mordant and went so far as to give a warning: "the wrath of the people is a powerful hurricane," whose "breath upsets thrones" and "causes crowns to fall from anointed heads."[30]

Rieger's speech sounded like the distant rumbling of a revolution. It was greeted with "stormy applause," and it needed but a firm stand on the part of the deputies to back it up and demonstrate to the government that there was a minimum ground which they were prepared to defend. However, the wrath of the people proved, when it came to deeds, anything but a hurricane. A few minutes after the speech, in an about-face almost beyond belief, a majority voted not to press Article One, but to shelve it for consideration in a later section of the constitution.[31] This was of course a complete victory for the government. In this fateful vote, the Left (the Germans) remained faithful to the principle and voted against shelving Article One. The Czech deputies deserted the principle in which they honestly believed. When the "chips were down," they went along with the government. More than any other single act, their vote on Article One mars their record in the Imperial Parliament. The Polish deputy Franciszek Smolka described their conduct fittingly in a letter to his wife: Rieger spoke very well, he wrote, "but what good does it do when afterwards all Czechs voted in the spirit of the government so that the whole of Rieger's speech looked like sheer comedy."[32] Little wonder that such a display of weakness only cemented the resolve of the government to reimpose absolutism; within ten days of the vote, the government made the final decision to dissolve Parliament and put it out of its misery altogether.[33] For a few more weeks Parliament lived on precariously. Then, on 7 March the emperor sent out two infantry companies to occupy the premises of the palace in which Parliament was housed; within a few hours police began to hunt down the deputies of the Left. An Imperial Decree issued at the same time (but predated to 4 March) declared the Imperial Parliament dissolved.

For the Czech deputies the dissolution was a defeat. In fact, it was worse than defeat: it was a stunning humiliation. It brought to ruin their whole calculated policy of giving parliamentary support to the government in return for possible political concessions for the Czech nation. Their support of the government, even amid clear signs of the government's drift into a policy of reaction, had the effect of abetting the forces of reaction and to that extent they contributed to the final collapse of constitutionalism. That the reaction would have triumphed without them – as it triumphed everywhere in Europe in the end – is clear enough. It is equally clear that it would have been vastly better for their prestige had that triumph occurred without their help.

30 *Verhandlungen*, IV, 354.
31 *Ibid.*, IV, 358.
32 V. Žáček, *Čechové a Poláci roku 1848*, II (Prague, 1948), 316.
33 *Ibid.*, 323.

Until the formation of the Schwarzenberg government, the cabinets had been moderate and the Czech deputies could justify supporting them. They could justify their support of the government against the Viennese revolution; given the dogmatic centralism and nationalist chauvinism of the Viennese radicals, they could not have acted otherwise. Yet, the defeat of the Viennese revolution stiffened the back of the reaction and brought new dangers to the liberal system. The new dangers were becoming ever more obvious under the Schwarzenberg government that took office after the revolution, and from the beginning of 1849 there could be no mistaking the anti-liberal course which this government followed. Despite the warning signs, the Czech deputies remained committed to the support of the government. The Czech radicals warned of the dangers of this course, but the warnings were disregarded. After the ill-fated vote on Article One, a Czech radical newspaper called the deputies to task: "Your weakness has become proverbial; unwittingly you sink further and further into the tentacles of ministers who will ill-reward you for your devotion."[34] It is probable that a few deputies would have wished to alter this course, but the prestige and the pressure of the leaders, notably Palacký, prevented them from doing so. A few Slavic deputies complained of "a tyrannical pressure exerted on them by the leaders," the leaders in question being Palacký, Antonín Strobach, and Brauner.[35]

To say that the Czech deputies supported the Schwarzenberg government is not to imply that during the same period they neglected the interests of the Czech nation. On the contrary, Havlíček, in his *Národní noviny*, the voice of the liberal leaders, subjected the government often to scathing criticism. Czech deputies frequently criticized the Schwarzenberg government on the floor of Parliament in their speeches and interpellations. Several times, they demanded that the government submit to the Parliament all the acts relating to the investigation of the June Uprising.[36] In response to Slovak complaints about national oppression by the imperial authorities, a parliamentary committee of three Czechs was chosen to probe the complaints; later, the Slavic parliamentary club (the Czechs were the dominant group in this club) dispatched on its own a three-man delegation, consisting of two Czechs and one South Slav, to take up the matter directly with the government.[37] The Slavic parliamentary club also submitted a memorandum to the government against the recruitment law and the manner in which it was being carried out.[38] These instances could be multipled.

Nevertheless, in instances of basic importance in which a vote was required the

34 *Noviny Lípy slovanské*, 14 Jan. 1849.
35 J. A. Helfert, *Geschichte Österreichs vom Ausgange des Wiener October-Aufstandes 1848*, iv/3 (Prague, 1886), 370.
36 *Verhandlungen*, iv, 540.
37 Helfert, *Geschichte Österreichs*, iv/3, 252–3.
38 Memorandum dated 28 Feb. 1849. Text in J. M. Černý, ed., *Boj za právo* (Prague, 1893), 529–31.

Czech deputies voted with the government, even when it meant a complete reversal of their public stance, as happened in the case of Article One. For their pro-government policy, they often had to endure the sneers of the Left, but they were sustained by the hope that at the end of the road there was a harvest of political rewards for the Czechs. Now the end of the road had been reached; and it proved a dead-end street, with no laurels and no rewards, only disappointment and bitterness. As Havlíček wrote after the dissolution: "We confess that ... the unexpected act of the government startled us so much that we still gaze, as though in a dream, at everything that is happening."[39]

It is only fair to note that after Parliament was dissolved the Czech deputies were the only parliamentary group to come to the defence of the Parliament and its record, in a protest issued on 15 March 1849. The majority of the thirty-four signatories of this document were Czech, and there were also a few members of other nationalities.[40] It may further be stressed that before dissolution, during the weeks of Parliament's dying agony, it is only from the Czech regions that this body received major expressions of confidence and support. The most outstanding of these was the "monster" petition of the "Slavic Linden," consisting of messages bearing a total of 40,595 signatures. It was received and gratefully acknowledged on 1 March, six days before dissolution.[41] The Prague Student Committee sent its own message of confidence, to which were added messages from a few Moravian communities.[42] Thus, it fell to the Czechs to rally to the Parliament in its hour of crisis. The message from the students was answered by the parliamentary president Smolka in a letter of thanks addressed to the Prague Student Committee and dated 6 March. When composing the letter, in Polish, Smolka could not know that this was the last official document to be written by him as president of the Imperial Parliament.[43]

39 NN, 10 March 1849.
40 Černý, Boj za právo, 592–5. However, Brauner's signature was absent from the list.
41 Verhandlungen, v, 252.
42 Helfert, Geschichte Österreichs, iv/3, 252.
43 Constitutionelles Blatt aus Böhmen, 11 March 1849.

America and the Beginnings of
Modern Czech Political Thought

JOSEF V. POLIŠENSKÝ

THE AIMS OF THIS ESSAY are very modest. Its origins go back to a reading of the article by Merle Curti and Kendall Birr entitled "The Immigrant and the American Image in Europe 1860–1914," which stresses the fact that the name "an American Century" would be most appropriate for the nineteenth because it was in that century that the common people of Europe saw in America the land of their dreams.[1] My essay is really only a report on the studies pursued in Czechoslovakia during the past twenty years concerning the history of the Czechs and Slovaks who left their old country for the New World. For technical reasons it concentrates especially on the years 1848–9, that is, on the period when the Czech nation initiated its political programme, with the backing of massive support from the middle classes.[2]

This does not mean, of course, that there was no interest in the New World long before this time. We know today that in the early sixteenth century the Czechs and Slovaks, in fact, displayed an interest in far-away islands and lands over the ocean

1 Merle Curti and Kendall Birr, "The Immigrant and the American Image in Europe 1860–1914," *The Mississippi Valley Historical Review*, XXXVII (1950), 203–30.
2 See also Rudolf Sturm, "Czech Opinion of America in the Mid-Nineteenth Century," in *The Czechoslovak Contribution to World Culture*, ed. Miloslav Rechcigl, Jr. (The Hague, 1964), 51–9.

earlier than many maritime nations of contemporary Europe, and that since the publication of *Spis o nových zemích a o novém světě* (Treatise on the New Lands and the New World) at Plzeň (Pilsen) in about 1508 by Bachelor Nicholas, known as "the Slovak," this interest has never faded. It is expressed in Czech cosmographic writings of the sixteenth and seventeenth centuries. We also know today from the Dutch archives that in the fourth decade of the seventeenth century several countrymen of Augustin Herrman, the founder of Bohemia Manor in Maryland and the first American cartographer, crossed the Atlantic in the services of the Dutch West-India company.[3]

We know too that Catholic missionaries, members of the Jesuit order, came to the Spanish-dominated regions of North America from 1680 on, and that the first attempt to organize the export of Bohemian products, especially Bohemian glass, was made by one of them, M. Sabel, in 1701–4.[4] From the middle of the eighteenth century the glass-exporting firms of north Bohemia had their factors and agents all over America, including Philadelphia and Baltimore, while the German-speaking Moravian Brethren, after a brief period in Georgia, became firmly settled in Pennsylvania.[5] The struggle of the American colonies for their independence was closely followed by the sympathetic public in central Europe, and the Bohemian "Jacobin" J. F. Opiz was an admirer of Abbé Raynal's *La Révolution en Amérique*, which was a much desired book in Prague in the 1770s and 1780s.[6] In contemporary libraries one can find the pamphlets of Thomas Paine and those of his adversaries John Adams and Edmund Burke, the essay of Crèvecœur, and the *Commentaries on the Constitution of the United States of America*.[7]

F. A. Steinský, professor of auxiliary historical sciences at the University of

3 The pioneering studies of O. Odložilík ("Vchynští ze Vchynic a Tetova v Nizozemí v XVI. a XVII. století ...," in *Friedrichův sborník* [Prague, n.d.], 291–309; "Poslední Smiřičtí," in *Pekařův sborník*, II [Prague, 1930], 70–87) on the Bohemian emigration of the seventeenth century have been continued in the last decade. Cf. S. Hart and J. V. Polišenský, "Praha a Amsterodam 17. a 18. století," *Československý časopis historický*, xv (1967), 827–47; and M. E. H. N. Mout, "Comenius en Amsterdam," Amsterdam Univ., unpublished dissertation (1967).

4 O. Odložilík, "Misioneros checos en México," *Boletín de la Sociedad mexicana de geografía y estadística* (México), LX (1945), 423–36. Cf. J. V. Polišenský, "Fuentes existentes en Checoslovaquia para la historia de América Latina," *Anales de la Universidad de Chile* (Santiago de Chile), CXXIII/133 (1965), 171–82.

5 The revival of interest in the Moravians, who were actually of German ethnic origin though remotely connected with the old Czech Unitas Fratrum, can be seen, for example, in T. Harry Williams, R. N. Current, and F. Freidel, *A History of the United States (to 1876)* (New York, 1960), 18, 20ff. See also John Taylor Hamilton and Kenneth Gardiner Hamilton, *History of the Moravian Church: The Renewed Unitas Fratrum, 1722–1957*, rev. ed. (Bethlehem, Pa., 1967).

6 This period (and the rest of this essay) is treated more fully in the author's study *America and Czechoslovakia. Their Contacts in the Past. Historical and Bibliographical Survey* (in preparation).

7 An inventory of Americana in Czechoslovak archives and libraries was included in the publi-

Prague, and J. Casanova, the librarian of Count Waldstein-Wartenberg, were among the acquaintances of Benjamin Franklin. Steinský used to send his more famous friend information about scientific life in the Bohemia of the Enlightenment regularly. Steinský had another correspondent in the liberated American colonies, J. Donat, who was a Bohemian-born factor of a north Bohemian export company. Donat's letters from 1790 to 1795 are letters of a "free-born American" poking fun at the unhappy civil servant of the Austrian absolute monarchy.[8] The first known description of the territory of the United States was written in June 1800, when J. C. Socher, a glass-merchant, active for several years in Mexico and Cuba, visited New York on his return journey and went from there to Philadelphia, which was still an important centre of trade relations between central Europe and America.[9] Of course, both Donat and Socher came from German-speaking regions of Bohemia, and the effect on the Czechs of any information they supplied could be but small.

Nevertheless, as we know, the situation was at that time undergoing change in Bohemia, and later in Moravia as well. The so-called national revival (renascence), i.e. the movement for the national emancipation of the Czechs, had begun. At first this was a movement among the intellectuals, influenced by both the Enlightenment and Romanticism, but later, from about the 1820s, it became closely connected with the rise of the middle classes both in the towns and in the countryside. Through the national renascence a new group of consumers was created for literature in the vernacular. It is difficult to decide whether the revival of interest in the "New World" had its basis in the older tradition, or whether this was a new phenomenon which was also manifested in the neighbouring German regions. *Maran a Onyra* (Maran and Onyra), an American story set in the period of the discovery of America, was published in 1791 by Prokop Šedivý, who also left a drama in manuscript entitled "Příchoz Němců z Ameriky" (The Coming of the Germans from America). A pioneering history of America was published in Bratislava by the Slovak geographer Ladislav Bartolomeides. Václav Kramerius, a very influential publisher of popular Czech literature and author of the Czech version of *John Smith's ... Truthful Travel Stories* (1798), published in Prague in 1803 his own essay on the discovery of America, *Historické vypsání* (Historical Narrative), which related "in what manner the fourth continent, America, was discovered through Columbus."[10]

---

cation *Otázky studia obecných dějin*, i–ii, Acta Univ. Carolinae, Historica (Prague, 1957, 1963). An English version will be published in volume iii of this publication.

8 A. Petráňová, "Z korespondence Fr. Steinského, prvního profesora pomocných věd historických na Karlově universitě," in *Vojtíškův sborník, Acta Univ. Carolinae, Philosophica et Historica*, ii (Prague, 1958), 101–12.

9 Remnants of Socher's correspondence are to be found today in the State Archives at Litoměřice-Děčín: Sources for the history of the Bohemian glass-trade.

10 For a survey of the first specimens of modern Czech and Slovak interest in America J. Jungmann's Appendix to his classic history of Czech literature (*Historie literatury české*) is still

When the first Czech learned journal, the *Časopis Českého musea* (Journal of the Bohemian Museum), started publication in 1827, Benjamin Franklin's appeal to educationalists was included. Indeed Franklin's works provided most influential reading material for the Czech common people; Czech patriots, especially Josef Jungmann, considered them of great value for a nation consisting of poor, or at best modest, hard-working people. Selected works of Benjamin Franklin were published by the Moravian patriot František Cyrill Kampelík in 1838.[11] Franklin fared much better than his compatriots Washington Irving and H. W. Longfellow, but their works were also translated from the end of the 1820s.

During the 1830s, Czech newspapers began to publish informative articles on America. The newspaper *Květy* (Flowers) in 1834 contained an article on Philadelphia, and other periodicals, such as the Journal of the Czech Museum and the *Česká včela* (The Czech Bee), followed suit. The first longer article on the contemporary United States was published in 1835 by the liberal publicist Jan Slavomír Tomíček. He wrote with admiration about American democracy and the republican constitution, which he mentioned as an example of this democracy. It was a courageous gesture, because the American republic was thus turned into a symbol of a completely different state and society from those of contemporary Austria. His attitude was similar to that of another refugee from Bohemia-Moravia, Karl Postl, *alias* Charles Sealsfield.[12]

Belief in the future of the United States, expressed in Tomíček's article, was shared by his collaborator on the periodical *Květy*, Jakub Malý. But Malý did not see only the positive side of contemporary America. In 1844 he published an article "Texas a Spojené státy severní Ameriky" (Texas and the United States of North America), in which he predicted almost exactly the direction of American expansion. He opposed the institution of slavery, too, in his article "Prodej černochův v N. Orleansu" (The Sale of Negroes in New Orleans), thus adding to the abolitionist note already expressed in an anonymous short story, called "Negr" (The Negro), issued for popular consumption by a small publisher, Landfras, at Jindřichův Hradec in 1834.[13] Somewhere between Tomíček, with his uncritical attitude, and Malý, and his criticism, stood Josef Benoni, who, at the threshold of the revolution of 1848, published in the magazine *Poutník* (The Pilgrim) a well-informed and informative essay "On America in General, and Especially the North American Communities." Benoni's essay included a historical survey "from the

---

useful. For John Smith's contemporaries and successors, see Z. Vančura, *Otcové poutníci a počátky americké literatury* (Prague, 1965).

11 Cf. J. Polišenský, *Benjamin Franklin a první americká revoluce* (Prague, 1956).

12 The best collection of these periodicals is to be found in the Library of the National Museum, Prague. See also B. Šindelář, "Příspěvek k otázce českého novodobého vystěhovalectví v epoše kapitalismu," *Sborník prací filosofické fakulty brněnské university* III, *Řada historická 1* (Brno, 1954), 18–43.

13 *Negr, Povídka z Večerního vyražení 1831* (Jindřichův Hradec, 1834).

discovery of America" up to 1776, and also gave basic information on the geography and constitution of the United States.[14]

Before 1848, it was risky to publish any commentary on political and social institutions, which might be taken as critical of the Austrian "establishment," and therefore not many appeared. But, if we take into account the newspapers and reviews published in German (the intelligentsia were still mostly bilingual, and German periodicals, especially those published in Brno, could print more outspoken articles than was allowed by the censorship in Prague), we can say that, slowly, a realistic picture of the United States of the Jacksonian era was emerging before the amazed eyes of the Czech reader. The positive aspects of American life were, for obvious reasons, stressed, the ideal America being a land of free farmers and small entrepreneurs, virtually independent and taking an active part in political life. The hated institution of slavery (by the end of the sixteenth century Czech translators of Jean de Léry's *Histoire d'un voyage faict en la terre du Brésil* [Description of Brasilia] were already defending the American Indians against the European conquerors), however, along with the expansion of the United States into Texas and the war against Mexico, prevented this "ideal" America from existing in the imagination of Czech readers. But the antithesis America–Austria was of political importance, and in the "revolutionary years" 1848–9, the American "model" of state and society was in popular use as a political weapon.[15]

Even the expansion of the United States, although this was clearly for them an unpopular movement, was used to advantage by would-be revolutionaries in central Europe. It was known that the United States supported, at least morally, the contemporary movements of European nations for liberty and national independence, and that some radical groups there were asking for military intervention in favour of the European revolutionaries. The leading Czech liberal publicist, Karel Havlíček-Borovský, accepted without reservation the American explanation of the annexation of Texas, and professed the belief that the United States had the task of spreading civilization across the American continent.

More important, the Czech press used the American example as an argument in discussions concerned with the political future of Austria. Radical and liberal newspapers and newspapermen saw in the United States an example that could be urged in favour of a federalization of Austria. Even government papers, such as *Pražské noviny* (Prague News) or the conservative *Vlastimil*, could not afford to write against this argument openly. Usually they pointed out that the United States was already far from revolutionary, and that its constitution was, in fact, a

14 J. Benoni, "O Americe vůbec a severoamerických obcích zvlášť," *Poutník* (1847). The much abused Jakub Malý had been publishing his remarkable articles in the periodicals *Česká včela, Květy*, etc. since 1844.

15 See J. Polišenský, "Der Ausgleich als historiographisches Problem," in *Sborník z konference o rakousko-uherském vyrovnání 1867* (Bratislava, in the press).

conservative one, and just for this reason a successful one. The government paper published in German, the *Prager Zeitung*, was, so far as we know, the only German paper to write about America in 1848–9, and it always did so in a negative way. According to its editors, any comparison of Austria with America was dangerous for the monarchy, and they warned against it. The attitude of the German-speaking press was logical: they could find in neighbouring Germany what the Czechs, as members of a suppressed nation, were seeking in France and America.[16]

The American example was quoted during the struggle for the self-government of urban and other communities and for the liberty of the press. With the help of this example publicists stressed the necessity of doing away with the dead weight of obsolete institutions, especially when they prevented free enterprise. On the other hand, conservatives either emphasized the fact that "American liberties" were successful because of the objective conditions – e.g., enough free soil, no struggle between nationalities – or, on the contrary, that the American way of life and government meant destruction, legal uncertainty, and danger to private property. In any case, in 1848–9 the existence of the American republic must have been very disagreeable to all defenders of the *ancien régime*.

The relation of the American republic to socialism aroused special interest. Czech writers usually understood by socialism French Utopian socialism. The only work of Engels known in Bohemia was his *Conditions of the Working-Class in England*, and the "revolutionary" Reader in History at the University of Prague in 1848–9, Anton Springer, was the first to bring more information to his audiences.[17] Commentaries interpreted the relation between American reality and socialism in very different ways. The radical *Pražský večerní list* (The Prague Evening Paper) went as far as to declare that the aims of socialism, Utopian socialism, were already realized within the framework of the United States. This was also the view of the conservative *Prager Zeitung*, with the difference, however, that this paper was of the opinion that the United States was a proof that socialism had failed, because it had reached the same situation as Europe, had the same social problems, and could not prevent the rise of the antagonistic social classes of capitalists and proletarians.[18]

The two political thinkers who in the years 1848–9 wrote about the future possibilities of the New World were the liberal publicist, Karel Havlíček-Borovský, and the liberal priest turned Utopian socialist, František Matouš Klácel.

Havlíček thought that the United States had already realized the ideals for whose achievement the peoples of central Europe were fighting in 1848. His con-

16 New works on the problems of Czech politics in Austria in 1848–9 are in preparation by A. Klíma and J. Polišenský.

17 J. Polišenský, "Historie a universita v době předbřeznové a v revolučním roce 1848," in *Vojtíškův sborník*, 113ff.

18 See J. Polišenský, "Rakousko, Prusko a Německo 1850–1866," *Československý časopis historický*, 1967/2, 249–62. See also Josef Kočí, *Emanuel Arnold* (Prague, 1964).

ception was far from any kind of radicalism. He was advocating the reception of everything positive that the American "model" could offer – especially since, in his view, democracy of the American type was the best safeguard against the danger of revolution and socialism. He was, of course, full of admiration for the American Revolution of the eighteenth century, but realistically he agreed also with the subsequent compromises which, according to him, had given rise to the United States.[19]

Klácel's conception of American democracy was, compared with the "political realism" of Havlíček, much more speculative and even more distant from reality. Klácel was persuaded that America would be the land where the real rebirth of human society would take place. According to him, the United States had already taken the first steps to achieve this goal. Political equality was the first step to the brotherhood of man and to a symbiosis of nationalities, and one could witness this in the United States. It was a picture of things to come all over the world. Klácel was not the only Forty-Eighter to share the romantic belief in an "American Utopia" and a "paradise amidst unspoiled nature." In the spring of 1848 a Viennese student hailing from Prague, Vojta Náprstek-Fingerhut (later founder of the Náprstek ethnographical museum in Prague), left turbulent central Europe for the United States, but before boarding his ship at Hamburg he sent an eloquent letter to his Prague friends saying: "I am leaving for America! I am going to the famous republic to get acquainted with the ideal for all development of human society – as I have longed to do for years ... A thorough acquaintance with the American republic, so far as state and society are concerned, will undoubtedly bring me much profit ..."[20]

Both Náprstek and Klácel dreamed of founding Czech settlements on American soil. Although Náprstek did not find the "American Utopia," he did indeed bring back to Prague valuable experiences and throughout the last four decades of the nineteenth century he tried to inform his fellow-countrymen of things American. In this he differed from the former missionary Ignác Stelzig or the former radical student Vilém Pflanzer, who came back from the United States as sceptical conservatives and acid critics of the land in which they had buried their youthful expectations.

We can sum up, therefore, by saying that in the middle of the nineteenth century the American conception of civilization had become, among the more or less revolutionized middle classes of central Europe, a powerful, although not a decisive political argument. It cannot be said that their image of the contemporary United States was a very concrete or a completely positive one. The expansionist tendencies and the attitude towards the Mexican and Negro populations were not favourably received by Czech publicists and men of letters.

Clearly, it might well be fruitful to view the (evidently very early) appreciation

19 See K. Kosík, *Čeští radikální demokraté* (Prague, 1953).
20 *Památce Vojty Náprstka*, ed. Renáta Tyršová (Prague, 1926), 7.

of the United States as something different from, something antagonistic to, previous European conceptions of civilization. The British and French "models" which came after the era of Dutch-Spanish antagonism, that is, in the latter half of the seventeenth century, survived the eighteenth. But henceforth to many persons only the United States of America represented a truly independent state and social organization.[21]

In 1848-9 this attitude did not greatly influence the outcome of the political struggle for a federalization of Austria. The people who were most influenced by the American type of government were radicals or liberals. The radicals were defeated in the streets of Prague and Vienna in June and September 1848 respectively. The liberal federalists were suppressed in Kroměříž (Kremsier) in the spring of 1849, and the conservative liberals, the party of the Stadions and Thuns, discovered very soon thereafter that they too had no chance against the forces of the *ancien régime*, the "military party" brought together in the Bohemian Army Corps during the forties under the command of Prince Alfred Windischgrätz. In the headquarters of Field-Marshal Radetzky in Lombardy in the spring months of 1848, Windischgrätz, Schwarzenberg, Sunstenau, Haynau, and Lobkowitz prepared a blueprint for the victory of counter-revolution in Austria. So far, the poet Franz Grillparzer was quite right when he said that the future of the monarchy lay with the army. Whether the future forged by the generals was a happy one for the Austrian nationalities appears now as very doubtful.[22]

During the 1850s, when immigration to the United States acquired a mass character, the nature of American-Czech relations was completely changed. The idea of a "New Country (Homeland)" across the Atlantic came slowly into being, and during the 1860s repeated attempts were made to organize Czech settlements on American soil. These attempts, connected with the activities of V. Náprstek, F. M. Klácel, and others, were unsuccessful. The Austrian government (but also the National party [i.e. Old Czechs] at home) and its Russian contact-men tried to prevent a mass emigration, or to direct it towards the Slavonic parts of Europe, and eventually towards some part of the Russian Empire. The plans for establishing a "New Czechia" on the banks of the Amur, however, were just as hopeless as those for the Utopian colonies in the Dakotas or in Nebraska. The Russian Imperial government was, in the end, little interested in bringing potential malcontents within its own borders.[23]

From the early 1860s, the Czech immigrants to the United States were rapidly

21 See, for example, Napoleon's remark to his Austrian "entourage" on his way to the Isle of Elba in the spring of 1814, in Karl Clam-Martinic, "Reise mit Kaiser Napoleon nach Elba, 1814," Clam-Martinic Family Archives, Central State Archives, Prague.
22 This will be shown in the monographs cited above in footnote 16.
23 See František Kutnar, *Počátky hromadného vystěhovalectví z Čech v období Bachova absolutismu* (Prague, 1964); and V. Mastný, "Statistika vystěhovalectví českého proletariátu do Spojených států," *Demografie*, 1962/3, 204ff.

gaining in importance. Their political programme was mostly the work of the Forty-Eighters and if the rank and file were not too interested in politics, the radicals were trying to help the work of the indefatigable Josef Václav Frič and his "Correspondence Tchèque." They also helped the young Josef Václav Sládek, another refugee from Austria in 1868, to get a first-hand knowledge of the American constitution – in the same way as Náprstek wanted to do twenty years earlier.[24] Soon afterwards, Czech working-class immigrants, with the benevolent help of the older generation, especially of Klácel, founded their own organizations, which for the two years of 1870–2 functioned in New York and Chicago as the only existing Czech sections of the First International.[25] Apart from these pioneers, the mass of Czech (and Slovak) immigrants also showed their loyalty to the abolitionist attitude of the "Old Country" and shed their blood for democratic ideals during the Civil War of 1861–5.[26]

By the end of the 1860s, however, Czech social and political life also underwent important changes. Although the *annus mirabilis* of 1868 did not bring the coveted liberty which a Czech-American had wished to Náprstek on that New Year's Day, it brought the Czech politicians massive support in the course of manifestations held all over Bohemia. It also gave them the opportunity to formulate their political programme. And this means, naturally, that one can no longer speak about the *beginnings* of modern Czech political thought, for Czech political thinking had already reached a further stage in its development.

24 Josef Polák, "Americká cesta Josefa Václava Sládka," *Acta Universitatis Palackianae Olomucensis, Philologica*, xix (Prague, 1966).
25 See J. Polišenský and J. Staněk, "Počátky české dělnické emigrace a české sekce I. Internacionály ve Spojených státech amerických," in *Počátky české a slovenské emigrace do USA* (Bratislava, 1970), 97–124.
26 See Josef Čermák, *Dějiny občanské války: S připojením zkušeností českých vojínů* (Chicago, 1899); Ella Lon, *Foreigners in the Union Army and Navy* (Baton Rouge, La., 1951).

The Hussite Movement in
the Historiography of the Czech Awakening

FREDERICK G. HEYMANN

DURING THE LONG PERIOD in the seventeenth and eighteenth centuries which in the Czech historical consciousness exists as the "Temno," the time of darkness, the Habsburg authorities and especially their strong instrument of counter-reformation, the Jesuit order, tried to suppress as far as possible the dangerous remembrance of the great revolutionary movement called Hussitism. One of the most decisive effects of the Thirty Years' War had been the complete defeat of those forces that, in defence of Bohemian Evangelism, had stood behind the rebellion of the Bohemian Estates against the emperors Matthias and Ferdinand II, and clearly the conquerors could not wish that the memory of an earlier rebellion fought against the Church of Rome and the Holy Roman Emperor of the time – and one that to a large extent had been successful – should be kept alive. One means of counteracting such an unwelcome development was the mass burning of books which, religious or otherwise, could be considered as causing doubts about the justice both of the policy of the Viennese authorities and of the counter-reformatory measures of the Jesuits and the Catholic church. But just as important as the disappearance of existing books was the need to prevent the appearance of new works which would in any way tend effectively to revive Hussite thoughts and traditions. A strict censorship was thus imposed, which, indeed, was not removed till 1848 (and later was temporarily re-established by the absolutist regime of Alexander Bach in the early 1850s). This supervision was considered all the more necessary since it was, after all, not quite possible to eliminate all writing on Bohemian history, whether old or new, and since the Hussite movement and its consequences could not simply be wiped out as if they had never existed. What was wanted was a presentation and interpretation of these great historical developments which would not encourage the people of Bohemia to identify themselves with the rebels of the fifteenth century.

Conveniently for the ruling powers some works were already in existence that presented, together with other material, the Hussite movement more or less in the spirit which the Viennese authorities favoured. Among them the most important, in terms of Bohemian historiography and up to a point also of their general influence, were the *Historia Bohemica* (Bohemian History) by Enea Silvio de' Piccolomini (Aeneas Sylvius, later Pope Pius II) and, quite as or even more famous, Václav Hájek of Libočany's *Kronika česká* (Bohemian Chronicle), which, in its original edition as well as in much-read translations into German and Latin, became for a long time the great standard work on the history of the Kingdom of Bohemia, to the extent that its author (who died in 1555) was flatteringly called the "Bohemian Livy." This latter work, though it was dedicated to King Ferdinand, nevertheless underwent (and passed) a careful scrutiny by a committee of prominent Czech Catholics appointed by the king. Throughout the sixteenth, seventeenth, and much of the eighteenth century it maintained its position and its amazing authority with, and its influence upon, all those authors who attempted to write the history of Bohemia, including even a few men possessing considerable gifts for historical study and presentation and a true love for their country. It took a long time before the weaknesses, failures, and distortions of this book were discovered, acknowledged, and slowly corrected. Indeed, it could almost be said that the process of shaking off the views of Hájek is the best indication of the development of a truly adequate Czech national historiography. And it was the treatment of the Hussite movement which presented this process most decisively and most significantly.

How can Hájek's work, especially in its treatment of Hussitism, be adequately characterized within the narrow framework of this brief study? As Hájek, though a Catholic, came from a family that had belonged to the Church of the Czech Brethren, and lived at a time when the Hussite-Utraquist church was still strong and influential (and in its more conservative "Old-Utraquist" wing quite acceptable to King Ferdinand), he did not present Jan Hus himself as a particularly bad or dangerous rebel. Indeed, both Hus and his friend Jerome (Jeroným) of Prague were presented in Hájek's book as personally decent men though on a wrong path, men whose death at Constance could at least be regretted.[1]

---

1 See Hájek, edition of 1541, 361ff. See also the presentation of Hájek's role in this context by Arnošt Kraus, *Husitství v literatuře, zejména německé* (Prague, 1917–24), I, 210ff. (cited as "Kraus" below); F. M. Bartoš, "Žižka v dějepisectví," *Sborník Žižkův 1424–1924*, ed. Rudolf Urbánek (Prague, 1924), 173–5 (cited as "Bartoš"); and F. Kavka, *Husitská revoluční tradice* (Prague, 1953), 64–6 (cited as "Kavka"). A small but in parts still useful sketch of Czech

Hájek begins to show his bitter antagonism against the Hussite movement only when he comes to the actual revolution, a movement which is personified in his eyes by Jan Žižka. It is characteristic that in his presentation of Žižka he is, in fact, much more hostile than Enea Silvio, who at least gives the great leader of Tábor and Oreb his due as a military genius.[2] For Hájek Žižka is nothing but a robber, a murderer, a destroyer, entirely responsible for any cruel deeds that occurred in the course of the Hussite revolt, all of which, so it appears from his description, were the work of the Hussites, and none the work of the German (and other) crusaders and invaders. Apart from such one-sided assertions the work is simply teeming with greater or smaller errors and distortions, as well as with inventions of details (including names). For some of these there is no basis in the sources which he used – or in some cases claimed to have used since there is sometimes reason to assume that he merely invented such "sources."

But it took a long time before these facts were recognized and before Hájek lost his prestige as the one great historian of his country. It was characteristic of the strength of Hájek's reputation that one of the few distinguished and patriotic Czech historians of the seventeenth century, the Jesuit Bohuslav Balbín (1621–88), used his work without any questioning of his scholarship,[3] and this even though he himself made some notable contributions to the publication of important source materials regarding Žižka. The same was true of Balbín's personal friend, the Prague canon and later suffragan bishop Thomas Pešina of Čechorod (1629–80). Both these men tried, without always paying full regard to the instructions coming from above, to paint a slightly less one-sided picture of the Hussite story, and cautiously to defend especially the "Hussite King" George of Poděbrady.[4] But their general treatment of the Hussite Revolution was still dominated by Hájek. The same was true even of a Lutheran historian, the Moravian-German Zacharias Theobald, whose *Hussitenkrieg* (The Hussite War; Nürnberg, 1621), with little regard to the author's religious confession, was strongly influenced by Hájek.[5]

The real break-through came from outside Bohemia, that is from outside the sphere of the Habsburgs' political and the Jesuits' spiritual domination, from regions where the Enlightenment was about to make its first appearance. Among the authors who, far from Bohemia, began to be interested in Hussite history we find two Huguenot ministers who both ended their careers as refugees in Berlin, the

---

historiography in English is Count Franz von Lützow's *Lectures on the Historians of Bohemia* (London, 1905).

2 See his *Historia Bohemica* (any of the many editions), chaps. 38, 40, 42, 44–6.

3 See, for example, Balbín's *Miscellanea historica regni Bohemiae*, III (Prague, 1681). There chapter 21, paragraphs VI and VII (pp. 255–62), is concerned with the Hussite age. Of fifty-five source references (only giving the names, nothing else), twenty-two refer to Hájek. The second most frequent reference is Zacharias Theobald, who, again, bases most of his information on Enea Silvio and Hájek. Otherwise see Kraus, II, 20–2, and Bartoš, 179–81.

4 See, for example, Pešina's *Mars moravicus* (Prague, 1677), 858–60.

5 See Kraus, I, 243–8.

capital of the newly established Kingdom of Prussia: Jacques Lenfant (1661–1724) and Isaac de Beausobre (1659–1738). Lenfant wrote a big work in two volumes called *Histoire de la guerre des Hussites et du Concile de Basle* (Amsterdam, 1731), but in its sources it did not go much beyond those used by Hájek and his followers. Not so Beausobre. His much shorter contribution, modestly called *Supplément à l'histoire de la guerre des Hussites de Mr. Lenfant* (Lausanne and Geneva, 1746), made, for the first time, fairly ample use of a Hussite source which, to this day, is of the greatest value and significance for our knowledge and understanding of the Hussite Revolution: the *Cronica Hussitica* of Laurence (Vavřinec) of Březová (mistakenly called by Beausobre "of Byzin").[6]

The strange thing is that this extremely important chronicle had not been unknown before. It had been available in several copies even though it did not appear in print until 1724, and then not in complete form. But Beausobre was the first who fully recognized the value of this work, and on this basis he succeeded in assuming a critical distance from the distorted picture based on Enea Silvio and especially on Hájek of Libočany. For the first time, we find in his book even a remarkably unprejudiced attempt at a critical analysis of the structure and thought of the radical movements that appeared within the framework of Hussitism, including Pikartism and Adamitism. He was the first who drew the attention of his readers to the strong possibility that many of the claims regarding the hateful and bloody deeds of those sectarians might have been invented by their enemies, above all by the monks. Here, of course, it is clearly the Huguenot speaking, with his attitude nourished by the ideas of early French Enlightenment.[7] Almost at the same time another Protestant minister and church historian, the Württemberg pietist Georg Cunrad Rieger, devoted a part of his lengthy history of the Church of the Czech Brethren to its Hussite antecedents, with a basic attitude very similar to that of Beausobre.[8]

The question arose: When would an independent, nation-conscious Czech historiography arise (which would necessarily have to put emphasis on the positive aspects of the Hussite movement)? The difficulties were considerable. The censorship was still functioning fully,[9] and as long as Hájek's authority was unshaken it was difficult to see how Czech historiography was to break free from its fetters, how

6 The latest (and only fully usable) edition was published by Jaroslav Goll in vol. v of *Fontes Rerum Bohemicarum* (Prague, 1893), 327–451 (under the name "Vavřince z Březové kronika husitská"). In the same volume there is a valuable introduction, also by Goll, pp. xx–xlii. František Palacký discussed the chronicler in his *Würdigung der alten böhmischen Geschichtsschreiber* (Prague, 1830), 202–17 (later quoted as *Würdigung*).

7 Yet his view is reflected in one of the most thorough and up-to-date modern treatments of the Taborite development, the *chef d'œuvre* of Josef Macek. See his *Tábor v husitském revolučním hnutí*, ii (Prague, 1955), 327, 355, and his publication of part of Beausobre's work in a Czech translation: *Rozprava o českých Adamitech* (Prague, 1954), with a postscript on Beausobre by Amedeo Molnár.

8 *Die alte und neue böhmische Brüder* [sic] (Züllichau, 1734–50). See also Bartoš, 184ff., for information concerning Rieger.

9 See, for this issue, Joseph F. Zacek's contribution in this volume.

it would feel the fresh winds of Western Enlightenment. There was, above all, the negative task of unmasking Hájek and other distorters of the facts, and, in order to make this possible, the need for collection and publication of important chronicles and other sources. The man who, in Bohemia, first made use of the somewhat less hopeless atmosphere of the Theresian age was the Piarist cleric Gelasius Dobner (1719–90). He subjected Hájek's work to a painstaking examination to which, according to Palacký, he devoted about twenty years.[10] Towards the end of his labours, in 1782, at a moment when Joseph II had become the sole ruler of his empire and a freer atmosphere – especially in relation to the religious situation – had begun to prevail, Dobner summarized his judgment as follows: "We have eventually come to the conclusion that Hájek's works abound in far more historical and elementary chronological errors than we had ever believed or could even have suspected."[11] Palacký praises Dobner especially for his critical sense and puts him far above his popular contemporary, the Jesuit historian František Pubička (Pubitschka) (1722–1807), author of a huge *Chronologische Geschichte von Böhmen* (Chronological History of Bohemia), again probably because Pubička still puts Hájek above Laurence of Březová and Beausobre. Yet Palacký blames Dobner for not using his high gifts earlier toward a constructive treatment of his country's history. For those years toward the turn of the century Palacký mentions, as giving promise of a better future for Bohemian historiography, the names of a number of distinguished men who had become members of the Royal Bohemian Society of Sciences (as it was known from 1784, although it had originally been founded as a private society in 1769).[12] Among its members was also František Martin Pelcl (Franz Martin Pelzel) (1734–1801), a man who is often considered as the last, indeed almost the only, predecessor of Palacký. Pelcl, who during his later years was professor of Czech language and literature at the University of Prague (which in the eighteenth century was still a German institution), published in 1774 his *Kurzgefasste Geschichte der Böhmen* (Concise History of the People of Bohemia) in two volumes. It went through four editions, the last one in 1817, long after his death.

Pelcl's treatment of the Hussite movement – which, as was usual at that time, he always called "der Hussitenkrieg," the Hussite War – is remarkably inconsistent. He speaks with great sympathy about Hus,[13] but the outbreak of the revolution appears to him like the eruption of an epidemic, a mass fever.[14] In his description of the fight between Hussites and Catholics he tries to take something like a neutral position, but his emotions appear anti-Hussite and especially anti-Taborite. He is

10 See his *Würdigung*, XIX–XXI, 279.
11 *Ibid.*, 284.
12 *Ibid.*, xxff. See J. F. Zacek, "The Virtuosi of Bohemia: The Royal Bohemian Society of Sciences," *East European Quarterly* (Boulder, Colorado), II/2 (June 1968), 147–59.
13 See Pelcl, *Kurzgefasste Geschichte der Böhmen*, I, 286–311 (edition of 1817).
14 *Ibid.*, 321ff.

always complaining about the fanaticism of the people and the sufferings which the country underwent as a result of those struggles. In Žižka he acknowledges the military genius. "He would," he says, "have been one of the greatest heroes of history if he had acted more humanely and had not raged against his own father-land."[15] Once he reaches the times of George (Jiří) of Poděbrady he very strongly takes the side of the Hussite king (whom he considers as the greatest ruler of his time) against the Papacy and the Catholic barons.[16] (References to the Jesuit Balbín made this easier, also, in relation to the censor.) In the preface to this work, Pelcl's patriotism seems to take him quite a step toward a positive stand in regard to the Hussites, or at least to some of their leaders. "Should not," he writes, "a Czech have the right to be proud of the heroism of his Žižka or his Prokop? True, they were Hussites, but even so they believed in Christ, and adored His Sacred Mother and Saint Wenceslas. Žižka even had a mass read to him every day in his encampment. Thus they are in this way superior to those heathen heroes whose deeds, without regard to their idolatry, are generally praised to high heaven." (This passage, incidentally, is omitted in the preface to the last, posthumous edition.)

Pelcl's understanding of Jan Hus and his historical role appears somewhat deepened in a later book on the reign of King Václav IV. This, however, was about the measure of his progress in the understanding of Hussitism. Of his last great work, the *Nová kronyka česká* (New Bohemian Chronicle), this time written in Czech, only the first three volumes appeared in print (1791–6); the fourth, which dealt with Czech history after Charles IV, was finished but, partly for censorship reasons, never published. The manuscript shows that Pelcl never quite overcame the powerful influence of Hájek, though he presented some new material, especially on Žižka. To the end his mind was torn – between the forces of national pride and a measure of historical understanding on one side, and dislike of the "lawlessness" of a revolution (fortified by worries about the censor) on the other.[17]

It was not a historian, at least not a man for whom history was the main subject of interest, who first understood, in a deeper sense, the enormous importance of the Hussite movement not only in Czech but even in European history. It was a philologist: Josef Dobrovský. There is one special subject to which, in the framework of the Hussite Revolution, he made a worth-while contribution: the history of the Pikarts and Adamites.[18] He succeeded at least in demonstrating some of the prejudices and distortions in what had long been considered as the most valuable source on these sects: the "Bohemian History" of Enea Silvio. But he also understood the deep connections between the religious and political history of Hussitism and the field in which he became the great pioneer: the systematic introduction of Slavonic

15 *Ibid.*, 374.
16 See, for example, *ibid.*, 475ff.
17 See the opinions of Kraus, II, 147ff., Bartoš, 186ff., and Kavka, 95–98.
18 *Geschichte der böhmischen Pickarden und Adamiten* ("Abhandlungen der kgl. böhmischen Gesellschaft der Wissenschaften," sec. 4, I; Prague, 1788), 300–43.

studies.[19] It is sadly ironical that he who did so much for the reawakening of interest in Czech language and literature was deeply pessimistic regarding its chances of a true revival.[20] However, he was not alone in this feeling of pessimism; some of the magnates who felt pride in the history of the Czech nation and were willing (e.g. in contributions to the Royal Bohemian Society) to help in recalling this great past shared his doubts concerning the future of Czech as an instrument of modern literary and historical expression. The man who (to some extent as a disciple of Dobrovský) refused to accept such pessimism and who indeed contributed more than anyone else to the cultural reawakening of Czech historical and political consciousness was František Palacký, one of the giants in the European historiography of the nineteenth century.

In the footsteps of Dobner Palacký, too, had to do a good deal of historiographical house-cleaning, in many fields and especially in that of the Hussite movement. His first substantial and important work, written for a prize competition to which the Royal Bohemian Society of Sciences had invited candidates in 1827, was published in 1830 under the title: *Würdigung der alten böhmischen Geschichtsschreiber* (Assessment of the Old Czech Historians). In it we find the beginnings of his philosophy of history, which to a very large extent centred in the history and significance of the Hussite movement.

As far as his historiographical battles are concerned there are three that deserve special mention: his critical reactions to two dead men, Enea Silvio and Hájek, and to one who was very much alive, the German professor of history at the University of Prague, Constantin Höfler.

The struggle with the two earlier historians, conducted mainly in his *Würdigung*, was relatively easy. Their once seemingly so unassailable position had already been shaken by such men as Dobner and by the more careful evaluation of such sources as the chronicle of Laurence of Březová. Even so Palacký had the opportunity of proving, in his criticism, mistaken or distorted facts or presentations which could be clearly confronted with the sources. In the case of Enea Silvio[21] these critical remarks almost all refer to Hussite history, in which the great humanist writer and cardinal (he wrote the *Historia* shortly before his elevation to the papal see) seemed especially competent.[22] As for Hájek, his fame, it can be said, received from Palacký its death stroke,[23] and I have not come across any attempt, from any side, to restore any part of it.

But the final historiographical struggle took place not at the beginning but towards the end of Palacký's career. In the year 1868, eight years before his death at

19 See Kavka, 99–103.
20 See, for example, Albert Pražák, *České obrození* (Prague, 1948), 37ff.
21 See *Würdigung*, 230–50.
22 Enea was, a good deal later, to find his defender in the person of Josef Pekař, with some – but only a limited – justification. See his *Žižka a jeho doba*, II (Prague, 1928), 119–29.
23 See *Würdigung*, 273–92.

the age of nearly seventy-eight, Palacký published a small book, again in German
– it was meant to reach a large public – called *Die Geschichte des Hussitenthums
und Professor Constantin Höfler* (The History of Hussitism and Professor C. H.). In
it he not only defended his own understanding of the Hussite movement (which had
taken a prominent place in his monumental "History of Bohemia"), but above all
tried to show that Höfler's understanding of this great historical development was
totally wrong, and that the German professor (he came originally from Bavaria and
never managed to learn the Czech language) was utterly incompetent in his function
as a palaeographer, as an editor of important source material, and in consequence
also as a historian. He had little difficulty in proving his charge regarding Höfler's
palaeographical incompetence. In going through six or seven Latin source publications he found about 500 errors in reading, a considerable proportion of which distorted the meaning of the text. It was a severe blow to Höfler (and unfortunately
for subsequent scholarship some of those faulty editions are to this day the only
ones available[24]).

The main question in this fiercely polemical discussion, however, remained open.
A considerable part of it was concerned with the issue of nationalism. Palacký felt
that the struggle between Czech and German (or Slav and German) and the defence of the Czechs against German expansionist tendencies were basic facts of
the history of Bohemia. Höfler, and with him some other German historians who
organized themselves in the Verein für Geschichte der Deutschen in Böhmen
(Society for the History of the Germans in Bohemia), answered, largely in the *Mitteilungen* (Publications) of this society. But Höfler had also tried to present Hus as
a fiercely anti-German nationalist, a charge against which Palacký, rightly, defended
him. The whole reproach of extreme and blind nationalism which Palacký and
Höfler hurled against the other's nation as a main reason for the Hussite Wars was
at least much exaggerated. Yet it is true that there had been a distinctly nationalist
element in the attitudes of both sides during the Hussite movement, although it was
probably stronger, and in terms of the historical development, further advanced
in the Czech camp, most of the Germans simply considering the majority of Czechs
as heretics who therefore had to be wiped out. Recent Czech historiography has
tended to reduce older, exaggerated claims regarding the dominant role of nationalism, and German scholars today (from both German republics) have contributed
valuable knowledge regarding the existence of Hussite movements among Germans
inside as well as outside Bohemia.[25] Indeed the Palacký-Höfler struggle was, as it

24 The most important among them is the Chronicle of Mikuláš of Pelhřimov, the Taborite
   bishop, contained in Höfler's *Geschichtsschreiber der husitischen Bewegung in Böhmen*
   ("Fontes Rerum Austriacarum," II, VI, VII; Vienna, 1856–66).
25 See Ferdinand Seibt, *Hussitica: Zur Struktur einer Revolution* (Cologne and Graz, 1965),
   passim, and especially 92–7; H. Köpstein, "Uber die Teilnahme von Deutschen an der hussit-
   ischen revolutionären Bewegung," in *Zeitschrift für Geschichtswissenschaft*, XI (1963),
   116–45; and most recently H. Heimpel, *Drei Inquisitionsverfahren aus dem Jahre 1425*
   ("Veröffentlichungen des Max-Planck-Instituts für Geschichte," 24; Göttingen, 1969).

were, a projection of the present into the past. It was particularly characteristic of the situation which obtained in Bohemia and Moravia after 1848 and after the demise of that early nineteenth-century movement which has been called *Böhmischer Landespatriotismus* (a patriotism shared temporarily by Bohemian Czechs and Germans and expressing love for the country rather than for the nation).

But nationalism was only one basic element in Palacký's understanding of the Hussite movement. To him the meaning of Czech history lay in the struggle for freedom not only against German attempts to dominate and suppress the Slavs and especially the Czechs, but also against religious and political absolutism.[26] Palacký, the heir of the tradition of the Czech Brethren, saw in the Hussite Revolution also a great idealistic movement. To some extent, however, Palacký found himself in a dilemma. By nature he was a conservative, the more so as he grew older, and he had not much sympathy for revolutions as such. He never forgot the help he received, in his plans for a great, up-to-date history of Bohemia, from the high nobility. He did, however, understand that revolutions are historically necessary, that in many cases true progress would not have been possible without them.[27] He himself had taken a notable (if far from radical) part in the political leadership of the Czechs during the revolution of 1848 and in the subsequent attempts (e.g. at the Reichstag of Kroměříž) to reach an ethnically just, and in many respects democratic reconstruction of the Habsburg Monarchy.[28] Thus, on the whole, his heart was on the side not only of Hus but also of the Hussites, occasionally even of the more radical Taborites. In addition, he saw (rightly, I believe) in the Hussite movement an extraordinarily close relationship with, indeed similarity to, the Protestant Reformation of the sixteenth century.[29] It seems almost comical that in this assumption his great enemy, Constantin Höfler, was essentially of the same opinion – only, of course, what in Palacký's eyes was a sign of greatness and progress in the Hussite movement was in Höfler's eyes the very opposite: an additional sinful responsibility for a deeply regrettable development, the destruction of religious union through the Protestant heresy.[30]

26 See, for example, his *Zur böhmischen Geschichtsschreibung* (Prague, 1871), 1.
27 On Palacký's attitude toward the historical phenomenon of revolutions see, for example, R. G. Plaschka, *Von Palacký bis Pekař* (Graz and Cologne, 1955), 17ff., and, in much more detail, J. F. Zacek's forthcoming book, *Palacký: The Historian as Scholar and Nationalist* (The Hague).
28 See Stanley Z. Pech, *The Czech Revolution of 1848* (Chapel Hill [North Carolina], 1969), 336ff.
29 See, for example, his German edition of the *Geschichte von Böhmen* of 1851, III/2, 294; also *Die Geschichte des Hussitenthums und Professor C. Höfler*, 160.
30 The radical condemnation of Hus himself and Hussitism as a movement made by leading Catholic historians of the nineteenth century is clearly shown in the case of Ludwig von Pastor. Pastor bases his judgment largely on Höfler, and although he has to admit that Höfler's source editions are inadequate he calls his writings *bahnbrechend*. (See Pastor's *Geschichte der Päpste*, published first in 1885, quoted here from the fifth edition of 1925, I, 168, 169 n. 3.) It is characteristic that even in his index Hus appears simply as "Johannes Hus, Irrlehrer" (*ibid.*, 878).

Palacký's main contribution to the history of the Hussite movement is, of course, contained not in those small but significant monographs but first of all in his enormously valuable source publications[31] and, secondly, in his *magnum opus*, called in its German edition *Geschichte von Böhmen* and in its Czech edition, more correctly, *Dějiny národu českého v Čechách a v Moravě* (History of the Czech Nation in Bohemia and Moravia).[32] It is almost a matter of course that this great classic, whose third part, devoted to the Hussite age, was written about one and a quarter centuries ago, cannot any longer be considered as up-to-date. The astonishing thing about it is the degree to which it is still valuable, quite apart from the influence it has had upon generation after generation of historians and other leading minds down to Tomáš G. Masaryk and Kamil Krofta. Because of their specific treatment of the Hussite age – which Palacký himself rightly considered as the most important phase of Czech history – the volumes devoted to it are probably those that are still most significant, despite the fact that this particular phase has been the subject of new studies and works ever since, not only in Czechoslovakia but also outside. It is impossible to present, within the framework of this short study, even a sketch of the treatment of the Hussite movement in Palacký's great work. Much that I have touched on before – Palacký's attitude to the phenomenon of revolutions, his emphasis on the early forms of nationalism, especially in regard to German-Czech antagonism, and the relationship between the Czech and the later German reformations – is developed in greater detail and depth in the great "History of Bohemia" than in the monographs discussed above.

Among those interpretations that are particularly characteristic of Palacký – and that cannot be accepted today to the same extent – is his claim that the Hussite movement is the first struggle in history fought out not for material gains but for ideas.[33] Palacký thinks in the first place of the ideas of religious reform, quite justifiably, and then of the ideas of freedom and equality, somewhat less convincingly. Fight for freedom: this is a rather elastic term which can probably be applied quite correctly in this connection. But there was surely less struggle for equality;

31 Among them the most important were: *Staří letopisové čeští od r. 1378 do 1527* (Old Czech Annalists), *Scriptores Rerum Bohemicarum*, III (Prague, 1829); *Archiv český*, a collection of historical documents in Czech, founded and for a long time edited by Palacký (Prague, 1840ff.), of the greatest importance; *Urkundliche Beiträge zur Geschichte des Hussitenkrieges*, 2 vols. (Prague, 1873), documents in languages other than Czech, mostly Latin and German; *Monumenta conciliarum generalium seculi decimi quinti; Concilium Basiliense*, 2 vols., with E. Birk (Vienna, 1857, 1873).

32 The first part of the "History of Bohemia" relating to the Hussite wars (vol. III, part 2; Prague, 1851) was the last to be published, first in German, then in Czech. Palacký then switched to the reverse procedure, writing the work in Czech and supervising and carefully editing the German text, which was translated by a man named Wenzig. The switch met at first with strong resistance from the Bohemian *Landesausschuss*, but Palacký remained firm. (See his *Zur böhmischen Geschichtsschreibung* [Prague, 1871], 125–30.) The Czech edition which received its final form in 1877 is somewhat differently organized and is spread over the whole of what was then called part III, consisting of three volumes.

33 See, for example, the German edition, III/3 (Prague, 1857), 229–30.

indeed the majority of the Czech people fighting on the side of the Chalice did not even think in these terms, though there were strong elements of a social revolution present in Tábor as well as in the New Town of Prague under the leadership of Jan Želivský. To some extent Palacký's treatment of this aspect of the revolution – he did, for example, give Želivský, the radical leader of the craft guilds and the poorer classes, a good deal of recognition[34] – makes him appear, as a historian, as less influenced by his own class standing than most of the European historians of his time (men such as Ranke or the older Guizot). Nevertheless his emphasis on the supposed striving for equality as one of the basic forces of the Hussite Revolution is doubtful, especially since he sees in this striving an old Czech, or Slavic, attitude which supposedly had been buried by the inequalities of the later Middle Ages merely through German influences which brought feudalism into Bohemia under the later Přemyslid kings.[35] This, of course, is an idealized image of the old Czechs or Slavs as a sociologically and ideologically purer race than their German contemporaries, an assumption no longer maintained by Czech historiography.

It is, of course, much easier for historians of the present day to be objective on these issues and to avoid nationalistic prejudice than it was in the mid-nineteenth century. The emphasis on the uniqueness of the Hussite movement, on its pioneering achievements, but also on the proved military capacity of the Czechs in the struggle with a numerically much superior enemy – all these features were particularly suited to combat the Czechs' feeling of inferiority in relation to the Germans, to strengthen their pride in the glorious past of the nation, and to revive their faith in the nation's future. If, in this process, there were some exaggerations in the work of the man who in such an impressive way combined the roles of historian, political philosopher, and political activist in a single person, then this is surely a venial sin, all the more so because there was so much effort from the other side to make Czech achievements appear insignificant in comparison with those of the Germans.

On the whole it is the early phase of the Hussite Revolution where Palacký's presentation, though still very much worth reading, has become outdated by later historical works. This is much less true for the later period, the one which follows the phase dominated by the genius of Žižka. It is not an accident that F. M. Bartoš, in the most recent treatment of the Hussite Revolution, has quoted Palacký far more frequently in his second volume (1426–37) than in the preceding one.[36] And in Western languages no work to this day has gone substantially beyond Palacký in the presentation of the post-Žižka period. This is also true of his treatment of the negotiations of the Czechs with the Council of Basel and of the origins of the Compacts.[37]

Palacký's treatment of Žižka the man has more historiographical than actual in-

---

34 *Ibid.*, III/2, 183–4.
35 See, for example, *ibid.*, III/3, 9.
36 See F. M. Bartoš, *Husitská revoluce* II: *Vláda bratrstev a její pád 1426–1437*/The Government of the Brotherhoods and Their Fall, 1426–1437 (Prague, 1966), *passim*.
37 See the first four chapters in III/3 of the German *Geschichte von Böhmen*.

terest. We have seen that most of the earlier historians had regarded Jan Žižka, apart from his generalship, as essentially a power of destruction. This, of course, was not Palacký's view; yet it cannot be said that he had very warm feelings for this man who (outside the field of religious thought and ideological development) was the greatest and the most effective of the Hussite leaders. Palacký emphasized Žižka's religious fanaticism, which he rightly considered as the prime motive for his harsh and often cruel treatment of the Catholic clergy as well as of the Hussites' most radical wing, the so-called Pikarts of Tábor. Furthermore, he did not admit that Žižka had any of the gifts that make a statesman, partly no doubt for the reason that his sources were especially meagre for the period 1423–4, a phase in which Žižka's political understanding and political role were particularly significant.[38] Palacký believed that not Žižka, but Žižka's chief competitor as a lay leader of Tábor, Mikuláš of Hus, might have been the Hussites' great political leader, if he had lived long enough (he died in 1420). This conclusion is somewhat surprising since of the two, Žižka and Mikuláš of Hus, the latter was, if anything, the more radical, a fact which would have made inter-Hussite cooperation more difficult than it in any case turned out to be.[39]

Even though Žižka's dominant personality did not awaken Palacký's general sympathy, he did admire him greatly as the man whose military genius saved his country and its religious reform against the repeated onslaughts from hostile neighbours. He analysed Žižka's work as a military organizer and a general with great precision and he combined this with remarkable insight into almost all the important changes that were taking place in the social and technical development of warfare at this time.

In this field, as in so many others, Palacký had only very limited help from the works of his predecessors, apart from Beausobre and Pelcl. (Pelcl, indeed, had planned a biography of Žižka but died before he could finish the project.) The most important of the earlier works which were of use to him is a collection of nine short articles with four appendices which Maximilian Millauer (1784–1840), professor of theology at the University of Prague and official historian of the (of course Catholic) theological faculty of that university, presented to the Royal Bohemian Society of Sciences.[40] Millauer's position in relation to the great warrior, and the revolution which he defended, is clearly expressed in the very first sentence of his study. "While Bohemia," he says, "can remember her [seinen] John Žižka, and the devastating efficacy which he displayed, only with deep distress, nevertheless he remains, in the framework of the history of our fatherland, an unforgettable man."[41]

The little work itself is, in the main, a collection of sources; it represents a first

38 See my John Žižka and the Hussite Revolution (Princeton, 1955), 401–4; also Bartoš, I, 192.
39 See on this Howard Kaminsky, A History of the Hussite Revolution (Berkeley and Los Angeles, 1937), 410ff., and my Žižka, chap. 12, pp. 186–98.
40 Diplomatisch-historische Aufsätze über Johann Žižka von Trocnow ("Abhandlungen der kgl. böhmischen Gesellschaft der Wissenschaften," new series, I; Prague, 1824).
41 Ibid., 3.

discussion, organized in an essentially scientific manner, of a number of problems connected with this historical figure. Indeed, the difficulties involved here are such that several issues have continued to remain subjects of debate, of disagreement, and of investigation to this day, and researchers have not always been able to go much further than Millauer in establishing absolute certainty. Among the problems contested are, for example, the origins and meaning of the name "Žižka";[42] the question of his age;[43] the significance of his coat of arms in documents where his seal, with that coat of arms, was used; his relationship, before the outbreak of the revolution, with King Václav IV; the place of his birth; his willingness to show repentance, in the name of his army, for sins (such as pillage and betrayal) committed at the conquest of Německý Brod;[44] and finally the date of his death.[45] What seems more important is that Millauer succeeded in finding and publishing four so far almost unknown letters and messages of Žižka,[46] thus increasing the number of significant titles of Žižka's correspondence from merely three (not counting his famous "Military Ordinance") to seven.[47] In recent times only two more have been discovered. In summary, it can be said that Millauer was the first who put research on Žižka, and with it research on the Hussite movement, on an essentially sober, scholarly basis, even though those short introductory words of his seemed to emphasize his continuing negative attitude (which incidentally, when

42 This question is most recently discussed, including sources and bibliography, in F. M. Bartoš, *Husitská revoluce*, I (Prague, 1965), 219–21. It does not appear to have been definitely solved.

43 Later scholars, though against considerable resistance, have tried to solve this problem by the assumption that the Jan Žižka who appears in the sources in 1378 and 1380 was not the Hussite leader at all but his father. This would make the historical Žižka at least twenty years younger and barely middle-aged at the time of his appearance in 1419. The last treatment of the issue (in much detail) is by Bartoš, *Husitská revoluce*, I, 42, in the appendix titled "Žižkův věk" (Žižka's Age), 216ff. The claim that the Žižka of the earliest documents was the general's father was first presented by V. V. Tomek in 1876. It was later supported by other historians, with Bartoš defending it in a number of publications. On the other side, H. Toman, J. Šusta, and J. Pekař maintained that Žižka, at the time of the outbreak of the revolution, was about sixty. I myself feel that this last assumption is the more likely (see my *Žižka*, 18–23), but in substance the question is as open as it was when Millauer presented it first as a problem.

44 See Žižka's letters in the appendix of my *Žižka*, 491ff. The meaning of the statement of collective repentance was put in doubt by Pekař, *Žižka a jeho doba*, II, 183. All other historians, earlier as well as later ones (including the present writer), have followed Millauer's interpretation.

45 On this issue many conflicting versions existed. Millauer's solution (12 October 1424) came very near the truth. The exact date is 11 October.

46 Millauer himself refers to five such documents already published, though not in one collection, but these include early documents which, in the view of later historians, are possibly documents of Žižka's father and in any case have nothing to do with Žižka's activities during the Hussite wars.

47 In their Czech original they are published by him on pp. 54–60, and German translations occur in various parts of the text.

combined with the clerical standpoint of the author, assured lenient treatment by the censor).

Palacký occasionally mentioned Millauer, whom, of course, he knew personally and whose work he could use. The two men probably had little liking for each other, and during the discussion in the Royal Bohemian Society concerning the publication of Palacký's *Würdigung* Millauer (who was by fourteen years Palacký's senior) presented some criticisms.[48] In actual fact Palacký's own production of basic documentary collections was, of course, infinitely more extensive and of far greater consequence than Millauer's.

Although Millauer's attitude to Žižka was scientific but cool and even Palacký retained, in relation to the great warrior, a measure of reserve, there were no such reservations in a little book which was published in 1850 and which, again because of earlier censorship difficulties, could not possibly have been published three years earlier. Its author was a young Moravian (thus a fellow-countryman of Palacký) named Jindřich Terebelský.[49] It contains only seventy-four pages. Of these, the concluding ones give the reader the wording of the Military Ordinance, and earlier ones quote several of his letters verbatim in the text. Since at this time Palacký's volume on the period of "the Hussite Wars" (vol. III, part II, published in its earlier, German edition only in 1851) was not yet available, it is difficult to say whether Terebelský had had any substantial access to Palacký's work and sources.[50] The importance of his book does not rest upon any new historical information – in this respect its contribution seems quite insignificant compared with Palacký's contemporary publication. It lies rather in the fact that for the first time Žižka, without any reservations, is presented not only as a gifted and victorious general but as a great man and true leader of his embattled nation, and thereby the whole Hussite movement is displayed in a most favourable light. Terebelský, whose work became quite popular, thus established a tradition which was to result in the extremely positive interpretation of Žižka's personality and work as a military and political leader in many publications, notably in one by Palacký's most immediate and at the time his greatest disciple, Václav Vladivoj Tomek.

Tomek's monumental history of Prague (in fact a history of Bohemia) and especially his biography of Žižka[51] seemed at the time to have established a valid and definite picture both of the great Hussite leader and of much of the Hussite Reformation and Revolution. Tomek's biography, of course, was in many ways a result of the work done during the later phases of the Czech awakening, though it can hardly be counted as belonging to it *stricto sensu*. This movement, by the early years of the

48 See J. Goll, *Vybrané spisy drobné*, I (Prague, 1928), 118ff.
49 *Život Jana Žižky z Trocnova, slovútného vůdce Táborských bratří* (Olomouc, 1850). In Bartoš's contribution to *Sborník Žižkův*, quoted repeatedly above, pp. 185ff., a couple of other related works are mentioned. But I have not had access to them.
50 Bartoš (in *Sborník Žižkův*, 191) takes this for granted.
51 *Jan Žižka* (Prague, 1879). (In German: *Johann Žižka, Versuch einer Biographie desselben* [Prague, 1882].)

last quarter of the nineteenth century, had already succeeded to an extent that made Czech fears (or the hopes of some strongly nationalist Germans) regarding a possible disappearance of the Czechs and of their culture as a living entity appear quite groundless – and even absurd.

A few words remain to be said about the further development of these historical problems. While Hussite historiography (overwhelmingly Czech, except for one German and one French writer[52]) continued to follow the tradition established in the course of the awakening (to which also the social philosopher, political leader, and later president, Tomáš G. Masaryk, subscribed), Tomek's view of Žižka became, in 1927 and the following years, the subject of a sharp attack at the hands of Josef Pekař, at that date often considered the greatest Czech historian of his time. In a huge work Pekař tried to "debunk" not only the figure of Žižka but along with him the whole significance of the Hussite Revolution as a European development of strongly progressive and positive values. This is not the place to go into the details of the often fierce debate which arose immediately out of Pekař's work.[53]

Today there is more agreement that the Hussite movement remains a high point not only of Czech but of European history and therefore, indeed, much more than an episode; and that it did pave the way for the reformations of the sixteenth century. This last fact was not accepted until recently by the international community of historians outside Bohemia. On the contrary, the influence of Hussitism on Luther and his reformation was either underrated or even totally neglected. But the Czech historiography of the time of the "Awakening" was well aware of it. Palacký, for instance, rightly criticized Ranke (for whom he had the greatest respect) for the fact that "he told the history of the German Reformation without even mentioning the preceding Czech Reformation." He added that "first by the Taborites, then by the Unity of the Czech Brethren, the basic teachings of Protestantism in their main features had already been developed long before Luther and Calvin."[54] This claim sounds like an expression, above all, of national pride, and indeed the strengthening of national consciousness was an important task of the "Awakening." Yet, as recent research on Luther's relation to Bohemia and the Hussite churches[55] shows, Palacký's view can well be defended.

52 Friedrich v. Bezold, *König Sigmund und die Reichskriege gegen die Hussiten*, 3 vols. (Munich, 1872–7), and *Zur Geschichte des Hussitenthums* (Munich, 1874); Ernest Denis, *Huss et la guerre des Hussites* (Paris, 1878).

53 The most important early answer was K. Krofta's *Žižka a husitská revoluce* (Prague, 1936). See in addition my *Žižka*, 444ff., no. 3. For post-1948 attacks on Pekař, see, for example, F. Kavka, *Husitská revoluční tradice* (Prague, 1953), 229ff., 251ff. Much more sophisticated, though no less sharp, is Macek's criticism; see his *Tábor v husitském revolučním hnutí* (Prague, 1955), I, 17ff.; II, 357ff. Finally see R. Kalivoda, *Husitská ideologie* (Prague, 1961), 426ff.

54 See his *Die Geschichte des Hussitenthums und Professor C. Höfler*, 160.

55 See, for example, the present writer's article, "The Impact of Martin Luther upon Bohemia," in *Central European History*, I/2 (June 1968), 107–30. References to the literature on Luther's relations with the Czechs can be found in its footnotes.

Masaryk's National Background

THOMAS D. MARZIK

IN 1918 Czechoslovakia emerged from the war-torn fabric of Austria-Hungary as one of the new nation states of east central Europe. Although it cannot be denied that the founder and first president of that state, Tomáš G. Masaryk, was a true national representative of the Czechs in 1918, it is also true that Masaryk's national background was not purely and simply Czech.

At least two factors are responsible for the considerable amount of confusion existing about Masaryk's national origins. The circumstances surrounding his birth – the period and place in which it occurred and the ethnic origins of his parents – admit of no simple, clear-cut description of his national background. Also, Masaryk's own statements about his national origins were themselves often ambiguous and contradictory.[1]

What makes a consideration of Masaryk's national background both interesting and relevant is his relationship with the Slavic inhabitants of Upper Hungary,[2] who formed an integral part of the first Czechoslovak Republic. As Czechoslovakia's

1 For a brief critical bibliographical survey of Masaryk's most important autobiographical writings, see Zdeněk Nejedlý, *T. G. Masaryk*, I/1 (Prague, 1930), 35–41.
2 Prior to 1918 the area inhabited by the Slovaks in the Hungarian Kingdom was known as Upper Hungary. The same geographical area has been referred to as Slovakia and Hungarian Slovakia. All three terms will be used interchangeably throughout this article.

president, Masaryk represented the Slovaks as well as the Czechs; and he claimed, as will be seen, that he received the right to call himself a Slovak through birth. During the period of the first Czechoslovak Republic the Czechs and Slovaks were officially considered not to be two separate nations but rather branches of one "Czechoslovak nation," a concept which has since been abandoned. The Czech-Slovak discords of the interwar years were reflected in Slovak attitudes toward Masaryk. Slovaks who supported Czech centralism and the Czechoslovak nation theory usually held Masaryk in high esteem and stressed his connections with the Slovaks; on the other hand, Slovak autonomists and separatists, who rejected "Czechoslovakism" as a Czech attempt to deny the existence of the Slovak nation and to "Czechize" the Slovaks, opposed Masaryk and minimized his Slovak ties. For representatives of the latter group, emotions rather than rational considerations sometimes seem to have taken precedence in deciding the question of Masaryk's ethnic relation to the Slovaks.[3] The extent to which Masaryk could be considered a Slovak, therefore, is a question which must be dealt with in any investigation of his national origins.

The following discussion is not an attempt to establish a national identity for Masaryk; such a task is unnecessary, for Masaryk's national identity was definitely that of a Czech. However, there are certain elements in his national background which were not Czech. By examining such factors as Masaryk's geographic and ethnic origins, his surname, his speech, and his national consciousness it will be possible to arrive at a more accurate description of his national background, especially with regard to its specifically Slovak aspects.

On 7 March 1850 Tomáš G. Masaryk was born on a Habsburg imperial estate in the town of Hodonín in southeastern Moravia. The fact that Masaryk was born in Moravia – and in a specific region of Moravia – presents the first difficulty in attempting to establish his national origin, because Moravia's geographic and political borders are not entirely identical with ethnic and linguistic boundaries. For centuries the margravate of Moravia belonged to the Czech crown, and its Slavic inhabitants shared with the Czechs of Bohemia a common destiny and language – Czech. Although the Moravians are considered to be Czechs from the point of view of nationality, they nevertheless are differentiated by a variety of dialects and ethnographic features which extend in a broad spectrum from the land of the Bohemian Czechs on their western border (Bohemia) to that of the Slovaks on their eastern border (Slovakia).

The transitional nature of linguistic and ethnographic types, which characterizes Moravia as a whole, is particularly complex in the immediate area of southeastern Moravia in which Masaryk was born and spent his early life; this area is adjacent to

3 After attempting to prove that Masaryk's ethnic origin was definitely non-Slovak, one American Slovak polemicist went so far as to assert: "The Slovaks will never *believe* [italics mine] that Thomas Garrigue Masaryk was a Slovak." Philip A. Hrobak, "Was T. G. Masaryk of Slovak Origin?," *Slovakia*, x/7 (Sept.–Dec. 1960), 12–13.

Slovakia and is known as Moravian Slovakia (Slovácko or Moravské Slovensko).[4] The inhabitants of this region, the so-called Moravian Slovaks, are a transitional group between the "Moravian Czechs" (a term I use here to denote the definitely Czech majority in Moravia) and the "Hungarian Slovaks" (a term I use here for the Slovaks in Upper Hungary and not, as is sometimes done, to refer to those who left this area to settle south of the Danube in ethnically Magyar territory). Their ancestors migrated from the mountains in nearby Slovakia to the Western Carpathians in the eleventh and twelfth centuries. To varying degrees they share with the Hungarian Slovaks certain linguistic and ethnographic characteristics; yet their centuries-long political and cultural association with the Moravian Czech groups have resulted in the absorption of more specifically Czech features in their speech, dress, and customs. Indeed, so inextricably mixed are the Czech and Slovak elements in Moravian Slovakia that a village might contain inhabitants whose dialect is more Czech than Slovak but whose costume is more Slovak than Czech. Hence the difficulty in classifying a person born in nineteenth-century Moravian Slovakia according to twentieth-century concepts of Czech and Slovak nationality. It would seem possible only to indicate those respects in which such a person can be considered to be more Czech than Slovak and vice versa.

Since it is difficult to determine whether individuals in the part of southeastern Moravia where Masaryk was born are decisively more Czech or more Slovak by nationality, it is impossible to ascertain Masaryk's national origin merely by reference to the place of his birth. Nonetheless, Masaryk might technically be called a Moravian or, more precisely, a Moravian Slovak, if these terms are interpreted in their geographic sense only.

The task of establishing Masaryk's ethnic origin by means of his parents' ethnic background is more difficult than might appear at first sight. Masaryk unwittingly made an observation about his own ethnic origin when he told Karel Čapek that "from the earliest times until now there has been a considerable mixing of races and nations. There is no such thing as so-called 'pure blood,' at least not in Europe."[5] Masaryk was definitely not the product of "pure blood." Most biographies say that he was the son of a Slovak father and a Czech mother. This oversimplification is, to some extent, valid; however, a more detailed analysis of the ethnic backgrounds of his parents must be made in order to describe his ethnic origin more accurately.

Masaryk himself claimed that by parentage and ancestry he was a Slovak.[6] This was certainly true as far as his father was concerned: "My father was a Slovak from

4 For information on Moravian Slovakia, see Lubor Niederle, ed., *Moravské Slovensko*, i and ii ("Národopis lidu československého," 1; Prague, 1922–3). Cf. also Jan Húsek, *Hranice mezi zemí Moravskoslezskou a Slovenskem* (Prague, 1932).
5 *Masaryk on Thought and Life: Conversations with Karel Čapek*, translated from the Czech by M. and R. Weatherall (London, 1938), 205.
6 Tomáš G. Masaryk, "Slovenské vzpomienky," *Slovenské hlasy*, no. 15 (22 Oct. 1917) as translated in Paul Selver, *Masaryk: A Biography* (London, 1940), 30. Hereafter this article will be referred to as "Vzpomienky."

Kopčany, and he spoke Slovak till his death."⁷ Although Josef Masaryk was a resident of Hodonín in Moravia at the time of his marriage, he had been born at Kopčany in Hungarian Slovakia on 25 February 1823, the youngest son of the Slovak peasants Ján and Anna (née Formánková) Masaryk. The Masaryk family had deep roots in the Kopčany-Holíč area of Slovakia traceable as far back as the seventeenth century.⁸ It was in Slovakia and among Hungarian Slovaks that Josef Masaryk spent the early years of his life. He found employment on the local imperial estates, but after some time he was transferred to the imperial estates at Hodonín, only a few miles away from his birth-place across the border between Slovakia and Moravia. Josef Masaryk served first as a groom, then as a coachman at Hodonín. It was there that he met Terezie Kropáčková, whom he married on 15 August 1849.

Although there is no doubt that Masaryk's father was a Slovak by birth⁹ and speech, the ethnic identity of Masaryk's mother is not so easily established. Masaryk himself was partially responsible for some of the confusion which has arisen concerning his mother's nationality. In his *curriculum vitae* written in 1875 he asserted that his mother was German.¹⁰ That rather startling statement was further qualified in one of Masaryk's later autobiographical writings:

... my mother's native place was Hustopeče, then a German parish, though already in my time most of the inhabitants could talk "Moravian." The family on my mother's side could talk "Moravian" well, because my mother's parents came from Haná ... I think that, by blood, I am a pure Slovak, without Magyar or German admixture, although when my mother was young she could speak German better than Czech. Later on she became completely Czech ...¹¹

7 *President Masaryk Tells His Story*, recounted by Karel Čapek, translated from the Czech (New York, 1935), 190. Hereafter this book will be referred to as "Čapek."
8 A genealogy of the Masaryk family can be found in Josef Pilnáček, *Rodokmen a vývod T. G. Masaryka* (n.p., 1927). It is quite possible that Josef Masaryk's ancestors were originally inhabitants of Moravian Slovakia and migrated to Hungarian Slovakia in the early part of the seventeenth century. Cf. *ibid.*, 3.
9 Although no concrete evidence has been found to support the contention, a rumour that Masaryk's natural father was actually Nathan Redlich – the grandfather of the Austrian historian Josef Redlich – has persisted among certain individuals. If such had been the case, then of course Masaryk could not have had any Slovak ethnic connection. For details on Masaryk's alleged illegitimacy, cf. Hrobak, "Was T. G. Masaryk of Slovak Origin?," 7–13; [Willy Lorenz], "Wer war Thomas G. Masaryk? Das Geheimnis seiner Abstammung," *Die Furche*, xiii/37 (14 Sept. 1957), 5; and Willy Lorenz, "Wer war Thomas Garrigue Masaryk? Das Rätsel seiner Abstammung," in *Virtute fideque. Festschrift für Dr. Otto von Habsburg zum 50. Geburtstag* (Vienna, 1965), 109–14.
10 Translated in Selver, 16. This *curriculum vitae* (dated 25 August 1875) was submitted by Masaryk to officials at the University of Vienna in applying for permission to take his doctoral examination. The document was reprinted both in the original German (pp. 9–17) and in a Czech translation (pp. 1–8) in Jaromír Doležal, *Masarykova cesta životem*, ii: *Masarykovy autobiografie a literární prvotiny* (Brno, 1921). It has been almost entirely translated into English in Selver, 15–25.
11 "Vzpomienky" in Selver, 30.

Despite Masaryk's explanation, it appears that Terezie Kropáčková was, for all practical purposes, a German at the time of her marriage. She was born in Husto-peče, a Moravian town northwest of Hodonín, on 4 August 1813 to Josef and Kate-řina (née Ruprechtová) Kropáček, a butcher and the daughter of the mayor of Hustopeče. Terezie's great-grandfather Kropáček had migrated from the Moravian village of Královo Pole just outside Brno to Hustopeče, where he married a native German of that town.[12] Successive intermarriages had resulted in the Germaniza-tion of the original Kropáček Slavic stock, so that Masaryk's mother was most pro-bably brought up as a German in Hustopeče. Furthermore, before she settled in Hodonín as a cook for a wealthy family there, Terezie Kropáčková had spent time as a servant in Vienna. It was probably only after her marriage to her Slovak hus-band that she was "Czechized," as Masaryk claimed, most likely through contact with the Czech-Slovak ethnic groups of southeastern Moravia.[13]

Masaryk's mother, therefore, must be considered to have been a German at the time of his birth; only in the sense that some of her ancestors were originally Czech and that she herself became "Czechized" in later life can she be said to have been a Czech.

Although it has little bearing on Masaryk's ethnic origins, it is nonetheless in-teresting to note that Masaryk considered the German-Czech part of his lineage more important than the Slovak part. In his conversations with Čapek Masaryk frankly admitted that his mother had more influence on him than his father had, adding "my father was gifted but simple, it was mother who ruled at home."[14] Perhaps it was her upbringing among urban-bred Germans that helped to account for the predominant influence which she exercised over her first son.

In any event, Masaryk's ethnic origin was mixed. He was Slovak through his father and more German than Czech through his mother; and although he con-sidered his mother's heritage the more important of the two, he never forgot or denied that he was by birth at least half Slovak.

The controversy concerning Masaryk's surname is another indication of the com-plexity of the question of Masaryk's national background. According to Czech orthography, the name should be spelled and pronounced "Masařík" instead of the more Slovak "Masaryk." Even after Masaryk had become president, his name was sometimes written in the Czech form outside of Czechoslovakia.[15] This is really

12 Nejedlý, I/1, 70.
13 In what manner and to what extent his mother "became completely Czech" were not explained by Masaryk.
14 Čapek, 14.
15 Jaromír Doležal, "Masaryk – Masařík," in *Masarykův sborník. Časopis pro studium života a díla T. G. Masaryka*, I: *1924–1925*, ed. V. K. Škrach (Prague, 1925), 317. The dispute over the correct spelling of Masaryk's name began at the end of the last century. Masaryk's politi-cal enemies continually attempted to discredit his Czech patriotism by claiming that he had changed his name, which they had assumed to have been originally purely Czech, in order to curry favour with Germans. Cf. Jan Herben, "Masaryk či Masařík," *Skizzář k Masarykovu životopisu* (Prague, 1930), 73–80. Dr. Doležal traced the spelling of the name "Masaryk" to its Slovak origins in order to dispel the confusion caused by the old controversy. The

not surprising, for Masaryk was plagued in his youth by the spelling of his name, as is attested to by numerous documents which contained variations in his surname. That confusion was due to two reasons: the requirements of the different Latin, Hungarian, Czech, and German orthographies and the mixture of Slovak and Czech dialects in southeastern Moravia which accounted for differences in pronunciation. A description of the evolution of Masaryk's surname into its final Slovak form provides an interesting insight into the problem of his national background.

Dr. Doležal found in the Kopčany-Holíč area of Slovakia (the birth-place of Masaryk's father) a total of eighty-two individuals between the years 1789 and 1823 with the following surname variations: Maszárik, Massarik, Maszarik, and Masarik. Except for minor orthographical accommodations, such as the Hungarian double consonant (sz = s), the Slovak name was consistently spelled with a simple "r" and never with the Czech fricative "ř."

Josef Masaryk's migration to Moravia produced a significant change in the official recording of his family name. In both the marriage and birth registries of the church in Hodonín the form "Massařik" appeared for the first time. The influence of the dialects in the Hodonín area was evident in the substitution of the Czech "ř" for the Slovak "r."

The further course of Masaryk's name transformation can be seen in his official school records. During the 1862-3 term at the Piarist school at Hustopeče his name was recorded as "Masařík," and that same spelling was retained at the gymnasium in Brno until the 1867-8 term. During the spring of 1868, however, Masaryk himself took an interest in the proper spelling of his name and established the form by which he was to be known from that time on:

In the documents which I hitherto possessed, the spelling of my name varied a good deal; Masařík, Massařík, Massarzik, etc., and the class-master, to whom I handed in my form of application for a scholarship, asked me for my baptismal certificate. At Easter I went to Hodonín, where from the parish records I could verify my name as I had heard it pronounced from my earliest days. The clerk gave me a baptismal certificate, and wrote my name phonetically, but not quite correctly, for I had always heard myself called Masárik, never Masarik or Masaryk. I asked him to keep to the original spelling of the name, for I was conscious of my Slovak origin.[16]

It is apparent that up until 1868 Masaryk was rather indifferent about the spelling of his name, which had been pronounced in his childhood in two ways: "Masárik" by his father and Slovak relatives and "Masařík" by some of his southeastern Moravian neighbours. The Moravians who recorded the name on documents usually wrote it according to Czech orthography and according to their own

---

results of his research were reported in the above-mentioned article (pp. 317-20), and my discussion is based mostly upon those findings.

16 "Vzpomienky" in Selver, 33, and in Doležal, *Masarykova cesta životem*, II, 22.

opinions as to how it should have been pronounced. When Masaryk opted for the more Slovak form with the simple "r" spelling, a "y" was substituted in place of the "i" as a sign to Czech-speakers that the "r" should not be pronounced as "ř." After 1868 the form "Masaryk" appeared quite regularly. It is found on a birth-baptismal certificate obtained by Masaryk from Hodonín in 1870,[17] and the records of Masaryk's years at the gymnasium in Vienna (1869–72) show either "Masaryk" or "Massaryk" (in German orthography the long ss = s). Despite the strong Czech dialectal influences in Moravia and despite the fact that Masaryk was to spend the major part of his life in Prague, he consciously adhered to the Slovak form of his surname.

A more important linguistic factor in Masaryk's national background is the question of his "native" or principal language. Owing to the fact that Masaryk was in a sense bilingual from his earliest years, the question of what he considered to be his native tongue has to be examined more closely.

A knowledge of German was one of Masaryk's first important acquisitions from his mother, who had been reared in German surroundings. He stated that at home he and his brothers prayed in German, adding: "... my mother had never learnt to pray in Czech and to the day of her death had only a German prayerbook, printed in Gothic characters. She never even tried to read Czech. My father knew German pretty well ... but we children never talked German to him, only to our mother. We also used to write to her in German."[18]

Masaryk's command of German, however, was quite limited in his early youth, a fact which caused problems for him at school, where German was the language of instruction. Concerning his experiences with German Masaryk told Čapek:

German I got to know as a small child, from my mother; but German was never a second mother tongue to me – of that I was well aware when I went to the German school at Hustopeče. The boys used to laugh at my German, and I had some difficulties with the lessons given in German which were only surmounted when I went to the high school, and even then did not vanish altogether. When I published my Suicide[19] a well-known German writer read it with particular attention to the style: he found about a dozen Slavisms in the book.[20]

It was only through higher education in German schools that Masaryk was able

---

17 A reproduction of that certificate, dated 3 September 1870, can be found in Doležal, "Masaryk – Masařík," 320.
18 "Vzpomienky" in Selver, 30.
19 This was Der Selbstmord als sociale Massenerscheinung der modernen Civilisation, Masaryk's qualifying dissertation for admission as lecturer in the philosophical faculty of the University of Vienna, which was published in 1881.
20 Čapek, 97. For another account by Masaryk of his acquaintance with and use of German, see Emil Ludwig, Defender of Democracy: Masaryk of Czechoslovakia (New York, 1936), 116–17.

to develop a facility in literary German; and although German was his mother's native tongue, that language was not considered by him to be his own.

The intermingling of Czech and Slovak elements in the dialects of Moravian Slovakia must be taken into account in considering the Slavic language which Masaryk used as a child. In the area where he was born and spent his childhood several dialects under the general heading of Moravian Slovak are spoken. Those dialects are transitional between definite Czech and Slovak dialects, and it is often difficult to determine whether a particular dialect is more Czech or more Slovak.[21] This confusion arising from the linguistic complexity of Moravian Slovakia was reflected in Masaryk's own evaluation of the Slavic language which he spoke in his early childhood.

Through his Slovak father Masaryk came into contact with Slovak, or at least a dialect which was more Slovak than Czech. According to Masaryk: "The influence of the Slovak language continued to assert itself in our family. My father never pronounced the Czech 'ř' sound and there were several current Slovak expressions which we always used. Except for the 'ř,' there is hardly any difference in these districts between Slovak and Moravian Slovak."[22]

Therefore, because of the difficulty in classifying the dialects of Moravian Slovakia as Czech or Slovak and the fact that Masaryk's earliest Slavic speech in his home was probably more Slovak than Czech as a result of his father's Slovak origin, Masaryk was to a certain extent justified in saying that he spoke Slovak as a child.[23] However, the influence of his father's more Slovak dialect was weakened by the periods spent by the family in villages northwest of Hodonín in which dialects more Czech than Slovak were spoken. Such, for example, was probably true of the village of Čejkovice, which Masaryk always considered to be the real home of his childhood.[24]

Masaryk once did proclaim: "... the Slovak language was a factor which helped fundamentally to shape the growth of my mind."[25] Exactly how that factor operated is not clear. It is true that elements of Slovak – certain expressions, vowel lengthenings, and a "soft" pronunciation – were to be found in his speech until his death, and Masaryk was able to deliver speeches written in literary Slovak;[26] nonetheless, Slovak, which he never learned as a literary language, was not for Masaryk

21 For information on this group of dialects, see Jaromír Bělič and Václav Křístek, *Moravsko-slovenská nářečí* (Olomouc, 1954). Bělič and Křístek consider the Moravian Slovak dialects to be Czech dialects; they are considered to be Slovak dialects by Václav Vážný, "Nářečí slovenská," in *Československá vlastivěda*, III: *Jazyk* (Prague, 1934), 219–310.
22 "Vzpomienky" in Selver, 31.
23 Čapek, 190.
24 *Ibid.*, 14. "At Čejkovice the dialect is different and so are the costumes" ("Vzpomienky" in Selver, 31).
25 "Vzpomienky" in Selver, 35.
26 Cf. Nejedlý, I/1, 105; Albert Pražák, *T. G. Masaryk a Slovensko* (Prague, 1937), 11; and Juraj Slávik, *Masaryk a Slovensko* (Perth Amboy, N.J., 1960), 11.

a principal language in his formative years, and it could be considered a native language of his only in a very narrow sense.

The other Slavic language with which Masaryk came into contact at an early age was Czech, or at least dialects which were more Czech than Slovak. When Masaryk recalled that at home they always spoke Czech[27] and that, as has been mentioned, his mother's family could speak "Moravian," he probably was referring to Moravian dialects which were more Czech than Slovak. The more Czech-speaking milieux northwest of Hodonín in which the young Masaryk grew up could not help having a forceful influence upon his speech outside the home.

Masaryk's inclination towards the use of Czech was further strengthened by his experiences in the schools which he attended. It was in Brno that he studied the Czech language formally, and he used it as the principal means of communication among the Moravian students with whom he associated. Masaryk described his "bilingualism" of that period to Čapek: "In German surroundings I talked Czech almost continuously, at my rooms, with my friends, in Czech circles; I heard German at school, and German was the language in which I gave my lessons; moreover the bulk of my reading was in German."[28]

Despite the fact that Masaryk's entire higher education in Vienna was conducted exclusively in German and German was his "official" language, Masaryk considered Czech to be more dear to him than German even at that time. His first published work – a series of articles entitled "Theorie a praksis" (Theory and Practice) – which appeared in the *Moravská orlice* (The Moravian Eagle) in 1876, was written in Czech; [29] and it was not until 1881 – after two or three more Czech articles – that his first German publication, his famous work on suicide, was printed. An indication of Masaryk's attachment to Czech is found in a letter to a friend in 1877 in which he wrote: "... there will not be a time in which I shall forget the language [Czech] which I have from youth considered to be my mother tongue."[30]

The affirmation of Czech over German as Masaryk's principal language was the result of a long process of evolution. Having begun life with exposure to German and Czech-Slovak dialects, Masaryk developed both German and Czech as literary languages through education and living among speakers of both. It was in Brno and Vienna – later to be reconfirmed in Prague – that the Czech language asserted its predominance in his personal life and interest.

The final consideration, that of Masaryk's own feeling of national consciousness,

27 "Vzpomienky" in Selver, 30.
28 Čapek, 97.
29 Although Masaryk's first publications were in Czech, his mastery of that language during the Vienna years was far from complete. Previous writings in Czech were rejected for publication, and Masaryk was uneasy about his own inadequacy in Czech. Cf. *ibid.*, 114, 130, and 141 and the quotation from a letter of 3 May 1876 to Leander Čech in Zdeněk Nejedlý, *T. G. Masaryk*, I/2 (Prague, 1931), 203.
30 As quoted in Nejedlý, I/2, 156.

is the most important factor of all, for it is precisely that which determined his national identity. At various times throughout his life Masaryk supplied different descriptions of his national identity. To Leander Čech he wrote in 1877: "Body and soul, I am a Czech ..."[31] At a political gathering in Brno in 1892 he exclaimed: "I am to the marrow of my bones a Moravian."[32] And in his memoirs of the First World War Masaryk stated that "as a Slovak by origin and tradition," his feelings were Slovak.[33] Despite these seemingly contradictory declarations, Masaryk did have a definite feeling of national consciousness, but, as in the case of his principal language, it was not a distinct reality nor was it clearly evident in his early childhood. It was the product of an evolutionary process which began in southeastern Moravia and which was finally realized in the city of Prague.

Masaryk, the founder of the Czechoslovak Republic, was in his earliest days neither an ardent Czech nor Slovak nationalist. "Until my fourteenth year," he once admitted, "I had no national consciousness at all. I regarded it as quite natural to speak two languages ..."[34] The reasons – beyond the obvious requirements of intellectual maturity – for that early lack of national consciousness are not difficult to explain. As has been mentioned, the southeastern part of Moravia where Masaryk spent his childhood was the home of a conglomeration of speakers of Slovak and Czech dialects in the villages and of German-speakers in the towns. The masses of the Moravian Slavs living there were not nationally conscious in twentieth-century terms. Because they were isolated from both Hungarian Slovakia and Bohemia, they had no feeling of identification with a national whole or fatherland, whether it be Bohemia, Slovakia, or perhaps even Moravia itself. The attachment of the people was to the village of their birth and the surrounding countryside, actually nothing more than an extremely limited regionalism.[35] In addition to the mixed national background of his parents the young Masaryk was further handicapped in developing any sort of national feeling, for in the years from 1850 to 1861 the Masaryk family changed places of residence no less than five times. As a result of the inability to strike deep roots among the Czech-Slovak groups in any locality, Masaryk could develop little more than "a feeling" for his own village of Čejkovice,[36] where he spent the most memorable part of his early life.

Despite the above-mentioned circumstances, there is reason to believe that some sort of rudimentary Slovak consciousness could have existed in Masaryk during his early youth, since it was at that time that he had the most direct and personal con-

31 *Ibid.*
32 Speech of 6 June 1892, as quoted in *Čas*, vi/24 (11 June 1892), 370.
33 Thomas Garrigue Masaryk, *The Making of a State: Memories and Observations, 1914–1918,* an English version, arranged and prepared with an introduction by Henry Wickham Steed (New York, 1927), 222.
34 "Vzpomienky" in Selver, 30–1.
35 Cf. Nejedlý, i/1, 106–8.
36 Čapek, 66.

tact with Slovaks. Masaryk's conversations with Čapek and especially his article "Slovenské vzpomienky" (Slovak Reminiscences)[37] contain references to certain early Slovak feelings which he claimed to have had. Concerning his first Slovak connections Masaryk said:

... I was never conscious of any difference between the Hungarian Slovaks and the Moravian Slovaks among whom I grew up. My grandmother in Kopčany used to bring me a pair of full white Slovak trousers as a present when she came to see us; I used to wear them at nights to go to bed in, because I was dressed "like a gentleman." My family was in constant touch with Kopčany and Holíč, and at Kopčany I often heard Hungarian spoken; a few Hungarian words would even crop up in our talk at home.[38]

Although Masaryk as a youth made no distinction between Hungarian and Moravian Slovaks, his earliest "Slovak" feelings should more accurately be considered as manifestations of a Moravian Slovak[39] rather than a specifically Hungarian Slovak consciousness, because of the fact that the young Masaryk's contact with Hungarian Slovaks was so limited. In addition, however, to visits among Slovak relatives in villages just beyond the border between Moravia and Slovakia, Masaryk in his youth did on at least three memorable occasions go further into the home area of the Hungarian Slovaks. When he was about eight years old his mother took him to a fair at Šaštín, a popular shrine in Slovakia.[40] Another visit to Slovakia which stuck out in Masaryk's mind took place during the Austro-Prussian War of 1866. A column of the retreating Austrian army marched into his village seeking directions to Hodonín. Masaryk and a friend guided the soldiers to that town and then crossed into Slovakia with them. After an adventure near Holíč, Masaryk proceeded all the way to Pressburg (Bratislava, the present-day capital of Slovakia). On the way home he stopped at Kopčany to see some of his relatives.[41] And, finally, once during his school days in Vienna Masaryk vacationed among Magyars in Hungary where

37 While in Russia during the First World War Masaryk wrote this article on the Slovak connections in his past for a Slovak newspaper in Petrograd. See *supra*, n. 6. The article was reprinted in Doležal, *Masarykova cesta životem*, II, 19–24, and most of it has been translated into English in Selver, 30–5. Since this article was written at a time when Masaryk was anxious to win adherents among Slovaks in Russia for his Czechoslovak programme, it is more than likely that the Slovak influences on his early life were not as extensive or intensive as this description might suggest. Furthermore, in this article – as well as in some of his other autobiographical writings – Masaryk did not take pains always to distinguish between Hungarian and Moravian Slovaks; thus, in many instances "Slovak" should read "Moravian Slovak."

38 Čapek, 190.

39 For a consideration of Masaryk's Moravian and Moravian Slovak consciousness and his connections with Moravia in general, see Miloslav Trapl, "Morava v životě a díle T. G. Masaryka (1850–1914)," *Časopis Matice moravské*, LXII/1 (1938), 1–89.

40 Čapek, 23.

41 *Ibid.*, 70–3.

he "searched for remains of the Great Moravian Empire." "At that time," he stated, "I studied closely the relation between Slovaks and Magyars, for in my own family there were people who had been completely Magyarized ..."[42] To what extent those visits to the land of the Slovaks affected Masaryk's early indentification with Hungarian Slovaks it is impossible to determine; the fact that they took place, however, does indicate that Masaryk was conscious of the existence of the Hungarian Slovaks and of their relation to his father's family.

It is, of course, interesting to note that Masaryk was not even aware of the Czechs of Bohemia in those early days. He told Čapek: "I knew nothing at all about Prague and Bohemia at that time. For the Slovaks in my part of the country, there was only one city – Vienna ... About Prague I learned for the first time from a children's book called *The Little One's Heritage*; there it described how a certain roving family drove in a cart to Prague, and how beautiful Prague was. I felt myself to be a Slovak."[43]

The young Masaryk's Moravian Slovak feelings were destined to change once he removed himself from Moravian Slovak surroundings. In the year 1865 Masaryk began studies at the gymnasium in Brno. He considered that date to be the birth of his national consciousness, for, as he explained to Čapek:

At Brno I began to understand my Czechdom: before that, at home, I had only felt a primitive kind of socialism.[44]

At that time, too, I had my first conflicts as a Czech. At school we were Czechs and Germans together, and naturally we quarreled and fought about the comparative excellences of our nations.[45]

Contact with German teachers and students could not help but compel the young, sensitive Masaryk to become aware of the sharp national distinction between the Germans and the Czechs in the bi-national capital of Moravia. Masaryk obviously first became conscious that he was not a German and then identified himself with the Moravian Czech students who became his close associates. His newly found national consciousness was manifested by his formal study of the Czech language in school, by his national designation as "*slavisch*" (which in Moravia meant Czech) in the academic registers,[46] and by the fact that in time he became the unofficial leader of the Czech students at the German gymnasium in Brno.[47] The seeds of Masaryk's future attraction to Prague were also sown at that time. As he later re-

42 "Vzpomienky" in Selver, 33. Cf. also Čapek, 160.
43 Čapek, 33–4.
44 *Ibid.*, 66. By "socialism" Masaryk probably meant the realization that the upper classes were German-speakers and the lower classes were Slav-speakers. Cf. "Vzpomienky" in Selver, 32.
45 Čapek, 64.
46 Nejedlý, I/1, 170.
47 Jan Herben, "Masarykovo dětství a jinošství," in *Česká mysl 1910: T. G. Masarykovi* (Prague, 1910), 96.

called: "Already then I realised how little I knew about Prague and Bohemia, and I read up all I could about Prague ..."[48]

In 1869 Masaryk was forced to leave Brno. He took up residence in Vienna and from 1869 to 1872 attended the academic gymnasum in that city in order to prepare for university studies. During his early stay there his national consciousness developed more quietly, more fully, and more permanently than in Brno, where there was much national tension. A definite sign of that consciousness was displayed in 1870 when he attempted to join the Czech Akademický spolek (Academic Society), a focal point for Czech and Moravian university students in Vienna. His membership in that organization had to be delayed, however, until he could qualify as a university student.

When enrolling at the University of Vienna in 1872 Masaryk listed his nationality as "*böhmisch.*"[49] He officially joined the Akademický spolek the very same year, registering himself there as "Vlastimil Masaryk"–his newly adopted Slavic forename (literally "lover of one's country") no doubt being a manifestation of intense national feeling. Masaryk found much time for the society. In 1875 he was elected chairman of the organization, and during his term of office he completely rejuvenated it and organized it into sections. In this manner Masaryk became acquainted with Czech and Moravian students in Vienna and strengthened his national consciousness as a Czech.

Vienna was, by that period, not easily accessible for the Hungarian Slovaks;[50] nonetheless, a few Slovak students were present in the imperial capital. The extent to which Masaryk came into contact with any of these students is uncertain.[51] Masaryk did, however, take some scholarly interest in his meagre Slovak heritage: "While in Vienna I examined the traces of the Slovaks who had lived there at different periods, such as the poet Kollár and the writer Kuzmány, who was the first, I believe, to attempt a Slovak novel."[52] Masaryk's acquaintance with the ideas of Jan Kollár, a Slovak Protestant who had been a leading figure in the Czech national awakening, was to influence his later political and historical writings. Undoubtedly part of Masaryk's research on Kollár was done for a speech which he delivered in

48 "Vzpomienky" in Selver, 33.
49 Herben, *Skizzář k Masarykovu životopisu*, 53.
50 Until the *Ausgleich* of 1867 the Slovaks had looked to Vienna for support in their opposition to Magyarization. As a result of the *Ausgleich* the Hungarian government in Budapest became solely responsible for the fate of Slovakia, which indeed did not possess any separate legal identity.
51 Two Slovak students, L'udevít Šimko and Michal Bodický, are reported to have attended lectures given by Masaryk in Vienna. Also, during the years 1879–82 the Slovak academic society Tatran, composed of Hungarian Slovak students in Vienna, was somehow associated with the Czech Akademický spolek. See Anton Štefánek, "Masaryk a Slovensko," in *Sborník přednášek o T. G. Masarykovi*, ed. Miloš Weingart (Prague, 1931), 211.
52 Čapek, 190.

1874 in connection with the Viennese Czech and Slovak community's celebration of the fiftieth anniversary of the publication of Kollár's most famous work, *Slávy dcera* (The Daughter of Sláva).[53]

Despite his superficial interest in Slovak historical personages, Masaryk certainly could not be considered a nationally conscious Slovak during his years in Vienna. His contact with Hungarian Slovaks and with life in Upper Hungary was extremely limited, if it existed at all. Slovak nationalism, which in itself was very weak, could hardly penetrate into Moravia or Vienna during that period. Masaryk's Slavic consciousness could not have been converted into a distinct Slovak consciousness under such unfavourable circumstances. The fact that Masaryk was born and brought up in Moravia – in the Austrian half of the empire – was crucial; for it meant a de facto exclusion from Hungarian Slovakia and an education among Czech-speaking Moravians, whose political and cultural orientation led to Prague through Vienna. Therefore, by the time Masaryk had reached Vienna any Slovak feelings which he might have had in his early youth would have yielded to the stronger Moravian-Czech inclination, inculcated in Brno and to be even more strongly fortified in Vienna. It was for Moravian journals that Masaryk wrote his first Czech articles, and it was toward Prague and the Czech national cause that he gravitated.

Masaryk's appointment to the Czech division of the University of Prague in 1882 was a confirmation of his Czech national consciousness which had grown to maturity during his years in Vienna. From that point on there was no turning back; Masaryk's role in history was to be that of a Czech. Masaryk's national consciousness as a Czech was something which could not have been entirely predicted by his birth; his Slavdom and his Czechdom were forged in the experiences and atmosphere in which he received his intellectual formation.

The preceding analysis of Masaryk's national background has yielded a complex set of conclusions. By geographic origin, Masaryk was Moravian or Moravian Slovak; by parentage, he was Slovak on his father's side and more German than Czech on his mother's side; by surname, he was Slovak; by speech, he was more Czech than German; and by acquired national consciousness, he was Czech. An accurate description of his national background must, therefore, include the Slovak and Moravian elements which were a definite part of it. Perhaps one of Masaryk's own descriptions of himself is the best that can be found: "I personally take the greatest delight in the fact that I am by birth a Moravian Slovak, by consciousness a Czech."[54]

The fact that Masaryk was born in Moravia of a Slovak father from whom he inherited a Slovak name was not without considerable significance. For the Slovaks in particular, Masaryk's early Slovak connections were extremely important; be-

53 Pražák, *T. G. Masaryk a Slovensko*, 11.
54 Speech in Chicago on 28 May 1918, as quoted from *Československá samostatnost*, iii/21 (26 June 1918) in Prokop Maxa, ed., *T. G. Masaryk: V boji za samostatnost* (Prague, 1927), 166.

cause of them Masaryk never forgot his father's fellow-countrymen in Upper Hungary. Furthermore, the Slovak and Moravian elements in Masaryk's early background enabled him to claim to be both a Slovak and a Moravian, and that fact was most useful to the future founder and first president of the Czechoslovak Republic when during the First World War he sought to unite Bohemia, Moravia, and Slovakia into a single political whole.[55] The accident of his birth in Czech-Slovak Moravian Slovakia made Masaryk and his programme of unity all the more attractive to the peoples involved – especially to those Czechs, Moravians, and Slovaks living abroad, upon whom Masaryk's independence and union movement heavily depended for support – because each group could identify itself with him in some respect. Masaryk was thus able to exclaim with truth during the war: "I am a living embodiment of this Czechoslovak programme ..."[56]

55 As Masaryk himself frankly admitted to Čapek: "It was a good thing, and one that stood me
     in good stead during the war, that I had been born half Slovak ..." (Čapek, 220).
56 "Vzpomienky" in Selver, 35.

The Politics of the Czech Eighties

H. GORDON SKILLING

THE RETURN OF CZECH REPRESENTATIVES to the Imperial Parliament (the Reichsrat) in 1879 marked a turning-point in Czech political life and began a new and significant phase in their political experience within the Habsburg Monarchy. In the decades since 1848, the Czechs had pursued a series of differing policies: a brief and abortive effort at revolution in that year; a few months of active participation, equally unsuccessful, in Austrian political life in 1848-9, and again in the early sixties; forced abstention from any political activity during the intervening absolutist period of the fifties; and, then, the long period of passive resistance from 1863 to 1879. During these later years, the Czechs had boycotted the imperial institutions in Vienna and, for most of the time, the Bohemian and Moravian diets, too, and, after 1867, had refused to recognize the validity of the constitutional framework established by the fundamental laws of that year. Then, during the eighties,[1] a new strategy of political action was embarked upon – that of participation in the Reichsrat and the diets and active cooperation with the existing Austrian political system. This momentous shift from "abstention" to "activism" was destined to have a lasting impact on Czech political consciousness and to exert a continuing influence on later phases of Czech political activity within Austria.

1 For our purposes, the "eighties" will be treated as extending from 1879, the beginning of "activism," to 1891, the year of the collapse of the Old Czechs, and as coinciding roughly with the regime of Count Eduard Taaffe as prime minister of Austria (1879-93).

The return to Vienna involved a recognition by the Czech leaders that passive resistance had been a failure.[2] This strategy, conducted under the banner of "Bohemian state right," had in fact not brought about any modification in the Austro-Hungarian dualist system, or in the centralism of the Austrian half of the monarchy. Moreover, their self-imposed exclusion from political activity had left the Czechs without any influence on the course of public affairs and had permitted the exclusive conduct of those affairs by the German "left" or *verfassungstreu* party.[3] With the decline in the fortunes of the German "left" at the end of the seventies, and the changing constellation of political forces resulting from the 1879 elections, there opened up an alternative possibility, namely, to take part in Austrian political life, to reap concrete advantages for the Czech cause and thus to strengthen the nation for greater achievements in the future. Once the decision was made to try this course, the Czechs emerged at once as a political factor of importance in Austrian politics, with a spokesman in the cabinet of Count Eduard Taaffe and with their representatives belonging to the parliamentary grouping, the "Iron Ring," on which the cabinet was based. As a result, the strategy pursued by the Czechs during the eighties achieved some solid gains, thus seeming to justify the policy of positive cooperation. Paradoxically, however, the decade witnessed the overwhelming defeat of the spokesmen of activism by the electorate, thus seeming to discredit this tactic and to justify the new alternative of opposition advanced by their rivals.

The eighties may be regarded then as a crucial transitional period in Czech political life and a time of gestation in their political thinking. It was a testing time for the strategy of positive work within the established institutions of the monarchy, and at the same time, the seed-time of an alternative tactic of parliamentary opposition. During this decade were crystallized many of the major issues which were to remain in the forefront of Czech and Austrian politics down to the collapse of the Habsburg Empire. During these years, too, the central points of conflict between Czech and German were sharply defined and the difficulty, if not the impossibility, of a mutual compromise of the opposing national viewpoints was made clearly evident. Above all, there evolved a fateful differentiation in Czech political ranks between the so-called Old and Young Czechs[4] who represented distinct and opposing conceptions of the Czech question and of the most effective strategy and tactics of political action.

2 The best treatment of passive resistance and the decision to abandon it is by Stanley Z. Pech, "Passive Resistance of the Czechs, 1863–1879," *Slavonic and East European Review*, xxxvi (June 1958), 434–52.
3 This included the moderate liberals, the more radical progressives, and the *verfassungstreu* nobility from Bohemia. The main group of the German left, representing the moderate or Austrian viewpoint, was at first known as the "Liberals"; after 1885, as the "German Austrians"; and after 1888, as the "United German Left." The much weaker, more radical or nationalist wing was represented at first by the "Progressives"; after 1885, by the "German Club"; and from 1888, by the "German National Union."
4 In terms of official party nomenclature, these two terms referred to the National party and the National Liberal party, respectively. See below pp. 273ff.

This critical period in Czech life has received surprisingly little attention from later scholars, whether Czech or foreign. The essential facts and the main events of the decade are, of course, familiar to all students of Czech political history.[5] During the first republic, those Czech scholars who concerned themselves with the decades prior to the First World War concentrated on editing letters and memoirs of the leading personalities and devoted attention to T. G. Masaryk and his role in preparing the way for national independence.[6] After 1948, Marxist scholars focused mainly on the economic and social development of the period and the rise of the social democratic movement.[7] General Czech histories have passed fleetingly by the events of the eighties, without indicating their significance.[8] Foreign scholars have dealt with this period largely as a phase of Austrian history, leaving the Czech aspects of the period often obscure.[9] Even works devoted to Czech history by eminent non-Czech specialists have given inadequate treatment of the politics of this decade.[10] In consequence, there exists almost no serious or systematic analysis of Czech politics in the eighties (or, for that matter, of subsequent decades),[11] and the era has

5 The fullest treatment continues to be that of Zdeněk Tobolka in vol. III of his *Politické dějiny československého národa od r. 1848 až do dnešní doby* (4 vols.; Prague, 1932–7). See also the earlier treatment in the two chapters by Karel Kramář on the Old and Young Czech periods in Z. Tobolka, ed., *Česká politika* (5 vols.; Prague, 1913), III.
6 See, for instance, J. Heidler, *Příspěvky k listáři dra F. L. Riegra* (2 vols.; Prague, 1924, 1926); F. Kameníček, *Paměti a listář Dra. Aloise Pražáka* (2 vols.; Prague, 1926–7); Z. V. Tobolka, ed., *JUDr. Jos. Kaizl: Z mého života* (3 vols.; Prague, 1909–14); Z. V. Tobolka, ed., *MUDr. Eduard Grégr: Denník* (2 vols.; Prague, 1908); Karel Mattuš, *Paměti, 1883–1913* (Prague, 1921). See also Jan Herben, *T. G. Masaryk* (2nd ed., 3 vols.; Prague, 1928–30); Jaromír Doležal, *Masarykova cesta životem* (2 vols.; Brno, 1920–1).
7 See M. Wolf, *Sociální a politické dějiny československé* (Prague, 1948); *Přehled československých dějin* (Prague, 1960). Jurij Křížek, however, in his *T. G. Masaryk a česká politika* (Prague, 1959), examines in great detail the role of the Realists within the framework of Czech politics of the time. Cf. an earlier Marxist essay by Jan Šverma, *Česká otázka ve světle marxismu* (Prague, 1933) published also in Šverma, *Vybrané spisy*, I (Prague, 1955).
8 See Kamil Krofta, *Dějiny československé* (Prague, 1946); *Československá vlastivěda* (Prague, 1929–36), IV; O. Odložilík, *Nástin československých dějin* (Prague, 1937; 4th ed., Prague, 1946).
9 See, for instance, A. J. P. Taylor, *The Habsburg Monarchy, 1815–1918* (London, 1942; 2nd ed. completely revised, London, 1948); Arthur J. May, *The Hapsburg Monarchy, 1867–1914* (Cambridge, Mass., 1951); Robert Kann, *The Multinational Empire* (2 vols.; New York, 1950); E. Wiskemann, *Czechs and Germans* (London, 1938). The fullest treatment of the eighties is by William A. Jenks, *Austria under the Iron Ring, 1879–1893* (Charlottesville, 1965). This volume deals with Czech politics more extensively, but without the use of sources in the Czech language.
10 R. W. Seton-Watson, *A History of the Czechs and Slovaks* (London, 1943); S. Harrison Thomson, *Czechoslovakia in European History* (Princeton, 1943; rev. ed. 1953); Hermann Münch, *Böhmische Tragödie* (Braunschweig, Berlin, Hamburg, 1949).
11 Almost alone stand the articles by Stanley Z. Pech on various aspects of Rieger's political life, in particular, "F. L. Rieger: The Road from Liberalism to Conservatism," *Journal of Central European Affairs*, XVII/1 (April 1957), 3–23; "František Ladislav Rieger: Some

traditionally been discussed in mainly negative terms, often through the eyes of contemporary critics.[12]

Certainly there was much that was repellent in the life of the time. In Masaryk's words, it was a period of "petty circumstances, petty means and petty people."[13] The overwhelming majority of the nation, deprived of the suffrage, could play in the theatre of Czech politics only the part of a more or less passive audience. The restricted stage was dominated, therefore, by the spokesmen of the narrow circles who were politically active – by František Ladislav Rieger, the rather tragic figure of a statesman *manqué*; a somewhat sinister *éminence grise*, Count Clam-Martinitz, the leading conservative noble; and the almost absurdly demagogic figures, the brothers Grégr, Eduard and Julius. None of these showed themselves to be masters in the art of politics, nor were the parties which they led models of political strategy. Action was concentrated on nationalistic issues, such as language rights, of interest mainly to the middle class, and neglected more pressing economic and social questions of concern to the broader masses. In many ways, the most interesting and potentially more important things were happening outside the sphere of politics as narrowly conceived, in the steady growth of the economic strength of the Czech bourgeoisie and the rise of an industrial working class and in the flowering of Czech cultural life, in music, literature, and the arts generally. Above all, the ferment of ideas at the Czech University and in intellectual circles was ultimately to have an enormous impact on Czech political thought and behaviour. Hovering in the wings were men such as Tomáš Masaryk, Josef Kaizl, and Karel Kramář, who were then active mainly in the intellectual realm, but were beginning to exert an influence on the margins of politics and were destined to be leading actors in the future.[14]

Nevertheless, it cannot be denied that what was happening on the main stage of Czech politics, in the Vienna Reichsrat and in the Bohemian Diet, was also of great

---

Critical Observations," *Canadian Slavonic Papers*, II (1957), 57–67. See also his unpublished PH.D. thesis, "The Role of František L. Rieger in Nineteenth Century Czech Political Development" (Univ. of Colorado, 1955).

12 See the works by T. G. Masaryk, *O naší nynější krisi: Pád strany staročeské a počátkové směrů nových* (Prague, 1895); *Česká otázka, Snahy a tužby národního obrození* (Prague, 1894); Josef Kaizl, *České myšlenky* (Prague, 1895); Karel Kramář, *Poznámky o české politice* (Prague, 1906); also in German, *Anmerkungen zur böhmischen Politik* (Vienna, 1906). Kaizl and Kramář, who later became leading Young Czechs, are more critical of the Old Czechs; Masaryk is critical of both Old and Young Czechs. See also the comments of the Old Czech, Albín Bráf, in Josef Gruber, ed., *Albín Bráf. Život a dílo* (5 vols.; Prague, 1922–4), especially "Paměti," I, 1–102 and his essay, "Listy politického kacíře" (Letters of a Political Heretic), v, 5–71. See also Jan Herben, *Deset let proti proudu, 1886–1896* (Prague, 1898), republished in Herben, *Kniha vzpomínek* (Prague, 1935–6) (references are to the latter).

13 Karel Čapek, *Hovory s T. G. Masarykem* (Prague, 1937), 93.

14 O. Odložilik has devoted several articles to Masaryk and the eighties and nineties. See "Enter Masaryk: A Prelude to His Political Career," *Journal of Central European Affairs*, X/1 (April 1950), 21–36; "T. G. Masaryk and the Czech 'Nineties,'" *The Spirit of Czechoslovakia* (London, 1945), VI/1, 10–12, 21; "Na předělu dob," *Zítřek* (1943), 2, 30–68.

258 / H. GORDON SKILLING

moment for the future.[15] The new policy of "activism" was later derisively called a policy of "crumbs."[16] Yet the "crumbs" were substantial ones and, taken together, represented significant advances for the Czechs. A major step was the establishment of a Czech university in Prague in 1881.[17] Although the Czechs had originally demanded "equality" at the existing single Charles-Ferdinand University, the creation of a separate university, with Czech as the exclusive language of instruction, was an event of far-reaching importance. Furthermore, the decade witnessed the building up of the Czech school system, both elementary and secondary, vocational and commercial as well as general. Although full equality was not achieved, the disproportion in the number of Czech and German schools was greatly reduced. The "crumbs" also included the expanded right of use of the Czech language in the courts and offices throughout Bohemia and Moravia, and the warding off of German demands for a legally entrenched German "state language." This widened employment of Czech in turn enhanced the opportunities of employment of Czech judges, lawyers, and officials in the public service of the two provinces. Not to be ignored was the new electoral regulation in 1882 which enabled the Czechs and the feudal nobility to attain for the first time a majority in the Bohemian Diet. These were solid and definite gains, less grandiose and romantic than the unattained goal of state right, but of real value to the nation. None of them would presumably have been attained if passive resistance had continued. When coupled with the significant economic and cultural advance achieved at this time, the eighties must be regarded, in spite of all the negative features, as a period of flourishing national development unequalled by any previous stage of the Czech national awakening.

There remains the paradox that the decade ended in political fiasco, in the repudiation of activism at the polls and the victory of a new tactic of radical opposition. The explanation of this puzzling consequence may be sought in the more or less objective and inescapable factors which formed the context of Czech political activity in the eighties and which indeed continued in later periods to exert a profound influence on Czech political life. Four such basic conditioning factors deserve examination: (1) the centralized character of Austria and its effect on Czech hopes for state right or autonomy, (2) the role of the imperial cabinet as personified by the prime minister, Count Taaffe, (3) the composition and the nature of the parlia-

---

15 Contrast the rather remarkable statement of Harrison Thomson (*Czechoslovakia in European History*, 1943 ed., 180) that the activity of the Czech delegates to the Vienna Parliament "was for the most part of little consequence." Seton Watson, in a fuller treatment, recognizes the gains made, but describes the eighties as "a period of disorientation" (*A History of the Czechs and Slovaks*, 224).

16 Rieger was reported to have said in May 1887, at a closed meeting of Czech deputies: "Since we did not succeed, by passive resistance, in achieving our rights at one stroke, we must now collect them in crumbs, even if we have to collect these crumbs under the table" (*Národní listy*, 12 May 1887). Rieger denied the accuracy of the report, but had used the term on another occasion in a letter to his wife. See below, p. 263.

17 See H. Gordon Skilling, "The Partition of the University in Prague," *The Slavonic and East European Review*, xxvii/69 (May 1949), 430–49.

mentary coalition, the Iron Ring, (4) the attitude of the German liberals and nationalists to Czech demands and the apparently unbridgeable gulf between Czech and German national goals. To these external factors, more or less beyond the control of the Czechs, there must be added another, apparently more subjective in character, but in fact reflecting the basic political forces already mentioned, namely, (5) the sharp division among the Czech political leaders themselves on fundamental issues of political strategy and tactics. It is the purpose of this essay to elucidate in general terms each of these elements of the situation and to assess the impact of the experiences of the eighties on the emerging political culture of the Czech nation.[18]

AUSTRIAN CENTRALISM AND BOHEMIAN STATE RIGHT

The Austro-Hungarian Compromise of 1867, which recognized the special position of Hungary and merged the Bohemian lands with the other Austrian crown-lands, dealt a severe blow at the traditional conception of Bohemia as a kingdom enjoying a special position of independence under the Habsburg crown, somewhat equivalent to that of Hungary. The December Constitution of the same year represented another step in the centuries-long tendency toward centralism in the Austrian half of the monarchy and negated still further the concept of Bohemia's statehood.[19] The constitution, although federal in form, was in reality highly centralist, with legislative and administrative power concentrated in the hands of the emperor and his cabinet, and of the Vienna Reichsrat. The other crown-lands, including Bohemia and Moravia, continued to exist as formal entities, with their own diets, but possessed a very restricted competence. Only Galicia, dominated by the Poles, was granted substantial home-rule.

Passive resistance by the Czechs had been an expression of their denial of both the legality and the justice of the 1867 system and of their continued hope for a change of course by the emperor in a direction more favourable to Bohemian state right (*České státní právo*, or *Böhmisches Staatsrecht*). This concept, in its earlier

---

18 Space prevents extensive documentation from the research on which this analysis is derived. As noted, there is no systematic treatment of Czech politics of this period, nor even adequate biographies of the principal participants, such as Rieger, the Grégrs, Clam Martinitz, and Taaffe. The most important primary sources are the collected letters and diaries of Rieger, Pražák, Mattuš, Kaizl, and Eduard Grégr, cited in n. 6. See also Arthur Skedl, *Der politische Nachlass des Grafen Eduard Taaffe* (Vienna, 1922). Another useful source is Adolf Srb, *Politické dějiny národa českého* (Prague, 1899). On the German side, see Ernst von Plener, *Erinnerungen* (3 vols.; Stuttgart, Leipzig, 1911, 1921); Paul Molisch, *Briefe zur deutschen Politik in Österreich von 1848 bis 1918* (Vienna and Leipzig, 1934). Another major source of information is the stenographic protocol of the Austrian Parliament and Bohemian Diet, and the main newspapers, especially *Národní listy, Politik* (in German), *Pokrok* and *Hlas národa, Čas* (from 1886), *Neue Freie Presse* and *Deutsche Zeitung*. For further bibliography and fuller treatment of the period, see the author's unpublished PH.D. thesis, "The German-Czech National Conflict in Bohemia, 1879–1893" (University of London, 1940).

19 The best analyses of the dual system and Austrian centralism continue to be Louis Eisenmann, *Le Compromis Austro-Hongrois de 1867* (Paris, 1904), and Josef Redlich, *Das österreichische Staats- und Reichsproblem* (Leipzig, 1920, 1926).

form, as expressed, for instance, in the Declaration of 1868, had asserted the unity and the independence of all three lands of the Bohemian crown (Bohemia, Moravia, and Silesia) and the need for a compromise with the monarchy endorsing this. When in 1871, during the regime of Count Karl Hohenwart, hopes were raised for such a compromise, the state right objective assumed more modest form. The Fundamental Articles adopted by the Bohemian Diet recognized the dualist system, accepted the December Constitution, and demanded an expanded autonomy for Bohemia only. The unity of the three lands was to be represented only in a proposed Bohemian Court Chancellor in Vienna and in the coronation ceremony of the monarch as king of the Bohemian lands. Even these modest hopes were soon dashed.[20] The return to Vienna in 1879 was an acknowledgment by the Czechs that state right could eventually be attained, if at all, only through participation in the Austrian system and in a form compatible with its main principles.

Participation in the imperial institutions emphasized sharply the inner ambiguity of the doctrine of Bohemian state right. To participate in the Reichsrat was to accept the legal facts of a system hitherto rejected and implicitly, therefore, to abandon the legal fiction of Bohemian statehood except in the narrow forms embodied in the 1867 constitution and as a goal for the future. The Czechs and the feudal nobles sought to conceal these implications of activism by making a state right declaration on the floor of the Austrian Parliament after their return. Modest and ambiguous, this statement seemed to represent little more than a claim for eventual constitutional revision in the form of a broadened autonomy of the kingdoms and lands. Count Taaffe, in granting the Czech spokesmen the opportunity to make their declaration, had not committed himself to an early restoration of Bohemian state right or even to a constitutional revision of an autonomist character.[21]

How far the Old Czechs had moved from the position of the sixties and seventies was suggested in 1885 when at the opening of a new parliamentary session they did not even repeat their declaration. Thereafter, their references to state right became more infrequent and vague. Rieger himself, in a statement in 1889, revealed how modest and attenuated was the substance then given to the traditional doctrine when he defined it as "the right to demand that that degree of autonomy which is allowed to us should now be expanded in a suitable, beneficial and harmless manner."[22] Even more significant, in spite of occasional demands for eventual constitutional revision embodying a greater degree of

20 See Eric Fischer, "The Negotiations for a National *Ausgleich* in Austria in 1871," *Journal of Central European Affairs*, II/2 (July 1942), 134–45.
21 See his speeches in the lower house on 30 October 1879 and 12 April 1880, *Stenographische Protokolle des Hauses der Abgeordneten des österreichischen Reichsrathes*, IX, 208 and X, 2198–200. See also Skedl, *Der politische Nachlass*, 249–50, 254–7.
22 See Rieger's speeches in the Bohemian Diet, 7 and 9 November 1889, *Böhmische Landtagsverhandlungen* (1889), 387ff. and 477ff.

autonomy and even definite references to expanded powers for the Diet in the educational and agricultural fields, not once did the Old Czech leaders submit a precise proposal for constitutional reform or expansion of autonomy. As we have noted earlier, they wished to attain other more specific ends that would not involve constitutional changes and were ready to postpone the achievement of broader constitutional objectives to a more distant future. The time was not ripe, said Rieger on more than one occasion, for state right demands. In the meantime, argued his close colleague Karel Mattuš, the task "was to strengthen ourselves politically and nationally, so that later we could easily proceed to a solution of the difficult state right tasks."[23]

This change in tactics by the Czech leadership, partially concealed as it was by the continued use of state right slogans, was bound to create dissatisfaction within the nation with the policy of activism and with the failure to attain the traditional goal.[24] This in turn provided the Young Czechs with a useful weapon against their political rivals. The Young Czechs, in the late 1870s, had been ready to recognize the futility of passive resistance as a means of attaining state right and had been vociferous protagonists of a return to Vienna. During the early eighties, although increasingly critical of Rieger's "opportunist" policy, the Young Czechs did not raise the state right issue. From 1885 on, however, the Grégrs began once again to assert the traditional doctrine, at first in the form of a demand for the coronation of the monarch as king of the Bohemian lands. Later, in 1889, in the Bohemian Diet, Julius Grégr launched a vigorous state right campaign in the style of the sixties and seventies using similar arguments in defence of Bohemian statehood. "The present constitution," declared Eduard Grégr, "was an unjust *octroi* ... an act of crying injustice and savage violence committed against the glorious Bohemian Kingdom and the Czech nation ..." "The only motive of the Czechs in entering the parliament," he continued, "was to sap and undermine this constitution hostile to us and finally to blow up this citadel, a prison for our nation."[25]

When the Young Czechs returned to Parliament as the leading Czech party in 1891, they made their own state right declaration comparable to that of the Old Czechs twelve years earlier. Their campaign had created a situation in which, as Rieger was forced to admit, "the idea of state right now moves the minds and hearts of the whole nation, even the lowest classes," and would "have to be satisfied somehow."[26] Yet the Young Czechs were caught in the same ambiguity of position as the Old Czechs, in the contradiction between their continued assertion of state right and their active participation in an "illegal" constitutional system. In his Diet speech just quoted, Grégr declared:

23 *Ibid.*, 9 November 1889, 462–6.
24 See Gruber, *Bráf*, I, 130; Tobolka, *Kaizl*, II, 531–43.
25 *Landtagsverhandlungen*, 7 November 1889, 394–407.
26 A letter of 7 September 1883, in Kameníček, *Paměti*, II, 414–6.

We recognize the present state laws, the present constitutional statutes as valid laws; ... we wish nothing more than, on this basis of law ..., to work in favour of our state right ... But, gentlemen, this does not mean that, when we adopt this standpoint of the existing valid laws, we are recognizing it; it means that standing in this Diet and in Parliament on the basis of the existing constitutional statutes, we, ourselves, do not recognize their authority and their legal validity, and we cannot admit that this is our law.

Moreover, in spite of their constant demands for state right, the Young Czechs gave little or no indication as to how and in what concrete form they proposed to achieve this traditional goal and failed to draft a precise constitutional programme of autonomy. Time was to reveal indeed that during their own period of positive activism in the nineties, they were to be as little able as the Old Czechs had been to achieve the goal of state right, or even a modest expansion of autonomy.

THE TAAFFE REGIME

The appointment of Count Taaffe as prime minister (minister-president) seemed to offer the Czechs favourable conditions for the attainment of some of their demands. The ministry described itself as one of "national conciliation"; its purpose was to implement, on the basis of the existing constitution, the principle of national equality proclaimed in Article XIX of the Constitution of 1867 and to work towards a compromise between Czechs and Germans.[27] True, Taaffe had sought to win some support from the German liberals by including several *verfassungstreu* ministers, such as Karl von Stremayr and Julius von Horst, in his cabinet. Although the prime minister, resisting Rieger's importuning before the Czech return to Parliament, had refused to make them any binding promises, he had, however, indicated his willingness to consider Czech claims when presented in an appropriate constitutional setting, and had included Alois Pražák, from Moravia, as Czech spokesman in the cabinet. When *verfassungstreu* opposition to Taaffe continued and Stremayr and Horst resigned from the cabinet in 1880, the government turned more and more to the coalition of the Right, of which the Czechs were a constituent part, for support. The situation, therefore, seemed relatively hopeful from the Czech point of view.

In fact, however, progress was slow and frustrating, owing in part to the personality and political style of Count Taaffe, and in part to the semi-absolutist nature of the Austrian system. Taaffe was first and foremost a servant of the emperor, a *Kaiserminister*, who had been appointed to meet the situation caused by German liberal opposition to the emperor's policies at the end of the seventies and to secure an alternative source of support for these policies and other needs of the state. As he himself often explained, his ministry was to be "above the parties."[28] It was designed, that is, to embody the emperor's will, and was not

27 Skedl, *Der politische Nachlass*, 400–4.
28 Taaffe's speech in the Reichsrat, 30 October 1879 (*Sten. Prot. des Hauses der Abgeordneten*, IX, 208).

bound to implement the wishes of the coalition or even of the individual members of the cabinet. When political expediency demanded it, concessions would be made to the individual parties, as part of the customary *Kuhhandel* (horsetrading) of Austrian politics, thus achieving a temporary solution in a given case and maintaining the regime in power. Moreover, in spite of the lip-service paid to "conciliation," Taaffe had no clear and consistent programme for the solution of the national conflicts with which he was faced. Although he saw the need for some concessions to the Czech viewpoint and did in fact make some, these were always partial and often ambiguous, and were usually balanced by concessions to the Germans, so that neither side was satisfied and the issues were not permanently settled. Although this was in some ways an appropriate policy in a state of many nationalities such as Austria, it was much more a reflection of Taaffe's tactic of playing one nationality and one party against another and thus "muddling through" (*fortwursteln*) the complicated issues of Austrian politics. His perhaps apocryphal statement of "keeping all the nations of Austria in a state of equal, well-tempered dissatisfaction" sums up the essence of his philosophy, or lack of it.[29]

The Czech leaders, faced for the first time directly with the exigencies of the imperial system and the peculiar methods of Taaffe, found their position a frustrating one. Frequently denied what they considered their legitimate demands and presented with unwelcome governmental measures, they were in many cases placed in the dilemma of deciding whether to support or oppose the regime. Rieger, the architect of the policy of positive cooperation, was annoyed and angered by Taaffe's behaviour and beset with doubts as to the efficacy of his policy. As early as 1881, he lamented that his *Opportunitätspolitik* (opportunist policy) had degenerated into an *Opatrnitätspolitik* (policy of caution).[30] In the same year, he told his wife: "Taaffe throws us little crumbs, as if to poultry. Some will say that he leads us by the nose, but we consciously let ourselves be led by the nose. Let someone advise us what else we should do. To overthrow Taaffe would be very easy if we knew what would come after."[31] In 1885 he complained of the government to his daughter: "They behave impertinently towards us – insultingly. They snub us and reject our complaints heedlessly, convinced that we do not dare proceed against the government and the Taaffe ministry."[32] His dissatisfaction extended sometimes to Pražák, in the ministry, and to Clam, who was even more wedded than he to the positive policy. In the later eighties, Rieger was frequently tempted to abandon the policy of cooperating with the government and to embark on a course of opposition.[33] In the end his better

29 A positive appraisal of Taaffe is given in the concluding chapter of Jenks, *Austria under the Iron Ring*, 304ff. More critical appraisals are given by Seton-Watson, *A History of the Czechs and Slovaks*, 223–4; Taylor, *The Habsburg Monarchy*, 194ff.; Münch, *Böhmische Tragödie*, 374ff.
30 Heidler, *Příspěvky*, II, 151. This is a play on the Czech word *opatrný* (cautious).
31 *Ibid.*, II, 158. 32 *Ibid.*, II, 261.
33 *Ibid.*, II, 321–2, 326–7, 333–4; Kameníček, *Paměti*, II, 301–5.

judgment and his caution convinced him that there was no alternative but to continue to support the regime. In a speech in 1887, he argued:

To overthrow the government would not perhaps be so difficult ... Our nation would not indeed perish through this ... A new persecution would, however, come and it is, therefore, necessary to consider which is better – to go forward, as hitherto, step by step, or to break away and embark on a sea without oars ...

I, therefore, prefer to choose to support the present government in the hope that it will be the defender of our right and that we shall get from it what we urgently need for our national progress.[34]

The more impatient Czechs became critical of Taaffe's policy and also of Rieger's cautious opportunism. For Eduard Grégr, indeed, the original purpose of the return to Vienna had been to continue resistance to the regime by means of opposition in Parliament. In the earlier years of activism, however, most Czechs, even the more radical, were ready reluctantly to go along with the official party policy and in fact did so. On specific issues there were increasing demands for a firmer attitude towards the regime and a greater unwillingness to support it on undesirable measures. The organ of the Young Czechs, *Národní listy*, denying that it advocated a breach with the government, wrote in 1883: "We wish that the Czech club should more skilfully and determinedly exploit its alliance with the government and the parliamentary majority, that it should free itself from subjugation to the government and to individual fractions and that it should make its own Czech policy and cease only to serve foreign interests."[35] In 1887, the same organ, taking a more radical stand, urged that the Right should place before Taaffe an agreed series of demands and, failing their immediate fulfilment, the Czechs should enter opposition.[36] Josef Kaizl, then an Old Czech, but critical of official Czech policy, put forward a similar view and ultimately resigned his parliamentary seat in protest at Old Czech policy. While denying that he wished to endanger the government and the majority, he expressed the wish:

that their maintenance should not be considered the beginning and end of Czech policy and the one condition and means of defence of our existence, and that if they did not already wish to satisfy us and if we are to receive, in place of the fulfilment of our just wishes, disregard and oppression, we should accept this the more willingly with sword in hand from an unfriendly government than with a smile of romantic melancholy from a so-called friendly government which we constantly support.[37]

34 See Srb, *Politické dějiny národa českého*, 694–5. Cf. a similar speech in 1888, quoted by H. Traub, *František Ladislav Rieger* (2nd ed.; Prague, 1922), 234–5.
35 Series of articles, *Národní listy*, 8, 11, 14 September 1883.
36 *Ibid.*, 11 October 1887.
37 Tobolka, *Kaizl: Z mého života*, ii, 411–15.

More and more often individual parliamentary deputies adopted a radical stance and, in spite of party discipline, voted against the government on specific issues which the parliamentary group had decided to support. In 1888, Czech ranks openly split and a small, separate Young Czech faction was formed in the Reichsrat. When the Young Czechs scored a victory in the Diet elections of 1889, Rieger's position became increasingly difficult. Imbued as he was with the feeling that opposition might perhaps be necessary, he used the growing radicalism of the Czech mood as a means of pressure on the government; in the end, however, he usually refrained from carrying through his threats of opposition, thus all the more discrediting his policy of cautious activism. Even in the years of his growing disillusionment, after 1890, and the overwhelming victory of the Young Czechs in the 1891 parliamentary elections, Rieger continued to support the government in spite of its unwillingness to meet any of his most urgent demands.

ALLIANCE WITH THE RIGHT

When the Czechs returned to Vienna in 1879, they did so in the company of the conservative wing of the Bohemian large landed estate-owners (*Grossgrundbesitzer*), headed by Count Heinrich Clam-Martinitz, with whom Rieger had been in close alliance ever since 1861. He had briefly shown signs of departing from this relationship in 1878 when he had had conversations in Emmersdorf with a number of German liberals concerning a possible return to Vienna and a Czech-German partnership.[38] Although these talks proved abortive, because of the opposition of the main German liberal leaders, the feudal nobles were so frightened by the prospect of a breach of the traditional alliance and a Czech return to Vienna in cooperation with the Germans, all to the detriment of the power and influence of the nobility, that they themselves concluded an electoral compromise with the liberal or *verfassungstreu* wing of the Bohemian *Grossgrundbesitzer* and committed themselves to abandon the policy of abstention. They then bent every effort to bring the Czechs back to Vienna in alliance with *them* and hence under *their* influence and thus to facilitate the formation of a conservative government and a conservative orientation of Austrian policy.[39] When in fact both the Czechs and the feudal nobles returned to the Reichsrat, the latter (nineteen members) formed a part of the common Czech parliamentary club (or caucus), along with the National party from Bohemia and the Czechs from Moravia, who numbered together thirty-five. A vice-presidency was reserved for the nobility and was occupied by Clam.

Rieger was well aware that the bulk of the feudal nobles had no real sympathy with the Czech national cause and "were Bohemians [*Böhmen*] and

38 For the Emmersdorf conference, see R. Charmatz, *Adolf Fischhof. Das Lebensbild eines österreichischen Politikers* (Stuttgart and Berlin, 1910), 316ff.; also Münch, *Böhmische Tragödie*, 397–9.
39 See Molisch, *Briefe*, cited above, 197–201, 204–7; Skedl, *Der politische Nachlass*, 377–90.

nothing more," defending state right in the interests, not of the nation, but of their class.[40] Nonetheless, they shared with him a common belief in Bohemian autonomy, a common social and political conservatism, and a common antipathy to extreme nationalism. Unity of action was possible as long as the nobility were ready to support at least the moderate objectives of the Czechs. Sometimes impatient with Clam's caution and moderation, Rieger nonetheless saw great advantages to the national cause in retaining his support and remained loyal to the alliance throughout the eighties. "The alliance with the nobility we need for the sake of the Court," he said. "If the nobles did not go with us, they would suspect us there as dangerous rebels and revolutionaries. Everything always depends for us on the favour of the emperor, and constitutionalism is only for appearances."[41]

The Young Czechs, on the other hand, had from the beginning of their political existence in 1874 objected to the alleged subjection of the national movement to what they called an "ultramontane" nobility, openly hostile to modern liberalism, lacking in national feeling, and seeking to serve their own "conservative, Tory and Catholic" ends.[42] After the return to Vienna, they became more than ever convinced that the Czech leaders were in fact subordinated to the nobility and were, therefore, forced to make serious sacrifices of national interests. "The whole delegation," wrote Grégr in his diary, "is hitched to the government carriage; Clam sits on the box-seat and whips them and they pull like blind men – for they do not know why – simply on the word of Clam that all will be well!"[43] The Young Czechs, and other more liberal elements of the Czech nation, found the link with the nobility increasingly unbearable and called for a more independent Czech policy.

The Czechs, after their entry into Parliament, also belonged to a broader alliance known as the Iron Ring, which brought together three main groups: the Czechs (fifty-four members), the Poles (fifty-seven), and the Hohenwart Right (fifty-three), made up mainly of German conservatives from the Alpine provinces and several small national groupings such as the Slovenes. This loose coalition was held together primarily by a common hostility to the German liberals and by a common allegiance to the idea of autonomy. When Taaffe failed to wean the German liberals away from their oppositional standpoint, this parliamentary "majority" of the Right provided him with his only reliable source of support for government measures. In theory it should have been capable of exerting counter-pressure on the government. Its ability to do so, however, was limited by the fact that it did not command a clear majority in the Reichsrat, having approximately 165 seats in a total of 353. Moreover, it had no common

40 Heidler, Příspěvky, II, 176 (letter of 23 February 1883).
41 Ibid., II, 424 (letter of 10 December 1889). Cf. p. 404.
42 Tobolka, Grégr: Denník, II, 51.
43 Ibid., II, 54–5.

programme, such as the Czechs had urged from the beginning, or even a clear agreement of mutual support for the aims of each group. The majority lived, therefore, a precarious life and had to be constructed anew in each case, thus making it more subject to the influence of the government than the reverse.

The other parties of the Right evinced some readiness to support moderate Czech demands, but such aid was uncertain and had to be won on each issue. In return, the Czechs had to offer support for the demands of the other members of the alliance and often felt they were being compelled to sacrifice too much for the sake of unity. This was all the more serious in view of the generally conservative nature of the coalition, and especially of the Hohenwart club. Proposals for school reform that came under discussion several times during the eighties presented the Czechs with difficult decisions as to whether to vote for German "clerical" bills requiring religious instruction in schools and shortening the period of school attendance. Although the feudal nobility and some of the Czechs were willing to do so, the more liberal Czechs, and especially the Young Czechs, balked at what they considered a sacrifice of principle. Disappointed with what they deemed the failure of their allies to support Czech needs and confronted with such distasteful demands from their allies, individual Czech representatives on more than one occasion broke ranks, voting against measures supported by the club officially and risking sanctions for their breach of club discipline.

Both Clam and Rieger remained convinced that alone the Czechs could achieve little or nothing and that only by backing their allies could they expect support for their own demands. They were also well aware that a failure to move with the Right on a given issue would endanger the existence of the government and might open up the way for a return of the German liberals to power. On more than one occasion Rieger's faith in his own tactics was put under severe strain, especially when it was subjected to the sharp censure of more radical Czechs. In the end, in spite of doubts and disappointments, he always convinced himself that there was no alternative.

In defending his policy on the school reform, for instance, in 1883, he argued:

It had to be considered which alternative would cause the greatest harm to our national interests – an eventual break-up of the Right, which would shake the ministry, or the acceptance of the school reform ... It was necessary to consider the important point that we wish to support them [the Germans from the Alps] sincerely in everything which constitutes a vital question for them and a real need of their people. Aside from the Poles and some elements of the Hohenwart club, we have in parliament no other allies than the conservative Germans from the Alpine provinces; we should achieve absolutely nothing if we did not show them by deed that, in case of need, we wish, even with some sacrifices, to be their loyal allies.[44]

44 Srb, *Politické dějiny národa českého*, 617–18.

Again, in 1887, Rieger explained his attitude in similar terms:

The representatives of the nation finally entered these parliaments [i.e. Diet and Reichsrat] and they succeeded in getting majorities, in the one by their alliance with the great landowners, in the other by their association with the Slavs and the loyally Austrian and autonomist elements. We cannot, of course, carry through here everything that we wish, nor can we do it at a stroke; as long, however, as we can win for our needs and justified claims majorities of the other clubs, we can at least achieve them slowly and piecemeal. To our dissenters, "all or nothing" is the word ... wherefore they advise us: "abandon your present allies, break up the whole of the present majority, and then things will move!" Yes, things will move − but how and whither? Does anyone think that the government would not easily create new majorities, if it wished, following the wish of the German-Austrian club, to oppress our nationality?[45]

For the Young Czechs, the Old Czech attitude to the Iron Ring was closely linked with that adopted toward the conservative nobility and the regime itself and confirmed their opinion that the official leadership was not showing enough independence of spirit. The organ of the radicals, *Národní listy*, for instance, assigned the blame for Czech failure to "the present direction of Czech policy, its lack of courage, its insufficiency of energy and of statesmanlike foresight, and its compliance with those in whose tow we find ourselves and for whom we have for all six years, and earlier, burned our fingers."[46] In 1887, a Young Czech manifesto charged the party with being submissive to allies in Parliament who had failed it, to the nobility who dominated the movement for their own reactionary ends, and to the government which ignored their just demands. The Young Czech recipe was, however, a somewhat vague one:

Freeing ourselves from subordination to unreliable elements, and casting off the chains of foreign influences, let us stand completely on our own feet so that, as an independent national party, we finally inaugurate again a Czech policy, a real national policy under the old honourable banner on which shines the indivisible slogan of Havlíček, Nationality and Freedom.[47]

Although this did not necessarily imply the need for breaking off relations with the allies on the Right, it reflected the Young Czech view that there were limits to the sacrifices they were ready to make for the maintenance of the coalition. When, after 1891, the Young Czechs entered Parliament as the majority party, they adopted a position of independence, without links either with the Bohemian nobility or with the parties of the Right, and by adopting an attitude of opposition to the government, they contributed decisively to the eventual fall of the Taaffe regime.

45 Letter to club members, 8 June 1887, Heidler, *Příspěvky*, ii, 308–12.
46 Series in *Národní listy*, 9 April and 26, 28 May 1885.
47 Srb, *Politické dějiny národa českého*, 689–94.

THE CZECH-GERMAN NATIONAL CONFLICT

Another formidable obstacle to the full achievement of Czech objectives was the attitude of the Germans, who, apart from the conservatives of the Alpine provinces, were unalterably opposed to the main demands raised by the Czechs. This was true of the more moderate and "Austrian" German liberals and their staunch allies of the *verfassungstreu* wing of the Bohemian landed nobility, as well as of the more nationally oriented Germans. Whether motivated primarily by the more "Austrian" desire to maintain the superior position of the Germans and their language as a requirement of Austrian unity, or by the more nationalist motive of protecting the position of the powerful German minority in Bohemia and Moravia, the Germans showed no readiness to yield the privileged positions inherited from the past and opposed all concessions to Czech demands by the Taaffe government. The Czechs, determined as they were to elevate their nation to a position of equality and to reduce the priority of Germandom both in Bohemia and Moravia and in Austria as a whole, showed no willingness to accept German counter-proposals. As a consequence, the unbridgeable chasm between Germans and Czechs on all basic questions constituted what seemed to be another unalterable feature of the political landscape.[48]

At least three major issues stood in the way of a genuine Czech-German compromise. One was the state right position of the Czechs, which the Germans considered to be in direct contradiction to the existing constitution. They were, moreover, hostile to any modification of the constitutional laws in the direction of autonomy, fearing that a federalized Austria would weaken the position of the Germans in the monarchy as a whole and would leave them as a helpless national minority in a Czech-dominated Bohemia. Although the Germans were ready to propose a wider autonomy for Galicia, Dalmatia, and other provinces, they did so only as a means of strengthening their position in the rest of Austria and, otherwise, were utterly opposed to any modification of the centralized Austrian system. In spite of the return to Vienna, the Germans remained convinced that the Czechs had not given up their ultimate state right objectives. They rejected even the more moderate version of autonomy advanced by the Old Czechs and, of course, were bitterly opposed to the more extreme demands of the Young Czechs. The prospect of a more powerful Bohemia, dominated by a Czech majority in the Diet, led them to submit the plan of partition (to be discussed below) and to abstain from the Diet during most of the eighties.

Secondly, on the language question the Czech and German views seemed equally

48 It is impossible to refer to the vast literature on the Czech-German conflict, mainly in the German language. Most useful are E. Herbst, *Das deutsche Sprachgebiet in Böhmen* (Prague, 1887); Heinrich Rauchberg, *Der nationale Besitzstand in Böhmen* (3 vols.; Leipzig, 1905); Alfred Fischel, *Materialien zur Sprachenfrage in Österreich* (2nd ed.; Brünn, 1910); K. G. Hugelmann, *Das Nationalitätsrecht des alten Österreich* (Vienna and Leipzig, 1934). The main Czech sources are the works cited in nn. 5, 12, and 18.

irreconcilable. The Czechs sought an expanded use of their language in offices and courts, thus modifying the dominant position of German and implementing the constitutional provisions for equality. In line with their conception of Bohemian unity, they interpreted equality to mean the right to employ Czech as a customary language in the external service throughout the whole of the province and, more than that, the expanded use of Czech even in the internal service.[49] This carried with it the implication that many, or all, officials and judges in Bohemia would have to know both languages. For the Germans, these demands were entirely unjustified constitutionally and were based on state right assumptions concerning the unity of Bohemia and the rights of the Czechs throughout the whole province. When the Stremayr ordinance of 1880 met the Czech demand in regard to the external service, the Germans, both moderate and radical, rejected it as ignoring the fact of the "closed German territory" in Bohemia where Czech, they argued, was not required in view of the over-whelming predominance of Germans in the population. Later, in 1886, in the Diet, the Czechs advanced more far-reaching proposals which would have made Czech the main language in the internal service of predominantly Czech regions and would have extended its use in other areas and in the provincial institutions in Prague. A decree issued by the minister of justice in 1886 fulfilled their wishes, at least in part, in the Prague High Court. This once again aroused the bitter hostility of all Germans, liberal and national, and was described as a threat to the rightful position of the German language and the very unity of the monarchy, paving the way for a federalized and Slav Austria. These dangers led the Germans to advance their own proposals for a legislative enactment of a German state language, which would have protected the traditional position of that language and maintained Austria as a German state. The exclusive use of German in the internal service was in their view a state necessity, as was its right to be used in external relations with citizens everywhere. For the Czechs, this codification of the privileges of German was an unacceptable petrification of the status quo which would have prevented the advance of Czech to an equal status.

A third issue pitted Czechs against Germans – the German proposal of "partition," which was designed to protect the German minority in Bohemia against the language and state right demands of the Czechs. The Germans, both liberal and nationalist, were, almost without exception, reconciled to the inevitability of the continued existence of a single Bohemian province. Partition, as advocated in successive projects, referred to more modest aims, in the first place the delimitation of the boundaries of the judicial and political districts so as to make them predominantly of one nationality, thus clearly defining the "closed German area" where the Czech language would not have to be used. In addition, the plan of

---

49 The distinction is between the relations of courts and offices directly with citizens (external service) and the inner official proceedings of these bodies (internal service).

partition came to include the division of provincial institutions, such as the High Court, and the Agricultural and School Councils, into national sections, and the setting up of national *curiae* in the Bohemian Diet armed with a veto in questions affecting national interests. These measures, it was believed, would insulate the German areas and the German official class against the worst implications of the Czech language proposals and would save the German minority from occupying a completely subordinate position in the provincial institutions, including the Diet. During most of the eighties, the Czechs were unalterably opposed to partition in any of its various forms, regarding it as an obstacle to the attainment of their language rights throughout the province, as well as a threat ultimately to the unity of Bohemia and a death-knell for Bohemian state right.

The eighties ended with an event that seemed to vindicate Taaffe's policy of conciliation – the decision to hold a conference of representatives of the Old Czechs, the Bohemian feudal nobility, and the United German Left (the main party of moderate Germans), together with delegates of the government, to seek a national compromise. The Vienna negotiations concluded their deliberations in early 1890 with a written agreement or compromise (the *Ausgleich* or *Punktace*) which has been treated by some authors as a major step towards national conciliation.[50] In fact, however, the Vienna Compromise was not a systematic adjustment of all the major issues in dispute, but a rather haphazard and fragmentary collection of mutual concessions, in the main favouring the German side.[51] Moreover, all the items of the agreement had to be implemented later by specific measures of the Reichsrat, government, or Diet, leaving, therefore, much room for subsequent manoeuvre and disagreement.

In the Compromise the issue of state right was put aside entirely and no reference was made even to an extension of Bohemian autonomy. On the language questions, many of the major issues were either postponed or dealt with in ambiguous fashion. The Czechs did not achieve recognition of the use of Czech in the internal service, or assurance of a general requirement of bilingualism of officials and judges, and were even brought to agree in principle to the eventual revision of the Stremayr ordinance. Their major gain was the agreement on a Diet electoral reform which would have assured them an increased majority. Through a misunderstanding, Rieger thought he had received a promise from the government of a widened use of Czech in the internal service of the courts,

---

50 Kann (*The Multinational Empire*, I, 201) calls the Vienna pact "a true compromise"; Arthur May (*The Hapsburg Monarchy*, 198) terms it "a promising set of accords."

51 The most thorough study of the Compromise is that by Karel Kazbunda, "Krise české politiky a vídeňská jednání o t. zv. punktace roku 1890," *Český časopis historický*, 40 (1934), 77–108, 310–46, 491–528; 41 (1935), 41–82, 294–320, 514–54. See the more recent study by Jenks, *Austria under the Iron Ring*, chap. 13, 239–74. The text of the agreement is given in Münch, *Böhmische Tragödie*, 401–3.

but the alleged promise was never implemented.[52] The Germans did not secure the immediate repeal of the Stremayr ordinance, but won the endorsement, even if in modified form, of their main objectives of national delimitation of the judicial and administrative districts and counties, as well as the division of the provincial institutions into sections and the introduction of national curiae in the Diet.

The Compromise was thus achieved only as a result of these far-reaching concessions by the Old Czechs to the Germans' viewpoint, without, however, any serious reciprocal actions by the latter. The Germans, moderate as well as nationalists, hailed the Compromise as a victory. It was not surprising that the Young Czechs, who were not represented at the negotiations, rejected what seemed to them to be an abandonment of traditional Czech claims without appropriate gains. It is doubtful, however, that their representation at the talks would have altered the final outcome. It would indeed more likely have prevented the attainment of an agreement in the first place. Although the Old Czechs were at first loyal to the Compromise and sought in vain for several years to secure a concession concerning the internal use of Czech, they, too, became progressively more and more disillusioned and ultimately turned against it. Young Czech opposition continued relentlessly, thus leading to the final collapse of the agreement and the fall of the Taaffe regime.

Had the Vienna Compromise represented a complete and genuine compromise between spokesmen who were fully representative of both nations, it might have planted the seeds of a parliamentary settlement, enforcing on the emperor and his advisers a solution of the national conflict attained by mutual agreement. In fact, the Compromise introduced no significant change in Austrian political procedures. For Taaffe, the negotiations were merely a continuation of the policy of *fortwursteln*, a means of providing an escape from a serious crisis, designed to break up the sharp opposition of the German left to his regime and to avert the incipient revolt of the Czechs against the Taaffe system. For the Old Czechs and their feudal allies, it was another step in their policy of opportunism by which they hoped to secure a few more concessions for the nation and thus strengthen their hands against the threat from the Young Czechs. For the moderate Germans, the Vienna conference yielded considerable gains, thus helping to counteract the propaganda of the German radicals and seeming to foreshadow a new trend of government policy facilitating the return of the Germans to power. In fact, as we have seen, the conference was founded on shifting sands and, brought about the reverse of all that was hoped for.

Was a compromise of Czech and German claims in Bohemia possible? Perhaps in theory a conciliation of such sharply conflicting viewpoints was not beyond the scope of human ingenuity. In subsequent decades, however, successive

52 See Kazbunda, "Krise české politiky," 518ff.; Heidler, *Příspěvky*, II, 433–4, 439–40; Mattuš, *Paměti*, 123–7.

governments and many German and Czech party leaders explored alternative routes to such a compromise, always without success. An agreement would have required a willingness on both sides to adjust to the views of the other and seek out a consensus based on mutual concessions. Extreme and diametrically opposed demands such as those of state right and Austrian centralism, a German state language and full bilingual equality for Czech, or far-reaching separation and complete provincial unity, would have had to be modified in the interests of agreement. Rieger had, by the end of the eighties, come to the conclusion that, without a major effort to meet the German viewpoint, a settlement in Bohemia was impossible and the ultimate attainment of Czech wishes, including state right, was excluded. As he put it in a speech in 1890: "State right does not have in any way to injure the rights of our German countrymen in our land, but on the contrary it has to assure their rights; I desire that we may achieve our state right in unity and in understanding with our German countrymen – otherwise, I think that we shall not achieve it."[53] This conciliatory position was in part a reaction to the growth of Young Czech radicalism and in part an expression of his growing conviction of the need to reach an agreement with the more moderate spokesmen of German nationalism. The latter, however, showed no signs of any willingness to meet Rieger half-way, although he later put aside his state right objectives. Even had a genuine compromise of moderate Germans and Czechs been reached, it might well have proved a pyrrhic victory, producing increased national extremism on the German as well as the Czech side, and leading to ultimate rejection by the radicals. Whatever the theoretical possibilities of ultimate agreement, the blunt fact remains that during the eighties there was no evidence of a serious basis for a genuine compromise beween the two nations.

CONFLICT OF OLD AND YOUNG CZECHS

Another crucial factor blocking the way to the success of the policy of activism was the progressive disintegration of Czech political unity as a result of the crystallization of two sharply opposed camps, commonly known as Old and Young Czechs. The traditional party, led by Palacký and Rieger from 1860, had been the National party. A division in Czech ranks had appeared as early as 1863 and had led to the formation of the National Liberal party (Young Czech) in 1874. The two parties, however, combined their forces in the 1879 elections and formed single parliamentary clubs in Diet and Reichsrat. In 1888, however, the Young Czechs formed a separate club of "independents" in Vienna. The conflict was, however, not merely a clash of separate parties or clubs, but represented a gradual process of differentiation between two opposing tendencies of thought and action. During most of the period, for instance, those who eventually became Young Czechs were members of the single Czech club and, even if reluctantly, accepted Old Czech leadership. Many Old Czechs shared their dissatisfaction

53 Speech of 31 May 1890, in Diet, *Landtagsverhandlungen (1890)*, 120ff.

with the achievements of activism and the leadership of Rieger and the nobility. When, at the end of the decade, the Young Czechs swept the field and became the main spokesmen of the nation, there soon appeared within their ranks equally serious differences on strategy and tactics which resembled the earlier division of Young and Old Czechs.

The differences were not therefore exclusively a conflict of two opposed parties. They represented in part a clash of two generations in Czech politics; in part a reflection of the character and temperament of the leading personalities on both sides. The differences were also, as we have seen, a product of the difficulties of the situation in which the Czechs found themselves and the varying assessments of the appropriate strategy and tactics that resulted. They also reflected differences of political approach, as Rieger and the Old Czechs tended more and more towards a conservative position and the Young Czechs espoused more liberal tendencies of thought.

Owing to the absence of a social class based on large-scale industry, commerce, and finance among the Czechs, and the exclusion of workers and most peasants from political activity, both the Old and Young Czech movements may be regarded as parties expressing the interests of the middle strata of the bourgoisie, with each tending to represent a different sector of the middle class.[54] The Old Czechs were identified with the more prosperous members of the nation: large landlords and farmers, successful businessmen and established professional persons, higher officials and leading local figures such as mayors and councillors. They aspired to be regarded as respectable elements, enjoying the confidence of the monarch and his entourage, and shunned the appearance of national or social radicalism which might spoil their prestige as loyal subjects and injure their political prospects. The Old Czechs were consciously and positively "Austrian" and royalist, ready to recognize the accomplished fact of Dualism and to accept the semi-constitutionalism and the "interest" representation of the Austrian system. They were quite willing to work closely with the conservative nobility

54 Tobolka, *Politické dějiny*, II, 358; *Masarykův slovník naučný* (Prague, 1938), v, 53. The customary Marxist view described the two parties as both representing the "bourgeoisie," and as essentially not differing from each other even in political strategy and tactics. See, for instance, *Přehled československých dějin* (Prague, 1960), II, part 1, 621–3, 649–51. Cf. Šverma, *Česká otázka*, I, 72–3. Křížek, however, distinguishes the two parties sharply, not only as representing different wings of the bourgeoisie, but also as advocating different tactics, radical and conservative. Masaryk and the Realists, according to Křížek, sought to overcome the split and to represent the common interests of the entire bourgeois class (*T. G. Masaryk*, 25–6 *et seq.*). Masaryk in his pre-war writings distinguished the Old and Young Czech as being more conservative and more "popular and democratic," respectively, the one embodying the tradition of Palacký, the other that of Havlíček (*Česká otázka*, 100–4). He later described "Old Czechism" as the "bankruptcy of the old bourgeois patriciate," and "Young Czechism" as "the party of newly rising classes, more rural, radical" (Čapek, *Hovory s T. G. Masarykem*, 110).

with whom they shared many common opinions. They were strongly opposed to anything but a modest expansion of the suffrage to enfranchise the lesser groups of the bourgeoisie and bitterly opposed universal suffrage which would give the vote to the working class. Their electoral manifestos and speeches dealt largely with constitutional and national questions and contained few proposals for social reform. Their social and political conservatism was coupled with a moderate nationalism which was ready to make compromises for the sake of the needs of the state and of the other nationalities and which sought to convince the ruling elements of Austria that the satisfaction of Czech demands was in the interests of the state and the dynasty. From this general moderateness of outlook developed their tactics of cautious opportunism, relying for success on careful parliamentary manoeuvres and bargains, and on private pressure on the court and the members of the cabinet.

The Young Czechs, on the other hand, tended to represent the "smaller" men of the community: tradespeople and craftsmen, the smaller peasants, teachers and lawyers, some professors and journalists, and some of the higher-paid workers. Although not republican or disloyal to Austria, the Young Czechs professed a more democratic and progressive attitude towards dynasty and state; they placed the nation at the top of their scale of political values. They were ready to challenge the established political forms such as the Dualist system and Austrian pseudo-parliamentarianism and advocated radical changes in existing institutions and procedures. Suspicious of the nobility, they were anxious to bring into politics, as part of the nation, the poorer classes, especially the working class, through universal suffrage. Their programme had a more pronounced social content than that of the Old Czechs, although their proposals were not radical. Theirs was a more extreme and chauvinist nationalism, refusing to admit the necessity for or advisability of compromise, and not hesitating to imply that an Austria which failed to satisfy Czech national needs did not deserve their allegiance. As we have seen, the Young Czechs objected to the Old Czechs' wary, opportunist reckoning with existing realities and were ready, if necessary, to fly in the face of the wishes of the emperor, the government, and their allies.

As was recognized by many contemporaries and as can be seen in retrospect, the conflicting standpoints of the two movements were not unnatural reflections of the basic realities of the contemporary political situation.[55] It *was* valuable, as Rieger believed, to win the confidence of the emperor, to convince him of the loyalty of the Czechs to the monarchy, and to persuade him of the value of a loyal Czech nation and a united Bohemian kingdom as a bulwark against the

55 For contemporary evaluations of Old and Young Czechs, see the works cited above, n. 12. In addition, see the penetrating analysis by Josef Kaizl, in his articles in Čas, 1, 8, and 15 June 1889, "Český klub na říšské radě" (The Czech Club in the Reichsrat), republished in Tobolka, Kaizl: Z mého života, II, 531–43.

future expansion of Germany. This could only be done by due regard for the emperor's wishes and for the needs of the state, and by demonstrating the ability of the Right to provide a stable, reliable parliamentary majority. It was above all necessary to refrain from criticism of foreign policy, such as Rieger had indulged in during the sixties.[56] It was equally necessary to neutralize the Hungarians, who exerted a decisive influence on Austrian affairs and might again, as in 1871, prevent the fulfilment of Czech claims. This could only be achieved by an acceptance of the permanence of Dualism. It was essential to win and deepen the confidence of the prime minister, Taaffe, and to strengthen the position of the Czechs in the legislative and administrative organs of the monarchy. It was necessary to diminish the hostility of the Germans, and, if possible, to get them to acquiesce in the satisfaction of Czech claims.

On the other hand, Old Czech tactics involved serious faults which were also clearly recognized at the time by contemporary critics. During the eighties the Czech club was a "government party," providing the regime with needed support on all crucial issues and in spite of heart-breaking discouragements, never severing its relations with Taaffe during his long tenure of office. Concessions were made to the government but without binding promises of rewards. Threats of opposition were sometimes made but never carried out, thus successively weakening their value. Sacrifices were made to allies without a clear understanding as to what they would do for the Czechs in return. Although the Czechs could achieve nothing on their own and had to avoid creating a parliamentary crisis on every issue, they were rightly criticized for never standing as firmly as the Poles or the German conservatives on issues of direct concern to them.[57]

Moreover, Old Czechs committed other errors which weakened their credibility and lessened the respect of their own nation. In the first place, they did not frankly explain that the state right struggle had for the time being been given up and that the new policy was designed to achieve less spectacular, more prosaic, gains. Nor did they fully make clear the difficulties of opportunism: the slowness of the advance and the sacrifices involved came consequently as a surprise to their followers. Out of this came the charge of "two-facedness." In Vienna the Old Czechs were "statesmen" recognizing the needs of the state, supporting the government loyally, and satisfying themselves with small gains: in Bohemia they were still radicals, speaking of state right as in the time of passive resistance.[58]

In the second place, the Old Czechs tended to assume that they were the infallible spokesmen of the nation and to denounce all dissidents as traitors to the national cause. They demanded an almost blind obedience from their followers and imposed a rigid discipline on the club. The continual breaking away of individual members was in part due to deep and basic differences on ques-

56 See the articles by Pech cited in n. 11.
57 Tobolka, *Kaizl*, II, 536, also 542.
58 *Ibid.*, 532; Kramář, *Poznámky*, 13–14.

tions of principle and tactics, but reflected a more serious malady resulting from the personal and doctrinal authoritarianism of the Old Czech leaders.[59]

Young Czech policy, too, had its merits and its defects. With other critics of the Old Czechs, they saw the need for more courage and independence in order to reap the full benefits of activism and to maintain the confidence of the nation in these tactics. It must be "a determined, consistent and sincere opportunism," Josef Kaizl urged.[60] As Karel Kramář expressed it in 1888, there was need of

a more honourable Czech policy ... : not to fear the fall of the ministry and the destruction of that fatal fiction that the Right makes us concessions out of love and that *only we* have an interest in its maintenance, from which flows the necessity of giving way at any price; absolute definiteness as to *what we must* get for our support of the government, as long as it is not possible to introduce the whole state right programme – especially a systematic plan for the expansion of autonomy ...[61]

It was in these respects that criticism of Old Czech tactics was well justified. "A policy of the free hand willing to support every government which is just to us and determined to combat every one which does not fulfill the duty of the state to the Czech nation," as Kramář urged at a later date,[62] might well have brought additional benefits to the Czechs in the first period of activism.

Yet the Young Czechs, repelled by the "realism" of the Old Czechs, turned to the opposite extreme – to a naive idealism which took no account of the difficulties of the Czech political position. They attached supreme value to uncompromising statements of maximum aims and rejected compromises or sacrifices for the sake of partial immediate advance. Eduard Grégr, before 1879, had himself argued in favour of an opportunist policy of winning allies in Vienna and had admitted the impossibility of achieving anything in isolation. In the eighties, Young Czech criticism of the official policy passed from constructive realism to futile demagogy. Discipline was denounced as dictatorship of the nobility; compromise and concession as lack of principle and betrayal; careful reckoning with the given circumstances as cowardice and conservatism. Most dishonest of all was the Young Czechs' manipulation of the state right tradition for party ends. Nor did they offer a distinctive national programme or indicate a clear alternative strategy for the more effective accomplishment of national objectives. "Grégr knew how to negate everything which the Old Czechs asserted, but did not think what he would do in their place," wrote Jan Herben.[63] The authoritarianism of the Old Czechs had its counterpart in a similar Young Czech authoritarianism –

59 Herben, *Kniha vzpomínek*, 189–93.
60 Tobolka, *Kaizl*, II, 542.
61 Letter to Kaizl, 14 November 1888, in Tobolka, *Kaizl*, II, 478–9 n. Italics in the original.
62 Kramář, *Poznámky*, 44–6.
63 Herben, *Kniha vzpomínek*, 311–14, 417–27.

a tendency of subordination to the policy dictated by Julius Grégr in his powerful, widely read organ, *Národní listy*.[64]

In conclusion, it is interesting to note that certain contemporaries, while recognizing the good and bad characteristics of each party, were of the opinion that both, in the given situation, were necessary. Thus, Kaizl, at first an Old Czech, then independent, finally a Young Czech, wrote to his constituents in 1889 that both parties and both "currents of political ideas" were of value. He expressed the task of the one party as follows:

to strengthen gradually our position through diligent, hard, prudent and skilful work and to prepare us for the greater struggles and the higher aims of the future. One means to this, but not the only one, is the maintenance of the alliance with the government and parliamentary parties as long as the visible national gains resulting for us from this are in general greater than the injuries coming from it.

The other (Young Czech) party's task was to prevent this opportunist (mercenary) policy, which works slowly and piecemeal, going too far; to spur it on to a quicker, more energetic tempo; to maintain the connection with the great aims of the time of passivity – the political autonomy of Bohemia and the freedom and full political authority of the people.[65]

In similar terms, the Young Czech, Gustav Eim, who, as Vienna correspondent of *Národní listy*, had done much to discredit Old Czech policy, but had begun at the end of the eighties to turn towards the Old Czechs, described the functions of the two parties as follows: "One acts in accordance with what can be and the other with what has to be. Some of us keep to practical possibility; others to absolute truth. The latter carry on a policy of principle and tenet and the others a policy of the moment, of opportunism, a policy *à propos*."[66]

As a result of the strengths and weaknesses of both parties, many persons chose to take up a position somewhat midway between them. This was true of a number of members of the Czech club who, although Young Czech at heart, remained for a long time in the club and criticized the independents for their extremism. Other younger men of distinction, destined later to emerge as political leaders of first magnitude, for instance, the so-called Realists – Kaizl, Kramář, and Masaryk – at first attempted to influence, and improve the quality of, both parties without joining either. Masaryk, for instance, argued strongly that it was necessary to "overcome both Old Czechism and Young Czechism."[67] When the question of joining one or the other party arose, the Realists were divided, Kaizl favouring union with the Old Czechs and a reform of this party, and Kramář, a union with the Young Czechs and the improvement of that party.

64 Tobolka, *Kaizl*, ɪɪ, 397.
65 *Ibid.*, 545–7.
66 J. Penížek ed., *Politické úvahy Gustava Eima* (Prague, 1897), 571–2.
67 Masaryk, *Naše nynější krise*, 107. See also Doležal, *Masarykova cesta životem*, ɪɪ, 28, 35.

Masaryk, in spite of severe doubts about both, negotiated with the Old Czechs, in vain, and then in the end joined the Young Czechs, only to break with them at a later period.[68]

CONCLUSION

As a national minority people within the Austrian Monarchy, the Czechs were faced with a continuing and painful dilemma. Two alternatives were in theory open to them: either to reject Austria entirely and by revolutionary or other means to separate from an alien system, or to accept Austria and work within this framework to attain at least minimum national goals. Revolutionary resistance to Austria, which more radical Czechs attempted on a small scale in 1848, was not seriously contemplated by Czech political leaders in the subsequent six decades of Austria's life and was in fact not a realistic option under existing circumstances. Once the Czechs had accommodated themselves with apparent finality to the Austrian framework of Czech political life, three alternative strategies of political action gradually crystallized. The first, passive resistance, was attempted without success until 1879 and was then abandoned in subsequent decades. The second, positive cooperation with the Austrian regime, was tried from 1879 to 1893, and then in diverse forms during most of the later years of the monarchy. Finally, parliamentary opposition, including radical obstruction of the procedures of the representative organs, was advocated in words in the eighties and in a limited degree carried out in action, and was implemented on a broader scale in later decades.

The eighties, like later stages through which Czechs passed in working out their fate within Austria, taught important lessons and exerted a striking influence on the future. This period demonstrated that a policy of positive cooperation with Austria, despite frustrations and sacrifices, could bear fruit in the form of concrete gains for the national cause. It is not surprising that the Young Czechs, who identified themselves at the time as radical critics of the opportunist policy, later resorted to a similar "step-by-step" tactic (*etapová taktika*) of their own and supplemented Old Czech achievements with additional gains.[69] Nor was it unnatural that such successes for the Czech cause confirmed the decision to abandon passive resistance, which was never again resorted to. More than that, the steady progress of the Czech nation could not help but produce a more positive attitude toward the Habsburg state, or at least a less reluctant acceptance of it. As a result, pro-Austrian sentiment was dominant among

68 The attitude of the Realists to the Old and Young Czechs and their negotiations with both have been described in detail by Herben, *Kniha vzpomínek*; Odložilík, in articles cited; and Křížek, *T. G. Masaryk*. Many documents concerning these events are given in Tobolka, *Kaizl*, II, 418ff.
69 For a defence of later Young Czech "opportunism," see Karel Kramář, *Poznámky*; J. Kaizl, *České myšlenky*; V. Škarda, "Dvacet pět let činné politiky" (Twenty-five Years of Active Policy), in M. Sísová, ed., *Výbor statí a řečí Dr. Václava Škardy* (Prague, 1912).

Czechs down to 1914, and hardly a single political personality espoused the idea of Czech independence.[70]

On the other hand, the experience of the eighties, which was repeated in different form in later decades, made it equally apparent that the Czechs were fated to live within a political framework that necessarily set strict limits to their freedom of action and to the degree to which their needs and wishes could be satisfied. By constant struggle, successes were registered, but only in the face of bitter resistance from opposing forces, such as the Germans, and never with enthusiasm by the ruling circles. In the eighties and subsequently, there was among Czechs always an undercurrent of disappointment and a growing disillusionment with the policy of activism. This helped to create a climate of dissatisfaction with the existing state and sowed the seeds of disaffection with the entire Austrian system. Although seldom explicitly formulated, these anti-Austrian feelings were sometimes implicitly intimated and, perhaps subconsciously, exerted a powerful influence on Czech thinking.

The eighties provide an instructive case study of particular forms of Czech adaptation to the realities of Austrian life and particular manifestations of the continuing dilemma of Czech politics. It would be an oversimplification to describe the period as "typical" of later decades of Czech political experience or as decisive in moulding Czech attitudes toward Austria.[71] After 1890, many new issues appeared in political life. New parties were formed, some with a class basis rather than with an exclusively national foundation. The objectives of Czech politics, while bearing some resemblance to those of the eighties, shifted. Yet always there was a somewhat similar dialectic of gains and frustrations, of positive and negative reactions, of pro-Austrian and anti-Austrian tendencies. The decision in 1918 to opt for independence was not inevitable, nor was it predetermined by the experiences of the eighties which, in any case, tended paradoxically in opposite directions. Yet the widespread dissatisfaction with the achievements of opportunism and the adoption of radical oppositional tactics and slogans had stimulated powerful forces which, in the favourable circum-

70 To this extent, the Marxists are right in stressing the *rakušanství* (Austrianism) of all pre-war Czech parties (Šverma, *Česká otázka*, I, 82–4). Harrison Thomson, without offering evidence, has argued that during the whole of this and subsequent periods, Czechs were seeking and preparing for political independence (*Czechoslovakia in European History*, 1943 ed., 189). A different viewpoint was expressed by Odložilík (*Nástin československých dějin*, 1937 ed., 79). He notes that the breaking of the links with the monarchy was, with rare exceptions, not generally advocated and that the conviction was widespread that in the given circumstances it was necessary to reckon with its existence.

71 Such a view was expressed by the Czech journalist J. Penížek, in his *Česká aktivita v létech 1878–1918* (2 vols.; Prague, 1930) where he wrote that the disappointment of the Czech nation in the Taaffe government led directly to the overthrow in 1918 and to independence (II, 155).

stances at the close of the First World War, contributed to the decision in favour of independence and ultimately overwhelmed the opposing tendencies toward loyalty and cooperation.[72]

72 Odložilík has argued that independence was not a fortunate accident, but was rooted deep in history, including the "school of political experience" from 1848 to 1918. "The conviction that they [Czechs and Slovaks] would not get far either by attending parliament and an activist policy, or by persistent and consistent opposition, and that only complete independence would bring liberation, had its best support in the bitter experiences of these times." (*Nastín*, 1946 ed., 146.)

Kramář, Kaizl, and the Hegemony of the Young Czech Party, 1891–1901

STANLEY B. WINTERS

IN NUMEROUS GENERAL HISTORIES of the Habsburg Monarchy and modern Czecho-slovakia the Young Czech party has fared poorly. This is understandable because history is rarely written from the standpoint of the loser, and the Young Czechs in the long run were losers. Their impressive electoral majorities in the 1890s dwindled by 1907 to less than a quarter of the Czech deputies victorious in Austria's first parliamentary election under universal, equal manhood suffrage. Even at its peak, from 1895 to 1897, the party only partly achieved its economic and cultural goals, and it failed completely in its maximal objective of autonomy for the Lands of the Bohemian Crown (Bohemia, Moravia, and Austrian Silesia) within a federal Cisleithanian Austria. Nevertheless, during the sixteen-year period in which it was predominant it was sufficiently strong to survive factionalism, official disfavour, and sharp competition from rival parties. Persons notable during the interwar Czechoslovak Republic such as President Tomáš G. Masaryk (1850–1937) served political apprenticeships in the party or in related groups. Karel Kramář (1860–1937), first prime minister under the republic, entered the Austrian Parliament as a Young Czech and after the turn of the century became the party's foremost spokesman.

The author expresses to the Newark College of Engineering and the National Endowment for the Humanities appreciation for funds which helped his research on this essay.

The Young Czech Party, officially the National Liberal party, was launched as an independent political force in 1874. It campaigned for democratic and liberal reforms and full national equality on a platform borrowed from various parties and interest groups including the small farmers, the dominant Old Czech party (officially the National party), business and industry, the nationalistic intelligentsia, and the Social Democrats. But with the development of a complex Czech social structure and political life, accompanying economic and cultural advances of the late 1890s and years following, which were expressed particularly in a pronounced rise in national self-consciousness, the Young Czech party found itself hard-pressed to please its constituent elements. The diverse groups which had united under its banner in the late 1880s and early 1890s, when it was storming the fortresses of privilege, melted away and it came increasingly to represent Czech financial, commercial, and industrial interests. Viewed within the broad framework of the Czech national renascence the party was an important force in the later stages of a transition in politics, social structure, and public opinion from an antiquated, narrowly based liberalism to an insurgent mass nationalism with strongly democratic overtones.

CZECH POLITICAL REALISM

The emergence of the Young Czech party as a powerful factor in Bohemian and Austrian politics was made possible by significant changes in Czech society that were well under way in the 1870s and continued into subsequent decades. In Bohemian towns and cities, and above all in the regional metropolis of Prague, changes were visible in population growth, expansion of the working class, and adoption by urban families of new styles of life according to nationality and social class.[1] In rural areas, meanwhile, Czech farmers organized for political action to protect themselves against harmful price fluctuations, periodic crises in sugar-beet production, and ruinous competition from United States and Hungarian grains.[2] The social mobility of the era was typified by the family of Petr Kramář (1834–1907), an enterprising nationalistic farmer from the Krkonoše mountain region in northern Bohemia who invested in a lucrative construction business. He made certain that his only son, Karel, received an education second to none of his compatriots. Young Karel Kramář attended the *gymnasium* in the Malá strana district of Prague, a school which educated many middle-class youths who later became civic and political leaders. He participated in patriotic demonstrations during the

1 Jan Havránek, "Social Classes, Nationality Ratios and Demographic Trends in Prague, 1880–1900," *Historica*, XIII (Prague, 1966), 171–208; *Atlas československých dějin*, ed. Jaroslav Purš (Prague, 1965), section 26; Jurij Křížek, "La crise du dualisme et le dernier Compromis austro-hongrois, 1897–1907," *Historica*, XII (Prague, 1966), esp. 85–105.

2 Kamil Krofta, *Dějiny selského stavu*, 2nd ed. (Prague, 1949), 436–8; Jan Havránek, "Die ökonomische und politische Lage der Bauernschaft in den böhmischen Ländern in den letzten Jahrzehnten des 19. Jahrhunderts," *Jahrbuch für Wirtschaftsgeschichte*, II (Berlin, 1966), 129ff.

Balkan crisis of the late 1870s and inclined, as did many fellow students, toward the Young Czech brand of militant nationalism.[3]

Upon graduation from the gymnasium, Kramář spent a year in western Europe studying at Berlin and Strasbourg and then studied history and law at the Charles-Ferdinand University in Prague, recently partitioned into Czech and German institutions, from which he was graduated in 1884 as Doctor of Jurisprudence. During the next two years he attended the École libre des sciences politiques in Paris (the first Czech to enrol there) and the University of Berlin, in the economics seminar of Professor Adolf Wagner (1835–1917), a leading *Kathedersozialist* and partisan of social reform on the Bismarckian model. Between 1886 and 1888 he joined public-minded Czech intellectuals in a circle which included the political economist Josef Kaizl (1854–1901) and the positivist social philosopher Tomáš G. Masaryk.

Kaizl came from a southern Bohemian family of minor officials and, like Kramář, studied in Strasbourg and Prague, where he combined law with political economy. He was named *docent* at the Charles-Ferdinand University in 1879 and four years later achieved a professorship. Practical politics attracted him. Joining the Old Czech party, he served as a deputy in Parliament (the Reichsrat) in Vienna from 1885 till 1887, when he resigned, ostensibly in protest against new governmental decrees on education, but actually as a result of disagreements with the party's conservative leadership.[4] Kaizl was a strong personality, independent in opinion, a representative of the anti-romantic outlook of the rising generation. A democratic moderate who looked askance at status based on hereditary privilege, he was also cool toward radicalism and violence. From 1883 onward he became friendly with Masaryk, but despite their mutual interests and collaboration there seems always to have been some rivalry between them.[5] Masaryk, professor of philosophy at the new Czech University since 1882, also inclined toward politics, but he was unable to get either an Old or Young Czech endorsement for his candidacy and hence had no parliamentary experience prior to 1891.[6] In association with these two learned, self-assured, and ambitious men, young Kramář was soon launched upon the political career for which he had been systematically prepared.

3 Karel Kramář, *Paměti*, 2nd ed., ed. Karel Hoch (Prague, 1938), 37–46; Vladimír Sís, *Karel Kramář, život a dílo: Skizza* (Prague, 1930), 13–21; Zdeněk Nejedlý, *T. G. Masaryk*, 4 vols. in 5 (Prague, 1930–7), II, 182.

4 Otakar Odložilík, "Enter Masaryk: A Prelude to His Political Career," *Journal of Central European Affairs*, x/1 (1950), 32.

5 Hugo Traub, "Kaizl a Masaryk," *Masarykův sborník*, III (Prague, 1929), 289–302; Albín Bráf, "Dr. Josef Kaizl," *Osvěta*, XXXI/ii, no. 10 (1901), 857–81.

6 Odložilík, "Enter Masaryk." There are no critical scholarly biographies of Masaryk in English. This middle stage in his career, extending from the mid-1880s, where Nejedlý's work leaves off, to the First World War, is usually superficially treated. The most detailed study of part of the period is Jurij Křížek, *T. G. Masaryk a česká politika* (Prague, 1959).

The events which catalysed the progressive intellectuals into political activity occurred in Bohemia in the 1880s in the setting of intense cultural ferment which engendered a hypersensitivity toward matters of Czech history and particularly where national honour was involved. At the new university, faculty and students divided into progressive and traditionalist factions,[7] while professors and politicians hotly debated the authenticity of literary manuscripts allegedly discovered by the romantic poet and scholar Václav Hanka (1791–1861), in a controversy that created lasting enmities. Masaryk, the historian Jaroslav Goll (1846–1929), the philologist Jan Gebauer (1838–1907), and other critics of the manuscripts were charged with treason by the leadership of both major Czech parties. Kaizl abstained from polemics but remained loyal to Masaryk and Goll, with whom he was editing an avant-garde scholarly periodical, *Athenaeum*. Kramář was not directly involved in the dispute but adopted a pragmatic position that foreshadowed his future approach to many issues. He respected the scholarly integrity of Masaryk and his colleagues and defended their right and duty to criticize; however, he felt that the manuscripts, even if they were forgeries as charged, had performed "a great, truly beneficent mission" for the nation and as forgeries were excusable because of the many historic crimes that had been committed against Czech culture.[8]

The prejudice and vindictiveness displayed in this dispute by the entrenched forces of the political and intellectual status quo challenged Masaryk, Kaizl, and Kramář to reform Czech public life along progressive and democratic lines. In the course of 1888 and 1889 they came to form a loose grouping whose political creed was known as Realism.[9] The Realists hoped to win a balance of power between the Old and Young Czechs, either by organizing an independent third party, an idea which was soon abandoned, or by supporting one of the two parties in exchange for revision of the party's programme according to Realist recommendations. The outcome, they hoped, would be an all-national coalition of the moderate liberal centre that could lead the Czech struggle for equality and autonomy in Austria. Other professional men associated with the Realists contributed money and articles to *Čas* (Time), a periodical converted into the Realist organ and published weekly. *Čas* influenced the educated public more than its modest press run of about 1300 copies might indicate. It scolded both Czech liberal parties for sacrificing national needs to narrow party interests. It attacked the government for denying full and equal rights to the Czechs and other Austrian Slavs. It criticized Czech conservatives and radicals alike for preventing national unity against German-Magyar economic competition and imperial German control of Austrian foreign policy.

7 František Kavka, ed., *Stručné dějiny university Karlovy* (Prague, 1964), 224ff., 243–6.
8 Kramář, *Paměti*, 80.
9 Křížek, *T. G. Masaryk a česká politika*, 39–70; Zdeněk V. Tobolka, *Politické dějiny československého národa od r. 1848 až do dnešní doby*, 4 vols. in 5 (Prague, 1932–7), iii/i, 275–92.

The Realists began their efforts at a time when the political leadership of the Czech nation by the "post-March" generation, in the ranks of the Old Czech party, showed signs of crisis. The party was incapable of modernizing its tactics and programme sufficiently to meet the growing challenge from the Young Czechs, whose mass base was enormously strengthened in the late 1880s when many small farmers turned to it in hopes of alleviating their production and marketing problems. In the landmark elections of July 1889 to the Bohemian Diet, the Young Czechs made substantial inroads at the Old Czechs' expense, although they still did not constitute a majority of the Czech deputies.[10] This was a great victory for two of the founders and leading personalities of the Young Czech party: Eduard Grégr (1829–1907), one-time medical scientist turned militant radical, and his brother Julius Grégr (1831–96), a proprietor and chief editor of the party organ, the influential Prague daily newspaper Národní listy (National Gazette).

Concerned over the repetitious, partisan campaign appeals of the major Czech parties and fearful of the growing influence of Young Czech radicals, in November 1890 the Realists issued "A Proposal for a People's Programme."[11] They stressed evolutionary progress through the cooperation of the ruling elements in Austria with various nationality and interest groups. Their demands included abolition of aristocratic privileges; broadening of educational opportunities, especially for women; equality of the Czech language with German in public and official usage; protection for Czech-owned enterprises against outside economic competition; updating and implementing of historic Czech claims of the indivisibility, unity, and autonomy of the Lands of the Bohemian Crown;[12] and equal rights for all nationalities within a federal Cisleithanian Austria. Essentially the programme voiced the Austro-Slavism enunciated by František Palacký in 1848 but modified in the light of four decades of sometimes bitter experience. Portions of the Realist programme were eventually incorporated into the Young Czech campaign platform in the parliamentary elections of 1891.

THE REALIST – YOUNG CZECH MERGER

The circumstance which facilitated Young Czech political hegemony was the transformation in national public opinion brought about by publication of the

10 Národní listy, xxix/181 (3 July 1889); Tobolka, Politické dějiny, 252f. When all returns were in, the Old Czechs outnumbered their rivals 58 to 39, but before the elections their advantage had been in the ratio of 9 to 1.

11 "Návrh programu lidového," Čas, iv (1890), 689–94.

12 The claim to the unity and autonomy of the Lands of the Bohemian Crown is expressed in the Czech phrase "České státní právo" or the German "Böhmisches Staatsrecht," hereinafter expressed as "state right." Not only was a historic charter or system of public law involved, but also a set of political demands advanced at one time or another by almost every Czech political party in the half-century preceding the First World War. On the political uses of state right, see the preceding essay by H. Gordon Skilling in this volume. On the legal and historic evolution of the concept, see Robert A. Kann, Das Nationalitätenproblem der Habsburgermonarchie, 2 vols. (Graz and Cologne, 1964), i, 149ff.

terms of the so-called Vienna Compromise of 1890 and expressed at the polls in the general parliamentary elections of the following year.[13] The Compromise was one of several adjustments in nationality relationships which various Austrian governments sponsored after the Austro-Hungarian Compromise (the *Ausgleich*) of 1867 had aroused Slav, and especially Czech, hostility toward the dual monarchy it created. Through the agreement reached between the Old Czechs and the Bohemian Germans in January 1890, the emperor and his minister-president Count Eduard Taaffe (1833–95) hoped to resolve these lingering hostilities in a manner favourable to the maintenance of the political status quo; namely, to bolster Taaffe's "Iron Ring" parliamentary coalition, already weakened in 1889 by the Old Czech set-back in the Diet elections, by reaching a settlement that would enhance the prestige of two other parties to the negotiations: the loyal, conservative Bohemian aristocracy and the Bohemian Germans, who would then end their three-year-old boycott of the Diet.

The Young Czechs stood apart from the Compromise negotiations, neither participating in them nor signing the final accord. They simply had not been invited, and even if they had, they might well have rejected the agreement in order to further differentiate themselves from their Old Czech rivals and capitalize on the public reaction. Indeed, once the full extent of the concessions made by the Old Czechs to German demands became known, Czech sentiment was galvanized along radical and nationalistic lines far beyond the expectations of the established political leadership. Vigorous protest demonstrations occurred from mid-January onward in Prague and in Czech areas of Bohemia. After some initial hesitancy, the Young Czechs took command of the protest movement, which was aggravated by Czech resentment over repressive police measures ordered by the royal governor of Bohemia, Count Franz Thun (1847–1916).[14] The Realists were slow to join the opposition. Their initial reaction was expressed by Kramář in *Čas*. He acknowledged the public's impatience with the Old Czechs but cautioned readers not to form hasty judgments against the Compromise that might foster "an undisciplined radicalism."[15] It was only after an interval of six months, during which the Realists discussed their potential relationship to the major parties, that they took a firm stand against the implementation of the Compromise and termed the Old Czechs incapable of further claiming to represent the nation.[16]

Although the Realists had now severed their links with the Old Czechs, they encountered several obstacles in attempting to reach an understanding with the Young Czechs. One was a journalistic feud between *Národní listy* and *Čas*, edited

---

13 Karel Kramář, *Anmerkungen zur böhmischen Politik* (Vienna, 1906), 5; Jan Havránek, "The Development of Czech Nationalism," *Austrian History Yearbook*, III/ii (Houston, 1967), 253.

14 Arthur Skedl, ed., *Der politische Nachlass des Grafen Eduard Taaffe* (Vienna, 1922), 474–80. On the press reaction see Karel Tůma, "Padesát let boje a práce," *Půl století "Národních listů" almanach: 1860–1910* (Prague, ca. 1910), 22–4.

15 Kramář, "Výhledy," *Čas*, IV (1890), 1–3.

16 Kramář, "Dopisy domácí i zahraničné," *Čas*, IV (1890), 441.

by Jan Herben (1857–1936), a follower of Masaryk. Another was a personal animosity between Masaryk and Julius Grégr dating to the controversy over the Hanka manuscripts. Kramář was determined to proceed, and Josef Kaizl came over to his side.[17] The quinquennial elections to Parliament were approaching; a Young Czech victory was in the air. Kaizl was interested in acquiring a stable party base to further his career, while Kramář, lacking only a few months of his thirtieth birthday, the minimum age for candidates, wanted a deputy's seat badly.

In the fall of 1890 Kramář was named titular editor of *Čas*, replacing Jan Herben as a sop to *Národní listy*. Then, at Kramář's initiative, a meeting was arranged between Masaryk and Julius Grégr. The two men outwardly buried past quarrels and agreed to the terms of a Realist merger with the party.[18] The settlement endowed the Young Czechs with respectability and expertise through association with a distinguished group of scholars, journalists, and other public figures. The Realists ostensibly secured a vehicle through which they could realize their political ideals and ambitions. The merger, however, left Kramář strangely disquieted. As the Realist most zealous for its consummation, he felt that his role in expediting it had been insufficiently acknowledged.[19] He resented entering the party as a rank-and-file member while Kaizl was appointed to the board of trustees and Masaryk to the executive committee. For the time being he buried his discontent in a spirited defence of the merger, warning the party that it had to take a different path than the Old Czechs or suffer the same fate.[20] The Realist–Young Czech *rapprochement*, it turned out, came not a moment too soon, for in January 1891 Parliament was dissolved and Minister-President Taaffe proclaimed new elections to be held in March.

The general parliamentary elections of 1891 form a watershed in Czech and Austrian history. They opened an era wherein parliamentary majorities shifted according to the specific issues affecting component parties, thus signalling the decline of a relatively stable governmental order. In Bohemia, the results established Young Czech supremacy; Old Czech control of national politics through the alliance of the urban patriciate with the conservative landowning aristocracy was destroyed. Taaffe was forced to woo the German Liberals, absent from government for over a decade, as replacements for the greatly diminished Old Czechs; in so doing, he strained his relations with one of the pillars of his regime, the Polish club from Galicia. An inkling of the extent of the set-back may be gleaned from

17 Josef Kaizl, *Z mého života*, ed. Z. V. Tobolka, 3 vols. in 4 (Prague, 1909–14), ii, 605f.; Křížek, *T. G. Masaryk a česká politika*, 143f.
18 Kramář, "Vstup realistů do strany mladočeské," *Půl století*, 49–53; also Jaroslav Chlubna, "Vstup realistů do mladočeské strany," *Národní myšlenka*, xiii (1935–6), 76–84.
19 Kramář, *Paměti*, 262, 277; Kamil Krofta, *Politická postava K. Kramáře* (Prague, 1930), 12, comments that Kramář played the key role in the merger negotiations.
20 Kramář, "Na nových drahách," *Čas*, iv (1890), 802. See Masaryk's similar warning: "We must put aside the policies of the Old Czechs, else the nation will put us aside as it did Dr. Rieger"; letter to Kramář, 28 July 1893, in Kramář, pozůstalost, Archiv Národního musea (hereinafter ANM), 2–3/6371–4.

the results of the voting among the Czechs of Bohemia; in urban curiae the Young Czechs won twenty-one seats with 57 per cent of the votes to twelve seats for the Old Czechs; in rural curiae the Young Czechs swept all sixteen seats with 58 per cent of the votes. Kramář ran successfully in a constituency in his native mountain region, Kaizl in a working-class neighbourhood in Prague, and Masaryk in an urban area in southwestern Bohemia. In return for the party's endorsement the three men accepted its regulations and by-laws. These required joining the party club in Parliament, adhering to its discipline, keeping club matters confidential, refraining from public attack upon fellow members, surrendering their seats in event of a split with their constituents, and resigning upon receipt of a government job or other emolument that made them dependent upon the regime in any way.[21] The strict discipline manifest in these regulations was perhaps due to the party's posture of unrelenting opposition to the established order; but this discipline proved difficult to enforce because of several deficiencies inherent in the party's organizational structure, which must be examined in greater detail.

Viewed in organizational terms, the Young Czech deputies' club in Vienna soon constituted a formidable new force in the party, rivalling in authority and prestige the executive committee in Prague. Hitherto the Prague group had exercised virtually sole decision-making power in the party. Its members were mainly lower middle-class politicians of radical bent, many of whom held seats in the Bohemian Diet and jobs in the party press, in private business, or in professions of modest status. The members of the deputies' club stood somewhat higher in regard to education and social position and inclined toward moderate, practical policies. They included seven lawyers, five university professors, four physicians, and four well-to-do farmers; some were also directors in banks and industries.[22] This dichotomy of social background and political outlook soon became a divisive factor. Kramář, as the youngest deputy in Parliament, was particularly sensitive to such distinctions. Self-confident and proud, cosmopolitan in education and manner, and of independent means through his father's business, he felt detached from the ebullient militancy of the Prague leadership and even superior to many of his associates in Vienna.[23] These sentiments, which could not be concealed, created a gap that took some years for Kramář to bridge, and then not fully. Kaizl and Masaryk, more experienced in the ways of the world, learned to live with the new situation, although they were not happy with it.

What was the inner nature of the party that now claimed to hold aloft the

21 The Young Czech party's regulations and by-laws are contained in various brochures, issued periodically and often without date or place of publication: *Stanovy klubu neodvislých poslanců českých v radě říšské*, 4 pp.; *Stanovy klubu svobodomyslných lidových poslanců v radě říšské*, 4 pp.; *Valný sjezd národní strany svobodomyslné* (1890–93), 4 pp. For copies of these items I am indebted to Dr. Jaromír Loužil, Director, Literární archiv, Památník národního písemnictví na Strahově (hereinafter abbreviated as LANM), in Prague.
22 Křížek, *T. G. Masaryk a česká politika*, 177; Michal Navrátil, *Čechové na říšské radě, 1879–1900* (Tábor, 1903), *passim*.
23 Kramář, *Paměti*, 274; Bedřich Hlaváč, "Vídeňské vzpomínky," ANM typescript, pp. 103–4.

290 / STANLEY B. WINTERS

banner of the Czech national movement? On the surface it was a coalition of elements from the Czech urban and farming middle classes which had temporarily united against the Germanizing tendencies of the Compromise of 1890. Paradoxically, this factor, which helped make the party's triumph possible, was also a source of weakness; for, once public attention shifted from the Compromise to other matters, the party was compelled to take stands that clarified its mission but antagonized many supporters. The party's recent and sudden growth also prevented it from consolidating its victory.[24] Internally, three main factions evolved after the 1891 elections. One faction, standing for large business interests, had realized that the Old Czech sun was setting and switched allegiance shortly before the elections. A second, coming from the sugar-beet farming areas, represented the rural bourgeoisie who had become politically active in the 1880s. A third, centring on the party's founders and pioneers, included small-town and Prague radical democrats grouped about *Národní listy*. Within this last faction there were subgroups which differed according to their degree of opposition to the government, relationship to the working class and smaller farmers, and involvement with anti-Semitism and extreme nationalism. The Realists occupied a special place in this constellation. They were distinguishable by their social reformism and tactical flexibility but exerted little influence in the party's executive committee and relied upon the deputies' club and *Čas* for support.

The most serious of these organizational and factional divisions was the one between the executive committee and the deputies' club, for it embodied both the ideological and social dichotomies. Responsibility for this division rested to a considerable extent with the opinions and policies of Julius Grégr and the powerful party organ he controlled. Grégr, and the Czech electorate, derived much of their knowledge about the parliamentary situation in Vienna from the dispatches of Gustav Eim (1849–97), a Young Czech deputy and Vienna correspondent for *Národní listy*, and an outstanding Czech journalist. Eim, whose enmity could affect a deputy's standing in the party,[25] grew increasingly in the 1890s to fear radical extremism and support evolutionary change in cooperation with constituted authority. According to Kramář, with whom Eim feuded several times before their relationship improved in the mid-1890s, Eim's dispatches led Grégr to discount the possibility of a constructive Czech parliamentary opposition to the Taaffe regime and to exaggerate the adverse effects upon the Czechs of a re-entry of the German Left into a working relationship with the government.[26] Grégr also alienated some of the Young Czech radicals by restraining the expression of Panslavic sentiments and attacks upon Austrian foreign policy in *Národní listy* as

24 Kramář, "Dějiny české politiky nové doby," *Česká politika*, ed. Z. V. Tobolka, 5 vols. in 6 (Prague, 1906–13), III, 528; Oskar Baron Parish, *Vzpomínky z doby Badeniho* (Prague, 1907), 3f.
25 Kramář, *Paměti*, 275; Tobolka, *Politické dějiny*, III/i, 250–2; Josef Holeček, *Tragédie Julia Grégra* (Prague, 1911–14), 385–97.
26 Kramář, *Paměti*, 284.

part of a secret pledge which he made under pressure from the governor, Count Thun.[27] Nor had Grégr been genuinely reconciled to the Realists. He feared they wanted to displace him from authority and substitute for *Národní listy* another newspaper as party organ.[28] Kramář and Kaizl respected Grégr's power in the party, but neither man reacted as negatively to him as Masaryk did. Kaizl, who found the party congenial to his aspirations, avoided any embroilment that might endanger his climb up the leadership ladder.[29] Although Kramář felt that the party sachems were slow to recognize his ability, he always observed party discipline, even in the face of personal attacks.[30] Masaryk, however, nourished Grégr's festering suspicions of his Czech patriotism and party loyalty by criticizing party strategy in public and through the columns of *Čas*. Tensions between Grégr and Masaryk, and among the Realists themselves, culminated in the summer of 1893, when Masaryk was condemned by the executive committee for conduct allegedly damaging to the party's welfare and prestige. When Masaryk appealed to Kaizl and Kramář for support, they declined in the interests of party solidarity and their own careers. In September he resigned his seats in Parliament and the Bohemian Diet.

Masaryk's withdrawal inevitably ended the Realists' collaboration and so the movement, in its original form, dissolved as a current in political thought and as a faction within the party. Kramář and Kaizl resigned from *Čas* and refused to participate in *Naše doba* (Our Era), a new periodical co-founded by Masaryk. Kaizl thereafter became the leading academic luminary in the Young Czech party; his prestige, coupled with his undeniable expertise in the organizational aspects of politics, soon won him a leadership role in both the Prague and Vienna groups. Kramář, liberated from Masaryk's friendly but paternal guidance, devoted himself more to politics and less to journalism. Before he could attain the party status he desired, however, he had to dispel distrust among some of the old-timers about his attitude and motives. His own faith in the party had been shaken by events in 1893,[31] which included not only certain irregularities surrounding the condemnation of Masaryk but also Young Czech involvement in violent protests against police repression and for democratic reforms, objectives which he favoured but

---

27 Letter of T. G. Masaryk, 29 January 1890, ANM 2–3/6331; Skedl, ed. *Der politische Nachlass des Grafen Eduard Taaffe*, 616.
28 See especially Masaryk's speech to his constituents in Strakonice, 22 September 1891, reprinted in *Čas*, v (1891), 622–9, in which he proposed that *Národní listy* be replaced as party organ by a new daily newspaper. Faced with such threats, Julius Grégr wanted to sever the newspaper's relationship to the party, but his brother Eduard argued against this on the grounds that the Realists would then seize the leadership of the party. See J. Grégr, pozůstalost, LANM no. 26, 25 March 1893. For this reference I am indebted to Mr. Bruce Garver of Yale University.
29 Kramář, *Paměti*, 92.
30 On his quarrels with G. Eim and J. Vašatý see B. Němec *et al.*, eds, *Sborník dra Karla Kramáře k jeho 70. narozeninám* (Prague, 1930), 353f.; also Kramář, *Paměti*, 294f., 301–5.
31 Kaizl, *Z mého života*, III/i, 259n.

means with which he disagreed. To secure another forum in which to vent his opinions, and to be closer to Prague, he ran for a seat in the Diet, winning a by-election in January 1894.

THE YOUNG CZECHS IN PARLIAMENTARY OPPOSITION

Notwithstanding the organizational problems cited above, the Young Czech deputies' club soon grasped the complexities of parliamentary affairs and became an asset to the party. The party's epochal election victory of 1891 affected the alignments within the new Chamber of Deputies which convened in April. The thirty-seven Young Czechs constituted themselves as "The Club of Independent Czech Deputies in Parliament." Reinforced by some liberal Slovenes and former Old Czechs, they became part of the opposition alongside thirty-one German radicals and Christian Socials. The pro-government Old Czech parliamentary club dissolved. Its eighteen deputies from the Bohemian aristocracy joined the conservative club of Count Karl Hohenwart (1824–99), and several Old Czechs from Bohemia joined ten from Moravia in a separate group. The other blocs in the 353-man chamber supported the government with varying degrees of loyalty and consistency depending as much upon their relations with each other as with the regime. The break-up of the "Iron Ring" coalition forced Minister-President Taaffe to depend upon the cooperation of the German liberal Left, in exchange for which he pledged to implement the provisions of the Vienna Compromise of 1890. Because of bitter Young Czech and popular opposition to the Compromise, however, he was unable to fulfil his promise, and support from the Left diminished. His makeshift regime entered a crisis in the fall of 1893, when he proposed to modify the electoral system in Cisleithanian Austria in order to bolster his majority in preparation for important debates on the state budget and the defence law. In October he submitted to Parliament a bill that would have amended the system by dropping the five-gulden requirement of 1882 and expanding the voting lists in the rural and urban curiae to include all eligible males thirty years and older. The number of voters would have increased from 1.7 million to 4.0 million or about one-third of the adult males in Austria. The bill, submitted without Taaffe's usual finesse, shocked the conservative parties, traditional bulwarks of his majority. Their negative reaction was the immediate cause for his government's downfall in November.

The Young Czechs wanted franchise reform in order to strengthen their nationalist demands by opening new channels of support from the Czech masses. They also wanted the reform to be of a nature and to be achieved in a manner that would profit them at the polls. For these reasons, and to fulfil their claims to be a democratic party, they advocated suffrage reform and other progressive demands in the legislative debates.[32] Kramář in January 1893 called for a general franchise

32 Jan Havránek, *Boj za všeobecné přímé a rovné hlasovací právo roku 1893* (Prague, 1964), 20–5.

reform to permit the working class to vote. On 17 March 1893, the party offered to Parliament the sweeping proposal of deputy Jan Slavík (1846–1910), which would have granted the direct, equal, and secret franchise to all males twenty-four years of age and older and enlarged the Chamber of Deputies to 400 members. The Slavík proposal had no chance of acceptance, but it kept alive the party's reputation as a progressive force, made some inroads upon the growing Social Democratic appeal to the masses, and foreshadowed reforms that were eventually enacted into law in 1907.

After the demise of the Taaffe government, the Young Czechs found new problems arising alongside unresolved old ones. Franchise reform dominated the agenda of the incoming Coalition government of Minister-President Prince Alfred Windischgrätz (1851–1927). Social Democracy was attracting a broad following, the farmers were tending toward independent political action, and Prague lay under martial law proclaimed in September as Governor Franz Thun's answer to militant Czech protest demonstrations. In the next few months the party met these problems by revising its parliamentary tactics and tightening its discipline. Under the Coalition the Young Czechs provided the core of the opposition along with the Christian Socials and the German nationalists. Eight Old Czechs from Moravia and ten South Slavs allied themselves with the party's parliamentary club, constituting in late November a "Slavic Opposition" group. Kramář justified the continued Czech opposition by charging the regime with lacking the will to implement a definite programme and with having no solutions to Czech demands other than police measures.[33]

The issue of franchise reform proved critical to the Coalition regime. Prince Windischgrätz proposed in February 1894 the creation of a fifth election curia of forty-three deputies from urban and rural districts, ten of them from Bohemia, while retaining in the other four curiae the principle of class representation based generally upon an individual's taxable wealth. The Slavic Opposition attacked the proposal as undemocratic, as did the Social Democrats, who were not yet represented in Parliament. The Czech wing of Social Democracy wanted to expose what it considered to be Young Czech exploitation of the franchise reform issue for demagogic party purposes and to neutralize middle-class influence among the workers.[34] Gustav Eim criticized preservation of the curia system, and Kramář assailed Parliament as a refuge "only of the privileged and those who just want to hold onto their privileges ..."[35] Despite these efforts the opposition could extract from Windischgrätz only a statement that he would not be swayed by street

33 *Stenographische Protokolle über die Sitzungen des Hauses der Abgeordneten des öster-reichischen Reichsrathes* (hereinafter s.p.a.), xi session, 16,345, 14 December 1894.

34 Hans Mommsen, *Die Sozialdemokratie und die Nationalitätenfrage im habsburgischen Vielvölkerstaat* (Vienna, 1963), i, 173–6.

35 s.p.a., xi, 19,050, 21 May 1895; Gustav Eim, *Politické úvahy*, ed. Josef Penížek (Prague, 1898), 463–98.

demonstrations. Until its downfall in June 1895 the Coalition government suffered heavily in repute, stability, and achievement by evading a democratic reform of the franchise.

Perhaps the most noteworthy feature of parliamentary sessions under the Coalition was the introduction by the opposition parties of the technique of obstructing business on the daily agenda in order to dramatize hostility to a particular bill. The use of obstructive tactics in Austrian legislatures was by no means novel. The most spectacular recent obstruction had occurred in the Bohemian Diet in May 1893. The Czechs then employed stormy measures to prevent consideration of a bill to delineate a judicial district in accordance with the provisions of the Compromise of 1890. The government acknowledged the opposition's strength by adjourning the Diet, to the chagrin of the Bohemian Germans. This lesson was not lost on the Germans, who turned the same weapon against the Czechs in 1897.

When an urgent motion by Kaizl on 21 May 1894 for a plenary debate on the franchise reform bill was rejected, the opposition began systematic obstruction of the proceedings in the Chamber of Deputies.[36] The government had received several hints of what was in store. Kramář warned Parliament in April that strong nationalist feeling in Bohemia might drive the Czech deputies into obstruction. He assailed as a frame-up the arrest of seventy-seven youths in the "Omladina" society, during martial law in Prague, on charges of sedition and treason,[37] and warned the government of possible Czech reprisals unless it granted concessions. His desire to head off a violent confrontation was consistent with his maturing political thought, which advocated transforming the Young Czech party into a stable, responsible organization capable of representing a popular national consensus. Such an outlook, according to Kramář, rather than a militant radicalism, would secure for the Czechs equal rights with the Austrian Germans and official recognition of the value of the Czech nation to the monarchy.[38] Kramář therefore opposed the use of obstructive tactics save in the direst emergency. He felt they unleashed radicalism and defaced the party's image among high officials whose favour was essential to progress.

Kramář made no secret of these opinions, which presented a target for extremists from both the radical and conservative wings. He shared this middle ground with Gustav Eim, whose interests now converged with his; but they both differed on the question with Josef Kaizl. Kaizl, usually a temperate politician, believed early in 1895 that obstructive tactics were justified by the intransigence of the Coalition and the continued martial law in Prague. Kaizl felt that unless the Young Czechs increased the tempo of their opposition they would lose mass sup-

36 Kramář, *Česká politika*, III, 547. On the problem of parliamentary obstruction see Berthold Sutter, *Die badenischen Sprachenverordnungen von 1897*, 2 vols. (Graz and Cologne, 1960–5), I, 264ff.

37 S.P.A., XI, 12,837, 6 April 1894.

38 See various articles by Kramář: "Co chceme?," *Čas*, III (1889), 1ff.; "Naše politické strany," *ibid.*, 37–40; "Slovo k studentstvu," *Čas*, VII (1893), 513–16.

port.[39] In late February he therefore urged the deputies' club to obstruct proceedings on legislation relating to political offenses, but because of opposition led by Kramář his proposal did not prevail.

Instead the Czech obstruction began over tax reform measures offered by the minister of finance Dr. Ernst Plener (1810–1908). When Dr. Plener's bill came up in March for discussion as a whole, the Young Czechs, at Kaizl's suggestion, decided to oppose it for alleged centralistic bias and favouritism toward big business. The Czechs did not wish to permit Dr. Plener, an outstanding German liberal and their most implacable foe in the cabinet, to gain a legislative victory. They began using concealed forms of obstruction involving strict interpretations of the rules of procedure. They hoped to delay passage of the bill until the fall session of Parliament, when franchise reform would be the first item on the agenda. By May 1895 the entire opposition was in full and open obstruction. Kramář refused to sanction the flagrant tactics used by some deputies, thereby incurring Kaizl's scorn.[40] Kramář felt the Coalition to be moribund and near death anyway; he feared the Germans would some day seize the two-edged sword of obstruction and use it against the Czechs. In the face of unrelenting opposition, Dr. Plener's bill never cleared the chamber.

PARTY REORGANIZATION

The dispute over tactics that was generated in the party's discussion on the obstruction disclosed a deeper problem involving not only the appeasement of militant and radical sentiment among party members and the public at large but also the price demanded, in the form of concessions from the government, before the party would abandon its opposition and independent attitude in Parliament. The party's leadership, realizing that at some point their opposition had to terminate, agreed that the concessions should be more substantial than those gained by the Old Czechs after their return to Parliament in 1879. But what should those concessions be? Opinions cut across the usual factional lines. Kaizl and Eduard Grégr would have settled for a federal reorganization of the Austro-Hungarian Empire that would have established territorial autonomy in the Lands of the Bohemian Crown. The militant nationalist deputy Jan Vašatý (1836–98) felt that a fair price would be the equal use of Czech as the "inner" language of administration (*innere Amtssprache*) in Bohemia. The progressive youth wing of the party and some radical deputies anticipated a crisis in foreign affairs during which the Czechs would assert their state right demands for the unity and autonomy of the Bohemian lands.[41]

Kramář's position was akin to Kaizl's but somewhat more flexible and prag-

39 Kaizl, Z mého života, III/i, 289ff., 328–31.
40 Ibid., 354; also Kramář, Anmerkungen, 27 (the date given as 1891 should read 1893).
41 Tobolka, Politické dějiny, III/i, 24–7. For Kramář's views see his "Federativné Rakousko," Čas, IV (1890), 694–701; also Das böhmische Staatsrecht (Vienna, 1896), esp. 50–69. Kaizl's concept is in Z mého života, III/i, 457–69.

matic. He was not ready under all circumstances to welcome a war or other grave crisis; he would first sever the Austrian alliance with Germany. Nor was he merely seeking concessions in language usage or territorial autonomy, although these were aspects of his position. He was mainly concerned with winning a share of political power and initiating a continuous process of change. His basic precondition for bringing the Czechs into a pro-government majority was the formation of a parliamentary coalition that would lead rather than be led, that would bargain as an equal with the minister-president (and ultimately with the emperor) and not, at their pleasure, merely pick up "crumbs from the table." He wanted a system of parliamentary government combining features of the British monarchy and the French Third Republic. In such a system the Czechs, with their population increase and rising tempo of economic growth, their national cohesiveness, wide literacy, and technical skills, would become the leading Slav nation in a predominantly Slavic Cisleithanian Austria. In practical terms, so far as his attitude toward ending Young Czech opposition to the regime was concerned, Kramář awaited a favourable occasion rather than a specific offer of concessions, although the two might occur simultaneously. Of course, the various outlooks within the party's leadership were perhaps not as sharp, unyielding, or fixed as might have been inferred from these observations. What is clear is that the party lacked an agreed policy on the problem, a deficiency that weakened its bargaining position and permitted a corroding factionalism to flourish.

The Young Czechs attempted to remedy these weaknesses in the summer and fall of 1894. The stimulus was their failure to free Prague from martial law despite vigorous protests in Parliament and the Diet. This failure encouraged radical elements in the party and in Bohemia. The party began to lose patience with the more extreme radicals, for it was far from being consciously revolutionary. Its rhetoric usually outstripped its willingness to act. Individual members who felt no obligation to party discipline constantly embarrassed it with incendiary remarks. These may once have suited the requisites of a minority party hungry for power but not those of the legitimate representative of the Czech nation. For example, in early April 1894 a group of militants, including Eduard Grégr and Jan Vašatý, spoke openly in Parliament against the Polish landlords in Galicia, the government, and worst of all the dynasty. The militants took umbrage when the deputies' club disclaimed any responsibility for their remarks. A move was soon launched in the club to expel the militants if they could not be restrained. Kramář and Kaizl, who favoured such steps, felt the party could not simultaneously combat the regime in Vienna, the Germans in Bohemia, and the radicals in its ranks.

The conflict between radicals and moderates arose in part from the growing competition for the allegiance of the masses, which the Young Czechs faced from forces arising on their left among the urban workers in the Social Democratic party and the rural small-holders in various agricultural societies. Perceiving this competition, radical Young Czechs began to lose faith in the capacity of a "responsible" party organization to achieve their millennial goals before its rivals did. The radicals disliked restraints, they resented discipline, and they feared hierarchical authority of any sort. Believing the Czechs could gain nothing in Vienna, they hoped to block Parliament's work, undermine its prestige, and at an opportune moment, perhaps even during a war, abandon it in favour of a swift and sweeping constitutional change that would achieve the historic state right of the Bohemian Crown at a single stroke.[42] The moderates, including Kramář, Kaizl, and Eim, realized that no government would cooperate with an unstable band of individuals linked merely by a common party label. Rather than favouring a return to the status of a government party held by the Old Czechs under former Minister-President Taaffe, they looked to the formation of a new parliamentary majority composed primarily of Slavic deputies but including reasonable Germans who might cooperate in reaching a genuine compromise in Bohemia. While these opinions circulated in 1894, the position taken by *Národní listy* was bound to be significant. It was still controlled by Julius Grégr, but he suffered from a crippling disease and could no longer be intimately involved in party affairs. In a showdown the newspaper was likely to support the party's majority so long as it preserved its status as party organ. One fact was clear: a substantial number of leading Young Czechs could no longer tolerate an undisciplined radical opposition in party ranks.

A fundamental reorganization of the Young Czech party began in July at Pardubice, outside the zone of martial law, at a meeting of Diet and parliamentary deputies. A resolution on reorganization passed there was unanimously approved at a closed meeting of the party's board of trustees in September at Nymburk.[43] Members of the radical wing and of progressive youth groups allied to the party were to have been present but at the last minute were excluded. The excuse was that such an arrangement violated party regulations; in reality, as Kramář pointed out and as the radicals themselves realized,[44] the gulf between them and the moderate majority had become unbridgeable. In discussing the resolution Kramář and Kaizl, who played leading roles, argued that Young Czech opposition to the government might have to terminate before the historic state right demands were fully achieved. They pressed, with only partial success, for adoption of a Realist concept that state right could be gained in gradual stages or perhaps not even at all in the absence of some grave political crisis.

The Nymburk meeting was therefore not so much concerned with the party's platform as it was with its internal unity and its tactical position vis-à-vis the

42 Tobolka, *Politické dějiny*, III/i, 82f.
43 On the congress see *ibid.*, III/ii, 83ff.; and *Přehled československých dějin*, 3 vols. in 4 (Prague, 1959–60), II/i, 660.
44 *Lidové noviny* (Brno), 1 April 1894, as quoted in *Čas*, VIII (1894), 211; Adolf Srb, *Politické dějiny národa českého*, 2 vols. (Prague, 1899–1901), I, 906n.

government and the other parties. The radical view that opposition was an end in itself was rejected in favour of a readiness to work under any circumstances that met the nation's needs as the party saw them. The Nymburk resolution accepted the principle of "responsible opposition" until the basis had been established for satisfying the demands of the Czech nation, and that basis was to be: "Sincere steps by the government for purposes of a state right settlement with the Bohemian Crown, for revision of the unjust electoral system in the Lands of the Bohemian Crown, and for introduction of equal rights by using Czech as an inner language in the courts and political administration."[45]

The resolution demanded the observance of discipline in party affairs by party journalists and supporters; disavowed the views of the progressive youth; kept open the doors to future cooperation with the Old Czechs and the Bohemian aristocracy, under Young Czech leadership; cold-shouldered clerical influence; and rejected the Social Democratic party's class concept of society while accepting its multinational approach to social and cultural problems. The Congress reaffirmed an executive committee decision of March 1891 which had granted tactical freedom to the deputies' club, save in direct negotiations with the government, when approval by the board of trustees would be required. The Nymburk resolution, as modified by a similar declaration approved in September 1897, became the theoretical basis for Young Czech strategy and tactics in the next decade. It vindicated the personal endeavours of Kramář and Kaizl against the extremist fringe and for a moderate party with a practical yet progressive programme. A year after Nymburk Kramář justified the decision by stating: "We know we will not reach our goals overnight; instead we rely upon more gradual progress," including preliminary steps toward the restoration of the state right and a settlement with the Bohemian Germans on a basis fair to both sides.[46] Kramář felt that Nymburk accelerated an inevitable process of political fragmentation, because "there could not be contained within one party all the social and political tendencies that normally grew among every people under modern conditions ..."[47]

After Nymburk the radicals split, some remaining within the party, their views somewhat toned down, others leaving to form rival parties. One of the new parties was the Radical Progressive Party of State Right, which voiced an anti-German brand of Czech national chauvinism.[48] Basically the splinter parties believed the Czechs should join no governmental majority that did not pledge itself in advance to alter the constitutional framework of the Austrian state. Nymburk signified that between two variant forms of Czech nationalism there now existed a firm division along organizational lines where none had existed before. The Young Czech party had made a choice: by disciplining its extremist wing it gained in pur-

45 Srb, *Politické dějiny*, ɪ, 907.
46 *Čas*, ɪx (1895), 461.
47 Kramář, *Česká politika*, ɪɪɪ, 563; *idem, Anmerkungen*, 9.
48 František Červinka, *Český nacionalismus v* xɪx. *století* (Prague, 1965), 167.

pose and cohesiveness. The split with the young generation, however, isolated the party from vital infusions of energy and ideas. The leading Young Czechs were in their mid-forties and fifties. The Grégr brothers were over sixty, Kaizl in 1894 was forty, and Kramář thirty-four. The academic intelligentsia was alienated because of Marasyk's withdrawal from the party and the anti-intellectual tone of the party press. In discouraging the dissenters and non-conformists, the Young Czechs lost the fervour and momentum typical of insurgent movements. Although Kramář himself many times had defended diversity of opinion on the floor of Parliament, he had fought long and hard to silence or expel the radicals. Like his party, he sacrificed principle to meet a practical political necessity.

ACCOMMODATION TO BADENI

During the ministry of Count Kazimierz Badeni (1846–1909), which after a brief caretaker government succeeded that of Prince Windischgrätz, the Young Czech party had its great opportunity of switching, under relatively favourable conditions, from a posture of opposition to one within a majority and of making concrete gains. The activities of Kramář, Kaizl, and the party between 1895 and 1897 reveal in microcosm the hopes and disappointments which many Czech politicians, especially of liberal persuasion, experienced in those eventful years.

Few Austrian ministers-president took office amid such anticipation as did Count Badeni in September 1895, and none departed, as he did twenty-seven months later, so engulfed by controversy and disillusion. At the outset, Badeni perceived Austria's overriding need to be the preservation of peace; he held that war would bring disaster to the multinational empire.[49] Keeping domestic social and political calm, in turn, would strengthen Austria's resistance to outside provocations that might lead to war. His cabinet of civil servants, in attempting to implement these assumptions, hewed to a policy of "the free hand": they wanted to lead Parliament independently of any party or bloc and not follow a majority; but they were not averse to enlightened reforms.

Badeni grew to appreciate with sympathy the Czech cause (although he apparently never fully grasped its complexities) through the counsel of a key adviser, Dr. Heinrich Halban (1845–1902).[50] Through Dr. Halban he was introduced to Gustav Eim, who became the contact between the minister-president and the Czech deputies during the pourparlers that led to their tentative cooperation. Halban believed that political conditions in Austria would remain unstable so long as the Czechs stayed in opposition. He thus stood at an opposite pole to Governor Count Franz Thun, who wanted to continue to repress the Czechs through surveillance and police action against manifestations of radicalism. Halban observed that Thun's martial law had actually stiffened Czech resistance; he wanted the

49 Wolfgang Rudert, Die Stellung des deutschen Reiches zur inner-österreichischen Lage, 1890–1900 (Leipzig, 1931), 59.
50 Kramář, Paměti, 84, 312; Tobolka, Politické dějiny, III/i, 89.

situation transformed so that the government could count upon Czech votes, in addition to Polish and German, to secure approval of its parliamentary programme. His ally, Eim, believed fulfilment of Czech state right hopes to be impossible under conditions of relative European stability such as had prevailed since conclusion of the Austro-German Alliance of 1879. Eim knew the practical issues requiring Czech support that confronted Minister-President Badeni: franchise reform, the Imperial Defence Law, renewal of the 1867 Ausgleich agreements with Hungary. He therefore reduced Czech demands to the one he thought most realizable, the one for which the Old Czechs had fought hardest – equality in the inner use of the Czech language with the German in government service in the Bohemian lands.

The initial Czech attitude toward Badeni was one of watchful waiting while remaining in the opposition. Although Badeni named no Czechs to his cabinet, he lifted the state of martial law in Prague and granted amnesty to political prisoners. But his refusal to propose constitutional changes in the status of Bohemia meant that the Czech deputies would remain in opposition, although they were less hostile than before. Gradually, almost inexorably, various tensions between Badeni and the Czech deputies began to diminish. In general elections to the Bohemian Diet in 1895 the Young Czechs swamped their rivals, winning eighty-nine seats to three Old Czechs, two Agrarians (their debut in the Diet), one Progressive, seventy great landowners, and sixty-two Bohemian Germans from various parties. The Young Czech party was now the largest in the Diet and sufficiently strong to compel government action in the case of Governor Franz Thun, who was, to the Czechs, the most hated official in Austria. Thun, realizing the embarrassment he was causing the regime, in January 1896 resigned from office.[51]

Before any real change could occur in the attitude of the Young Czechs toward the government, several key deputies had to be converted from a feeling of scepticism to one of support. Eim tried without success to get Eduard Grégr to co-operate with Minister-President Badeni and then turned for help to Kramář and Kaizl. Kramář was easily persuaded but had to move cautiously so as not to endanger his hard-won and still provisional status in the party. Kaizl agreed to go along after several meetings with Badeni and after receiving confidential assurances that Badeni, to secure a *rapprochement*, would not only remove Governor Thun from office but also establish a Czech university in Moravia, equalize the use of Czech with German in Bohemian courts and government agencies, and name a cabinet minister from Bohemia to fill a vacant post. Badeni hoped that after these measures had been taken, the Young Czechs would abandon the opposition and enter a coalition assembled from the German Left, the Bohemian conservative great landowners, the Poles, and the Czechs. After this, he promised, he would appoint as additional cabinet members a Bohemian Czech, probably Kaizl

51 On Thun see Albín Bráf, *Život a dílo*, ed. Josef Gruber, 5 vols. (Prague, 1922–4), I, 61–78; Srb, *Politické dějiny*, II, 48f.; S.P.A., XI, 21,963–4, 10 December 1895.

himself, and a Bohemian German from the ranks of the liberal wing of the great landowners' party.

Kramář and Kaizl furthered these preliminary understandings in parliamentary speeches that combined faint praise for Badeni with requests for specific concessions. The two Czechs differed at this time, however, in the significance they attached to the state right demands. Kramář, fresh from writing an important brochure on the subject (České státní právo; in German, Das böhmische Staatsrecht [Vienna, 1896]), believed that they could now be achieved in a single act, through a change in the Basic State Laws (Staatsgrundgesetze, i.e. Constitution) of 1867. He also felt that the Bohemian Germans would require no compensation for such an action because they had long benefited unfairly at Czech expense; that it was the government's duty, as impartial arbiter, to equalize the position of the two nationalities so that they could freely negotiate a genuine Bohemian compromise.[52] Kaizl was prepared to be more conciliatory. Although he paid lip-service to the state right programme, he believed it could be achieved only after initial steps involving concessions to the Czechs in language usage, education, and the judiciary had been taken. He was willing to appease the Germans by conceding their demand for districts delineated along linguistic lines so long as there were equal facilities and opportunities for both nationalities in the schools and government offices.[53] These differences in emphasis and interpretation between men who had collaborated for years exemplify the complex problems with which the Young Czechs had to grapple in striving for consensus. They also perhaps illustrate an emerging rivalry for supreme leadership in the party between the two members of the middle generation best equipped by education and talent to assume that responsibility. The issue was seemingly resolved in February 1896 when Kaizl, over the objections of party militants, secured approval in the deputies' club of an interpretation of the original Nymburk resolution to the effect that a key phrase in the resolution implied a step-by-step procedure for achieving the state right demands.

The next major event in the evolution of the relationship between the Czechs and the Badeni regime was passage of the electoral reform law of 1896. Badeni's bill was a compromise designed to broaden the franchise while retaining the inequitable curia system of voting in order to defend the political status quo. He achieved this by adding a fifth curia, open to all able-bodied men twenty-four years and older. The Czech wing of the All-Austrian Social Democratic Party opposed the bill, but Viktor Adler (1852–1919), founder of the party, called it an opening wedge toward a more democratic reform.[54] The Young Czechs at first opposed the bill because it fell far short of their avowed commitment to universal, equal, direct manhood suffrage and left the Germans, numerically a minority in

52 s.p.a., xi, 21,961–6, 10 December 1895.
53 Kaizl, Z mého života, iii/i, 468; also Václav Škarda, "Politika etapová a základní názor strany svobodomyslné na českou politiku," Česká revue, iii/i (1898), 536–51.
54 Mommsen, Die Sozialdemokratie, i, 177.

Cisleithanian Austria, still a majority in Parliament. Kaizl and Eim worked inde-
fatigably to persuade the deputies' club to support Badeni's bill. The militants
held out for universal equal suffrage, while a small group opposed any reform
whatsoever. By a split vote the club decided in March 1896 to press for the original proposal of Young Czech deputy Jan Slavík, made in 1893, and, failing that,
to support Badeni by voting with the majority. This was a victory for the opportunistic moderates, who marshalled impressive arguments for the bill: it extended
the suffrage to 3.5 million new voters; it introduced universal suffrage in the new
fifth curia; a more democratic reform was then unfeasible; and it was going to pass
anyway.[55] Badeni personally intervened to solicit Czech backing, implying that
without it he would become utterly dependent upon the German Left or would
have to resign.

The club's decision pleased few constituents back in Bohemia. The deputies
were blasted by the Old Czechs for sacrificing the state right, by the radicals for
not fighting to the bitter end, and by the Social Democrats for "betraying the
masses." The franchise reform was approved on 7 May 1896, by a vote of 234 to
19 with the Czech deputies badly divided. Before voting they proclaimed they
were not ending their opposition or expressing confidence in the regime. Of the
Young Czechs present, twenty-one voted in favour, including Kramář, Kaizl, and
Eim; fifteen voted against, among them Eduard Grégr and Jan Vašatý, with others
such as Josef Herold (1850–1908), club chairman, deliberately absent. Forecasts
in *Čas* and the Social Democratic press that the deputies' club was disintegrat-
ing[56] turned out to be wishful thinking, but the actual consequences were almost
as serious. The reform in the fifth curia enabled the All-Austrian Social Democratic party to differentiate itself once and for all from the middle-class parties of
the various nationalities from which it drew its membership. The new law strengthened parties such as the Social Democrats and the Agrarians, which were based
largely on economic and social-class interests rather than on nationality or historic
factors.[57] Badeni's measure therefore encouraged forces inimical to the Young
Czech party which eventually destroyed its claims to represent the interests of
the entire Czech nation.

BADENI'S LANGUAGE ORDINANCE

The year 1897 was decisive not only for the Czechs but also for the other nationalities of Austria, and the fateful arena was Parliament. The new Parliament which

55 Kramář, *Česká politika*, iii, 579; Kaizl, *Z mého života*, iii/i, 502–4.
56 *Čas*, x (1896), 305f.; *Česká stráž* (iii/15, 11 April 1896) a Social Democratic organ, also
claimed a Young Czech debacle.
57 The various rural groups that later formed the Czech Agrarian party were still allied at this
time to the Young Czechs. See, for example, an open letter affirming the alliance signed by
250 agrarians on 5 December 1896; also the Young Czech executive committee statement of
14 December 1896, announcing the formation of a new agrarian committee "to have henceforth full participation in all matters relating to the political leadership of the party"; both
items in Engel, pozůstalost, LANM 6P74/6R80.

assembled in March differed in composition from the previous one. At general elections held earlier in the month the Young Czechs won sixty-three seats to became the largest single party in the chamber. They ran candidates from all electoral districts and in the new fifth curia, which they refused to concede to the Social Democrats. Kramář handily defeated two rivals in his rural constituency and Kaizl triumphed in Prague. There were now eighty-seven deputies of Czech nationality, not counting five Social Democrats, representing the Bohemian lands. There was significantly a strengthening of the radical German nationalist parties in Bohemia (Progressives, Pan-Germans, People's party) and an upsurge for the Christian Socials in Lower Austria.

After the opening of the parliamentary session, the government assumed toward the issues of increased crown-land autonomy and fulfilment of the Bohemian state right a bland attitude that irritated many Czech deputies and caused them to suspect Badeni's intentions. The minister-president had no interest either in decentralizing authority or in encouraging the formation of a conservative, federalist coalition resembling the Right Wing of Minister-President Taaffe's era. Needing Czech votes for the renewal of the Ausgleich agreements and seeing some justice in certain Czech demands,[58] Badeni calculated that he could base his government on the Czechs, the Poles and Ruthenes from Galicia, the South Slavs, the Italians, and as many liberal Germans as would back him; but defections thwarted his plan and he commenced legislative activity lacking a firm majority. Actually he feared that too strong a majority might diminish his power and freedom of action. The conservatives, notably the great landowners and the deputies' club of former Minister-President Count Hohenwart, opened negotiations with the Poles and others for the resurrection of a right wing coalition.[59] Many Young Czechs who were wary of Badeni leaned toward such a united front, including Emanuel Engel (1844–1907), president of the party; Josef Herold, chairman of the deputies' club; and Bedřich Pacák (1846–1914), member of a small inner circle.

Kramář was instrumental, along with Kaizl, who now basically concurred in his tactics, in influencing Young Czech policy. Placing full confidence in Badeni, Kramář in the winter of 1896-7 succeeded Gustav Eim, who died in February, as go-between for Badeni and the Czech deputies. Kramář opposed revival of the Right as bound to weaken the party's influence and expose it to charges of surrendering to aristocratic leadership similar to those levelled against the Old

58 "As a good Pole he felt the humiliation which the Czech people experienced upon being denied the natural right of every people to have officials conducting business in its own language," according to Kramář, Česká politika, III, 582.

59 Kramář, Anmerkungen, 22. The terms "Right" and "Left" in Austrian parliamentary usage were relative, denoting a party's relationship to the government and the parliamentary majority. Until 1891 the groups in the Right majority (the "Iron Ring") included the Poles, the Old Czechs, the Clerical Conservatives, and the South Slavs. Basically they endorsed federalist, non-centralist proposals under the leadership of the largely supranational aristocracy.

Czechs in 1890.[60] At a meeting of the Czech deputies, he and Kaizl got a provisional agreement to support Badeni; however, party president Engel (whether intentionally or not is unclear) nonetheless pledged Young Czech solidarity with the incipient Right coalition. Kramář hurriedly assured Badeni that there was no double-cross, and Kaizl disclaimed the validity of Engel's action.[61] But damage was done: Badeni's confidence in the Czechs was shaken, and the party's chronic problem of lack of unity was again revealed.

Then on 5 April the government published its language ordinances for Bohemia; those for Moravia followed on 22 April. Their appearance signified for Austria the dawn of an era in which extreme nationalism overshadowed other factors.[62] The force of the protests unleashed by various opposition political parties rendered parliamentary government, never very robust, inoperative and crushed the hopes of the Austrian Slavs that the monarchy would finally implement the theoretical equality of rights proclaimed in the Basic State Laws of 1867. Two events coincided to produce this explosive reaction. One was the creation of the Right coalition, conservative, autonomist, and pro-Slavic, "an unexpected, dreadful blow" to the Germans,[63] which revived their fears of an anti-German trend in policy. The other was publication of the language ordinances, which, in requiring the use of both Czech and German in the inner administration, decisively rejected long-standing German opposition to this practice, threatened the near-monopoly of Germans in high civil service jobs in Bohemia, and vindicated the lengthy Czech struggle for linguistic equality.[64]

An influential element in the process by which the parliamentary obstruction of 1897 brought Badeni's ministry to its knees was the role played by the Young Czechs, and Kramář in particular. The process unfolded in two stages, the first of which, from late 1895 to the spring of 1897, involved the party in negotiations with Badeni over the details of the ordinances and the respect to be accorded the

60 Kaizl, Z mého života, III/i, 579; Čas, IX (1895), 460f.

61 Kaizl, Z mého života, III/i, 579.

62 Hugo Hantsch, Die Geschichte Österreichs, 3rd ed., 2 vols. (Graz and Cologne, 1959–62), II, 443.

63 Kramář, Anmerkungen, 26; Karel Mattuš, Paměti (Prague, 1921), 159.

64 The ordinances obligated five ministries (Interior, Justice, Finance, Commerce and Trade, and Agriculture) to conduct all administrative business in either Czech or German as requested by a petitioner at the outset of a complaint. In business not initiated by a party to a complaint or by the original petitioner, both Czech and German could be used "according to the nature of the case." Most controversial was a requirement that all civil servants in Bohemia and Moravia would have to offer, no later than 1 July, 1901, evidence of a command of Czech and German or face dismissal. Sutter, Die badenischen Sprachenverordnungen, I, 128ff., traces the preliminary work on the preparation of the ordinances from a viewpoint favourable to the Germans. See Hermann Münch, Böhmische Tragödie (Braunschweig, 1949), 700–26, for a survey of the legal evolution of the language question. On the situation in the civil service in Bohemia and Moravia consult Péter Hanák, ed., Die nationale Frage in der österreichisch-ungarischen Monarchie, 1900–1918 (Budapest, 1966), 329f.

opinions of the Bohemian Germans. Matters went far from smoothly: each concession to the Czechs was regarded by the Germans as cause for a counter-concession; news leaks and loose talk by Czech deputies privy to confidential details bred rumours and tensions;[65] and even relations between Kramář and Kaizl suffered. Before Julius Grégr's death in October 1896 Kaizl had become de facto party leader. Kramář was a natural contender for the position of second in authority. Kaizl seems to have been ruffled by Kramář's swift rise in party affairs and a concomitant increase in his self-esteem.[66] Although their close collaboration continued, a note of rivalry was now present.

After the government had prepared the final draft of the language ordinances, a residue of Czech discontent remained. Having failed to win the precise wording they wanted in certain vital clauses in the ordinances, the Young Czechs made their support of the government contingent upon the satisfaction of about three-dozen demands which they presented at the end of March to the astonishment of the cabinet.[67] The demands, covering many aspects of educational, political, and economic life in the Lands of the Bohemian Crown, had been drafted at the insistence of party moderates who feared that language concessions alone would be insufficient to appease the growing militancy of the Czech people. Some demands were not within the government's competence, and others were impossible to fulfil at once. Word of the demands reached the German press, which charged Badeni and the Czechs with betrayal and requested new negotiations.[68]

Badeni rejected most of the demands, temporized on others, and reiterated that the Czechs were obligated to support him. The deputies now faced a question they had dreaded having to answer since assuming national leadership six years earlier: whether to abandon the opposition by adopting a "positive policy" of cooperating with the regime in exchange for specific, limited gains or to press for complete realization of the state right programme. Some party members, nurtured on radicalism and opposition, could not easily surrender their beliefs; others feared that Czech public opinion would react unfavourably to their alliance with some of the conservative parties supporting the government. The deputies were exhausted from their long, tiring, and unrewarding oppositional struggle.[69] The majority of them, lacking the courage to implement party slogans, therefore capitulated, and Kaizl and Kramář committed the party's support, providing the

65 Kramář, *Česká politika*, III, 585; Kaizl, *Z mého života*, III/i 551, 587n.
66 Kaizl, *Z mého života*, III/i, 553, 558.
67 Kramář, *Anmerkungen*, 20f.; Sutter, *Die badenischen Sprachenverordnungen*, I, 192ff.; Tobolka, *Politické dějiny*, III/ii, 146ff.
68 The Bohemian Germans, apart from doubts about specific provisions of the ordinances, wanted them to be part of a larger settlement of Bohemian problems to be negotiated directly with the Czechs and not through government mediation. The Czechs, in general, favoured such negotiations but only after conditions between the two nationalities had been equalized, so that they could bargain as equals.
69 Kramář, *Česká politika*, III, 593f.; Kaizl, *Z mého života*, III/i, 408f.

language ordinances were promptly issued. This decision was, however, kept from the electorate, who continued to believe that the deputies retained their traditional freedom of tactical manoeuvre.[70]

BADENI'S STORMY DOWNFALL

The second and climactic stage of Young Czech activity in 1897, from April to November, was determined by forces over which the party had no control: namely, the German nationalist resistance and the spread of that resistance from Vienna to all of Cisleithanian Austria. When the opposition parties failed to win cancellation of the language ordinances through normal parliamentary methods, they began in late April to obstruct the order of business with various procedural devices, facilitated in their task, perhaps unwittingly, by the Speaker of the Chamber of Deputies, Dr. Theodor Kathrein (1842–1916), an experienced parliamentarian who wanted to minimize the conflict at all cost. Serving with Kathrein on the newly elected presidium were the first deputy speaker, Dawid Abrahamowicz (1839–1926), a Polish landowner, and the second deputy speaker, Karel Kramář. Kramář was nominated by the Young Czechs as a candidate for the position after Kaizl, who was awaiting an appointment by Badeni as a cabinet minister, had declined.[71] This was one of several distinctions which Kramář achieved at this period in his career. In 1896 he was elected to the joint Austro-Hungarian Delegations, thereby receiving an outlet for his foreign policy views. In September 1897, after Kathrein's resignation, Abrahamowicz was elected Speaker and Kramář first deputy. Then in October Kramář became chairman of the parliamentary budget committee. No other Young Czech could match Kramář in influence during this meteoric rise to prominence, but his ascendancy was short-lived.

As the German opposition became increasingly stubborn, the Czech deputies' club proved unable to preserve sufficient unity and discipline to provide the regime with a suitable counterweight. In late April, when a bloc of club moderates cool toward Badeni won over about half of the Czech deputies and launched a sharp struggle over club policy, Kramář complained to Kaizl: "Everything goes differently than we had imagined ... I view Badeni's situation quite pessimistically."[72] Orderly procedure in the chamber became difficult to sustain after a genuinely stormy outburst occurred in mid-May. Kramář was at the hub of events, chairing sessions in the chamber, labouring to bring order out of chaos, and transmitting information to Badeni, Kaizl, and others. At this time Kramář conceived a plan to end the obstruction through government intervention of a far-reaching

70 Kramář noted that "it was essential to handle very coolly the matter of revealing Badeni's intentions regarding our people"; see *Česká politika*, III, 594; also *Přehled československých dějin*, II/i, 661.

71 Kaizl, *Z mého života*, III/i, 581; Gustav Kolmer, *Parlament und Verfassung in Österreich, 1848–1904*, 8 vols. (Vienna and Leipzig, 1902–14), VI, 219; ANM, "Protokol 4. schůze klubu svobodomyslných poslanců na radě říšské konané dne 6. dubna 1897," ms.

72 Kaizl, *Z mého života*, III/i, 587n.

nature, involving the exercise of emergency powers under Article 14 of Basic State Law 141 of 1867 – Concerning Imperial Representation (*Reichsvertretung*).[73] But Badeni was interested in breaking the opposition through parliamentary means, not through emergency decrees (*octroi*). When Parliament was closed on 2 June he got cabinet approval to conclude, rather than to adjourn, the session, the first such action in twenty-eight years of Austrian legislative history. He hoped for a cooling-off period and a fresh start in the fall with a new order of business on the legislative agenda. Actually, the minister-president's policy, and that of the Young Czechs, had reached a dead end.

Badeni's expectations of an interval of decompression proved illusory. The German deputies aroused their constituents to the government's unjust language ordinances, while the Czechs publicized the German threat to their rights. By July some Bohemian towns resembled armed camps, with violence erupting between Czechs and Germans. Kramář and Kaizl utilized the recess to enlighten their constituents, to urge Kramář's plan for government intervention upon high officials, and to rally the party to Badeni's side. The revived Right Wing was the only significant parliamentary force opposed to German extremism, and Kramář publicly hinted that a Young Czech alliance with the Right might be necessary.[74] He still entertained hopes of negotiating a settlement with German moderates but ruled out any dealings with extremists such as the Pan-Germans. He, Kaizl, and other partisans of this approach were accused by critics of wanting to sacrifice national interests for petty concessions; for example, *Čas* compared the Young Czech position to that of the Old Czechs in accepting the Compromise of 1890.[75] Badeni was unable to convene the leaders of the various Czech and German parties, as Taaffe had done, in order to settle their differences. Methods which under calm conditions might have brought some results now met with hostility. In mid-summer Kaizl fell ill from nervous tension and anaemia and stayed at various Bohemian health resorts, unable to return to Prague and Vienna until late November. This was a misfortune for the party and especially for Kramář, who, despite some differences with Kaizl, relied heavily upon his colleague's advice.

With the new parliamentary session imminent, in early September Badeni revised his strategy and reached a *modus operandi* with the Right parties (the Poles and Ruthenes, the Christian Socials, and great landowners, the Catholic People's party, and several other groups) whereby they would support the renewal of the Ausgleich with Hungary. The Young Czechs, in line with Kramář's wishes, agreed to cooperate with the Right, a decision that reversed their policy of the previous years of unrelenting opposition. Indeed, the polarization of forces along nationalist

---

73 *Ibid.*, 411, 615; Tobolka, *Politické dějiny*, III/ii, 158. The law provided the government with authority to issue provisional decrees which would have the force of law between parliamentary sessions so long as they were speedily ratified at the following session.

74 *Čas*, XI (1897), 394; Sís, *Karel Kramář*, 111.

75 *Čas*, XI (1897), 544.

lines left them no alternative if they wished to salvage part of their programme.[76] But they withheld complete support of Badeni pending fulfilment, within four weeks, of the three-dozen demands submitted in March. Kramář criticized this ultimatum for placing immediate objectives above what he considered the party's, and the nation's, best long-range interests.[77] However, Badeni conceded nothing to the Young Czechs until early November, when, in a deteriorating situation, he consented to several demands in return for Czech votes on the Ausgleich renewal. This pledge mollified the deputies, but Badeni was unable to keep it, and the party was left empty-handed.

A grave deficiency in Badeni's new strategy was the vulnerability of the Right coalition to pressure, one instance being the vacillation of the Catholic People's party due to increasing German nationalist agitation in party strongholds in the Alpine regions and the Tyrol. Another weakness was a shortage of time because of the deadline for renewing the Ausgleich. Recognizing this, the opposition, notably the German Progressives and the German People's party, planned to obstruct the Ausgleich on the assumption that if it were not renewed by year's end, Badeni would have to resign and his language ordinances could be revoked under his successor. The Young Czechs remained in association with the Right but were impelled to retain some tactical mobility, a policy that was reaffirmed at the party's congress in Prague in late September. When Kramář's fears that pressure from party militants might alter this course proved groundless, he hailed the congress as "a final liberation, a definite emancipation from the superficial, empty radicalism of bygone years," and a logical conclusion to the reorganization begun at Nymburk.[78] He also welcomed the German obstruction as pushing Austria toward a revision of the pro-German centralistic system and the creation of a federal administration more equitable to the Czechs; but his optimism was hollow, for actual events ran counter to his hopes.

Parliamentary obstruction in October mounted as the roll-calls and recesses escalated into filibusters and choruses of shouts and insults. Badeni retained the emperor's confidence and might have survived had he kept presence of mind and prepared adequate measures in advance.[79] This he apparently failed to do before the show-down arrived in November, after the Hungarian Parliament had approved the Ausgleich renewal and the leaders of the Right coalition decided to force it through the obstruction. The Speaker of the chamber, Dr. Kathrein, refused to cooperate and resigned, leaving the presidium in the hands of the two Slav deputy speakers, Dawid Abrahamowicz and Kramář, and giving the German nationalists cause to see it as a hostile weapon. The presidium now became a

76 Kramář, *Anmerkungen*, 22f.
77 *Česká politika*, III, 603f; Tobolka, *Politické dějiny*, III/ii, 173.
78 Kramář, "Po sjezdu důvěrníků," *Česká revue*, I/i (1897–8), 1; Kaizl, *Z mého života*, III/i, 658n. The steps taken to smother dissension at the congress are discussed in Engel's letter to Škarda of 23 August 1897, in Václav Škarda, pozůstalost, ANM.
79 Tobolka, *Politické dějiny*, III/ii, 175.

major target for the onslaughts of the opposition. Public opinion in German-speaking areas of Austria grew more inflamed, while expressions of sympathy poured in from Imperial Germany.[80] The Czechs reacted vigorously to these attacks, and other Austrian Slavs supported them. But *Čas*, mouthpiece for Masaryk and Jan Herben, shed crocodile tears for the deputies' club, reporting that the Young Czechs were "peevish and surly" over the behaviour of certain members: "Dr. Kramář, in particular, does not ascend in the esteem of his colleagues to the same degree that he ascends hourly in Parliament."[81]

As the deadline approached for passage of the Ausgleich renewal, opposition in the chamber reached the point where the presidium was assaulted, deputies traded blows, and a German brandished a knife at Czechs and Poles. Badeni and leaders of the Right thereupon decided that the renewal could be forced through only by a change in the standing order of the agenda approved by the majority. Kramář defended this controversial decision[82] because he felt circumstances warranted emergency action. He and Abrahamowicz asked Badeni to station a guard inside the chamber to ensure uninterrupted debate, but Badeni refused, saying that this was the prerogative of the parliamentary majority. "The Right Wing waited for the government, the government for the Right Wing, until catastrophe came."[83] Then Kramář urged Badeni to suspend Parliament for two days, to use emergency powers to change the order of the agenda, and to enact the Ausgleich through emergency decree, reconvening Parliament to ratify these actions. But Badeni wanted help from the Right majority, and the Right responded with a proposal to exclude obstructive deputies submitted by the conservative great landowner, Count Julius Falkenhayn (1829–99), and approved on 25 November with Kramář calling for a show of hands amid a great tumult. The Young Czechs wanted to amend the *Lex Falkenhayn* so as to limit the force that it authorized to be used against offending deputies, but they failed. The next day the presidium employed the new weapon at its disposal and ordered unruly deputies to be excluded. The Social Democrats immediately joined the opposition, bringing with them not only the moral righteousness of the underprivileged but also the legions they could summon to the streets. Badeni then took the explosive step of using police to clear the chamber of thirteen unruly Pan-Germans and Social Democrats. Kramář approved of this measure and wanted even stricter ones taken.[84]

80 Jiří Kořalka, *Všeněmecký svaz a česká otázka koncem 19. století* (Prague, 1963), 48; *idem*, "La montée du pangermanisme et l'Autriche-Hongrie," *Historica*, x (Prague, 1965), 234ff. Kořalka sees the Badeni crisis as the culmination of a surge of German chauvinism that had lasting impact upon central Europe.

81 *Čas*, xi (1897), 738. The article noted that Kaizl's continuing absence was meeting with disfavour and that even Herold, the club chairman, was under fire. On 14 September Engel cautioned Kramář: "You are not on the presidium as an individual person but as the representative of the club ..."; ANM 2–3/1612–13.

82 Kann, *Das Nationalitätenproblem*, i, 196; Mommsen, *Die Sozialdemokratie*, i, 285.

83 Kramář, *Česká politika*, iii, 608.

84 *Ibid.*, 609; *Anmerkungen*, 30.

But he blundered when, presiding during an uproar in the session of 26 November, he ordered an adjournment through a misunderstanding of a message from Abrahamowicz and to the distress of the Right, which had hoped to vote on the Ausgleich that same day.

Given this reprieve the opposition scaled new heights, spreading to the public squares of dozens of Austrian towns and villages. The Christian Socials and the Catholic People's party deserted the Right. Public officials warned that matters were getting out of control; indeed, a revolutionary potential entered the situation.[85] Kramář decided not to persevere in a hopeless cause. He presided in the chamber on 27 November merely to close the session. Badeni resigned later that day and was succeeded as minister-president by Baron Paul Gautsch (1851–1918). Under Gautsch in February 1898, the ordinances were slightly modified in favour of the Germans. In October 1899, during the brief ministry of Count Manfred Clary (1852–1928), the regulations governing language usage in Bohemia reverted to those that had existed since 1880, that is, prior to Badeni's. This represented a total defeat for the Young Czechs on an issue over which they had waged their bitterest struggle.

EROSION OF YOUNG CZECH STRENGTH

The events of 1897 rocked the Young Czech party but did not shatter it. Yet its decline began at that time and was reflected in the growing strength of other parties that were founded in the next few years. The gravest threat to the Young Czech middle-class base of support was posed by the Czech Agrarian party, an amalgam of rural action groups, once allied to the Young Czechs, that ran candidates in by-elections in 1899 and 1900. The mushroom growth of the Agrarians, who attracted middling corn and sugar-beet farmers in central Bohemia, became a real problem to the Young Czechs in 1901. At parliamentary elections in January, the Agrarians won eight seats while the Young Czechs dropped eight below their previous total. At Diet elections that fall, the Agrarians jumped from two to twenty-one seats, gaining 37 per cent of the votes cast in the rural curiae, while the Young Czechs won sixty-eight seats, a decline of twenty-three.[86] The Agrarains thus made their political debut in a fashion reminiscent of 1889, when a rebellion by the rural bourgeoisie gave the Young Czechs their initial foothold at the expense of the dominant Old Czechs.

The Young Czech party's organization and leadership, meanwhile, underwent

---

85 Mattuš, *Paměti*, 159; *Čas*, xi (1897), 771; Paul Molisch, ed., *Briefe zur deutschen Politik in Österreich von 1848 bis 1918* (Vienna and Leipzig, 1934), 357.

86 Jan Havránek, "Die ökonomische und politische Lage der Bauernschaft in den böhmischen Ländern in den letzten Jahrzehnten des 19. Jahrhunderts," *Jahrbuch für Wirtschaftsgeschichte*, pt. ii (Berlin), 133. The French consul in Prague attributed the setback to "the unduly opportunistic and selfish policy of Kaizl, Kramář, Engel, and Pacák"; see Pavla Horská, "Česká otázka v Rakousko-Uhersku 1897–1914 ve světle zpráv francouzských zastupitelských úřadů," *Československý časopis historický*, xv/3 (1967), 456.

various changes, none sufficient to reverse the party's fortunes. During the 1890s the party erected a comprehensive organizational structure that at the top included a governing board of trustees and an executive committee and below them numerous regional, district, and special interest (i.e., women, students, and workers) clubs. Within this structure, which was far more sophisticated than anything the Old Czechs had ever created, the parliamentary deputies' club in Vienna gradually intruded until it assumed the preponderant role in dealings with the central government. This role was facilitated by a growing interconnection between the executive committee and the deputies through persons such as Kaizl and party president Emanuel Engel who held dual party and elective public offices. The party commanded an extensive newspaper network consisting of *Národní listy* and several dozen regional newspapers, some of which were personal organs for party leaders. Although factionalism and petty jealousies hampered the smooth functioning of this apparatus, it served adequately until the early twentieth century, when the Young Czechs, faced with stern competition at the polls and the prospect of a genuine universal suffrage reform, made an effort to update and revitalize it.[87]

So far as leadership was concerned, the party suffered from problems such as a shortage of really competent persons, the loss of some leaders through government appointments, personality clashes, and disagreements on policy. The party was unable, and to a certain extent unwilling, to perpetuate the Czech liberal tradition of elevating one pre-eminent figure as a national leader, as the Old Czechs had done with František Palacký and František L. Rieger. It was common knowledge within the party that several members aspired to this lofty status; Kaizl seemed a possible contender in the mid-1890s. In March 1898, however, Kaizl was named minister of finance in the cabinet of Count Franz Thun, becoming the first Young Czech to enter the cabinet and the holder of the highest office yet achieved by a Czech. For several reasons this appointment injured Kaizl's reputation:[88] Minister-President Thun had never been forgiven by the Czechs for his repressive measures as royal governor of Bohemia; also Kaizl made his decision unilaterally, informing only a few close friends but never seeking formal party approval. The militant Eduard Grégr and *Národní listy* assailed him for betraying the state right programme, and in fact Kaizl had become progressively disillusioned with it. His appointment symbolized his growing personal conservatism and the party's new *hoffähig* status. He had come to fear above all the rise of aggressive German nationalism of the type which had burgeoned during the Badeni crisis in reaction to Czech demands and government concessions. He accepted the conventional view that foreign policy was solely the business of the emperor and the foreign minister; he even censured Kramář for stirring up official

87 Letter of V. Škarda to Kramář, 11 January 1901, ANM 2–4/220–1; letter of P. Grégr to Kramář, 19 February 1906, ANM/2016–19.
88 Kaizl, Z *mého života*, III/i, 730; Tobolka, *Politické dějiny*, III/ii, 201, 222ff.

disfavour with an article criticizing Austrian membership in the Triple Alliance that appeared in a French periodical.[89] In a certain sense, Kaizl sacrificed much political capital to assume a government position from which he could aid the Czech cause largely through such discreet actions as placing Czechs in the upper echelons of the central bureaucracy in Vienna. Behind the scenes he continued to influence the party by advising close friends like Václav Škarda (1861–1912), chairman of the executive committee; Bedřich Pacák; and Emanuel Engel, who belonged to a small oligarchy that actually ran the party at that time. Kaizl's death in 1901 at the age of forty-seven robbed the party of a mature and inde-fatigable worker, but one who lacked the magnetism, daring, and perhaps the integrity necessary to inspire an entire nation.

Kramář, in contrast to Kaizl, operated as a lone wolf on the periphery of the party's decision-making oligarchy. He was respected for courage, knowledge, and honesty, perhaps even a bit feared for aggressive self-confidence, but vanity pre-vented him from developing genuine tact and a proper sense of timing. He nursed a lasting resentment over the role of scapegoat which he bore after Badeni's collapse;[90] however, his recovery was helped by his relative youth and the retire-ment, death, or cooptation of leading Young Czechs. The Badeni crisis convinced Kramář irrevocably that the monarchy would never make genuine structural changes toward equalizing the conditions of the Czechs and the other Austrian Slavs with the ruling Germans and Magyars until it sundered the diplomatic alliance with Germany. He turned his attention increasingly toward foreign policy, but this aspect of his career, and of the party's evolution, belongs to another era.

The activities of the Young Czech party at its zenith may have produced no startling or fundamental benefits for the Czech nation, but the responsibility for failure was not the party's alone. In justice to the party, it must be acknowledged that it operated within an inherited framework of institutions and modes of thought that could not easily be transformed. The party's hegemony was due to special circumstances: a restricted franchise, an aura of being a democratic "all-national" party, and lack of competition from rivals. Once these circumstances altered, the party lost some of the elements which had joined it during the opposition to the Compromise of 1890. The continuous development of class differences and special interests within Czech society in the 1890's prevented the party from satisfying all these elements. Marginal peasants and small farmers had different interests than large-scale agricultural entrepreneurs. The Czech industrial and financial bour-geoisie felt that their personal enrichment would serve the national cause, as ex-pressed in Emanuel Engel's remark that twenty Czech millionaire manufacturers would benefit the nation more than the best language ordinances.[91] The working

89 Kaizl, Z mého života, iii/i, 879.
90 Ibid.; Kramář, Anmerkungen, 29.
91 Samostatnost, 29 August 1903, quoted Engel as saying this during an interview reported originally in the St. Petersburg Viedomosti.

class naturally enlisted in the camp of Social Democracy when it became politically active in the 1890s. Facing such diversity, no party could long have maintained pervasive control.

The Young Czechs, nevertheless, might have managed their affairs more skilfully than they did. The party's programme concentrated on outdated state right demands that were unrealistic in the new era of mass nationalism. Its economic and social demands were limited largely to those that benefited the middle class. The parliamentary deputies' club lacked confidence in the electorate and even in the party membership and withheld information on its activities in Vienna. Unrelenting party opposition to the government was perhaps essential to defend the nation against pro-German measures, but such opposition denied the party any possibility of success on a broad scale. Individual deputies of course managed to attend to specific grievances of individual constituents, and this kind of achievement was one of the keys to the party's operation. By the time Young Czech policies changed to the "free hand" and then to tentative cooperation under Badeni, the numerically large deputies' club no longer represented the sentiments of the working masses on the threshold of active political participation, if it ever had. Factionalism and lack of discipline springing from personal as well as political causes sapped the party's energy. The Young Czech leaders were impelled by the changing dynamics of their social base to seek an accommodation with their critics. They chose reconciliation with the Right rather than with the Left, keeping open the door to cooperation with the Old Czechs, and to a limited extent with the aristocracy, while closing it to radical nationalists and socialists. At Nymburk in 1894 they virtually destroyed the left wing within the party only to see it reappear in the form of rival splinter groups and eventually full-fledged parties. The left wing, in turn, assailed every Young Czech attempt at a "positive policy" as capitulation. This highlighted the party's dilemma of having to win specific gains on the one hand, while mouthing the militant slogans of insurgent nationalism on the other. The gulf between Young Czech words and deeds was apparent.

To overcome these obstacles was difficult in itself; it was impossible without a party leader who was master of the political art. There were dedicated and able men in the Young Czech ranks. None produced any new ideas or inspiring conceptions.[92] The party as a whole prepared no just and practical solutions to the national and constitutional questions, but at that time no other Austrian party did so either. In practical terms, this programmatic deficiency resulted in the party's oscillation between an obstruction (1893, 1894, 1900) that negated the parliamentary process and a hard-headed quest for concessions that acknowleged the status quo. This

92 Masaryk's studies on Czech political development (*Česká otázka, Naše nynější krise,* and *Karel Havlíček*) appeared after he had left the Young Czech party. Kaizl accepted the "establishment" too much to challenge its basic assumptions. Kramář realized his potential as a critic primarily in the field of foreign policy and then in an impractical form that depended too heavily upon a supposedly liberalized tsarist Russia.

persistent instability and opportunism hurt the party's public image among the progressive youth and the urban working class, the bearers of the most militant anti-"establishment" sentiments in the 1890s.

The Young Czechs held a great responsibility as representatives of the most mature, the most literate, and the wealthiest people among the Slavs of Austria. To their credit, they officially rejected the spurious doctrines of anti-Semitism and national chauvinism. They stood fast against Germanization. They fought stalwartly for universal equal suffrage. They introduced a generation to the realities of practical politics. And they defended the interests of the Czech nation while the imperceptible, ongoing forces of economic and cultural change were shaping the national consciousness for great trials to come.

Selected Bibliography of the Publications of Otakar Odložilík

The following abbreviations have been used below:

ČMM *Časopis Matice moravské* (Brno)
JCEA *Journal of Central European Affairs* (Boulder, Colorado)
SEER *Slavonic and East European Review* (London)
VKČSN *Věstník Královské české společnosti nauk* (Prague)

1923

'Jednota bratří Habrovanských,' *Český časopis historický* (Prague), vol. xxix,
  pp. 1–70, 301–57
'K otázce rodiště Husova,' *Otavan* (Písek), vol. vii, pp. 147–9

1924

Jan Milíč z Kroměříže, Kroměříž, 28 pp.
Mistr Štěpán z Kolína, Prague, 73 pp.
'Utrakvistická postilla z r. 1540,' VKČSN, ser. i, vol. for 1924, no. iii, 30 pp.

1925

'Dvě písně z r. 1848,' *Sborník Matice slovenskej* (Turčiansky Sv. Martin), vol. iii,
  pp. 145–8
'Husovy oslavy 1915,' *Národní osvobození* (Prague), no. 183
'K sedmdesátinám Jindř. Vančury,' *Národní osvobození*, no. 237
'Listy Kašpara Fejérpatakyho a Ctiboha Zocha Karlu Havlíčkovi,' *Sborník Matice
  slovenskej*, vol. iii, pp. 148–51
'Několik písní z r. 1848,' *Časopis Společnosti přátel starožitností českých* (Prague),
  vol. 33, pp. 138–44

'Nová literatura o Jednotě bratrské,' *Naše věda* (Prague), vol. vii, pp. 9–25
'Příspěvky ke sporu o rodiště Husovo,' *Otavan*, vol. ix, pp. 19–21
'Světový význam husitství,' *Přerod* (Prague), vol. iv, pp. 81–2, 98–100
'Der Wiederhall der Lehre Zwinglis in Mähren,' *Zwingliana* (Zürich), vol. iv, no. 9, pp. 227–76
'Z počátků husitství na Moravě. Šimon z Tišnova a Jan Vavřincův z Račic,' čmm, vol. 49, pp. 1–170
'Z redaktorské činnosti J. Nerudy,' *Lumír* (Prague), vol. 52, pp. 546–50
'Žeň literární Žižkova jubilea,' *Jihočeský přehled* (Č. Budějovice), vol. i, pp. 265–70

1926
'Dva listy Dra Jana Kozánka z r. 1848,' čmm, vol. 50, pp. 680–8
'J. K. Tyl za bouří svatodušních,' *Plzeňsko* (Plzeň), vol. viii, pp. 26–8
'Leták M. Štěpána z Kolína o pronásledování kněží z r. 1393,' vкčsn, ser. i, vol. for 1926, no. i, 48 pp.
'Madame de Staël et la police autrichienne en 1808,' *Revue française de Prague* (Prague), vol. v, pp. 31–4
(Ed.) *Matěje z Janova 'Regulae veteris et novi testamenti,'* vol. v: *De corpore Christi*, Prague, xxxii + 432 pp.
'Palacký in München. Unbekannte Dokumenten,' *Prager Presse* (Prague), no. 134; Supplement: Dichtung und Welt, no. 20
'Palackýs Berufung zum Minister im Jahre 1848,' *Prager Presse*, no. 143
'Palacký v rodinném kruhu,' *Československá republika* (Prague), no. 143
'Pokus o soudní vyšetřování Palackého v r. 1848,' *Národní osvobození*, no. 143
'Z jubilejní literatury o Žižkovi,' *Naše věda*, vol. viii, pp. 12–39

1927
'Milan Prelog, *Slavenska renesansa 1780–1848*, Zagreb, 1924,' čmm, vol. 51, pp. 329–47
'Neue Dokumente über den Prager Slavenkongress,' *Prager Presse*, no. 285

1928
(Ed.) 'Bratra Jana Blahoslava Přerovského spis O původu Jednoty bratrské a řádu v ní,' vкčsn, ser. i, vol. for 1928, no. vii, 71 pp.
'Daniel Arnošt Jablonský a Lužičtí Srbové,' in *Z dějin východní Evropy a Slovanstva. Sborník věnovaný Jaroslavu Bidlovi*, Prague, pp. 331–9
'Komenský a Harvardská kolej,' čmm, vol. 52, pp. 349–60
'Proč byl G. A. Lindner přeložen z Jičína do Celje,' *Národní osvobození*, no. 74
'Slovanský sjezd a svatodušní bouře 1848,' *Slovanský přehled* (Prague), vol. xx, pp. 408–25
'Z pansofických studií J. A. Komenského. Kritická studie o zlomku dosud neznámého pansofického spisu,' čmm, vol. 52, pp. 125–98
(Ed.) *Jan Blahoslav: O původu Jednoty bratrské a řádu v ní*, Prague, 211 pp.

1929

'Čeští exulanti v Berlíně a Lešno, *Reformační sborník* (Prague), vol. III, pp. 22–4
'Dobrovský a anglický slavista John Bowring,' in *Josef Dobrovský, 1753–1829.*
    Sborník statí k stému výročí smrti Josefa Dobrovského, Prague, pp. 252–8
'Good King Wenceslas: A Historical Sketch,' SEER, vol. VIII, pp. 120–30
'Die Hinterlassenschaft Jablonskýs,' *Slavische Rundschau* (Prague), vol. I, pp.
    411–12
'Hus, Jan, in *Nordisk Familjebok*, 3rd ed., Stockholm, vol. x, col. 147–8
'Husiter. Husitkrigen (1419–34),' in *Nordisk Familjebok*, vol. x, col. 159–61
'Karel Kadlec,' SEER, vol. VIII, pp. 204–5
'Komenského poselství k milostivému létu 1631–32,' ČMM, vol. 53, pp. 289–319
'Komenský a anglický parlament,' pp. 249–70 in *Českou minulostí. Práce věnované*
    profesoru Karlovy university Václavu Novotnému jeho žáky k šedesátým
    narozeninám (eds. Otakar Odložilík, Jaroslav Prokeš, Rudolf Urbánek), Prague,
    391 pp.
'New Light upon Comenius,' SEER, vol. VII, pp. 453–7
'Vyšetřovací komise z r. 1848 a jejich registratura,' *Sborník archivu Ministerstva*
    vnitra (Prague), vol. II, pp. 1–90
'Wycliffe's Influence upon Central and Eastern Europe,' SEER, vol. VII, pp. 634–48

1930

'Comenius and Christian Unity,' SEER, vol. IX, pp. 79–93
'Moravští exulanti Jiří a Jan Veselští-Laetové,' ČMM, vol. 54, pp. 79–182
'Návštěva perského cestovatele v Novém Jičíně r. 1590,' ČMM, vol. 54, pp. 377–8
'O anglických podobiznách Komenského,' in *Přátelé čsl. starožitností svému učiteli.*
    K. šedesátinám univ. prof. Dr. J. V. Šimáka. Příloha Časopisu Společnosti přátel
    starožitností československých, vol. 38, no. 2/3, pp. 136–40
'Poslední Smiřičtí,' in *Od pravěku k dnešku. Sborník prací z dějin československých.*
    K šedesátým narozeninám Josefa Pekaře, Prague, pt. 2, pp. 70–88
'Šedesátiny prof. Bohumila Navrátila,' *Lidové noviny* (Brno), no. 94

1931

'Alfons Šťastný na prahu veřejné činnosti,' *Časopis pro dějiny venkova* (Prague),
    vol. XVIII, pp. 89–103
'Aug. Neumann: *Nové prameny k dějinám husitství na Moravě*, Olomouc, 1930,'
    ČMM, vol. 55, pp. 221–44
'Bratří na Slovensku,' ČMM, vol. 55, pp. 329–70
'Daniel Vetter a jeho cesta na Island,' ČMM, vol. 55, pp. 75–94
'Vchynští ze Vchynic a Tetova v Nizozemí v XVI. a XVII. století. Příspěvky k
    dějinám rodu,' in *Sborník prací věnovaných prof. dru Gustavu Friedrichovi*
    k šedesátým narozeninám 1871–1931, Prague, pp. 291–309

'Z anglických archivů a knihoven,' *Časopis archivní školy* (Prague), vol. VIII, pp. 93–138

'Zápas o bratrskou školu v Třebíči 1557,' ČMM, vol. 55, pp. 186–9

1932

Contributions to *Československá vlastivěda*, vol. IV, *Dějiny*, Prague: Doba stará, III. Rozmach české říše do vymření Přemyslovců, pp. 61–79. Doba stará, IV. Léta nejistoty.–Panování Jana Lucemburského (1306–46), pp. 80–98. Doba střední, I. Rozkvět národního života za Karla IV. a Václava IV., pp. 99–162. Doba střední, III. Rozkvět a zánik reformace, pp. 341–490

'Gustav Adolf und die Hoffnungen der tschechischen Emigration,' *Prager Presse*, no. 313

'Jan Filiczki z Filic a jeho čeští přátelé,' in *K dějinám československým v období humanismu. Sborník prací věnovaných J. B. Novákovi k šedesátým narozeninám*, Prague, pp. 431–42

'Komenský v Groningen r. 1656,' *Archiv pro badání o životě a spisech J. A. Komenského* (Brno), vol. XIII, pp. 93–5

'Václav Novotný, 1869–1932,' ČMM, vol. 56, pp. 343–68

'Za Václavem Novotným,' *Naše doba* (Prague), vol. 39, pp. 612–15

'Ze zápasů pobělohorské emigrace,' ČMM, vol. 56, pp. 1–58, 369–88

'Z korespondence pobělohorské emigrace z let 1621–1624,' VKČSN, ser. I, vol. for 1932, no. II, 198 pp.

1933

'An Attempt to Reconcile the Protestant Churches in the XVIIIth Century (As Discussed between Archbishop W. Wake and D. E. Jabłoński),' in VIIᵉ *Congrès international des sciences historiques. Résumés des communications présentées au congrès*, Warsaw, vol. I, pp. 260–4

'Berlínský rukopis kroniky Pulkavovy,' *Časopis archivní školy*, vol. IX/X, pp. 98–107

'Husyci na brzegu Bałtyku w 1433 roku,' *Rocznik Gdański* (Danzig), vol. VII, pp. 81–125

'M. Jan z Rokycan a Jednota bratrská,' *Kalich* (Rokycany), pp. 9–14

1934

'Česká emigrace,' in *Doba bělohorská a Albrecht z Valdštejna. Sborník osmi statí* (ed. J. Prokeš), Prague, pp. 85–117

'Lipany na soudu historiků,' *Lidové noviny*, vol. XXIX, 30.5.1934

'Petr Chelčický,' in *Tvůrcové dějin* (ed. K. Stloukal), Prague, vol. II, pp. 528–36

'Politické a hospodářské poměry po Bílé hoře,' in *Doba bělohorská a Albrecht z Valdštejna*, pp. 61–84

'Protestant Reunion in the 18th Century. Archbishop W. Wake and D. E. Jablonski,' SEER, vol. XIII, pp. 119–26

'Ze zápasů pobělohorské emigrace,' pt. 3, ČMM, vol. 57, pp. 59–157
Žižkovo vítězství u Hořic 1423, Prague. 16 pp., 1 map. 'Průvodce po bojištích a vojenských památnostech ČSR,' no. 9
Zkáza Nymburka za války třicetileté, Nymburk, 20 pp.
'Zeň šedesátníkova (Josef Šusta),' *Nové Čechy* (Prague), vol. XVII, pp. 49–55

1935
'Cesty z Čech a Moravy do Vel. Britanie v letech 1563–1620,' ČMM, vol. 59, pp. 241–320
'Jan Blahoslav,' in *Tvůrcové dějin*, vol. III, pp. 125–131
'Wyclif and Bohemia,' VKČSN, ser. I, vol. for 1935, no. I. 14 pp.

1936
'Bohumil Navrátil, 1870–1936,' ČMM, vol. 60, pp. 417–54
Karel starší ze Žerotína, 1564–1636, Prague, 197 pp.
'Komenský und das Harvard College,' *Prager Presse*, 3.9.1936

1937
'La carrière et l'œuvre de Joseph Pekař,' *L'Europe centrale* (Prague), 6.2.1937
'Dva listy Komenského gdanskému kazateli Arn. Andreae,' *Archiv pro badání o životě a spisech J. A. Komenského*, vol. XIV, pp. 3–6
'Karel of Žerotín and the English Court, 1564–1636,' SEER, vol. XV, pp. 413–25
'Nástin československých dějin,' in *Sborník "Poznání,"* Prague, vol. II, 96 pp. Reprinted separately as 2nd edition with minor alterations and an index, Prague, 132 pp. Third edition, London, 1942 (1943 on wrapper), 132 pp.
'Příspěvky z Anglie na stavbu Salvátorského chrámu,' *Reformační sborník*, vol. VI, pp. 127–8
'Václav Novotný, učitel a buditel,' *Časopis Národního musea* (Prague), vol. 111, pp. 177–85
Wyclif and Bohemia. Two essays, Prague, 60 pp.

1938
'Jaroslav Bidlo,' SEER, vol. XVI, pp. 696–8
Mistr Jan Campanus, Prague, 1938, 48 pp. (Reprint of an article in *Zvon*, vol. 38)
Odvěký úděl. Úvaha z října 1938, Prague, 30 pp.
'O německé historiografii v Československu,' in *První sjezd československých historiků 1937. Přednášky a debaty*, Prague, pp. 109–16
'Political Thought in Bohemia in the Early 17th Century,' *Bulletin of the International Committee of Historical Sciences* (Paris), vol. X, pp. 635–7
'Stát český a uherský,' in *Dějiny lidstva* (ed. Josef Šusta), Prague, vol. V, pp. 201–26

1939

'Bohemian Protestants and the Calvinist Churches,' *Church History* (Chicago), vol. VIII, pp. 342–55

'Gustav Adolf a česká otázka,' in Nil Ahnlund, *Gustav Adolf král švédský*, transl. from Swedish, Prague, pp. 250–64

'Nizozemí a Anglie v první polovici 17 věku,' in *Dějiny lidstva*, vol. VI, pp. 15–60

'Pobělohorská emigrace,' in *Co daly naše země Evropě a lidstvu* (ed. Vilém Mathesius), vol. I, Prague, pp. 170–6 (2nd ed., 1940)

1940

'Anežka ze Štítného-Kralovna Mab-Kateřina ze Žerotína, roz. z Valdštejna,' in *Královny, kněžny a velké ženy české* (ed. K. Stloukal), Prague, pp. 138–42, 281–7, 288–93 (2nd ed. 1941)

'Hus and the Czech Nation,' *The Spirit of Czechoslovakia* (London), vol. I, no. I, pp. 3–4

'Jan Máchal–Arne Novák–Josef Matoušek,' SEER, vol. XIX, pp. 311–15

'Two Reformation Leaders of the Unitas Fratrum,' *Church History*, vol. IX, pp. 253–63

'We Live in the Seventeenth Century,' *The Educational Forum* (New York), vol. V, pp. 5–16

1941

'Clio in Chains: Czech Historiography, 1939–1940,' SEER, vol. XX, pp. 330–7

'Comenius in London,' *The Spirit of Czechoslovakia*, vol. II, no. 9–10, pp. 4 and 16

'A Czech Plan for a Danubian Federation – 1848,' JCEA, vol. I, pp. 253–74

'Czechoslovak Resistance,' *New Europe* (New York), vol. I, pp. 65–7

'George of Poděbrady and Bohemia to the Pacification of Silesia – 1459,' *University of Colorado Studies* (Boulder), vol. I, pp. 265–88

'Old Facts in New Perspective,' *New Europe*, vol. I, pp. 289–91

'Problems of the Reign of George of Poděbrady,' SEER, vol. XX, pp. 206–22

'Twilight or Dawn for the Small Nations,' JCEA, vol. I, pp. 45–54

Vzkříšení mateřštiny, New York, 20 pp.

1942

'Braving the Tyrant,' *The American-Czechoslovak Fellowship* (Chicago), vol. I, pp. 74–7

'Czechoslovak Writers Fight On,' *Books Abroad* (Norman, Okla.), vol. XVI, pp. 380–4

'A Czech Pioneer,' *The American-Czechoslovak Fellowship*, vol. I, pp. 16–19

'The Glory and Martyrdom of Czechoslovak Schools,' in *The Way of Light*, Chicago, pp. 5–19

Jan Amos Komenský (Comenius), Chicago, 34 pp. Reprinted under the title

'Comenius' Life and Work in its Historical Setting,' in *The Teacher of Nations* (ed. Joseph Needham), Cambridge, pp. 41–60

'Mezi včerejškem a dneškem,' *Zítřek* (New York), vol. I, pp. 20–38.

'The Plight of the Czechoslovak Youth,' *The American-Czechoslovak Fellowship*, vol. I, pp. 29–38

'Traditio Lampadis,' *The American-Czechoslovak Fellowship*, vol. II, pp. 47–57

'Undaunted Czechoslovakia,' *Congressional Record* (Washington, D.C.), vol. 88, pt. 10 (Sept. 23, 1942), pp. A 3395–97

'The Wave of the Past,' *New Europe*, vol. II, pp. 35–7

1943

'Bohemia and Poland in Medieval Plans of European Organization,' *Quarterly Bulletin of the Polish Institute* (New York), vol. I, pp. 432–9. Spanish version: 'Bohemia y Polonia en los planes medievales de organización Europea,' *La revista de estudios eslavos* (Mexico City), vol. I (1947), pp. 39–44

'Na předělu dob,' *Zítřek*, vol. II, pp. 30–68

'Nationality North of the Danube,' *The Antioch Review* (Yellow Springs), vol. III, pp. 106–16. Reprinted in *Democratic Postwar Reconstruction in Central Eastern Europe*, Yellow Springs, pp. 28–34

'The Pattern of Education in Central and Eastern Europe,' *New Europe*, vol. III, pp. 22–3. Also separately in *The Central and Eastern European Planning Board Pamphlet Series*, no. 5, pp. 4–8

'Universities at Crossroads,' *Bulletin of the Masaryk Institute* (New York), vol. I, no. 5, pp. 1–5

1944

'The Czechoslovak Tradition of Friendship with Russia,' *The Spirit of Czechoslovakia*, vol. V, no. I, pp. 12–14

'Education for Peace,' in *Proceedings of the International Student Assembly*, Oxford, pp. 128–30

'The Foundations of Czechoslovak Foreign Policy,' *The Spirit of Czechoslovakia*, vol. V, no. 2, pp. 31–4

Povstalec a emigrant. Kapitoly z dějin třicetileté války, London, 80 pp.

'The Rights and Wrongs of a Controversy,' *The Central European Observer* (London), vol. XXI, pp. 302–3

'Tvář Ameriky,' *Zítřek*, vol. III, pp. 16–39. Reprinted in *Svazky* (Prague), no. 93, 1946

1945

'Components of the Czechoslovak Tradition,' SEER, London, vol. XXIII, pp. 97–106. Reprinted in *Czechoslovak Inheritance*, Calcutta, pp. 20–38

'Czech Missionaries in New Spain,' *The Hispanic American Historical Review*

(Durham, N.C.), vol. xxv, pp. 428–54. Czech version: 'Čeští misionáři v Mexiku,' *Obzor* (London), vol. I, (1944), pp. 53–60. Spanish translation: 'Misioneros checos en Mexico,' *Boletino de la sociedad mexicana de geografia y estadistica* (Mexico City), vol. 60 (1945), pp. 423–36

'Is a Mediator Needed?,' *Bulletin of the Masaryk Institute*, vol. III, no. 7, pp. 1–7

Maják nad vodami, London, 14 pp.

'Masaryk and the Czech Nineties,' *The Spirit of Czechoslovakia*, vol. VI, no. 1, pp. 10–12

'On the Threshold of a New Era,' *The Norseman* (London), vol. III, pp. 26–33. Reprinted in *Czechoslovak Inheritance*, pp. 5–19

S druhého břehu (with J. L. Hromádka), 1st ed., New York (2nd. ed., Prague, 1946): Otakar Odložilík's essays, pp. 151–269

Tři stati o české otázce, London, 27 pp.

1946

'Anglické a americké práce o slovanských dějinách z let 1939–1946,' *Český časopis historický*, vol. 47, pp. 124–46

'Palacký o pravém lidství,' *Křesťanská revue* (Prague), vol. XIII, pp. 104–10

'Prague,' SEER, vol. XXIII–XXIV, pp. 81–91. Also separately: *Prague through the Ages*, Prague, 1948, 16 pp.

'Studentům na uvítanou,' *Křesťanská revue*, vol. XIII, pp. 151–6

'V zrcadle vzpomínek,' in *In memoriam MUDr Jana Vignatiho*, Brno, pp. 14–21

'Známe se?,' *Křesťanská revue*, vol. XIII, pp. 54–60

1947

'Budoucnost naší vzdělanosti,' *Křesťanská revue*, vol. XIV, pp. 6–10

'Dějinné panorama,' *Křesťanská revue*, vol. XIV, pp. 71–4

Na kroměřížském sněmu 1848 a 1849, Prague, 1947, 42 pp.

'Problémy novějších moravských dějin,' ČMM, vol. 67, pp. 203–21

'Vrak Evropy,' *Křesťanská revue*, vol. XIV, 168–72

1948

'Beneš of Czechoslovakia,' *Queen's Quarterly* (Kingston, Ont.), vol. 55, pp. 377–89

'Dvě doby Karlovy university,' *Naše doba*, vol. 54, pp. 289–92

'Kam se obrátí Německo,' *Křesťanská revue*, vol. xv, pp. 4–11

Karlova universita, 1348–1948, Prague, 78 pp. Also in English, French and Russian translations

'The Peace of Westphalia 1648,' *The Contemporary Review* (London), vol. 174, pp. 361–5

'Storm over the Danube,' JCEA, vol. VIII, pp. 129–38. Reprinted in *The Making of Modern Europe* (ed. Herman Ausubel), New York, 1951, vol. II, pp. 656–67

1949

'Commemorating T. G. Masaryk,' *Bulletin of the Masaryk Institute*, Special issue, March 1949, 4 pp.

'Edward Beneš' Memoirs,' JCEA, vol. VIII, pp. 412–20

1950

'Central Europe,' *Columbia Journal of International Affairs* (New York), vol. IV, pp. 29–32

'Concerning Munich and the Ides of March,' JCEA, vol. IX, pp. 419–28

'Enter Masaryk: A Prologue to His Political Career,' JCEA, vol. X, pp. 21–36

T. G. Masaryk, 1850–1950, Chicago, 56 pp. (in Czech)

'T. G. Masaryk in the Past and Present,' in *Tributes to T. G. Masaryk*, London, pp. 12–14

'Thirty Years of Central European Exchanges,' *Institute of International Education Bulletin* (New York), vol. XXV, pp. 6–7

'The Way of Democracy in Central Europe,' *The Australian Quarterly* (Sydney), vol. XXII, pp. 91–103

1951

'Masaryk's Idea of Democracy,' *University of Toronto Quarterly* (Toronto), vol. XXI, pp. 1–13. Also published separately by the Masaryk Institute (New York), 1952

1952

'Modern Czechoslovak Historiography,' SEER, vol. XXX, pp. 376–92

1953

'The Czechs on the Eve of the 1848 Revolution,' *Harvard Slavic Studies* (Cambridge, Mass.), vol. I, pp. 179–217

Jan Hus, Chicago, 64 pp. (in Czech)

1954

'From Velehrad to Olomouc,' *Harvard Slavic Studies*, vol. II, pp. 75–90

Listy z dějin rodného kraje, New York, 35 pp.

1955

'The Poet's Way,' in *Poetae in Exilio* (ed. Peeter Arumaa and Robert Vlach), Stockholm, pp. 12–16

1956

'The Chapel of Bethlehem in Prague,' *Studien zur älteren Geschichte Osteuropa*, pt. I, in *Wiener Archiv für Geschichte des Slawentums und Osteuropa*, vol. II, pp. 125–41

'Mickiewicz among the Czechs and Slovaks,' in *Adam Mickiewicz in World Literature* (ed. Wacław Lednicki), Berkeley and Los Angeles, pp. 437–68

1957

'Charles IV et son époque,' *Comité d'études culturelles franco-tchécoslovaque: Bulletin* (Paris), no. 2, pp. 3–19

'The Contest for East Central Europe in the Eleventh Century,' *The Polish Review* (New York), vol. II, pp. 3–17

'Edvard Beneš on Munich Days,' JCEA, vol. XVI, 384–93

1958

'Congresses of Slavic Youth, 1890–1892,' *The Annals of the Ukrainian Academy of Arts and Sciences in the U.S.* (New York), vol. VI, pp. 1327–57

Obrázky z dvou světů, Philadelphia and Lund, 156 pp.

1959

'The Slavic Congress of 1848,' *The Polish Review*, vol. IV, pp. 3–15

1962

Vzpomínky a ohlasy, Philadelphia, 124 pp.

1963

'Bohemia (History to 1740),' in *Encyclopaedia Britannica*, Chicago, vol. III, pp. 846–51

'Rembrandt's Polish Nobleman,' *The Polish Review*, vol. VIII, pp. 3–32

'Russia and Czech National Aspirations,' JCEA, vol. XXII, pp. 407–39

1964

Jednota bratrská a reformovaní francouzského jazyka, Philadelphia, 140 pp.

'Prague and Cracow Scholars in the Fifteenth Century,' *The Polish Review*, vol. IX, pp. 19–29

1965

The Hussite King: Bohemia in European Affairs, 1440–1471, New Brunswick (New Jersey), 337 pp.

1966

'Thomas Seget: A Scottish Friend of Szymon Szymonowicz,' *The Polish Review*, vol. XI, pp. 1–37

'Die Wittenberger Philippisten und die Brüderunität,' *Ost und West in der Geschichte des Denkens und der kulturellen Beziehungen* (ed. W. Steinitz et al.), Berlin, pp. 106–18

1967

'The Czechs,' in *The Immigrants' Influence on Wilson's Peace Policies* (ed. J. P. O'Grady), Lexington (Kentucky), pp. 204–23

1968

'Recent Studies in Czech Humanism,' *Renaissance Quarterly* (New York), vol. xxi, pp. 248–53

'Úvaha s trochou vzpomínek,' in *Padesát let: Soubor vzpomínek a úvah o Masarykově republice* (eds. Ivan Herben and František Třešňák), Toronto, pp. 5–8

1969

'Josef Matoušek,' *Proměny* (New York), vol. vi, no. 4, pp. 17–23

'Václav Hollar v Antverpách,' *Proměny*, vol. vi, no. 2, pp. 40–4

INDEX

Abhandlungen der gelehrten Privatgesellschaft, 55, 60
Abrahamowicz, D., 306, 308, 310
academies, *see* Societies
Acta Eruditorum, 55
Adamites, 227
Adams, J., 216
Adler, V., 301
Aehrenthal, Baron, 196
Agrarian Party (Czech), 300, 302, 310
Andrássy, Count, 62
Andrian-Werburg, V. von, 159
anti-Semitism, 152n., 157, 163, 188, 193, 290, 314
Aranitskii, S., 185, 186
archaeology, 71, 72
Aretino, L., 108
art, 8, 30, 257
artisans, and Czech national renascence, 39–42 *passim*, 47, 49, 50, 52, 234, 275

Athenaeum, 285
Auden, W. H., 32
Augsburger Allgemeine Zeitung, 118
Austria, Lower, 152n.
Austro-Hungarian Compromise (Ausgleich) of 1867, and Bohemia, 259, 287, 300, 303, 307–10 *passim*
Austro-Hungarian Monarchy
– and Germany, 4, 148, 158, 161, 177, 285, 296, 312
– German provinces, German-speaking population of: and Austrian Parliament, 203, 204, 209, 213, 266, 267, 268, 290, 292, 293, 295, 300, 302, 304, 306, 308, 309, 310; and Czechs after 1879, 269–73 *passim*, 290–4 *passim*, 297, 298; and Masaryk's ancestry, 243, 252; and Slavs in 1848–9, 4, 169, 181, 194, 199, 200, 203; and "Viennese radical-ism," 204, 205, 209

– historians on, 67
– Parliament of, national representation in, 203
– Parliament of, and Czechs: in 1848–9, 202–14 passim; after 1879, 4, 152n., 257–78; after 1891, 284, 288, 289, 300–3 passim; electoral reform of, 292–5 passim, 300–2 passim, 311; and revolution of 1848–9, 165, 166; see also under national groups
– Polish attitudes to, 192; see also Poland and Austrian Parliament
– revolution of 1848–9 in, 129, 151, 157, 168, 169, 197, 202–14 passim, 222
– and serfdom, 206
– and Slav Congress (1848), 182, 184, 189, 194, 199, 200
– Slav groups in, 57n., 58; political attitudes of: to 1848, 131–3 passim; in 1848–9, 182, 188, 192, 198, 200; and Parliament, 203
– Slovak attitudes to: to 1848, 140–2 passim; in 1848–9, 181, 182
Austro-Hungarian Monarchy, court and government of
– attitude to Bohemia and Czechs before 1848, 59, 65, 95–112, 128, 156; in 1848–9, 163–6 passim, 170, 178, 183, 189, 190, 205; 1850–79, 69–72 passim; after 1879, 4, 6, 255, 262–8 passim; see also Censorship
– attitude to Hungary, 169, 196, 205, 207, 276
– Czech attitudes to: before 1848, 23, 65, 122, 123, 126, 139, 140, 141, 142, 152, 153, see also Austro-Slavism; in 1848–9, 129, 165, 167, 177, 182, 183, 185, 187, 189, 194, 202–14 passim; 1850–79, 67; 1879–91, 257–81 passim; after 1891, 282–314 passim
Austro-Slavism, 24, 57n., 58, 65, 72, 101n., 142, 157, 162, 165, 175, 182, 184, 201, 205, 208

Bach, A. von, 6, 67, 69, 71, 72, 169, 206n., 224
Badeni, Count K., 299–313 passim
Balbín, B., 226, 228
Bartolomeides, L., 217
Bartoš, F. M., 234, 236n.
Basel, Council of, 234
Batthyány, Count J., 188, 196
Bäuerle, A., 26
Bautzen, 87, 92; gymnasium at, 76, 81–3 passim; library of Maćica Serbska, 88
Bavaria, 29, 71, 111n., 164, 232
Beausobre, I. de, 227, 228, 235
Beck, A. J., 183
Belgium, 29, 148, 150, 152
Bělič, J., 246n.
Benoni, J., 218
Béranger, P. J. de, 11
Berlin, 150, 169, 283
Berliner Zeitungshalle, 165n.
Bernolák, A., 58, 67, 133n., 136n., 139
Berwiński, R., 187
Bezold, F. von, 238
Bibles: Czech, 57; Slavonic, 22, 103; Krumlov Bible, 67
Biblioteka Warszawska, 66
Biesiadecki, W., 193
Birke, E., 174
Birr, K., 215
Bismarck, Prince O. von, 149n., 172n.
Bleiweis, J., 184
Boček, A., 101
Bodianskii, O. M., 80, 184
Bodický, M., 251n.
Bohemia
– Czech patriots in (1827–48), 33–52 passim

– Diet of, 202, 254, 257, 260, 261, 262, 268, 269, 271, 273, 286, 289, 292, 294, 310
– Estates of, 105, 106, 110, 153, 154n., 224
– Germans in, 51; cultural influence of, 55, 57, 89, 117n., 131, 250, 270; political attitudes of: to 1848, 153; in 1848–9, 159, 166, 170, 178, 190; after 1879, 269, 301, 304, 305, 307
Bohemia, 27, 117n.
Bohemian Brethren (Unitas Fratrum), 20, 216n.
Bohemian Museum, 53–5 *passim*, 58, 59, 85, 93, 154, *see also Časopis Českého musea*, Matice česká
Bohemian state right, 255, 259, 260, 262, 266, 271, 273, 276, 277, 286n., 295, 300–3 *passim*
Böhmische Gesellschaft der Wissenschaften, 56
"Böhmischer Landespatriotismus," 232
Bolzano, B., 164n.
Borkowski, L. D., 191
Bosnia, 179, *see also* South Slavs
botany, 68
Böttiger [Böttinger?], K. A., 99
Brabec, M. K., 180
Bracciolini, P., 108–10 *passim*
Brandl, V., 19, 20, 21
Bratislava, 58, 191, 217, 249; Diet at, 176, 177; literary societies at, 58; lyceum at, 135
Brauner, F. A., 125n., 179, 180, 188, 193; in Austrian Parliament, 206, 210n., 213, 214n.
Breslau, *see* Wrocław
Britain, 27, 296; and Czech national renascence, 55, 148, 168; influence on Czech literature, 11, 65, 68, 71
Brno, 18, 187, 219, 243, 247, 248;

Franciscium, 59; gymnasium at, 244, 250, 251, 252
Brussels, 148, 150, 152
Bulgaria, 179
Bürger, G. A., 11
burghers, *see* middle class
Burke, E., 216

Caf, O., 184, 197, 198
Calvin, J., 238
Čapek, K., 241, 243, 245, 247, 249, 253n.
cartography, 67, 79, 216
Čas, 12, 285, 287, 288, 290, 291, 302, 307, 309
Casanova, J., 217
Časopis Českého musea, 34, 35, 36, 54n., 62, 63, 64, 69n., 70, 87, 103n., 139n., 218
Časopis Matice moravské, 54n.
Časopis Musea království českého, 60n.
Časopis Narodního musea, 60n.
Časopis pro katolické duchovenstvo, 113
Časopis Společnosti vlastenského museum v Čechách, 60, 97, 102
Catholic Union (Ireland), 127
Catholics, Catholicism: in Austrian Parliament, 204; and censorship, 104, 107, 108; Czech, and national renascence, 57, 58, 167; and historiography, 225; and Lusatian Serbs, 74, 86; mediaeval, 229, 235; and Slovaks, 133n., 135, 136, 139, 143, 144; *see also* Jesuits
Čech, 28, 30–1
Čech, 114
Čech, L., 248
Čech, S., 7
Čechoslav, 114
Čejka, J., 64, 69
Čejkovice, 246, 248
Čelakovský, F. L., 7, 10, 11, 154; and Czech language, 132; and Matice

česká, 64, 66, 71; as editor, 114; and
Lusatian Serbs, 83–4, 89, 91n.; and
1848–9, 184; death of, 70, 93
Celje, 66
censorship: Austro-Hungarian, 6, 149;
and Czech national renascence, 68, 71,
95–112, 128n., 156, 219, 224, 225,
227, 229; German, 149, 151n., 160
Červenák, B. P., 82n.
Černín, Count E., 99
Černín, family of, 62
Černý, A., 88
Česká společnost nauk, see Böhmische
Gesellschaft der Wissenschaften
Česká včela, 114, 116, 117, 118, 218,
219n.
České Budějovice, 50, 51
Český Repeal, 179
Chalupný, E., 44
Charles iv, Emperor, 103
Chateaubriand, F. R., Vicomte de, 10,
12, 28
Chlumčanský, Prince V. L., 62n.
Chotek, Count K., 98, 103, 106, 107
Christian Social Party (Austrian), 303,
307, 310
Cieszkowski, A., 187
C. k. vlastenecká hospodářská společnost,
56
C. k. vlastenecké noviny, 57
Clam-Martinic (Martinitz), family of, 62
Clam-Martinitz, Count H., 257, 263, 265,
266, 267
Clary, Count M., 310
Classicism, 5, 8, 10, 11; neo-classicism, 8,
9, 12
clergy: and censorship, 102; and historio-
graphy, 224; and national renascence,
36, 40, 42–5 passim, 51, 52, 62, 81, 87,
90, 113, 134, 135, 184; and socialism,
220
Committee for Scholarly Fostering of

Czech Language, see Sbor k
vědeckému vzdělávání řeči a literatury
české
composers, Czech, 27, 32, 87n.
Constance, Council of, 108, 225
Constitution, Die, 188
Copenhagen, 66, 71
Cosmas Pragensis, 28–32
Cracow, 192, 200; Society of Learning,
71; tomb of Kościuszko, 121; Univer-
sity Library, 66
Crèvecoeur, M.-G. J. de, 216
Croatia, Croats, 132, 141; Croatian
matica, 58n., 66; national renascence,
57n., 89, 161n.; and 1848, 177–9 pas-
sim, 191, 193–8 passim, 207, 208n.
Croatian Society of St. Jerome, 58n.
Curti, M. E., 215
Curtius, E. R., 30, 31
Cybulski, W., 184
Cyril and Methodius, SS., 104, 139
Czartoryski, Prince A., 186n., 196
Czech Brethren, church of, 225, 227, 232,
238
Czech language, 138, 246; promotion of,
53, 54, 56, 60, 63, 65, 66, 70, 119; in
Russia, 114; use of, 4, 5, 34, 49, 61, 66,
77, 82, 95, 143, 230, 258, 270, 271,
272, 286, 295, 300, 301, 304, 310; see
also Dobrovský, Orthography
Czech literature: anthology of (ed.
Palacký), 68; and learned societies, 56,
see also Matice česká; Old Czech, 29–
30, 32, 60; history and periodization of,
3–13, 27, 67; religious, 34; translations,
5, 10, 12, 28, 31, 32, 60, 68; see also
individual authors
Czech national anthem, 26–8, 30–2, 88n.
Czech nobility, see Nobility
Czechoslovak historiography, see Historiography
Czechoslovakia, Republic of, 172

Czechs: and Germans, 146–75 *passim*, 177, 178, 190, 231–3, 234, 262, 269–73; and Lusatian Serbs, 78, 81, 83, 87, 91–3 *passim*; and Magyars, 208, 276; in New World, 215–23; and Poles, 121; and Russians, 144; and Slovaks, 131–45; *see also* Old Czechs, Young Czechs
Czoernig, C. J., 100

Dalmatia, Dalmatians, 187, 198, 269
Darowski, M., 187
Dědictví svatojanské, 34, 40, 57
Dědictví svatováclavské, 57n.
De Léry, J., 219
Demidov, N. P., 184
demography: Czech, 283; emigration to New World, 216, 222; Lusatian Serb, 74–5n., 80n.; Slav, 79
Denis, E., 238
Derzhavin, G. R., 9
De Sauvigné, G. de B., 149n.
Deym, Count F., 153; and 1848, 180, 186, 188, 191
Deym, V., 200
dictionaries, 56, 61, 63, 64, 78n.; *see also* Rieger
Dobblhoff, A. Freiherr von, 153, 190
Dobner, G., 21, 102, 228, 230
Dobrovský, J.: birth of, 16n.; Brandl on, 19, 21; and Czech language, 17, 18, 20, 132; and "Czech Society," 56; and Czechs, 16, 17; Dolanský on, 22; as editor, 28; and Enlightenment, 20–2; and German language, 17, 20, 24; and Goethe, 15–16; and Habsburgs, 23–4; Havránek on, 22; and historicism, 20–2, 24; and humanism, 20; and Hungary, 16; and Josephinism, 24; and Lusatian Serbs, 79, 85, 86; Machovec on, 22–4; Marxist interpretation of, 22–3; Masaryk on, 19–21; Novák on, 21–2; and Palacký, 60; Palacký on,

15–18; portrait of, 15; and Slavonic languages, 17, 18; and Slavs, 19, 20; on St. Václav, 102; death of, 15
Dobrzański, J., 184–6 *passim*, 193
Dolanský, J., 22
Doležal, J., 243n., 244
Dolni Karlovci, 184
Donat, J., 217
Doucha, F., 68, 91; and Lusatian Serbs, 86, 87, 88, 89
Dragoni-Křenovský, J., 194
Drahomíra, 102
Dresden, 90, 97, 155n.
Durych, F., 21
Dvoráček, J., 185, 186
Dvořak, A., 27
Dvůr Králové (Königinhof), 85; *Královédvorský rukopis*, 10, 12
Działynski, Count T. A., 184

Ebert, K. E., 101
economic development (Bohemia), 154n., 156, 257
Edinburgh, 57
education, 267; Czech, 4, 5, 51, 61, 66, 67, 114, 119, 258, 271, 286; gymnasia, 70, 71; industrial schools, 35, 40, 119, 120; rural schools, 126; Slovak, 58, 72, 135; *see also* Schoolteachers, Societies, Students, *and individual universities*
Eichhorn, J. G., 97
Eim, G., 278, 290, 293, 294, 297, 299, 300, 302, 303
Eisenmann, L., 147n.
Emmersdorf, 265
encyclopaedia, Czech, 54, 61, 67
Engel, E., 303, 304, 308n., 309n., 311, 312
Engels, F., 220
Enlightenment, 55, 227, 228; in central Europe, 5, 9, 20–2, 24, 75, 125n., 133, 217

Erben, K. J., 11, 27, 109; and Lusatian
  Serbs, 86; and Matice česká, 64, 70,
  72; and 1848, 179, 180, 186, 187, 188,
  191, 193
Eszterházy, Prince P., 196
ethnography, 11, 78, 85

Falkenhayn, Count J., 309
farmers, 283, 286, 289, 290, 310, 312
Ferdinand I, Emperor, 63, 65, 106, 107,
  166, 170, 211
Ferdinand II, Emperor, 224, 225
Fidlovačka, 27
Fingerhut, F., 182
Flajšhans, V., 3
folk literature: Lusatian Serb, 78, 81, 85;
  Russian, 85
folklore, 8; Czech, 11, 30; Lusatian Serb,
  78, 81
folk songs: Czech, 125n.; Lusatian Serb,
  77, 78, 80, 81, 84, 87–8; Slovak, 80
France, 57, 103, 115, 152, 155n., 284,
  296; revolution of 1848 in, 157; and
  Czech national renascence, 148, 168
Francis I, Emperor, 59, 63, 65, 96, 97,
  106
Francis Joseph, Emperor, 166, 169, 170,
  172, 197, 199, 200, 201, 210, 212,
  259, 262, 272, 275, 276, 287, 308
Frankfurt, 152, 160, 164n., 199, see also
  Vorparlament
Franklin, B., 217, 218
Franz Karl, Archduke, 65
Frederick William IV, King of Prussia, 150
Freiligrath, F., 176
Freimuthige, Der, 189
Freytag, G., 151, 172n.
Frič, J. V., 7, 62, 64, 70, 91n., 178, 182,
  223
Friedland, Duke and Duchy of, 100,
  105n.
Frinta, A., 88

Furstenberg, Prince K. E. von, 56; family
  of, 62

Gabriel, J. A., 182
Gaj, L., 58, 132, 178, 184, 187, 191, 197
Galicia, 178, 189, 192, 193, 196, 204,
  207n., 259, 269, 288, 296
Gauč, V., 179, 181n.
Gautsch, Baron P., 310
Gazeta Krakowska, 184
Gebauer, J., 285
Gelehrte Privatgesellschaft, 55
geography, 67, 72, 217
geology, 71
George (Jiří) of Poděbrady, King of
  Bohemia, vi, 71, 226, 229
German language, 63; used by Czechs,
  17, 56, 59, 60, 68n., 118, 219; used by
  Lusatian Serbs, 75, 91, 92, 93; used by
  Masaryk, 245, 247; used by Slovaks,
  82; as official language in Bohemia, 4,
  5, 119, 248, 258, 270, 286; see also
  Dictionaries, Orthography
German literature, 11, 15–16, 20, 114,
  222
Germanistenverein, 184
German National Union, 255n.
Germans, Germany, and Czechs: to 1620,
  231, 233, 234, 238; before 1848, 146–
  57, 161; in 1848–9, 157–72, 177, 178,
  179, 180; after 1870, 151
Germans, Germany, Confederation, 4,
  129, 177, 178; National Socialist, 173
Germans: in Bohemia, see Bohemia
  (Germans in); and Lusatian Serbs, 74,
  75
Germany, East, historiography in, 175
Gesellschaft des Vaterländischen
  Museums in Böhmen, 59
glass, 216, 217
Goethe, J. W. von, 15, 16, 99
Gogol, N., 115

Goll, J., 285
Göttingen, University of, 97
Gray, T., 11
Graz, 69, 194, 197; Johanneum, 59
Great Moravian Empire, 139, 250
Grégr, E., 257, 261, 262, 264, 266, 277, 286, 295, 296, 299, 300, 302, 311
Grégr, J., 257, 261, 278, 286, 288, 290, 297, 299, 305
Grigorovich, V. I., 184
Grenzboten, Die, 118, 146–75
Grillparzer, F., 222
Grimm, J. L. C. and W. C., 11
Grzybowski, W., 180, 183, 186
Guizot, F. P. G., 234
Gyarmat, 16n.

Haase, B., 117, 185n.
Haase, O., 117
Habsburgs, see Austro-Hungarian Monarchy
Hadžić-Svetić, J., 58
Hájek, V., of Libočany, 225–30 passim
Hajnec, L., 85n.
Halban, H., 299
Hálek, V., 11, 12, 13
Halle, University of, 79, 81, 82
Hanka, V., 16, 28, 168, 285; and censorship, 102–3, 104; as editor, 68; and forged ms. of Dvůr Králové, 10, 85, 288; and Lusatian Serbs, 86, 89; and Matice česká, 62, 64; and 1848, 183, 184, 186, 188; death of, 86n., 93
Hardenberg, K. A., 154n.
Harrach, family of, 62n.
Hartmann, M., 153
Haupt, L., 78n.
Havlíček, F., 206
Havlíček-Borovský, K., 91, 111; in Austrian Parliament, 206; and Austro-Hungarian Monarchy, 122–4, 129, 142; and constitutional government, 127–8,

130; early career of, 115–17; on Czecho-Slovak unity, 142, 143, 144, 145; on education, 119–20, 126; and Ireland, 126–7; as journalist, 7, 114, 204, 205, 210, 213, 214, 219, 220, 221; on peasant question, 124–6; on Russia, 142; and Slav idea, 120–4, 268; and 1848, 180, 192, 193
Havránek, B., 22
Haynau, Baron J. J. von, 222
Heine, H., 11
Helcel, A. Z., 184
Herben, J., 12, 277, 288, 309
Herder, J. G. von, 20, 55, 56, 89, 171
Heritage of St. Jan Nepomuk, see Dědictví svatojanské
Heritage of St. Václav, see Dědictví svatováclavské
Herold, J., 302, 303
Herrman, A., 216
Heyde, J., 128
Heyduk, A., 12
Hildprandt, Baron R., 181, 185, 186
historiography: Austrian, 155n.; Czecho-slovak, 6, 7, 159n., 173–5, 256, 274n.; on Czechs and U.S.A., 215–23; German, 155n.; on Hussites, 224–38
Hlahol society, 72
Hlasové, 143
Hoch, Captain J., 106n.
Hodonín, 240, 244, 245, 246, 249
Hodža, M. M., 135, 138n.
Höfler, C., 230, 231, 232
Hohenwart, Count K., 260, 266, 267, 292, 303
Holíč, 242, 244, 249
Hollý, J., 10
Holovatskii, I., 194
Holovna Rada Rus'ka, 184
Holy Roman Empire, and Hussites, 224, 225
Hoppe, C. G., 98n.

Hormayr, J. Freiherr von, 111n.
Horn, U., 126n., 153
Horst, J. von, 262
Hradec Králové, 50, 63, 117n.; theological seminary at, 50
Huguenots, 226, 227
Hungarians and Austrian Parliament, 207, 208, 209
Hungary, 10, 16, 18; Magyar Academy, 62; Magyar language, use of, 134; Magyar National Museum, 59; and Russia, 122; and Slovakia, 134, 139, 140; and revolution of 1848–9, 167, 169, 176–81 passim, 188–99 passim; see also Austro-Hungarian Monarchy, Nobility, Pest, Serbs
Hungary, Upper, see Slovakia
Hurban, J. M., 135, 143
Hus, J.: Odložilík on, vi; Palacký on, 68n., 69n., 104, 107, 108, 109; other historians on, 71, 225, 228, 231
Hussites, Hussitism, vi, 20, 60, 139, 224–38
Hustopeče, 242–5 passim

Ignaz, Knight of Born, 55
Illyrians, see South Slavs
Innsbruck, 164, 197
intelligentsia: and Czech national renascence, 39–52 passim, 62, 87, 88, 131; Slav, 132, 133; Slovak, 136
International, First, 223
Ireland, national movement in, 126–7
Iron Ring, 255, 259, 266, 268, 287, 292, 303n.
Irving, W., 218
Italy, 303; national movement in, 129, 161n., 201

Jahrbücher für slawische Literatur ..., 86, 92, 151n.
Jakubec, J., 4, 5, 23, 72

Jan of Štěkna, 104
Jaroš, F. S. Kř., 181
Jawornik, P., 184
Jelačić, Baron J., 207
Jeroným (Jerome) of Prague, 108, 110, 225
Jesuits, 57n., 139, 216, 224, 226, 228
Jews, see anti-Semitism
Jezbera, F., 93
Jindřichův, Hradec, 218
Jindy a nyní, 114
Jirásek, A., 72
Johann, Archduke, 59
Jordan, J. P., 77n., 86, 91, 92, 94n., 105, 151n., 179, 180, 183, 186–99 passim
Joseph II, Emperor, 24, 56, 155, 156, 228; historians on, 21, 23; reforms of, 59, 124n., 139; Josephinism, 20, 24, 153, 156
Journal des sçavans, 55
Jungmann, J., 10, 16, 17, 19, 93–94n., 154, 218; Czech-German dictionary, 63, 68; and Czech language, 4, 20, 54; and Czech literature, 68, 132; and Havlíček-Borovský, 115, 123; and Matice česká, 60, 62, 63, 66, 67, 68; and translations into Czech, 10, 12, 28, 68, 85n.

Kaizl, J., 257, 264, 277, 278, 288, 289, 291, 295–312 passim
Kampelík, F. C., 218
Karadžić, V., 58, 178
Karlsruhe, 152
Károlyi, Count G., 62
Kašpar, K. H., 180, 191
Kassovsky, Professor, 184
Katherin of Sagan or Zaháň, 62n.
Kathrein, T., 306, 308
Katkov, M. N., 184
Kaunic, Count M., 62n.
Kavka, F., 175

Kazinczy, F., 135
Keil, E. and Co., 151n.
Khevenmüller, General F. von, 170
Kiev, 66
Kinský, Prince F., 62n.
Kinský, R., 60
Kinzelberg, K., 182
Klácel, F. M., 220–3 passim
Klaudy, K. L., 206n.
Kleinert, V., 182
Klodziński, A., 184
Klopstock, F. G., 9
Klucký, L., 184
Knoll, J. L., 106
Kocor, K. A., 87
Kohn, H., 172, 173
Kojsević, 184
Kollár, J., 23, 62, 138, 142n., 154; and
    Czech language, 20; early poetry of,
    10; and Havlíček-Borovský, 115, 121;
    and Lusatian Serbs, 81–2, 89; and
    Masaryk, 251; and nationalism, 137;
    and Palacký, 100–1, 111n., and "Slav
    reciprocity," 7, 19, 20, 121; Slávy
    dcera, 18, 80, 101, 132, 252; and
    Slovak language, 82, 144; and 1848,
    184; death of, 93
Kolovrat, family of, 62
Kolovrat, Count F. A., 59, 98
Kolovrat-Krakovský, A., Archbishop of
    Prague, 62
Kolovrat-Krakovský, Count H., 64, 181,
    185, 186, 196
Königlich-böhmische Gesellschaft der
    Wissenschaften, see Kralovská česká
    společnost nauk
Konstitutioneller Verein, 178
Kopčany, 242, 244, 249
Kopitar, B. [J.], 17, 22, 99, 101n., 104
Köpl, K., 96n., 105n.
Kořalka, J., 309n.
Kornel, V., of Všehrd, 67, 102, 103

Kościuszko, T., 121
Kossuth, L., 134, 135, 177
Koubek, P. J., 128n.
Kozler, P., 198
Krakovský, family of, 62
Královédvorský rukopis, 10, 12
Královo Pole, 243
Kralovská česká společnost nauk, 6, 7,
    56, 65, 71, 103, 104, 154, 228, 230,
    235, 237; "Transactions" of, 104
Kramář, K., 257, 277, 278, 283–5, 287–
    312 passim
Kramář, P., 283
Kramerius, V. M., 56, 57, 217
Krauss, P. Freiherr von, 169, 190
Krawc, B., 87n.
Krejčí, J., 71
Křístek, V., 246
Kristián of Valdštejn, Count, 69
Křížek, J., 274n.
Krofta, K., 233
Krok, 28, 31
Krok, 114
Kroměříž (Kremsier), Parliament at, 69,
    166, 167n., 170, 210–11, 222, 232
Kropáček, J., 243
Kropáček, K., 243
Kropáčková, T., 242
Krumlov, see Bible
Kübeck, K. Freiherr von, 167n.
Kubelík, 27
Kukuljević-Sakcinski, I., 179, 180
Kuranda, I., 146–75 passim; death of, 151
Kurelac, F., 178
Kuzmanić, A., 184, 187, 198
Kuzmány, K., 251
Květy, 28, 88, 114, 123n., 218, 219n.

Ladislav Posthumous, 69n.
Lamartine, A. de, 168
Lamberg, Count F., 209
Lambl, K. J., 182, 193

Lamennais, H. F. R. de, 115
Landfras, A. J., 218
Latin America, 217
Latin language, 18; use of by Czechs, 8, 28–30; use of in Hungary and Slovakia, 10, 134, 140; use of by Slav Congress, 185
Latin literature, 29–31 *passim*, 68, 257
Latour, Count T., 190, 209, 210
Laurence (Vavřinec) of Březová, 227, 228, 230
law, 67, 103; lawyers, 45, 49, 50, 258, 270, 271, 275, 289
Łaz (Lohsa), 75, 84
Léger, L., 111n.
Leibniz, G. W., 22
Leipzig, 55, 118; University of, 76, 83, 150, 151n., 175
Lenfant, J., 227
Leopold II, Emperor, 23, 24
Lhotsky, A., 155n.
Libelt, K., 187
liberalism: Austrian, 147, 152, 158; Czech, 91, 141, 142, 144, 218, 267, *see also* Young Czechs; German, 75, 90, 141, 146–75 *passim*, 265, 266, 267; Hungarian, 176
libraries: American, 148; Austrian, 65; Czech, 65, 114; English, 57; Slavonic, 76, 77, 78, 80; Slovak, 71
Libuše, 30, 32
Liège, 29
Linda, J., 10, 11, 28
Linz, 197
Lipiński, T., 184
Lipski, W., 187
Liptovský Svätý Mikuláš, 191
Literary Foundation, Czech, *see* Matice česká
Literata slavica societas, 58
Lithuania, Lithuanians, 122
Litoměřice: archives at, 217n.; seminary at, 50

Ljetopis of Serbian Matice, 58
Lobkovic, family of, 62
Lobkowitz (Lobkovic), 222
Löhner, L. von, 208
Lomonosov, M. V., 9
London: Royal Society, 55; University of, 175
Longfellow, H. W., 218
Loos, D., 182
Lubjenski, H., 94n.
Lubomirski, J., 184–7 *passim*
Lusatia, Upper, 76
Lusatian Serbs, 74–94 *passim*; language and literature, 74, 77, 78, 81, 83, 87, 88, 183; and 1848, 90–1, 179
Luther, M., 238
Lutheran Church in Slovakia, 133n., 134, 135, 136
Łužičan, 93
Lwów, 121, 178, 194; Ossolineum, 66, 71; *see also* Polish National Committee

Macaulay, Lord, 168
Macek, J., 227n.
Mácha, K. H., 6, 12, 13, 27
Machovec, M., 22–5 *passim*
Maćica Serbska, 58n., 88–91
Macierz polska, 58n.
Macpherson, J., 11
Magyars, *see* Hungarians
Majer, M., 184
Malevsky, 184
Malinowski, M., 184
Malisz, K., 182, 186, 187
Malý, J., 123, 218
Mareš, B., 27
Maria Theresa, Empress, 21, 139
Marie Anna, Empress, 65
Marienbad, 27
Marx, K.: and Czechs, 165n.; *see also* Historiography (Czechoslovak)
Masaryk, A., 242
Masaryk, Jan, 242

Masaryk, Josef, 241–2, 244
Masaryk, President T. G., vi, 7, 12, 23,
 130, 174, 175, 233, 238; ancestry of,
 240–3; career of, 257, 278, 279, 282,
 284, 285, 288, 289, 291, 299, 309; and
 Czech national renascence, 19–20;
 historians on, 256; on Czech history,
 257, 274n., 313n.; languages spoken
 by, 245–7 *passim*; name of, 243–5;
 national background of, 239–53;
 national consciousness of, 248–52; on
 suicide, 245, 247
Matěj of Janov, 104
Matica dalmatinska, 58n.
Matica hrvatska, 58n.
Matica ilirska, 58n., 89
Matica slovenska, 58n.
Matica srbska, 58, 89
Matice česká: foundation of, 40, 53–5,
 58n., 60; flourishing of, 61, 64–8;
 decline of, 61, 69–72; and Austro-
 Slavism, 58, 65; and cartography, 67;
 and Czech-Slovak unity, 142; and
 fostering of Czech language, 53–5, 61,
 65, 66, 70; and fostering of Czech
 literature, 61, 65, 66, 68, 70–2 *passim*;
 and foreign institutions, 61, 66, 70, 72;
 funds of, 61–2, 65, 70; and Hanka, 68;
 and Havlíček-Borovský, 117; and
 Jungmann, 63, 64, 68; and Krejčí, 71;
 and Lusatian Serbs, 89; membership of,
 34, 61, 62, 64, 65, 70; and Odložilík,
 54n.; organization of, 60, 61–4, 70; and
 Palacký, 53–5, 63, 64, 65, 68, 69, 71,
 103n.; and Presl, 68; publications of,
 53n, 62, 63–8 *passim*, 70; and Purkyně,
 71; and religion, 71; and 1848–9, 68;
 and Šafařík, 63, 64, 68; and "Slavic
 reciprocity," 66, 72, 73; and Tomek,
 71; and Tyl, 116
Matice lidu, 72
Matice moravská, 54n., 58n., 66
Matthias, Emperor, 224

Mattuš, K., 261
Medau, K., 117
Meissner, A., 153
Menzel, W. I., 184
merchants, *see* middle class
Měšťanská beseda, 180, 182, 184
Metternich, Prince C.: government of,
 59, 69; and censorship, 96–7, 108,
 111n., 149; and Czechs, 106, 149n.;
 fall of, 129, 148, 158, 176
Mickiewicz, A., 115, 184
middle class: Czech (Bohemian), 39–44
 passim, 52, 118, 154n., 156, 182, 204,
 234, 257, 274, 290, 312, 313; German,
 170; Slovak, 136
Miklosich (Miklosić), F., 198
Mikuláš of Hus, 235
Mikuláš of Pelhřimov, 231n.
Milíč, J., of Kroměříž, 104
Millauer, M., 235–7 *passim*
Milton, J., 68
Mitrowsky, Count A. F., 106
Mnouček, P., 181
Mohl, R., 152
Montenegro, 179
*Monatschrift der Gesellschaft des
 vaterländischen Museums in Böhmen,*
 59, 97
Moraczewski, J., 179
Moravia, 217, 237, 240–1, 262, 263, 300,
 304; and Austrian Parliament, 203,
 204, 292, 293; Diet of, 203n., 254;
 Estates of, 138; and Masaryk, 240–3,
 244, 248; and Matice česká, 72;
 national renascence in, 35, 218; and
 1848, 179, 185, 187, 188, 193, 194,
 198; *see also* Matice moravská
Moravia, margravate of, 240
Moravian Brethren, 216
Moravian Slovakia, 241, 246, 250, 252
Moravská orlice, 247
Moscow: Imperial Society of History and
 Antiquities, 66; University of, 115

Mosen, J., 121n.
Muczkowski, J., 184
Munich: Collegium Carolinum, 174;
  Royal Academy, 66, 71
Muršec, J., 184, 197, 198
music: Czech, 27, 32, 87n., 101, 257;
  Lusatian, 87n.; see also Folk songs,
  Hlahol
myth, mythology: Czech, 11, 30, 125n.;
  Russian, 104; Slavonic, 22

Namier, Sir L., 158
Napoleon I, Emperor of the French, 222n.
Náprstek-Fingerhut, V., 221–3 passim
Národní listy, 91n., 264, 268, 278, 286–
  91 passim, 297, 311
Národní noviny, 118n., 129, 180, 182,
  186, 188, 192, 213
Národní výbor, 178, 180
Naše doba, 291
National Liberal Party, see Young Czechs
National Party (Czech), 222, 265, 273;
  see also Palacký, Rieger
Nebeský, V. B., 70
Němcová, B., 11
Německý Brod, 115, 116, 235
Neruda, J., 6, 12, 13
Netherlands, 216
Neue rheinische Zeitung, 165n.
Neuretter, M., 117n.
Nicholas I, Tsar, 114, 144
Nicholas, Bachelor, "the Slovak," 216
Niederle, L., 72
nobility: Czech (Bohemian), 59, 62, 64,
  95, 100, 116, 125n., 126, 129, 153n.,
  154n., 180, 181, 182, 188, 204, 230,
  232, 260, 265, 266, 267, 268, 269, 271,
  272, 274, 287, 292, 300; German, 153,
  169; Lusatian Serb, 81; Magyar, 62n.;
  Polish, 62n., 121, 135, 296, 306;
  Russian, 121; Slovak, 81, 135, 136, 140
Norbert, J., Knight of Neuberg, 64, 69,

70, 180–8 passim, 191, 193, 196–200
  passim
Nostic, family of, 62n.
Nostitz-Rieneck, Count F. A., 59
Novák, A., 5, 7–10, 13, 21–2
Novák, J. V., 5, 7–10, 13
Novi Sad, 58, 64, 111n., 177, 193
Novine Dalmatinske-Horvatske-
  Slavonske, 179
Novotný, J., 139n.
Nowy Sącz (Sandecki), 193
Nymburk, Young Czechs at, 297, 298,
  301, 308, 313

Obrenović, Prince M., 65
O'Connell, D., 126–7
Odložilík, Professor O., v–vii, 54n., 148,
  173, 280n., 281n.
officials: Austrian, 270, 271; Czech, and
  national renascence, 36, 40–8 passim,
  50, 52, 62, 204, 274; in Austrian civil
  service, 258
Ohéral, P. J., 184, 187, 188
Old Czechs, 111, 255, 260, 261, 262, 264,
  268, 269, 271–9 passim, 283, 284,
  287–90 passim, 293, 297–300 passim,
  303, 307, 310, 311
Olomouc, 210; Generalseminar at, 24;
  Societas incognitorum, 55
"Omladina," 294
Ondříček, I., 27
Opiz, J. F., 216
Oreb, 226
Orol Tatránski, 135, 137
orthography: Cyrillic, 93n.; Czech, 74,
  103, 243, 244; German, 244; Hun-
  garian, 244; Lusatian Serb, 74, 77, 78,
  83; Slavonic, 22; Slovak, 133n., 139,
  243–5 passim
Ossian, 11
Ostdeutsche Post, 160
Österreichischdeutsche Zeitung, Die, 189

Pacák, B., 303, 312

Paine, T., 216

Palacký, F.: in Austrian Parliament, 206, 207, 210, 213; and Austro-Slavism, 142, 161, 172; and censorship, 96–112; and Czech-Slovak unity, 139, 140, 144; and Dobrovský, 15–18, 23, 60; as editor, 60, 67, 68; and Goethe, 15, 16; and Havlíček-Borovský, 117–18; and Professor C. Höfler, 231; as official historiographer, 105–6; and historiography, 60, 227n., 228, 230–8 passim; "History of Czech Nation," 67, 68, 71, 88, 89, 96, 105–10, 154, 233; and literature, 10; and Lusatian Serbs, 89, 92, 105; and Matice česká, 53–5, 62, 70; on the nation, 140; Nováks on, 7; political activity of, 91, 111, 311; Předchůdcové husitství v Čechách, 104; and revolution of 1848–9, 69, 147, 159, 163, 165, 166, 168, 177, 180, 183–92 passim, 197, 199, 200, 232, 286; and Šafařík, 58, 64; and Serbs, 58; and Slovaks, 58; and Smoler, 88, 89; and Sternberg, 60, 99; death of, 88n.

Palacký, M., 111n.

Palkovič, J., 58, 135

Palmer, R. R., 153

Památky archaeologické a místopisné, 72

Pan-German Party, 303

Panić, M., 182, 186

"Panrussism," 122

Panslavism, 7, 10, 28, 91, 92, 96, 120–3, 132n., 135, 177, 181, 185, 195, 290

Papić, M., 185, 186

Pardubice, 297

Paris, 152, 284

Pastor, L. von, 232n.

Páta, J., 88, 92

Patera, A., 86n., 93

Paulický, J. F., 63

Paumann, A., 69

Pavlović, T., 184, 187

peasants: Czech (Bohemian), 40, 42, 44, 47, 48, 49, 50, 62, 125, 154n., 204, 206, 207, 275; Lusatian Serb, 75, 76, 81, 87, 90; Polish, 193; Slovak, 136; see also Farmers

Pekař, J., 230n., 236n., 238

Pelcl (Pelzel), F. M., 21, 28, 56, 228, 229, 235

Penížek, J., 280n.

People's Party (German), 303, 307, 308, 310

Pertz, G. H., 154n.

Pešina, T., Bishop of Čechorod, 226

Pest, 58, 59, 81, 89, 100, 187, 209

Petrasch, J. Freiherr von, 55

Pflanzer, V., 221

Pfleger-Moravský, G., 12

physicians, 45, 48–50 passim, 289

Piarists, 228, 244

Piccolomini, E. S. de, see Pius II

Pietism, 227

Pikartism, 227, 229, 235

Pillersdorf, F., 183, 190, 191, 196

Pinkas, A., 211

Píšek, J. K., 27

Pius II, Pope, 109, 225, 226, 227, 229, 230

Pius IX, Pope, 129

Plener, E., 295

Plzeň, 57, 216

Podlipský (?), J., 101n.

Pogodin, M. P., 184

Pohl, J. V., 18

Polabian Slavs, 80

Polák, M., 9

Poland, Polish: and Austrian Parliament, 204, 212, 266, 267, 276, 288, 299, 300, 303, 307, 309; language, 74, 76, 115; literature, 115; national movement, 121; publications, 66; revolt of 1830 in, 5, 121, 144; and 1848, 176, 178, 179,

181–9 passim, 191–200 passim; see also Nobility
Polish National Committee (Lwów), 178, 186n., 187, 191, 193, 194, 199
Polish National Committee (Poznań), 179, 180, 184, 187, 192, 194
police, see Austro-Hungarian Monarchy (court and government of), Censorship
Popović, M., 184
Popović, S., 198
Pospíšil, J., 63, 117n.
Postęp, 194
Postl, K. (Sealsfield, C.), 218
Poutník, 117n., 218
Poznań, 176, 178, 179, see also Polish National Committee
Prager gelehrte Nachrichten, 55
Prager Zeitung, 117n., 162n., 220
Prague, 4, 5, 39, 40, 47, 57n., 64, 81, 84, 86, 88, 147, 153, 217, 219, 283; and Hussites, 234; and 1848, 4, 159, 161, 162–9 passim, 178, 202; in 1879–91, 294, 296, 300, 303; Academy at, see Královská česká společnost nauk; Archbishopric of, 113; Baths of St. Václav, 159n., 163, 181; Charles University, 44, 48, 49, 65, 106, 115, 159n., 163n., 167, 216, 217, 220, 228, 230, 235, 252, 258, 284; Czech university, 257, 258, 285; High Court, 270, 271; 12-volume history of, by Tomek, 71; Hradčany, 170; Jewish ghetto, 157; learned societies in, 55, 56; seminaries in, 86, 115; Slavonic monastery, 103; Soldiers' Hospital, 65; theatres, 59, 69, 70; Wimmerovy sady, 27; Žofínský ostrov, 199; see also Bohemian Museum, Slav Congress
Pražák, A., 141n., 262, 263
Pražské noviny, 91, 111n., 113, 114, 117–19 passim, 121n., 123, 128, 129, 219

Pražský večerní list, 220
Prelog, M., 183
Přemysl Ottokar II, King of Bohemia, 68n., 161
Přemyslids, 30, 234
Presl, J. S., 54, 60, 62, 68, 70, 167
Privatgesellschaft patriotischer Kunstfreunde, see Společnost vlasteneckých přatel umění
Progressive Party (German), 303, 308
Prokop, St., 103, 229
Protestantism, 76, 232; and Czechs, 64, 107, 224, 225; and Germans, 227; and Lusatian Serbs, 74, 86; and Slovaks, 58, 135, 144; see also Hussitism, Lutheran Church, Moravian Brethren, Unitas Fratrum
proverbs, 78, 81
Průmyslová jednota, 119, 128
Prussia, 154n., 227; 1848 revolution in, 90, 176, 178; and Czechs, 83, 148, 164; and Lusatian Serbs, 74, 75, 76, 80, 89, 91
Prziemysl (Primizl), 30
Pubička (Pubitschka), F., 105, 228
Puchmajer, A., 9, 57
Pulszky, F., 134
Purkyně, J. E., 64, 70, 71, 76, 83, 89, 184

Raczyński, R., 187
Rada Narodowa, see Polish National Committee (Lwów)
Radetzky, Count J. J., Field-Marshal, 222
Radical Progressive Party of State Right (Czech), 298, 300
Radnice, 57
Rank, J., 153, 156
Ranke, L. von, 147, 148, 234, 238
Rapant, D., 134n.
Rath, R. G., 150n.
Raupach, H., 173
Rayevskii, M. F., 184

Raynal, Abbé, 216
Realism (literary), 5–12 passim, 115;
  pre-realism, 9, 12; (political), 278, 286,
  287, 288, 290, 291, 297
Redlich, N., 242n.
Regino, Abbot of Prüm, 29
Reichsrat, see Austro-Hungarian
  Monarchy (Parliament of)
"Repeal," 126, 127
revolution of 1848, 4, 6, 34, 65, 68, 146–
  75 passim, 176–201 passim; see also
  under individual countries
Richter, P., 182
Rieger, F. L., 35, 62, 67, 72, 101n., 166,
  172, 311; and 1848, 180, 186, 188, 191,
  193, 199, 200; and Austrian Parliament,
  206, 207, 208, 210n., 211, 212; and
  period 1879–91, 257, 260–76 passim
Rieger, G. C., 227
Riegrův naučný slovník, 35
Romanticism, 5, 8, 9, 11, 12, 16, 28, 75,
  100, 131, 217
Rothfels, H., 147, 158n.
Rott, V. J., 182
Rozličnosti, see Pražské noviny
Rozmaitošci, 66
Rumania, Rumanians, 141, 177
Rummerskirch, Count, 181, 185, 186
Russia, Russian, 83, 102, 121, 122; and
  Czechs, 136, 148, 222; Czechs on,
  133; folklore, 11; language, 93n., 115;
  literature, 9, 85, 115; Masaryk in,
  249n.; and Matice česká, 65; and revo-
  lution of 1848, 167, 179, 183, 184, 195;
  see also Moscow, St. Petersburg
Ruthenia, Ruthenians (Ukraine,
  Ukrainians), 122; and Matice česká,
  66; and 1848, 179, 184, 185, 192–4
  passim, 198, 199; and 1879–91, 303,
  307
Ruthenian Society of St. Basil, 58n.
Rychnov, 50

Rypota, J., 181
Rzewuski, Count L., 194

Sabel, M., 216
Sacher-Masoch, L. von, 69
Šafařík, P. J., 168; and Austrian
  Parliament, 69; and censorship, 101n.,
  102, 105, 109, 111n.; and Czech
  language, 20, 82; as editor, 63, 68; and
  Havlíček-Borovský, 115; and literature,
  10, 154; and Lusatian Serbs, 79, 80, 89;
  and Matice česká, 67; and Palacký, 58;
  as political journalist, 7, 142n.; and
  1848, 180–97 passim, 200; and Slovak
  language, 144; Slovanské starožitnosti,
  63, 68, 79, 132; Slovanský národopis,
  79; death of, 93
St. Petersburg: Academy of Sciences, 71;
  Archaeological Society, 66
Salm-Reiferscheid, Count H. von, 18
Sám, 114
Sand, G., 11
Sapieha, Prince L., 196
Šaštín, 249
Sawiczewski, F., 184
Saxony, 74–6 passim, 89, 164; and 1848
  revolution, 90, 91, 179
Sbor k vědeckému vzdělávání řeči a
  literatury české, 54, 55
Scheiner, G. F. von, 108, 109
Schiller, F. von, 151
Schilling, E., 180; "Schilling committee,"
  178–80 passim, 192
Schmidt, J., 151, 163, 164n., 165
schoolteachers: and Czech national
  renascence, 43, 45, 81, 87–8, 90, 120;
  and Parliament, 204; and Young
  Czechs, 275
Schwarzenberg, Prince F., 147n., 166n.,
  168, 211
Schwarzenberg, Prince J., 62n., 69

science, 217; *see also under individual sciences*

Scott, Sir W., 65

Šedivý, P., 217

Sedlnitzky, Count J., and censorship, 98, 101n., 102–3, 106, 107, 110, 111n.

Šembera, A. V., 87n.

Serbe, Der, 197n.

Serbia, Serbs, 141; and Matice česká, 65; nationalism in, 57n., 89; and 1848, 179, 182, 184, 191, 193, 195, 197, 198; Hungarian Serbs and 1848, 177, 178, 187; *see also* Matica srbska

serfdom: in Austro-Hungarian Monarchy, 206, 207; in Bohemia, 100, 124–5, 154n.

Shevyrev, S., 115

Silesia: and Austrian Parliament, 203, 204; and 1848, 179, 185, 198

Šimko, L., 251n.

Škarda, V., 308n., 312

Škroup, F., 27

Sládek, J. V., 223

Slaný, 50

Slav Congress (1848), 69n., 91, 134, 144, 147, 163; preparatory committee of, 176–201; *see also* Panslavism

slavery (U.S.A.), 218, 219

Slávia (Slavonic Brotherhood), 66, 182

Slavík, J., 180, 293, 302

Slavonic rite, 104

Slavonic studies in Prague, 64

Slavophiles, Slavophilism, 76, 123

Slavs, *see* Austro-Hungarian Monarchy (Slav groups in), Panslavism, *and under individual nations*

Slovak Society of St. Adalbert, 58n.

Slovakia, Slovaks: and Austro-Hungarian Monarchy, 14, 213; and Hungarians, 134, 135; language, 8, 58, 66, 67, 82, 144, 242, 247; second Czech-Slovak linguistic split, 133–45; libraries, 71;

literature, 10, 71, 217; and Lusatian Serbs, 81–3; and Masaryk, 239–53; and Matice česká, 72; and national renascence, 58, 94, *see also* Kollár, Štúr; in New World, 215–23; and Protestantism, 58, 134, 135, 144; and 1848 revolution, 177–9 *passim*, 191, 198; schools, 58, 72; societies, 58

Slovan, 118n.

Slovanská lípa, 181, 182

Slovanska orlice, 179

Slovene Society of St. Hermangoras, 57n., 58n.

Slovenes, Slovenia, 57n., 132; and Austrian Parliament, 266, 292; and 1848, 177, 184, 197, 198

Slovenija, 197

Slovenské pohledy, 145

Slovenskje národňje novini, 135

Šmejkal, J. V., 27

Smetana, A., 163n.

Smetana, B., 32, 87n.

Smetana, J. F., 66

Smoler, J. E., 74–94 *passim*

Smolka, F., 212, 214

Socher, J. C., 217

Social Democrats: All-Austrian, 301; Czech, 283, 293, 296, 298, 302, 303, 309, 312

socialism, 6, 220, 250, 256; *see also* Social Democrats

Société slave (Paris), 191

societies: academies, 6, 7, 56, 62, 65, 66, 71, 103, 104, 154; artists', 72; choral, 72; gymnastic, 72; learned, 55, 56, 58, 59; literary, 55, 58, 59; publishing, 57; reading, 57, 150n; *see also* Matice česká *etc.*

Society for Lusatian Language and History (Wrocław), 76

Sokol, 72

Sommaruga, F. Freiherr von, 190

Soukromná společnost učená, *see* Gelehrte Privatgesellschaft
South Slav Academy, 62
South Slavs, 57n., 122, 132; and 1848, 182, 185, 187, 193, 195, 198, 213; in 1879–91, 293, 303; *see also* Serbs etc.
Spinka, V., 117n.
Spohr, L., 101
Společnost česká, 54, 63
Společnost vlasteneckých přatel umění, 56
Společnost vlastenského museum v Čechách, *see* Gesellschaft des Vaterländischen Museums in Böhmen
Spolek literatury slovenské, 58
Springer, A., 220
Srbik, H., Ritter von, 149
Sremski Karlovci, 193, 196
Sreznevskii, I. I., 136, 184
Stadion, Count J. F., 62n., 211, 222
Stalin, J. V., 22
Staněk, J., 138n.
Staněk, V., 64, 69, 84
Stein, K. Freiherr von, 154n.
Steinský, F. A., 216, 217
Stelzig, I., 221
Stephan, Archduke, 65, 107, 110
Sternberg, Count F., 60
Sternberg, Count K., 59, 62, 98, 99, 102
Sternberg, family of, 62
Stift, Freiherr von, 153
Stillfried, Baron von, 80
Štítný, T., 67
Štorch, K. B., 180, 188
Strahov, 15
Strakatý, K., 27
Stralsund, 57
Strasbourg, 284
Strauss, D. F., 152
Strejček, F., 27
Stremayr, K. V., 262; ordinance of, 270–2 *passim*
Strobach, A., 183, 213

Strossmayer, J. G., Bishop of Djakovo, 62
students: Austrian, 209; and Czech national renascence, 36, 40, 42, 44, 45, 48–52 *passim*, 90, 221; membership of Matice česká, 62; political societies, 76, 214, 251; *see also* Slávia
Štulc, V. S., 180, 186, 188
Štúr, L., 67, 71, 79, 82, 178–88 *passim*; and Lusatian Serbs, 82ff.; and Slovak national renascence, 135–45; death of, 93
Stuttgart, 152
Sudeten Germans, 163n., 174
Sunstenau, 222
Šusta, J., 236n.
Svatobor, 72
Světlá, K., 11, 12
Svoboda, K., 182
Sylvius, A., *see* Pius II
Széchenyi, Count I., 62, 135

Taaffe, Count E.: government of, 4, 254n., 255, 258, 260, 262–6 *passim*, 269, 271, 272, 276, 287–92 *passim*, 297, 303, 307; fall of, 268, 272, 293
Tábor, Taborites, 226, 228, 231n., 232, 234, 235, 238
Tatra Mts., 144
Technologie, 113n., 119n.
Telegraph, 152
Terebelský, J., 237
Thám, V., 9, 12
theatre: Czech (Bohemian), 59, 69, 70, 92n., 114; Lusatian Serb, 92n.
Theobold, Z., 226
Theocritus, concept of *locus amoenus*, 30, 31, 32
Thirty Years' War, 224
Thomson, S. H., 280n.
Thun, Count F., 287, 291, 293, 299, 300, 311

Thun, J. M., 184n., 186, 188, 192, 196, 197, 200, 222
Thun, Count L., 64, 134, 188, 190, 197, 199, 222
Thun, family of, 62
Tkadlík, F., 15
Tobolka, Z., 196
Toman, H., 236n.
Tomek, V. V.: and censorship, 109, 110; and Matice česká, 64, 66, 67, 70, 72; and 1848, 186; as historian, 71, 236n., 237, 238
Tomíček, J. S., 218
Transylvania, 177
Traub, H., 196
Trautmannsdorf, Prince F., 62n.
Trnava, 58, 133n.
Trojan, A. P., 206
Tübingen, University of, 152
Tygodnik, 66
Tyl, J. K., 28–31 passim, 114, 154; and Czech national anthem, 26–8, 30–2; and Havlíček-Borovský, 116–17, 120; and Matice česká, 65, 116
Tyrol, 308

Ukraine, see Ruthenia
Umelěcká beseda, 72
Ungar, K., 21
Uniate church, 122, 184
Unitas Fratrum, 20, 216n.
United States of America, 66; and central Europe, 150n., 283; and Czech thought, 215–23
universities, see under name of town
Utraquists, 103, 225; Old Utraquists, 225
Uvarov, Count S. S., 65, 184

Václav, St., 229; Palacký on, 102
Václav IV, King of Bohemia, 229, 236
Valdštein, Count K., 181
Valdštein, Count V., 181, 185, 186, 196

Vašatý, J., 295, 296, 302
Vay, Count, 62
Večerní vyražení, 40, 42
Verein für Geschichte der Deutschen in Böhmen, 231
Vetterlová, J., 117n.
Vienna, 26, 152, 160; and Compromise of 1890, 271, 272, 287, 290, 292, 307, 312; Congress of 1815, 131; Imperial Academy of Science, 65; Imperial Court Library, 65; Imperial Hospital, 65; and Matice česká, 62, 69; Masaryk in, 245, 247, 251; Protestant Theological Seminary, 66; reading societies, 57; and 1848 revolution, 151, 165, 169, 178, 197; theatre, 152; University of, 106, 152, 242n., 251; see also Austro-Hungarian Monarchy (German provinces)
Villani, K. I., 180, 188
Vinařický, K. A., 68, 94n.
Virgil, 29, 30, 68
Vladislav II (Jagiełło), King of Bohemia, 100, 103
Vlastimil, 219
Vlček, J., 4
Vocel, J. E.: and Matice česká, 64, 66, 69, 70; and 1848 revolution, 179–84 passim, 186, 188
Vodek, J., 182
Vodička, F., 11n.
Voigt, A., 21
Vojtěch, J., 57, 104
Voltaire, F. M. A. de, 115
Vorparlament (1848), 147, 151, 158, 159, 163, 164–5, 177, 179, 204, 205
Vratislav, Count J., 62n.
Vraz, S., 132, 184, 187, 197

Wächter, K. G. von, 180
Wagner, A., 284

Waldhauser, K., 104

Waldstein-Wartenberg, Count, 217

Walewski, A., 196

Wallenstein, Count A. von (afterwards Duke of Mecklenburg and Prince of Friedland), 100, 105n.

Walter, F., 149n.

Walzel, O., 5

Wárko, J. A., 85

Washington, Smithsonian Institution, 66

Wellek, R., 8

Wenzig, T., 233n.

Wiener Schnellpost, 194

Wiener Zeitung, 189

Windischgrätz, Prince Alfred, Field-Marshal (1787–1862), 147, 164, 170, 201, 209, 210, 222

Windischgrätz, Prince Alfred (1851–1927), 293, 299

Wiszniewski, M., 184

Wolański, T., 184, 193

Wolff, C., 22

women's movement, 204, 286

working class, 257, 283, 312; and Czech national renascence, 42, 62, 119; emigration of, 223; and Parliament, 204, 205, 274, 275; and socialism, 220; unrest among, 156, 209

Wrocław: Slav Congress at, 186, 187, 194, 195; Slavonic library (of Purkyně) at, 76, 77, 78, 80; University of, 76, 80, 83, 84

Württemberg, 227

Young, J., 11

Young Austria, 152n.

Young Germany, 11

Young Czechs, 255, 261–9 *passim*, 272, 273–9; after 1891, 282–314 *passim*

Záborský, J., 82n.

Žáček, V., 196

Zach, F., 191, 199

Zagreb, 89, 176, 179, 187, 191, 192, 193, 196

Zap, K. V., 72; and revolution of 1848, 179, 180, 184–9 *passim*, 194–8 *passim*

Zay, Count K., 135

Zbyszewski, W., 191

Zejler, H., 94n.

Želivský, J., 234

Ziemiałkowski, F., 187

Zimmermann, J. V., 100

Ziva, 71, 72

Žižka, J.: historians on, 226, 229, 234–7 *passim*; death of, 69n.

Znojmo, 30

Zollverein, 156

Zora Dalmatinska, 187, 198

Zubritskii, D. I., 184

Zvolen, 136n.